NOTES FOR TRAVELLERS IN EGYPT

This encyclopaedic work on ancient Egypt was specially commissioned by Thomas Cook for their Egyptian tours. Today, it is unrivalled as a reliable general source for those interested in any aspect of Egypt, including early excavations, the Nile, Egyptian writing, ancient buildings, cities and kings.

E. A. Wallis Budge, author of many books on Egyptology, was once Keeper of Egyptian and Assyrian antiques in the British Museum.

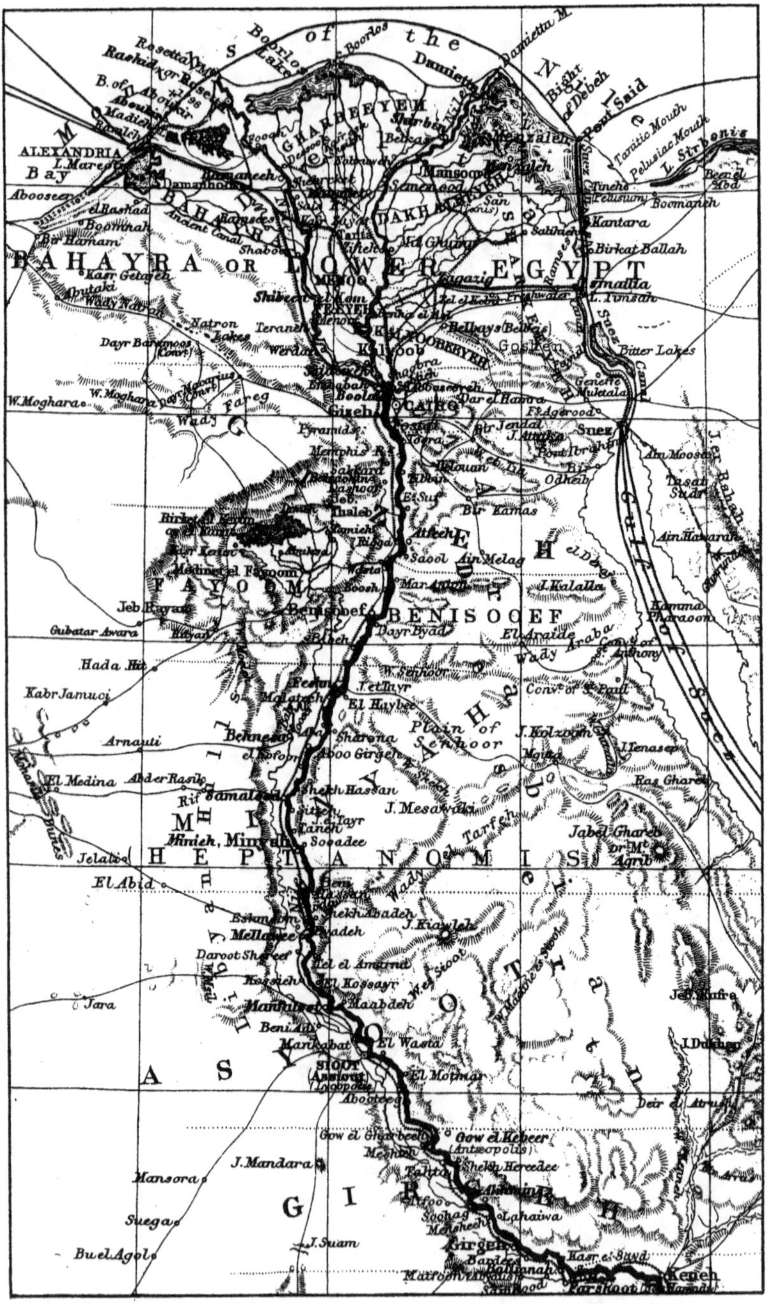

MAP OF COOK'S STEAMER AN

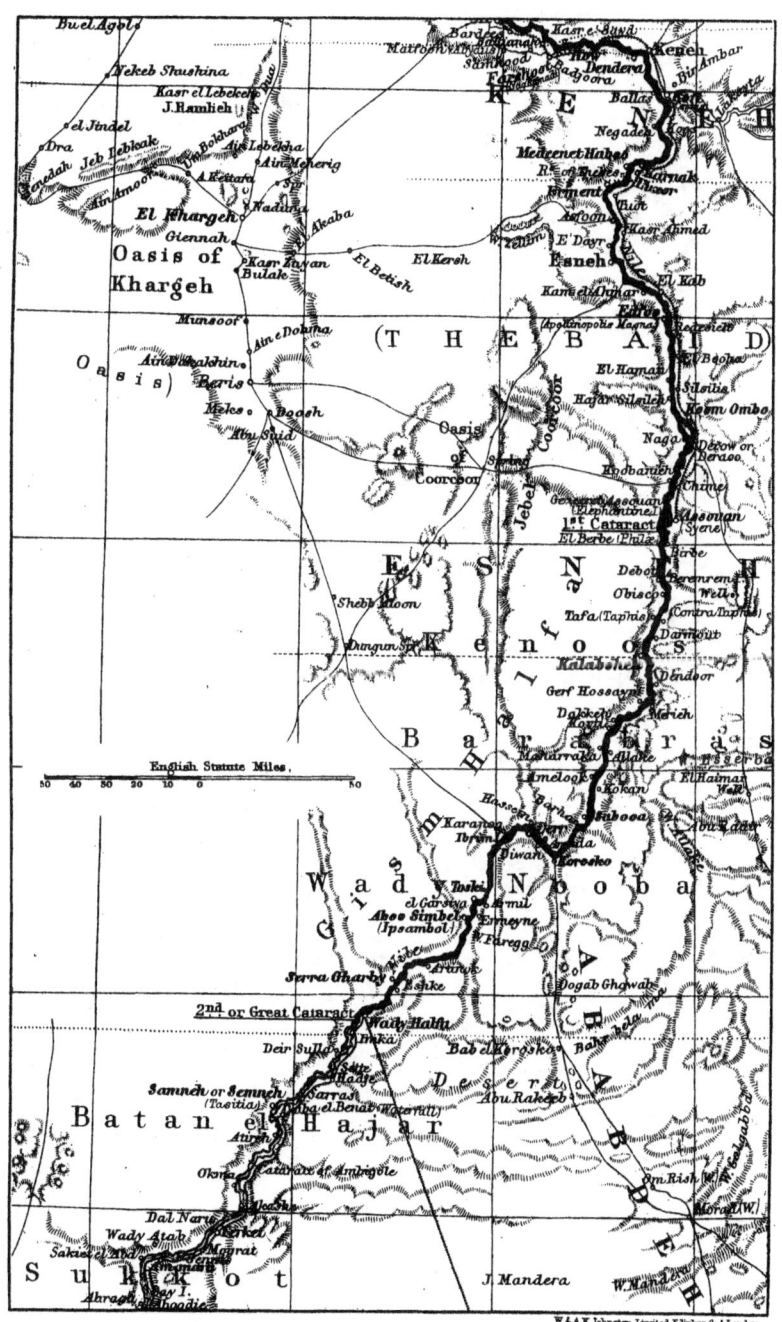

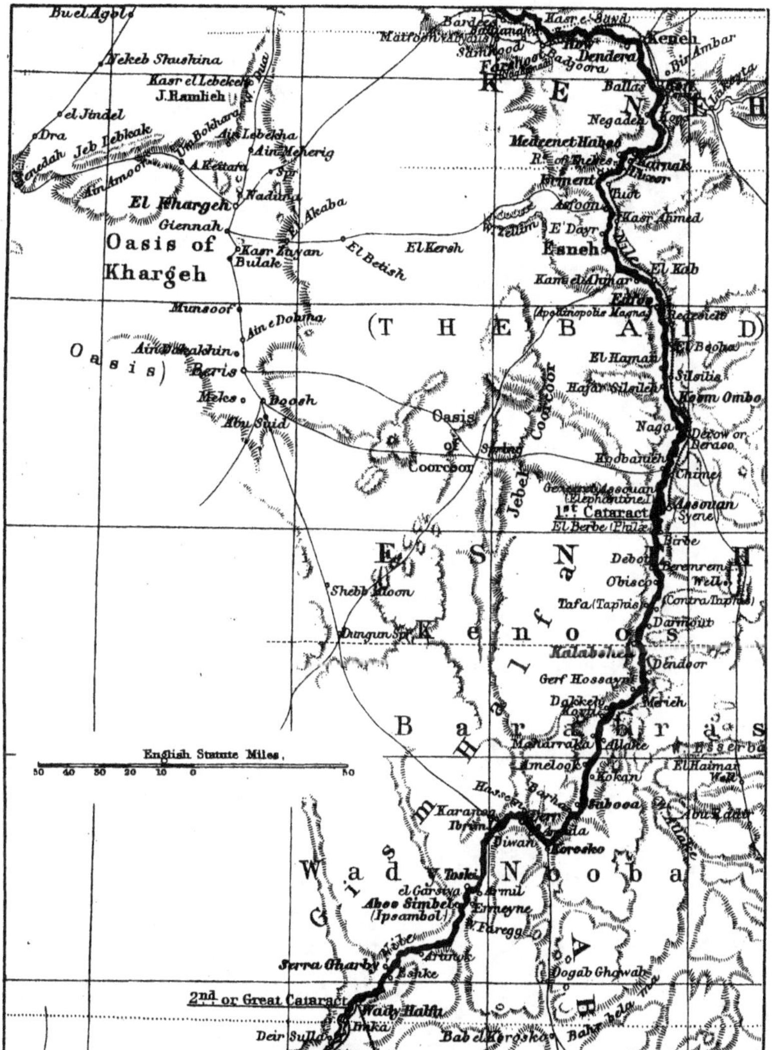

W. & A. K. Johnston Limited Edinburgh & London.

BEAH SERVICE ON THE NILE

NOTES FOR TRAVELLERS IN EGYPT

E. A. WALLIS BUDGE

Routledge
Taylor & Francis Group
LONDON AND NEW YORK

First published in 2004 by
Kegan Paul International

This edition first published in 2011 by
Routledge
2 Park Square, Milton Park, Abingdon, Oxfordshire OX14 4RN

Simultaneously published in the USA and Canada
by Routledge
711 Third Avenue, New York, NY 10017

First issued in paperback 2016

Routledge is an imprint of the Taylor and Francis Group, an informa business

British Library Cataloguing in Publication Data
A catalogue record for this book is available from the British Library

ISBN 13: 978-1-138-97730-3 (pbk)
ISBN 13: 978-0-7103-0954-9 (hbk)

Publisher's Note
The publisher has gone to great lengths to ensure the quality of this reprint but points out that some imperfections in the original copies may be apparent. The publisher has made every effort to contact original copyright holders and would welcome correspondence from those they have been unable to trace.

INTRODUCTION.

Having for some years felt the insufficiency of the information given by Dragomans to travellers on the Nile, and finding with one or two striking exceptions how limited is their knowledge of facts relating to the history of the antiquities in Upper Egypt, Messrs. Thos. Cook and Son have arranged with Dr. E. A. Wallis Budge to compile the following pages, which they have much pleasure in presenting to every passenger under their Nile arrangements on their Tourist Steamers and Dhahabiyyahs. In this way passengers will no longer be liable to be misled (unintentionally) by Dragomans, but will be able at their leisure to prepare themselves for what they have to see, and thus by an agreeable study add to the interest with which their visits to the various places are made.

PREFACE TO THE SEVENTH EDITION.

The short descriptions of the principal Egyptian monuments on each side of the Nile between Cairo and Kharṭûm, printed in the following pages, are not in any way intended to form a "Guide to Egypt." They are drawn up for the use of those travellers who have a very few weeks to spend in Egypt, and who wish to carry away from that country some of the more important facts connected with the fast-perishing remains of one of the most interesting and ancient civilizations that has been developed on the face of the earth. The existing guide books are too full, and they contain too many details for such travellers. Experience has shown that the greater number of travellers in Egypt are more interested in the remains and civilization of the ancient Egyptians than in the history of Egypt under the rule of the Persians, Ptolemies, Romans, Arabs, and Turks. It is for this reason that no attempt has been made to describe, otherwise than in the briefest manner possible, its history under these foreign rulers, and only such facts connected with them as are absolutely necessary for a right understanding of its monuments have been inserted.

In addition to such descriptions, a few chapters have been added on the history of the country during the rule of the Pharaohs, and on its people, and their buildings, their religion, and their methods of writing. The lists of hieroglyphic characters and their phonetic values, printed on pp. 133–139, will, it is hoped, be useful to those who may wish to spell out the royal names on tombs, and temples, and the commoner words which occur in the inscriptions.

In transcribing Arabic names of places, the system in general use throughout Europe has been employed, but well-known names like "Cairo," "Luxor," etc., have not been altered. Similarly, the ordinary well-known forms of Egyptian proper names such as "Rameses," "Amenophis," "Hophra," etc., have been used in preference to the more correct transcriptions, "Rā-messu," "Ȧmen-ḥetep," and "Uaḥ-ȧb-Rā."

The dates assigned to the Egyptian kings are those of the late Dr. Heinrich Brugsch, who based his calculations on the assumption that the average duration of a generation was thirty-three years. Hence it will be readily understood that the date assigned to Rameses II. (B.C. 1333), for instance, is only approximately correct. In recent years many attempts have been made to reduce the length of the historic period of Egypt, and to prove that the reigns of the historic kings of Egypt were considerably antedated by the early Egyptologists. Recent excavations, however, have shown that the historical Egyptians and their immediate ancestors have occupied the Nile Valley for many thousands of years, and even if Manetho's list of kings were to be proved incorrect in every particular, and the total years of the reigns of the historical kings be reduced by 1500 years, the great antiquity of Egyptian civilization cannot be doubted.

In the last two editions of "Nile Notes," considerable alterations and additions have been made. As a result of recent excavations many of the articles have been entirely re-written, and a brief descrption of the antiquities between Wâdî Ḥalfah and Kharṭûm has been included. So much general interest has been aroused in the Copts and Muḥammadans, that additional chapters on the religious history of these peoples have been added. In deference to many suggestions, the summary of the events which have taken place in Egypt under British influence has been considerably amplified, and the short chapter on "Progress in Egypt" will prove to what excellent purpose Lord Cromer has toiled in that land. The notes on the history and development of the idea of the Mahdi among the Muḥammadans, will, it is hoped, explain to the reader, who has not found time to examine into the Arabic sources, how religious fanaticism, acting on the minds of people who have been the victims of a long course of systematic misgovernment and oppression, has overthrown kings and deluged whole countries with blood. In compiling certain sections of this work for facts and figures I have drawn frequently from Lord Cromer's official Despatches, and from the reports and works of Sir William Garstin, K.C.M.G., Major H. G. Lyons, R.E., Major Willcocks, C.M.G., and other officials in the service of the Egyptian Government. The works of Sir F. R. Wingate, K.C.B., etc., Sir Rudolf von Slatin Pâsha, K.C.B., Father Ohrwalder, and Mr. Royle have supplied many facts concerning Mahdiism and the reconquest of the Sûdân, and from Edward Lane's "Modern Egyptians" I have derived much information concerning phases of modern Egyptian life which have now passed away.

During recent years the positions of many of the antiquities exhibited in the Gîzeh Museum have been changed frequently, and no Guide, not even that issued by the officials of the institution, correctly described the places where all the objects could be found for more than a few months at a time. It is understood that at the present moment a number of the antiquities are packed up awaiting removal to the new Museum at Cairo, and as it is, therefore, impossible to make a complete description of the contents of the Gîzeh Museum, Messrs. Thos. Cook and Son have decided to reprint the description which appeared in the sixth edition of "Nile Notes." When the antiquities have been re-arranged in their new home, a new and full account of them will, it is hoped, be included in the future editions of this work.

E. A. WALLIS BUDGE.

June 16, 1902.

CONTENTS.

	PAGE
Map of Egypt	
Introduction	v
Preface to the Seventh Edition	vii–x
Excavations in 1901–02	xvii–xxvi
Egyptian History and its sources	1
Historical Summary—	
Ancient Empire	10
Middle Empire	13
New Empire	16
Persians	19
Macedonians	19
Ptolemies	19
Romans	21
The Byzantines	24
Muḥammadans	26
Dates assigned to the Egyptian Dynasties by Egyptologists	50
Progress in Egypt under British Rule	51
The Country of Egypt	57
The Nomes of Egypt	61
The Ancient Egyptians	64
The Nile	73
The Oases	94
Ancient Egyptian Buildings, Sculpture, Painting, etc.	98
Egyptian Writing	121
A list of some Hieroglyphic Signs	133
Arabic Alphabet	139
Coptic Alphabet	140
Egyptian Months	141

	PAGE
The Religion and Gods of Egypt	143
The Modern Egyptians	191
Sketch of Coptic History	200
The Arabs, Muḥammad, etc.	211
Alexandria	247
The Pharos	248
Pompey's Pillar	251
Cleopatra's Needles	251
Catacombs	252
Damanhûr	253
Kafr ez-Zaiyât	254
Ṭanṭa	254
Benha el-'Asal	254
Rosetta Stone	255
Suez and the Suez Canal	256
Shibîn el-Ḳanâṭir	261
Zaḳâzîḳ and Tell-Basṭa	262–264
Abu Ḥammâd	264
Tell el-Kebîr	264
Maḥsamah	264
Isma'îlîya	265
Nefîsheh	265
Tanis	265–267
Cairo	268
Coptic Churches	269
Mosques	273
Tombs of the Khalifs	278
Tombs of the Mamelukes	278
The Citadel	278
Joseph's Well	279
The Library	279
Ezbekîyeh Garden	279
The Nilometer at Rôḍa	280
Heliopolis	281
The Pyramids of Gîzeh	283

PAGE

The Great Pyramid 285
The Second Pyramid 289
The Third Pyramid 291
The Sphinx 294
The Temple of the Sphinx 295
The Tomb of Numbers 295
Campbell's Tomb 296
The Pyramids of Abu-Roâsh 296
The Pyramids of Abuṣir 296
Bedrashên, Memphis, and Saḳḳârah 298
The Statue of Rameses II. 301
The Step Pyramid 302
Pyramid of Unȧs 303
Pyramid of Tetȧ 303
Pyramid of Pepi I. 304
The Serapeum 305
The Tomb of Thi 307
Mariette's House 310
The Pyramids of Dahshûr 311
The Quarries of Ma'ṣara and Ṭurra 319
The Pyramid of Mêdûm 319
Upper Egypt Railway 321
Wasṭa and the Fayyûm 325
Aṭfîḥ 329
Beni Suwêf 329
Maghâghah 330
Cynopolis 331
Convent of the Pulley... 332
Minyeh... 333
Beni Hasân 334
Rôḍa 343
Melâwî 345
Haggi Ḳandîl 345
Gebel Abu Faḍah 348
Manfalûṭ 348

	PAGE
Asyûṭ	349
Abu Tîg	350
Ṭahṭah	351
Sûhâg	351
The White and Red Monasteries	351–353
Akhmîm, Menshiah, Girgeh	353
Abydos	355
Temple of Seti I.	357
Temple of Rameses II.	360
Farshûṭ	363
Nag' Ḥamâdî	363
Ḳaṣr eṣ-Ṣayyâd...	363
Ḳeneh	363
The Temple of Denderah	364
Ḳufṭ	367
Ḳûs	368
Naḳadah	368
Luxor and Thebes	370
The Temple of Luxor	374
The Temple at Karnak	381
The Temple at Ḳûrnah	392
The Ramesseum	392
The Colossi of Amenophis III.	394
Medînet Habû	395
The Temple of Rameses III.	396
Dêr el-Baḥari	403
Dêr el-Medînet	411
The Discovery of Royal Mummies at Dêr el-Baḥari	412
The Tombs of the Kings—	
Tomb of Seti I.	418
Tomb of Rameses III.	420
Tomb of Rameses IV	420
Tomb of Rameses VI.	420
Tomb of Rameses IX.	420
Tomb of Rameses I.	421

PAGE
Tomb of Thothmes III. 421
Tomb of Amenophis II. 421
Tomb of Rechmá-Rā 422
Tomb of Nekht 422
Erment 432
Gebelên 432
Esneh 433
El-Kâb 435
Edfû 438
Hagar Silsileh 439
Kom Ombo 439
Aswân 444
Elephantine 445
The First Cataract 453
Philæ 455
The Nile between the First and Second Cataracts ... 466
Dabôd 467
Ḳartassi 467
Wâdi Tâfah 468
Kalâbshah 468
Bêt el-Walî 468
Dendûr 469
Gerf-Hussên 469
Dakkeh 470
Kubân 471
Kûrta 472
Miḥarrakah 472
Wâdi Sebûa 472
Korosko 473
Amada 473
Dêrr 474
Abû-Simbel 474
Map of the Country south of Wâdî Ḥalfah 480
Wâdî Ḥalfah 480
Wâdî Ḥalfah to Kharṭûm 481–518

	PAGE
Sûdân Military Railway	485
Sarras, Semneh, Kummeh	489
Mughrat Wells, Akasheh, Ferket, Kosheh, Sai, Amârah	491
Sedênga, Suarda, Gebel Dûsh, Soleb, Sesebi, Dalgo, Tombos	492
Al-Ḥafîr, New Donḳola or Ḳaṣr Donḳola	493
Old Donḳola	494
Abu Gûs, Al-Dabbah, Ḳûrṭa	495
Kurru, Zuma, Tanḳassi	496
Marawî and Gebel Barkal	497
Nuri	502
Fourth Cataract	503
Abu Ḥamed	504
Berber	505
Atbara	506
Meroë	507
Shendi	513
Nâga	514
Ben Nâga	514
Muṣawwarât aṣ-Ṣufra	515
Omdurmân	516
Kharṭûm and Tuti Island	517
List of Hieroglyphic names of Kings	519
Gîzeh Museum	555
Rôda Gauge	628
Index	629

EXCAVATIONS IN 1901–02.

The principal excavations carried on in Upper Egypt during the winter of 1900–01 are those of Mr. Garstang at Bêt Ḳhallâf, Messrs. Reisner, Mace, and Lithgow, on a site opposite the town of Girgeh, and of Professor Petrie at Abydos. The village of Bêt Khallâf lies about nine miles west of Girgeh, on the skirt of the desert, and some distance to the north of it Mr. Garstang began to work; in the course of his excavations he discovered several maṣṭaba tombs of the Early Empire. Three miles south-west of Bêt Khallâf, in the desert, he discovered in 1900–01 the two large maṣṭaba tombs of KHET-NETER and ḤEN NEKHT, kings of the IIIrd Dynasty. The first of these names is the Horus name of the well-known king Tcheser, who built a pyramid at Saḳḳâra, and is famous as the king who reigned over Egypt during a famine which lasted seven years. The skeleton of ḤEN-NEKHT was discovered in his tomb at Bêt Khallâf, and it is evident that the king was a man of extraordinary stature; Egyptian tradition has preserved many stories of kings of gigantic height, *e.g.*, Osiris and Sesostris were said to be 8 cubits 6 palms and 3 fingers in height, and Sesochris was said to be 5 cubits high, and 3 cubits broad. The maṣṭaba of Tcheser is a very imposing building, and the labour expended in constructing it was enormous, for the interior is hewn out of the limestone to a depth which is almost equal to the height of the brick building above ground; it is well worth visiting and should be ascended: the descent into the interior, however, is unsafe, and without suitable tackle should not be attempted. Between the royal maṣṭabas and the neighbouring village of Bêt Da'ûd lies an interesting tomb of an early ḥā prince; it is approached by means of an inclined plane and is worth a visit.

Mr. Reisner excavated on sites of the predynastic period, and of the IVth Dynasty, and of the period following the VIth Dynasty. His works have been carried out with great care, and when his results are published, it will probably be found necessary to revise some of the existing ideas on the subject of the development of Egyptian civilization in the light of his discoveries. Professor Petrie, it is understood, has been excavating within the area of the Temple of Osiris at Arâbat al-Madfûnah, north of the Temple of Rameses II. at Abydos, and is said to have discovered predynastic tombs on the slope of Kôm es-Sulṭân. In Lower Egypt excavations have been carried out by the German Archæological Mission, under the direction of Dr. Borchardt, at Abuṣîr, near Gîzeh, with successful results.

THE RECENTLY DISCOVERED CATACOMB AT ALEXANDRIA.

In the year 1900 a magnificent tomb of the Roman period was discovered at Kôm esh-Shuḳâfa, near Pompey's Pillar, in the quarry at this place, by some workmen, and thanks to the exertions of Dr. Botti, the Director of the Museum at Alexandria, this extremely interesting monument has been preserved in the state in which it was found. The tomb is divided into three stages, which descend into the living rock. It is entered by means of a circular staircase (A), which has been more or less restored, and when the visitor has passed through a narrow way with a semicircular recess (B) on each side, he arrives at a large rotunda (C) with a circular gallery (DDDD), out of which open a series of chambers (EEEE) which appear to have been dedicated to the worship of the dead. On the right the two chambers contain niches and sarcophagi; on the left is a large rectangular chamber, the roof of which is supported by four pillars, and it contains three tables hewn out of the solid rock,

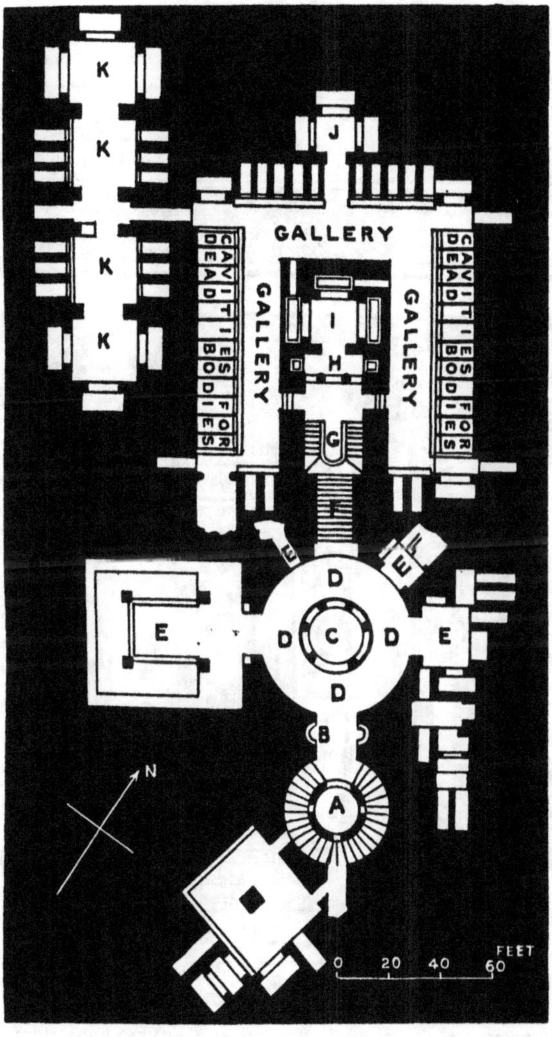

A Circular staircase (entrance). B Corridor with semicircular recesses. C Rotunda. D Circular gallery. F Staircase to second stage. G Entrance to third stage. H Ante-chamber. I Funeral chamber. J Sarcophagus chamber. K Funeral chambers with cavities for dead bodies.

THE PRONAOS AND ENTRANCE TO THE FUNERAL CHAMBER.

which were used for festival purposes by the relatives and friends of the dead who assembled there at certain times during the year. From the circular gallery a staircase leads to the second stage of the tomb, which contains the chief sarcophagus chamber; but a little way down it forks, and passes round the entrance (G) to the third or lowest stage of the tomb. The ante-chamber (H) of the tomb, or pronaos, contains two Egyptian columns which support a cornice ornamented with the winged solar disk, hawks, etc., in relief. In each of the side walls of the chamber is a niche, in the form of an Egyptian pylon; that on the right contains the statue of a man, that on the left the statue of a woman. It has been thought that these niches are ancient openings in the walls which were closed up for the purpose of receiving the statues. The door of the actual funeral chamber (I) is ornamented with the winged solar disk, and a cornice of uræi; on each side of the door, on a pylon-shaped pedestal, is a large serpent wearing the double crown , and with each are the caduceus of Hermes, and the thyrsus of Dionysos. These serpents are probably intended to represent the goddesses Uatchet and Nekhebet. Above each serpent is a circular shield with a Gorgon's head. The roof of the funeral chamber is vaulted, and the stone is of the colour of old gold; at each corner is a pilaster with a composite capital. In each of the three sides is a niche containing a sarcophagus, which is hewn out of the solid rock; the fronts of the three sarcophagi are ornamented with festoons of vine leaves and bunches of grapes, the heads of bulls, heads of Medusa, etc. Curiously enough no one seems to have been laid in them. In the principal relief of the right niche we see the figure of a king, or prince, wearing the crowns of the South and North, making an offering of a deep collar or breastplate to the Apis Bull, which stands on a pylon-shaped pedestal, and has a disk between its horns; behind Apis stands Isis with a solar disk encircled by a uræus upon her head, and holding in her right hand the feather of Maāt. The walls of the niches are ornamented with figures of Egyptian gods, and in the central niche is a scene in which the mummy of the deceased is represented lying upon its bier. The bier has the usual form , but above the lion's head is the Atef crown of Osiris, and at the feet is the feather of Maāt. By the side of the bier stands Anubis, with the solar disk and uræi  on his head; at the head of the bier stands Thoth, and at the feet is Horus, and under the bier are vases containing the intestines of the deceased dedicated to Qebḥsennuf (hawk-headed), Mesthȧ (human headed), and Ḥāpi (ape-headed). To the right and left of the door are figures of:—1. Anubis, standing upright, in human form, jackal-headed, with a solar disk on his head; his right hand rests upon the edge of a shield which stands on the ground by his side, and in his left he clasps a spear. Round his neck and shoulder hangs a belt from which is suspended a short sword. 2. Set (?), in the form of a human body with arms and hands of a man, and the head and tail of a crocodile; in his right hand he clasps a spear, and in the left the end of a cloak.

Round the funeral chamber in which these reliefs occur, on three sides, is a comparatively spacious gallery, in the walls of which are hollowed-out cavities, each large enough to hold three dead bodies; there are traces of names of those who were buried in them. At the north-west corner of this gallery is a corridor which leads into four other chambers, two of which have in them niches for sarcophagi, and two are provided with cavities wherein bodies might be laid on stone slabs at intervals, one above the other. We have already mentioned a third stage of the tomb, which was approached by an entrance situated just below the place where the staircase leading from the first to the second stage forked; this is now filled with water, and cannot be investigated. The tomb is the most interesting of all the tombs of the Roman period which have been found in Alexandria, and is very instructive. It is, unfortunately, impossible to assign an exact date to it, but it was probably built in the first century B.C. or the first century A.D. The name of the man for whom it was built is unknown, but it is clear that he was of high rank, and there is no doubt that his religion was *au fond* Egyptian. The artistic treatment of the figures of the gods, and of the walls, pillars, etc., exhibits strong Roman influence, and the mixture of the two styles of funereal art is better illustrated in this tomb than in any other of the period to which it belongs. It is hard to explain why the sarcophagi in the niches of the main funeral chamber have not been occupied by the people for whom they were intended, and it is difficult to understand why others were made in other chambers of the tomb whilst these remained empty. It would appear that the tomb was made for the head of a large and powerful family, the members of which respected the places that had been left for certain members of it, and judging from the amount of space for burial which was actually occupied, we are justified in thinking that the tomb was used as a private mausoleum for about 150 or 200 years.

THE SÛDÂN IN 1901.

The revenue of the Sûdân was £E238,500, and the expenditure £E403,000; the revenue for the past three years was:—

	£E.
1899	126,500
1900	157,000
1901	238,500

In 1881 the amount of gum exported was 150,861

kantars (the *kantars* = 99·05 lbs.); in 1901 it was 170,781 *kantars*; the amount exported in 1900 was 60,912 *kantars*, and in 1899 41,963 *kantars*. The military charge on the Sûdân has been reduced from £E222,000 to £E122,000, and the general contribution of the Egyptian treasury to make good the Sûdân deficit, both civil and military, has been reduced from about £E417,000 in 1901 to about £E390,000 in 1902. The total receipts of the Sûdân railways were £E165,000, the working expenses being £E124,000; 6,703 passengers were carried in 1900, and 8,265 in 1901; 27,555 tons of goods were carried in 1900, and 63,874 in 1901. The imports are valued at £E370,852, and consist of:—

	Tons.	Value (£E).
Cotton stuffs	1,387	217,482
Flour	431	6,034
Rice	76	760
Spirits	250	8,400
Provisions	163	6,520
Sugar	1,733	19,687
Perfumes	7	2,800
Soap	117	3,217
Oil	98	2,352
Tallow	7	230
Dates	851	6,195
Tea	26	2,912
Petroleum	90	583
Tobacco	115	31,280
Miscellaneous	1,950	62,400
	7,301	370,852

On telegraphs the estimated revenue was £E4,500, and the expenditure £E15,000; had the Government telegrams been charged at the ordinary rates, the deficit of £E10,500 would have been turned into a surplus of about £E6,000. A new telegraph line from Suakin to Erkourt, a distance of 40 miles, has been constructed. The net revenue of the Post Office was rather less than £E5,000.

A tract of country about 300 miles long, and from 100 to 150 miles broad, has been made into a game preserve; it lies between the Blue and White Niles, the Sobat River, and the Abyssinian frontier. The wild animals killed under license in 1901 numbered 842. Small civil hospitals have been established at Omdurmân, Kharṭûm, Ḥalfa, Berber, Dongola, Suakin, and Kassala. On Military and Civil Works £E68,000 were spent, exclusive of £25,000 for barracks to house a British battalion at Kharṭûm, a charge which is borne by the British Government. The Gordon College will be finished in the present year (1902), and a primary school of 170 boys will be established in it. The material condition of the people has greatly improved. The population of Dongola in 1901 showed an increase of 14,046 over 1900; of this increase, 12,899 are children. "The point of chief importance in connexion with the government of the Sûdân since its reoccupation has been to avoid serious fiscal and administrative errors at starting, which it might possibly have been difficult to rectify later. I think it may be said that no such errors have been committed. The form of government is suitable to the present very backward condition of the country. It is not a military government, if I understand the use of that very vague and indefinite expression. It is a government which endeavours to carry out the ordinary principles of civil administration through the agency of a number of carefully selected officials, most of whom are military officers. It is only necessary to read the reports . . . . to be convinced that . . . . the spirit which inspires the whole administration is, in its essence, not military, but civil. . . . Under all the circumstances of the case, the existing machine of government, taken as a whole, is probably as good as any that could be devised. Save in some few very remote localities, life and property may be said to be everywhere secure. The ordinary principles of civil and criminal justice are applied throughout by far the greater part of the country In the second place, so far as I can gather, the people seem contented. Their contentment rests, I believe, on two main grounds. First, there has been no interference with their religion or religious customs; secondly, they are not overtaxed. . . . . A somewhat long experience of the East has led me to attach more importance to low taxation than to reforms, however necessary these may, from the European point of view, appear. As the revenue grows, and as funds become available, these various reforms will be accomplished in the Soudan, as they have for the most part been already accomplished in Egypt, though I do not doubt that the process of reformation will be relatively slow. . . . The main requirement of the Soudan, for the moment, is, as I have already mentioned, the improvement of its communications, and notably the establishment of connexion by rail between the Nile Valley and the Red Sea. When the Engineer officers can report with confidence as to the best method of attaining this latter object, the funds necessary for the execution of the work shall be forthcoming, and the very important question of the labour, through the agency of which the railway shall be constructed, will be fully considered." See the Earl of Cromer in his Report on *Egypt and the Soudan* in 1901, Egypt, No. 1 (1902), pp. 75, 76.

NOTES FOR TRAVELLERS IN EGYPT.

EGYPTIAN HISTORY.

The history of Egypt is the oldest history known to us. It is true that the earliest of the Babylonian kings whose names are known lived very little later than the earliest kings of Egypt, nevertheless our knowledge of the early Egyptian is greater than of the early Babylonian kings. A large portion of Egyptian history can be constructed from the native records of the Egyptians, and it is now possible to correct and modify many of the statements upon this subject made by Herodotus, Diodorus Siculus and other classical authors. The native and other documents from which Egyptian history is obtained are:—

I. **Lists of Kings** found in the **Turin Papyrus,** the **Tablet of Abydos,** the **Tablet of Ṣaḳḳâra,** and the **Tablet of Karnak.** The Turin papyrus contained a complete list of kings, beginning with the god-kings and continuing down to the end of the rule of the Hyksos, about B.C. 1700. The name of each king during this period, together with the length of his reign in years, months and days, was given, and it would have been, beyond all doubt, the most valuable of all documents for the chronology of the oldest period of Egyptian history, if scholars had been able to make use of it in the perfect condition in which it was discovered. When it arrived in Turin, however, it was found to be broken into more than one hundred and fifty fragments. So far back as 1824, Champollion recognized the true value of the fragments, and placed some of them in their chronological order. Its evidence is of the greatest importance for the history of the XIIIth and XIVth dynasties, because in this section the papyrus is tolerably perfect; for the earlier dynasties it is of very little use.

On the monuments each Egyptian king has usually two names, the prenomen and the nomen; each of these is contained in a cartouche.* Thus the prenomen of Thothmes III. is 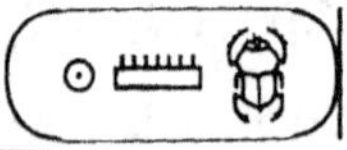 Rā-men-Kheper, and his nomen is  Teḥuti-mes. Rā-men-Kheper means something like "Rā (the Sun-god) establishes becoming or existence"; Teḥuti-mes means "born of Thoth," or "Thoth's son." These names are quite distinct from his titles. Before the prenomen comes the title  *suten net* (or *bàt*), † "King of the North and South," and after it comes  *sa Rā*, "son of the Sun," preceding the nomen. Each prenomen has a meaning, but it is at times difficult to render it exactly in English. Every king styled himself king of "the North and South," and "son of the Sun." The first title is sometimes varied by "Beautiful

* Cartouche is the name which is usually given to the oval , in which the name of a royal person is enclosed.

† The ordinary word for "king" is  *suten.* The word Pharaoh, פַּרְעֹה, which the Hebrews called the kings of Egypt, is derived from the Egyptian  *per āa,* otherwise written 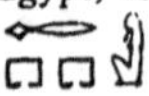 or 

god, lord of the two earths."* In the earliest times the kings were named after some attribute possessed by them ; thus Menȧ, the first king of Egypt, is the "firm" or "established." In the Turin Papyrus only the prenomens of the kings are given, but its statements are confirmed and amplified by the other lists.

The **Tablet of Abydos**† was discovered by Dümichen in the temple of Osiris at Abydos, during M. Mariette's excavations there in 1864. This list gives us the names of seventy-five kings, beginning with Menȧ or Menes, and ending with Seti I., the father of Rameses II.; it is not a complete list, and it would seem as if the scribe who drew up the list only inserted such names as he considered worthy of living for ever. The **Tablet of Ṣaḳḳâra** ‡ was discovered at Ṣaḳḳâra by Mariette, in the grave of a dignitary who lived during the reign of Rameses II. In spite of a break in it, and some orthographical errors, it is a valuable list; it gives the names of forty-seven kings, and it agrees very closely with the Abydos list. It is a curious fact that it begins with the name of Mer-ba-pen, the sixth king of the Ist dynasty. The **Tablet of Karnak** was discovered at Karnak by Burton, and was taken to Paris by Prisse. It

* Some kings had a large number of titles. Thus Thothmes III. is styled "Horus, mighty bull, diademed with law, the lord, maker of things, Rā-men-kheper," etc., etc. He is also called : , "King of the North and South, mighty of terror in all lands"; , "Horus, exalted one of the white crown, beloved of Rā"; 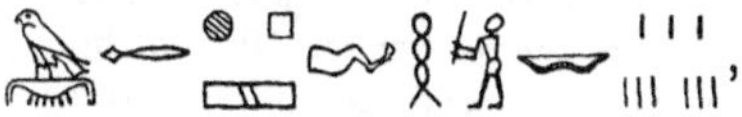, "Golden Horus, mighty of valour, smiter of the Nine Bows," etc.

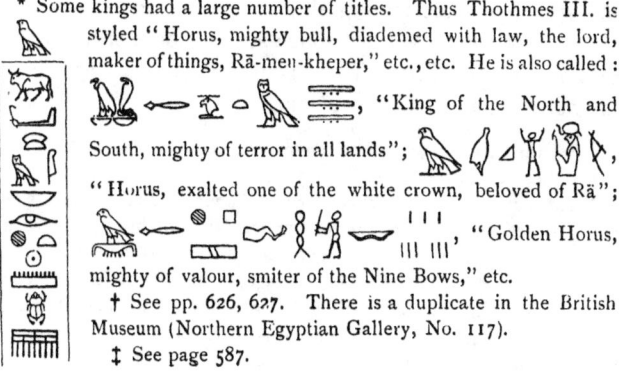

† See pp. 626, 627. There is a duplicate in the British Museum (Northern Egyptian Gallery, No. 117).

‡ See page 587.

was drawn up in the time of Thothmes III., and contains the names of sixty-one of his ancestors. They are not arranged in any chronological order, but the tablet is of the highest historical importance, for it records the names of some of the rulers from the XIIIth to the XVIIth dynasties, and gives the names of those of the XIth dynasty more completely than any other list.

II. Annals of Egyptian Kings inscribed upon the walls of temples, obelisks, and buildings. The narrative of such inscriptions is very simple, and practically these records merely represent itineraries in which the names of conquered and tributary lands and people are given; incidentally facts of interest are noted down. As the day and month and regnal years of the king by whom these expeditions were undertaken are generally given, these inscriptions throw much light on history. The lists of tribute are also useful, for they show what the products of the various countries were. The poetical version* of the history of the famous battle of Rameses II. against the Kheta by the poet Pen-ta-urt is a pleasant variety of historical narrative. The inscription on the Stele† of Piānkhi, the Ethiopian conqueror of Egypt, is decidedly remarkable for the minute details of his fights, the speeches made by himself and his conquered foes, and the mention of many facts‡ which are not commonly noticed by Egyptian annalists. The vigour and poetical nature of the narrative are also very striking.

* See the notice of the official Egyptian account on page 478.

† Preserved at Gîzeh. See page 583.

‡ For example, it is stated that when Piānkhi had taken possession of the storehouses and treasury of Nemart (Nimrod) his foe, he went afterwards into the stables, and found that the horses there had been kept short of food. Bursting into a rage, he turned to Nimrod and said, "By my life, by my darling Rā, who revives my nostrils with life, to have kept my horses hungry is more heinous in my sight than any other offence which thou hast committed against me." Mariette, *Monuments Divers*, pl. 3, ll. 65, 66.

III. Historical Stelæ and Papyri, which briefly relate in chronological order the various expeditions undertaken by the king for whom they were made. Egyptian kings occasionally caused summaries of their principal conquests and of the chief events of their reign to be drawn up; examples of these are (*a*) the stele of Thothmes III.,* and (*b*) the last section of the great **Harris Papyrus,** in which Rameses III. reviews all the good works which he has brought to a successful issue to the glory of the gods of Egypt and for the benefit of her inhabitants. This wonderful papyrus measures 135 feet by 17 inches, and was found in a box in the temple at Medînet Habû, built by Rameses III.; it is now in the British Museum.

IV. Decrees, Scarabs, Statues of Kings and Private Persons are fruitful sources of information about historical, religious, and chronological subjects.

V. Biblical notices about Egypt and allusions to events of Egyptian history.

VI. The Cuneiform Inscriptions. In 1887 about 310 tablets† inscribed in cuneiform were found at Tell el-Amarna. The inscriptions relate to a period of Egyptian history which falls in the fifteenth century B.C., and they are letters from the kings of Babylon, and cities of Mesopotamia and Phœnicia relating to marriages, offensive and defensive alliances, military matters, etc., etc., and reports on the rebellions and wars which took place at that time, addressed to Amenophis III. and to his son Khut-en-âten or Amenophis IV. The Babylonian king who writes is called Kurigalzu. Thothmes III. had carried his victorious arms into Mesopotamia, and one of his successors, Amenophis III., delighted to go there and shoot the lions

* Preserved at Gîzeh; see page 587.

† See the description of the Gîzeh Museum, pp. 592–595.

with which the country abounded. During one of these hunting expeditions he fell in love with the lady Thi (in cuneiform Ti-i-e), the daughter of Iuȧa and Thuȧa, and married her, and he brought her to Egypt, with another wife named Kilḳipa (in cuneiform Gi-lu-khi-pa), accompanied by 317 of her attendants. It will require time to settle the historical and philological difficulties which are raised by these tablets, but the examination of them already made has thrown most valuable light upon the social condition of Egypt and of other countries. One of the tablets is written in the language of Mitani, and others are inscribed with cuneiform characters in a language which is at present unknown; and some of them have dockets in hieratic which state from what country they were brought. The discovery of these tablets shows that there must have been people at the court of Amenophis III. who understood the cuneiform characters, and that the officers in command over towns in Phœnicia subject to the rule of Egypt could, when occasion required, write their despatches in cuneiform. The greater part of these tablets are now in the Museums of London and Berlin, some are at the Gîzeh Museum, and a few are in private hands. Summaries of the contents of those preserved in the British Museum are given in the *Tell el-Amarna Tablets* (Bezold—Budge), London, 1892; and for translations of most of the tablets of the "find," see the *Tell el-Amarna Letters*, by H. Winckler, London and Berlin, 1894.

The Assyrian kings Sennacherib, Esarhaddon, and Assurbanipal marched against Egypt; Tirhakah defeated Sennacherib at Eltekeh, but was defeated by Esarhaddon, the son of Sennacherib, who drove him back into Ethiopia. Esarhaddon's son, Assurbanipal, also attacked Tirhakah and defeated him. Thebes was captured, and Egypt was divided into twenty-two provinces, over some of which Assyrian viceroys were placed. A fragment of a Babylonian tablet states that Nebuchadnezzar II. marched into Egypt.

VII. The Greek and Roman writers upon Egypt are many; and of these the best known are Herodotus, Manetho, and Diodorus Siculus. **Herodotus** devotes the whole of the second and the beginning of the third book of his work to a history of Egypt and the Egyptians, and his is the oldest Greek treatise on the subject known to us. In spite of the attacks made upon his work during the last few years, the evidence of the hieroglyphic inscriptions which are being deciphered year after year shows that on the whole his work is trustworthy. A work more valuable than that of Herodotus is the Egyptian history of **Manetho** (still living in B.C. 271) of Sebennytus, who is said by Plutarch to have been a contemporary of Ptolemy I.; his work, however, was written during the reign of Ptolemy II. Philadelphus (B.C. 286–247). According to words put into his mouth, he was chief priest and scribe in one of the temples of Egypt, and he appears to have been perfectly acquainted with the ancient Egyptian language and literature. He had also had the benefit of a Greek education, and was therefore peculiarly fitted to draw up in Greek for Ptolemy Philadelphus a history of Egypt and her religion. The remains of the great Egyptian history of Manetho are preserved in the polemical treatise of Josephus against Apion, in which a series of passages of Egyptian history from the XVth to the XIXth dynasties is given, and in the list of the dynasties, together with the number of years of the reign of each king, given by Africanus and Eusebius on his authority. At the beginning of his work Manetho gives a list of gods and demi-gods who ruled over Egypt before Menes, the first human king of Egypt; the thirty dynasties known to us he divides into three sections:—I–XI, XII–XIX, and XX–XXX. **Diodorus Siculus,** who visited Egypt about B.C. 57, wrote a history of the country, its people and its religion, based chiefly upon the works of Herodotus and Hekatæus. He was not so able a writer nor so accurate an observer as Herodotus, and his work contains many blunders. Other important ancient writers on Egypt are Strabo,* Chaeremon,† Josephus,‡ Plutarch§ and Horapollo.||

According to Manetho, there reigned over Egypt before Menȧ, or Menes, the first mortal king of that country, a number of beings who may be identified with the Shesu Ḥeru, or "followers of Horus"; of their deeds and history nothing is known. Some have believed that during their rule Egypt was divided into two parts, each ruled by its own king; and others have thought that the whole of Upper and Lower Egypt was divided into a large series of small, independent principalities, which were united under one head in the person of Menes. There is, however, no support to be obtained from the inscriptions for either of these theories. The kings of Egypt following after the mythical period are divided into thirty dynasties. For the sake of convenience, Egyptian history is divided into three periods:—I, the **Ancient Empire,** which includes the first eleven dynasties; II, the **Middle Empire,** which includes the next nine dynasties (XIIth–XXth); and, III, the **New Empire,** which includes the remaining ten dynasties, XXIst–XXXth, one being Persian. The rule of the Saïte kings was followed by that of the **Persians, Macedonians, Ptolemies** and **Romans.** The rule of the **Arabs** which began A.D. 641, ended A.D. 1517, when the country was conquered by the **Turks**; since this time Egypt has been nominally a pashalik of Turkey.

* About A.D. 15. † About A.D. 50. ‡ About A.D. 75. § About A.D. 100. || About A.D. 400.

The date assigned to the first dynasty is variously given by different scholars: by Champollion-Figeac it is B.C. 5867, by Böckh 5702, by Bunsen 3623, by Lepsius 3892, by Lieblein 3893, by Mariette 5004, and by Brugsch 4400. As far as can be seen, there is much to be said in favour of that given by Brugsch, and his dates are adopted throughout in this book.

HISTORICAL SUMMARY.

ANCIENT EMPIRE.

Dynasty I, from This.

B.C.

4400. **Menȧ,*** the first human king of Egypt, founded Memphis, having turned aside the course of the Nile, and established a temple service there.

4366. **Tetȧ,** wrote a book on anatomy, and continued buildings at Memphis.

4266. **Semti** . Some papyri say that the 64th Chapter of the Book of the Dead was "found" in his time.

Dynasty II, from This.

4133. **Neter-baiu,†** in whose reign an earthquake swallowed up many people at Bubastis.

4100. **Kakau,** in whose days the worship of Apis at Memphis, and that of Mnevis at Heliopolis, was continued.

4066. **Ba-en-neter,** in whose reign, according to John of Antioch, the Nile flowed with honey for eleven days. During the reign of this king the succession of females to the throne of Egypt was declared valid.

4000. **Senṭ.** Sepulchral stelæ of this king's priests are preserved at Oxford and at Gîzeh; see page 572.

—— **Nefer-ka-Seker,** in whose reign an eclipse appears to be mentioned.

Dynasty III, from Memphis.

3900. **Tcheser,** the builder of the famous "Step Pyramid" at Saḳḳâra.

* See under Abydos, page 356. † Or 

Dynasty IV, from Memphis.

B.C.

3766. **Seneferu.** Important contemporaneous monuments of this king exist. During his reign the copper mines of Wâdî Ma'ârah were worked. He built the pyramid of Mêdûm.

3733. **Khufu** (Cheops), who fought with the people of Sinai; he built the first pyramid of Gîzeh.

3666. **Khā-f-Rā** (Chephren), the builder of the second pyramid at Gîzeh.

3633. **Men-kau-Rā** (Mycerinus), the builder of the third pyramid at Gîzeh. The fragments of his coffin are in the British Museum. Some copies of the Book of the Dead say that the 64th chapter of that work was compiled during the reign of this king.

Dynasty V, from Elephantine.

3533. **Saḥu-Rā,** the builder of a pyramid at Abuṣîr.

3443. **Rā-en-user,** the builder of a pyramid at Abuṣîr.

3366. **Ṭeṭ-ka-Rā.** The Precepts of Ptaḥ-ḥetep were written during the reign of this king.

3333. **Unȧs,** whose pyramid at Saḳḳâra was explored in 1881.

Dynasty VI, from Memphis.

3266. **Tetȧ,** the builder of a pyramid at Ṣaḳḳâra.

3233. Pepi-meri-Rā, the builder of a pyramid at Ṣaḳḳâra.

3200. Mer-en-Rā.

3166. Nefer-ka-Rā.

3133 (?). Nit-ȧqert (Nitocris), "the beautiful woman with rosy cheeks."

3100. *Dynasties VII and X, from Memphis.*

Nefer-ka.

Nefer-Seḥ . . . .

Ȧb.

Nefer-kau-Rā.

Kharthi.

B.C.
3033. Nefer-ka-Rā.
3000. Nefer-ka-Rā-Nebi.
2966. Ṭeṭ-ka-Rā-. . . . .
2933. Nefer-ka-Rā-Khenṭu.
2900. Mer-en-Ḥeru.
2866. Se-nefer-ka-Rā.
2833. Ka-en-Rā.
2800. Nefer-ka-Rā-Tererl.
2766. Nefer-ka-Rā-Ḥeru.
2733. Nefer-ka-Rā Pepi Seneb.
2700. Nefer-ka-Rā-Ānnu.
2633. Nefer-kau-Rā.
2600. Nefer-kau-Ḥeru.
2533. Nefer-åri-ka-Rā.*

Dynasty XI, from Diospolis, or Thebes.

It is not at present possible to arrange in chronological order the names of the kings of this dynasty, although several of them are well known. Names common to several of them are **Åntef** and **Menthu-ḥetep.** Some of the kings appear to have ruled for long periods, but their reigns were on the whole uneventful; the burial place of the kings of this dynasty is at Drah abu'l-Neḳḳah.

2500. **Se-ānkh-ka-Rā.** This king is known to us through an inscription at Ḥamâmât, which states that he sent an expedition to the land of Punt; this shows that at that early date an active trade must have been carried on across the Arabian desert between Egypt and Arabia. The other kings of the XIth dynasty bore the names of Åntef-āa, Ån-åntef, Åmentuf, Ån-āa, and Mentu-ḥetep. Se-ānkh-ka-Rā appears to have been the immediate predecessor of the XIIth dynasty.

* These names are obtained from the TABLET OF ABYDOS; see page 3.

MIDDLE EMPIRE.

B.C. *Dynasty XII, from Diospolis, or Thebes.*

2466. **Åmenemḥāt I.** ascended the throne of Egypt after hard fighting; he conquered the Uaua, a Libyan tribe that lived near Korosko in Nubia, and wrote a series of instructions for his son Usertsen I. The story of Senehet was written during this reign.

2433. **Usertsen I.** made war against the tribes of Ethiopia; he erected granite obelisks and built largely at Heliopolis. He and his father built pyramids at Lisht, a necropolis situated about 30 miles south of Cairo.

2400. **Åmenemḥāt II.** Khnemu-ḥetep, son of Neḥerå, whose tomb is at Beni-hasân, lived during the reign of this king.

2366. **Usertsen II.** He built a pyramid at Illahûn.

2333. **Usertsen III.**

2300. Åmenemḥāt III. During this king's reign special attention was paid to the rise of the Nile, and canals were dug and sluices made for irrigating the country; in this reign the famous Lake Moeris, in the district called by the Arabs El-Fayyûm,* was built. The rise of the Nile was marked on the rocks at Semneh, about thirty-five miles above the second cataract, and the inscriptions are visible to this day. He built a pyramid at Ḥawâra and the Labyrinth.

2266. **Åmenemḥāt IV.**

2233. *Dynasties XIII–XVII. The so-called Hyksos Period.*

According to Manetho these dynasties were as follows:—

Dynasty	XIII,	from Thebes,	60	kings	in	453	years.
,,	XIV,	,, Xoïs,†	76	,,	,,	484	,,
,,	XV,	Hyksos,	6	,,	,,	260	,,
,,	XVI,	,,	10	,,	,,	251	,,
,,	XVII,	from Thebes,	10	,,	,,	10	,,

* In Arabic الفيوم, from the Coptic ⲪⲒⲞⲘ, "the lake."

† A town in the Delta.

Unfortunately there are no monuments whereby we can correct or modify these figures. The number of years assigned to the rule of the XIIIth and XIVth dynasties seems excessive. The Hyksos appear to have made their way from the countries in and to the west of Mesopotamia into Egypt. They joined with their countrymen, who had already settled in the Delta, and were able to defeat the native kings; it is thought that their rule lasted 500 years, and that Joseph arrived in Egypt towards the end of this period. The name Hyksos is derived from the Egyptian  *Ḥequ Shaȧsu*, i.e., "princes of the Shasu," or nomad tribes on the east and north-east of Egypt. The principal Hyksos kings of the XVIth dynasty are Ȧpepȧ I. and Ȧpepȧ II.; Nubti and the native Egyptian princes ruled under them. Under Se-qenen-Rā, a Theban ruler of the XVIIth dynasty, a war broke out between the Egyptians and the Hyksos, which continued for many years, and resulted in the expulsion of the foreign rulers.

Dynasty XVIII, from Thebes.

B.C.

1700. **Ȧāḥmes I.,** who re-established the independence of Egypt.

1666. **Ȧmen-ḥetep**(Amenophis) I.

1633. **Teḥuti-mes** (Thothmes) I.

1600. " " II.

1600. { **Ḥāt-shepset,** sister of Thothmes II. She sent an expedition to Punt.
Teḥuti-mes (Thothmes) III. made victorious expeditions into Mesopotamia. He was one of the greatest kings that ever ruled over Egypt. }

1566. **Ȧmen-ḥetep II.**

1533. **Teḥuti-mes IV.**

1500. **Åmen-ḥetep III.** warred successfully in the lands to the south of Egypt and in Asia. He made it a custom to go into Mesopotamia to shoot lions, and, while there he married a sister and daughter of Tushratta, the king of Mitani, and a sister and a daughter of Kadashman-Bêl (?), king of Karaduniyash; he afterwards made proposals of marriage for another daughter of this latter king called Sukharti. The correspondence and despatches from kings of Babylon, Mesopotamia, and Phœnicia were found in 1887 at Tell el-Amarna, and large portions of them are now preserved in the Museums of London, Berlin, and Gîzeh.

Åmen-ḥetep IV. or Khu-en-Åten ("brilliance, or glory of the solar disk"), the founder of the city Khu-åten, the ruins of which are called Tell el-Amarna, and of the heresy of the disk-worshippers. He was succeeded by a few kings who held the same religious opinions as himself.

B.C. *Dynasty XIX, from Thebes.*

1400. **Rameses I.**

1366. **Seti I.** conquered the rebellious tribes in Western Asia, and built the Memnonium at Abydos. He was famous as a builder, and attended with great care to the material welfare of his kingdom. He is said to have built a canal from the Nile to the Red Sea.

1333. **Rameses II.** subjugated Nubia and Mesopotamia. He was a great builder, and a liberal patron of the arts and sciences; learned men like Pentaurt were attached to his court. He is famous as one of the oppressors of the Israelites.

1300. **Seti Meneptaḥ I.** is thought to have been the Pharaoh of the Exodus; his mummy was found in the tomb of Amenophis II. at Thebes.

NEW EMPIRE.

Dynasty XX, from Thebes.

1200. **Rameses III.** was famous for his buildings, and for the splendid gifts which he made to the temples of Thebes, Abydos and Heliopolis. His reign represented an era of great commercial prosperity.

1166–1133. **Rameses IV.–XII.**

Dynasty XXI, from Tanis and Thebes.

B.C.	I. Tanis.	II. Thebes.
1100–1000.	Sa-Mentu.	**Ḥer-Ḥeru,** the first priest-king.
	Pasebkhānu I.	Pi-ānkhi.
	Åmen-em-åpt.	Pai-net'em I–III.
	Pasebkhānu II.	

Dynasty XXII, Libyans who ruled the country from Bubastis (Tell-Basṭa).

966. **Shashanq** (Shishak) I. (see 1 Kings, xiv. 25–28; 2 Chron., xii. 2–13) besieged Jerusalem, and having conquered it, pillaged the Temple and carried away much spoil.

933. Uasarken I.
900. Takeleth I.
866. Uasarken II.
833. Shashanq II.
Takeleth II.
Shashanq III.
800. Pamai
Shashanq IV.

Under the rule of these kings Egypt finally lost most of her foreign possessions, and the feebleness of their rule made her an easy prey for the warlike.

Dynasty XXIII, from Tanis.

766. Peṭā-Bast.
Uasarken III.

Dynasty XXIV, from Saïs (Sâ el-Ḥagar).

733. **Bak-en-ren-f** (Bocchoris).

Dynasty XXV, from Ethiopia.

B.C.

700. **Shabaka (Sabaco).** See 2 Kings, xvii. 4.
Shabataka.

693. Taharqa (Tirhakah, 2 Kings, xix. 9) is famous for having conquered Sennacherib and delivered Hezekiah; he was, however, defeated by Esarhaddon and Assurbanipal, the son and grandson of Sennacherib. Tirhakah's son-in-law, Urdamanah, was also defeated by the Assyrians.

Dynasty XXVI, from Saïs.

666. **Psemthek I.** (Psammetichus) allowed Greeks to settle in the Delta, and employed Greek soldiers to fight for him.

612. **Nekau II. (Necho)** defeated Josiah, king of Judah, and was defeated by Nebuchadnezzar II. son of Nabopolassar, king of Babylon. See 2 Kings, xxiii. 29 ff; Jeremiah xlvi. 2.

596. **Psammetichus II.**

591. **Uaḥ-àb-Rā, Apries (Hophra** of the Bible, Gr. Apries) marched to the help of Zedekiah, king of Judah, who was defeated by Nebuchadnezzar II. His army rebelled against him, and he was dethroned; Amāsis, a general in his army, then succeeded to the throne. See Jeremiah, xliv. 30.

572. **Àāḥmes** or **Amāsis II.** favoured the Greeks, and granted them many privileges; in his reign Naucratis became a great city.

528. **Psammetichus III.** was defeated at Pelusium by Cambyses the Persian, and taken prisoner; he was afterwards slain for rebellion against the Persians.

Dynasty XXVII, from Persia.

527. **Cambyses** marched against the Ethiopians and the inhabitants of the Oases.

B.C.

521. **Darius I. (Hystaspes)** endeavoured to open up the ancient routes of commerce; he established a coinage, and adopted a conciliatory and tolerant system of government, and favoured all attempts to promote the welfare of Egypt.

486. **Xerxes I.**

465. **Artaxerxes I.**, during whose reign the Egyptians revolted, headed by Amyrtæus.

425. **Darius II. (Nothus)**, during whose reign the Egyptians revolted successfully, and a second Amyrtæus became king of Egypt.

405. **Artaxerxes II.**

Dynasty XXVIII, from Saïs.

Ȧmen-ruṭ (Amyrtæus), reigned six years.

Dynasty XXIX, from Mendes.

399. Naifāauruṭ I.
393. Haḳar.
380. P-se-mut.
379. Naifāauruṭ II.

Dynasty XXX, from Sebennytus.

378. **Nekht-Ḥeru-ḥeb (Nectanebus I.)** defeated the Persians at Mendes.

360. **T'e-ḥer** surrendered to the Persians.

358. **Nekht-neb-f (Nectanebus II.)** devoted himself to the pursuit of magic, and neglected his empire; when Artaxerxes III. (Ochus) marched against him, he fled from his kingdom, and the Persians again ruled Egypt.

B.C.

PERSIANS.

340. **Artaxerxes III.** (Ochus).

338. Arses.

336. Darius III. (Codomannus) conquered by Alexande the Great at Issus.

MACEDONIANS.

332. **Alexander the Great** founded Alexandria. He showed his toleration of the Egyptian religion by sacrificing to the god Åmen of Libya.

PTOLEMIES.*

323. **Ptolemy I. Soter,** son of Lagus, became king of Egypt after Alexander's death. He founded the famous Alexandrian Library, and encouraged learned Greeks to make Alexandria their home; he died B.C. 284.

285. **Ptolemy II. Philadelphus** built the Pharos, founded Berenice and Arsinoë, caused Manetho's Egyptian history to be compiled, and the Greek version of the Old Testament (Septuagint) to be made.

247. **Ptolemy III. Euergetes I.** The stele of Canopus † was set up in the ninth year of his reign; he obtained possession of all Syria, and was a patron of the arts and sciences.

* For the chronology of the Ptolemies, see Lepsius, *Königsbuch*, Synoptische Tafeln 9.

† This important stele, preserved at Gîzeh, see page 590, is inscribed in hieroglyphics, Greek and demotic with a decree made at Canopus by the priesthood, assembled there from all parts of Egypt, in honour of Ptolemy III. It mentions the great benefits which he had conferred upon Egypt, and states what festivals are to be celebrated in his honour and in that of Berenice, etc., and concludes with a resolution ordering that a copy of this inscription in hieroglyphics, Greek and demotic shall be placed in every large temple of Egypt. Two other copies of this work are known.

B.C.

222. **Ptolemy IV. Philopator** defeated Antiochus, and founded the temple at Edfû.

205. **Ptolemy V. Epiphanes.** During his reign the help of the Romans against Antiochus was asked for by the Egyptians. Coelesyria and Palestine were lost to Egypt. He was poisoned B.C. 182, and his son Ptolemy VI. Philometor, died in that same year. The Rosetta Stone was set up in the eighth year of the reign of this king.

— **Ptolemy VI. Philometor** did not reign a full year.

181. **Ptolemy VII. Eupator** was taken prisoner at Pelusium by Antiochus IV., B.C. 171, and died B.C. 146. He reigned alone at first, then conjointly (B.C. 170—165) with Ptolemy IX. Euergetes II. (also called Physcon), and finally having gone to Rome on account of his quarrel with Physcon, he reigned as sole monarch of Egypt (B.C. 165). Physcon was overthrown B.C. 132, reigned again B.C. 125, and died B.C. 117.

170. **Ptolemy VIII. Neos Philopator** is murdered by Physcon.

146. **Ptolemy IX. Euergetes II. (Physcon).**

117. **Ptolemy X. Soter II.** Philometor II. (Lathyrus), reigns jointly with Cleopatra III. Ptolemy X. is banished (B.C. 106), his brother Ptolemy XI. Alexander I. is made co-regent, but afterwards banished (B.C. 89) and slain (B.C. 87); Ptolemy X. is recalled, and dies B.C. 81.

88. **Ptolemy XI. Alexander I.** is killed.

81. Ptolemy XII. Alexander II. is slain.

81. **Ptolemy XIII.** Neos Dionysos (Auletes), ascends the throne; dies B.C. 52.

B.C.

52. **Ptolemy XIV.** Dionysos II. and Cleopatra VII. are, according to the will of Ptolemy XIII., to marry each other; the Roman senate to be their guardian. Ptolemy XIV. banishes Cleopatra, and is a party to the murder of Pompey, their guardian, who visits Egypt after his defeat at Pharsalia. Cæsar arrives in Egypt to support Cleopatra (B.C. 48); Ptolemy XIV. is drowned; **Ptolemy XV.**, brother of Cleopatra VII., is appointed her co-regent by Cæsar (B.C. 47); he is murdered at her wish, and her son by Cæsar, **Ptolemy XVI.** Cæsarion, is named co-regent (B.C. 45).

42. **Antony** orders **Cleopatra** to appear before him, and is seduced by her charms; he kills himself, and Cleopatra dies by the bite of an asp. Egypt becomes a Roman province B.C. 30.

ROMANS.

Cæsar Augustus becomes master of the Roman Empire. Cornelius Gallus is the first prefect of Egypt. Under the third prefect, Aelius Gallus, Candace, queen of the Ethiopians, invades Egypt, but is defeated.

In the consulship of Marcus Silanus and Lucius Norbanus, Germanicus set out (A.D. 19) for Egypt to study its antiquities. His ostensible motive, however, was solicitude for the province. He sailed up the Nile from the city of Canopus, which was founded by the Spartans because Canopus, pilot of one of their ships, had been buried there, when Menelaus on his return to Greece was driven into a distant sea and to the shores of Libya. "Next he visited the vast ruins of ancient Thebes. There yet remained on the towering piles Egyptian inscriptions, with a complete account of the city's past grandeur.

One of the aged priests, who was desired to interpret the language of his country, related how once there had dwelt in Thebes 700,000 men of military age, and how with such an army Rhamses conquered Libya, Ethiopia, Media, Persia, Bactria, and Scythia, and held under his sway the countries inhabited by the Syrians, Armenians, and their neighbours, the Cappadocians, from the Bithynian to the Lycian Sea. There was also to be read what tributes were imposed on these nations, the weight of silver and gold, the tale of arms and horses, the gifts of ivory and of perfumes to the temples, and the amount of grain and supplies furnished by each people, a revenue as magnificent as is now exacted by the might of Parthia or the power of Rome. But Germanicus also bestowed attention on other wonders. Chief of these were the stone image of Memnon, which, when struck by the sun's rays, gives out the sound of a human voice; the pyramids, rising up like mountains amid almost impassable wastes of shifting sand; raised by the emulation and vast wealth of kings; the lake (*i.e.*, Moeris) hollowed out of the earth to be a receptacle for the Nile's overflow; and elsewhere the river's narrow channel and profound depth which no line of the explorer can penetrate. He then came to Elephantine and Syene, formerly the limits of the Roman empire, which now extends to the Red Sea."—*Tacitus*, book ii., §§ 59–61 (Church and Brodribb).

A.D.

14. **Tiberius.** In his reign Germanicus visited Egypt.

37. **Caligula.** In his reign a persecution of the Jews took place.

41. **Claudius.**

55. **Nero.** In his reign Christianity was first preached in Egypt by Saint Mark. The Blemmyes made raids upon the southern frontier of Egypt.

69. **Vespasian.** Jerusalem destroyed A.D. 70.

A.D.

82. **Domitian** causes temples to Isis and Serapis to be built at Rome.

98. **Trajan.** The Nile and Red Sea Canal (Amnis Trajânus) re-opened.

117. **Hadrian.** Visited Egypt twice.

138. **Antoninus Pius.**

161. **Marcus Aurelius** caused the famous *Itinerary* to be made.

180. **Commodus.**

193. **Septimius Severus.**

211. Caracalla visited Egypt, and caused a large number of young men to be massacred at Alexandria.

217. **Macrinus.**

218. **Elagabalus.**

249. **Decius.** Christians persecuted.

253. **Valerianus.** Christians persecuted.

260. **Gallienus.** Persecution of Christians stayed. Zenobia, Queen of Palmyra, invades Egypt A.D. 268.

270. **Aurelian.** Zenobia becomes Queen of Egypt for a short time, but is dethroned A.D. 273.

276. **Probus.**

284. **Diocletian.** "**Pompey's Pillar**" erected A.D. 302, persecution of Christians A.D. 304. The Copts date the era of the Martyrs from the day of Diocletian's accession to the throne (August 29).

324. **Constantine the Great,** the Christian Emperor, in whose reign, A.D. 325, the Council of Nicæa was held. At this council it was decided that Christ and His Father were of one and the *same* nature, as taught by Athanasius; and the doctrine of

A.D.

and recent title of mother of God, which had been insensibly adopted since the origin of the Arian controversy. From the pulpit of Constantinople, a friend of the patriarch,* and afterwards the patriarch himself, repeatedly preached against the use, or the abuse, of a word unknown to the apostles, unauthorized by the church, and which could only tend to alarm the timorous, to mislead the simple, to amuse the profane, and to justify, by a seeming resemblance, the old genealogy of Olympus. In his calmer moments Nestorius confessed, that it might be tolerated or excused by the union of the two natures, and the communication of their *idioms* (*i.e.*, a transfer of properties of each nature to the other—of infinity to man, passibility to God, etc.): but he was exasperated, by contradiction, to disclaim the worship of a newborn, an infant Deity, to draw his inadequate similes from the conjugal or civil partnerships of life, and to describe the manhood of Christ, as the robe, the instrument, the tabernacle of his Godhead."—Gibbon, *Decline and Fall*, chap. 47.

450. **Marcianus.** The Monophysite doctrine of Eutyches was condemned at the Council of Chalcedon, A.D. 451. Eutyches, from the one person of Christ, inferred also one nature, viz., the Divine—the human having been absorbed into it. Silko invaded Egypt with his Nubian followers.

474. **Zeno.** He issued the *Henoticon*, an edict which, while affirming the Incarnation, made no attempt to decide the difficult question whether Christ possessed a single or a double nature.

* Anastasius of Antioch, who said, "Let no one call Mary *Theotokos;* for Mary was but a woman; and it is impossible that God should be born of a woman."—Socrates, *Eccles. Hist.*, Bk. VII., chap. xxxii.

A.D.

491. **Anastasius.**

527. **Justinian.** The Monophysites separated from the Melkites, or "Royalists," and chose their own patriarch; they were afterwards called Copts, القُبْط.*

610. **Heraclius.** The Persians under Chosroes held Egypt for ten years; they were expelled by Heraclius A.D. 629.

MUḤAMMADANS.

640. **'Amr ibn al-'Aṣi** conquers Egypt. 'Amr began his expedition against Egypt with about 4,000 men, but the Khalîfa Omar sent him reinforcements, and by the time the famous general arrived at 'Arîsh his army numbered 16,000 men. Having vanquished the garrison at Pelusium, he marched along the Pelusiac branch of the Nile, and passed by way of Bubastis to Heliopolis. A truce of four days was obtained for George, the Maḳawḳas, the governor of Upper Egypt, by the Coptic Patriarch Benjamin, and it seems that the Egyptian official, who was a Jacobite Copt, and a hater of the ruling class in Egypt, greatly aided the Arab general. The Arabs moved on towards Memphis, and soon after, under Zubêr, 'Amr's colleague, made a general assault upon the fortress of Babylon, scaled the walls, and so became masters of the capital of Upper Egypt. George, the Maḳawḳas, arranged the details of the capitulation, and a capitation tax of two dînârs for every male adult, besides other payments. 'Amr then marched on Alexandria, and as the Greeks took to their

* The name given to the native Christians of Egypt by the Arabs, from ⲔⲨⲠⲦⲀⲒⲞⲤ for Αἰγύπτιος.

ships and fled, George, the Maḳawḳas, who had gone to Alexandria after the fall of Babylon, offered to capitulate on the same terms as he had made for that city. 'Amr returned to Memphis, and made the head-quarters of the army at Fosṭâṭ, near which the modern town of Cairo has grown up. 'Amr refused to possess himself of any land, and he was not even given a site whereon to build a house. One of his most useful works was to re-open the old canal which ran from Belbês through the Wâdî Ṭûmîlât to the Bitter Lakes, and thence to the Red Sea; by this means it was possible to convey corn which had been loaded into ships at Memphis from that city into Yenbô, the port of Medîna in Arabia, without transhipment. This canal was in use for about eighty years, when it became silted up. After the second siege of Alexandria (A.D. 646) the Arabs made Fosṭaṭ the capital of Egypt.

A.D.

644. 'Othmân.

750. Merwân II., the last of the 'Omayyade dynasty, was put to death in Egypt.

750–870. The 'Abbasides rule over Egypt.

786. Harûn ar-Rashîd.

813. Mâmûn visited Egypt, and opened the Great Pyramid.

870. Aḥmad ibn-Ṭulûn governs Egypt.

884. Khamârûyeh enlarges Fosṭâṭ.

969–1171. The Fâṭimites govern Egypt, with Maṣr el-Ḳâhira * (Cairo) as their residence.

975. Al-'Azîz, son of Mu'izz, great grandson of 'Obêdallâh.

996. Ḥâkim, son of 'Azîz, founder of the Druses. This remarkable prince wished to be considered God incarnate.

* القَاهِرَة

A.D.

1020. Ẓâhir, son of Ḥâkim.

1036. Abu Tamîm el-Mustanṣir.

1094. Musta'li, son of el-Mustanṣir, captured Jerusalem (A.D. 1096), but was defeated by the Crusaders under Godfrey de Bouillon.

1160. 'Aḍîd Ledînallâh, the last of the Fâṭimites.

1171. Ṣalâḥeddîn (Saladin) defeated the Crusaders at Ḥittîn, and recaptured Jerusalem.

1193. Melik al-'Adîl.

1218. Melik al-Kâmil, the builder of Manṣûrah.

1240. Melik aṣ-Ṣâleḥ, the usurper, captured Jerusalem, Damascus, and Ascalon. Louis IX. of France, attacked and captured Damietta, but was made prisoner at Manṣûrah, with all his army.

1250–1380. The Baḥrite Mamelukes.

1260. Bêbars.

1277. Ḳalâûn.

1291. Al-Ashraf Khalîl captured Acre.

1346. Ḥasan.

1382–1517. Burgite or Circassian Mamelukes.

1382. Barḳûḳ.

1422. Bursbey.

1468. Ḳâit Bey.

1501. Al-Ghûri.

1517. Ṭûmân Bey is deposed by Selim I. of Constantinople, and Egypt becomes a Turkish Pashalik. Soon after his conquest of Egypt, Selim divided the country into twenty-four provinces, over each of which he appointed a local governor; these governors were placed in subjection to a Pâsha, who, with the help of a council of seven Turkish officials, ruled the country. One of the twenty-four governors was elected to the important office of "Shêkh al-balad," or governor of the metropolis, a post which was greatly coveted by his colleagues

A. D.

when they saw what frequent opportunities were enjoyed by him of "squeezing" the natives, and of making himself a rich man. This system worked well for a time, but as the power of Turkey declined, so the power of her nominees the Pâshas of Egypt declined, and at length the twenty-four local governors became the actual rulers of Egypt, for the revenues of the country were in their hands, and they paid the Turkish Pâsha his salary.

1771. 'Ali Bey, a slave, obtains great power in Egypt. He was accused of entering into a conspiracy against the Sulṭân at Constantinople, and a messenger was sent to Egypt to bring back 'Ali Bey's head. 'Ali caught and slew the messenger, and having called his colleagues together, drove out the Pâsha and
1772. declared Egypt independent He was poisoned by Muḥammad abu-Dhabad, a man on whom he had showered favours.

1773. Ismâ'îl, Ibrâhîm, and Murâd strive for the mastery over Egypt. When Murâd became ruler, a Turkish army invaded Egypt and seized Cairo, and at-
1790. tempted to follow the rebel (Murâd) into Upper Egypt

1798. **Napoleon Bonaparte** lands near Alexandria with an army of 36,000 men (July 1); storming of Alexandria (July 5); Murâd meets the French in battle at Embâbeh, opposite Cairo, with 60,000 men, but is beaten, and about 15,000 of his men are killed. This fight is commonly called the **Battle of the Pyramids**. A few days later Nelson destroyed the French fleet in Abuḳîr Bay.

1799. Destruction of the Turkish army by the French at Abuḳîr.

1800. Sir Sydney Smith signs a treaty at Al-'Arîsh granting General Kléber's army permission to leave Egypt

A.D. (February 24), but as he had to admit later that he had exceeded his powers, and that the British Government demanded the surrender of the whole French army as prisoners of war, Gen. Kléber attacked the Turks at the village of Maṭarîyeh and is said to have routed 70,000 men, an army six times as large as his own. A few months later Kléber was assassinated, and General Menou became commander-in-chief of the French army in Egypt.

1801. Sir Ralph Abercromby lands at Abuḳîr Bay with 17,000 men (March 8); battle of Alexandria and defeat of the French (March 21); the French capitulate at Cairo (June 27); the French capitulate at Alexandria (August 30); evacuation of Egypt by the French (September).

1803. England restores Egypt to the Turks. As soon as the English left Egypt, severe conflicts took place between two Turkish parties in the country, the Albanians and the Ghuzz; to the former belonged Muḥammad 'Ali.

1805. **Muḥammad Ali** is elected Pâsha of Egypt by the people. His election was afterwards confirmed by the Porte. He was born at Cavalla, a small town on the sea-coast of Albania, in 1769, and he served in the Turkish army at an early age. He was sent with a body of troops to fight against the French, and enjoyed at that time the rank of major (*bimbashi*); he married the daughter of the governor of his native town, and by her had three sons, Ibrâhîm, Ṭusûn, and Ismâ'îl.

1807. General Fraser arrives at Alexandria with 5,000 British troops (March 17), but being unsuccessful in his mission, he evacuated Alexandria on September 14.

A.D.

1811. Assassination of the Mamelukes by Muḥammad 'Ali. These unfortunate men were invited by Muḥammad Ali to attend the investiture of his son Ṭusûn with a garment of state at the Citadel on March 1. When they arrived they were graciously received and led into the Citadel, but as soon as they were inside the gates were closed and Muḥammad 'Ali's soldiers opened fire upon them; about 470 of the Beys and their followers were murdered, and of all who entered only one is said to have escaped.

1820. Expedition to the Sûdân led by Ismâ'îl, who was burned to death by an Arab shêkh called Nimr (1822).

1821. Muḥammad 'Ali sends about 8,000 troops to assist the Turks against the Greeks. In 1824 a false Mahdi appeared near Thebes, with about 25,000 followers, but nearly all of them were massacred by the Government troops.

1831. Invasion of Syria by Ibrâhîm, son of Muḥammad 'Ali. Acre was invested on November 29, but was not captured until May 27, 1832. Ibrâhîm was victorious at Emesa on July 8, he defeated Rashîd Pâsha, and destroyed the Turkish fleet so completely that Constantinople was in imminent danger of capture. In 1833 the whole of Syria was ceded to Muḥammad 'Ali, and the rule of his son Ibrâhîm was firm but just. In 1839 war again broke out between the Turks and Egyptians, and two years later Syria was given back to the former. In 1847 Muhammad 'Ali visited Ḉonstantinople, and soon after his reasoning powers became impaired.

1848. **Ibrâhîm** is appointed to rule Egypt on account of his father's failing health. He died after the reign of a few months, but Muḥammad did not

A.D. die until August 3, 1849. Muḥammad 'Ali was
1849. an able ruler, and one who had the interest of his country at heart. He created an army and a navy, and established equitable laws for collecting the revenues; he founded colleges of various kinds, and also the famous Bûlâk printing press. There is no doubt that but for the obstacles placed in his way by the British Government, and its interference, he would have freed Egypt entirely from Turkish misrule. His health and spirits were broken by England when she reduced his army to 18,000 men and forbade him to employ his fleet, which rotted away as it lay inactive at Alexandria.

1849. **'Abbâs** Pâsha, the son of Ṭusûn, the son of Muḥammad 'Ali, succeeds Ibrâhîm. He was an incapable ruler, and is said to have been strangled at Benha in July, 1854.

1854. **Sa'îd** Pâsha, the fourth son of Muḥammad 'Ali, becomes ruler of Egypt. Though not a strong ruler, he was a just man, and he will be chiefly remembered for having abolished a number of cruel monopolies. In many particulars he sought to carry out his father's plans, and first and foremost among these must be mentioned the building of railways in the Delta, and the enlarging of the canals with the view of improving irrigation and of facilitating communication. He it was who supported the project of making the Suez Canal, and he gave M. de Lesseps the concession for it. He founded the Bûlâḳ Museum, and encouraged excavations on the sites of the ancient cities of Egypt.

1863. **Ismâ'îl,** son of Ibrâhîm Pâsha, and grandson ot Muḥammad 'Ali, becomes the ruler of Egypt; he was born in 1830, and by a decree of the Sulṭân,

A.D.
1863. dated May 14, 1867, was made "Khĕdîve"* of Egypt. In the early years of the rule of this remarkable man everything seemed to go well, and the material welfare of the country of Egypt appeared to be secured. Apparently Ismâ'îl was straining every nerve to rule his country according to Western ideas of justice and progress. Railways were built, schools were opened, trade of every kind was fostered, and agriculture, upon which the prosperity of Egypt depends, was encouraged to a remarkable degree. The making of the Suez Canal, which was begun in 1859, was carried on with great zeal under his auspices (as well as the Fresh Water Canal, which was begun in 1858 and finished in 1863), and the work was successfully accomplished in 1869. But the various enterprises in which he embarked cost
1875. large sums of money, and towards the end of 1875 his liabilities amounted to £77,667,569 sterling. The salaries of the officials were in arrear, and the Treasury bills were shunned by all. In this year he sold 176,602 Suez Canal shares to the British Government for £3,976,582 sterling; these shares
1878. are now worth over 25 millions sterling. In 1878 M. Waddington, the French Minister of Foreign Affairs, urged Lord Derby to co-operate with France in an attempt to put the finances of Egypt on a sounder base, and a Commission of Inquiry was instituted by the Decree of March 30, under the presidency of Mr. Rivers Wilson. In April Ismâ'îl was obliged to find the sum of £1,200,000 to pay the May coupon of the Unified Debt, and

* The Arabic form of the title is خُدَيْوِيّ *Khudêwîy.*

A.D.
1878. it is said that he did so by the familiar process of "squeezing" the native. The labours of the Commission proved that "the land tenures were so arranged that the wealthier proprietors evaded a great portion of the land tax, and the system of forced labour was applied in a way which was ruinous to the country." (Royle, *Egyptian Campaigns*, p. 6.) Ismâ'îl had built himself palaces everywhere, and he and his family had become possessed of one-fifth of the best of the land of Egypt. The taxes were collected with great cruelty and injury to the native, and peculation and bribery were rampant everywhere. In August of this year a Cabinet was formed with Nubar Pâsha at the head, with Rivers Wilson as Minister of Finance, and M. de Blignières as Minister of Public Works. At this time Ismâ'îl announced that he was, in future, determined to rule the country through a Council of Ministers. It must be remembered that the debt of Egypt at this time was about £90,000,000. On February 18th,
1879. 1879, Nubar Pâsha and his Cabinet were, owing to the machinations of Ismâ'îl, mobbed by about 2,500 officers and men at the Ministry of Finance, but at the critical moment Ismâ'îl himself appeared, and the uproar ceased. At the same time, however, he told the European Consuls-General that unless more power were given to him he would not be answerable for what might happen. Soon after this he issued a Decree to raise the number of men in the army to 60,000, and in April he reduced the interest on the Debt. When Nubar Pâsha resigned his office, Ismâ'îl appointed his own son Tawfîḳ as Prime Minister, but soon after this he dismissed the whole Cabinet and appointed

A.D.

1879. a set of native Ministers with Sherîf Pâsha as Prime Minister. As the result of this truly Oriental proceeding England and France, after much hesitation, demanded the deposition of Ismâ'îl from the Sulṭân. About this time Ismâ'îl sent large bribes to the Sulṭân, but these availed him nothing, and on June 25th Mr. Lascelles, the British Consul-General, and M. Tricon, the French Consul-General, together with Sherîf Pâsha, waited upon Ismâ'îl to inform him that he must at once abdicate in obedience to the orders of his sovereign master, the Sulṭân, which had been received from Constantinople. Ismâ'îl of course refused to do this, but about 10.30 a.m. a telegram addressed to Ismâ'îl Pâsha, late Khedive of Egypt, was received at the Abdîn Palace, and it was taken to him by Sherîf Pâsha, who called upon his master to resign in favour of **Tawfîḳ** Pâsha. Almost at the same hour Tawfîḳ received at the Isma'îlîyyeh Palace a telegram addressed to Muḥammad Tawfîḳ, Khedive of Egypt, and when he went to the Abdîn Palace with Sherîf Pâsha, who had come from there to tell him about the telegram to Ismâ'îl, he found his father ready to salute and to wish him better fortune than he himself had enjoyed. On Monday, the 30th of June, Ismâ'îl left Egypt in the Khedivial yacht for Smyrna, taking with him a large sum of money and about 300 women; in 1887 he settled in Constantinople, where he died in 1895. Under Tawfîḳ's rule the Control was restored, and on September 4 Rîaz Pâsha became Prime Minister.

1880. Commission of Liquidation appointed, and a number of reforms, including a reduction of the taxes, are made.

A.D.

1881. A rebellion headed by Aḥmad Arabi or "**Arabi Pâsha**" and others breaks out. Arabi was born in the year 1840 in Lower Egypt, and was the son of a peasant farmer. He offended Ismâ'îl, and was accused of malpractices and misappropriation of army stores, but this the despot forgave him, and promoted him to the rank of colonel, and gave him a royal slave to wife. Arabi was the leader of a secret society, the aim of which was to free Egypt from foreign interference and control, and to increase the army, and make Tawfîḳ appoint an Egyptian to the office of Minister of War in the place of Osman Rifki. These facts coming to the notice of the authorities, Arabi and two of his colleagues were ordered to be arrested, and when this had been done, and they had been taken to the barracks in Cairo for examination, the soldiers who were in their companies rushed into the rooms and rescued them. The rebel officers and men next went to the palace where Tawfîḳ was, and compelled him to grant their requests, and to do away with the cause of their dissatisfaction.

1881. On February 2 of this year Tawfîḳ was called upon to form a new Cabinet, and Arabi became Minister of War, and Maḥmûd Sami was appointed President of the Council; Arabi was created a Pâsha by the Sulṭân and his power became paramount. In May a serious dispute arose between Arabi and his colleagues and the Khedive; and on the 19th and 20th three British and three French vessels arrived at Alexandria. On May 25th the Consuls-General of England and France demanded the resignation of Maḥmûd Sami's Cabinet, and the retirement of Arabi from the

A.D.
1881. country. These demands were conceded on the following day, but shortly after Tawfîḳ reinstated Arabi, with the view of maintaining order and the tranquillity of the country. "On June 3 three more British and three more French warships arrived at Alexandria. On June 11 a serious riot broke out at Alexandria; and the British Consul was stoned and nearly beaten to death, and Mr. Ribton, a missionary, and a British naval officer and two seamen were actually killed." The massacre had been threatened by Maḥmûd Sami, and the riot was pre-arranged, and the native police and soldiery were parties to the murders of the Europeans which took place on that day; Mr. Royle (*Egyptian Campaigns*, p. 54) estimates the number of Europeans killed at 150. On June 25 the Sulṭân decorated Arabi with the Grand Order of the Medjidieh! On July 11 at 7 a.m. the **bombardment of Alexandria** was begun by H.M.S. "Alexandra" firing a shell into the newly made fortifications of the city, and the other British ships, "Inflexible," "Superb," "Sultan," "Téméraire," "Invincible," "Monarch," and "Penelope," soon after opened fire. After the bombardment was over the city was plundered and set on fire by the natives, and an idea of the damage done may be gained from the fact that the Commission of Indemnities awarded the claimants the sum of £4,341,011 sterling (Royle, *op. cit.*, p. 102). On July 14th British seamen were landed to protect the city, and on the 15th many forts were occupied by them. Early in August Arabi was removed from his post, and he at once began to prepare to resist the English soldiers who were known to be on their way to

A.D.

1881. Egypt; on August 15 Sir Garnet Wolseley arrived in Egypt; on the 18th the British fleet arrived at Port Ṣa'îd; on the 20th the British seized the Suez Canal, and the British Government was declared by M. de Lesseps to have paid to him £100,000 for loss of business! (Royle, *op. cit.*, p. 152). On September 13 Sir Garnet Wolseley was victorious at Tell el-Kebîr, at a cost of about 460 British officers and men; the Egyptians lost about 2,000, and several hundreds were wounded. On the 15th Cairo was occupied by the British, and the 10,000 Egyptian soldiers there submitted without fighting. On December 26th Arabi left Egypt for exile in Ceylon.

1883. A rebellion led by the **Mahdi** breaks out in the Sûdân. The Mahdi was one Muḥammad Aḥmad, a carpenter, who was born between 1840 and 1850; his native village was situated near the Island of Argo, in the province of Donḳola, and though poor, his parents declared that they belonged to the *Ashraf*, or "nobility," and claimed to be descendants of Muḥammad the Prophet. His father was a religious teacher, and had taught him to read and write. He studied at Berber under Muḥammad al-Khên, and later at Kharṭûm under the famous Shêkh Muḥammad Sherîf, and when he became a man he led a life of great asceticism on the Island of Abba in the White Nile. His piety and learning secured for him a great reputation in the Sûdân, and the greater number of the inhabitants sided with him in a serious quarrel which he had with Muḥammad Sherîf. He wandered about preaching against the Christians, and he declared that the decay in the Muḥammadan religion was due to the contact of Arabs

A.D.

1883. with Christians, that true faith was dead, and that he was deputed by God to restore it. He then attached a number of important people to himself, and having retired to Abba Island, he declared himself to be the "Mahdi," or the being whose advent had been foretold by Muḥammadan writers, who would restore the religion of the Arabs to its former purity. In July, 1881, Rauf Pâsha, the Governor-General of the Sûdân, sent for him to come to Kharṭûm, but the Mahdi refused, and six weeks later he and his followers defeated the Government troops which had been sent to bring him, and slew half of them. In December he defeated Rashîd Bey, the Governor of Fashôda, and slew nearly all the 400 soldiers which he had with him at Geddîn. In April, 1882, Giegler Pâsha, the temporary Governor-General, next attacked the Mahdi, and under his able generalship considerable loss was inflicted on the rebels; but on June 7 the Mahdi and his Dervishes massacred the combined forces of 'Abd-Allah and Yussuf Pâsha, and in September he besieged El-Obêd, which capitulated on January 17, 1883. In the same month Colonel **W. Hicks,** a retired Indian officer, was appointed head of the Army in the Sûdân, and on February 7 he left Cairo for Kharṭûm *viâ* Berber, which he reached on March 1; in April he set out against the Dervishes, and on the last day of the month he defeated about 4,000 of them and killed about 500. On September 9 he set out with reinforcements for Duêm, intending to recapture El-Obêd, but early in November the Mahdi attacked his force of about 10,000 men with some thousands of soldiers from the old Egyptian Army, near Lake Rahad, it is said, and the gallant Englishman and his officers and men, who were suffering greatly from want of water, having been led into an ambush, were cut to pieces.

A.D. Thus the Mahdi became master of the Sûdân.

1884. In February Baker Pâsha set out with about 3,800 men to relieve Sinkat, but his motley troops were defeated at Tokar, and about 2,400 of them slain, and thousands of rifles and much ammunition fell into the hands of the Dervishes. In January of this year **Charles George Gordon** (born January 28, 1833, murdered at Kharṭûm on the night of January 26, 1885) was sent to Kharṭûm to arrange for the evacuation of the Sûdân; he left Cairo on January 26 and arrived there on February 18. On February 28, General Graham defeated the Dervishes at **El-teb,** and nearly 1,000 of them were slain. On March 13 he defeated **Osman Diḳna's*** army at **Tamaai** and killed about 2,500 of his men; Osman's camp was burnt, and several hundred thousand of the cartridges which had been taken from Baker Pâsha were destroyed. On the 27th, Tamanib was occupied by Graham and then burnt. About the middle of April the Mahdi began to besiege Gordon in Kharṭûm, and preparations for a relief expedition were begun in England in May; this expedition was placed (August 26) under Sir Garnet Wolseley, who decided to attempt to reach Kharṭûm by ascending the Nile. This route made it necessary to travel 1,700 miles against the stream, and six cataracts, and other natural barriers, made the progress extremely slow; General Sir F. Stephenson, the highest authority on the subject,

* *i.e.*, "Osman of the beard"; he is the son of a Turkish merchant and slave dealer who settled in the Eastern Sûdân early in the XIXth century.

A.D.
1884. advised the route *viâ* Sawwaḳîn (Suâkin) and Berber, and by it troops could have entered Kharṭûm some months before Gordon was murdered. On the other hand it has been urged that, as the town of Berber surrendered on May 26, the main reason for an advance along the Suâkin-Berber road was taken away (*Sudan Campaign*, Pt. I, p. 25). The expedition consisted of 7,000 men, and all of them had reached Wâdî Ḥalfa by the end of November. On December 2, the troops at Donḳola set out for Korti, which was reached by Sir Herbert Stewart on the 13th of the same month. Here it was decided to send a part of the force to Kharṭûm across the desert, *viâ* Matemmah, and a part by way of the river. On December 30, Sir Herbert Stewart set out with about 1,100 officers
1885. and men, and on January 2 he seized the Gakdul Wells, 95 miles from Korti; after one day he returned with the greater part of his force to Korti (January 5) to fetch further supplies, having left 400 men at Gakdul to build forts and to guard the wells. On the 8th, he again set out for Gakdul, and on the 16th he reached a spot about four miles from the wells of **Abu Klea**,* and 23 miles from Matemmah; next day the famous battle of Abu Klea was fought, and 1,500 British soldiers defeated 11,000 Dervishes. The Dervishes succeeded in breaking the British square, but every one of them who got in was killed, and 1,100 of their dead were counted near it; their number of wounded was admitted by them to have been very large. On the 18th General

* More correctly Abu Tliḥ ابو طليح, *i.e.*, a place abounding in acacia trees.

A.D.

1885. Stewart moved on towards Matemmah and, after a march which lasted all day and all night, again fought the Dervishes on the 19th, and killed or wounded 800; in this fight, however, he received the wound of which he died. On the 20th **Abu Kru,** or Gubat, was occupied by the British: on the 21st Sir Charles Wilson attempted to take Matemmah, but the force at his command was insufficient for the purpose. On the 22nd the British soldiers began to build two forts at Abu Kru; on the 23rd Sir C. Wilson began to make the steamers ready to go to Kharṭûm; and on the 24th he set out with two steamers and twenty men. Four days later he came to Tuti Island and found that Kharṭûm was in the hands of the Mahdi, whereupon he ordered his vessels to turn and run down the river with all speed; when they were out of the reach of the enemy's fire, Sir C. Wilson stopped them and sent out messengers to learn what had happened, and it was found that Kharṭûm had fallen on the night of the 26th, and that Gordon had been murdered a little before sunrise on the 27th. His head was cut off and taken to the Mahdi, but his body was left in the garden for a whole day, and thousands of Dervishes came and plunged their spears into it; later the head was thrown into a well. On February 13 the British troops, including those which had marched with General Buller to Gubat, retreated to Abu Klea, and a fortnight later they set out for Korti, which they reached on March 1. The portion of the British troops which attempted to reach Khartûm by river left Korti on December 28, 1884, and reached Berti on February 1, 1885, and on the 9th was fought the battle of

A.D.
1885. Kirbekan, in which General Earle was shot dead On the 17th the house, palm trees, and water-wheels of Sulêmân Wad Gamr, who murdered Colonel Stewart, were destroyed, and on the 24th, orders having been received to withdraw, the river column made ready to return to Korti, which was reached on the 8th of March. When it was seen that Lord Wolseley's expedition had failed to bring Gordon from Kharṭûm, it was decided by the British Government to break the power of Osman Diḳna, and with this object in view the Suâkin Expedition was planned. On February 17, 1885, the British Government made a contract with Messrs. Lucas and Aird to construct a railway of 4 feet 8½ inches gauge from Suâkin to Berber. On the 20th General Graham was placed in command of the Suâkin Field Force, which consisted of about 10,500 officers and men. On March 20 General Graham fought an action at Hashin, and two days later a fierce fight took place at Tofrik, between Suâkin and Tamaai. General McNeill was attacked by about 3,000 Dervishes, of whom 1,000 were killed, but the British loss was, relatively, considerable. In May the British Government recalled Graham's expedition, and abandoned the making of the railway to Berber, and thus Osman Diḳna was again able to boast that he had driven the English out of the country (Royle, *Sudan Campaigns*, p. 436). On June 22, the **death of the Mahdi** occurred; he was succeeded by 'Abd-Allah, better known as the "**Khalîfa.**" In July the last of the British troops of Lord Wolseley's expedition left Donḳola; by the end of September nearly the whole country as far north as Wâdi Ḥalfa was in the hands of the Mahdi, and

it was seen that, unless checked, the Dervishes would invade Egypt. General Sir F. Stephenson and General Sir Francis Grenfell attacked them at Kosheh and Ginnis on December 30, and about 1,000 of the Mahdi's troops were killed and wounded.

A.D.

1886. Towards the close of this year Osman Diḳna withdrew from Suâkin to Omdurmân, partly because the Arabs about Suâkin had defeated his troops and occupied Tamaai, and partly because he hoped for much benefit from the Mahdi's attack on Egypt.

1887. In June, Osman Diḳna returned to Suâkin with about 2,000 Baggara Dervishes, but failed to move the people of the country; in the following month he returned to Omdurmân, but hearing that the Egyptian garrison at Suâkin had been reduced, he returned with 5,000 men and determined to capture the city.

1888. On January 17, Colonel (now Lord) Kitchener, at the head of some friendly Arabs, attacked and captured the Dervish camp, but eventually the Dervishes re-formed and turned the Egyptian victory into a defeat. On December 20, General Grenfell, with reinforcements, attacked Osman Diḳna's troops and killed and wounded 500 of them.

1889. In April Wad en-Negûmi had advanced as far north as Hafîr with about 5,000 men, and another 1,000 were at Sarras, only about 33 miles south of Wâdi Ḥalfa. On July 1, Colonel Wodehouse, with about 2,000 Egyptian soldiers, defeated the Dervishes, under Wad en-Negûmi, at Argîn, near Wâdi Ḥalfa, killing 900 and taking 500 prisoners. On the 5th, General Grenfell left Cairo for the south with reinforcements, and made arrangements to meet the attack of Wad en-Negûmi, who, undaunted by his defeat at Argîn, was marching north; and on August 1 this redoubtable warrior

A.D.
1889. collected his force of 3,300 men and 4,000 followers on the hills to the south of Tushki, or Toski. On the 3rd General Grenfell disposed his British and Egyptian troops in such a way as to check the advance of Wad en-Negûmi, who, however, only wished to get away and not to fight. He was at length forced to fight, and he fought bravely, but General Grenfell's tactics were so thoroughly well planned and carried out, that the Dervish force was completely routed and destroyed. About 1,200 were killed and 4,000 were taken prisoners, and the Egyptian loss only amounted to 25 killed and 140 wounded. The effect on the country was marvellous, for, as Mr. Royle says (*op. cit.*, p. 485), "the victory of Toski marked the turning point in the invasion, and was a shock to the cause of Mahdism which it took years to recover." The Dervish reinforcements beat a hasty retreat, and the Mahdi suspended all further operations for the invasion of Egypt.

1890. Osman Diḳna continued to make raids upon Suâkin from Tokar.

1891. In January Colonel (now Sir C.) Holled-Smith set out to attack Osman Diḳna, and on February 19 he routed the enemy at Tokar, killing 700 men.

1892–1895. Osman Diḳna continued to harass the Arabs round Suâkin, and made raids wherever he thought he had any chance of success. On January 7, 1892, the Khedive, Tawfîk Pâsha, died after a short illness at Ḥelwân, and he was succeeded by his eldest son, **Abbâs II. Hilmy**; the Imperial Firman from the Porte confirming his succession cost about £6,154, and was read on April 14.

1896. In the early part of this year Osman Diḳna's forces were attacked and defeated with great loss by

A. D.

1896. Colonel Lloyd, Major Sydney, and Captain Fenwick. On February 29 the Italians were defeated with severe loss at Adowa, and the Italian garrison at Kassala was in imminent danger from the Dervishes. With a view of assisting Italy by making it necessary for the Dervishes to turn their attention elsewhere, the British Government determined to advance to Akasheh and Donḳola. In the hands of General Kitchener, who had succeeded General Grenfell as Sirdar of the Egyptian Army in April, 1892, the conduct of the new Sûdân Expedition was placed. On March 21 he left Cairo for the south, and the first serious skirmish between the Dervishes and Egyptians took place on May 1. Early in June the Sirdar divided his forces, and one column marched upon **Ferket** by way of the river, and another across the desert. On June 7 the two columns joined hands, and a fierce fight ensued. The Sirdar's arrangements were so skilfully made and carried out, that the Dervishes were utterly routed; they lost about 1,000 killed and wounded, and 500 were made prisoners. Among the killed were about forty of their chief men. The Egyptian loss was 100 killed and wounded. On September 19 the Sirdar occupied Hafîr after a fight, and four days later the Egyptian troops entered Donḳola; Debbeh, Korti, and Marawî were next occupied, and the country as far as the foot of the Fourth Cataract was once more in the hands of the Egyptians.

1897. Early in this year the decision to make the Wâdi Ḥalfa and Abu-Ḥamed Railway was arrived at, for the Sirdar regarded it as absolutely necessary; by this route nearly 350 miles of difficult river transport would be avoided. When the railway had

A.D.

1897. advanced considerably more than half way to Abu Ḥamed, General Hunter marched from Marawî to Abu Ḥamed and defeated the Dervishes, who held it in force, and occupied it on August 7. Of the Dervish garrison of 1,500 men, about 1,300 were killed and wounded. Soon afterwards the Dervishes evacuated Berber, which was entered by General Hunter on September 13. On October 31 the railway reached Abu-Ḥamed.

1898. On April 8th, Good Friday, the Sirdar utterly defeated the great Dervish force under Maḥmûd at the **Battle of the Atbara**; the Dervish loss was about 3,000 killed, and 2,000 were taken prisoners, while the Sirdar's loss was under 600 killed and wounded. The forces engaged on each side were about 14,000. On September 2nd the capture of Omdurmân and the **defeat of the Khalîfa** 'Abdu-Allahi were accomplished by the Sirdar. The Khalîfa's forces numbered at least 50,000, and those of the Sirdar about 22,000. The Dervish loss was at least 11,000 killed and 16,000 wounded, and over 4,000 were made prisoners; the Sirdar's loss was rather more than 400 killed and wounded. The Khalîfa escaped and fled south, having first taken care to bury his treasure; the body of the Mahdi was removed from its tomb, and burnt, and the ashes were thrown into the Nile; the head is said to be buried at Wâdi Ḥalfa. The tomb was destroyed because, if left untouched, it would always have formed a centre for religious fanaticism and sedition. On Sunday, September 4, the Sirdar held a memorial service for General Gordon at Kharṭûm, when the British and Egyptian flags were hoisted. On the 19th the Sirdar hoisted the Egyptian flag at Fashôda, which had been occupied by Major Marchand, the head of a French expedition, who sought to claim as a right a position on the Nile on behalf of France.

A.D.

1899.* In January General Kitchener set out to catch the Khalîfa, who had fled towards Kordofân, but his expedition failed for want of water. In November it was said that the Khalîfa was at Gebel Geddîr, which lay to the north-west of Fashôda, on the west bank of the Nile, and about 160 miles from the river. The Sirdar pursued with a large force, but the Khalîfa fled towards Khartûm. On November 22 Colonel (now Sir) F. R. Wingate (now Sirdar of the Egyptian army) pursued him to Abba Island on the Nile, and learning that he was encamped at Umm Dabrikât, attacked him on the 24th. After a fierce but short fight in the early morning, Colonel Wingate defeated the Khalîfa, killing over 1,000 of his men, and taking prisoners 3,000. The Khalîfa met his fate like a man, and seeing that all was lost, seated himself upon a sheepskin with his chief Emîrs, and with them fell riddled with bullets. The Egyptian loss was 15 killed and wounded. The death of the Khalîfa was the death-blow to Mahdism.

---

*On March 4 of this year, Mr. John M. Cook, the late head of the firm of Thomas Cook and Son, died at Walton-on-Thames. The services which he rendered to the Egyptian Government were very considerable. In the Gordon Relief Expedition his firm transported from Asyût to Wâdî Ḥalfa, a distance of about 550 miles, Lord Wolseley's entire force, which consisted of 11,000 British and 7,000 Egyptian troops, 800 whalers, and 130,000 tons of stores and war materials. In 1885, 1886, and 1896 his firm again rendered invaluable services to the Government, and one is tempted to regret,

A.D.

1900. In January Osman Diḳna was in hiding near Tokar, and Muḥammad 'Ali, the loyal Gamilab Shêkh, found that he had entered his country. Major Burges and Aḥmad Bey, left Suâkin on January 8 and 10 respectively, and a few days later they arrived at the Warriba range, which about 90 miles to the south-west of Suâkin; and there Osman was seen apparently waiting to partake of a meal from a recently killed sheep. At the sight of his pursuers he fled up a hill, but was soon caught, and was despatched from Suâkin in the S.S. "Behera," and arrived at Suez on January 25, *en route* for Rosetta, where he now lies in prison. On September 25 Slatin Pâsha was appointed British Inspector of the Sûdân. On November 2 Major Hobbs opened a branch of the Bank of Egypt at Kharṭûm.

1902. On February 4 Kaimakam Matthews reported that the Ṣudd would be cleared from Baḥral-Jabal by about March 1.

---

with Mr. Royle (*The Egyptian Campaigns*, p. 554), that, in view of the melancholy failure of the Gordon Relief Expedition, his contract did not include the rescue of Gordon and the Sûdân garrisons. He transported the wounded to Cairo by water after the battle of Tell el-Kebîr, and when the British Army in Egypt was decimated with enteric fever, conveyed the convalescents by special steamers up the Nile, and made no charge in either case except the actual cost of running the steamers. He was greatly beloved by the natives, and the Luxor Hospital, which he founded, is one of the many evidences of the interest which he took in their welfare. Thousands of natives were employed in his service, and it would be difficult to estimate the benefits which accrued indirectly to hundreds of families in all parts of the country through his energy and foresight.

Dates assigned to the Egyptian Dynasties by Egyptologists.

Dynasty.		Champollion-Figeac.	Lepsius (in 1858).	Brugsch (in 1877).	Mariette.
I.	B.C.	5,867	3,892	4,400	5,004
II.		5,615	3,639	4,133	4,751
III.		5,318	3,338	3,966	4,449
IV.		5,121	3,124	3,733	4,235
V.		4,673	2,840	3,566	3,951
VI.		4,425	2,744	3,300	3,703
VII.		4,222	2,592	3,100	3,500
VIII.		4,147	2,522	—	3,500
IX.		4,047	2,674	—	3,358
X.		3,947	2,565	—	3,249
XI.		3,762	2,423	—	3,064
XII.		3,703	2,380	2,466	2,851
XIII.		3,417	2,136	2,235	—
XIV.		3,004	2,167	—	2,398
XV.		2,520	2,101	—	2,214
XVI.		2,270	1,842	—	—
XVII.		2,082	1,684	—	—
XVIII.		1,822	1,591	1,700	1,703
XIX.		1,473	1,443	1,400	1,462
XX.		1,279	1,269	1,200	1,288
XXI.		1,101	1,091	1,100	1,110
XXII.		971	961	966	980
XXIII.		851	787	766	810
XXIV.		762	729	733	721
XXV.		718	716	700	715
XXVI.		674	685	666	665
XXVII.		524	525	527	527
XXVIII.		404	525	—	406
XXIX.		398	399	399	399
XXX.		377	378	378	378
XXXI.		339	340	340	340

PROGRESS IN EGYPT UNDER BRITISH RULE.

The progress made in Egypt since the country passed under the rule of the British is astonishing, even to those who knew its wonderfully recuperative powers. Its material prosperity is so great and advances with such rapid strides that it is difficult to understand its miserable and bankrupt condition at the time of Arabi Pâsha's rebellion. A journey through the country reveals the fact that for one beast seen in the fields at that time, ten may now be counted, for the peasant farmer need not now fear the sudden descent of arbitrary tax-gatherers who would carry off the occupants of his fields and byres. In the towns and villages the houses are better built and kept in better repair, for their owners need not fear that the laying on of a coat of paint or whitewash will be taken as evidence that they possess superfluous cash, and so bring down upon themselves a visit from the local revenue officer and increased taxation. The water supply is regulated with justice, and the peasant obtains his due as surely and as regularly as the Pâsha, and it is now impossible for any large landowner to irrigate his garden at the expense of the parched plots of his poor neighbours. One of the greatest boons which Britain has conferred upon the Egyptian is the abolition of the **Corvée.** The work to be done by the corvée was of two kinds, viz., (1) to make and upkeep earthworks, *i.e.*, to cut and clean canals, etc., (2) to protect the river banks during the inundation. The liability of the Egyptian male to be called upon to do work of the former class was abolished in 1889, and although it costs Egypt £420,000 per annum to do without forced labour, it is admitted on all hands that the expenditure is justified. Under the old system the most shameful abuses crept in, and hundreds of the official classes had their houses built, canals cut and cleaned, and estates watered entirely by the corvée. The iniquity of the system was that it pressed hardest upon the poorest classes. Mr. Willcocks, of the Egyptian Irrigation Department, first showed that by adopting improved methods the necessity for much of the labour was done away with, and its abolition is one of Viscount Cromer's most brilliant achievements. It must not be forgotten that men have to be called out each year to protect the river banks in time of flood, and that all the inhabitants may be called out in any sudden emergency, the following figures give the numbers for the last few years of those called out :—

1891	...	...	...	...	...	44,962
1892	...	...	...	...	...	84,391
1893	...	...	...	...	...	32,752
1894	...	...	...	...	...	49,448
1895	...	...	...	...	...	36,982
1896	...	...	...	...	...	25,794
1897	...	...	...	...	...	11,069
1898	...	...	...	...	...	10,079
1899	...	...	...	...	...	7,893
1900	...	...	...	...	...	14,180
1900	...	...	...	...	...	8,763*

The official returns show the increase in the **revenue** during the last ten years :—

						£E
1890	...	...	...	...	...	10,237,000
1891	...	...	...	...	...	10,539,000
1892	...	...	...	...	...	10,297,000
1893	...	...	...	...	...	10,242,000
1894	...	...	...	...	...	10,161,000
1895	...	...	...	...	...	10,431,000
1896	...	...	..	...	...	10,694,000
1897	...	...	...	...	...	11,093,000
1898	...	...	...	...	...	11,132,000
1899	...	...	...	...	...	11,200,000
1900	...	...	...	...	...	11,663,000
1901	...	...	...	.	...	12,160,000

* Parliamentary Papers, Egypt No. 1, 1900, p. 19; Egypt No. 1, 1902, p 24.

This has been the case notwithstanding that a considerable diminution in taxation has been effected; the taxation per head of the population was in 1881 £1 2*s.* 2*d.*, and that of the debt £14 8*s.* 9*d.*; in 1897 the corresponding figures were 17*s.* 9*d.* and £10 0*s.* 2*d.* (Mr. Dawkins, in Milner, *England in Egypt*, p. 384). Between 1890 and 1901 taxes to the extent of £E1,408,000 per annum have been remitted. The following, taken from the Parliamentary Papers (1896, No. 1, p. 3, etc.), will show the amounts of **surplus** and **deficit** between 1883 and 1901—

	Surplus. £ E.	Deficit. £ E.		Surplus. £ E.	Deficit. £ E.
1883	—	920,000	1893	720,000	—
1884	—	460,000	1894	785,000	—
1885	—	697,000	1895	1,088,000	—
1886	—	684,000	1896	690,000	—
1887	111,000	—	1897	630,000	—
1888	—	1,000	1898	1,376,000	—
1889	160,000	—	1899	1,848,000	—
1890	591,000	—	1900	559,000	—
1891	951,000	—	1901	764,000	—
1892	769,000	—			

The financial situation on December 30, 1901, may be thus summarised:—

The **National Debt** £E.103,710,000, but £E.7,273,000 of this sum was held by the Commissioners of the Public Debt. There is no floating debt. The General **Reserve Fund** amounted to £E.3,795,000; the Special Reserve Fund to £E.1,287,000; and the accumulated Conversion Economies amounted to £E.4,485,000. The Economies Fund "is invested in Egyptian bonds, and Egypt is therefore becoming *pro tanto* the holder of her own debt. But to buy up your debts at a premium of 8 per cent., instead of paying them off at par, a premium continually forced up by further obligatory purchases on your own part, is extravagant finance. It is an extravagance forced on Egypt by international conventions, for which, in the present case, the word 'France' might be used"

(Dawkins, *op. cit.*, p. 302). The sum of £E.2,500,000 which was spent on the Sûdân Expedition in 1896-98 may be regarded as a good investment, for as assets Egypt has 760 miles of railway, with an adequate number of engines, rolling-stock, etc.; 2,000 miles of telegraph line, six new gun-boats, barges, etc., *and* the whole Sûdân (Kitchener's speech in London, Nov. 4, 1898). **Railways** in 1899 brought in £E.1,222,000. The cost of the repairs to the Embâbeh Bridge has been very large. The bridge was built by a French firm for £E.80,000, but £E.43,000 (!) more has had to be spent upon it before it was safe for traffic. **Telegraphs** brought in £E.64,000; **salt**, under the new regulations, brought in £E.223,000; **customs** £E.2,563,193, being £145,218 in excess of the revenue in 1900. The revenue from this last source has, therefore, increased greatly for the amount collected in 1889 only amounted to £E.1,027,000. The value of the **Imports** in 1901 was £E.15,245,000, which is £E.1,133,000 more than the figure for 1900; and the value of the **Exports** was £E.15,730,000, a decrease of £E.1,036,000 over 1900. The **Post Office** yields a net revenue to the Government of £E.28,000. The total number of persons confined in prisons in 1901 was 9,357; 11 cases of prosecution for **slave dealing** were carried on in 1900; 23,447 cases were treated in the Government hospitals; 357,000 successful vaccinations were made in 1900; 80,011 legal cases were brought before Native Tribunals; the system of Village Justice evolved by Lord Cromer and his legal advisers has proved to be a great success; the powers of the Mixed Tribunals have been modified, and considerable alterations have been made in the application of Muḥammadan Law. In **Education** great strides have been made. In 1887 only 1,919 pupils were under the direct management of the Department of Public Instruction; in 1898 the number had grown to 19,684, and in 1899 to

23,390. The school fees in 1887 were £E.9,000, and in 1899 £E.36,000. It is a remarkable fact that the percentage of Muḥammadan pupils in schools and colleges under the Department is less than the percentage of the Muḥammadans in the total population, while the percentage of Coptic pupils in the same schools is almost treble the percentage of Copts throughout Egypt. Thus Muḥammadans form 93 per cent. of the total population, and the number of their children in the schools forms 78 per cent. of the pupils; the Copts form 6 per cent. of the total population, but the number of their children in the schools forms 17 per cent. of the pupils. At the beginning of the British occupation of Egypt the principal European language taught in the Government schools was French; English was either altogether neglected or was very badly taught. The schools of the American Missionaries were the only places where English was taught, and the splendid services rendered by these institutions in this respect must not be forgotten. Until the last few years nearly every railway, postal, or telegraph official in Egypt who possessed any competent knowledge of the English language owed his instruction to the American missionaries. The following figures illustrate the growth of the study of English in Government schools:—

	English.	French.
1889	1,063 ...	2,994
1890	1,747 ...	3,199
1891	2,032 ...	2,852
1892	2,237 ...	2,864
1893	2,434 ...	2,585
1894	2,669 ...	3,748
1895	2,665 ...	3,417
1896	2,800 ...	3,363
1897	3,058 ...	3,150
1898	3,859 ...	1,881
1899	4,401 ...	1,210

Thus in 1899 about 78 per cent. of the pupils were studying English and 22 per cent. French; in 1889 the figures were 26 per cent. and 74 per cent. respectively. In 1884 about 360,000 tons of **coal** were imported at Alexandria, and 726,000 at Port Ṣa'îd; in 1901 these numbers had risen to 867,150 and 228,865 tons respectively. In January, 1882, "Egyptian Unifieds" were quoted at 61⅛, and in January, 1901, at 106½. Worthy of mention too is the success of the societies which have been established in Cairo, Alexandria, and Port Ṣa'îd for the prevention of cruelty to animals. In Cairo 1,178 animals were treated in the infirmary in 1900, in Alexandria 2,384, and in Port Sa'îd 159; it is good to learn that Lord Cromer thinks the action of these societies is causing a steady improvement in the condition of the animals employed in the towns where the societies exist. The productive and recuperative powers of Egypt have been proverbial from time out of mind, but the most sanguine reformer of Egypt in 1883 could never have expected that the last year of the century would have witnessed such a state of prosperity in the country as now exists. This is due entirely to the fidelity with which the civil and military officials have performed their duties, and to the carrying out of the consistent and wise policy which was inaugurated by Viscount Cromer, whose strong hand has ceaselessly guided and supported every work which tended to the welfare and prosperity of Egypt.

Ceiling ornament at Philæ.

THE COUNTRY OF EGYPT.

Geology.—In ancient days Egypt proper terminated at Aswân (Syene), but now the term Egypt includes that portion of the Nile valley which lies between the Mediterranean and Wâdî Ḥalfa, *i.e.*, between 22° and 31° 30′ N. latitude. According to Major H. G. Lyons,* Director-General of Surveys of Egypt, the country consists chiefly of a series of sedimentary deposits of Cretaceous and Tertiary ages, which have been laid down upon the uneven and eroded surface of a great mass of crystalline rocks, which come to the surface on the edge of the eastern desert and also cover large areas of it. The direction of the Nile Valley is generally north and south, and is due to the great earth movements which took place in Miocene times; indeed, the Nile Valley itself has been determined by a line of fracture which is traceable from the sea nearly to the First Cataract. Into this valley in late Miocene or early Pliocene times the sea penetrated at least as far as Esneh, and laid down thick deposits of sand and gravel on the floor of the valley and up to the foot of the cliffs bounding it, while the tributary streams, fed by a rainfall much heavier than that of to-day, brought down masses of detritus from the limestone plateaux and piled them up along the margins of the valley. A subsequent rise of the area converted this "fiord" into a river valley, and the deposition of the Nile mud and the formation of cultivable land began. The crystalline rocks occur at Aswân, Kalâbsheh, Wâdî Ḥalfa, and other points further south, forming cataracts and gorges. East and north-east of Ḳeneh

* I quote from his description of the geology of Egypt written for Major Willcocks, C.M.G., and printed in *Egyptian Irrigation*, 2nd edition, London, 1899.

their base is a gneiss, overlaid by mica, talc, and chlorite schists, and above these is a thick volcanic series, into which intrudes a gray hornblendic granite, and also a later red granite. The best known of these is the red hornblendic granite of Aswân, which was largely used by the Egyptians for temples, statues, etc., and also the fine porphyry, much used by the Roman emperors. The tops of such rocks rise to the surface of the ground at Aswân, Kalâbsheh, and Wâdî Ḥalfa. In Nubia nearly the whole of the eroded surface of the crystalline rocks has been overlaid by a yellowish sandstone, which at its base usually becomes a quartz conglomerate. Above these lies a large series of green and gray clays with thick band of soft white limestone. Next comes an immense thickness of soft white limestone, which forms the cliffs of the Nile Valley from Luxor to Cairo, and furnishes almost the whole of the building stone in Egypt. These strata have been greatly affected by the great earth movements of the Miocene period, which resulted in the formation of the Red Sea, Gulf of Suez, Gulf of Aqaba, the Jordan Valley, and the Nile Valley, and the salts of the Wâdî Naṭrûn are due to the shore lagunes when they existed there. As a result of this, thick deposits of sand and gravel were laid down, which to-day underlie the later Nile mud deposits and which furnish a good water supply. After this, climatic conditions analogous to those of to-day seem to have soon set in, and river deposits of dark sandy mud were laid down, which were at levels considerably above the deposits of to-day. Nile mud with shells similar to those now existing occurs in Nubia at 30 metres, and in Egypt at lesser heights, above the present Nile flood level. To-day the Nile is depositing in its bed at the rate of about 0·12 metre per century. At Benha, Maḥallat Rûḥ (in the Ṭanṭa district), and Ḳalyûb (all in the Delta), the thickness of the layer of Nile mud is 17, 18, and 12·5 metres respectively; while at Zaḳâziḳ, Beni Suwêf, and Suhâg (all in the Nile Valley), it is 33·11 and 17 metres respectively. Between the First and Second Cataracts the proportion of sandstone to granite is about 9 to 1, and good granite is only met with at Kalâbsheh, where the pass is about 168 yards wide, and the depth of water at *low* Nile about 111 feet. No fossils whatever are found in the Nubian sandstone. From Abû Simbel northwards the valley is bounded on the left by the high limestone plateau called by the Arabs Sinn al-Kiddâb, which, at this point, is more than 50 miles distant from the river, and it gradually approaches the stream until at Aswân it is only 25 miles distant, and at Gebelên it marches with the river. There is a similar plateau between Gebelên and Esneh. At the First Cataract there is an extensive outcrop of granite and quartz diorite. Between Aswân and a little south of Esneh the river flows between sandstone hills, except at the plains of Kom Ombos and Edfu; these plains were originally ancient deltas of rivers coming down from the high ranges which skirt the Red Sea. In the Kom Ombos plain the Nile deposit is about 80 feet above the maximum flood level of to-day. At Ra'âmah, about 38 miles north of Aswân, limestone is met with, and immediately north of it is the sandstone of Silsileh. The channel at Silsileh does not represent the original bed of the Nile, for it is only a branch of it; the true channel, which was nearly a mile wide and 50 feet deep, lies on the right of the hill in which the quarries are, and is now buried under mud and silt. There was never a cataract at Silsileh. At Luxor the Nile again enters low denuded plains, and a part of the plateau of the Sinn al-Kiddâb lies on its left; the plateau again appears at Ḳeneh, and from this place to Cairo the river flows between limestone hills. At Ḳeneh the lower Londinian formation dips below the level of the Nile deposit, and the upper Londinian formation monopolises the whole section of the limestone as far as a point midway between Asyûṭ and Minyeh; here the lower Parisian strata appear on the tops of the plateaux, and the upper Londinian strata finally disappear a little to the north of Minyeh. The lower Parisian formation is now generally met with as far as Cairo.

The Ancient Egyptians called Egypt *Baq* or *Baqet*; *Ta-merȧ*; and *Qemt*. Baq seems to refer to Egypt as the olive-producing country, and Ta-merȧ as the land of the inundation; the name by which it is most commonly called in the inscriptions is Qem, *i.e.*, "Black," from the darkness of its soil. It was also called the "land of the sycamore," and the "land of the eye of Horus" (*i.e.*, the Sun). It was divided by the Egyptians into two parts: I. Upper Egypt *Ta-res* or *Ta-qemā*, "the southern land"; and II. Lower Egypt, *Ta-meḥ*, "the northern land." The kings of Egypt styled themselves *suten net* (or *bȧt*), "king of the North and South," and *neb taui*, "lord of two earths."* The country was divided into nomes, the number of which is variously given; the list given by some of the classical authorities contains thirty-six, but judging by the monuments the number was nearer forty. The nome (*ḥesp*) was divided into four parts; 1, the capital town (*nut*); 2, the cultivated land; 3, the marshes, which could only at times be used for purposes of cultivation; and 4, the canals, which had to be kept clear and provided with sluices, etc., for irrigation purposes. During the rule of the Greeks Egypt was divided into three parts: Upper, Central, and

* As ruler of the two countries, each king wore the crown, which was made up of, the *teśer*, or red crown, representing the northern part of Egypt, and, the *ḥet'*, or white crown, representing the southern part of Egypt.

Lower Egypt; Central Egypt consisted of seven nomes, and was called **Heptanomis.**

LIST OF NOMES OF EGYPT—UPPER EGYPT.

	Nome.	Capital.	Divinity.
1.	Ta-Kens.	Ābu (Elephantine), in later times Nubt (Ombos).	Khnemu.
2.	Tes-Ḥeru.	Ṭeb (Apollinopolis magna, Arab. Uṭfu or Edfû).	Ḥeru - Beḥu tet.
3.	Ten.	Nekheb (Eileithyia), in later times Sene (Latopolis), Esneh.	Nekheb.
4.	Uast.	Uast (Thebes), in later times Hermonthis.	Åmen-Rā.
5.	Ḥerui.	Kebti (Coptos).	Åmsu.
6.	Āa-ti.	Taenterer (Denderah).	Hathor (Ḥet Ḥert).
7.	Sekhem.	Ḥa (Diospolis parva).	Hathor.
8.	Åbṭ.	Åbṭu (Abydos), in earlier times Teni (This).	Anḥur.
9.	Åmsu.	Åpu (Panopolis).	Åmsu.
10.	Uat'et.	Ṭebu (Aphroditopolis).	Hathor.
11.	Set.	Shasḥetep (Hypsele).	Khnemu.
12.	Ṭuf.	Nen-ent-bak (Antaeopolis).	Horus.
13.	Atefkhent.	Saiut (Lycopolis, Arab Sîûṭ).	Åp-uat.
14.	Atef-peḥ.	Kesi (Cusae).	Hathor.
15.	Un.	Khemennu (Hermopolis).	Thoth.
16.	Meḥ-maḥet.	Ḥebennu (Hipponon).	Horus.
17.	. . . .	Kasa (Cynonpolis).	Anubis.
18.	Sapet.	Ḥa-suten (Alabastronpolis).	Anubis.
19.	Uab.	Pa-mat'et (Oxyrhynchos).	Set.
20.	Am-khent.	Khenensu (Heracleopolis magna).	Ḥeru-shefi.

	Nome.	Capital.	Divinity.
21.	Am-peḥ.	Se-men Ḥeru.	Khnemu.
22.	Maten.	Ṭep-âḥet (Aphroditopolis).	Hathor.

LOWER EGYPT.

	Nome.	Capital.	Divinity.
1.	Aneb-ḥet'.	Men-nefer (Memphis).	Ptaḥ.
2.	Aā.	Sekhem (Letopolis).	Ḥeru-ur.
3.	Àment.	Nenten-Ḥapi (Apis).	Ḥathor-nub
4.	Sepi-res.	T'eka (Canopus).	Àmen-Rā.
5.	Sepi-emḥet.	Sa (Sais).	Neit.
6.	Kaset	Khesun (Xoïs).	Àmen-Rā.
7.	. . . Àment.	Sent-Nefer (Metelis).	Ḥu.
8.	. . . Àbṭet.	T'ukot (Sethroë).	Atmu.
9.	At'i.	Per-Àusàr (Busiris).	Osiris.
10.	Kakem.	Ḥataḥeràb (Athribis).	Ḥeru-khenti khati.
11.	Kaḥebes.	Kaḥebes (Kabasos).	Isis.
12.	Kat'eb.	T'eb-neter (Sebennythos).	Anḥur
13.	Ḥakaṭ.	Ànnu (Heliopolis).	Rā.
14.	Khent-àbeṭ.	T'an (Tanis).	Horus.
15.	Teḥuti.	Pa-Teḥuti (Hermopolis).	Thoth.
16.	Khar.	Pabaneb-ṭeṭ (Mendes).	Ba-neb-ṭeṭ
17.	Sam-beḥutet.	Pa-khen-en-Àmen (Diospolis).	Àmen-Rā.
18.	Amchent.	Pa-Bast (Bubastis).	Bast.
19.	Am-peḥ.	Pa-Uat' (Buto).	Uat'.
20.	Sept.	Kesem (Phakussa).	Sept.

Lower Egypt is divided into six provinces :—

1. **Baḥêrah,** with seven districts ; capital, Damanhûr Population (including the Oasis of Sîwa, 7,200), 631,225.
2. **Ḳalyubîyah,** with three districts ; capital, Benha. Population, 371,465.
3. **Sharḳîyah,** with six districts ; capital, Zaḳâziḳ. Population, 749,130.

4. **Daḳhalîyah,** with six districts; capital, Manṣûrah. Population, 736,708.
5. **Menûfîyah,** with five districts; capital, Menûf. Population, 864,206.
6. **Gharbîyah,** with eleven districts; capital, Tanṭa. Population, 1,297,656.

Upper Egypt is divided into seven districts:—

1. **Gîzeh,** with four districts; capital, Gîzeh. Population, 401,634.
2. **Beni-Suwêf,** with three districts; capital, Beni-Suêf. Population, 314,454.
3. **Minyeh,** with eight districts; capital, Minyeh. Population (including the Oasis of Baḥrîyah (6,082), and the Oasis of Farâfra (542)), 548,632.
4. **Asyûṭ,** with nine districts; capital, Asyût. Population (including the Oasis of Dâkhlah (17,090), and the Oasis of Khargah (7,220)), 782,720.
5. **Girgeh,** with five districts; capital, Ṣûhag. Population, 668,011.
6. **Ḳeneh,** with seven districts: capital, Ḳeneh. Population, 711,457.
7. **Fayyûm,** with three districts; capital, Wasṭa. Population, 371,006.

Large towns like Alexandria, Port Sa'îd, Suez, Cairo, Damietta, and El'arîsh are governed by native rulers.

In ancient days the population of Egypt proper is said to have been from seven and a half to nine millions; at the present time (1900) it is probably well over ten millions. The population of the provinces south of Egypt, which originally belonged to her, has never been accurately ascertained. The country on each side of the Baḥr el-Abyaḍ is very thickly peopled; it is generally thought that the population of this and the other provinces which belonged to Egypt in the time of Ismâ'îl amounts to about ten millions.

THE ANCIENT EGYPTIANS.

The Egyptians, whom the sculptures and monuments made known to us as being among the most ancient inhabitants of the country, belong, according to some, to the Caucasian race, and according to others, to the Libyan. The original home of the invaders was, probably, Asia, and they made their way across Mesopotamia and Arabia, and across the Isthmus of Suez into Egypt. It has been suggested that they sailed across the Indian Ocean and up the Red Sea, on the western shore of which they landed; that they came viâ Arabia is more probable. It is, however, very doubtful if a people, who lived in the middle of a huge land like central Asia, would have enough experience to make and handle ships sufficiently large to cross such seas. No period can be fixed for the arrival of the new-comers from the East into Egypt; we are, however, justified in assuming that it took place long before B.C. 5000.

When the people from the East had made their way into Egypt, they found there aboriginal races, one with a dark, and one with a fair skin. The Egyptians generally called their land 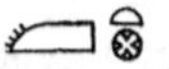 Qemt, *i.e.*, "black"; and if the dark, rich colour of the cultivated land of Egypt be considered, the appropriateness of the term is evident. The hieroglyphic which is read *Qem*, is the skin of a crocodile, and we know from Horapollo (ed. Cory, p. 87), that this sign was used to express anything of a dark colour.* The name "Ham" is given to Egypt by the

* "To denote *darkness*, they represent the TAIL OF A CROCODILE, for by no other means does the crocodile inflict death and destruction on any animal which it may have caught than by first striking it with its tail, and rendering it incapable of motion."

Bible; this word may be compared with the Coptic ⲕⲏⲙⲉ, ⲕⲏⲙⲓ or ⲭⲏⲙⲓ. The children of Ham are said to be Cush, Mizraim, Put, and Canaan. The second of these, Miṣraim, is the name given to Egypt by the Hebrews. The dual form of the word, which means "the double Miṣor," probably has reference to the "two lands" (in Egypt. 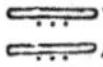), over which the Egyptian kings, in their inscriptions, proclaimed their rule. The descendants of Cush are represented on the monuments by the inhabitants of Nubia and the negro tribes which live to the south of that country. In the earliest times the descendants of Cush appear to have had the same religion as the Egyptians. The Put of the Bible is thought by some to be represented by the land of Punt, or spice-land, of the monuments. The people of Punt appear to have dwelt on both sides of the Red Sea to the south of Egypt and on the Somâli coast, and as far back as B.C. 2500 a large trade was carried on between them and the Egyptians; it is thought that the Egyptians regarded them as kinsmen. The aboriginal inhabitants of Phœnicia were probably the kinsfolk of the descendants of Miṣraim, called by the Bible Canaanites. Diodorus and some other classical authorities tell us that Egypt was colonized from Ethiopia; for this view, however, there is no support. The civilization, religion, art of building, etc., of the Ethiopians are all of Egyptian origin, and in this, as in so many other points relating to the history of Egypt, the Greeks were either misinformed, or they misunderstood what they were told.

An examination of the painted representations of the Egyptians by native artists shows us that the pure Egyptian was of slender make, with broad shoulders, long hands and feet, and sinewy legs and arms. His forehead was high, his chin square, his eyes large, his cheeks full, his mouth wide, his lips full, and his nose short and rounded. His jaws protruded slightly, and his hair was smooth and fine. The evidence of the pictures on the tombs is supported and confirmed by the skulls and bones of mummies which anthropologists have examined and measured during the last few years; hence all attempts to prove that the Egyptian is of negro origin are overthrown at the outset by facts which cannot be controverted. In cases where the Egyptians intermarried with people of Semitic origin, we find aquiline noses.* One of the most remarkable things connected with the Egyptians of to-day is the fact that a very large number of them have reproduced, without the slightest alteration, many of the personal features of their ancestors who lived seven thousand years ago. The traveller is often accompanied on a visit to a tomb of the Ancient Empire by a modern Egyptian who, in his attitudes, form, and face, is a veritable reproduction of the hereditary nobleman who built the tomb which he is examining. It may be that no invading race has ever found itself physically able to reproduce persistently its own characteristics for any important length of time, or it may be that the absorption of such races by intermarriage with the natives, together with the influence

* A very good example of this is seen in the black granite head of the statue of Osorkon II., presented to the British Museum (No. 1063) by the Committee of the Egypt Exploration Fund. The lower part of the nose is broken away, but enough of the upper part remains to show what was its original angle. It was confidently asserted that this head belonged to a statue of one of the so-called Hyksos kings, but the assertion was not supported by any trustworthy evidence. The face and features are those of a man whose ancestors were Semites and Egyptians, and men with similar countenances are to be seen in the desert to the south-east of Palestine to this day. A clinching proof that the statue is not that of a Hyksos king was brought forward by Prof. Lanzone of Turin, who, in 1890, had in his possession a small statue of Osorkon II., having precisely the same face and features. The XXIInd dynasty, to which this king belonged, were Semites, as their names show, and they were always regarded by the Egyptians as foreigners, and , the determinative of a man from a foreign country, was placed after each of their names.

of the climate, has made such characteristics disappear; the fact, however, remains, that the physical type of the Egyptian fellâḥ is exactly what it was in the earliest dynasties. The invasions of the Babylonians, Hyksos, Ethiopians (including negro races), Assyrians, Persians, Greeks, Romans, Arabs, and Turks, have had no permanent effect either on their physical or mental characteristics. The Egyptian has seen the civilizations of all these nations rise up, progress, flourish, decay, and pass away; he has been influenced from time to time by their religious views and learning; he has been the servant of each of them in turn, and has paid tribute to them all; he has, nevertheless, survived all of them save one. It will, of course, be understood that the inhabitants of the towns form a class quite distinct from the Egyptians of the country; the townsfolk represent a mixture of many nationalities, and their character and features change according to the exigencies of the time and circumstances in which they live and the influence of the ruling power.

In recent years, thanks chiefly to the excavations and labours of M. J. de Morgan,* formerly Director of the Gîzeh Museum, very considerable light has been thrown upon the autochthones of Egypt, and the results of his work may be here briefly summarised. At the end of 1894 M. de Morgan made excavations at Al-'Amrah, a place which is situated a few miles to the south of Abydos, where he found a number of what are now rightly called **pre-dynastic tombs.** The tombs were in the form of oval pits from three to five feet deep, and in these bodies had been laid on their left side with their legs doubled up in such wise that the knees were almost on a level with the chin. The head was bent forwards slightly, and the fore-

* M. Amélineau has described the excavations which he made at 'Amrah and other places in his *Les Nouvelles Fouilles d'Abydos*, Angers, 1896, and in subsequent publications.

arms were laid in such a position that the hands, one resting upon the other, might be in front of the face. Round the body were a number of large and small vases filled with burnt bones, etc., and quite close to it were red and black vases, stone pots, figures of fish in schist, worked or unworked flints, alabaster objects like mace-heads, shell bracelets, etc. In tombs of this class, objects in bronze were rarely found, a fact which proves that the metal was not common when the tombs were made. Most of the tombs are, according to M. de Morgan, the sepulchres of neolithic man in Egypt, but some of them seem to belong to the transition period between the stone and the bronze age. The bodies found in the tombs seem to have been treated with salt and some preparation of bitumen, and if this be so they are probably the oldest mummified remains known.

During the winter of 1894–5, Prof. Petrie carried on excavations along the edge of the desert between Ballas and Naḳâda, about 30 miles north of Thebes. He stated that, in the course of his work, he found a maṣṭăba pyramid, similar to that of Ṣaḳḳâra, and a number of tombs of the IVth, Vth, and VIth dynasties; the pyramid, and all the tombs save one, had been plundered in ancient days. He believed his main discovery to be that of "a fresh and hitherto unsuspected race, who had nothing of the Egyptian civilization." The early announcements of his discovery stated that they were cannibals. According to Prof. Petrie, they lived after the rule of the IVth dynasty, and before that of the XIIth. "This new race must therefore be the people who overthrew the first great civilization of Egypt at the fall of the VIth dynasty, and who were in turn overthrown by the rise of the XIth dynasty at Thebes. As the Xth dynasty in Middle Egypt was contemporary with the greater part of the XIth dynasty, this limits the new race to the age of the VIIth to the IXth dynasty (about 3000 B.C.), who ruled only in Middle Egypt, and of whom no trace has been yet found, except a few small objects and a tomb at Siut. The extent to which Egypt was subdued by these people is indicated by their remains being found between Gebelen and Abydos, over rather more than a hundred miles of the Nile valley . . . . . . The invaders completely expelled the Egyptians." Their graves were square pits, measuring usually 6 × 4 × 5 feet. "The body was invariably laid in a contracted position, with the head to the south, face west, and on the left side . . . . . A regular ceremonial system is observable . . . . . . From the uniformity of the details it is clear that a system of belief was in full force."*

In March, 1897, M. de Morgan decided to excavate the pre-dynastic cemeteries of Upper Egypt, and began to work at Naḳâdah near the site of Prof. Petrie's labours two years before; two cemeteries were chosen for examination, the one, to the south, belonging to the indigenous peoples of Egypt, and the other, to the north, containing burials of ancient Egyptians. After a short time he discovered to the north of the northern necropolis, the remains of a monument, built of unbaked bricks, which had been destroyed by fire. From the fact that all the jars and objects which had been placed in the building were broken, it was clear that he had come upon a tomb belonging to an extremely ancient period; in the tombs of the neolithic period the vessels, etc., are found whole. The building contained 21 chambers, and was undoubtedly a royal tomb, judging from the abundance of the offerings which had been placed in them; it was rectangular in shape, and measured 54 metres by 27 metres, and its main sides were oriented at an angle of 15° E. of the magnetic north. Close by this tomb was another, which had been wrecked and spoiled in modern times.

* Quoted from Petrie, *Catalogue of a Collection of Egyptian Antiquities*, London, 1895.

Among the objects found in the chambers of the larger monument were fragments of vases and vessels made of various kinds of hard stone, alabaster, etc., flint knives, ivory vases and plaques, terra-cotta vases and vessels, etc., many of which were inscribed. The large mud sealings of the wine jars bore impressions of inscribed seals, and these proved beyond a doubt that the building wherein they were found was a royal one. An examination of the tombs of less importance close by led to conclusions of a far-reaching and important character. M. de Morgan was accompanied in his work by the eminent German Egyptologist, Prof. A. Wiedemann, and by M. Jéquier, and he thus had the benefit of trained, expert opinion on philological problems, which his own profession of mathematician and civil engineer had left him no time to study exhaustively. Briefly, the conclusions arrived at after an examination of a large number of tombs of the same class as those excavated by Prof. Petrie were as follows :—(1) The people to whom the tombs belong occupied not a small portion of, but the *whole* valley of the Nile. (2) Their manners, customs, industries, and abilities were *different from those of the Egyptians, and physically the two peoples had nothing in common.* (3) The people called the "new race" by Prof. Petrie were the inhabitants of Egypt *long before those whom we call Egyptians*; and it was from them that the Egyptians of dynastic times learned many of their industries, etc.; in other words, the Egyptians borrowed a great deal from these their predecessors in the valley of the Nile. "La *new race* de M. Flinders Petrie devient donc une véritable *old race*, celle des aborigènes, que les Égyptiens pharaoniques rencontrèrent quand ils envahirent l'Égypte";* in fact, the "new race" were of the highest antiquity in Egypt, which they had occupied

* De Morgan, *Recherches sur les Origines de l'Égypte*, Paris, 1897.

some thousands of years before the time of Menes. The graves excavated by M. de Morgan show that the dead were buried in three ways, *i.e.*, with the bones separated one from another, or with the complete skeleton bent up in a position similar to that of a child before birth, or with the whole body buried and then burnt in the tomb. Each method is different from that employed by the Egyptians, among whom every effort was made to bury the dead in as perfect a form as possible, for they believed that the continuance of the future life of the dead depended upon it. In the religious texts of the Egyptians there are frequent allusions to the customs of dismemberment, and decapitation, and burning of the dead, which prove, if proof be needed, that such things were customary long before their time, and that the Egyptians on their arrival in Egypt adopted gradually certain of the funeral customs and beliefs of the autochthones, but considerably modified others.

It has not yet been definitely decided to what race the people who were buried in such graves were related, but there are many grounds for thinking that they were either members of a tribe of the Taḥennu, or Thaḥennu, who are often mentioned in the texts of historical kings, or were akin to them. Pictures of them show that they were people with light skins, blue eyes, and fair hair, and although in historic times the tribes certainly lived to the north-west of Lower Egypt, we know that in the VIth dynasty they possessed settlements as far to the south as Nubia. The name commonly given to the Taḥennu is "Libyans," and the known facts point to the conclusion that some tribe, or group of tribes, of the Libyans formed the autochthones of Egypt. The Libyans seem to have been conquered by a race that invaded and reduced Egypt to slavery, and when the foreign kings began to reign over Egypt the conquered people formed the inferior portion of the population. It is still a subject open to debate where the invaders came from; some think they were of Asiatic origin and entered Egypt by way of the Isthmus of Suez; others think that they came from the south, that is to say, from Ethiopia (compare Ezekiel xxix. 14, where the home of the Egyptians is said to be Pathros, *i.e.*, the Egyptian *Pa-ta-reset* ); and others believe they made their way up or across the Red Sea to Ḳuṣêr (القصير), a port for the ships coming from Yaman, and across the Eastern Desert to Coptos on the Nile. But by which road they entered Egypt is, relatively, of little importance; that they came primarily from the East is beyond dispute. All the known evidence contradicts the theory that Arabia was the home of the invaders of Egypt, and although there are many striking resemblances between the art of the statues and other objects which have been excavated at Tell Lo and other ancient sites in Southern Babylonia in recent years, and pre-dynastic and early dynastic objects found by Messrs. de Morgan, Amélineau, and Petrie at Abydos and Naḳâdah, they do not in the writer's opinion prove conclusively that the invaders of Egypt and the Babylonians were of the same race. The culture and civilization of the Babylonians between B.C. 6000 and B.C. 2300 were derived from their Sumerian conquerors, whose method of writing, and much of their learning and literature the Babylonians adopted, modified, and then assimilated. There is no evidence to show that the invaders of Egypt were kinsfolk of the Babylonians, but there are very strong probabilities that the civilizations of both peoples sprang from a common stock; what that stock was, or where the race lived, or when its cognate peoples took possession of Southern Babylonia and of Egypt, no one can at present say with certainty.

THE NILE.

The source of the Nile was discovered by Captains Grant and Speke and Sir Samuel Baker, who made out that its parents are the Albert Nyanza and Victoria Nyanza;* into the latter the Tangourie River, which rises a few degrees to the south of the Equator, empties itself. Lake Victoria is situated on the Equator in the region of perpetual rains, and it is also fed by springs and tributaries like the Tangourie River. Strictly speaking, the Nile is formed by the junction, at 15° 34′ N. lat., and 30° 30′ 58″ E. long., of two great tributaries called respectively the Baḥr al-Azraḳ, *i.e.*, the "lurid" or Blue Nile, and the Baḥr al-Abyaḍ, *i.e.*, the "clear," or White Nile. From Lake Victoria to Kharṭûm the distance by river is about 2,185 miles; from Kharṭûm to Aswân is 1,130 miles; and from Aswân to the sea about 750 miles more, so that if we include the length of any of the larger tributaries of Lake Victoria in the length of the Nile, we may say that this wonderful river is about 4,100 miles long. The White Nile

* Nyanza means "Lake."

is so called because of the fine, whitish clay which colours its waters. It is broader and deeper than the eastern arm, and it brings down a much larger volume of water; the ancients appear to have regarded it as the true Nile. There can, however, be no doubt that either the Blue Nile or the Atbara is the true Nile, for during their rapid courses from the Abyssinian mountains they carry down with them all the rich mud which, during the lapse of ages, has been spread over the land on each side of its course, and which has formed the land of Egypt. In truth, Egypt is the gift of the Blue Nile and the Atbara. Lake Victoria lies about 3,675 feet above the sea, and is 1,625 feet higher than Lake Albert, and when the river leaves the lake it is about 1,300 feet wide*; at the Ripon Falls it drops about 13 feet. Between the Victoria and Albert Lakes, a distance of 300 miles, the White Nile, known here as the "Somerset," passes through a number of swamps, and then flows into the N.E. corner of Lake Albert; from Lake Albert it flows in a broad, deep, and almost level stream for a distance of 125 miles to the Fola Falls, a little to the north of Duffilé, at which point the river is nearly 300 feet wide, and becomes almost a torrent. Flowing on to Lado, about 125 miles from Duffilé, the river becomes only 6½ feet deep in the winter at low water, and 15 feet in flood. From Lado to Bôhr, a distance of about 75 miles, the river has a rapid fall and keeps to one channel, but from Bôhr, to the mouth of the Gazelle River (a distance of about 235 miles), the stream passes through many channels. Here are the large masses of living vegetation which are commonly called "Sudd," and which form almost insuperable barriers to navigation. The Gazelle River flows into the Nile on its west, and 60 miles further north the Sobat (or Sawbat)

* I am indebted for a number of the facts here given to Mr. Willcocks exhaustive work, "*Egyptian Irrigation*," London, 1899, p. 27 ff.

River flows into it from the east or right bank. From the latter river to Kharṭûm, a distance of about 560 miles, the White Nile flows slowly in a stream about 6½ feet deep, and considerably more than a mile wide. At Kharṭûm, where the Blue Nile from Abyssinia joins the White Nile, the river is about 1,270 feet above sea-level. The Blue Nile, which is about 840 miles long, is almost clear in summer, but from June to October its water is of a reddish-brown colour, and is highly charged with alluvium. The greenish colour which is sometimes observed in the Nile far to the north is due to the decaying vegetation which is brought down by the White Nile. About 56 miles below Kharṭûm is the **Sixth Cataract,** and 145 miles lower down the river Atbara flows into the Nile on the east or right bank. The Atbara rises in the Abyssinian mountains, and its waters bring down with them a large quantity of volcanic dust, which is an excellent fertilizing element; after the Atbara the Nile on its journey north receives no other tributary. About 32 miles below the Atbara is the **Fifth Cataract,** which is over 100 miles in length; between the southern and the northern end the Nile drops about 205 feet. About 60 miles lower down begins the **Fourth Cataract,** which is 66 miles long; between the southern and the northern end the Nile drops 160 feet. About 195 miles lower down begins the **Third Cataract,** which is 45 miles long; between the southern and the northern end the river drops 36 feet. The **Second Cataract** begins about 70 miles lower down; it is 125 miles long, and between its two ends the river drops about 213 feet. At Semneh, which is rather more than 35 miles south of Wâdî Ḥalfa, are the rocks where the late Dr. Lepsius discovered the gauges which were cut by order of the kings of the XIIth dynasty, about B.C. 2300, and these show that the Nile flood recorded there was 26 feet higher than any flood of to-day. The eminent irrigation authority,

Mr. Willcocks, thinks that the Nile could very easily be barred by a dam at Semneh, and it is possible that Åmen-em-ḥāt III. tried to build one there in the hope of forming a reservoir. The distance between the Second and First Cataract is about 210 miles, and the stream is usually about 1,630 feet wide. The **First Cataract** is about three miles long, and between Philæ at the southern end, and Aswân at the northern end the river drops over 16 feet. From Aswân to the Barrage, a little to the north of Cairo, the length of the river is about 600 miles, and its mean width is 3,000 feet.

Sketch showing the height of the Nile above mean sea-level at different points of its course.

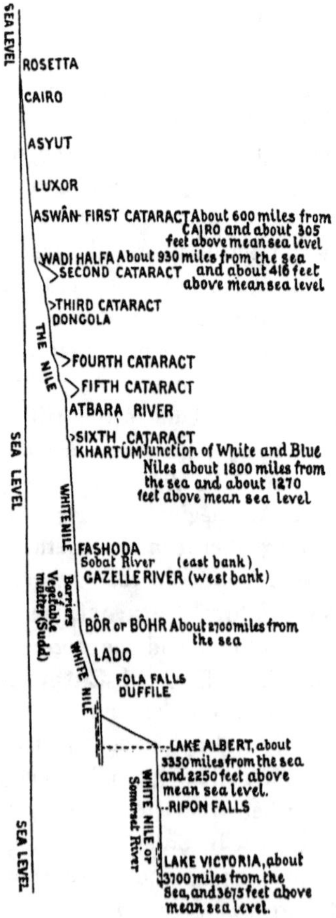

The ancient Egyptians kept careful record of the height of the Nile in flood, and numbers of ancient Nilometers have been found, *e.g.*, at Philæ, Elephantine, Edfu, Esneh, Karnak, etc., from the readings of which it is possible to determine the rate of the rise of the bed of the Nile. According to a calculation quoted by Mr. Willcocks, between A.D. 200 and A.D. 1800 the banks and bed of the Nile have risen 2·11 metres, or 0·132 metre per 100 years. When the famous Nilometer at Rôḍa (*see* page 280) was constructed, a reading of 16 cubits meant the lowest level at which flood irrigation could be ensured everywhere. The level of to-day is 20½ cubits on the Nilometer, and the difference between them is 1·22 metre; according to these data the rise is 12 centimetres per 100 years (Willcocks, *op. cit.*, p. 32). A little to the north of Cairo the Nile splits up into the Rosetta and Damietta branches, each of which is about 140 miles long; the mean width of the former branch is 1,630 feet, and that of the latter, 870 feet. In ancient days the Nile emptied its waters into the sea by seven mouths, viz., the Pelusiac, Tanitic, Mendesian, Phatnitic, Sebennytic, Bolbitic, and the Canopic. In flood time the waters of the Nile take 50 days to flow from Lake Victoria to the sea, and at low water 90 days;—From Lake Victoria to Lake Albert 8 days, Lake Albert to Lado 5 days, Lado to Kharṭûm 20 days, Kharṭûm to Aswân 10 days, Aswân to Cairo 5 days, Cairo to the sea 2 days; at low water the times are 8, 5, 36, 26, 12 and 3 days respectively.

The width of the Nile valley varies from 4 to 10 miles in Nubia, and from 15 to 30 in Egypt. The width of the strip of cultivated land on each bank in Nubia is sometimes only a few feet, and even in Egypt proper, when taken together, it is never more than 8 or 9 miles. The Delta is, in its widest part, about 90 miles across from east to west, and the distance of the apex from the sea is also 90 miles. The Nile drains an area of 3,110,000 square kilometres. The **inundation** is caused by the rains which fall in the country round about Lake Victoria and in the Abyssinian mountains; in the former the rainy season lasts from February to November, with one maximum in April and another in October, and in the latter there are light rains in January and February, and heavy rains from the middle of April to September, with a maximum in

August. In April the heavy rains near Lado force down the green water of the swamps, and about April 15 the Nile has begun to rise at this place; this rise is felt at Kharṭûm about May 20, and at Aswân about June 10, and the green water announcing this rise is seen at Cairo about June 20. About June 5 the Blue Nile begins to rise quickly, and it reaches its ordinary maximum by August 25; its red, muddy water reaches Aswân about July 15, and Cairo 10 days later. When once the red water has appeared the rise of the Nile is rapid, for the Atbara is in flood shortly after the Blue Nile; the Atbara flood begins early in July and is at its highest about August 20. The Nile continues to rise until the middle of September, when it remains stationary for a period of about three weeks, sometimes a little less. In October it rises again, and attains its highest level. From this period it begins to subside, and, though it rises yet once more, and reaches occasionally its former highest point, it sinks steadily until the month of June, when it is again at its lowest level. Thus it is clear that the Sobat, Blue Nile, and Atbara rivers supply the waters of the inundation, and that the White Nile supplies Egypt for the rest of the year. The ordinary maximum discharge of the Nile at Aswân is 10,000 cubic metres per second, and the ordinary minimum discharge 410 cubic metres per second; the ordinary maximum discharge at Cairo is 7,600 cubic metres per second, and the ordinary minimum discharge 380 cubic metres per second.

The **irrigation** of Egypt is gauged by the height of the river at Aswân. When the maximum rise of the river is only 21 feet there will be famine in parts of Upper Egypt; when the rise is between 21 and 23 feet much of the land of Upper Egypt will be imperfectly watered; when the rise is between 23 feet 6 inches and 25 feet certain lands will only be watered with difficulty; when the rise is between 25 feet and 26 feet 6 inches the whole country can be watered; when the rise is between 26 feet 6 inches and 28 feet the country will be flooded; and any rise beyond the last figure will spell misery and the ruin of many. The slope of water surface of the Nile is in summer $\frac{1}{13000}$, and in flood $\frac{1}{12200}$; the cubic contents of the trough of the Nile between Aswân and Cairo are 7,000,000,000 cubic metres; direct **irrigation** between these places takes 50 cubic metres per second, **evaporation** 130, and **absorption** 400. The amount of **water discharged** by the Nile into the sea is 65,000,000,000 cubic metres per annum, and in an average year the amount of **solid matter carried** by the Nile to the sea is 36,600,000 tons.

The **dykes**, or embankments, which kept the waters of the Nile in check, and regulated their distribution over the lands, were in Pharaonic days maintained in a state of efficiency by public funds, and, in the time of the Romans, any person found destroying a dyke was either condemned to hard labour in the public works or mines, or to be branded and sent to one of the Oases. If we accept the statements of Strabo, we may believe that the ancient system of irrigation was so perfect that the varying height of the inundation caused but little inconvenience to the inhabitants of Egypt, as far as the results of agricultural labours were concerned, though an unusually high Nile would of course wash away whole villages and drown much cattle. If the statements made by ancient writers be compared with facts ascertained in modern times, it will be seen that the actual height of the inundation is the same now as it always was, and that it maintains the same proportion to the land it irrigates. From what has been said above it will be evident that the Nile is the chief physical characteristic of Egypt, and as such it has excited the surprise, wonder, admiration, and reverence of countless generations of men. Without it Egypt would have been a desert, and uninhabitable to any but nomad tribes; it has always formed the water supply of the whole country, and the existence of men and animals has depended entirely upon the existence of the river in all ages. The Nile was the highway of Egypt, and to it the Egyptians owed their wealth and prosperity, and their importance as owners of a great corn producing country among the peoples of the ancient world. In the earliest times the rulers of Egypt gave their deepest attention to the irrigation of the country, and no efforts were spared to obtain the best agricultural results by means of canals and embankments. It seems that each village or city or district was responsible for the maintenance of its river banks in good order, but details as to the way in which the work was carried out are wanting. Under despotic rulers the banks must always have been maintained by forced labour, and the cutting and cleaning of the canals and reservoirs was, of course, carried out by the same means. As long as everyone was made to take a share in such labour the hardship was not great, for all were interested in the irrigation of the country, but it will be readily seen that under a despotic government or a corrupt administration certain individuals would be exempted from the performance of such labour at the expense of the other members of the community. Also, forced labour gangs would, by bribing the officials, be made to do work which ought to be done at the expense of private individuals, and members of such gangs who had no friends or influence among the official classes would be kept at forced labour practically the whole year round. Whatever may have happened in early times, this was certainly the case in Egypt until the British began to gain power, and all the work done in connexion with the cleaning of canals, and the protecting of the banks during the inundation, and the strengthening of the dykes, was done by forced labour or **corvée.** Sa'îd Pâsha used the corvée in making the Suez Canal, and Ismâ'îl Pâsha boldly used it in digging a canal in Upper Egypt, the chief object of which was to water his own private estates. The high officials exempted their own tenants and co-religionists from the corvée, and made the wretched *fellaḥîn* do the work for them. The corvée had to work for nine months of the year, and they had to provide spades, and baskets, and food; their place of abode was changed almost daily, and they had to sleep on the ground. During the inundation they had to live on the river bank, and to provide the materials for the protection of the bank on each side of the Nile. Every male between 15 and 50 years of age was liable to serve in the corvée, and each quarter of the male population was expected to serve for 45 days during the summer. In 1881 nearly one-half of the men who were liable had succeeded in freeing themselves from their duty. In a decree dated January 25, 1881 (see the text in Willcocks, *op. cit.*, p. 402), the terms on which certain privileged classes could redeem their tenants from the corvée are set forth, but as no penalties were laid down for those who neither sent men nor paid the redemption tax, every man of any position freed himself from the liability, and the whole of the forced labour fell on the poorer classes. In 1885 Sir Evelyn Baring (Lord Cromer) approved of an advance of £30,000, with the view of trying to substitute hand labour by contract for the corvée, and the experiment was a success. A year later, a quarter of a million was granted towards the relief of the corvée, and for the first time in Egyptian history, the State paid towards the up-keep of the canals and river banks of the country. The total relief of the earthwork maintenance corvée costs the State £420,000 a year. In December, 1889, the corvée was abolished as far as the clearance of canals and repairs of banks was concerned, and the Public Works Department undertook to do all the repairs; but the corvée for the protection of the Nile banks during the inundation could not be abolished, and a certain number of men have to be called out each year. In 1899 the Nile was abnormally low, and it in many respects resembled that of 1888; in 1899, however, only 10,079 were called out per 100 days (which is the lowest number on record), while in 1888 the number was 58,788 men per 100 days (Cromer, *Report*, Egypt No. 1 (1900), p. 19). The abolition of the earthworks corvée is due entirely to the exertions of Viscount Cromer and the officials of the Irrigation Department, who have toiled unceasingly for years to remove an infamous burden from the shoulders of the men who were the least able to bear it.

Sir Samuel Baker (*Albert Nyanza*, vol. ii. p. 331) and many other travellers have described the masses of vegetation, both living and dead, which in parts of the White Nile, *e.g.*, Baḥr el-Ghazal, completely obstruct the fairway of the river. These masses, or blocks of **sudd*** as they are called, are often of very considerable length, and where they exist the river becomes practically a mere swamp. Sir Samuel describes one which was three-quarters of a mile wide; it was perfectly firm, and was already overgrown with high reeds and grass. The graves of the people who had died of the plague were actually upon it. When the Nile stream approached this vegetable dam it plunged beneath it by a subterranean channel with a rush like a cataract. From time to time these dams are added to by small islands of vegetation, which drift down upon them, and trees and dead crocodiles, and hippopotami, help to make the mass more dense. Sudd is met with between Shambe (lat. 7° 5′ 53″ north) and the Sobat River (lat. 9° 22′ 8″ north), or a distance of 250 miles, and on the White Nile between Lake No and the Sobat River. See "Report on the Soudan," by Sir W. Garstin, K.C.M.G., London, 1899. With the view of opening the White Nile to navigation, the Egyptian Government, in 1899, voted the

* Arab. سَدّ *sadd*, or سُدّ *sudd;* plural أَسْدَاد.

sum of £E.10,000 for cutting the *sudd* between Lake No and Shambe, and a party of 700 men, 4 officers, with 4 steamers, left Omdurmân in December, 1899, to carry out the work. The blocks of *sudd* were nine in number. The grass and dry vegetation upon them were set fire to, and when they were burnt, the blocks were cut gradually into sections, each of which had to be towed away by a steamer, by means of a steel hawser. The *sudd* cutting party was under the command of Major Peake, who, according to a telegram of May 17th, from Cairo, stated that the White Nile was then clear as far as Bedden, and that Sir W. Garstin's orders had been effectively carried out. When the *sudd* was removed, a vast amount of stagnant water was set free, and as a result the fish died in large numbers in the lower reaches of the river.

The **Barrage** or **Barrages**. From time immemorial the Nile has been allowed to water the land of Egypt according to its own will and pleasure, and there are no records to show that any ruler of Egypt seriously undertook to regulate the supply of water to the cultivable lands by means of dams or reservoirs. The river has been allowed to waste itself for thousands of years, and it was not until the present century that any attempt was made to keep the Nile and its branches within bounds. It is recorded by Clot Bey (Willcocks, *op. cit.*, p. 257; R. H. Brown, *History of the Barrage*, p. 1; Milner, *England in Egypt*, p. 239) that Napoleon I. saw the necessity of some means of regulating the supply of water to the Rosetta and Damietta branches of the Nile, with the view of letting the whole of it flow first down one branch and then down the other, thus doubling the effect of the inundation in flood. In 1833 Muḥammad 'Ali blocked the head of the Rosetta branch with a stone dam, which made the Nile stream flow into the Damietta branch, wherefrom all the large canals in the Delta drew their supply. Linant Pâsha, seeing the serious effect which would be produced upon Alexandria and the Eastern Delta if this action were continued, remonstrated with his master, and proposed as an alternative the construction of a Barrage across the head of each branch, about six miles below the bifurcation of the river. This proposal was approved by Muḥammad 'Ali, and when informed by Linant Pâsha of the amount of stone, etc., which would be required, promptly ordered it to be taken from the Pyramids, and only relinquished this plan when it was proved to him that stone could be got at a cheaper rate from the quarries at Cairo. The work was begun in 1833, and was continued until 1835, but towards the end of this year it was carried on with less vigour, and soon after it was entirely stopped. For seven years the old system of clearing out the canals by the corvée was revived, and nothing more was done. In 1842 Mougel, a French engineer, proposed a system of Barrages, to which was united a series of fortifications which were to be built at the bifurcation of the river, and the idea pleased Muḥammad 'Ali, who ordered the work to be undertaken at once. The Damietta Barrage was begun in 1843, and the Rosetta Barrage in 1847. The work was hurried on so fast that it was badly done, and the disrepute into which Mougel's magnificent scheme fell in later years was due to his master's impatience and interference with his plans. In 1853, the new Viceroy, 'Abbâs Pâsha, dismissed Mougel, being dissatisfied with the rate of progress made, and Mazhar Bey was ordered to finish the Barrages on Mougel's plans. Commissions sat on the matter, and although the defects of the work already done were well known, no attempt was made to remedy them, and the Barrages were finished in 1861. They had cost £1,800,000, exclusive of the corvée, and the fortifications, etc., cost £2,000,000 more. These works form the famous "Barrage," which lies about fourteen miles to the north of Cairo; the Rosetta

Barrage has 61 arches and two locks, and is about 1,512 feet long; the Damietta Barrage has 61 arches (originally 71) and two locks, and is about 1,730 feet long. In 1863 the gates of the Rosetta Barrage were closed, so that more water might be turned into the Damietta branch, and cracks promptly appeared in the structure. In 1867 ten openings or arches of the Rosetta Barrage separated themselves from the rest of the work, and moved out of their places. In 1876, Mr. (late Sir) John Fowler reported on the Barrage, and he proved that the floor and foundations were cracked, that the latter were too shallow, and that £1,200,000 would have to be spent to make the work fit for any useful purpose; General Rundall, R.E., also reported on the Barrage, and estimated that it could be made serviceable for £500,000, and described how the repairs were to be carried out*. Finally, in 1883, Rousseau Pâsha, Director General of Public Works, declared that the Barrage could only be used as a distributor of the river discharge between the two branches, and that to make it fit for this purpose it would be necessary to spend about £400,000 upon it. With the failure of the Barrage to do its work, the supply of water in the canals naturally failed, and the Egyptian Government had to pay a Company £26,000 per annum to pump water into one canal only; and when Sir Colin Scott Moncrieff, in 1883, came to Egypt, ministers were solemnly thinking of adopting a scheme for pumping water into all the canals in the Delta. The engines were to cost £E.700,000, and the annual cost was to be about £250,000; and "the Egyptian Government was actually on the verge of trying to *lift* the whole river" (Milner, *op. cit.*, p. 242).

* Major H. Brown (*op. cit.*, p. 94) says "the manner of restoring the Barrage as recommended by General Rundall is very nearly that which was actually adopted, and further, the cost of the restoration was correctly estimated."

The English ministers set aside this scheme at once, and directed Mr. Willcocks to test the capacity of the Barrage and its power to hold up water. These instructions were carried out, and it was found that parts of the structure had not been finished, and that the Damietta section had never been provided with gates. At the cost of about £26,000 he effected such important repairs, that he was able to hold up water to the depth of nearly four feet more than had ever been possible before, and the cotton crop in 1884 amounted to 3,630,000 ḳanṭars (1 ḳanṭar = 101¼ lbs.), as against that of 1879, at that time the highest known, which amounted to 3,186,600 ḳanṭars. The work was a great triumph, and Mr. Willcocks continued his experiments in 1885 with even greater success. It now became possible to consider the systematic repair of the Barrage, and the complete restoration of this fine work was begun in 1886, and finished at a cost of about £472,000 in 1891 at which time it was able to hold up a head of about 13 feet of water. Thus Mougel's Barrage was made a success, and it would be difficult to describe the greatness of the benefit which the English officials conferred upon Egypt by making it perform the work intended. Now during the years while the Barrage was an object of ridicule, the position of Mougel Bey went from bad to worse, and at length he became extremely poor and forgotten; the Egyptian Government had visited upon him the sins of Muḥammad 'Ali, who had made the Barrage a failure by his haste and impatience, and had left him unprovided for, and the French Government had done nothing for him. At the moment when Sir Colin Moncrieff was planning the restoration of the Barrage, the poor old man, broken down by grief and semi-starvation, was brought to his notice, and he left no stone unturned until the Egyptian Government bestowed an adequate pension upon him, and lifted him out of the reach of want.

But although the Barrage is now doing splendid work,

it does not even now store all the water which is required for the cotton and other crops in the summer throughout Egypt, not to mention the water which is necessary for new plantations. This fact has been borne in mind for many years past, and Sir William Garstin and Mr. Willcocks have been giving their most earnest attention to the finding of some means whereby the lands which are at present waste may be brought under cultivation. Speaking broadly, the cultivated land in Egypt is now producing nearly all it is capable of, and as the revenue of the country depends upon agricultural prosperity, little more revenue is to be expected until more land is brought under irrigation. As Sir Alfred Milner says, "In Egypt prosperity and water go hand in hand." After much thought the English engineers of the Irrigation Department decided that the only way to provide more water, and so increase the revenue, was to build a huge reservoir, preferably at Aswân. Statistics prepared by Mr. Willcocks (*op. cit.*, p. 428), show that about *one-third* of the land in Egypt is undeveloped, that nearly the whole of this undeveloped land lies in the perennially irrigated tracts, and that the summer supply of water is not sufficient for perennial irrigation. There are about 2,000,000 acres of waste land in Egypt, and to redeem these and water all the cultivable land, 6,000,000,000 cubic metres of water will be required. The proposal to build the **Aswân Reservoir** was opposed violently by archæologists, because, according to the original plans, the beautiful temple at Philæ would have been submerged annually and finally destroyed by the water. Instead of holding up the water at a level of 114 metres above mean sea level, Sir W. Garstin reduced the level to 106 metres, which satisfied most people; but Mr. Willcocks thinks (p. 437) that "this action of the archæologists has hurt the reservoir and will not in the end save the temple." After some difficulties as to ways and means, Messrs. Aird and Co. signed a contract with the Egyptian Government, undertaking to build the Aswân Dam and supplementary works for the sum of £2,000,000; the works are to be completed in 1903, Messrs. Aird will receive no payment until that date, when the debt is to be paid off in 30 half-yearly annuities of £78,613. The canals and drains, which form an important part of the scheme, are to be made within the five years in which Messrs. Aird are building the dam, and will cost about £2,000,000 sterling more. When the works are completed, it is calculated that the revenues of the country will be increased by about £2,750,000, and while they are in progress Egypt pays nothing.

The **Aswân Dam** stands in the First Cataract, a few miles south of Aswân. It is designed to hold up water to a level of 106 metres above mean sea level, or rather more than 20 metres above the low-water level of the Nile at site. Its total length will be 2,156 yards, with a width at crest of 26·4 feet. The width of the base at the deepest portion will be 82·5 feet, and the height of the work at the deepest spot will be 92·4 feet. The dam will be pierced by 180 openings, or under-sluices, of which 140 are 23·1 feet by 6·6 feet, and 40 are 18·2 feet by 6 6 feet, provided with gates. Three locks will be built, and a navigation channel made on the west of the river. The **Asyûṭ Dam** will be what is called an open Barrage, and will consist of 111 bays or openings, each 16·5 feet wide, and each bay will be provided with regulating gates. The total length of the work will be 903 yards, and a lock 53 feet wide will be built on the west bank, large enough to pass the largest tourist boat plying on the river. Both works were begun by Messrs. Aird in 1898.

The ancient Egyptians called the Nile Ḥāp, or Ḥāpi 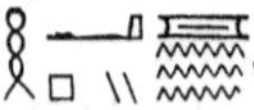, and the Arabs call it "Baḥr," which is a term applied to any large mass of natural water, whether sea, lake, or river. As the Egyptians divided their country into north and south, even so they conceived the existence of two Niles, which they called "Ḥāp reset" , the "South Nile," and "Ḥāp meḥet" 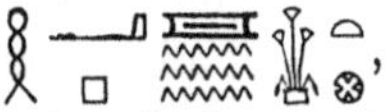, the "North Nile." Both Niles were represented by men bearing upon their heads the plant which was characteristic of the region through which that Nile flowed; thus , the papyrus plant, represented the country of the south where the papyrus grew, and , the lotus plant, typified the country of the north, *i.e.*, the Delta, where the lotus grew. The god of one Nile was coloured red and the god of the other a greenish-blue; it has been thought that these colours have reference to the colour of the waters of the Nile after and before the inundation. The ancient Egyptians seem to have had no knowledge of the source of the Nile, and in late times it was thought that the river sprang out of the

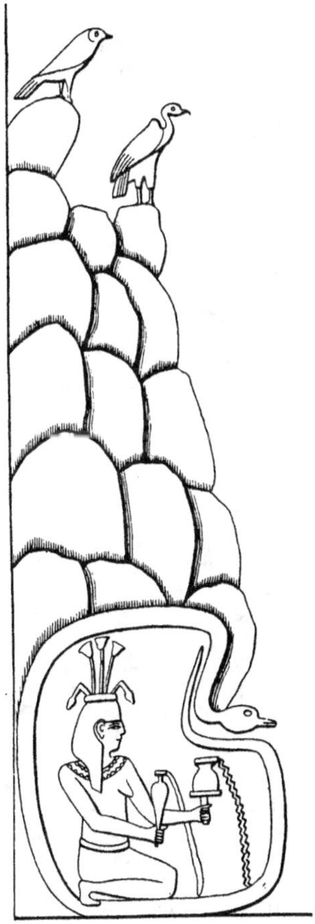

The Source of the Nile at Philæ.
(From Rosellini.)

ground between two mountains which lay between the Island of Elephantine and Philæ. Herodotus tells us that these mountains were called Κρῶφι and Μῶφι, in which some have sought to identify the Egyptian words Qer-Ḥāpi 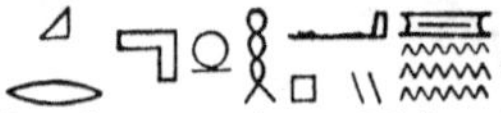, and Mu-Ḥāpi 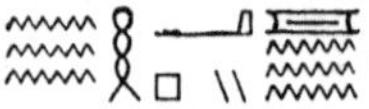. In the temple at Philæ is a very interesting relief in which an attempt is made to depict the source of the Nile of the South. Here we see a huge mass of rocks piled one upon the other, and standing on the top of them are a vulture and a hawk; beneath the mass of rocks is a serpent, within the coil of which kneels the Nile god of the South with a cluster of papyrus plants upon his head. In his hand he holds two vases, out of which he is pouring water. The reverence paid to the Nile was very great from the earliest period, for the Egyptians recognized that their health, happiness, and wealth depended upon its waters. The god of the Nile was addressed as the "Father of the gods," and we are told in a hymn that if he were to fail, "the

The Nile god pouring water over the soul of Osiris. (From Rosellini.)

gods would fall down headlong, and men would perish"; his majesty was considered to be so great that it is said of him, "he cannot be sculptured in stone; he is not to be seen in the statues on which are set the crowns of the South and of the North; neither service nor oblations can be offered unto him in person; and he cannot be brought forth from his secret habitations; the place where he dwelleth is unknown; he is not to be found in the shrines whereon are inscriptions; no habitation is large enough to hold him; and he cannot be imagined by thee in thy heart." This extract is sufficient to show that the Egyptians ascribed to the god of the Nile many of the attributes of God.

Among the festivals of the ancient Egyptians that which was celebrated in honour of the Nile was of prime importance. It was believed that unless the prescribed ceremonies were performed at the right season, in the proper manner, by a duly qualified person or persons, the Nile would refuse to rise and water their lands. The festival was celebrated by all classes with the greatest honour and magnificence when the river began to rise at the summer solstice, and the rejoicings were proportionate to the height of the rise. Statues of the Nile-god were carried about through the towns and villages, so that all men might honour him and pray to him. The ancient Egyptian festival finds its equivalent among the Muḥammadans in that which is celebrated by them on the 11th day of the Coptic month Paoni, *i.e.*, June 17, and is called **Lêtet al-Nuḳṭa,** or the "Night of the Drop," because it is believed that a miraculous drop then falls into the Nile and causes its rise. The astrologers and soothsayers pretend to be able to state the exact moment when the drop is to fall. Many of the Egyptians spend this night in the open air, usually on the banks of the Nile, and Mr. Lane says (*Modern Egyptians*, vol. II., p. 224) that the women observe a curious custom. After sunset they place as many lumps of dough on the terrace as there are persons in the house, and each person puts his or her mark upon one of them; on the following morning each looks at the lump of dough upon which he set his mark the evening before, and if any lump be found to be cracked, it is held to be a sign that the life of the person whom it represents will soon come to an end. About a fortnight later, criers begin to go about in the streets and proclaim the height of the daily rise of the river, each being usually accompanied by a boy; they are listened to with respect, but no one believes the statements they make about the height of the rise. The criers converse with the boys that are with them, and invoke blessings upon the houses of the people before which they stand, the object being, of course, that alms may be given to them. A little before the middle of August, the criers, accompanied by little boys carrying coloured flags, announce the "Completion of the Nile," *i.e.*, that the water reaches to the mark of the 16th cubit on the Nilometer. According to an old law the land tax cannot be exacted until the Nile rises to this height, and it is said that in old days the Government officials used to deceive the people regularly as to the height of the Nile, and demanded the tax when it was not due. The day after this announcement is made, the **Cutting of the Dam** at Fum al-Khalîg, in Cairo, takes place. This dam is made yearly near the mouth of the Khalîg Canal, and the top of it rises to the height of about 22 or 23 feet above the level of the Nile at its lowest; a short distance in front of the dam is heaped up a conical mound of earth called the *arûsa* or "bride," in allusion to the young virgin who, in ancient days, was cast into the river as a sacrifice, in order to obtain a plentiful inundation. This mound is always washed away before the dam is cut. At sunrise, on the day following the "completion" of the Nile, the thickness of the dam is thinned by workmen, and at length a boat is rowed against it, and breaking the dam passes through with the current. The ceremony attracts large crowds, and is usually accompanied by singing, dancing and fireworks.

Between Wâdi Ḥalfa and Cairo there are, on the right bank of the Nile, 312 towns and villages, and the cultivated land amounts to 381,000 feddâns*; between the same limits, on the left bank, are 1,058 towns and villages with 1,638,000 feddâns of cultivated land. The province of the Fayyûm contains 85 towns and villages, with 328,000 feddâns of cultivated land; the whole Delta contains 847 towns and villages, with 1,430,000 feddâns; east of the Delta are 1,017 towns and villages, with 1,271,000 feddâns; west of the Delta are 367 towns and villages, with 601,000 feddâns; the Isthmus of Suez contains 6 towns and villages, with 1,000 feddâns. Egypt contains an amount of land suitable for cultivation which is equal to about 8,000,000 feddâns, or 33,607 square kilomètres, or 12,976 square miles. The cultivated area of Egypt is about 5,650,000 feddâns, or 23,735 square kilomètres, the proportion for Lower and Upper Egypt being 3,303,000 feddâns, with a population of 5,675,109 inhabitants, and 2,347,000 feddâns, with a population of 4,058,296 inhabitants. That is to say, for every 127 inhabitants there are 100 feddâns of cultivated land. According to Mr. Willcocks (*Egyptian Irrigation*, p. 17) the summer crops for the whole of Egypt cover 2,046,500 acres, and yield £15,177,500; the flood crops cover 1,510,000 acres, and yield £6,870,000; and the winter crops cover 4,260,000 acres, and yield £17,013,000; the whole area of 5,750,000 acres has a gross yield of £39,060,500, or £7 per acre.

* The *faddân* or *feddân*, Arab. فَدَّان is the amount of land which a pair of oxen can plough in a day. The feddân contains 4,200 square metres, or about 5,082 square yards, and = rather less than one-fortieth part of an acre.

THE OASES.

In connection with the Nile may be fittingly mentioned the Oases, for it is probable that, in addition to the springs which are found in these natural depressions in the desert, a quantity of water finds its way to them by underground channels from the Nile. The Egyptian for an oasis was 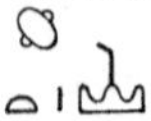 ut, or perhaps uḥet; from this was derived the Coptic ⲟⲩⲁϩⲉ, and the Arabic واح (plur. واحات). In Ptolemaïc times *seven* oases were enumerated,* and their hieroglyphic names are as follows:—

1. KENEMET 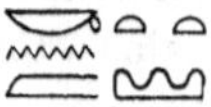, or 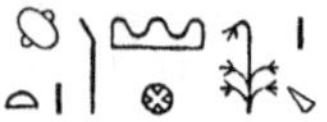 *Ut-res* "Oasis of the South."
2. TCHESTCHESET 
3. TA-ÅḤET 
4. UT-MEḤT 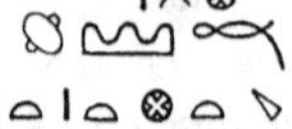 "Oasis of the North."
5. SEKHET-ÅMIT 
6. UT 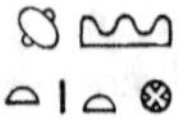
7. SEKHET-ḤEMAM 

1. The **Oasis of Kenemet** is called to-day **Al-Khârgeh,** and lies almost due west of the town of Esneh, at a distance of about four days' journey; it is best known by the name of the "Great Oasis." Population in 1897, 7,200. The name "Oasis of the South" was given to it to distinguish it from the "Oasis of the North." The ancient name of the chief town was Hebt, , and the principal object of interest in the

* The texts are given by Dümichen in *Die Oasen der Libyschen Wüste*; Strassburg, 1877.

Oasis is the ruined ancient Egyptian temple, wherein the god Åmen-Rā was worshipped. The temple was founded by Darius I. Hystaspes (B.C. 521–486), and finished by Darius II. Nothus (B.C. 425–405), and restored by Nectanebus I. (B.C. 378–360), the first king of the XXXth dynasty. The scenes on the walls represent these kings making offerings and adoring a number of the great gods and goddesses of Egypt, *e.g.*, Åmen-Rā, Mut, Temu, Uatchit, Menthu, Rā-Harmachis, Khensu, Khnemu, Isis, Osiris, Anḥur-Shu, Nephthys, etc. Among the inscriptions worthy of special interest are the famous Hymn to the Sun-god which was inscribed on the walls of a small chamber in the temple, and a text written in the so-called enigmatical writing. It is interesting to note too the rare prenomen 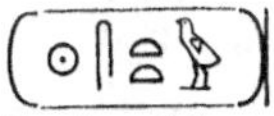 Settu-Rā, which is here applied to one of the Darius kings (Brugsch, *Reise*, pl. VIII.). In other parts of the Oasis are a number of ruins of Roman and Christian buildings, and, as political offenders were banished there by the various rulers of Egypt, and Christians fled there for refuge, this is not to be wondered at; the ruins of a Roman fort suggest that the Oasis was used for garrison purposes at one period.

2. The **Oasis of Tchestcheset** is called to-day **Dâkhel**, and lies to the west of Al-Khârgeh, at a distance of about four days' journey; it is best known by the name of Oasis Minor. Population in 1897, 17,090. The chief town of this Oasis was called 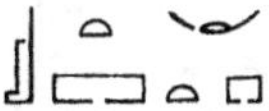 Åuset Åāḥet, "the seat of the Moon-god," and the principal object of worship was the god Åmen-Rā,  "Åmen-Rā, lord of the country of the Moon." The ruins prove that the temple was founded and restored by Titus and other Roman Emperors.

3. The **Oasis of Farâfra** lies to the north-west of the Great Oasis, and there seems to be little doubt that it

represents the Ta-âḥet of the Egyptian texts; it lies about half-way between the Oasis of Baḥriyeh and Dâkhel. Population, 1897, 542. The god worshipped there was called 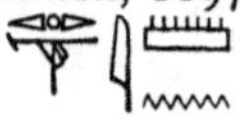 Âmsu-Âmen.

4. The **Oasis of Baḥrîyeh** lies to the north-east of the Oases of Farâfra and Dâkhel, at a distance of about four days' journey from the Fayyûm. The ruins there belong chiefly to the Roman period. The Arabic name "Northern Oasis" seems to be a translation of its old Egyptian name, "Oasis of the North." Population in 1897, 6,082.

5. The **Oasis of Sîwa,** better known by the name of the Oasis of Jupiter Ammon, is the most northerly of all the Oases, and lies west of Cairo at a distance of about sixteen days' journey. Population in 1897, 5,200. The god worshipped there was Âmen-Rā. The name given to it by the Egyptians, Sekhet-Âmit, means the "field of the palm trees," and the many thousands of loads of dates which are exported annually justify the selection of this name. In very early times a temple dedicated to the god Ammon or Âmen stood here, and the reputation of its priests was so wide-spread that it tempted Alexander the Great to visit it in order that he might consult the famous oracle. Christianity is said to have been preached in this oasis by one of the Apostles.

6. The **Oasis.** This oasis has not been identified, but it lay most probably at no great distance from the Oasis of Sîwa, and it may have formed part of the Sekhet-Âmit. Dümichen suggests (*op. cit.*, p. 33) that it may be the Oasis of Araj, which is a journey of two days from Sîwa.

7. **Sekhet-ḥemam,** or the "Salt-field," is no doubt to be identified with the Wâdî Naṭrûn or Natron Valley.

The determinative of the word for oasis in Egyptian () indicates that the inhabitants of the oases were not Egyptians, but it is quite certain that as early as the time of Thothmes III. the inhabitants paid tribute to the kings of Egypt. Rameses the Great kept a number of troops stationed in the largest of the oases, and it is probably from the officers and soldiers who went there from Egypt, that the inhabitants learned to know and worship Egyptian gods. Between the oases and Egypt there must have been a very considerable trade, for the wine of Kenem, and the dates of Sekhet-Åmit, and the salt of Sekhet-ḥemam, were famous throughout the Nile Valley of Egypt.

ANCIENT EGYPTIAN BUILDINGS, SCULPTURE, PAINTING, ETC.

The oldest buildings in Egypt are **Tombs,** and whether large or small they reflect in every age the religious ideas of those who built them. The excavations made in recent years show that the Egyptian tomb in the first instance was an oval hollow, either dug in the sand, or roughly cut in the limestone, and when the body had been laid therein, it was covered over with sand. It was, however, soon found that the wild animals scratched away the sand, and dragged out the bodies and devoured them; to prevent this the friends of the dead laid slabs of stone loosely over the hollow in the ground. As time went on these slabs of stone were better fitted and plaster was used to keep them together, and finally the sides and bottom of the grave were lined with mud bricks or stone slabs. Thus the stone (or brick) lined grave is the oldest building in Egypt, and the Egyptians made it as a result of their belief in the resurrection of the body. But even at this early period there must have been numbers of the dead who were laid to their rest in the sand. After a further lapse of time and as a result of the development of religious ideas, men began to raise stone structures over the graves, whereon they might lay their offerings to the dead, and hold some kind of intercourse with them. What the earliest structures were like we do not know, but in the earlier part of the historic period the kings, and nobles, and high officials, were buried in chambers cut in the solid rock several yards below the surface of the ground, and rectangular chambers made of stones were built over them. The tops of such structures were perfectly flat, and the sides sloped outwards very slightly; a building of this kind is commonly called **Maṣṭăba,** because it resembles a bench. They did not resemble portions of pyramids, but, as Mariette said, a maṣṭăba somewhat resembles a section cut horizontally out of an obelisk, supposing the obelisk to have a rectangular base. The walls are of varying thickness, and few are built in exactly the same way; it is a common characteristic of them all that the cores are made of very poor materials. It is hard to understand why the builders, who gave so much time and attention and labour to such buildings, did not go a step further and build their walls solidly throughout. Maṣṭăba tombs were oriented towards the north. They vary in length and breadth, but all consist of a hall for prayer and sacrifice, of a shaft or pit leading to the chamber where the mummy lies, and of the mummy chamber. The entrance to the maṣṭăba is through an opening on the eastern side, and this opening is often quite plain. Above the opening is a lintel, a portion of which is rounded, and here is found the name of the deceased; occasionally the opening is sunk in the wall to a considerable depth, and a kind of small portico, with square pillars, appears in front. The interior of the maṣṭăba may be divided into chambers, the number of these varying according to the size of the monument and the fancy of the builder; usually, however, a maṣṭăba contains only one. On the ground inside a stele, or tombstone, which always faces the east, is found; at its foot stands an altar or table intended for offerings, and near it is a chamber in which a statue of the deceased was placed. The pit leading to the mummy chamber was square or

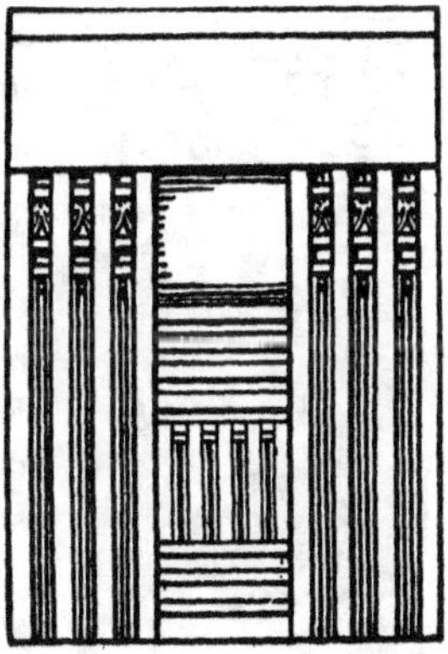

Door from a maṣṭăba tomb at Memphis.
(After *Prisse d'Avennes.*)

rectangular, and, when the dead body had been laid away in its coffin or sarcophagus, was filled up once and for all. The maṣṭăbas were built in rows and stood close together, having narrow passages between them.

Contemporary with the maṣṭăbas are the tombs which were built in the form of **pyramids,** but which preserved all the main features of the maṣṭăba as far as religious ideas were concerned. For various reasons it was found impossible to build a hall inside a great pyramid sufficiently large to accommodate all those who would bring offerings and pray for the deceased buried below; therefore a hall was built outside in the form of a chapel. Instead of descending perpendicularly, the shaft which led to the mummy chamber beneath the pyramid is sometimes diagonal, in which case heavy sarcophagi were more easily lowered down it. It is probable that **step-pyramids,** which are after all only modifications of maṣṭăbas, are older than the true pyramid, and it is also probable that they fell into disuse because they could be more easily wrecked. Well built stone pyramids with the steps

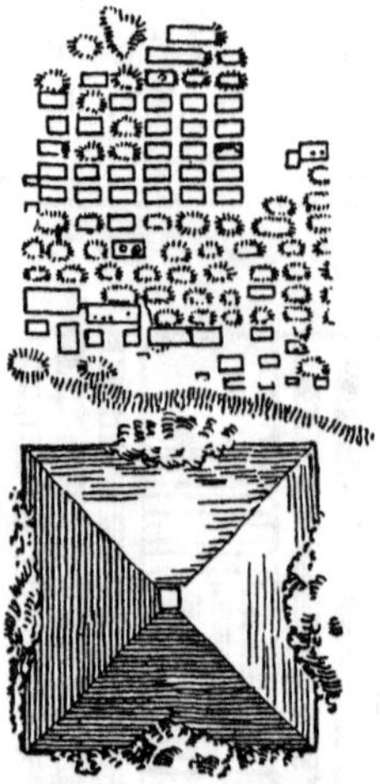

Royal pyramid with rows of maṣṭăba tombs behind it.

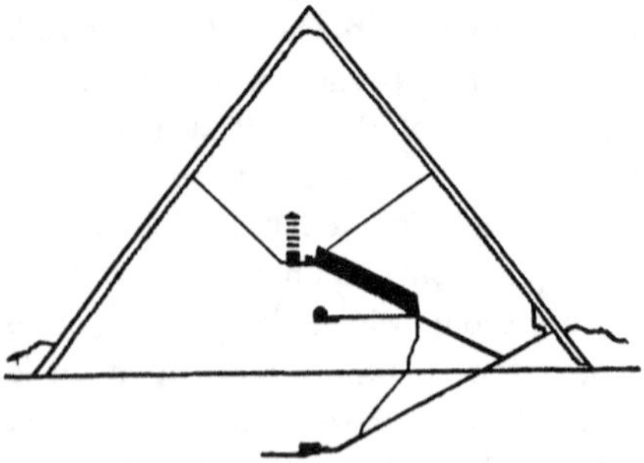

The Great Pyramid, showing passages and mummy chambers.

filled up by stones that fitted closely have proved to be almost indestructible, especially if built on a grand scale. Examples of the step-pyramid are found at Ṣaḳḳâra and Mêdûm, in Egypt, and at Gebel Barkal, Nûri, and to the east of the

The Step Pyramid at Ṣaḳḳâra.
(From a photograph by A. Beato of Luxor.)

site of the ancient city of Meroë, where Candace ruled; the so-called Blunted Pyramid at Dahshûr is the unique example of a most unusual type of pyramid, for about half way up the side of each face the inclination changes, and while the lower portion of the face forms an angle of 54° 11′ with the horizon, the angle which the upper portion makes with the horizon is only 42° 59′. The pyramids of the Sûdân form a class by themselves. The outsides are built of well cut stones, carefully laid in their places, but the

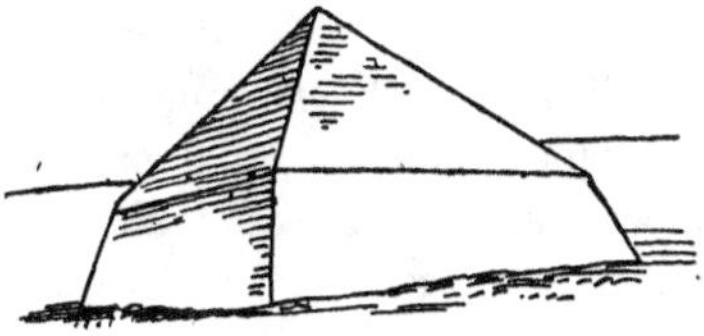

The Blunted Pyramid at Dahshûr.

insides are filled with masons' rubbish and sand. In the upper part of the east face is an opening, and the door faces the east nearly. Each has a chapel, or hall for offerings, in front of it. The stone pyramid was, in the Early Empire, usually the tomb of a king or royal personage, but in later times both kings and priestly or military officials, while adopting the form, built their tombs of brick; this class formed the next development in the architecture of the tomb, and is characteristic of the XIIth and following dynasties. The pyramidal tombs of this period are usually from fifteen to twenty feet high, and the bricks are made of unbaked mud; when they stood anywhere on ground which was tolerably level they were surrounded by a wall. On one side of the pyramid is a sepulchral stele or a small rectangular building which served the purpose of the chapel to a large pyramid, for here the funeral ceremonies were performed, and offerings made, and prayers said on behalf of the dead. The oldest examples of this class of tomb are at Abydos; they date from the VIth to the XIIth dynasty.

Pyramid and chapel at Gebel Barkal.
(After *Prisse d'Avennes.*)

The next step in the development of the tomb was the building it in the mountains on one side or the other of the Nile, where the hall, shaft, and mummy chamber, were hewn out of the living rock. A small portico is often formed by means of two or more square or rectangular pillars cut out of the rock, also an entablature which consists of an architrave and a kind of cornice. When space permitted a portion of the hill or mountain immediately in front of the tomb was levelled, and served to accommodate the visitors who went to the tomb. Passing between the pillars we enter the rock-hewn chamber, usually with square pillars, where, in a niche, was a statue of the deceased; as the double (*ka*) was supposed to dwell in the statue of a man, this arrangement was excellent for enabling the deceased to see the offerings that were made in his chapel, and for hearing the prayers said. This niche is the equivalent of the *serdâb* in the maṣṭăba tomb. In a corner of the hall or chapel, or, if there be more than one hall, in the hall most remote, is the entrance to the square pit which leads to the mummy chamber. The best examples of tombs of this period are at Beni-Ḥasan and Aswân, and at each place there are many really fine tombs. At Aswân is a very interesting flight of steps, up which coffins and sarcophagi were dragged from the level of the river into the tombs, and it is probable that a similar arrangement was provided wherever rock-hewn tombs were made in the side of a steep, high hill. The rock-hewn tomb was very popular in Egypt among high military and priestly officials, and this is hardly to be wondered at, for a body carefully buried therein would be extremely difficult to find when once the opening of the tomb had been blocked up. Coming to the period of the XVIIIth and four following dynasties, we find that it became the fashion among kings and royal personages to have magnificent tombs with long corridors and numerous chambers hewn out of the solid rock; and as the kings of this period reigned at Thebes, the Theban mountains were literally turned into a cemetery. In various parts of the rocky ground on the western bank the priests and high officials caused magnificent tombs to be hewn, and, although the fundamental ideas which guided the builders of the pyramid and maṣṭăba tombs were still all-powerful, the shape, the disposition of the chambers, the ornamentation, and texts inscribed upon the walls show that many new religious ideas had sprung into being in the mind of the Egyptian. The tombs of the kings at Thebes are the best examples of the royal tombs of the period, and in them all we have the equivalents of the hall, the stele, the *serdâb*, the statue, the shaft or pit, and the mummy-chamber; there is, however, one great difference. In the Theban mountains it was found to be impossible to build chapels of a size proportionate to the tombs hewn within them, therefore the kings decided to have their funeral chapels built on the level ground near the river, where they were easy of access, and where there was abundant room for crowds of people to make their offerings to their kings, and to pray for them. In them also the religious were free to worship the gods they loved, as well as perform commemoration services, and in this way temples like the Ramesseum acquired a double character. As every man seems to have had his tomb prepared according to his own plans, it follows as a matter of course that in details hardly any two tombs are alike; nevertheless the central ideas of providing for the hiding of the body and for the supply of suitable offerings at regular intervals for the *ka* of the deceased were never lost sight of. The tombs constructed under the rule of the priests of Amen are inferior to those made in the time of the great Theban kings. In the XXVIth dynasty an attempt was made to revive the funeral ceremonies of the Early Empire, and, in consequence, a number of modifications were made in the internal arrangement of the subterranean rooms, etc.; but very soon the old ideas reasserted themselves, and the Egyptians who could afford to hew sepulchres out of the rocks adopted the class of tomb in general use at the time.

It has been said above that the oldest buildings in Egypt are tombs, and although the necessary evidence, in the shape of ruins, which would prove the great antiquity of the use of temples in Egypt, is not forthcoming, we are fully justified in assuming that, after

an open courtyard; (3) a hypostyle hall; and (4) a shrine, which could be completely cut off from the rest of the temple, and a number of chambers intended to hold statues or emblems of the gods. The first pylon was approached by a broad path, or **dromos**, on each side of which were arranged, at regular intervals, stone figures of ram-headed or human-headed sphinxes, mounted on pedestals, and having their heads turned towards the axis of the path. The length of the path varies, but the longest known is that which leads from Luxor to Karnak, and which is more than a mile and a quarter long. It is probable that the sphinxes were intended either to contain or to represent guardian spirits. The temple buildings were enclosed within a wall of unbaked mud bricks, but the avenue of sphinxes was *outside* this wall. The **pylon** consists of a large rectangular doorway and two high massive towers, built with sides which slope towards a common centre, and it forms, probably, one of the most prominent characteristics of the Egyptian temple buildings. On festal occasions the towers were ornamented by a number of painted poles, from which flew coloured streamers or flags. At each side of the doorway of the pylon stood a colossal figure of the king in granite, limestone, or sandstone, and a granite obelisk, mounted on a pedestal of suitable dimensions, and colossal statues were sometimes also placed in front of the towers of the pylon. The open **court** was furnished with a **colonnade** on three sides, and it is probable that those who sold objects used by the worshippers had their stalls situated in it; both this court and the **hypostyle hall** beyond it, which was entered through the doorway of another pylon, were thronged on festal occasions, and in one or both the animals intended for slaughter were offered up. All that part of the temple which lay beyond the hypostyle hall was probably reserved for the use of the priests and the performance of the sacred ceremonies in connection with the worship of the god. In the most holy part of the **shrine**,

tombs, the building of temples for the safe-keeping of the statues of the gods, and for their worship, would form the next subject of earnest consideration in the minds of the people of that country. In fact, as soon as the Egyptian arrived at any comparatively advanced stage of civilization, he would set to work to build "a house of God" 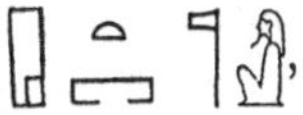, or **temple**, suitable to the rank and position of this god in the land. That the pre-dynastic and early dynastic Egyptians believed in numbers of gods goes without saying; unfortunately, however, their houses, or *temples*, were built of such fragile materials that even the sites of them are unknown. It has been thought that the earliest temples of the Egyptians were built of wood, that bricks formed the next material employed, and that stone was employed last of all. The earliest stone temples were probably contemporary with the earliest of the maṣṭăba tombs, but what such temples were like we shall never know, for they were at a very remote period restored, or enlarged, or reconstructed out of existence. One thing about them, however, is certain: the sites of the principal temples have remained unchanged. The sanctuaries of Heliopolis, Memphis, Abydos, Thebes, and other cities were the abodes of gods probably ten thousand years ago. The names and characteristics of the gods worshipped in them have changed, no doubt, and dozens of buildings have, successively, been erected upon them, but the sites must always have enjoyed a solid reputation for holiness, even though the histories or legends which gave them their reputations have been forgotten. The earliest known temple in Egypt is the granite and limestone **Temple of the Sphinx**, which was discovered by Mariette in 1853, and which lies about 130 feet to the south-east of the right foot of the Sphinx at Gîzeh. The following plan (after Perrot and Chipiez) will illustrate its arrangement:—The room or hall (A), with six square granite pillars, measures about 32 feet by 23 feet, and the pillars are about 16 feet 6 inches high, and 4 feet square. The room or hall (B), which opens out of this, runs from east to west, and measures about 56 feet by 30 feet; the granite pillars here are ten in number. To the east of the smaller hall is a corridor (C), having a room at each end, and near the opening into it is a well, wherein a number of statues of king Chephren were found by Mariette. In the room (D), which is entered from the small hall, mummies were probably kept, and when we bear in mind the well, or pit, in the hall (C), it seems not unlikely that this massive little temple was originally nothing more than a royal funeral chapel. The pillars are without any ornament or decoration, and the walls have neither bas-reliefs nor paintings on them; the outsides of the walls are, however, ornamented with vertical and horizontal channels only, and resemble the outside of a sarcophagus of the early maṣṭăba period. Strictly speaking, the idea of the temple, such as we see at Karnak and elsewhere, was not imagined in the Early Empire, and the Temple of the Sphinx is the most complete example known of those that were built between B.C. 4500 and B.C. 2500. Of the temples which were built in Egypt between B.C. 2500 and B.C. 1700, we have very few remains, but it is certain that the great kings of the XIIth dynasty restored the temples which had been erected

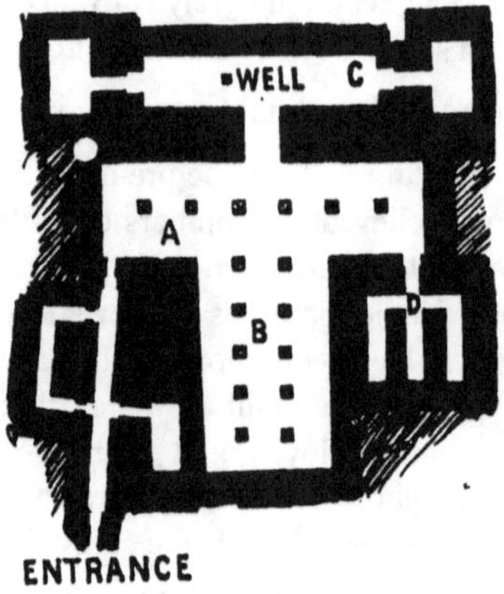

The Temple of the Sphinx.

on historic sites by their predecessors, and it is probable that they built new ones. There are many reasons for believing that the temples of the XIIth dynasty were large, beautiful, and richly decorated, among the chief of these being the fact that beautifully painted rock-hewn tombs were executed at this period. Now the public temples, especially if they had been originally funeral chapels, must have been as grand and beautiful as the chapels of private individuals. We know, too, that the XIIth dynasty temples must have been of very considerable size, otherwise the huge granite obelisks which were set up before them would have looked absurdly out of proportion, and the pylons would have dwarfed the rest of the buildings on the site. Belonging to this period, and worthy of special note, are the ruins of the little temple which the Åmen-em-ḥāt and Usertsen kings built at Karnak in honour of the god Åmen; this temple formed the nucleus of all the buildings which the succeeding kings of Egypt vied with each other in raising upon that site. From about B.C. 1700 to B.C. 1400, a favourite form of temple was a rectangular building with a colonnade running round all four sides; a parapet, which rested upon the severely plain square pillars that supported the roof, was one of its prominent features. The temple was entered through a door at the east end, which was usually approached by steps. At the top of the steps on each side was a pillar with a decorated capital, and between these pillars the two leaves of a door were hung; immediately opposite to them was the door of the temple building leading to the shrine, and it also was provided with swinging leaves that were probably plated with *smu* metal or copper. The shrine was, of course, at the other end of the building. At a later time, when all the chief characteristics of such a temple were changed, the interior was divided into three parts, a portico, a pronaos, and a shrine. Under the kings of the XIXth dynasty the temple buildings consisted of:—(1) Pylons; (2)

and jealously guarded, was the statue, or boat, or emblem of the god, which was only looked upon by the high priest, or by some extremely privileged visitor, about once a year. It was kept inside a sacred ark or tabernacle, made of precious wood or metal, elaborately painted and gilded and worked, and was provided with doors and bolts. In the ground outside the temple-walls, but within the surrounding mud-brick wall, lay the sacred lake or lakes, wherein the devout bathed, and in the waters of which the processions of the sacred boats took place. Speaking generally, the above is a brief description of the principal characteristics of Egyptian temples, and it applies to those that were built or restored between B.C. 1370 and B.C. 200. About the latter date many of the small temples built by the Ptolemies are only modified copies of the small temples of the latter part of the XVIIIth dynasty. An examination of a number of temples will show the visitor to Egypt that in comparatively minor matters each temple possesses characteristics which are peculiar to itself. Thus in the temple at Luxor the open court and the rest of the temple are connected by means of a long, narrow courtyard, which is wanting in many temples; and at Abydos, because there was no room to build all the various parts of the temple in a straight line as usual, the portion which contains the sanctuary has been built to the side of one end of it. Before passing on to other matters, mention must be made of temples which were hewn out of the rock, and of this class, which is a very small one, those of Bêt el-Wali and Abu Simbel in Nubia are the finest specimens. The other temples in Nubia, and those in the Eastern Sûdân, form a class by themselves, and although of those the sites are of a venerable antiquity, the greater number of the buildings belong to the Ptolemaïc period. At Gebel Barkal, parts of the largest temple there are probably as old as the XVIIIth dynasty, and the general teaching of Egyptian history would lead us not to expect to find any ruins older than the time of Amenophis I. In outlying districts the Egyptian temple served both as a place of worship and a place of refuge, and in many respects the building became half temple, half fortress.

The **ornamentation of tombs and temples** varied at different periods. The earliest tombs are almost bare in every part, and contain nothing but a few brief inscriptions. Later the inscriptions were multiplied, and human and animal figures, either cut in low relief or painted in *tempera*, began to fill the walls and to cover the sides of the rectangular pillars which supported the roof.

Scene from the Wall of a Tomb. Deceased fowling.

Still later, every available space in the tomb was filled with scenes most elaborately drawn and painted in vivid colours, and the ceilings were ornamented with geometrical patterns and designs, edged with floral and other borders. As time went on it seemed to be the aim of the funeral artist to make

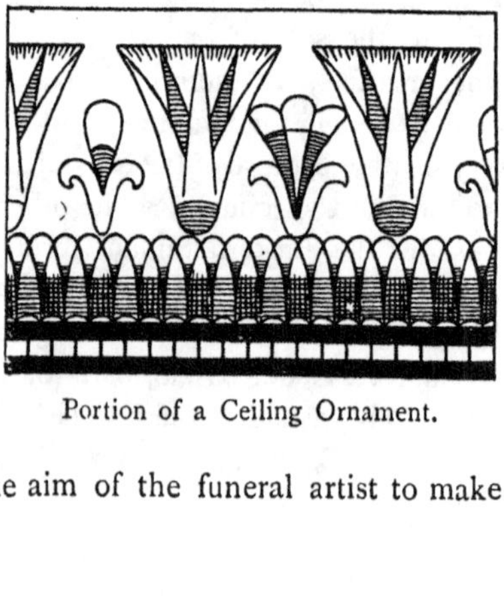

Portion of a Ceiling Ornament.

the walls of the tomb to reproduce scenes of all the principal events which had occurred in the life of the deceased, and to describe his wealth and power. But under the rule of the Theban kings of the XVIIIth dynasty, it became the fashion with many to make such painted scenes and the accompanying descriptive texts subordinate to religious inscriptions, and many tombs are almost entirely covered with extracts from the Book of the Dead, or from works of a similar character, and with scenes illustrative of them. The earliest temples were, probably, without ornamentation of any kind, but when it became the fashion to decorate the tombs with bas-reliefs, or painted scenes, the walls and pillars of the temples were treated in the same manner. In the XVIIIth and following dynasties the outsides of the walls of temples were covered with inscriptions and scenes which recorded the victories of the king or kings who built them, and the insides were decorated with figures of the gods and of the king performing religious ceremonies; later, both the insides and outsides of the walls were devoted to representations of colossal figures of the king slaughtering rebels in masses, and to religious scenes.

The **Palace** and the **House**. The palace of an Egyptian king was enclosed within a wall like a temple, and was often built of stone; unfortunately, however, the ruins of the royal residences known to us, with but one or two exceptions, do not permit the laying down of any general rule about their construction. It is probable that kings often lived in buildings attached to the temples, and in this case the style of the palace would resemble that of the temple. The entrance into the outside grounds was made through a pylon, and the building which formed the palace consisted of large numbers of rooms, lighted by means of grating-work windows, grouped round open courts, which were separated from each other by pylons. Some rooms were set apart for state receptions and ceremonies, others for the sleeping apartments of the male members of the household, and others for the royal ladies. The servants, and others who were not in close attendance on the family, lived and slept outside the palace proper, but within the grounds, in small chambers built against the surrounding wall. In some part of the grounds spice, incense, and fruit trees grew, and one or two ponds, or small lakes, with reedy margins, afforded excellent cover for water fowl. The private house was a rectangular building of two storeys with a flat roof, the whole being made of unbaked mud bricks, with the exception of the lintels of the doors. A man of means enclosed his house and a piece of ground within a wall, and then he had space enough to build a portico, or colonnade, before his house, where he could find shelter from the sun, and lay out a courtyard. A portion of the enclosed space was laid out as gardens or planted with trees, a lake or fountain of water was made near the house, and the servants or slaves, and others, lived in small buildings, or booths, not very far from the house. In fact, the house and garden of a Theban gentleman or high official must have resembled closely the house and courtyard, and garden, with its fountain of running water and scented trees, of a Muḥammadan gentleman of Damascus, or Cairo, or any other flourishing city in the beginning of the Middle Ages. The courtyard was then, as now, probably tiled, and the outside walls of the house painted in one or two bright colours; the internal decorations of the walls and ceilings consisted of some intricate geometrical design, elaborately painted in several bright colours. The Egyptian house must always have been a comparatively simple building, for its owner really only needed shelter from the cold by night, and a shady place wherein to sit or sleep in the afternoons. The peasant farmer's house was a small, strong building, with a courtyard large enough to hold his cattle and granaries wherein to stock his grain. His living and sleeping rooms were usually low and small, but, judging by the models of houses which are to be seen in our museums, he often sat on the roof in a sort of small summerhouse, where he could catch the breeze; the roof was approached by means of a flight of steps. The cooking for his house was done in the courtyard by his wives and female slaves.

Among miscellaneous Egyptian buildings must be mentioned the fortified or fenced cities, which were very numerous, and were surrounded by thick walls and guarded by gates; in fact, any place where many men of means had assembled and accumulated wealth had to be fortified in order that their possessions might be defended against the attacks of marauding tribes. The fortresses at Semneh, in Nubia, and El-kab, in Upper Egypt, are excellent examples of such buildings, and the ruins of them prove that the Egyptians were skilful military architects, and that they not only knew how to choose a site for a fort, but how to erect on it a strong building. In places where they had the choice of more than one site they invariably selected the best, and they seem instinctively to have availed themselves of every advantage which the natural position of that site gave them. The space here available will not permit of any attempt being made to describe methods of construction and cognate matters, but attention must be called to the fact that the Egyptian architects did not pay sufficient attention either to the making of foundations, or to the roofing of their temples. The expert researches made by Mr. Somers Clarke at El-kab, Karnak, Dêr el-baḥarî, and other sites, have revealed some very curious facts about the scantiness and insecurity of the foundations of columns, etc., and the wonder is that the temples have stood so long in the condition in which we now find them. The whole civilized world laments the falling of eleven pillars at Karnak in

1899, but an examination of the foundations shows that in the first place they were too small, and in the second that the materials of which they were made had been thrown into them in a reckless fashion. The question that now arises is, "Are the foundations of all the columns of Egyptian temples as badly made?" and none but an expert can answer it satisfactorily. It is clear that we owe the preservation of most of the temples to the heaps of rubbish which had covered them up, and it is equally clear that no one should be allowed to remove such heaps from precious ruins except under the advice of some competent architect or engineer. The field of Egyptology is so large in these days, that the archæologist cannot expect to become a skilled engineer, still less ought he to take upon himself the risk of destroying the ruins of buildings which form part of the scientific heritage not of the Egyptians only, but of the present and future civilized nations of the world.

The **Pillar*** and the **Column,*** after the walls, are perhaps the most prominent features of the Egyptian building. The oldest pillars were square, and generally monolithic, and the sides were either parallel or slightly sloping upwards; frequently they had neither base nor capital. In the Early Empire they were not decorated in any way, but in the Middle Empire the sides were ornamented with scenes and inscriptions, or with bas-reliefs, or with figures of gods in very high relief, and the capitals with Hathor heads and sistra. The **"Osirian Pillar,"** *i.e.*, a pillar with an upright colossal figure of Osiris in high relief on one side of it, is seen to advantage both in the second court in the temple of Medînet Habu, and in the rock-hewn temple at Abu Simbel; in the Sûdân the god chosen to decorate

* For fuller information on these subjects the reader is referred to Perrot and Chipiez, *L'Égypte*, p. 346, ff., and for examples to Prisse d'Avennes, *Histoire de l'Art*, to which excellent work I am indebted for the illustrations here given.

rectangular pillars was Bes, as may be seen from the ruins of the temples at Gebel Barkal and Ben-Nâga. A variety of the rectangular pillar is the **pillar stele,** of which examples are to be found at Karnak, but it seems never to have been used as an actual support. Out of the rectangular pillar a new variety was made by cutting off the four angles; thus the pillar had *eight* sides instead of four; when it was desired to make the appearance of the new variety of pillar lighter still, the eight angles were cut off, and the pillar now had *sixteen* sides. Examples of both kinds of pillar will be found in the same tomb at Beni Ḥasan. To these new forms, which are called polygonal, polyhedral or prismatic, bases and capitals were added, and thus they came to be compared with certain Greek pillars and so called **Proto-Doric.** Another interesting variety of the rectangular pillar is found at Beni Ḥasan, and is called cruciform. The **column** has many

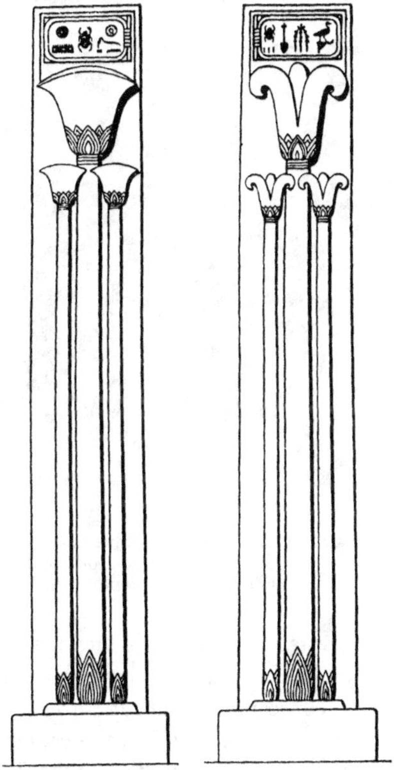

Pillar stelae inscribed with the names of Thothmes III., XVIIIth dynasty.

varieties, but all have the same characteristics; it has a base, and a capital, which is surmounted by a rectangular slab of stone, whereon the framework of the

Entrance to the tomb of Khnemu-ḥetep II. at Beni Ḥasan, with Proto-Doric pillars.
(From a photograph by A. Beato of Luxor.)

roof rests. The capitals are of several kinds. The bud capital, the cup capital, the palm capital. A curious variety of the cup capital occurs at Karnak, where in a part of the building of Thothmes III. the capitals are in the form of inverted cups. In the time of the Ptolemies the architect or master-mason made many variations in the details of the capitals, and frequently with very pleasing results; the authorities, however, do not seem to be agreed as to the canon of proportion employed.

It is at present impossible to gauge by years the antiquity of the period when the Egyptians began to be skilled in the art of **sculpture** and the making of bas-reliefs, but it is certain that in pre-dynastic times they possessed marvellous skill in working the hardest kinds of stone, and in the early dynasties they were masters in the art of painting statues to resemble their living originals. In estimating the character of Egyptian sculpture, it must be remembered that many statues and bas-reliefs were executed almost mechanically, and probably at a fixed rate, to satisfy conventional requirements; in such work the best skill is not to be looked for. Speaking generally, the sculptor's art seemed to culminate between the middle of the IVth and the end of the Vth dynasty. At this period statues and bas-reliefs, and the hieroglyphics of inscriptions, both raised and incuse, possessed a fidelity to life, an attention to detail, and a

Pillar with figures of Amenophis III. and the goddess Hathor.

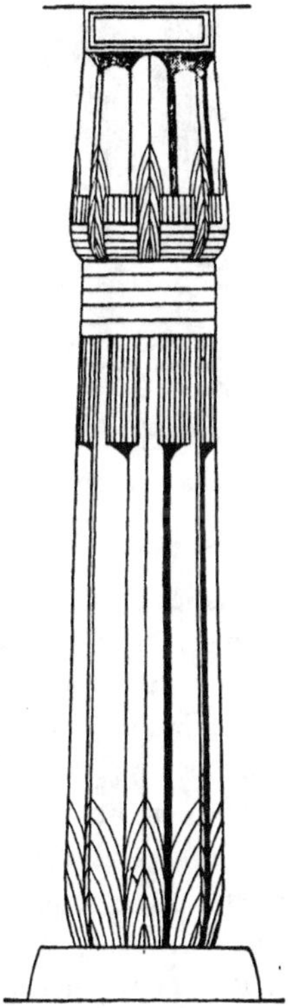

Column with lotus capital.

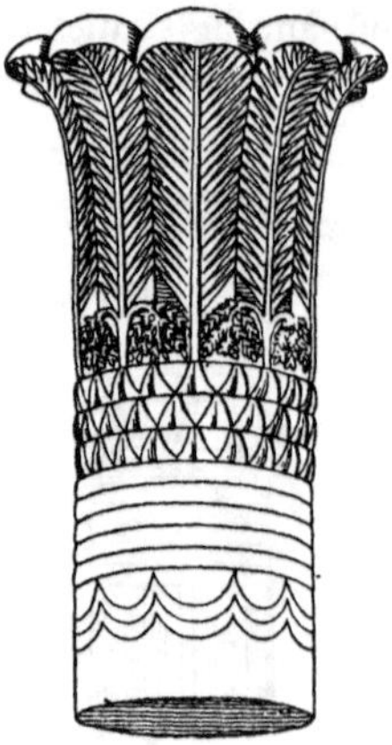

Palm-leaf capital.

Hathor-headed capital.

spirit of repose and dignity which are lacking in the work of later periods. The Egyptians themselves thought this, for in the XXVIth dynasty, when the Saïte kings attempted to revive the dying arts of sculpture and painting, they took the works of the great artists of the IVth and Vth dynasties as their models. The men who made them were no mere hirelings, and their work shows that they tried to represent men and things as they saw them; the unbiassed will probably admit that they succeeded admirably in doing this. In the Gîzeh Museum are fine series of examples of statues, etc., of this period, which testify to the great skill of the Egyptian artists, both as sculptors and

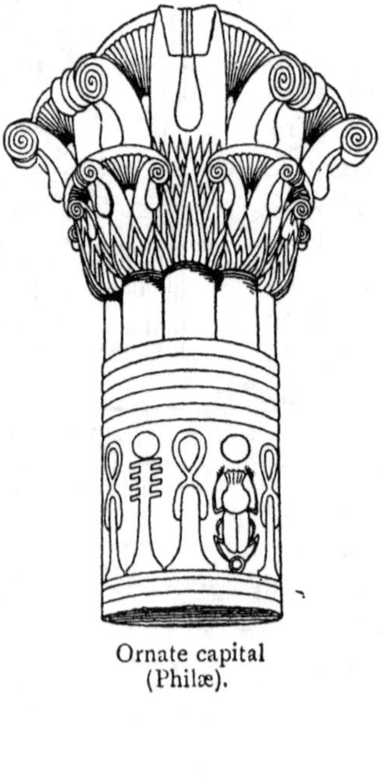

Ornate capital (Philæ).

painters. It seems that the earliest statues were made of wood, like the earliest temples and other buildings, and as rare specimens of artistic work in wood the reader should note the panels from the tomb of Ḥesi at Ṣaḳḳâra, which were made about B.C. 3,600; these panels are now in the Gîzeh Museum, and they are undoubtedly the finest known examples of that particular class of work. It is, as a rule, to the private tombs that we must look for the best examples of artistic work of all kinds, for the individual was more free to follow his own dictates in the selection of both subject and artist than the royal personage, who was practically obliged to employ court draughtsmen, court artists, and court sculptors.

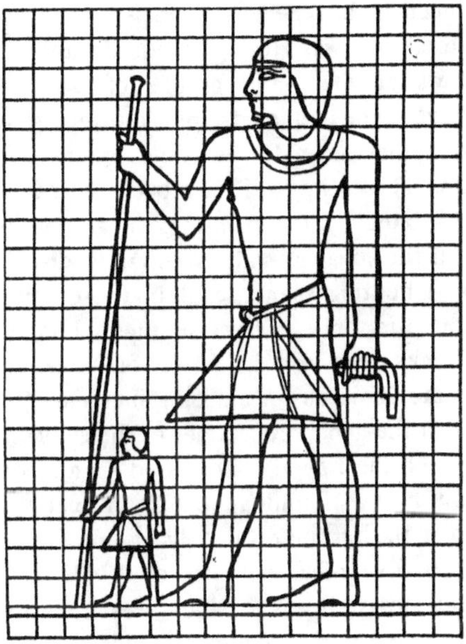

Canon of proportion.

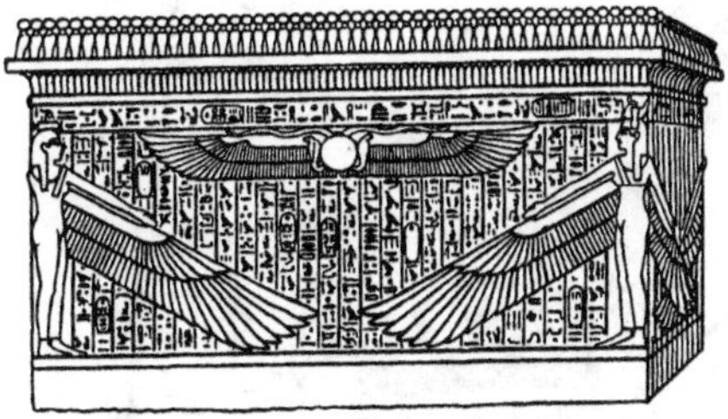

Sarcophagus of King Ai, XVIIIth dynasty.

In **bas-reliefs** and painted scenes, much of the artistic effect is lost because perspective was either not understood, or was little practised, and as a result where rows of men, and groups of animals or objects, etc., have to be depicted, they are represented in such a way that they seem to be standing one above the other or upon the other. The artist's skill in drawing which is exhibited by the paintings in all periods is marvellous, but the greatest skill is certainly displayed in the fishing and hunting scenes, and in those which are commonly found in tombs. Even in these, however, the artist often breaks away from his fetters of conventionality, and depicts some ludicrous or amusing incident quite out of keeping with the general character of the subject. The sense of fun which the Egyptian possessed in all periods of his history must have found an outlet in many comic sketches on papyri, but unfortunately besides the so-called satirical papyri very few examples of such have come down to us; touches of realism which western artists would not have included in their compositions occur every here and there, but these are due rather to an attempt to be true to nature than to depraved ideas.

The Lion and the Unicorn playing draughts. From a "Satirical" papyrus in the British Museum.

EGYPTIAN WRITING.

The system of writing employed by the earliest inhabitants of the Valley of the Nile known to us was entirely pictorial, and had much in common with the pictorial writing of the Chinese and the ancient people who migrated into Babylonia from the East. There appears to be no inscription in which pictorial characters are used entirely, for the earliest inscriptions now known to us contain alphabetic characters. Inscriptions upon statues, coffins, tombs, temples, etc., in which figures or representations of objects are employed, are usually termed 'Hieroglyphic' (from the Greek ἱερογλυφικός); for writing on papyri a cursive form of hieroglyphic called 'Hieratic' (from the Greek ἱερατικός) was employed by the priests, who, at times, also used hieroglyphic; a third kind of writing, consisting of purely conventional modifications of hieratic characters, which preserve little of the original form, was employed for social and business purposes; it is called demotic (from the Greek δημοτικός). The following will show the different forms of the characters in the three styles of writing—

I. HIERATIC.

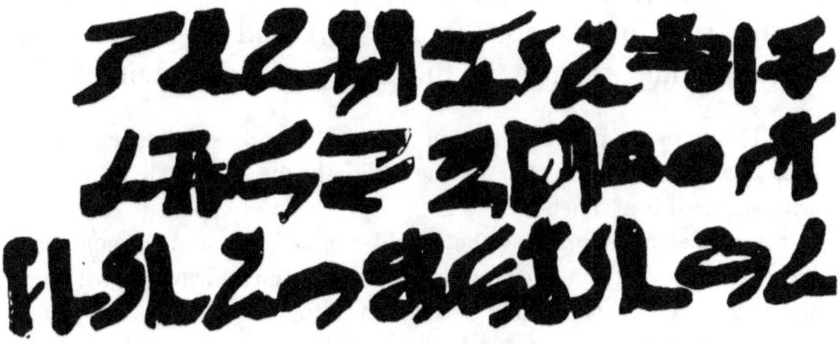

II. Hieroglyphic Transcript of No. I.

III. Demotic.

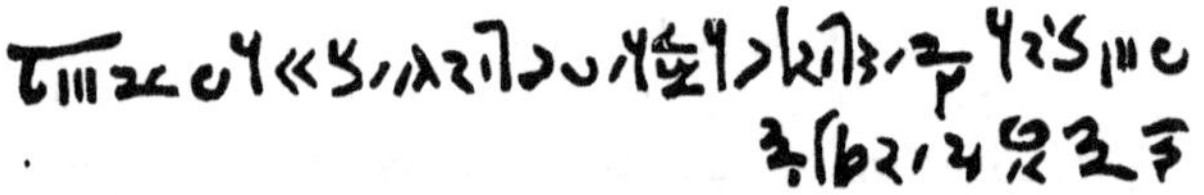

IV. Hieroglyphic Transcript of No. III.

No. I is copied from the Prisse * papyrus (Maxims of Ptaḥ-ḥetep, p. V. l. 1), and is transcribed and translated as follows :—

àb temu àn seχa - nef sef
.... the heart fails, not remembers he yesterday.
qes men-f en āuu bu nefer χeper em-
The body suffers it in [its] entirety, happiness becomes
bu [*bàn*]
wretchedness.†

No. III. is copied from the demotic version inscribed on the stele of Canopus (see p. 19), and No. IV. is the corresponding passage in the hieroglyphic version of the

* This papyrus is the oldest in the world, and was written about B.C. 2500 ; it was presented to the Bibliothèque Nationale by Prisse, who acquired it at Thebes.

† Ptaḥ-ḥetep is lamenting the troubles of old age, and the complete passage runs : "The understanding perisheth, an old man remembers not yesterday. The body becometh altogether pain ; happiness turneth into wretchedness ; and taste vanisheth away."

Decree. The transliteration of the Demotic, according to Hess (*Roman von Stne Ha-m-us*, p. 80), is:—*p-ḥon nuter . . . . . ua n-n-uêb' ent sâtp er-p-ma uêb er-ube p-gi-n-er mnḫ n-n-nuter'*, "a prophet, or one of the priests who are selected for the sanctuary to perform the dressing of the gods." The transliteration of the hieroglyphic text is: *ḥen neter erpu uā àmθ ābu setep er āb-ur àu smā er māret neteru em sati-sen.*

The earliest hieroglyphic inscriptions are the names of the kings of the first dynasty which have been found at Naḳâda and Abydos. The oldest hieratic inscription is that contained in the famous Prisse papyrus which records the advice of Ptaḥ-ḥetep to his son. It dates from the XIth or XIIth dynasty. The demotic writing appears to have come into use about B.C. 900. Hieroglyphics were used until the third century after Christ, and hieratic and demotic for at least a century later. The inscriptions on the Rosetta and Canopus stelæ are written in hieroglyphic, demotic, and Greek characters. The Egyptians inscribed, wrote, or painted inscriptions upon almost every kind of substance, but the material most used by them for their histories, and religious and other works was papyrus. Sections from the stem of the papyrus plant were carefully cut, and the layers were taken off, pressed flat, and several of them gummed one over the other transversely; thus almost any length of papyrus for writing upon could be made. The longest known is the great Harris papyrus, No. 1; it measures 135 feet by 17 inches. The scribe wrote upon the papyrus with reeds, and the inks were principally made of vegetable colours. Black and red are the commonest colours used, but some papyri are painted with as many as eleven or thirteen. The scribe's palette was a rectangular piece of wood varying from six to thirteen inches long by two, or two and a half, inches wide. In the middle was a hollow for holding the reeds, and at one end were the circular or oval cavities in which the colours were placed.

At the beginning of the Greek rule over Egypt, the knowledge of the ancient Egyptian language began to decline, and the language of Greece began to modify and eventually to supersede that of Egypt. When we consider that Ptolemy I., Soter, succeeded in attracting to Alexandria a large number of the greatest Greek scholars of the day, such as Euclid the mathematician, Stilpo of Megara, Theodorus of Cyrene and Diodorus Cronus the philosophers, Zenodotus the grammarian, Philetas the poet from Cos, and many others, this is not to be wondered at. The founding of the great Alexandrian Library and Museum, and the endowment of these institutions for the support of a number of the most eminent Greek philosophers and scholars, was an act of far-sighted policy on the part of Ptolemy I., whose aim was to make the learning and language of the Greeks to become dominant in Egypt. Little by little the principal posts in the Government were monopolised by the Greeks, and little by little the Egyptians became servants and slaves to their intellectually superior masters. In respect to their language, "the Egyptians were not prohibited from making use, so far as it seemed requisite according to ritual or otherwise appropriate, of the native language and of its time-hallowed written signs; in this old home, moreover, of the use of writing in ordinary intercourse the native language, alone familiar to the great public, and the usual writing must necessarily have been allowed not merely in the case of private contracts, but even as regards tax-receipts and similar documents. But this was a concession, and the ruling Hellenism strove to enlarge its domain." Mommsen, *The Provinces of the Roman Empire*, Vol. II., p. 243. It is true that Ptolemy II., Philadelphus, employed the famous Manetho (*i.e.*, , Mer-en-Teḥuti, 'beloved of Thoth') to draw up a history of Egypt, and an account of the ancient Egyptian religion from the papyri and other native records; but it is also true that during the reigns of these two Ptolemies the Egyptians were firmly kept in obscurity, and that the ancient priest-college of Heliopolis was suppressed. A century or two after the Christian era, Greek had obtained such a hold upon the inhabitants of Egypt that the Egyptian Christians, the followers and disciples of St. Mark, were obliged to use the Greek alphabet to write down the Egyptian, that is to say, Coptic translation of the books of the Old and New Testaments. The letters ϣ, *sh*, ϥ, *f*, ϧ, χ, ϩ, *ḥ*, ϭ, *č*, ϫ, *ḳ*, were added from the demotic forms of hieratic characters to represent sounds which were unknown in the Greek language. During the Greek rule over Egypt many of the hieroglyphic characters had new phonetic values given to them; by this time the knowledge of hieroglyphic writing had practically died out.

The history of the decipherment of hieroglyphics is of great interest, but no thorough account of it can be given here; only the most important facts connected with it can be mentioned. During the XVIth–XVIIIth centuries many attempts were made by scholars to interpret the hieroglyphic inscriptions then known to the world, but they resulted in nothing useful. The fact is that they did not understand the nature of the problem to be solved, and they failed to perceive the use of the same hieroglyphic character as a phonetic or determinative in the same inscription. In 1799, a French officer discovered at Bolbitane or Rosetta a basalt slab inscribed in the hieroglyphic, demotic, and Greek characters; it was shortly after captured by the English army, and taken to London, where it was carefully examined by Dr. Thomas Young.*

* Thomas Young was born at Milverton, in Somersetshire, on the 13th of June, 1773; both his parents were Quakers. At the age of fourteen he is said to have been versed in Greek, Latin, French,

The Society of Antiquaries published a fac-simile of the inscription, which was distributed among scholars, and Silvestre de Sacy and Akerblad made some useful discoveries about certain parts of the demotic version of the inscription. Dr. Young was enabled, ten years after, to make translations of the three inscriptions, and the results of his studies were published in 1821. In 1822 M. Champollion * (Le Jeune) published a translation of the same inscriptions, and was enabled to make out something like an alphabet. There appears to be no doubt that he was greatly helped by the publications and labours of Young, who had succeeded in grouping certain words in demotic, and in assigning accurate values to some of the hieroglyphic characters used in writing the names of the Greek rulers of Egypt. Young made many mistakes, but some of his work was of value, Champollion, to whom the credit of definitely settling the phonetic values of several signs really belongs, had been carefully grounded in the Coptic language, and was therefore enabled with little difficulty to recognize the hieroglyphic forms of the words which were familiar to him in Coptic; Young had no such advantage. Champollion's system was subjected to many attacks, but little by little it gained ground, and the labours of other scholars have

Italian, Hebrew, Persian and Arabic. He took his degree of M.D. in July, 1796, in 1802 he was appointed professor of natural philosophy at the Royal Institution, and in 1810 he was elected physician to St. George's Hospital. He was not, however, a popular physician. He died on the 10th of May, 1829.

* Jean François Champollion le Jeune was born at Figeac, department du Lot, in 1796. He was educated at Grenoble, and afterwards at Paris, where he devoted himself to the study of Coptic. In the year 1824 he was ordered by Charles X. to visit all the important collections of Egyptian antiquities in Europe. On his return he was appointed Director of the Louvre. In 1828 he was sent on a scientific mission to Egypt, and was afterwards made professor of Egyptian antiquities at the Collège de France. He died in 1831.

proved that he was right. The other early workers in the field of hieroglyphics were Dr. Samuel Birch in England; Dr. Lepsius in Germany, and MM. Rosellini and Salvolini in Italy. The study of hieroglyphics has become comparatively general, and each year sees books of texts published, learned papers on Egyptian grammar written, and translations made into the various European languages.

In hieroglyphic inscriptions the signs are used in two ways: I, IDEOGRAPHIC, II, PHONETIC. In the ideographic system a word is expressed by a picture or *ideograph* thus:  *mu*, 'water'; in the phonetic system the same word is written  *m* + *u*, no regard being paid to the fact that  represents an owl and  a rope, for their sounds only are needed. Similarly  *emsuḥ* is a 'crocodile' in the ideographic system, but phonetically it is written  *m* + *s* + *u* + *ḥ*. The ideographic system is probably older than the phonetic.

PHONETIC signs are: I, ALPHABETIC, as  *m*,  *s*,  *u*; or II, SYLLABIC, as  *mer*,  *χeper*,  *ḥetep*. The sign  *χeper* can be written 1, ; 2, ; 3, ; 4, ; the sign  *nefer* can be written 1, ; 2, ; 3, 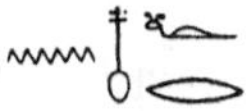; 4, ; 5, . The scribes took pains to represent the exact value of these syllabic signs in order that no mistake might be made.

The IDEOGRAPHIC signs are also used as determinatives, and are placed after words written phonetically to determine their meaning. For example, *nem* means 'to sleep' 'to walk,' 'to go back,' 'to become infirm' 'tongue,' and 'again'; without a determinative the meaning of this word in a sentence would be easily mistaken. DETERMINATIVES are of two kinds: I, *ideographic*, and II, *generic*. Thus after  *màu*, 'cat,' a cat, , was written; this is an *ideographic* determinative. After  *ḳerḥ*, 'darkness,' the night sky with a star in it, 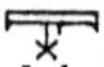, was written; this is a *generic* determinative. A word has frequently more than one determinative; for example, in the word  *bāḥ*, 'to overflow,'  is a determinative of the sound *bāḥ*;  is a determinative of water,  of a lake or collection of water, and  of ground. The list of hieroglyphic signs with their phonetic values given on pp. 133–138 will be of use in reading kings' names, etc.; for convenience, however, the hieroglyphic alphabet is added here. The system of transliteration of Egyptian characters used in this book is that most generally adopted.

	*a*	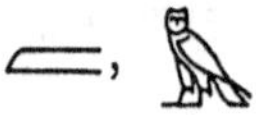	*m*
	*à*	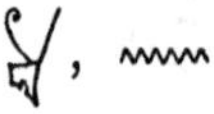	*n*
	*ā*	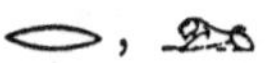	*r* or *l*
	*i*		*h*
	*u*		*ḥ*
	*b*		*χ (kh)*
	*p*	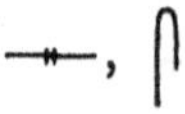	*s*
	*f*		*sh*

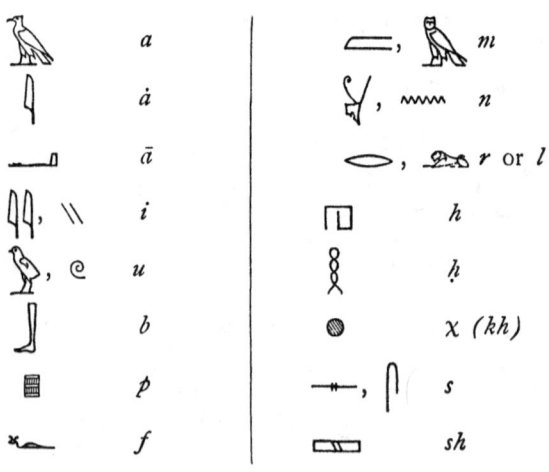

	*k*		*t*
	*q*		*ṭ*
	*ḳ*	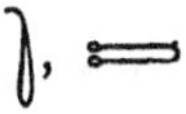	*θ* (*th*)

 *t'* (like *ch* in child)

The number of hieroglyphic characters is about two thousand.

NUMBERS.

 uā, *one*	 paut *or* psṭ, *nine*
 sen, *two*	 met, *ten*
 khemet, *three*	 t'aut, *twenty*
 fṭu, *four*	 māb, *thirty*
 ṭua, *five*	 śaā, *a hundred*
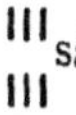 sȧs (?), *six*	 kha, *a thousand*
 sekhef, *seven*	 t'ebā, *ten thousand*
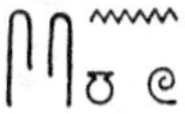 khemennu, *eight*	 ḥefnu, *a hundred thousand*

 ḥeḥ, *a million*

The forms of the numbers 40, 50, 60, 70, 80 and 90 are not known exactly.

Hieroglyphic inscriptions are usually to be read in the opposite direction to which the characters face; there is however no hard and fast rule in this matter. On the papyri they are read in various directions, and there are instances in which the ancient copyist mistook the end of a chapter for its beginning, and copied the whole of it in the reverse order. Some inscriptions are to be read in perpendicular lines.

The following transliterated and translated extract from the first page of the "Tale of the Two Brothers" will explain the foregoing statements.

1. 

àr ementuf χertu sen sen

There were once on a time brothers two [the children]

en uā muθet en uā àtf

of one mother and of one father;

Ànpu ren pa āa àu Batau

Anubis was the name of the elder, was Bata

ren pa šeràu χer àr

the name of the younger. Now as regards

Ànpu su χeri per χeri ḥemt

Anpu, he possessed a house [and] had a wife,

2. 

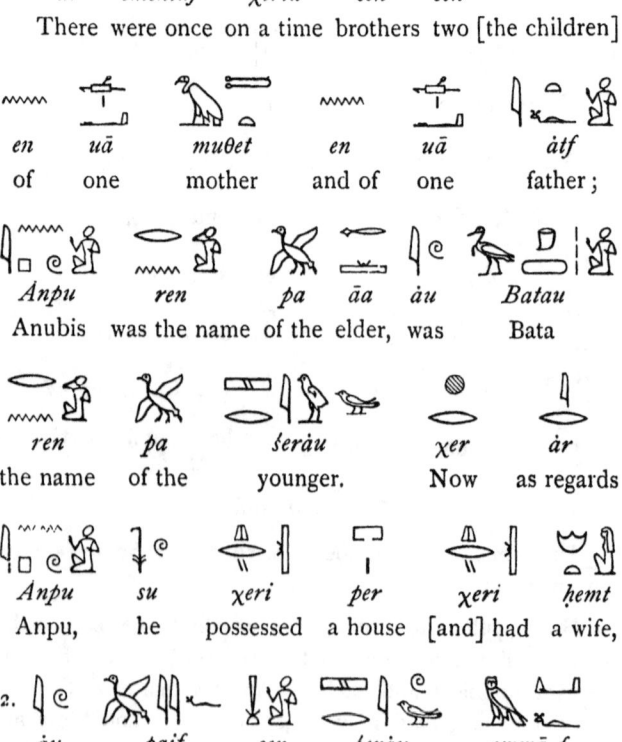

àu paif sen šeràu emmā-f

[and] was his brother younger [living] with him

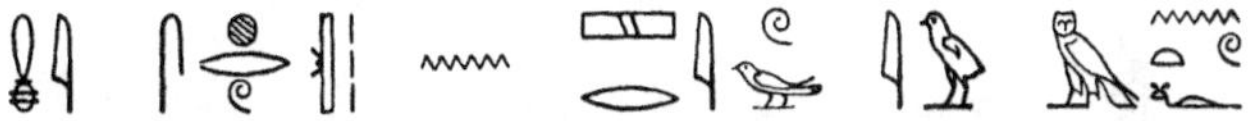

mȧ *seχeru* *en* *śerȧu* *ȧu* *ementuf*

after the manner of a servant, for it was he

ȧ *ȧritu-nef* *ḥebsu* *ȧuf* *ḥer* *seśem*

who made the clothes, it was he who followed

em-sa *nai-f* *ȧaut* *er* *seχet*

after his [Anpu's] cattle in the fields,

3· 

ȧu *ementuf* *ȧ* *ȧritu* *seka*

he it was who did the ploughing,

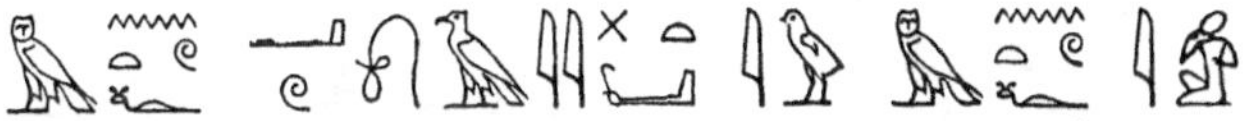

ementuf *āuuait* *ȧu* *ementuf* *ȧ*

he it was who laboured, he it was who

ȧritu-nef *ȧput* *neb* *enti* *em*

performed the duties all which were [connected] with

seχet *ȧs-tu* *ȧu* *pa* *śerȧu*

the fields; and behold was the young man

4· 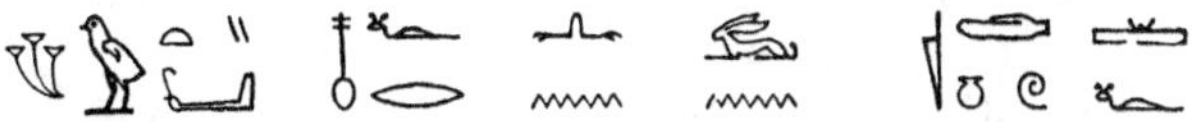

ḥenuti *nefer* *ȧn* *un* *qeṭenu-f*

a farmer excellent, not existed the like of him

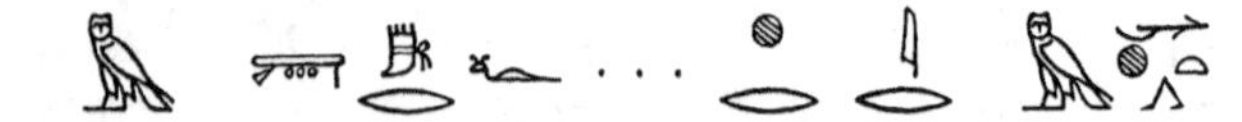

em *ta* *t'er-f* . . . *χer* *ȧr* *emχet*

in the land the whole of it . . . Now thus it was during

hru *qennu* *ḥer-sa* *enen* *ȧu*

days many upon those [days] that

5.

paif *sen* *śerȧu* *emsa* *naif*

was his brother younger following after his

ȧaut *em* *paif* *seχeru* *enti*

cattle according to his wont of

hru *neb* *ementuf* *ḥer* *uāu* (or *beḥāu*) *er*

every day, and he returned to

pai-f *per* *er* *tennu* *ruha*

his house every evening, and

6.

ȧuf *ȧtep* *em* *simu* *neb*

he was laden with vegetables of all kinds

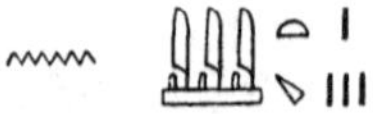

en *seχet*

of the fields.

A List of some of the Principal Hieroglyphic Signs and their Phonetic Values.

Men and Women.

ȧn	āχ	ȧm	śeps
ḥa	qa	ȧr	ȧmen
ur	qeṭ	sa	āb
ser	seḥer	fa	χer
ȧθi	tut	ḥeḥ	ḥenen
ȧau	ȧ	ḥeḥ	maāt

beq

Limbs, &c., of Men.

ṭep, t'at'a	ḥu	χu	sem
ḥrȧ, ḥer	sept	t'eser	seśem
ȧnem	ka	χen	ȧn
ut'a	χen	t	śes
tȧa	ȧn, ȧt	t'ebā	tet *or* θeθ
ȧn	ā	ka, met baḥ	reṭ
ȧri	mā	sem	b
ȧr, sa	neχt	i	āā, āu
r or l	ṭā	seb	

ANIMALS.

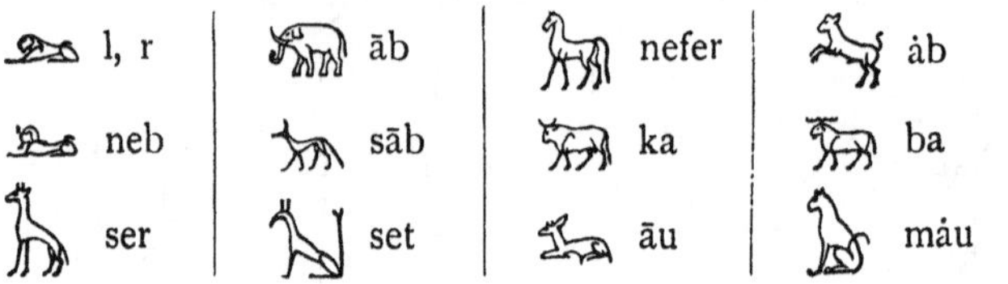

l, r	āb	nefer	ȧb
neb	sāb	ka	ba
ser	set	āu	mȧu

LIMBS, &c., OF ANIMALS.

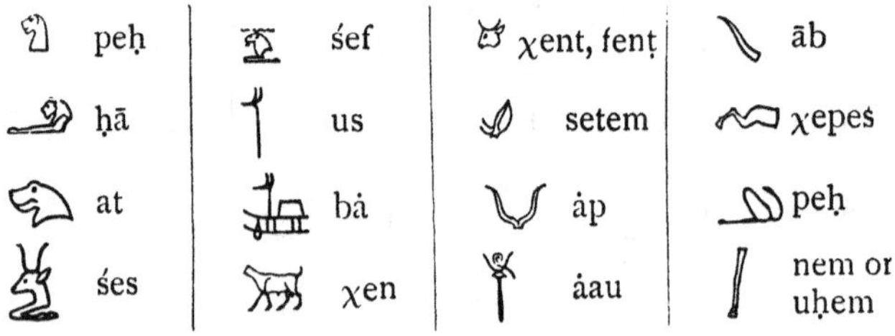

peḥ	śef	χent, fenṭ	āb
ḥā	us	setem	χepeś
at	bȧ	ȧp	peḥ
śes	χen	ȧau	nem or uḥem

BIRDS.

Ḥeru, bak	ur	m	u
ba	ba	neḥ	pa
χu	mut	qem	ten
āq	sa	ti	reχ
śerȧ	mer	a	t'a
			senṭ

PARTS OF BIRDS.

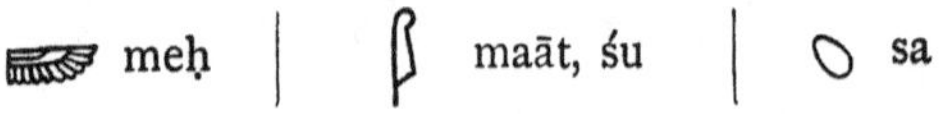

meḥ	maāt, śu	sa

FISH.

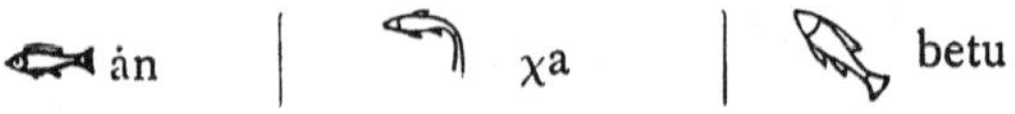

ȧn	χa	betu

REPTILES.

sebek	t′	f
ḥefen	āf, net, χeb seχet, bȧt	χeper
serq′	qem	

TREES AND PLANTS.

ȧm	net′em	su	i
χet	uat′	resu	mes
ḥen	χa	qemā	ḥet′
un	meḥ	renp	sen
uaḥ	ḥa	śa	ḥen
sek	neχeb	seχet	ȧs
bener	enen	ȧ	t′er

CELESTIAL OBJECTS.

pet, ḥer	rā	χā	seb, ṭua
θeḥen	χu	ȧāḥ	

OBJECTS OF EARTH.

ta	ṭu	set, semt	ȧner

WATER.

mu	n	ś	mer	āh

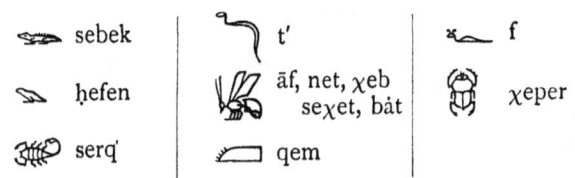

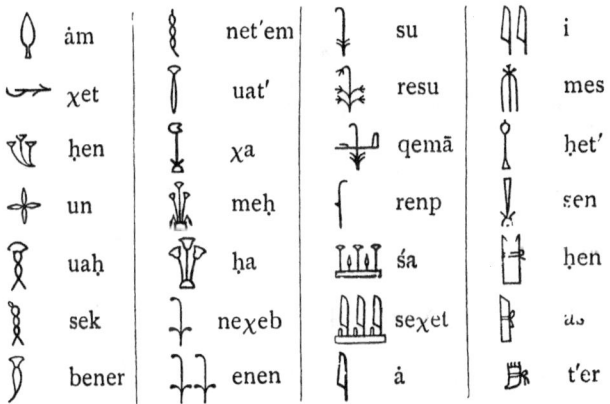

Building.

	nu		seḥ		ā		ṭeṭ
	per		ḥeb		s		ȧs, or ȧst
	ḥet		ȧneb		ȧn		

Arms, etc.

	neter		ma		s		net'
	ṭes ṭem		meḥ		ām, t'ā, qem		āb or ḥem
	sem		śeṭ		set'eb		menχ
	nemmat		χu		χen		χa
	seq		ṭem		ut		sa
	ṭep		ḥeq		meṭ		sma
	āa		āu		θ		setp
	uā		uas		t'a		ut'ā
	peṭ		seχem		men		θ
	śemer		χerp		θes, res		mer
	āḥa		ȧmen		āb, qes, ḳen		
	qeṭ		āb		seḥ		

Musical Instruments.

nefer	seχem	maāt
ḥes	men	sa

Crowns.

ḥet'	meḥ	seχet
net, bȧt	śu	atf

Cords.

qes, śes	ut, ḥeseb	nes	ṭeb
śen	u	āṭ	nub
reṭ	set	θes	χaker
śen	ua	net	śen
ḥ	setchaut seχet	sa	sāḥ
menχ	mer	āper	ānχ

Mathematical Figures.

χ	ḥu	h	ḥer
sep	sepṭ	mer	t'eṭ
paut	ṭā	rer	qen, t'at'a
t	p	ṭeben	ȧmsu
χemt	ḥāp	ren	ȧp
q	× uu, ur, śes	tenȧ, peχ	

Vases, etc.

nu	qebḥ	ta	χer
χnem	ḥen	ta	k
ȧb	mȧ	ḥetep	neb
ḥes	āu, āb	ȧa	ḥeb
χent	ba	ḳ	nā, ān

Ships, etc.

χent	ḥem	seśep	ȧmaχ
ȧm	nef	āu	ȧm
uā, beḥā	āḥā	ḥer, māten	χesef
χer, ḥep	χent	tem	seχt

Determinatives.

to call	of women	of birds
to pray	of birth	of goddesses
to rejoice	to see	of trees
to dance	of strength	of grain
to plough	to give	of heaven
foes	to walk, stand	of light
of men	of flesh	of country
of gods	to breathe, smell	of towns

DETERMINATIVES—*continued.*

	of iron		of metals		of festival
	of water				of unguents
	of houses		writing, computation, knowledge, and abstract ideas		of roads
	of writing				of ships
	of ground		of fire		of winds

THE ARABIC ALPHABET.

Elif	ا	*a*	Zäd	ض	*ḍ* aspirated
Bâ	ب	*b*	Tâ	ط	*ṭ* palatal
Tâ	ت	*t*	Zâ	ظ	*ẓ* palatal
Thâ	ث	*th* = *θ*	‘Ain †	ع	
Gîm	ج	*g* (like *g* in *gin*)*	Ghain	غ	*g* guttural ‡
Hâ	ح	*ḥ* (a smooth guttural aspirate)	Fâ	ف	*f*
Khâ	خ	*ch* (like *ch* in *loch*)	Ḳâf	ق	*ḳ* guttural
Dâl	د	*d*	Kâf	ك	*k*
Zâl	ذ	*th* (like *th* in *that*)	Lâm	ل	*l*
Râ	ر	*r*	Mîm	م	*m*
Zây	ز	*z*	Nûn	ن	*n*
Sîn	س	*s*	Hâ	ه	*h*
Shîn	ش	*sh* (like *sh* in *shut*)	Wâw	و	*w*
Ṣad	ص	*ṣ* (like *ss* in *hiss*)	Yâ	ى	*y*

* Pronounced hard in Egypt.

† Usually unpronounceable by Europeans.

‡ Accompanied by a rattling sound.

The Coptic Alphabet (31 letters).

ⲁ	*a*	ⲙ	*m*	ⲯ	*ps*
ⲃ	*b*	ⲛ	*n*	ⲱ	*ô*
ⲅ	*g*	ⲝ	*x* or *ks*	ϣ	*sh*
ⲇ	*d*	ⲟ	*o*	ϥ	*f*
ⲉ	*e*	ⲡ	*p*	ϧ	χ or *ch*
ⲍ	*z*	ⲣ	*r*	ϩ	*ḥ*
ⲏ	*ê*	ⲥ	*s*	ϫ	*ğ*
ⲑ	*th*	ⲧ	*t*	ϭ	*c*
ⲓ	*i*	ⲩ	*y*	ϯ†	*ti*
ⲕ	*k*	ⲫ	*ph*		
ⲗ	*l*	ⲭ	*ch*		

* In the Boheiric dialect there are thirty-two.

† Six letters of the Coptic alphabet are modifications of the forms of Egyptian characters in demotic. *See* p. 125. The names of the letters in Coptic are ⲁⲗⲫⲁ, ⲃⲓⲇⲁ, ⲅⲁⲙⲙⲁ, ⲇⲁⲗⲇⲁ, ⲉⲓ, ⲍⲓⲧⲁ, ⲏⲧⲁ, ⲑⲓⲧⲁ, ⲓⲁⲩⲧⲁ, ⲕⲁⲡⲡⲁ, ⲗⲁⲩⲗⲁ, ⲙⲓ, ⲛⲓ, ⲝⲓ, ⲟ, ⲡⲓ, ⲣⲟ, ⲥⲓⲙⲁ, ⲧⲁⲩ, ⲩⲉ (ϩⲉ), ⲫⲓ, ⲭⲓ, ⲯⲓ, ⲁⲩ, ϣⲉⲓ, ϥⲉⲓ, ϧⲉⲓ, ϩⲟⲣⲓ, ϫⲁⲛϫⲓⲁ, ϭⲓⲙⲁ, ϯ.

Names of the Months.

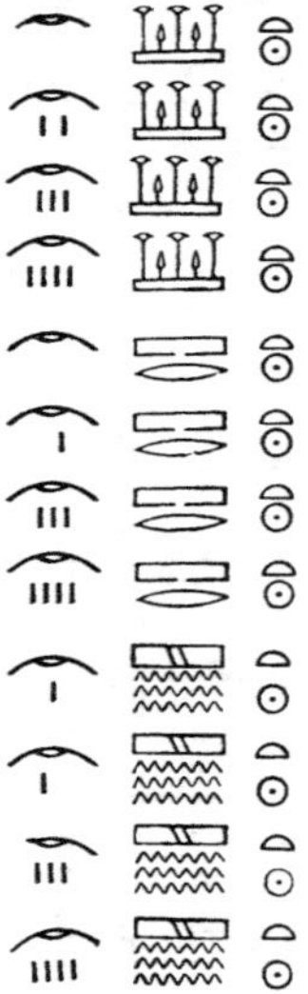

Egyptian.		Alexandrian Months (Coptic Forms).		
ȧbeṭ uā śat	Month one of sowing	ⲑⲱⲟⲩⲧ	August	29 *
ȧbeṭ sen śat	Month two of sowing	ⲡⲁⲟⲡⲓ	September	28
ȧbeṭ chemt śat	Month three of sowing	ⲁⲑⲱⲣ	October	28
ȧbeṭ fṭu śat	Month four of sowing	ⲭⲟⲓⲁⲕ	November	27
ȧbeṭ uā pert	Month one of growing	ⲧⲱⲃⲓ	December	27
ȧbeṭ sen pert	Month two of growing	ⲙⲉⲭⲓⲣ	January	26
ȧbeṭ chemt pert	Month three of growing	ⲫⲁⲙⲉⲛⲱⲑ	February	25
ȧbeṭ fṭu pert	Month four of growing	ⲫⲁⲣⲙⲟⲩⲑⲓ	March	27
ȧbeṭ uā śet	Month one of inundation	ⲡⲁⲭⲟⲛ	April	26
ȧbeṭ sen śet	Month two of inundation	ⲡⲁⲱⲛⲓ	May	26
ȧbeṭ chemt śet	Month three of inundation	ⲉⲡⲏⲡ	June	25
ȧbeṭ fṭu śet	Month four of inundation	ⲙⲉⲥⲱⲣⲏ	July	25

* The days for the beginnings of these months were first fixed at Alexandria about B.C. 30.

The ancient Egyptians had: I. the vague or civil year, which consisted of 365 days; it was divided into twelve months of thirty days each, and five intercalary days were added at the end; II. the Sothic year of 365¼ days. The first year of a Sothic period began with the rising of Sirius or the dog-star, on the 1st of the month Thoth, when it coincided with the beginning of the inundation; III. the Egyptian solar year,* which was treated as if it were a quarter of a day shorter than the Sothic year, an error which corrected itself in 1460 fixed years or 1461 vague years. The true year was estimated approximately by the conjunction of the sun with Sirius. Dr. Brugsch thinks (*Egypt under the Pharaohs*, Vol. I., p. 176) that as early as B.C. 2500 *five* different forms of the year were already in use, and that the "little year' corresponded with the lunar year, and the "great year" with a lunar year having intercalated days. Each month was dedicated to a god.† The Egyptians dated their stelæ and documents by the day of the month and the year of the king who was reigning at the time. The Copts first dated their documents according to the years of the INDICTION; the indictions were periods of fifteen years, and the first began A.D. 312. In later times the Copts made use of the era of the Martyrs, which was reckoned from the 29th of August, A.D. 284. About the ninth century after Christ they began to adopt the Muḥammadan era of the Hijrah or "flight," which was reckoned from A.D. 622.

* It was practically the same as the civil year.

† Some of the Coptic names of the months show that they have been derived from the ancient Egyptian: thus Thôth is from , *Teḥuti*, Pachôn from  *Khensu*, Athôr from , *Ḥet-Ḥeru*, Mesôre from  *mes-Ḥeru*, "the birth of Horus" festival, etc. The Copts have I. an agricultural year, and II. an ecclesiastical year; the latter consists of twelve months of thirty days, with a thirteenth month called Nissi of five or six intercalary days.

THE RELIGION AND GODS OF ANCIENT EGYPT.

The religion of the ancient Egyptians is one of the most difficult problems of Egyptology, and though a great deal has been written about it during the last few years, and many difficulties have been satisfactorily explained, there still remain unanswered a large number of questions connected with it. In all religious texts the reader is always assumed to have a knowledge of the subject treated of by the writer, and no definite statement is made on the subject concerning which very little, comparatively, is known by students to-day. For example, in the texts inscribed inside the pyramids of Unȧs, Tetȧ, and Pepi (B.C. 3300-3233), we are brought face to face with religious compositions which mention the acts and relationships of the gods, and refer to beliefs, and give instructions for the performance of certain acts of ritual which are nowhere explained. It will be remembered that Ptolemy II. Philadelphus instructed Manetho to draw up a history of the religion of the ancient Egyptians. If such a work was needed by the cultured Greek who lived when the religion of ancient Egypt, though much modified, was still in existence, how much more is it needed now? The main beliefs of the Egyptian religion were always the same. The attributes of one god were applied to another, or one god was confused with another; the cult of one god declined in favour of another, or new gods arose and became popular, but the fundamentals of the religion of Egypt remained unchanged. Still, it is asserted by some that the religion of the Early Empire was simpler than that of the Middle and New Empires, in which the nature and mutual relationships of the gods were discussed and theogonies formulated. Many of the gods of Egypt were the everlasting and unalterable powers of nature. The oldest god of Egypt is Ḥeru, and his symbol was a hawk. The great Sun-god Rā, or Åmen-Rā, as he was called in the Middle Empire, was said to be the maker of all things; the various gods Horus, Åtmu, etc., were merely forms of him. Rā was self-begotten, and hymns to him never cease to proclaim his absolute and perfect unity in terms which resemble those of the Hebrew Scriptures. It will be seen from the translation of a hymn given in the following pages that he is made to possess every attribute, natural and spiritual, which Christian peoples ascribe to God Almighty, and there is no doubt that long before this hymn was written, the Egyptians had formulated a belief in One God, who was almighty and was self-existent. The material symbol of God was the sun, who was personified under the form of Rā, or later Amen-Rā; and although Osiris, who was an indigenous Libyan (?) god, is far older than Rā in Egypt, Rā was declared to have been the father of Osiris, and Osiris was his only son. Osiris was of divine origin, and he reigned wisely and well on earth, but at length he was slain and mutilated by Set, the personification of the powers of darkness. But he rose from the dead, and became the god of the underworld and of the beings who were therein. Because he suffered, died, and rose from the dead, he became the type of the **Resurrection** to the Egyptians, who based all their hopes of everlasting life upon the belief that Osiris was immortal and eternal. When, where, or how this belief arose cannot be said, but, however far back we go in dynastic, and even pre-dynastic, times in Egypt, we find evidences that the belief in the resurrection and eternal life was universal. Under the earliest dynasties tombs * were built in order that the bodies placed in them might be preserved until the Resurrection should take place. It is clear from the papyri that man was supposed to possess a body,  *khat*, a soul,  *ba*, a "double,"  *ka*, an intelligence,  *khu*, a shadow  *khaibit*, a form,  *sekhem*, a heart,  *àb*, a name,  *ren*, and a spiritual body,  *sāḥ*. The body, freed from all its most corruptible portions, was preserved by being filled with bitumen, spices, and aromatic drugs, and having been swathed with many a fold of linen, and protected by amulets and religious texts, awaited in its tomb the visit of its soul.

Of the funeral procession we are able to gain some idea from the vignettes which are given in hieroglyphic copies of the Book of the Dead. In the centre of p. 147 the dead man is seen lying on a bier in a chest mounted on a boat with runners, which is drawn by oxen. In the rear is a sepulchral ark or chest surmounted by a figure of Anubis, the god of the dead. In front of the boat are a group of

* "Les belles tombes que l'on admire dans les plaine de Thèbes et de Saḳḳârah ne sont donc pas dues à l'orgueil de ceux qui les ont érigées. Une pensée plus large a présidé à leur construction. Plus les matériaux sont énormes, plus on est sûr que les promesses faites par la religion recevront leur exécution. En ces sens, les Pyramides ne sont pas des monuments 'de la vaine ostentation des rois'; elles sont des obstacles impossibles à renverser, et les preuves gigantesques d'un dogme consolant." (Mariette, *Notices des Principaux Monuments*, p. 44.)

women (p. 148) beating their faces and wailing, and a youth carrying the staff, chair, and box of the deceased. At the head of the procession is the *kher ḥeb* or master of funereal ceremonies, who reads from an open roll of papyrus the funereal service. The scene on page 148 represents the ceremony of "opening the mouth," which takes place at the door of the tomb. Before the tomb stands the mummy of Hu-nefer to receive the final honours; behind him, and embracing him, stands Anubis, the god of the dead, and at his feet in front kneel his wife Nasha and her daughter to take a last farewell of the body. By the side of a table of offerings stand three priests: the *sem* priest, who wears a panther's skin, holding in his right hand a libation vase, and in the left a censer; a priest who offers vases of unguents to the deceased; and a priest who holds in one hand the instrument *ur-ḥeka*  with which he is about to touch the eyes and mouth of the mummy, and in the other the instrument  for "opening the mouth." On the rounded stele , at the door of the tomb, is inscribed:—"Hail, Osiris, chief of Amenta, the lord of eternity, spreading out in everlastingness, lord of adorations, chief of the cycle of his gods; and hail, Anubis [dweller] in the tomb, great god, chief of the divine dwelling. May they grant that I may go in and come out from the underworld; that I may follow Osiris in all his festivals at the beginning of the year; that I may receive cakes, and that I may come forth in the presence of [Osiris], I the *ka* of Osiris, the greatly favoured of his god, Hu-nefer."

In the lower register are a cow and calf, a priest holding a vase , a priest carrying a haunch of a bull , a table of offerings, a sepulchral box , and a table upon which are arranged the instruments employed in the ceremony of

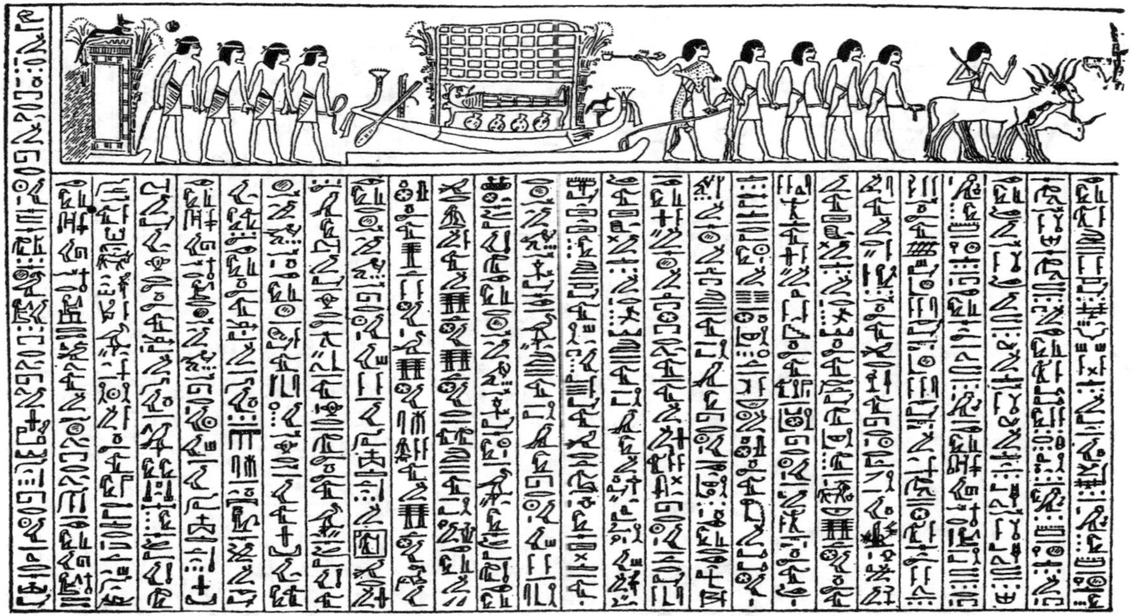

An Egyptian Funeral Procession. The hieroglyphic text beneath is the First Chapter of the Book of the Dead. (From British Museum Papyrus, No. 9901.)

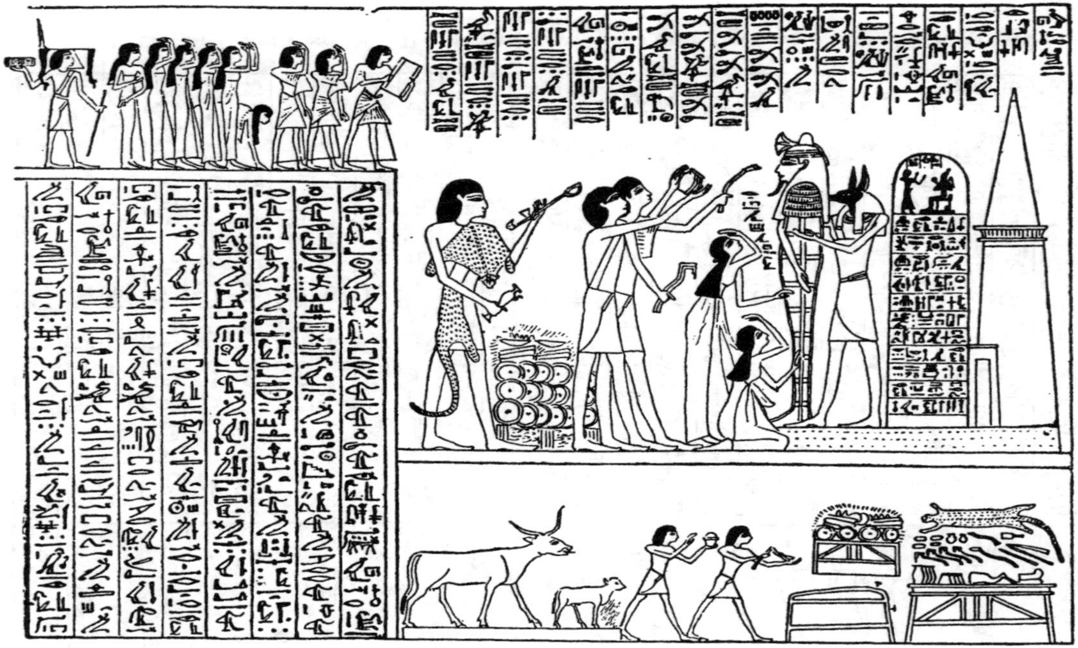

An Egyptian Funeral Procession and the Performance of the Ceremony of "Opening the Mouth" at the Door of the Tomb. (From British Museum Papyrus, No. [illegible].)

opening the mouth, *viz.*, the *Pesh-en-kef*, the haunch, the libation vases, the feather, the instruments, the *ur-ḥeka*, the boxes of purification, the bandlet, *etc.*

After the death of a man it was thought that he was taken into the hall of the god Osiris, judge of the dead, and that his conscience, symbolized by the heart, was weighed in the balance before him. An excellent idea of what the Egyptians believed in this matter may be gathered from the two following scenes in the Papyrus of Ani. Ani and his wife Thuthu are entering the **Hall of Double Truth**, wherein the heart is to be weighed against the feather, emblematic of Right and Truth, or Law. This ceremony is being performed in the presence of the gods "Ḥeru-khuti (Harmachis) the great god within his boat"; Temu; Shu; "Tefnut, lady of heaven,"; Seb; "Nut, lady of heaven,"; Isis; Nephthys; "Horus, the great god,"; "Hathor, lady of Amenta,"; Ḥu; and Sa. Upon the beam of the scales is the dog-headed ape, the companion or attendant of Thoth, "the scribe of the gods." The god Anubis, jackal-headed, is kneeling to examine the indicator of the balance, which is suspended from a projection made in the form of. The inscription above the head of Anubis reads:—"Saith he

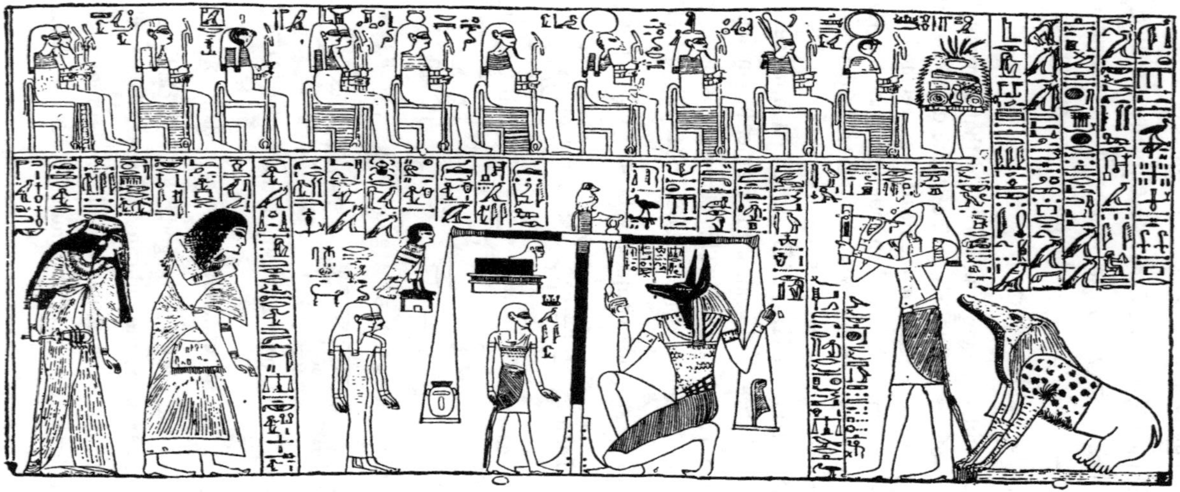

THE HEART OF ANI BEING WEIGHED IN THE BALANCE.

(From British Museum Papyrus, No. 10,470.)

Horus introducing Ani to the God Osiris.

(From British Museum Papyrus, No. 10,470.)

who is in the abode of the dead, 'Turn thy face, O just and righteous weigher [who weighest] the heart in the balance, to stablish it.'" Facing Anubis, a god of the dead, stands Ani's "Luck" or "Destiny," *Shai* , and above is a human-headed object resting upon a pylon which is supposed to be connected with the place where he was born. Behind these stand the goddesses Meskhenet  and Renenet , who were the deities who presided over the birth and education of children. Near these is the soul of Ani in the form of a human-headed bird , standing upon a pylon . On the right of the balance, behind Anubis, stands Thoth, the scribe of the gods, with his reed-pen and palette containing black and red ink, with which to record the result of the trial. Behind Thoth is the female monster Āmām 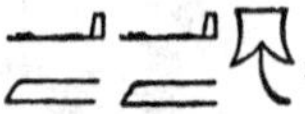, the "Devourer," called also Ām-mit  , the "Eater of the Dead." She has the fore-part of a crocodile, the hind-quarters of a hippopotamus, and the middle part of a lion. Ani says:—

"My heart my mother, my heart my mother, my heart my coming into being. May there be no resistance to me in [my] judgment; may there be no opposition to me from the divine chiefs; may there be no parting of thee from me in the presence of him who keepeth the scales! Thou art my *ka* (double) within my body which knitteth and strengtheneth my limbs. Mayest thou come forth to the place of happiness to which we advance. May the divine chiefs (*Shenit*) not make my name to stink, and may no lies be spoken against me in the presence of the god. It is good for thee to hear [glad tidings of joy at the weighing of words. May no false accusation be made against me in the presence of the great god. Verily, exceedingly mighty shalt thou be when thou risest]."

Thoth, the righteous judge of the great cycle of the gods who are in the presence of the god Osiris, saith, "Hear ye this judgment. The heart of Osiris hath in very truth been weighed and his soul hath stood as a witness for him; his trial in the Great Balance is true. There hath not been found any wickedness in him; he hath not wasted the offerings in the temples; he hath not harmed any by his works; and he uttered not evil reports while he was upon earth."

Next the great cycle of the gods reply to Thoth dwelling in Khemennu (Hermopolis): "That which cometh forth from thy mouth cannot be gainsaid. Osiris, the scribe Ani, the victorious one in judgment, is just and righteous. He hath not committed sin, neither hath he done evil against us. The Devourer shall not be allowed to prevail over him; he shall be allowed to enter into the presence of the god Osiris, and offerings of meat and drink shall be given unto him, together with an abiding habitation in Sekhet-ḥetepu, as unto the followers of Horus."

In the second part of this scene we have Ani being led into the presence of the god Osiris. On the left the hawk-headed god Horus , the son of Isis, wearing the crowns of the North and South , holding Ani by the hand, leads him into the presence of "Osiris, the lord of eternity,"  *Ȧusȧr neb t'etta.* This god is seated within a shrine in the form of a funereal chest, and he wears the *atef* crown , with plumes; at the back of his neck hangs a *menȧt* , the emblem of joy and

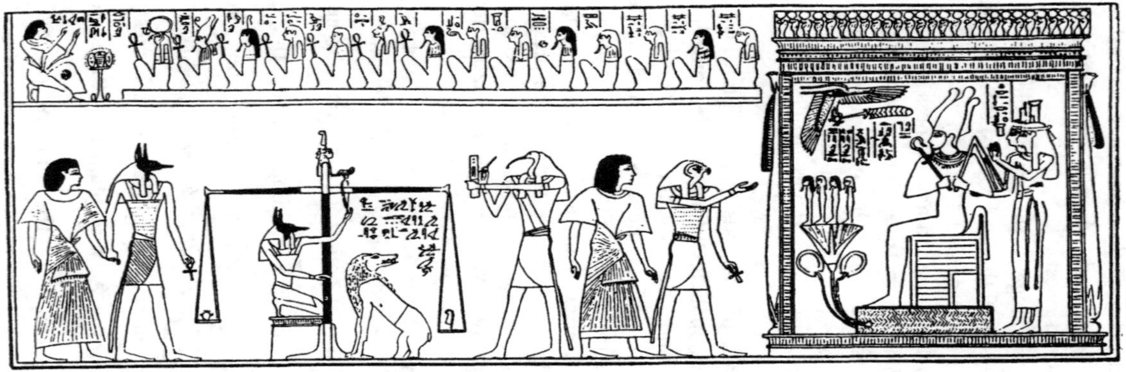

Scene of the Weighing of the Heart in the Hall of Osiris.

(From British Museum Papyrus, No. 9,901.)

Here it will be noticed that the details of the Judgment Scene are different from those given in the Papyrus of Ani. Thus Meskhenet, Renenet, Meskhen, Shai, and the soul of the deceased are omitted; the pillar of the balance is surmounted by a head of the goddess Maāt; the wife of the deceased is omitted, and the throne of Osiris is set upon water.

happiness. In his hands he holds the crook , sceptre , and the flail , emblems of rule, sovereignty and dominion. On the side of his throne are depicted the doors of the tomb with bolts, . Behind him stand Nephthys on his right and Isis on his left. Standing upon a lotus flower which springs from the ground, are the four deities generally known as "the children of Horus" (or Osiris); they represent the cardinal points. The first, Mesthȧ , has the head of a man ; the second, Ḥāpi , the head of an ape ; the third, Ṭuamāutef , the head of a jackal ; and the fourth, Qebḥsennuf, , the head of a hawk . Suspended near the lotus flower is a bullock's hide, into which the deceased, or the person who represented him at funereal ceremonies, was supposed to enter. The roof of the shrine rests upon pillars with lotus capitals, and is ornamented with a cornice of uræi; the hawk-headed figure above represents the god Horus-Sepṭ or Horus-Seker.

At the foot of steps leading to the throne of Osiris, kneels Ani upon a mat made of fresh reeds; his right hand is raised in adoration, and in his left he holds the *kherp* sceptre . He wears a whitened wig surmounted by a "cone," the signification of which is unknown. Round his neck is the collar . Close by are a table of offerings of meat, fruit, flowers, *etc.*, and a number of vases containing wine, beer, unguents, , , , *etc.*; with these are trussed ducks , flowers , cakes and loaves of bread , , , *etc.* The inscription above the table of offerings reads, "Osiris, the scribe Ani." . The inscription above Ani reads: "O Lord of Amenta (the underworld), I am in thy presence. There is no sin in my body, I have uttered no lie wilfully, and I have done nothing with a double motive. Grant that I may be like unto those favoured beings who [stand] about thee, and that I may be an Osiris greatly favoured of the beautiful god and beloved of the lord of the world—[I] who am in truth a royal scribe loving him, Ani, victorious in judgment before the god Osiris."

To Osiris Horus says:—"I have come to thee, O Unnefer, and I have brought the Osiris Ani to thee. His heart is righteous coming forth from the balance, and it hath not committed sin against any god or any goddess. Thoth hath weighed it according to the directions spoken to him by the cycle of the gods; and it is very true and righteous. Grant unto him offerings of meat and drink, permit him to enter into the presence of Osiris, and grant that he may be like unto the followers of Horus for ever."

An interesting vignette in the papyrus of Neb-seni (British Museum, No. 9,900) shows the deceased being weighed against his own heart in the presence of the god Osiris:

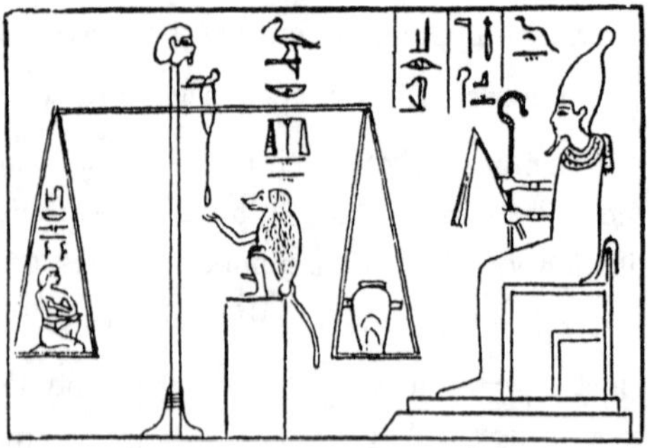

If the result of the weighing of the heart was unfavourable, the Devourer stepped forward and claimed the dead man as his. Annihilation was the result.

The following is a specimen of the hymns which the deceased addresses to Rā :—

A HYMN TO RĀ [TO BE SUNG] WHEN HE RISETH IN THE EASTERN SKY.

(*From British Museum Papyrus, No.* 9,901.)

"Homage to thee, O thou who art Rā when thou risest and Tmu when thou settest. Thou risest, thou risest; thou shinest, thou shinest, O thou who art crowned king of the gods. Thou art the lord of heaven, thou art the lord of earth, thou art the creator of those who dwell in the heights, and of those who dwell in the depths. Thou art the ONE god who came into being in the beginning of time. Thou didst create the earth, thou didst fashion man, thou didst make the watery abyss of the sky, thou didst form Ḥāpi (Nile); thou art the maker of all streams and of the great deep, and thou givest life to all that is therein. Thou hast knit together the mountains, thou, thou hast made mankind and the beasts of the field, thou hast created the heavens and the earth. Worshipped be thou whom the goddess Maāt embraceth at morn and at eve. Thou stridest across the sky with heart expanded with joy; the Lake of Tchestches is at peace. The fiend Nȧk hath fallen and his two arms are cut off. The boat of the rising sun hath a fair wind, and the heart of him that is in its shrine rejoiceth. Thou art crowned with a heavenly form, thou the Only ONE art provided [with all things]. Rā cometh forth from Nu (sky) in triumph. O thou mighty youth, thou everlasting son, self-begotten, who didst give birth to thyself; O thou mighty One of myriad forms and aspects, King of the world, Prince of Ȧnnu (Heliopolis), lord of eternity, and ruler of the everlasting, the company of the gods rejoice when thou risest, and when thou sailest across the sky, O thou who art exalted in the *sektet* boat. Homage to thee, O Ȧmen-Rā, thou who dost rest upon Maāt, thou who passest over heaven, [from] every face that seeth thee. Thou dost wax great as thy Majesty doth advance, and thy rays are upon all faces. Thou art unknown and inscrutable . . . . ; thou art the Only One. [Men] praise thee in thy name [Rā], and they swear by thee, for thou art lord over them. Thou hast heard with thine ears and thou hast seen with thine eyes. Millions of years have gone over the world; those through which thou hast passed I cannot count. Thy heart hath decreed a day of happiness in thy name [of Rā]. Thou dost pass over and travellest through untold spaces of millions and hundreds of thousands of years, thou settest in peace and thou steerest thy way across the watery abyss to the place which thou lovest; this thou doest in one little moment of time, and thou dost sink down and make an end of the hours. Hail my lord, thou that passest through eternity and whose being is everlasting. Hail thou Disk, lord of beams of light, thou risest and thou makest all mankind to live. Grant thou that I may behold thee at dawn each day."

From the scene on p. 159, we may form an idea of how the deceased was supposed to employ his time in the "islands of the blessed," which the Egyptians called "Sekhet-Ḥetepu." Here we have an estate intersected by canals of waters. To the left in the upper division are three pools called Qenqenet, Ȧnttenet and Nut-ur. Beneath is the legend:—"The being in peace in the Fields of Air (?).' Before three gods who are described as "gods of the horizon" is an altar with flowers, "an offering to the great god, the lord of heaven." On a pylon stands a hawk. Next we see the deceased making an offering of incense to his own soul in the form of a human-headed hawk . In a boat,

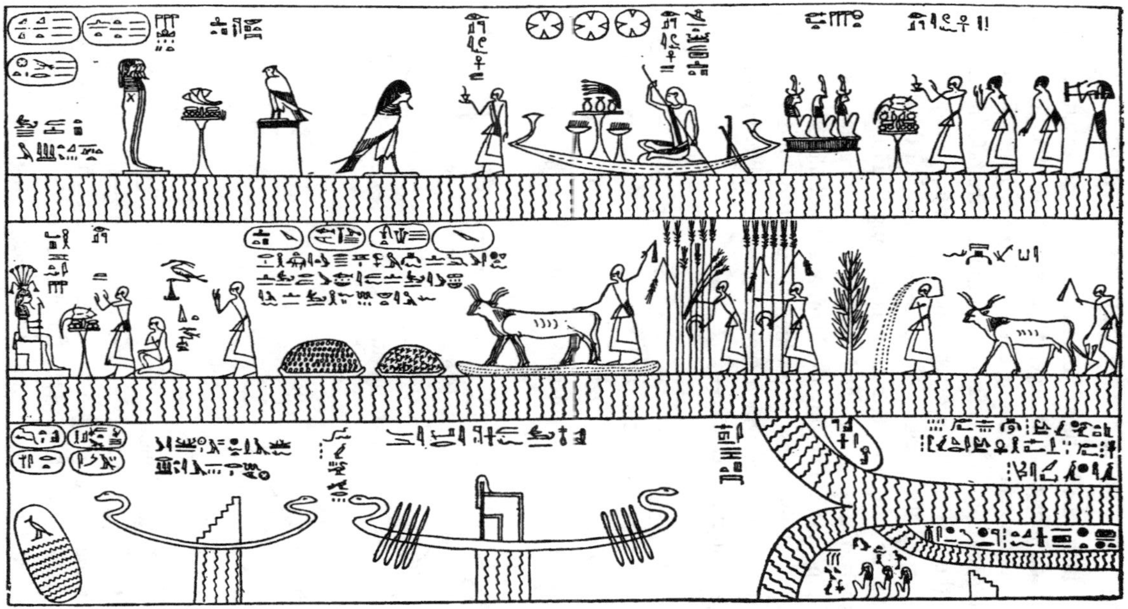

The Sekhet-Ḥetepu or Elysian Fields of the Egyptians.

in which stand tables of offerings, sits the deceased paddling himself along. The legend reads, "Osiris, the living one, the victorious one sailing over the Lake of Peace." Behind, the deceased and his father and mother are offering incense to the "great cycle of the gods"; close by stands Thoth the scribe of the gods. In the second division the deceased, with his father and mother, is adoring "Ḥāpi (Nile), the father of the gods," and we see him ploughing, sowing, reaping and winnowing the luxuriant wheat along a track by the canal the "length of which is one thousand measures, and the width of which cannot be told." The legend says concerning this canal:—

àn	*un*	*remu*	*neb*	*àm-f*	*àn*	*un*
"Not	exist	fishes	any	in it,	not	exist

àu	*neb*	*àm-f*	*àr.*	*un*	*ḥefi*
àu fishes	any	in it,	not	exist	{ worms snakes

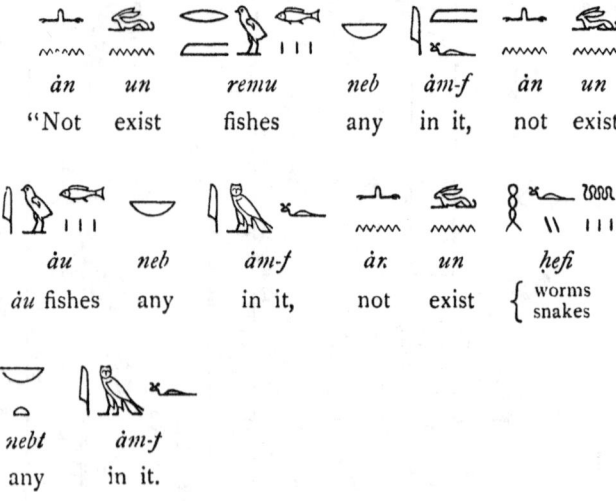

nebt	*àm-f*
any	in it.

In the third division are:—five islands (?); "the boat of Rā-Harmachis when he goeth forth to Sekhet-Àanre"; a boat the master of which is the god Un-nefer; and three small divisions formed by the "water of the sky." In the first are "beatified beings seven cubits high, and wheat three cubits high for spiritual beings who are made perfect"; the second is the place where the gods refresh themselves; and in the third live the gods Seb, Shu and Tefnut.

After death the soul of the dead man was supposed to have many enemies to combat, just as the sun was supposed to spend the time between his setting and rising in fighting the powers of mist, darkness, and night. These he vanquished by the knowledge and use of certain "words of power." The deceased was also supposed to be condemned to perform field labours in the nether-world, but to avoid this, stone, wooden, or Egyptian porcelain figures

THE SOUL REVISITING THE BODY IN THE TOMB.
(From the Papyrus of Neb-seni, British Museum, No. 9,900.)

were placed in his tomb to do the work for him. After undergoing all these troubles and trials the soul went into the abode of beatified spirits, and there did everything wished by it, and remained in bliss until it rejoined its body in the tomb. During its wanderings it might make its transformations into a phœnix (*bennu*), a heron, a swallow, a snake, a crocodile, etc.

In the Hall of Osiris the soul was supposed to affirm before the Forty-Two gods that it had not committed any of the forty-two sins which are detailed in good papyri at full length as follows :—

1. O thou that stridest, coming forth from Heliopolis, I have done no wrong.*
2. O thou that embracest flame, coming forth from Kher-āba, I have not committed theft.
3. O Fenṭiu, who comest forth from Hermopolis, I have committed no act of violence.
4. O Eater of Shadows, who comest forth from Qernet, I have never slain men.
5. O Neḥa-ḥrȧ, who comest forth from Re-stau, I have never filched from the measures of corn.
6. O ye double lions, who come forth from the sky, I have committed no fault.
7. O Eyes of Flame, who come forth from Seaut, I have never stolen the property of the gods.
8. O Neba (*i.e.*, Fire), who comest forth in retreating, I have never spoken falsehood.
9. O Seizer of Bones, who comest forth from Suten-ḥenen, I have never stolen food to eat.
10. O Breath of Flame, who comest forth from the Ḥet-ka-Ptaḥ (Memphis), I have spoken no evil.
11. O Qererti, who comest forth from the underworld, I have committed no act of uncleanness.
12. O thou god whose face is turned behind thee, who comest forth from thy shrine, I have never caused any one to weep tears of sadness.
13. O Basti, who comest forth from the tomb (?), I have never eaten my heart (*i.e.*, lied).

* From the Papyrus of Ani, Brit. Mus. No. 10,470, plates 31, 32. For a complete translation of the 125th Chapter of the *Book of the Dead*, of which this extract forms part, see my *Papyrus of Ani*, London, 1895, p. 344 ff. The forty-two negative declarations are commonly called the "Negative Confession."

14. O Legs of Flame, who come forth from the darkness of night, I have never made an attack upon any man.

15. O Eater of Blood, who comest forth from the block of sacrifice, I have never meditated upon iniquity.

16. O Eater of the intestines, who comest forth from the Abode of the Thirty, I have never stolen tilled ground.

17. O Lord of Law, who comest forth from the abode of Law, I have never entered into a conspiracy.

18. O thou that stridest backwards, who comest forth from Bubastis, I have never accused any man of crime.

19. O Serṭiu, who comest forth from Heliopolis, I have never been angry without cause.

20. O god of two-fold evil, who comest forth from the nome Atchi,* I have never committed adultery.

21. O Uamemti, who comest forth from Khebt, I have never committed adultery.

22. O thou that observest what hath been brought into the Temple of Åmsu, I have never defiled myself.

23. O ye Chiefs, who come forth from the persea trees, I have never caused terror.

24. O Khemi, who comest forth from Ḳu, I have never transgressed.

25. O Reciter of words, who comest forth from Urit, I have never spoken in hot anger.

26. O Babe, who comest forth from Uab,† I have never made my ear (*literally*, face) deaf to the sound of words of truth.

27. O Kenememti, who comest forth from Kenemmet, I have never uttered curses.

28. O thou that bringest thy offering, who comest forth from Seut, I have never put out my hand in a quarrel.

* The ninth nome of Lower Egypt.

† The 19th nome of Upper Egypt, capital Oxyrhynchos.

29. O thou that orderest words, who comest forth from Unaset, I have never been an excitable and contentious person.
30. O Lord of [various] aspects, who comest forth from Netchefet, I have never been precipitate in judgment.
31. O Sekheriu, who comest forth from Uten, I have never stirred up conspiracy.
32. O Lord of the double horns, who comest forth from Senti, I have never multiplied my words against those of others.
33. O Nefer-Temu, who comest forth from Ḥet-ka-Ptaḥ (Memphis), I have never meditated evil, and I have never done evil.
34. O Temu in his seasons, who comest forth from Ṭaṭṭu, I have never committed an act of wrong against the king.
35. O thou that workest in thy heart, who comest forth from Sahu, I have never turned running water out of its course.
36. O Akhi, who comest forth from Nu, I have never been arrogant in speech.
37. O thou who verdifiest mankind, who comest from Seu, I have never blasphemed God.
38. O Neḥebka, who comest forth from thy shrine, I have never committed fraud.
39. O thou who art dowered with splendours, who comest forth from thy shrine, I have never defrauded the gods of their offerings.
40. O Ser-ṭep, who comest forth from [thy] shrine, I have never robbed the dead.
41. O thou that bringest thy arm, who comest forth from the place of double truth, I have never robbed the child nor defiled the god of [my] town.
42. O Illuminator of the lands, who comest forth from Tashe (Fayyûm), I have never slain the animals sacred to the gods.

It is tolerably evident then that grand tombs were not built as mere objects of pride, but as "everlasting habitations" which would serve to preserve the body from decay, and keep it ready to be re-inhabited by the soul at the proper season. Greek authors have written much about the beliefs of the Egyptians; but the greater number of their statements are to be received with caution. They wrote down what they were told, but were frequently misinformed.

The papyri which have come down to us show that the moral conceptions of the Egyptians were of a very high order: and works like the Maxims of Ptaḥ-ḥetep and the Maxims of Ani* show clearly that a man's duty to his god and to his fellow-man was laid down in a distinct manner. Such works will compare very favourably with the Proverbs of Solomon and the Wisdom of Jesus the son of Sirach.

The religious literature of the Egyptians includes a large number of works, of which the most important is the collection of chapters generally called the **Book of the Dead**; in Egyptian its name is *per em hru*, "Coming forth by day." Selections from this work were written in the hieratic character upon coffins as early as the XIIth dynasty (B.C. 2500), and this practice was continued down to the second century of our era. The walls of tombs were covered with extracts from it, and scribes and people of rank had buried with them large rolls of papyrus inscribed with its principal chapters, and ornamented with vignettes explanatory of the text which ran beneath. Some of the chapters in the work are of very great antiquity; and as far back as B.C. 3500 the text was so old that the scribes could not understand it all. Many parts of it are obscure, and some corrupt; but the discovery from time to time of ancient papyri with accurate readings tends to clear up many doubtful points, and to bring out the right meaning of certain parts of the work.

* See page 597.

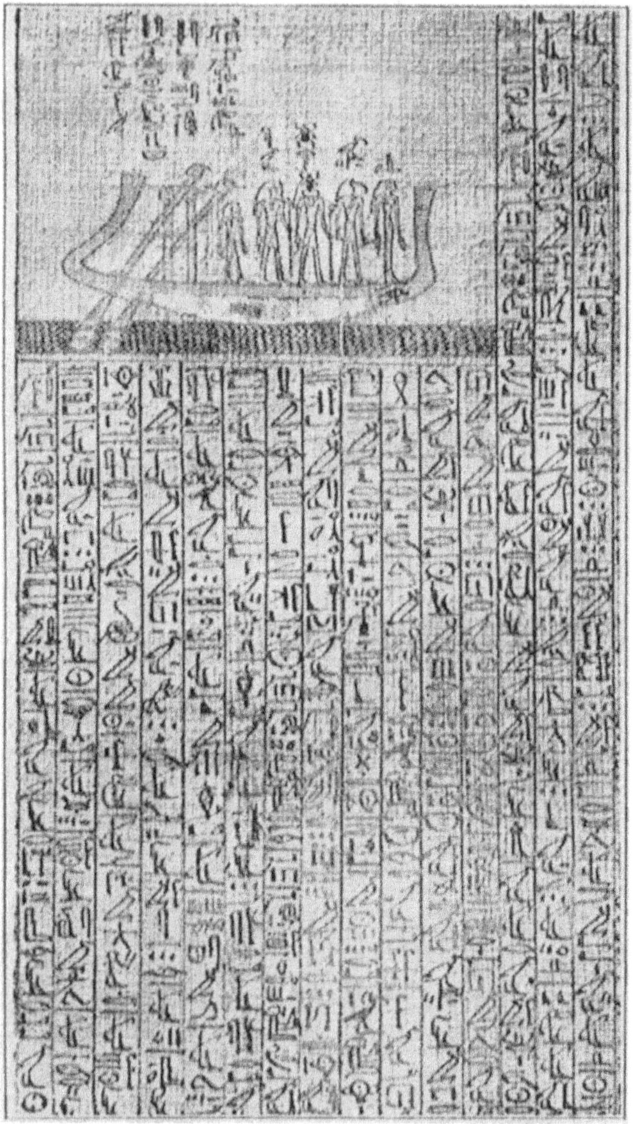

Vignette and Chapter of the Book of the Dead.
F(rom the Papyrus of Nu in the British Museum. Early XVIIIth dynasty.)

The following is a list of the most important gods with their names in hieroglyphics; it will be readily seen how very many of them are merely forms of the sun-god Rā, and how many of them have the same attributes :—

Khnemu,* the 'Moulder,' 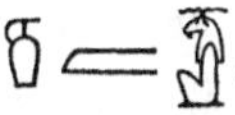, is represented with the head of a ram, and is one of the oldest gods of the Egyptian religion. He was thought to possess some of the attributes of Åmen, Rā, and Ptaḥ, and shared with the last-named god the attribute of "maker of mankind." At Philæ he is represented making man out of clay on a potter's wheel. Khnemu put together the scattered limbs of the dead body of Osiris, and it was he who constructed the beautiful woman who became the wife of Bata in the Tale of the Two Brothers. Like Åmen-Rā he is said to be the father of the gods. His cult had great vogue in the regions round about the first cataract, where he was always associated with Āneq and Sati. In bas-reliefs he is usually coloured green, and wears the *atef* crown† with uræi, etc.

KHNEMU.

* The authorities for the figures of the gods are given by Lanzone in his *Dizionario di Mitologia Egizia.*

† The following are the crowns most commonly met with on the monuments :—

Ptaḥ, the 'Blacksmith,' one of the oldest of the gods, was honoured with a temple and worshipped at Memphis from the time of the Ist dynasty. He is said to be the father of the gods, who came forth from his eye, and of men, who came forth from his mouth. He is represented in the form of a mummy, and he holds a sceptre composed of *usr*, 'strength,' *ānkh*, 'life,' and *ṭeṭ*, 'stability.' In connection with the **resurrection** and the nether-world, he is called PTAḤ-SEKER-ÅSÅR, and is then represented as a little squat boy, at times wearing a beetle on his head. He is at times represented with Isis and Nephthys, and then appears to be a form of Osiris.

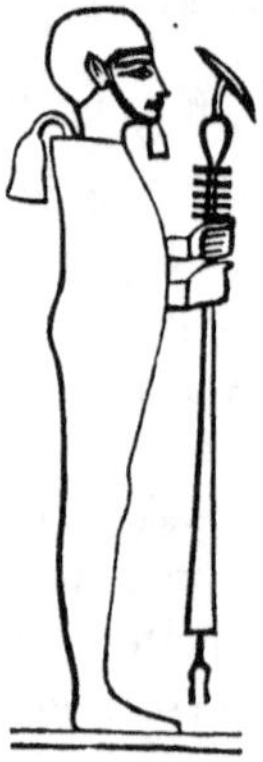

PTAḤ.

Temu, or ÅTMU, a form of the Sun-god, was the 'Closer' of the day or night.

TEMU.

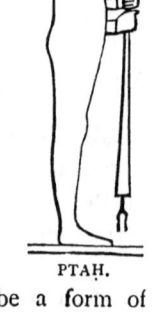

MUT.

Mut, the 'Mother,' was one of the divinities of the Theban triad; she was supposed to represent Nature, the mother of all things.

Kheperà, the 'Creator,' was associated with Ptaḥ, and was supposed to be the god who caused himself to come into existence. He is represented with a beetle for his head. He was supposed to be the father of the gods and creator of the universe, and his attributes were ascribed to Rā under the Middle Empire; he was the father of Shu and Tefnut.

Bast was principally worshipped in Lower Egypt at Bubastis, where a magnificent temple was built in her honour (see p. 263); she is represented with the head of a cat, and was associated with Ptaḥ. Her sister goddess was **Sekhet,** who had the head of a lion, and typified the scorching heat of the sun.

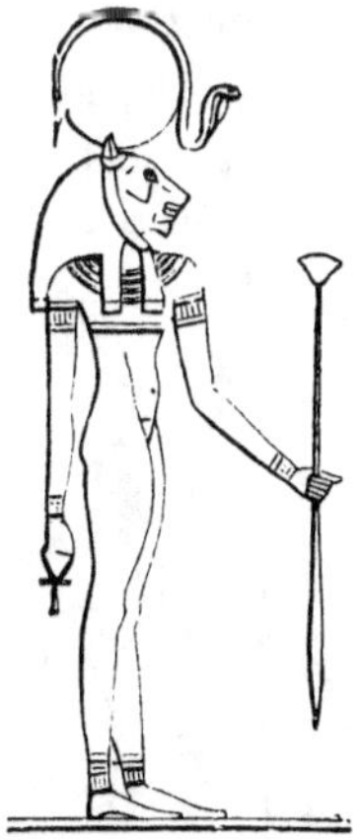

BAST.

NIT.

Nit was in late times made to be a counterpart of Mut and Hathor. She was the goddess of hunting, and is represented holding bows and arrows; her cult is older than the Ist dynasty.

Ra, , the Sun-god, was the creator of gods and men; his emblem was the sun's disk. His worship was very ancient, and he was said to be the offspring of Nut, or the sky. He assumed the forms of several other gods, and is at times represented by the lion, cat, and hawk. In papyri and on bas-reliefs he is represented with the head of a hawk and wearing a disk, in front of which is an uræus . He was particularly adored at Thebes. When he rose in the morning he was called Ḥeru-khuti or Harmachis; and at night, when he set, he was called Åtmu, or 'the closer.' During the night he was supposed to be engaged in fighting Āpep, the serpent, who, at the head of a large army of fiends, personifications of mist, darkness, and cloud, tried to overthrow him. The battle was fought daily, but Rā always conquered, and appeared day after day in the sky.

Horus, , Ḥeru, is the morning sun, and is also represented as having the head of a hawk; he was said to be the son of Isis and Osiris, and is usually called the "avenger of his father," in reference to his defeat of Set.

RĀ.

HORU

Åmen-Rā, **Mut**, and **Khonsu** formed the great triad of Thebes. Åmen-Rā was said to be the son of Ptaḥ, and he seems to have usurped the attributes of many of the gods. The word Åmen means 'hidden.' His chief titles were "lord of the thrones of the two lands," and "king of the gods." He is represented as wearing horns and feathers, and holding 'rule,' 'dominion,' 'power,' and 'stability.' The god **Åmsu** was a form of Åmen-Rā. The exalted position which Åmen-Rā, originally a mere local deity, occupied at Thebes, will be best understood from the translation of a hymn to him written in hieratic during the XVIIIth or XIXth dynasty:—

ÅMEN-RĀ.

"Hymn * to Åmen-Rā, the bull in Heliopolis, president of all the gods, beautiful god, beloved one, the giver of the life of all warmth to all beautiful cattle!

"Hail to thee, Åmen-Rā, lord of the thrones of the two lands, at the head of the Åpts.† The bull of his mother, at the head of his fields, the extender of footsteps, at the head of the "land of the South," ‡ lord of the Mat'au, § prince of Araby, lord of the sky, eldest son of earth, lord

* A French version of this hymn is given by Grébaut in his *Hymne à Ammon-Rā*, Paris, 1875. The hieratic text is published by Mariette, *Les Papyrus Égyptiens de Musée du Boulaq*, pl. 11–13.

† The great temple at Karnak.

‡ Ethiopia and Asia.

§ A country in Asia.

of things which exist, establisher of things, establisher of all things.

"One in his times, as among the gods. Beautiful bull of the cycle of the gods, president of all the gods, lord of Law, father of the gods, maker of men, creator of beasts, lord of things which exist, creator of the staff of life, maker of the green food which makes cattle to live. Form made by Ptaḥ, beautiful child, beloved one. The gods make adorations to him, the maker of things which are below, and of things which are above. He shines on the two lands sailing through the sky in peace. King of the South and North, the SUN (Rā), whose word is law, prince of the world! The mighty of valour, the lord of terror, the chief who makes the earth like unto himself. How very many more are his forms than those of any (other) god! The gods rejoice in his beauties, and they make praises to him in the two great horizons, at (his) risings in the double horizon of flame. The gods love the smell of him when he, the eldest born of the dew,* comes from Araby, when he traverses the land of the Mat'au, the beautiful face coming from Neter-ta.† The gods cast themselves down before his feet when they recognize their lord in his majesty, the lord of fear, the mighty one of victory, the mighty of Will, the master of diadems, the verdifier of offerings (?), the maker of *t'efau* food.

"Adorations to thee, O thou maker of the gods, who hast stretched out the heavens and founded the earth! The untiring watcher, Åmsu-Åmen, lord of eternity, maker of everlasting, to whom adorations are made (literally, lord of adorations), at the head of the Åpts, established with two horns, beautiful of aspects; the lord of the uræus crown,

* Compare Psalm cx. 3.

† *I.e.*, "Divine land," a name frequently given on the monuments to indicate the lands which lie to the south of Egypt between the Nile and the Red Sea.

exalted of plumes, beautiful of tiara, exalted of the white crown; the serpent *meḥen* and the two uræi are the (ornaments) of his face; the double crown, helmet and cap are his decorations in (his) temple. Beautiful of face he receives the *atef* crown ; beloved of the south and north is he, he is master of the *sekhti* crown . He receives the âmsu sceptre , (and is) lord of the. . . . . . and of the whip. Beautiful prince, rising with the white crown  lord of rays, creator of light! The gods give acclamations to him, and he stretches out his hands to him that loves him. The flame makes his enemies fall, his eye overthrows the rebels, it thrusts its copper lance into the sky and makes the serpent Nȧk* vomit what it has swallowed.

* Nȧk is one of the names of Āpep, the demon of mist, cloud, and night, who was supposed to swallow up the sun daily; he was the enemy, *par excellence*, whom the Sun-god Rā was supposed to fight against and overcome. Āpep was represented under the form of a serpent with knives stuck in his back 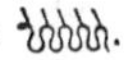. Compare the following extract from the service for his destruction which was recited daily in the temple of Amen-Rā, at Thebes: "Fall down upon thy face, Āpep, enemy of Rā! The flame coming forth from the eye of Horus comes against thee, a mighty flame which comes forth from the eye of Horus comes against thee. Thou art thrust down into the flame of fire which rushes out against thee, a flame which is fatal to thy soul, thy intelligence, thy words of power, thy body and thy shade. The flame prevails over thee, it drives darts into thy soul, it makes an end of whatever thou hast, and sends goads into thy form. Thou hast fallen by the eye of Horus, which is mighty over its enemy, which devours thee, and which leads on the mighty flame against thee; the eye of Rā prevails over thee, the flame devours thee, and nothing of thee remains. Get thee back, thou art hacked in pieces, thy soul is parched, thy name is buried in oblivion, silence covers it, it is overthrown; thou art put an end to and buried under threefold oblivion. Get thee back, retreat thou, thou art cut in pieces and removed from him that is in his shrine. O Āpep, thou doubly crushed one, an end to thee, an end to thee! Mayest thou never rise up again! The eye of Horus prevails over thee

"Hail to thee, Rā, lord of Law, whose shrine is hidden, master of the gods, the god Kheperȧ in his boat; by the sending forth of (his) word the gods sprang into existence. Hail god Ȧtmu, maker of mortals. However many are their forms he causes them to live, he makes different the colour of one man from another. He hears the prayer of him that is oppressed, he is kind of heart to him that calls unto him, he delivers him that is afraid from him that is strong of heart, he judges between the mighty and the weak.

"The lord of intelligence, knowledge (?) is the utterance of his mouth. The Nile cometh by his will, the greatly beloved lord of the palm tree comes to make mortals live. Making advance every work, acting in the sky, he makes to come into existence the sweet things of the daylight; the gods rejoice in his beauties, and their hearts live when they see him. O Rā, adored in the Ȧpts, mighty one of risings in the shrine; O Ȧni,* lord of the festival of the new moon, who makest the six days' festival and the festival of the last quarter of the moon; O prince, life, health, and strength! lord of all the gods, whose appearances are in the horizon, president of the ancestors of Ȧuḳer;† his name is hidden from his children in his name 'Ȧmen.'

"Hail to thee, O thou who art in peace, lord of dilation of heart (*i.e.*, joy), crowned form, lord of the *ureret* crown, exalted of the plumes, beautiful of tiara, exalted of the white crown, the gods love to look upon thee; the double crown of Upper and Lower Egypt is established upon thy brow. Beloved art thou in passing through the two lands.

and devours thee daily, according to that which Rā decreed should be done to thee. Thou art thrown down into the flame of fire which feeds upon thee; thou art condemned to the fire of the eye of Horus which devours thee, thy soul, thy body, thy intelligence and thy shade."—British Museum Papyrus, 10,188, col. xxiv.

* , a form of Rā.

† A common name for a necropolis.

Thou sendest forth rays in rising from thy two beautiful eyes. The *pāt* (ancestors, *i.e.*, the dead) are in raptures of delight when thou shinest, the cattle become languid when thou shinest in full strength; thou art loved when thou art in the sky of the south, thou art esteemed pleasant in the sky of the north. Thy beauties seize and carry away all hearts, the love of thee makes the arms drop; thy beautiful creation makes the hands tremble, and (all) hearts to melt at the sight of thee.

"O Form, ONE, creator of all things, O ONE, ONLY, maker of existences! Men came forth from his two eyes, the gods sprang into existence at the utterance of his mouth. He maketh the green herb to make cattle live, and the staff of life for the (use of) man. He maketh the fishes to live in the rivers, the winged fowl in the sky; he giveth the breath of life to (the germ) in the egg, he maketh birds of all kinds to live, and likewise the reptiles that creep and fly; he causeth the rats to live in their holes, and the birds that are on every green twig. Hail to thee, O maker of all these things, thou ONLY ONE.

"He is of many forms in his might! He watches all people who sleep, he seeks the good for his brute creation. O Åmen, establisher of all things, Åtmu and Harmachis,* all people adore thee, saying, 'Praise to thee because of thy resting among us; homage to thee because thou hast created us.' All creatures say 'Hail to thee,' and all lands praise thee; from the height of the sky, to the breadth of the earth, and to the depths of the sea art thou praised. The gods bow down before thy majesty to exalt the Will of their creator; they rejoice when they meet their begetter, and say to thee, Come in peace, O father of the fathers of all the gods, who hast spread out the sky and hast founded the earth, maker of things which are,

* These three names are the names of the Sun-god at mid-day, evening and morning respectively.

creator of things which exist, prince, life, health, strength; president of the gods. We adore thy will, inasmuch as thou hast made us, thou hast made (us) and given us birth, and we give praises to thee by reason of thy resting with us.

"Hail to thee, maker of all things, lord of Law, father of the gods, maker of men, creator of animals, lord of grain, making to live the cattle of the hills! Hail Åmen, bull, beautiful of face, beloved in the Apts, mighty of risings in the shrine, doubly crowned in Heliopolis, thou judge of Horus and Set in the great hall.* President of the great cycle of the gods, ONLY ONE,† without his second, at the head of the Åpts, Åni at the head of the cycle of his gods, living in Law every day, the double horizoned Horus of the East! He has created the mountain (or earth), the silver, the gold, and genuine lapis-lazuli at his Will . . . . Incense and fresh *ānti* ‡ are prepared for thy nostrils, O beautiful face, coming from the land of the Māt'au, Åmen-Rā, lord of the thrones of the two lands, at the head of the Apts, Åni at the head of his shrine. King, ONE among the gods, myriad are his names, how many are they is not known; shining in the eastern horizon and setting in the western horizon, overthrowing his enemies by his birth at dawn every day. Thoth exalts his two eyes, and makes him to set in his splendours; the gods rejoice in his beauties which those who are in his . . . . . . exalt. Lord of the *sekti* § boat, and of the *āṭet* || boat, which travel over the sky for thee in peace. Thy sailors rejoice when they see Nåk overthrown, his limbs stabbed with the knife, the fire devouring him, his foul soul beaten out of his foul body, and his feet carried away. The gods rejoice, Rā is satisfied,

* See page 184.

† Compare "The Lord our God is ONE," Deut. vi. 4.

‡ A perfume brought into Egypt from the East.

§ The boat in which Rā sailed to his place of setting in the West.

|| The boat in which Rā sailed from his place of rising in the East.

Heliopolis is glad, the enemies of Åtmu are overthrown, and the heart of Nebt-ānkh * is happy because the enemies of her lord are overthrown. The gods of Kher-āba are rejoicing, those who dwell in the shrines are making obeisance when they see him mighty in his strength (?) Form (?) of the gods of law, lord of the Åpts in thy name of 'maker of Law.' Lord of *t'efau* food, bull . . . . . . in thy name of 'Åmen bull of his mother.' Maker of mortals, making . . . . . become, maker of all things that are in thy name of Atmu Kheperå. Mighty Law making the body festal, beautiful of face, making festal the breast. Form of attributes (?), lofty of diadem; the two uræi fly by his forehead. The hearts of the *pätu* go forth to him, and unborn generations turn to him; by his coming he maketh festal the two lands. Hail to thee, Åmen-Rā, lord of the thrones of the two lands! his town loves his shining."

Another hymn to Åmen-Rā reads as follows:—

1. Hail, prince coming forth from the womb!
2. Hail, eldest son of primeval matter!
3. Hail, lord of multitudes of aspects and evolutions!
4. Hail, golden circle in the temples!
5. Hail, lord of time and bestower of years!
6. Hail, lord of life for all eternity!
7. Hail, lord of myriads and millions!
8. Hail, thou who shinest in rising and setting!
9. Hail, thou who makest beings joyful!
10. Hail, thou lord of terror, thou fearful one!
11. Hail, lord of multitudes of aspects and divinities!
12. Hail, thou who art crowned with the white crown; thou master of the *urerer* crown!
13. Hail, thou sacred baby of Horus, praise!
14. Hail, son of Rā who sittest in the boat of millions of years!
15. Hail, restful leader, come to thy hidden places!

* *I.e.*, "the lady of life," a name of Isis.

16. Hail, lord of terror, self-produced !
17. Hail, thou restful of heart, come to thy town !
18. Hail, thou that causest cries of joy, come to thy town !
19. Hail, thou darling of the gods and goddesses !
20. Hail, thou dipper in the sea, come to thy temple !
21. Hail, thou who art in the Nether-world, come to thy offerings !
22. Hail, thou that protectest them, come to thy temple !
23. Hail, Moon-god, growing from a crescent into an illuminated disk !
24. Hail, sacred flower of the mighty house !
25. Hail, thou that bringest the sacred cordage of the Sekti* boat !
26. Hail, thou lord of the Ḥennu† boat who becomest young again in the hidden place !
27. Hail, thou perfect soul in the Nether-world !
28. Hail, thou sacred visitor of the north and south !
29. Hail, thou hidden one, unknown to mankind !
30. Hail, thou illuminator of him that is in the Nether world, that causest him to see the disk !

* The *Sektet* 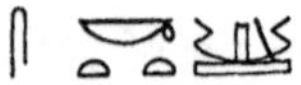 was the boat of the sun in the morning, just as the *Māti*  was the boat of the sun in the evening. A hymn to the sun-god says :—

χā - k *em* *ṭuau* *em* *sekti*
Risest thou in the morning in the *sekti* boat ;

ḥetep-k *em* *māti* *em* *mā̆ser*
Settest thou in the *māti* boat in the evening.

† The *ḥennu* 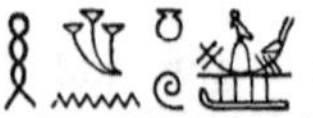 was the boat which was drawn around the sanctuaries of the temples at dawn. Drawings of it are given by Lanzone, *Dizionario*, plates CCLXV-CCLXVII.

31. Hail, lord of the *atef* crown, thou mighty one in Ḥet-suten-ḥenen ! *
32. Hail, mighty one of terror !
33. Hail, thou that risest in Thebes, flourishing for ever !
34. Hail, Åmen-Rā, king of the gods, who makest thy limbs to grow in rising and setting !
35. Hail, ... offerings and oblations in Ru-stau (*i.e.*, the passages of the tomb) !
36. Hail, thou that placest the uræus upon the head of its lord!
37. Hail, stablisher of the earth upon its foundations !
38. Hail, opener of the mouth of the four mighty gods who are in the Nether-world !
39. Hail, thou living soul of Osiris, who art diademed with the moon !
40. Hail, thou that hidest thy body in the great coffin at Heliopolis !
41. Hail, hidden one, mighty one, Osiris in the Netherworld !
42. Hail, thou that unitest his soul to heaven, thine enemy is fallen !

Isis, , Åset, the mother of Horus and wife of **Osiris**, , Åsår, was the daughter of Nut, or the sky; she married her brother Osiris. Her sister **Nephthys** and her brother **Set** likewise married one another. This last couple conspired against Isis and Osiris, and Set, having induced his brother Osiris to enter a box, closed the lid down and threw it into the Nile; the box was carried down by the river and finally cast up on the sea shore. Set, having found the box once more, cut the body of Osiris into fourteen pieces, which he cast over the length and breadth of the land. As soon as

ISIS.

* Heracleopolis, the metropolis of the 20th nome of Upper Egypt.

Isis heard what had happened, she went about seeking for the pieces, and built a temple over each one; she found all save one. Osiris, however, had become king of the nether-world, and vengeance was taken by his son Horus upon his brother Set. Osiris is usually represented in the form of a mummy, holding in his hands 𓌀 'dominion,' ☥ 'life,' 𓍪 'rule,' and 𓌂 'power.' He is called 'the lord of Abydos,' 'lord of the holy land, lord of eternity and prince of everlasting,' 'the president of the gods,' 'the head of the corridor of the tomb,' 'bull of the west,' 'judge of the dead,' etc., etc.

The writers of Egyptian mythological texts always assume their readers to possess a knowledge of the history of the murder of Osiris by Set, and of the wanderings and troubles of his disconsolate wife Isis. The following extracts from Plutarch's work on the subject will supply certain information not given in the Egyptian texts.

"Osiris, being now become king of Egypt, applied himself towards civilizing his countrymen by turning them from their former indigent and barbarous course of life; he moreover taught them how to cultivate and improve the fruits of the earth; he gave them a body of laws to regulate their conduct by, and instructed them in that reverence and worship which they were to pay to the gods; with the same good disposition he afterwards travelled over the rest of the world, inducing the people everywhere to submit to his discipline; not indeed compelling them by force of arms, but persuading them to yield to the strength of his reasons, which were conveyed to them in the most agreeable manner, in hymns and songs accompanied with instruments of music; from

OSIRIS.

which last circumstance the Greeks conclude him to have been the same person with their Dionysus or Bacchus. During the absence of Osiris from his kingdom, Typhon had no opportunity of making any innovations in the State, Isis being extremely vigilant in the government, and always upon her guard. After his return, however, having first persuaded seventy-two other persons to join with him in the conspiracy, together with a certain queen of Ethiopia named Aso, who chanced to be in Egypt at that time, he contrived a proper stratagem to execute his base designs. For having privily taken the measure of Osiris's body, he caused a chest to be made exactly of the same size with it, as beautiful as might be, and set off with all the ornaments of art. This chest he brought into his banqueting room; where after it had been much admired by all who were present, Typhon, as it were in jest, promised to give it to any one of them whose body upon trial it might be found to fit. Upon this the whole company, one after another, go into it. But as it did not fit any of them, last of all Osiris lays himself down in it; upon which the conspirators immediately ran together, clapped the cover upon it, then fastened it down on the outside with nails, pouring likewise melted lead over it. After this they carried it away to the river-side, and conveyed it to the sea by the Tanaïtic mouth of the Nile; which, for this reason, is still held in the utmost abomination by the Egyptians, and never named by them but with proper marks of detestation. These things, say they, were thus executed upon the 17th day of the month Athôr, when the sun was in Scorpio, in the 28th year of Osiris's reign; though there are others who tell us that he was no more than twenty-eight years old at this time.

"The first who knew of the accident which had befallen their king, were the Pans and Satyrs who inhabited the country round Khemmis (Panopolis or Aḥmîm), and they immediately acquainting the people with the news, gave the first occasion to the name of Panic Terrors, which has ever since been made use of to signify any sudden affright or amazement of a multitude. As to Isis, as soon as the report reached her, she immediately cut off one of the locks of her hair, and put on mourning apparel upon the very spot where she then happened to be, which accordingly from this accident has ever since been called Coptos, or the *City of Mourning*, though some are of opinion that this word rather signifies *Deprivation.* After this she wandered everywhere about the country full of disquietude and perplexity in search of the chest, enquiring of every person she met with, even of some children whom she chanced to see, whether they knew what was become of it. Now it so happened that these children had seen what Typhon's accomplices had done with the body, and accordingly acquainted her by what mouth of the Nile it had been conveyed into the sea . . . . .

"At length she received more particular news of the chest, that it had been carried by the waves of the sea to the coast of Byblos, and there gently lodged in the branches of a bush of Tamarisk, which in a short time had shot up into a large and beautiful tree, growing round the chest and enclosing it on every side, so that it was not to be seen; and further, that the king of the country, amazed at its unusual size, had cut the tree down, and made that part of the trunk wherein the chest was concealed a pillar to support the roof of his house. These things, say they, being made known to Isis in an extraordinary manner, by the report of demons, she immediately went to Byblos;* where, setting herself down by the side of a fountain, she refused to speak to any body excepting only to the queen's women who chanced to be there; these she saluted and caressed in the kindest manner possible, plaiting their hair for them, and transmitting

* *I.e.*, the papyrus swamps.

into them part of that wonderfully grateful odour which issued from her own body . . . . . The queen therefore sent for her to court, and after a further acquaintance with her, made her nurse to one of her sons . . . . . The goddess, discovering herself, requested that the pillar which supported the roof of the king's house might be given to her; which she accordingly took down, and then easily cutting it open, after she had taken out what she wanted, she wrapt up the remainder of the trunk in fine linen, and pouring perfumed oil upon it, delivered it into the hands of the king and queen . . . . . . When this was done, she threw herself upon the chest, making at the same time such a loud and terrible lamentation over it as frighted the younger of the king's sons who heard her out of his life. But the elder of them she took with her, and set sail with the chest for Egypt . . . . .

"No sooner was she arrived in a desert place, where she imagined herself to be alone, but she presently opened the chest, and laying her face upon her dead husband's, embraced his corpse, and wept bitterly.

"Isis intending a visit to her son Horus, who was brought up at Butus, deposited the chest in the meanwhile in a remote and unfrequented place; Typhon, however, as he was one night hunting by the light of the moon accidentally met with it; and knowing the body which was enclosed in it, tore it into several pieces, fourteen in all, dispersing them up and down in different parts of the country. Upon being made acquainted with this event, Isis once more sets out in search of the scattered fragments of her husband's body, making use of a boat made of the reed papyrus in order the more easily to pass through the lower and fenny parts of the country. For which reason, say they, the crocodile never touches any persons who sail in this sort of vessel, as either fearing the anger of the goddess, or else respecting it on account of its having once carried her. To this occasion, therefore, it is to be imputed that there are so many different sepulchres of Osiris shewn in Egypt; for we are told that wherever Isis met with any of the scattered limbs of her husband, she there buried it. There are others, however, who contradict this relation, and tell us that this variety of sepulchres was owing rather to the policy of the queen, who, instead of the real body, as was pretended, presented these several cities with the image only of her husband; and that she did this not only to render the honours which would by this means be paid to his memory more extensive, but likewise that she might hereby elude the malicious search of Typhon; who, if he got the better of Horus in the war wherein they were going to be engaged, distracted by this multiplicity of sepulchres, might despair of being able to find the true one. . . . . . .

"After these things Osiris, returning from the other world, appeared to his son Horus, encouraged him to the battle, and at the same time instructed him in the exercise of arms. He then asked him, 'what he thought the most glorious action a man could perform?' to which Horus replied, 'to revenge the injuries offered to his father and mother.' This reply much rejoiced Osiris . . . . We are moreover told that amongst the great numbers who were continually deserting from Typhon's party was the goddess Thoueris, and that a serpent pursuing her as she was coming over to Horus, was slain by his soldiers. Afterwards it came to a battle between them, which lasted many days; but victory at length inclined to Horus, Typhon himself being taken prisoner. Isis, however, to whose custody he was committed, was so far from putting him to death, that she even loosed his bonds and set him at liberty. This action of his mother so extremely incensed Horus, that he laid hands upon her and pulled off the ensign of royalty which she wore on her head; and instead thereof Hermes clapt on an helmet made in the shape of an ox's head.

. . . . After this there were two other battles fought between them, in both of which Typhon had the worst. . . . . . .

"Such, then, are the principal circumstances of this famous story, the more harsh and shocking parts of it, such as the cutting in pieces of Horus and the beheading of Isis, being omitted." (Plutarch, *De Iside et Osiride*, xii–xx. Squire's translation.)

The following is an extract from a hymn addressed to Osiris by Isis and Nephthys (Brit. Mus. Papyrus No. 10,188):—

"O beloved of his father, lord of rejoicings, thou delightest the hearts of the cycle of the gods, and thou illuminatest thy house with thy beauties; the cycle of the gods fear thy power, the earth trembleth through fear of thee.

I am thy wife who maketh thy protection, the sister who protecteth her brother; come, let me see thee, O lord of my love.

O twice exalted one, mighty of attributes, come, let me see thee; O baby who advancest, child, come, let me see thee.

Countries and regions weep for thee, the zones weep for thee as if thou wert Sesheta, heaven and earth weep for thee, inasmuch as thou art greater than the gods; may there be no cessation of the glorifying of thy *Ka*.

Come to thy temple, be not afraid, thy son Horus embraces the circuit of heaven.

O thou sovereign, who makest afraid, be not afraid. Thy son Horus avenges thee and overthrows for thee the fiends and the devils.

Hail, lord, follow after me with thy radiance, let me see thee daily; the smell of thy flesh is like that of Punt (*i.e.*, the spice land of Arabia).

Thou art adored by the venerable women, in peace; the entire cycle of the gods rejoice.

Come thou to thy wife in peace, her heart flutters through her love for thee, she will embrace thee and not let thee depart from her; her heart is oppressed because of her anxiety to see thee and thy beauties. She has made an end of preparations for thee in the secret house; she has destroyed the pain which is in thy limbs and the sickness as if it never existed. Life is given to thee by the most excellent wife.

Hail, thou protectest the inundation in the fields of Aphroditopolis this day.

The cow (*i.e.*, Isis) weeps aloud for thee with her voice, thy love is the limit of her desire. Her heart flutters because thou art shut up from her.

She would embrace thy body with both arms and would come to thee quickly.

She avenges thee on account of what was done to thee, she makes sound for thee thy flesh on thy bones, she attaches thy nose to thy face for thee, she gathers together for thee all thy bones."

In the calendar of the lucky and unlucky days of the Egyptian year, the directions concerning the 26th day of the month of Thoth, which is marked , or "thrice unlucky," say, "Do nothing at all on this day, for it is the day on which Horus fought against Set. Standing on the soles of their feet they aimed blows at each other like men, and they became like two bears of hell, lords of Kher-āba. They passed three days and three nights in this manner, after which Isis made their weapons fall. Horus fell down, crying out, 'I am thy son Horus,' and Isis cried to the weapons, saying, 'Away, away, from my son Horus' . . . . Her brother Set fell down and cried out, saying, 'Help, help!' Isis cried out to the weapons, 'Fall down.' Set cried out several times, 'Do I not wish to honour my mother's brother?' and Isis cried out to the weapons, 'Fall down—set my elder brother free'; then the weapons fell away from him. And Horus and Set stood up like two men, and each paid no attention to what they had said. And the majesty of Horus was enraged against his mother Isis like a panther of the south, and she fled before him. On that day a terrible struggle took place, and Horus cut off the head of Isis; and Thoth transformed this head by his incantations, and put it on her again in the form of a head of a cow." (Chabas, *Le Calendrier*, p. 29.)

Nephthys, , Nebt-ḥet, sister of Osiris and Isis, is generally represented standing at the bier of Osiris lamenting him. One myth relates that Osiris mistook her for Isis, and that ANUBIS, the god of the dead, was the result of the union.

Set, , the god of evil, appears to have been worshipped in the earliest times. He was the opponent of Horus in a three days' battle, at the end of which he was defeated. He was worshipped by the Hyksos, and also by the Kheta; but in the later days of the Egyptian empire he was supposed to be the god of evil, and was considered to be the chief fiend and rebel against the sun-god Rā.

Anubis, , Ȧnpu, the god of the dead, is usually represented with the head of a jackal.

Seb, , or Ḳeb, was the husband of Nut, and father of Osiris and the other gods of that cycle.

NEBT-ḤET.

ANUBIS.

SEB, or ḲEB.

Thoth, , Teḥuti, 'the measurer,' was the scribe of the gods, and the measurer of time and inventor of numbers. In the judgment hall of Osiris he stands by the side of the balance holding a palette and reed ready to record the result of the weighing as announced by the dog-headed ape which sits on the middle of the beam of the scales. In one aspect he is the god of the moon, and is represented with the head of an ibis.

TEḤUTI.

KHONSU.

Khonsu, , was associated with Ȧmen-Rā and Mut in the Theban triad. He was the god of the moon, and is represented as hawk-headed and wearing the lunar disk and crescent. His second name was Nefer-ḥetep, and he was worshipped with great honour at Thebes.

Sebek, , the crocodile-headed god, was worshipped at Kom-Ombos and in the Fayyûm.

Ī-em-ḥetep (Imouthis), , was the son of Ptaḥ.

Shu, [hieroglyphs], and **Tefnut**, [hieroglyphs], were the parents of Seb and Nut, and were the personifications of sunlight and moisture respectively.

Athor, or **Hathor**, [hieroglyphs], Ḥet-Ḥeru, 'the house of Horus,' is identified with Nut, the sky, or place in which she brought forth and suckled Horus. She was the wife of Ȧtmu, a form of Rā. She is represented as a woman wearing a headdress in the shape of a vulture, and above it a disk and horns. She is called 'mistress of the gods,' 'lady of the sycamore,' 'lady of the west,' and 'Hathor of Thebes.' She is the female power of nature, and has some of the attributes of Isis, Nut, and Mut. She is often represented under the form of a cow coming out of the Theban hills.

HATHOR.

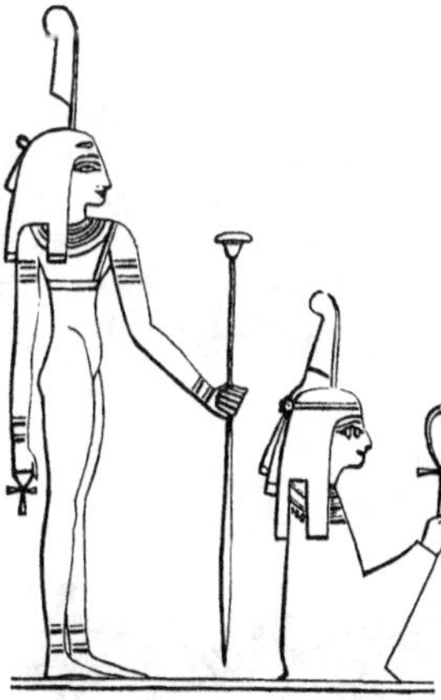

MAȦT.

Maāt, [hieroglyphs], the goddess of 'Law,' was the eye of the Sun-god Rā; she is represented as wearing the feather [hieroglyph], emblematic of law [hieroglyph].

Ḥāpi, , the god of the Nile, is represented wearing a cluster of flowers on his head ; he is coloured red and green, probably to represent the colours of the water of the Nile immediately before and just after the beginning of the inundation.

Serapis, *i.e.*, Osiris-Apis, , was a god introduced into Egypt during the reign of the Ptolemies;* he is represented with the head of a bull wearing a disk and uræus. He is said to be the second son of Ptaḥ. The worship of Apis at Memphis goes back to the earliest times; the Serapeum, discovered there by M. Mariette, contained the tombs of Apis bulls from the time of Amenophis III. (about B.C. 1550) down to the time of the Roman Empire. See page 306.

* ". . . . . the Lagids, as well as the Seleucids, were careful of disturbing the foundations of the old religion of the country; . . . . . they introduced . . . . . the Greek god of the lower world, Pluto, into the native worship, under the hitherto little mentioned name of the Egyptian god Serapis, and then gradually transferred to this the old Osiris worship." (Mommsen, *Provinces of the Roman Empire*, Vol. II., p. 265.)

THE MODERN EGYPTIANS.

The total population of Egypt proper was on June 1, 1897, 9,734,405, of whom 112,526 were foreigners.

In a country where an increase in population always means an increase in taxation, it is quite impossible to obtain an accurate census. As far back as the time of David * the idea of "numbering the people" has been unpopular in the East.

It is exceedingly difficult to obtain an exact idea of what the population of Egypt actually was in Pharaonic times, for the inscriptions tell us nothing. Herodotus gives us no information on this matter, but Diodorus tells us that it amounted to 7,000,000 in ancient times. The priests at Thebes informed Germanicus, A.D. 19, that in the times of Rameses II. the country contained 700,000 † fighting men; it will also be remembered that the Bible states that the "children of Israel journeyed from Rameses to Succoth, about six hundred thousand on foot that were men, beside children. And a mixed multitude went up also with them." Exodus xii. 37, 38. In the time of Vespasian 7,500,000 persons paid poll-tax; we may assume that about 500,000 were exempt, and therefore there must have been at least 8,000,000 of people in Egypt, without reckoning slaves. (Mommsen, *Provinces of Rome*, Vol. II., p. 258.) It is probable, however, that the population of Egypt under the rule of the Pharaohs has been greatly exaggerated, chiefly because no accurate data were at hand whereby errors might be corrected. During the occupation of the country by the French in 1798–1801 it was said to be 2,460,200; Sir

* "And Satan stood up against Israel, and moved David to number Israel." 1 Chronicles xxi. 1.

† "Septigenta milia aetate militari." Tacitus, *Annals*, Bk. ii., 60.

Gardner Wilkinson, however, set it down at as low a figure as 1,500,000. In 1821 the population numbered 2,536,400, and in 1846 it had risen to 4,476,440. Another census was ordered by Khedivial decree on December 2, 1881, and it was completed on May 3, 1882. According to the official statement published in the *Recensement Général de l'Égypte*, at Cairo, in 1884, it amounted in 1882 to 6,806,381 persons, of whom 3,216,847 were men, and 3,252,869 were women. Of the 6,806,381 persons, 6,708,185 were inhabitants of the country, and 98,196 were nomads. It showed that there were in the total 245,779 Bedâwin and 90,886 foreigners.

According to the census of 1897 the population in Lower Egypt was 5,676,109, and in Upper Egypt, 4,058,296. The distribution of the population in the cities having governors and in the provinces is as follows:—

Cairo, 570,062; Alexandria, 319,766; Port Sa'îd and Canal, 50,179; Suez, 24,970; Damietta, 43,751; El-'Arîsh, 16,991; Beḥêreh, 631,225; Sherḳîyeh, 749,130; Daḳhalîyeh, 736,708; Gharbîyeh, 1,297,656; Ḳalyûb, 371,465; Menûf, 864,206; Asyûṭ, 782,720; Beni-Suwêf, 314,454; Fayyûm, 371,006; Gîzeh, 401,634; Minyeh, 548,632; Girgeh, 688,011; Ḳeneh, 711,457; Nubia, 240,382. In the Oasis of Sîwa, 5,000; Oasis of Baḥrîyah, 6,082; Oasis of Farâfra, 542; Oasis of Dâkhleh, 17,090; Oasis of Khargah, 7,200; Donḳola, 56,426; Sawwâḳîn, 15,713. The males numbered 4,947,850, and the females, 4,786,555. The number of houses occupied was 1,422,302. The increase in the population since 1882 is 43 per cent. The Muslims number 8,978,775; Jews, 25,200; Christians (of all sects), 730,162. Males and females able to read and write were 467,886; and 9,266,519 were illiterate.

The population of Egypt to-day comprises the Fellâḥîn, Copts, Bedâwin, Jews, Turks, Negroes, Nubians and people from Abyssinia, Armenians and Europeans.

The **Fellaḥîn** amount to about four-fifths of the entire

population of Egypt, and are chiefly employed in agricultural pursuits. In physical type they greatly resemble the ancient Egyptians as depicted on the monuments. Their complexion is dark; they have straight eyebrows, high cheek bones, flat noses with low bridges, slightly protruding jaws, broad shoulders, large mouths and full lips. The colour of their skin becomes darker as the south is approached. The whole of the cultivation of Egypt is in the hands of the fellaḥîn.

The **Copts** * are also direct descendants from the ancient Egyptians, and inhabit chiefly the cities of Upper Egypt, such as Asyûṭ and Aḥmîm. The name Copt is derived from قبط *Ḳubṭ*, the Arabic form of the Coptic form of the Greek name for Egyptian, Αἰγύπτιος; it may be mentioned, in passing, that Αἴγυπτος, Egypt, is thought by some to be derived from an ancient Egyptian name for Memphis, Ḥet-ka-Ptaḥ, "The house of the genius of Ptaḥ." The number of Copts in Egypt to-day is estimated at about 608,000, and the greater number of them are engaged in the trades of goldsmiths, clothworkers, etc.; a respectable body of clerks and accountants in the postal, telegraph and government offices in Egypt, is drawn from their community. They are clever with their fingers, and are capable of rapid education up to a certain point; beyond this they rarely go. Physically, they are of a finer type than the fellâḥîn; their heads are longer and their features are more European.

The Copts are famous in ecclesiastical history for having embraced with extraordinary zeal and rapidity the doctrines of Christianity as preached by St. Mark at Alexandria. Before the end of the third century A.D. Egypt was filled with hundreds of thousands of ascetics, monks, recluses, and solitaries who had thrown over their own weird and

* A sketch of their history is given elsewhere in this work (*see* pp. 200-210).

confused religious beliefs and embraced Christianity; they then retired to the mountains and deserts of their country to dedicate their lives to the service of the Christians' God. The Egyptians, their ancestors, who lived sixteen hundred years before Christ, had already arrived at the conception of a god who was one in his person, but who manifested himself in the world under many forms and many names. The Greeks and the Romans, who successively held Egypt, caused many changes to come over the native religion of the country which they governed; and since the conflicting myths and theories taught to the people of Egypt under their rule had bewildered their minds and confused their beliefs, they gladly accepted the simple teaching of Christ's Apostle as a veritable gift of God. Their religious belief took the form of that of Eutyches (died after 451), who sacrificed the "distinction of the two natures in Christ to the unity of the person to such an extent as to make the incarnation an absorption of the human nature by the divine, or a deification of human nature, even of the body." In other words, they believed that Christ had but one composite nature, and for this reason they were called Monophysites; in their liturgies they stated that God had been crucified. They formed a part of the Alexandrian Church until the Council of Chalcedon, A.D. 451, when it was laid down that Christ had a *double* nature—human and divine—but after this date they separated themselves from it, and were accounted heretics by it, because they obstinately refused to give up their belief in the *one* divine nature of Christ which embraced and included the human. To the sect of Monophysites or Eutychians the Copts still belong. The orthodox church of Alexandria and its heretical offshoot continued to discuss with anger and tumult the subtle points of their different opinions, until the fifth Œcumenical Council, held at Constantinople A.D. 553, made some concessions to the Monophysite party Shortly after, however, new dissensions arose which so weakened the orthodox church that the Monophysite party hailed with gladness the arrival of the arms of Muḥammad the Prophet, and joined its forces with his that they might destroy the power of their theological opponents. After 'Amr had made himself master of Egypt (A.D. 640), he appointed the Copts to positions of dignity and wealth; finding, however, that they were unworthy of his confidence, they were degraded, and finally persecuted with vigour. From the time of Cyril, Patriarch of Alexandria, A.D. 1235 and onwards, but little is known of the history of the Coptic Church. The Copt of to-day usually troubles himself little about theological matters; in certain cases, however, he affirms with considerable firmness the doctrine of the "one nature."

The knowledge of the Coptic language is, generally speaking, extinct; it is exceedingly doubtful if three Coptic scholars, in the Western sense of the word, exist even among the priests. The language spoken by them is Arabic, and though copies of parts of the Bible are found in churches and private houses, they are usually accompanied by an Arabic version of the Coptic text, which is more usually read than the Coptic. The Bible, in all or part, was translated from Greek into Coptic in the third century of our era; some, however, think that the translation was not made until the eighth century. The versions of the principal books of the Old and the whole of the New Testament, together with lives of saints, monks and martyrs, form the greater part of Coptic literature. The Coptic language is, at base, a dialect of ancient Egyptian; many of the nouns and verbs found in the hieroglyphic texts remain unchanged in Coptic, and a large number of others can, by making proper allowance for phonetic decay and dialectic differences, be identified without difficulty. The Copts used the Greek alphabet to write down their language, but found it necessary to borrow six* signs from the demotic forms of ancient Egyptian characters to express the sounds which they found unrepresented in Greek. The dialect of Upper Egypt is called "Sahidic"† or Theban, and that of Lower Egypt "Memphitic."‡ During the last few years the study of Coptic has revived among European scholars, but this is partly owing to the fact that the importance of a knowledge of the language, as a preliminary to the study of hieroglyphics, has been at length recognized. The Roman Propagandist Tuki published during the last century some valuable works; in spite, however, of the activity of scholars and the enterprise of publishers, it still costs nearly £5 to purchase a copy of as much of the Memphitic Coptic version of the Bible as has come down to us.

The **Bedâwin** are represented by the various Arabic-speaking and Muḥammadan tribes, who live in the deserts which lie on each side of the Nile; they amount in number to about 250,000. The Bisharîn, Hadendoa, and Ababdeh tribes, who speak a language (called 'to bedhawîyyeh') which is like ancient Egyptian in some respects, and who live in the most southern part of Upper Egypt, Nubia, and Abyssinia, are included among this number. Among these

* These signs are:
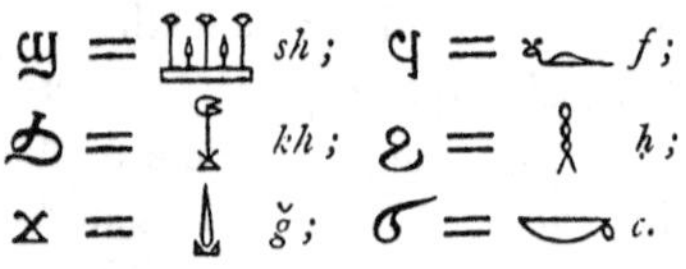
ϣ = sh;
ϥ = f;
ϧ = kh;
ϩ = ḥ;
ϫ = ğ;
ϭ = c.

† This is the older and richer dialect of Coptic, which was spoken from Minyeh to Aswân.

‡ More correctly called Boheiric, from the province of Boheirâ in the Delta; the name Bashmuric has been wrongly applied to this dialect, but as it appears to have been exclusively the language of Memphis, it may be styled "Middle Egyptian." The dialect of Bushmûr on the Lake of Menzaleh appears to have become extinct about A.D. 900, and to have left no traces of itself behind. See Stern, *Kopt. Gram.*, p. 1.

three tribes the institutions of Muḥammad are not observed with any great strictness. When the Bedâwin settle down to village or town life, they appear to lose all the bravery and fine qualities of independent manhood which characterize them when they live in their home, the desert.

The inhabitants of Cairo, Alexandria, and other large towns form a class of people quite distinct from the other inhabitants of Egypt ; in Alexandria there is a very large Greek element, and in Cairo the number of Turks is very great. In the bazaars of Cairo one may see the offspring of marriages between members of nearly every European nation and Egyptian or Nubian women, the colour of their skins varying from a dark brick-red to nearly white. The shopkeepers are fully alive to their opportunities of making money, and would, beyond doubt, become rich but for their natural indolence and belief in fate. Whatever they appear or however much they may mask their belief in the Muḥammadan religion, it must never be forgotten that they have the greatest dislike to every religion but their own. The love of gain alone causes them to submit to the remarks made upon them by Europeans, and to suffer their entrance and sojourning among them.

The **Nubians** or Berbers, as they are sometimes called, inhabit the tract of land which extends from Aswân or Syene to the fourth cataract. The word Nubia appears to be derived from *nub*, 'gold,' because Nubia was a gold-producing country. The word Berber is considered to mean 'barbarian' by some, and to be also of Egyptian origin. They speak a language which is allied to some of the North African tongues, and rarely speak Arabic well. The Nubians found in Egypt are generally doorkeepers and domestic servants, who can usually be depended upon for their honesty and obedience.

The **Negroes** form a large part of the non-native population of Egypt, and are employed by natives to perform hard work, or are held by them as slaves. They are Muḥammadans by religion, and come from the countries known by the name of Sûdân. Negro women make good and faithful servants.

The Syrian Christians who have settled down in Egypt are generally known by the name of **Levantines.** They are shrewd business men, and the facility and rapidity with which they learn European languages place them in positions of trust and emolument.

The **Turks** form a comparatively small portion of the population of Egypt, but many civil and military appointments are, or were, in their hands. Many of them are the children of Circassian slaves. The merchants are famous for their civility to foreigners and their keen eye to business.

The **Armenians** and **Jews** form a small but important part of the inhabitants in the large towns of Egypt. The former are famous for their linguistic attainments and wealth; the latter have blue eyes, fair hair and skin, and busy themselves in mercantile pursuits and the business of bankers and money-changing.

The European population in Egypt consists of Greeks, 38,175; Italians, 24,467; English, 19,557; French, 14,155; Austrians, 7,117; Russians, 3,193; Germans, 1,277; Spaniards, 765; Swiss, 472; Americans, 291; Belgians, 256; Dutch, 247; Portuguese, 151; Swedes, 107; Danes, 72; Persians, 1,301; Miscellaneous, 923. The greater part of the business of Alexandria is in the hands of the Greek merchants, many of whom are famous for their wealth. It is said that the Greek community contributes most largely to the crime in the country, but if the size of that community be taken into account, it will be found that this statement is not strictly true. The enterprise and good business habits of the Greeks in Alexandria have made it the great city that it is. The French, Austrian, German, and English nations are likewise represented there, and in Cairo, by several first-rate business houses. The destructive fanaticism peculiar to the Muḥammadan mind, so common in the far east parts of Mesopotamia, seems to be non-existent in Egypt ; such fanaticism as exists is, no doubt, kept in check by the presence of Europeans, and all the different peoples live side by side in a most peaceable manner. The great benefit derived by Egypt from the immigration of Europeans during the last few years is evident from the increased material prosperity of the country, and the administration of equitable laws which has obtained. The European element in Egypt now contributes to the revenue in taxation a considerable sum annually.

SKETCH OF COPTIC HISTORY.

About A.D. 64 St. Mark made Ananius patriarch of Alexandria, and he also appointed to the church there twelve presbyters, from whom a successor to Ananius was to be elected; the patriarch was at that time called Bâbâ or Pâpâ. Ananius was succeeded by Minius or Philetius (A.D. 87), who was succeeded by Cerdo (A.D. 99), during whose rule a fierce persecution of the Christians took place by the order of Hadrian; his successor was Primus (A.D. 110), during whose rule the persecution of Hadrian was continued. This emperor caused the Christians to be massacred in large numbers, and well nigh exterminated them in Egypt; he destroyed also the Christian churches in Jerusalem. After Primus came Justus (A.D. 118), Eumenius (A.D. 133), Marcianus (A.D. 143), Claudianus (A.D. 153), Agrippinus (A.D. 167), Julianus (A.D. 179), Demetrius (A.D. 190), during whose rule Severianus slaughtered large numbers of the Christians in Egypt, and overthrew their churches. This persecution was continued in the time of Theoclas (A.D. 231), but was relaxed in that of Cæsar Philippus. During the rule of Dionysius (A.D. 244) the Christians in Egypt suffered much at the hands of Decius; about this time St. Anthony the Great retired to the desert and taught men to lead there an ascetic life. After Maximus (A.D. 266) Theonas became patriarch (A.D. 282); under his rule a church in honour of the Virgin Mary was built at Alexandria, and the Christians worshipped therein openly; his successor Peter (A.D. 289) was slain in Alexandria, and his disciple Achillas (A.D. 295) who was elected patriarch after him, only sat for six months. The persecution of the Christians by Diocletian was very severe, and the Copts commemorate it by dating their documents according to the "Era of the Martyrs," which was made to begin with the day of the Emperor's accession to the throne, *i.e.*, August 29, 284. Under the patriarch Alexander (A.D. 295) the great Arian controversy took place. **Arius** was born in the north of Libya about A.D. 256, and was ordained deacon and presbyter by the patriarchs Peter and Achillas respectively; with Achillas he was a candidate for the patriarchate. He taught that God is eternal, unchangeable, good, wise, and unbegotten; that He created the world not directly, but by means of the Logos, who was created for this express purpose; that the Son of God was created before all time, and before the world, and before all created things in it, and was in every respect the perfect image of the Father; and that He created the world and became in this sense God and the Logos. Christ, however, Arius declared to be a creature, and not eternal, and not unchangeable, and further declared that there was a time when He did not exist, and that He was not made of the essence of His Father, but out of nothing. Arius ascribed to Christ a human body with an animal soul, and not a rational soul. The controversy between Arius and the patriarch Alexander began in 318, and lasted, with brief intervals, for nearly one hundred years. Arius was excommunicated in 321 by one hundred bishops, and again at the Œcumenical Council of Nicæa in 325, and was banished by Constantine. In 331 Constantine ordered that he be restored to the communion of the Church, but Athanasius refused to receive him. Five years later Constantine repeated his order, but Arius died on the Saturday preceding the Sunday on which it was arranged that he should be received into the communion of the Church His death was attributed by some to poison, but, judging by the account given by Socrates and Sozomen, he seems to have perished by a violent attack of cholera.

Alexander was followed in the patriarchate by Athanasius (A.D. 326), who succeeded in making many thousands of Jews profess Christianity; during his rule Julian began to persecute the Christians severely, but under Jovianus the banished bishops were restored to their sees. A little before his death Athanasius fell into great disfavour with the Alexandrians, and they tried to kill him; the aged patriarch fled, and Lucius, an Arian, was made to occupy the patriarchal throne. A few months later Lucius was excommunicated, and Athanasius was brought back, and continued to be patriarch until his death. Athanasius was succeeded by Peter (A.D. 372), Timothy (A.D. 380), Theophilus (A.D. 385), and Cyril (A.D. 412); under the rule of Cyril the Nestorian heresy broke out. Nestorius was patriarch of Constantinople A.D. 428–431, and he held the view that Mary the Virgin should not be called "God-bearer," because she was but a woman, and it was impossible that God should be born of a woman. Nestorius was excommunicated and banished, and is said to have died at Akhmîm in Upper Egypt. The next patriarch of Alexandria was **Dioscorus** (A.D. 444), who was appointed by Theodosius, and he taught that Christ was one substance out of two substances, one person out of two persons, one nature out of two natures, and one will out of two wills, but Marcianus held the view that the Messiah was two substances, two natures, and two wills in one person. To discuss this question a new Council was called together at Chalcedon on the 8th of October, 451; it was attended by 634 bishops, who advised Dioscorus to agree with the views of the king. As a result of this Council the Christians were divided into **Melkites,** *i.e.* Royalists, or those who accepted the views of Marcianus, and **Jacobites,** *i.e.*, those who held the opinion of Dioscorus and his party. Dioscorus was succeeded by Proterius (Melkite), Timothy (Jacobite), Severus, Peter (A.D. 477), Athanasius (A.D. 486), John

(A.D. 498), John (A.D. 505), Dioscorus (A.D. 526), Theodosius (A.D. 545), Peter (A.D. 548), Damianus (A.D. 555), Anastasius (A.D. 604), Andronicus (A.D. 609), and Benjamin (A.D. 615).

About this time, Makrîzî declares, the land of Egypt was full of Christians, but they were divided both as regards race and religion. On the one side there were about 300,000 men who were attached to the service of the Government, their religious views being Melkite, and on the other were the rest of the inhabitants of Egypt, who were Jacobites. Each side hated the other, and the religious views of each prevented inter-marriage, and often led to murders and massacres. This state of affairs facilitated the task of 'Amr ibn al-'Âṣi, who set out from Syria to conquer Egypt in 638; he captured Pelusium without difficulty and marched on Memphis, which he besieged for seven months. The famous Fortress of Babylon was bravely defended by the Greeks or royalist soldiers, and although their efforts were apparently well supported by the soldiers generally, there is no doubt that the Jacobites were tired of the Byzantine rule, and that they were anxious to make terms with 'Amr and his Muḥammadan troops. One of the chief officers of state at that time was the Maḳawḳas,* "the prince of the Copts," a Jacobite, whose sympathies had been alienated from his royalist masters. He had great influence in the country, and all the evidence goes to show that he used it against his employers; be this as it may, he used his position as governor of Babylon to negotiate terms of peace with 'Amr, and just as the city was on the point of being overrun by the Arabs, he bought off the disaster by agreeing to pay a tax of two dînârs on every male, and to submit to the other impositions which 'Amr had laid upon vanquished peoples. In return for the help of the Jacobites, the Arabs supported them against the

* *i.e.*, George, the son of Menas, the μεγαυχής.

Melkites or Royalists, and for nearly one hundred years a Jacobite sat on the patriarchal throne at Alexandria. Benjamin, who was patriarch at the time of the conquest of Egypt by the Arabs, died A.D. 663, and he was succeeded by Agathon, Isaac (A.D. 680), Simon the Syrian (A.D. 693), and Alexander (A.D. 704). During the rule of this patriarch the Coptic Church suffered greatly at the hands of the Arab governors, for the patriarch himself was twice made to pay 6,000 dînârs, and a census of the monks having been taken, a tax of one dînâr was levied on each monk. The Copts were next stripped of their possessions, and every monk had his name branded on his hand, and the name of his convent and his number; any monk who had not this brand upon him had his hand cut off. In the monasteries those who were without the brand were either beaten to death or beheaded, and the crosses and pictures were destroyed, the images were broken and the churches pulled down. Every Christian and every animal possessed by him were branded with a number. The next patriarch was Cosmas (A.D. 722), and he was followed by Theodore (A.D. 727), and by Michael (A.D. 735), in whose days fighting went on continually between the Copts and Arabs; Mirwân burnt Old Cairo and the growing crops round about. During the patriarchate of Amba Mîna (A.D. 766), the churches in Cairo were wrecked or burnt, and the Christians were obliged to eat the bodies of their dead. Amba Mîna was followed by John (A.D. 775), Mark (A.D. 795), James (A.D. 826), Simon (A.D. 844), and Joseph (A.D. 849). About this period it was ordered that the Christians should only ride mules and asses; that the men should wear a girdle, use saddles with wooden stirrups, and wear patches of different colours on their garments; that the women should wear veils of yellow coloured stuff, and abstain from putting on girdles. Their graves were to be made level with the earth, they were to light no fire on the road on a journey, the cross was not to be exhibited in their public services, figures of devils were to be placed over the doors of their houses, etc. From the time of Joseph to that of Zacharias (A.D. 1002) the condition of the Christians became steadily worse, but in many cases they were themselves the cause of their misfortunes. The Muḥammadans employed them in official positions, sometimes of a very important character, and the Copts used every opportunity to harm their masters and to plot against them. The Muḥammadans retaliated, and not content with robbing and murdering the wretched Christians, they sacked, pillaged and burnt their churches and convents, and made such harassing regulations that life for the Copts became well-nigh unendurable. Each man had to wear, hanging from his neck, a wooden cross, weighing at least ten pounds; his head shawl and turban were to be black; his goods were to be sold at auction and the proceeds handed to the Arabs; and every man was obliged to wear a cross when he went to the bath. After Zacharias the patriarchal throne was occupied by Sanutius (1029), who was followed by Christodoulos (1049), Cyril (1078), Michael (1093), Macarius (1103), Gabriel (1131), Michael (1146), John (1147), Mark (1163), John (1180), David (1235), and Athanasius (1251). In the days of this last the tax upon the Christians was doubled, and every man was ordered to make way for a Muḥammadan on horseback; besides this, owing to a quarrel which took place between a Christian official and a Muḥammadan, a fierce onslaught was made upon the Copts, large numbers of them were slain, and their houses were sacked and burnt. An order was issued that all the Copts should either embrace Islâm or suffer death, and many of them did become Muḥammadans; many Christian churches were either pulled down or turned into mosques at this time. Soon afterwards an order was promulgated that the Christians should wear blue and the Jews yellow turbans; disobedience was to be followed by the confiscation of their property and death. A few years later, according to a prearranged plan, all the Christian churches were destroyed in one day, the excuse given being the arrogance and luxury of the Copts. The mob attacked the Copts in the streets, and beat them and robbed them, and lit fires to burn them in; the house of any Christian which happened to stand a little higher than those of his neighbours was promptly pulled down. In Upper Egypt all the churches were destroyed, and in one town more than 450 Christians embraced Muḥammadanism in one day; intermarriage between the Copts and Arabs became the order of the day, and though the persecutions became fewer and less violent, the Copts lost gradually whatever riches and power they once possessed. After Athanasius, Gabriel became patriarch (1260), and he was followed by John (1262), Theodosius (1294), and John (1300), during whose patriarchate another severe persecution of the Copts broke out, and two of their churches were closed for nearly two years. From about 1350 to the middle of the 19th century the position of the Coptic Church has been one of weakness and poverty, but this is not to be wondered at if the peculiar characteristics of Coptic ecclesiastical officials be taken into account. In recent years, however, thanks to the labours of the American Missionaries, their children have become educated, and now the parents are beginning to see that the foolish and obstinate policy of their clergy which was in vogue in olden times can no longer be perservered in with personal success or benefit to the community.

In **personal appearance** the Copts resemble the ancient Egyptians as known to us by the monuments, but there are some remarkable differences in their features, which are due to intermarriage with Arabs and Ethiopians, and other tribes of the Eastern Sûdân. In Lower Egypt the Copts closely resemble the Arabs, to whom their best families are nearly related. The hair is black and often curly, the eyes are large, black, and elongated; the nose is straight, but flat at the end; the lips are often thick, and the complexion varies from a pale yellow colour to a dark brown. The women blacken their eyelids with stibium, and stain their nails with *ḥenna*, and tattoo their faces with the cross and other devices. The Copts usually wear garments made of dark coloured stuffs, and their turbans, in the cities, are generally black or blue in colour; in this respect they seem to have adopted the colours for their dress which were prescribed by the sumptuary laws of their Arab conquerors in days of old. The Coptic women veil their faces in public and in the presence of men, but in recent years this custom has been considerably relaxed; unmarried women generally wear white veils, and married women black.

The head of the Coptic Church is the Patriarch of Alexandria, but he now lives in Cairo. He is usually chosen from the monks of the Monastery of Saint Anthony in the desert near the Red Sea; he must be unmarried, and he ought to live a life of great austerity. The bishops are twelve in number, and although they need not of necessity be monks, they must lead very strict lives. The priests are ordained either by the patriarch or by a bishop, and they must not be under thirty-three years of age at the time of ordination. A priest must either be unmarried, or a man who has married one wife, a virgin, and he must have married her before he was ordained; he may not marry a second time. The deacon is either an unmarried man, or one who has only once married, the woman being a virgin; a second marriage costs him his office. The Copts baptize their children, believing that the Holy Ghost descends upon them during the ceremony, and they attach the greatest importance to baptism, for it is thought that unbaptized children will be blind in the world to come.

Boys are baptized when forty days old, and girls at the age of eighty days, but in the event of serious illness or impending death, the ceremony of baptism may be performed at any time. At baptism the sign of the cross is made on the forehead of the child, who is immersed three times in consecrated water, into which three kinds of holy oil have been poured.

The Copts, like the ancient Egyptians, circumcise their children, but they do not seem to attach any special religious importance to the ceremony, which may be performed at any time between the ages of two and twenty; it is, no doubt, a survival of the blood offering which every male had to make to the tribal god, but to the Copts, as to many other peoples, it has lost its true significance. The Copts have always maintained **schools** for their boys, but until recent years very few girls or women could read. The boys were taught the Psalms, Gospels, and Epistles in Arabic, and then the Gospels and Epistles in Coptic; but although prayers are said publicly and privately in Coptic, it is very doubtful if three per cent. of those who say them have any exact knowledge of their meaning. Coptic children are exceedingly intelligent, and the boys and young men make excellent clerks in Government offices, being especially quick and skilful at figures; indeed they have inherited many of the qualities of their ancestors, the scribes of the Pharaohs. At the present time they owe their ability to perform the duties of their appointments entirely to the American Missionaries, who have taught them English, and educated them on modern lines, and helped them to lead lives based upon a high standard of public and private morality. All classes of Egyptian society are deeply anxious to have their children well educated, but no community in Egypt is so largely represented in the Government schools, in proportion to population, as the Copts. The proportion of Muḥammadans in the entire population is 92 per cent., and of the Copts 6 per cent.; yet the proportion of Coptic pupils in the Government schools is 17 per cent., and that of the Muḥammadans 78 per cent. (Viscount Cromer, *Egypt*, No. 1, 1900, p. 35.)

Like Jews and Muslims, the Copts say **prayers** seven times daily, *i.e.*, at daybreak, and at the third, sixth, ninth, eleventh, and twelfth hours, and at midnight; whilst praying they face the east, and many people wash before praying. The service in **church** usually begins at daybreak and lasts three hours; the clergy, choir, and prominent members of the congregation occupy the part of the church next to that containing the altar, the ordinary members of the congregation occupy a second compartment, and the women, who sit by themselves, a third; and each compartment is separated from the other by a screen with one or more doors. The churches contain no images, but pictures of the saints are common. The men remove their shoes from their feet at the door, and each uses a crutch to lean upon, as he stands during the greater part of the service. The Copts make use of **confession**, which is obligatory before the receiving of the Eucharist, and they observe the following fasts:—(1) The Fast of Nineveh, which is observed a week before Lent, three days and three nights. (2) The Great Fast (*i.e.*, Lent), fifty-five days. (3) The Fast of the Nativity, twenty-eight days. (4) The Fast of the Apostles, the length of which varies. (5) The Fast of the Virgin, fifteen days. The festivals are seven in number, and at the celebration of the Festival of the Baptism of Christ the boys and men dip themselves in a stream or in the river, and as each does this, one of his friends says, "Plunge, as thy father and grandfather plunged, and remove Al-Islâm from thy heart." The Copts may contract **marriages** with members of their own community only; he who would marry a woman belonging to another sect must either adopt her religion or marry her by a civil rite, which the Church does not acknowledge. The betrothal is brought about by an agent, or go-between, who arranges the details of the wedding contract in the presence of a priest; two-thirds of the dowry are paid at this time, and when the business part of the ceremony is concluded all present say the Lord's Prayer three times. As with the Muḥammadans, the bridegroom rarely sees his bride's face until marriage; the marriage rejoicings usually occupy about eight days, and nearly all Coptic marriages take place on a Saturday night.* The service in the church is a lengthy one, and the priest, or Patriarch, administers the Eucharist to the bridegroom and bride. After marriage the bride does not leave her house until after the birth of her first child, but it is said that in recent years the observance of this, and of many another marriage custom, is not so strict as formerly. Divorce can be readily obtained for adultery on the part of the wife, but it is also granted for much less grave causes. In burying their dead the Copts follow, in many respects, the custom of the country, and women wail in the house of the dead for three days; the friends and relatives of the dead visit the graves three times a year, *i.e.*, on the festivals of the Nativity and Baptism and Resurrection of our Lord. After each visit the well-to-do give alms to the poor in the shape of food, and in this matter they seem to follow unconsciously the customs of their ancestors, the ancient Egyptians.

* The marriage ceremonies are fully described in Lane, *Modern Egyptians*, vol. II., p. 291 *ff.*, to which work I am indebted for many of the facts given above.

THE ARABS, MUḤAMMAD, AND MUḤAMMADANISM.

The home of the Arabs is the peninsula of Arabia, which is about 1,450 miles long and 700 wide; the greater part of the country is desert and mountain, and only in the south-west portion of it are perennial streams found. The Arabs are Semites, and the modern descendants of them trace their origin to the Hebrews through Kâhtân, who is identified with Joktan, the son of Eber, and to Adnân, the direct descendant of Ishmael, the son of Abraham and Hagar. The kingdoms of Yaman and Hijâz were founded by Yârab and Yorhom, sons of Kâhtân. The provinces of Sâba and Hadhramaut were ruled by princes of the tribe of Himyar, whose kingdoms lasted two or three thousand years. In the third century before Christ a terrible calamity befell the Arabs, for the great dam which Sâba, the builder of Saba and Mareb, built to hold up the rain water and mountain springs, suddenly burst, and the widespread ruin brought by the flood which was thus let loose on the plains caused eight great Arab tribes to leave their country. The water is said to have been held up to a height of about 180 feet, and the people felt so sure of the security of the dam that they built their houses upon it. In the second century after Christ the Arabs migrated northwards and established petty kingdoms at Palmyra* and al-Ḥîra,† and came at times into conflict with the Roman authorities in Syria and with the Persian powers in Eastern Mesopotamia. The Arabs of Palmyra embraced Christianity in the time of Constantine, but those of al-Hîra did not accept it until after A.D. 550; the Arabs of the desert, however, continued to be for the

* The Arabs of Palmyra were descended from the tribe of Azd.

† The Arabs of al-Ḥîra were descended from Kâhtân.

most part idolaters. The rule of the Himyar princes came to an end in the first half of the VIth century of our era, when the king of Ethiopia overthrew a base usurper called Dhu-Nuwâs, who inflicted tortures of the worst description on the Christians, and who is said to have destroyed 20,000 of them; the Ethiopian rule was of short duration, for before the end of the century the Persians were masters of the country. Strictly speaking, the Arabs, as a nation, have never been conquered, and no ruler has ever been able to make his authority effective in all parts of their dominions. In pre-Muḥammadan times, which the Arabs call "Jâhilîyah," جَاهِلِيَّة, *i.e.*, the "epoch of ignorance," their religion was the grossest idolatry, and the dominant phase of it was the religion of **Sabaism.** They believed in One God, but worshipped the stars, planets, and angels. They prayed three times a day, and fasted three times a year, they offered up sacrifices, they went on a pilgrimage to a place near Harran, and they held in great honour the temple at Mecca, and the Pyramids of Egypt, believing these last to be the tombs of Seth and of his sons Enoch and Sabi. Three great powers worshipped by the whole nation were Lât, Al-Uzza, and Manât; the Ḳur'ân (Koran) mentions five very ancient idols, viz., Wadd, Sawâ'â, Yaghûth, Ya'ûḳ, and Nasra. The first of these had the form of a man, the second that of a woman, the third that of a lion, the fourth that of a horse, and the fifth that of an eagle. Sabaism taught that the souls of the wicked will be punished for 9,000 ages, but that after that period they will obtain mercy. Many Arabs, however, believed neither in the creation nor in the resurrection, and attributed all things to the operations of nature. Magianism, of Persian origin, found many followers in Arabia, but Judaism and Christianity exerted a profound influence upon the religion of the Arabs. The Arabs prided themselves upon their skill in oratory and in making poetry, and in the arts of war, and they made a boast of their hospitality; but they always had the character of being fierce, cruel, and vindictive, generous to friends, but implacable to foes, and addicted to robbery and rapine.

Muḥammad, commonly known as the "Prophet," was born at Mecca on August 20, A.D. 570; his mother was called Amîna, and his father 'Abd-Allah, and his ancestors were men of high rank in the city of Mecca, many of them holding offices in connection with the temple there. His parents were poor, and Muḥammad's inheritance consisted of five camels, a flock of goats, and a slave girl. He was suckled by Thuêba and Ḥalîma, and reared by his grandfather 'Abd al-Muṭṭalib, and was instructed in the trade of merchant by his uncle Abu Ṭâlib. At the age of six his mother took him to Medîna, but on the way home she died; at the age of twelve (A.D. 582), Abû Ṭâlib took him to Syria. At the age of twenty he visited the Fair at Okas, three days to the east of Mecca, where he heard the great Arab poets declaim their compositions, and met numbers of Christians and Jews. In 595 he began to do business as a merchant on behalf of Khadîjah, a wealthy lady of the Koreish tribe, and his trafficking was successful; soon after his return from Syria, this lady, who was about forty years of age, determined to marry him, and the ceremony was performed by Khadîjah's father, whom she had made drunk for the purpose. By this marriage he had two sons and four daughters. In 605 the great Ka'ba was built, and the lot fell upon Muḥammad to build the famous Black Stone into its eastern corner, where it may be kissed by all who visit it. When he arrived at the age of 40 he began to formulate a system for the reform of the religion of the Arabs, and he became convinced that he was destined by God to carry out that reform; at times, however, he was very despondent, and he often meditated suicide, from which Khadîjah dissuaded him. About this time he declared that Gabriel appeared to him and entrusted to him the divine mission of reforming the religion of the Arabs. When Muḥammad was 45 years old he had collected a sufficiently large number of influential converts about him to provoke great opposition and persecution in and about Mecca, and in 615 the **first Ḥijra,** or "flight," to Abyssinia took place. At this time Muḥammad relaxed his exertions somewhat, for he became doubtful about the value of his mission, and seemed to be willing to tolerate the worship of idols. In December, 619, his beloved wife Khâdijah died, aged 70, and about a month later Abu Ṭâlib, his uncle, also died, and in the midst of these afflictions Muḥammad had the vexation of seeing that his converts were not increasing in number. In 620 he set out to call Taif to repentance, but he was expelled from the city; a few weeks later he married a widow called Sawda, and betrothed himself to 'Aisha, the daughter of Abu Bakr, a child of six or seven years of age. In the same year Muḥammad made converts at Medîna, a city which lies about 250 miles to the north of Mecca, and on June 20, A.D. 622, the year on which the Arabs base their chronology, the **Second Hijra** or "Flight" to Medîna took place. He arrived in that city on June 28, and at once began to build a mosque on the spot where his camel Al-Kaswa had knelt down. At the age of 53 he married 'Aisha, aged 10, and it is said that the bride carried her toys to her husband's house, and that at times he joined in her games. In 623 he ceased to pray towards Jerusalem, and ordered his followers to pray towards the Ka'ba at Mecca; in this year the battle of Badr was fought, in which he vanquished his opponents in Mecca. In 624 his power and influence continued to grow, and he married Ḥafsa, the daughter of 'Omar. In 625 was fought the battle of Uhud, in which Muḥammad was wounded, and a number of powerful Jews were expelled from Medîna. In January, 626, he married Zênab, the daughter of Khuzêma, and a month later Umm-Salma, the widow of Abu-Salma; in June he married Zênab bint-Jahsh, who was divorced by her husband Zêd, the adopted son of Muḥammad, and later in the year he married a seventh wife, called Juwêrya. In 627 Medîna was besieged, and the Beni-Kurèba were massacred, and Muḥammad's power and influence continued to increase; the people of Mecca then began to come to terms with him. In 628 he despatched letters to Heraclius, and to the king of Persia, and to the governors of Yaman, Egypt, and Abyssinia, calling upon them to acknowledge the divine mission of Muḥammad. In the same year he betrothed himself to Umm-Ḥabûba, and conquered Khêbar, where he married Safia, the bride of Kinâna; and the Jews bribed a sorcerer to bewitch Muḥummad by tying knots of his hairs upon a palm branch, which was sunk in a well, and he is said to have begun to waste away. But the archangel Gabriel revealed the matter to him, and when the branch had been taken out of the well and the hairs untied he recovered his health. Soon after this he went to Mecca and married Mêmûna, and his power increased in the city; in 630 he conquered the city and destroyed the idols, and was successful in many raids which he made upon the tribes who had not acknowledged his divine mission. At this time George the Maḳawḳas sent to him from Egypt two sisters called Shirîn and Maryam (Mary); the latter Muḥammad married, and she bore him a son called Ibrahîm, who, however, died in June or July, 631. In this year many tribes sent envoys to Muḥammad tendering their submission, and among them were men who represented the Christian Arabs; the answer given to the latter proves that Muḥammad only tolerated the Christian religion, and that he expected the children of Christians to be brought up in the faith of Al-Islâm. In 632 Muḥammad ordered an expedition against Syria, but he died early in the month of

June. In **personal appearance** he was of medium height, and he had an upright carriage until his later years, when he began to stoop, and he walked fast. He laughed often and had a ready wit and a good memory; his manners were pleasing, and he was exceedingly gracious to inferiors. Of learning he had none, and he could neither read nor write. He was slow and dignified of speech, and prudent in judgment. He was not ashamed to mend his own clothes and shoes, and his humility was so great that he would ride upon an ass. He ate with his thumb and the first and second fingers, and he greatly liked bread cooked with meat, dates dressed with milk and butter, pumpkins, cucumbers, and undried dates; onions and garlic he abhorred. His garments were of different colours, but he loved white, although he was very fond of striped stuffs; it is said that he once gave seventeen camels for a single garment. His hair was long, like his beard, but he clipped his moustache; he painted his eyelids with antimony, and greatly loved musk, ambergris, and camphor burnt on sweet-smelling woods. His life was simple, but his disposition was sensual, and his polygamous inclinations sorely tried the convictions of his followers. He was a staunch friend to his friends, and a bitter foe to his enemies, whom he often treated with great cruelty; he had the reputation for sincerity, but at times he behaved with cunning and meanness; his urbanity hid a determination which few realized, and the sword was the real cause of the conversion of the nations to his views. The religion which he preached was, and is, intolerant and fanatical, and, although it has made millions of men believe in one God, and renounce the worship of idols, and abhor wine and strong drink, it has set the seal of his approval upon the unbridled gratification of sensual appetites, and has given polygamy and divorce a religious status and wide-spread popularity.

Al-Ḳur'ân* (the Koran, or Coran) is the name given to the revelations or instructions which Muḥammad declared had been sent to him from God by the archangel Gabriel. During the lifetime of Muḥammad these revelations were written upon skins, shoulder-bones of camels and goats, palm leaves, slices of stone, or anything which was convenient for writing upon, and then committed to memory by every true believer; they thus took the place of the poetical compositions which the Arabs had, from time immemorial, been accustomed to learn by heart. It is tolerably certain that copies of the revelations were multiplied as soon as they were uttered by the Prophet, and their number must have been considerable. On the death of the Prophet, the Arabs of the south revolted, and Abu-Bakr was obliged to suppress the rebellion with a strong hand, but the false prophet Musailima had many adherents, and the fight was fierce and bloody, and many of those who best knew the Ḳur'ân were slain. At this time the various sections of the book were not arranged in any order, and 'Omar, fearing that certain sections might be lost, advised Abu-Bakr to have all the revelations gathered together into one book. This was A.D. 633. By Abu-Bakr's orders, a young man called Zêd ibn-Thâbit, who had been Muḥammad's secretary and had learned Syriac and Hebrew, was entrusted with the task, and he collected the sections from every conceivable source, and made a fair copy of them in the order in which they have come down to us. This copy was given by 'Omar, the successor of Abu-Bakr, to his daughter Ḥafṣa, one of the widows of the Prophet. Before long, however, variations sprang up in the copies which were made from that of Ḥafṣa, and these variations became so numerous, and caused such serious disputes, that the Khalif 'Othmân ordered Zêd ibn-Thâbit and three men of the Koreish tribe to prepare a new recen-

* The word means "the reading," or "what ought to be read."

sion of the Ḳur'ân. At length the new recension was finished, and copies were sent to Kûfa, Baṣra, Damascus, Mecca and Medîna, and all the pre-existing versions were ruthlessly burnt. Ḥafṣa's copy was restored to her, but it was afterwards destroyed by Merwân, the governor of Medîna. The Arabs regard the language of the Ḳur'ân as extremely pure, and incomparable for beauty and eloquence; it is also thought to be under God's special protection, and therefore to be incorruptible. To explain the existence of slight variations, it was declared that the book was revealed in seven distinct dialects. The Ḳur'ân contains 114 sections, each of which is called a *sûra;* some were revealed at Mecca, and others at Medîna, and others were revealed partly at Mecca and partly at Medîna. The number of verses in the whole book is given as 6,000, or 6,214, or 6,219, or 6,225, or 6,226, or 6,236, according to the authority followed; the number of words is said to be 77,639, or 99,464; and the number of letters 323,015, or 330,113, for, like the Jews,* the Arabs counted the letters of their Scriptures. At the head of each section, after the title, come the words, "In the Name of God, the Merciful, the Compassionate," which formula, Sale thinks, was borrowed from the Magians. That Muḥammad, assisted by his friends, composed the Ḳur'ân is certain, yet his followers declare that the first transcript of it existed in heaven, written upon the "Preserved Table" or Tablet from all eternity, and that it subsists in the very essence of God. A copy on paper was sent down to the lowest heaven by Gabriel, who revealed it to the Prophet piecemeal, but showed him the whole book, bound in silk and set with the gold and precious stones of Paradise, once a year. Hence the Ḳur'ân is held in the greatest reverence by the Muḥam-

* The number of times which each letter occurs in the Hebrew Bible will be found in the *Massoreth ha-Massoreth* of Elias Levita (ed. Ginsburg), p. 271 *ff.*

madans, who are said never to touch it unless they are ceremonially pure.

The Muḥammadans divide their religion, which they call "**Islâm,**" into two parts, i.e., *Imân*, faith, or theory, and *Dîn*, religion, or practice; it is built on five fundamental points, one belonging to faith and four to practice. The confession of faith is, "There is no god but God," and "Muḥammad is the Apostle of God." Under this point the Arabs comprehend:—1. Belief in God; 2. In His Angels; 3. In His Scriptures; 4. In His Prophets; 5. In the Resurrection and Day of Judgment; 6. In God's absolute decree and predetermination both of good and evil. The four points of practice are:—1. Prayer and ablutions; 2. Alms; 3. Fasting; 4. Pilgrimage to Mecca.

1. The **belief in God** is thus expressed:—"Say, God is one God; the eternal God; he begetteth not, neither is he begotten; and there is not any one like unto him" (*Sura* cxii).

2. The **Angels** are beings of light who neither eat nor drink, and who are without sex; they are without sin, and perform God's behests in heaven and upon earth, and adore Him. There are four Archangels, Gabriel, Michael, Azraêl, the angel of death, and Isrâfêl, the angel who will sound the trumpet at the end of the world. Every believer is attended by two angels, one writing down his good actions, and the other his evil actions; the guardian angels are variously said to be five, sixty, or a hundred and sixty. The angels Munkar and Nakîr examine the dead, and torture the wicked in their graves. The **Jinn** were created before Adam, and are beings of fire, who eat and drink and marry; they include Jann, Satans, 'Afrîts, and Mârids. The head of them is 'Azâzêl or Iblîs, who was cast out of heaven because he refused to worship Adam.

3. The **Scriptures** are the uncreated word of God which He revealed to His Prophets; of these alone remain,

but in a corrupt state, the Pentateuch of Moses, the Psalms of David, the Gospels of Christ, and the Ḳur'ân, which surpasses in excellence all other revelations. Ten books were given to Adam, fifty to Seth, thirty to Enoch, and ten to Abraham, but all these are lost.

4. The **Prophets** are in number 124,000 or 224,000, of whom 313 were Apostles; among the Apostles of special importance are Adam, Noah, Abraham, Moses, Jesus Christ, and Muḥammad, who is declared to be the last, and greatest, and most excellent of them all. It is admitted that Christ is the Word of God, and the Messiah, but the Muḥammadans deny that He is the Son of God.

5. **Resurrection** and day of judgment. When the body is laid in the grave two angels, called **Munkar and Nakîr,** appear there, and make the dead man sit upright, and question him as to his faith; if the answers are satisfactory he is allowed to rest in peace, but if not the angels beat him on the temples with iron maces, and having heaped earth upon the body, it is gnawed by ninety-nine dragons, each having seven heads. All good Muḥammadans have their graves made hollow and two stones placed in a suitable position for the two angels to sit upon. The souls of the just when taken from their bodies by the angel of death may be borne to heaven, but various opinions exist on this point. Some think that the souls remain near the graves either for seven days or for a longer period; others think they exist with Adam in the lowest heaven; others that they live in the trumpet which is to wake the dead; and others that they dwell in the forms of white birds under the throne of God. The souls of the wicked having been rejected by heaven and by this earth are taken down to the seventh earth, and thrown into a dungeon under a green rock, or under the Devil's jaw, where they will be tortured until called upon to rejoin their bodies. Muḥammadans generally believe in the resurrec-

tion both of the body and of the soul. All parts of the bodies of the dead will decay except the cuckoo bone (coccyx), wherefrom the whole body shall be renewed, and this renewal shall take place through a rain of forty days, which shall cover the earth to a depth of twelve cubits, and cause the bodies to sprout like plants. The time when the resurrection is to take place is known only to God. The first blast of the trumpet will shake heaven and earth; the second will cause all living creatures to die, the last being the angel of death; and the third, which is to take place forty years after the second, will raise the dead, Muḥammad being the first to rise. The general resurrection will include animals. Some say the day of judgment will last 1,000 years, and others 50,000; the place of judgment will be the earth, and Muḥammad is to be the intercessor with God on behalf of man. A book wherein is written an account of his actions will be given to each man, and all things will be weighed in a balance; the judgment over, the souls of the good will turn to a road on the right, and those of the bad to a road on the left. All will, however, have to pass over the bridge Al-Sirât, which is laid over the midst of hell, and is finer than a hair, and sharper than the edge of a sword; the good will have no difficulty in passing over this, but the wicked will fall from it and meet their doom in Gehenna, which is divided into seven stories, one below the other. Between hell and paradise is a partition or gulf, which is not, however, so wide that the blessed and the damned cannot discourse together. The blessed will drink out of a lake, the water of which comes from paradise, and is whiter than milk, and sweeter in smell than musk. Paradise was created before the world, and is situated above the seven heavens, near the throne of God; its earth is made of fine wheat flour, or musk, or saffron; its stones are pearls; its walls are inlaid with gold and silver; and the trunks of all its trees are of gold. Therein is the Ṭûba tree, laden with every kind of fruit, and it will supply the true believer with everything he needs, *i.e.*, meat, drink, raiment, horses to ride, etc. The rivers flow with milk, wine, and honey, and the fountains are innumerable. The women of Paradise, the Ḥûr al-'uyûn (Houris), who will be given to the believers, are made of pure musk, and are free from all the defects of earthly women; they live in hollow pearls, which are sixty miles long, and sixty miles wide. The beings in Paradise will never grow old, and they will always remain in the prime and vigour of a man thirty years of age; when they enter Paradise, they will be of the same stature as Adam, *i.e.*, sixty cubits, or 110 feet high. Women who have lived good lives upon earth will live in Paradise in an abode specially set apart for them.

6. **Predestination**. God's decree, whether concerning evil or good, is absolute; and whatever hath come or will come to pass hath been irrevocably fixed from all eternity. A man's fate cannot, either by wisdom or foresight, be avoided.

Concerning the four points of practice :—

1. **Prayer** and **ablutions**. Prayer is the prop of religion and the key of Paradise, and the pious Muḥammadan prays at least five times a day:—Between daybreak and sunrise; 2. In the early afternoon; 3. In the afternoon before sunset; 4. In the evening after sunset; and 5. Before the first watch of the night. Notice is given from the mosques of the times of prayer daily; because the day begins with sunset, the time of which changes daily, and every believer is expected to prepare for prayer as soon as he hears the voice of the crier from the mosque. The prayers recited are those ordained by God and those ordained by the Prophet; some are said sitting, some standing upright, and some with the head bent. Before praying a man must wash his hands, mouth, nostrils, face and

arms, each three times, and then the upper part of the head, the beard, ears, neck and feet, each once. Muḥammad is said to have declared that "the practice of religion is founded on cleanliness," which is one half of the faith and the key of prayer, without which it will not be heard by God; and also that "there could be no good in that religion wherein was no prayer." When praying the Muḥammadans turn the face towards the temple at Mecca, and in mosques and public inns the direction of that city is always indicated by a niche which is called Ḳibla or Miḥrâb, and all prayer is held to be in vain unless it be said with a humble, penitent, and sincere heart. Muḥammadans never pray clad in fine clothes, nor do they pray in public with women.

2. **Almsgiving.** Alms are of two kinds, obligatory and voluntary, and they are regarded as of great assistance in causing God to hear prayer; it has been said by one of the Khâlifs that "prayer carries us half-way to God, fasting brings us to the door of his palace, and alms procure us admission." Alms are to be given of cattle, money, corn, fruits, and merchandise sold, and one-fortieth part must be given either in money or kind of everything received.

3. **Fasting.** The three degrees of fasting are:—1. The restraining of the lusts of the body; 2. The restraining of the members of the body from sin; and 3. The fasting of the heart from worldly cares, and compelling the mind to dwell upon God. The Muḥammadan must abstain from eating and drinking, and any physical indulgence, every day during the month of Ramaḍân from dawn until sunset, unless physically incapacitated; it is said that this month was chosen as the month for fasting because in it the Ḳur'ân was sent down from heaven. Strict Muḥammadans suffer nothing to enter their mouths during the day, and regard the fast as broken if a man smell perfumes, or bathe, or swallow

his spittle, or kiss or touch a woman, or smoke; on and after sunset they eat and drink as they please.

4. **The Pilgrimage to Mecca.** Every Muḥammadan must undertake a pilgrimage to Mecca at least once in his life, for Muḥammad is said to have declared that he who does not do so may as well die a Jew or a Christian. The object of the pilgrimage is to visit the **Ka'ba** and perform certain ceremonies there. This building is rectangular, and the famous **Black Stone**,* set in silver, is built into its south-eastern corner; the stone measures about 6 inches by 8, and is of a reddish-black colour. It is said to have fallen from Paradise to earth with Adam, and to have been miraculously preserved during the deluge, and given to Abraham by Gabriel when he built the Ka'ba. When a pilgrim has arrived near Mecca he removes his ordinary clothes and puts on a woollen tunic about his loins, and a woollen shawl about his shoulders, and very loose slippers. He then goes round the Ka'ba seven times, and each time he passes he must either kiss the Black Stone or touch it; he must next pass seven times between the low hills Ṣafâ and Merwâ, partly running and partly walking, in memory of Hagar's hurried steps as she wandered up and down seeking water for Ishmael; he must next go to Mount 'Arafât, near Mecca, and pray there and listen to a discourse until sunset; and the day following he must go to the valley of Mîna and cast seven stones at certain marks. This last act is the "stoning of the Devil," and is done in imitation of Abraham, who cast stones at the great Enemy because he tempted or disturbed him when praying while preparing to offer up his son Isaac. When the stoning is done the pilgrims slay animals in the valley of Mîna, and make a great feast, and give gifts to the poor, and when they have shaved their heads and pared their nails the

* A view of this stone is given in Sir William Muir's *Life of Mahomet*, p. 27.

pilgrimage is considered to have been performed. The various ceremonies of the pilgrimage described above are extremely ancient, and are admitted by the Muḥammadans to be the product of the "time of ignorance"; at one epoch each had a special signification, which may or may not have been understood by the Prophet. He, though wishing to do so, had no power to abolish them, but he certainly succeeded in depriving them of meaning, and now these rites have no signification whatever.

The Ḳur'ân prohibits the drinking of **wine** and all intoxicating liquors in these words:—"O true believers, surely wine, and lots, and images, and divining arrows are an abomination of the work of Satan; therefore avoid ye them, that ye may prosper"; and again, "They will ask thee concerning wine and lots: Answer, in both there is great sin, and also some things of use unto men; but their sinfulness is greater than their use." Strict Muḥammadans abjure the use of **opium** and **ḥashîsh,** or Indian hemp (*cannabis Indica*), which when taken in excess practically makes a man mad,* and they are bidden to avoid all gaming and gambling, and divination and magic. Tobacco is used freely everywhere, and of course coffee, but many learned Muḥammadans have doubted the legality of the use of either of these. When not corrupted by intercourse with Western peoples, the Muḥammadans are probably the most abstemious people in the East. The duties of a man to his neighbour are laid down at length by Muḥammadan teachers, and in great detail, and we may see from the Ḳur'ân that the observance of most of the virtues beloved by Western nations is also strictly inculcated by them. In the matter of **Polygamy** and **Divorce,** however, their morality is exceedingly lax, and there is no doubt that the

* In 1898 over ten *tons* were seized by the coast-guard at or near Alexandria, and in 1899 about 900 persons were fined for selling the drug, and the dens kept by 310 persons were closed.

domestic habits of the Arab nations have seriously hampered their progress among the peoples of the earth. Muḥammad said, "If ye fear that ye shall not act with equity towards orphans [of the female sex], take in marriage of such [other] women as please you, two, or three, or four," (Sûra IV); but the example which he himself set was an unfortunate one, and has been the cause of much misery to the Arabs. Among poor folk want of means is the great deterrent to polygamy, and many men, therefore, marry only one wife; but the laws relating to divorce are so loose, that a man with money can generally find or buy an excuse for getting rid of his wife and for taking a new one. The children of concubines or slaves are held to be legitimate, and the Prophet did a good deed when he put a stop to the inhuman custom among the pagan Arabs of burying their daughters alive. It is said that the girl who was intended to die was allowed to live until she was six years old, when she was perfumed and dressed in fine raiment, and taken to a pit dug for that purpose; the father then stood behind her, and pushed her in, and had the pit filled up at once. The punishment for **murder** is death, but it may, if all parties concerned agree, be compounded by the payment of money, and by the freeing of a Muḥammadan from captivity; **Manslaughter** may be compounded by a fine and by the freeing of a Muḥammadan from captivity. **Theft,** if the object stolen be worth more than £2, is punished by the loss of a member:—for the first offence, the right hand; for the second, the left foot; for the third, the left hand; for the fourth, the right foot. In recent years beating and hard labour have taken the place of the punishment of mutilation. **Adultery** is punished by death by stoning if the charge against the woman be established by four eye-witnesses; the extreme penalty of the law is, naturally, carried out but rarely. **Drunkenness** is punished by flogging. **Blasphemy** of God, or Christ, or

Muḥammad, is ordered to be punished by death; the same punishment has been inflicted upon women for **Apostasy.**

The **Festivals** of the Muḥammadans are thus classified by Mr. Lane (*op. cit.*, vol. II, p. 145, ff.):—

1. To the first ten days of the month Muḥarram, which is the first month of the Muḥammadan year, special importance is attached, and great rejoicing takes place in them; but of all days the tenth is the most honoured. Water which has been blessed is sold freely as a charm against the evil eye, and the Jinn are supposed to visit men and women by night during this period of ten days. On the tenth day of Muḥarram the meeting between Adam and Eve took place after they had been cast out of Paradise; on this day Noah left the ark, and the Prophet's grandson, Al-Ḥusên, was slain at the battle of Kerbela. The pagan Arabs fasted on this day, and many Muḥammadans follow their example, and it is unlucky to make a marriage contract in this month.

2. About the end of the second month (Ṣafar), the return of the **Mecca Caravan** is celebrated. When the main body of the Caravan is yet some days' journey distant, two Arabs, mounted on swift dromedaries, hurry on to the Citadel at Cairo to announce the day of its arrival. Many pious people go as much as a three days' journey to meet the Caravan, and carry with them gifts of raiment and food for the pilgrims, and donkeys on which certain of them may ride. When the Caravan arrives it is greeted with shouts of joy and music in honour of those who have returned, and weeping and wailing for those who have left their bones on the way. It is considered a most meritorious thing for a man or woman to die when making the "Ḥagg"* or Pilgrimage to Mecca, and many sick folk make arrangements to set out on the road to Mecca, full well knowing that they will die on the road. Some years ago, when the

* Thus pronounced in Egypt.

Indian Pilgrims, who sailed from Bombay, were not so well looked after as they are now, the number of those who died on the ships and were buried at sea was considerable. The pilgrims bring back, as gifts for their friends, holy water from the Sacred Well of Zamzam, from which Hagar gave Ishmael water to drink, pieces of the covering of the Ka'ba, which is renewed yearly, cakes of dust from the Prophet's tomb, frankincense, palm fibres for washing the body, combs and rosaries of the wood of aloes, tooth sticks and eye paint. A prominent object in the Caravan is the Maḥmil, to which great reverence is paid. It is a square framework of wood with a pyramidal top; on the top, and at each corner, is a silver-gilt ball with a crescent. The framework is covered with black brocade, richly marked in gold, and ornamented with tassels; there is nothing inside the Maḥmil, but two copies of the Ḳur'ân, one on a scroll and one in book form, are attached to the outside of it. When the Maḥmil reaches the Citadel it is saluted with twelve guns.

3. At the beginning of Rabî' al-awwal (the third month), the Mûlid al-Nebi, or Birthday of the Prophet, is commemorated. The rejoicings begin on the third day of the month, and for nine days and nine nights the people indulge in singing and dancing and festivities of every kind, the streets are illuminated by night, and processions of Dervishes go about through the streets by day and by night. Mr. Lane once heard the sweetmeat sellers crying out when this festival was being celebrated, "A grain of salt in the eye of him who doth not bless the Prophet," probably a warning to Jews and Christians to keep away. He was also fortunate enough to see the Shêkh of the Sa'dîyeh Dervishes ride over the bodies of a large number of them. Some sixty of these lay down upon the ground side by side as closely as possible, their backs being upwards, their legs extended, and their arms placed beneath their foreheads.

None of the men were hurt, a fact which they attributed to the prayers which they had said the day before. This ceremony is called **Doseh,** and during its performance those trodden upon continued to utter the name "Allah," or God.

4. In the fourth month, Rabî' al-tâni, fifteen days and fourteen nights are spent in celebrating the festival of the **Mûlid al-Ḥasanên**, or the birthday of Al-Ḥusên, whose head is buried in the Mosque of the Ḥasanên.

5. In the middle of the seventh month, Regeb, the birthday of Zênab, the granddaughter of the Prophet, is celebrated; and on the 27th of the month the festival of the ascension of the Prophet is celebrated. He is said to have been carried from Mecca to Jerusalam, and from Jerusalem to heaven, and having held converse with God, to have returned to Mecca in one night!

6. On the first or second Wednesday of the eighth month, Sha'bân, the birthday of Imâm Shafêi is celebrated, and the cemetery called the Karâfeh becomes the scene of great festivities. Above the dome of the mosque of the Imâm a metal boat is placed, and it is said to turn about even in the absence of wind, and according to the direction in which it turns, good or evil is foretold. The eve of the fifteenth day of this month is held in great reverence, because the fate of every man during the year ensuing is decided. The lote tree of Paradise contains as many leaves as there are human beings in the world, and on each leaf is written the name of a man or woman; shortly after sunset this tree is shaken, when numbers of its leaves fall, and those whose names are written on the fallen leaves will die in the ensuing year. Pious Muḥammadans pass this night in solemn prayer.

The ninth month, **Ramaḍân,** is observed as a month of fasting; when this month falls in the summer time the Muḥammadans suffer greatly from both hunger and thirst.

Mr. Lane calculates that the time during which the daily fast is kept varies from 12 h. 5 m. to 16 h. 14 m. The effect of the fast upon the country is, practically, to turn night into day, for nearly all the shops are kept open at night, and the streets are thronged, and the stranger sometimes finds it difficult to believe that the fasting is as rigorous as it undoubtedly is. The 27th night of the month is called the Lêlet al-Ḳadr, or "**Night of Power,**" and is held to be "better than a thousand months," for in it the Ḳur'ân is said to have been sent down to Muḥammad. On this night the angels bring blessings to the faithful, and as the gates of heaven are then open, it is believed that prayer will certainly find admission. Salt water is said to become sweet during that night, and some people keep a vessel of salt water before them and taste it evening after evening, that when it becomes sweet they may be certain that they are observing the Night of Power.

On the first three days of the tenth month, Shawwâl, the **Lesser Festival,** or **Ramaḍân Bairam** is kept with great rejoicing; it marks the end of the fast of Ramaḍân. When friends meet in the street they embrace and kiss each other, and the women visit the graves of their relatives and lay broken palm branches and sweet basil upon them; during this festival many put on new clothes, and presents of every kind are given and received by members of all classes.

A few days later the **Kiswah,** or Covering of the Ka'ba, followed by the Maḥmil, is conveyed from the Citadel, where it is manufactured at the Sulṭân's expense, to the Mosque of the Ḥasanên, and the occasion is looked upon by everyone as a festival. The Kiswah is of black brocade covered with inscriptions, and having a broad band at the edge of each side ornamented with inscriptions worked in gold; the covering and its band are each woven in four pieces, which are afterwards sewn together. The Veil which covers the door of the Ka'ba is made of richly worked black brocade and is lined with green silk, while the Kiswah is only lined with cotton. A Covering and a Veil are taken to the Ka'ba yearly by the great Mecca Caravan, and the old ones, which have become spoiled by rain and dust, are cut up in pieces and sold to the pilgrims. On the 23rd of the month Shawwâl the procession of the officers and the escort of the Mecca Caravan pass from the Citadel through the streets of the metropolis to a plain to the north of the city called Ḥaṣwa (*i.e.*, pebbly); on the 25th it proceeds to the Birket al-Ḥagg, or Pilgrim Lake, about eleven miles from the city, and on the 27th the caravan starts for Mecca. The journey to Mecca occupies usually about 37 days, but those who like to travel leisurely take longer; this city is about 45 miles, and is almost due east, from Jiddah on the Red Sea.

On the tenth of the month Dhul-ḥiggah, *i.e.*, the month of the Pilgrimage and the last of the Muḥammadan year, the **Great Festival** begins; it is observed in much the same way as the Little Festival, and lasts three or four days.

Muḥammadan **sects.** The Muḥammadans of Egypt, and of many other parts of the Turkish Empire may be described as **orthodox,** for they base their public and private life upon the teaching of Muḥammad, and upon the traditions handed down by his early disciples, and upon the decisions which they promulgated. Among these, however, there are four chief sects, the Ḥanafites, the Shâfe'ites, the Malekites, and the Ḥambalites, which, though agreeing as regards fundamentals of faith, differ in matters of detail. Speaking generally, the Ḥanafites may be said to follow their own opinions in many matters of faith instead of those of the Prophet, while the other three sects follow the traditions of Muḥammad. The founders of the sects were Abu Ḥanîfa, born at Kûfa, A.H. 80; Shâfe'i, born at Gaza or Askelon, A.H. 150; Malek, born at

Medîna about A.H. 94; and Ḥambal, born either at Merv or Baghdad. The **heterodox** among the Arabs are called Shî'ites,* and are regarded with detestation by the Sunnites or traditionalists, who declare that they may just as well not be Muḥammadans at all, because they are doomed to eternal punishment. Among the heterodox some rejected all eternal attributes of God; others disputed about the essence of God; others declared that God could not have made unbelievers; others held that there were two Gods, the one, the most high God, being eternal, and the other, Christ, being non-eternal; others denied everlasting punishment; others said that God could be a liar; others denied the absoluteness of predestination, and endowed men with free-will; others distinguished the attributes of God from His essence; others taught anthropomorphism pure and simple, and ascribed to God a material body; and within a comparatively short time after the death of the Prophet, **Ṣûfism,** or the doctrine of Divine love, with which were mingled mysticism and asceticism, attained great influence over the minds of the Persian Muḥammadans, and its followers became a very large sect.

The **Mahdi.** From what has been said above it will be evident to the reader that the Arabs were always divided into sects which disputed among themselves about questions of religion, especially about those which savoured of mysticism and dogma. When the Arabs embraced the doctrines of Muḥammad the Prophet, they carried into their new religion many ideas, and beliefs, and customs, which even that masterful man was unable to set aside. Muḥammad the "illiterate," as his followers love to call him, permitted them to believe whatever did not interfere with the supremacy of his own views, and he himself borrowed most of his doctrines and mythology from the Jews and Christians and Persians.

* Most Persians are Shî'ites.

In Judaism and Zoroastrianism there was a common idea that the world had fallen into an evil condition, that religion had been corrupted, that all men were exceedingly wicked, and that only a supernatural being, who was to come at the end of time, could put all things right; this being the Jews called the Messiah, and the Persians Sooshyant; the Jews said he was to be the son of David, and the Persians said he was to be the son of Zoroaster. Muḥammad the Prophet admitted that Jesus Christ was a prophet, and declared him to be the greatest of the prophets of the old dispensation; but he regarded Him as inferior to the line of prophets of which he himself was the first, and said He would only be the servant, or vicar, of the supernatural personage who was to come in the last days, and who was to right all things, namely, the **Mahdi.** The word Mahdi means he who is directed (or led) [by God]. According to Muḥammad, Jesus was to destroy Antichrist and convert Christians to the religion of Islâm! The Mahdi was to be a descendant of the Prophet through 'Ali, the cousin of Muḥammad, who had given him his daughter Fâtima to wife.

When the Persians were conquered by the Muḥammadans, they accepted the religion and doctrines of the Prophet, but they adopted the view that his legitimate successor (Khalîfa) was his son-in-law 'Ali, and that the first three khalîfas, Abu-Bakr, 'Omar, and 'Othman were impostors, who had seized the Khalifate by intrigue. Thus the Muḥammadan world was split up into two parties, the **Sunnites,** or "traditionalists," who acknowledge the first three Khalifs, and the **Shî'ites,** or **Imamians**, who reject them. 'Ali was declared to be divine by his adherents even during his lifetime, and when he and his sons Ḥasan and Ḥusên had been murdered by the 'Omeyyad usurpers, his life and deeds appealed in a remarkable manner to the imagination of the Persians, and, remembering that the

Prophet had declared that the Mahdi should spring from his own family, they accepted and promulgated the view that he was to be among the descendants of 'Ali. There have been many who assumed the title "Mahdi," but the first of these was "Muḥammad, the son of the Hanefite," *i.e.*, the son of 'Ali by another wife, and he was practically made to adopt it by a cunning man called Mukhtâr. Mahdi after Mahdi appeared in the Muḥammadan world, but when the eleventh Imâm had come to an end, that is to say, had been murdered—the true Mahdi was to be the twelfth—and left no successor, men began to fall into despair. At the end of the VIIIth century a schism among the Shî'ites took place, and a large, wealthy body of men, who called themselves Ismaelites (from Ismâ'îl, the son of Ja'fâr), left them; the leader of the new sect was a Persian dentist called 'Obêdallâh, who sent messengers to Arabia and the north of Africa to announce the advent of the Mahdi, *i.e.*, himself. 'Obêdallâh, moreover, declared himself to be a descendant of 'Ali, and with this prestige in 908 he succeeded in founding a dynasty in North Africa, having overthrown the reigning Aghlabite king there. He also founded the city of Mahdîya. In 925 'Obêdallâh attempted to overrun Egypt, but he was defeated, and it was not until 969 that the Fâṭimites succeeded in conquering Egypt, which they did under Jôhar, the general of Mu'izz, the great grandson of 'Obêdallâh, who founded the city of Cairo and assumed the title of Khâlifa. Thus a Mahdi made himself master of nearly all North Africa and of Egypt, and his dynasty ruled the last named country for well nigh 200 years.* The next great Mahdi was Muḥammad ibn-Tûmurt, of the tribe of Masmûda, and a native of Morocco, whose followers, known by the name of "Almohades," conquered Spain and ruled it during the XIIth century. The idea of the Mahdi still lives in Northern

* A.D. 972–1172.

Africa, and without taking into account the Mahdi of the Senûsi (see Wingate, *Mahdiism*,* p. 2 ff.), who always calls himself "Muḥammad al-Mahdi," it is said that at the present time another Mahdi is waiting at Massa in Morocco to declare himself to the world. In 1666 a Mahdi called Sabbatai Zevi made his appearance in Turkey, but he disgraced himself by submitting to become a servant of the Sulṭân Muḥammad IV. Another appeared at Adrianople in 1694, but he was eventually exiled to Lemnos. In 1799 a Mahdi from Tripoli appeared in Egypt, but he was killed in a fight with the French at Damanhûr.

Muḥammad Aḥmad, the Mahdi who in recent years set the Sûdân in a blaze, was born near Donḳola either in 1843 or 1848; his father's name was 'Abd-allâhi, and that of his mother Amína. Thus Aḥmad's parents bore the same names as those of the Prophet. His family were boat builders on the White Nile, and he worked at the same trade when a boy. When twelve years of age he knew the Kur'ân by heart, and when twenty-two years old he settled down in the Island of Abba in the White Nile, and meditated there for fifteen years. He lived in a hole in the ground, and fasted and prayed, and his reputation for sanctity spread over the whole country; his followers and disciples increased so fast and in such numbers that at length he declared himself to be the Mahdi. Like his predecessors, he sent forth envoys to all parts to declare his divine mission. In 1881 he and his dervishes cut to pieces 200 soldiers who had been sent to seize him; and a few months later, at the head of 50,000 rebels, he defeated and slew at Gebel Gaddîr nearly 7,000 Egyptian troops. These victories gave him a reputation for invincibility, and thousands of men in all parts of the Sûdân could not help

* On Mahdiism generally, see Querry, *Recueil des lois Chyites*, vol. I.; Gobineau, *Religions*, p. 340 ff.; De Slane, *Ibn-Khaldur*, vol. III., p. 496; Darmesteter, *The Mahdi*, London, 1885.

believing in his pretensions when they saw city after city fall into his hands. Few now doubted that he was the twelfth and last Imâm, and his adoption of the Shî'ite views, and his calling his followers by the Persian name "Darwîsh,"* made men to assume the heavenly character of his work. On November 5, 1883, he annihilated Hicks Pâsha's army, and Al-'Obêd and the neighbouring country fell into the Mahdi's hands. On December 16 Slatin Pâsha surrendered to him, and on January 15, 1884, the valuable province of Darfûr became a part of the rebel's kingdom. In February General Gordon arrived in Kharṭûm on his fatal mission, having on his way thither, unfortunately, told the Mudîr of Berber and the Ĕmir of Matammah that he was going to remove the Egyptian garrisons; this became noised abroad, and many people, when they learned that the Egyptian Government was going to abandon the Sûdân, joined the Mahdi. Thus fate played into the Mahdi's hands. The next city to fall was Berber, Gordon's troops having been defeated on March 16. On October 23 the Mahdi arrived in Omdurmân, being well aware of Gordon's desperate condition through the correspondence which had been captured in the steamer *Abbas*. This unfortunate steamer was wrecked on the Fourth Cataract, and Colonel Stewart was betrayed and murdered there; all letters and papers found in the baggage were sent to the Mahdi. On Sunday night, January 26, the Mahdi attacked Kharṭûm and entered the town, and a little before sunrise on the Monday General Gordon was murdered; and in a few days 50,000 Dervishes looted the town and destroyed 10,000 men, women, and children. As a proof of the admiration for General Gordon felt by even his bitterest foes, it is sufficient to quote a common saying in the Sûdân, "Had Gordon been one of us, he would have been a perfect man." After the capture

* دَرْوِيش, a mendicant monk

of Kharṭûm, no one doubted the divine mission of the Mahdi, and his word and power became absolute. He now gave himself up to a life of ease and luxury. He who had professed himself satisfied with *one* coarse garment, and had lived in a hole in the ground, and slept upon a straw mat, and fasted and well-nigh starved himself, now dressed himself in shirts and trousers of silk and in the daintiest fabrics of the East, and lived in a large, fine house, and slept upon the best bed that Kharṭûm could produce, and ate dainties and drank immoderately. Father Ohrwalder tells us that he had his clothes perfumed before he put them on, and that his wives anointed his body with the expensive unguent called "Sandalia," musk, and the oil of roses. He had four lawful wives, and an unlimited number of concubines, among whom were representatives from almost every tribe in the Sûdân; with these were a number of little Turkish girls of eight years of age, for the Mahdi's sensuality spared no one. He would recline in his house on a splendid carpet, with his head on a pillow of gold brocade, with as many as thirty women in attendance upon him; some would fan him with great ostrich feathers, others would rub his hands and feet as he slept, and 'Aisha, his chief wife, would cover his head and neck with loving embraces. His blessing was sought for by tens of thousands of men and women, and the earth touched by his foot was held to be holy. His life of ease, however, was his undoing, and a few months after the fall of Kharṭum he became ill, and his disease progressed with such rapidity that he died on June 22, 1885, some say of heart disease, others of poison. When the Mahdi died his sway was absolute over about 2,000,000 square miles of north-east Africa, and his dominions reached from the Baḥr al-Ghazal to Wâdi Ḥalfa, and from Darfûr to the Red Sea. The Mahdi was a tall, broad-shouldered man, strongly built, and of a light brown colour; his head was large, and he wore a black beard. His eyes were black and sparkling, his nose and mouth were well shaped, and he had a V-shaped aperture between his two front teeth which is always regarded as a sign of good luck in the Sûdân; on each cheek were the three slits seen on faces everywhere in the Sûdân.

The Mahdi's successor was Sayyid 'Abd-Allahi, the son of Muḥammad al-Taki, a member of the Taaisha section of the Baḳḳâra tribe, and he was a native of the south-western part of Darfûr; he is better known, however, as the **Khalîfa,** which he was specially appointed to be by the Mahdi. As brief notices of the defeats of his generals and of his own defeat and death are given elsewhere (see pp. 43–49), they need not appear here. He is described by Slatin Pâsha as having been a powerfully built man of a suspicious, resolute, cruel, tyrannical, vain disposition, hasty in temper, and unscrupulous in action. His belief in his own powers was unbounded, and he took the credit for everything that succeeded. He had four legal wives and a large number of concubines, who were kept under the charge of a free woman; at intervals he held a sort of review of all his ladies, and dismissed numbers of them as presents to his friends. His chief wife was called Sahra, with whom he quarrelled on the subject of food; she wished him to keep to the kind of food which he ate in his early days, and he wished to indulge in Egyptian and Turkish dishes. Twice he gave her letters of separation, and twice he revoked them. A detailed sketch of his life is given by Slatin Pâsha in his *Fire and Sword*, p. 514 ff.; and the horrors of his rule are graphically described by Father Ohrwalder in *Ten Years' Captivity* (14th edition), p. 455 ff.

Birth, Marriage, and **Death** among the Muḥammadans. When a child is born, the call to prayer must be pronounced in his right ear by a male as soon as possible, for only by this can the child be preserved from the influence of the evil spirits. The father names the boy, and the mother the girl, and no ceremony takes place at the naming of children. A surname is often added indicating relationship, or a title of honour, or the origin, family, birthplace, sect, or trade; a surname of any kind usually follows the proper name. When about two years old a boy's head is shaved, but two tufts of hair are left, one on the crown and another on the forehead; girls' heads are rarely shaved. Young children of well-to-do people are often dressed like those of beggars, and their faces are rarely washed, because the parents fear lest the **Evil Eye** be cast upon them. Boys* are circumcised at the age of five or six years, and the ceremony is usually made an occasion of joyful display. The boy is dressed as a girl and wears a red turban, and he rides a horse and frequently covers part of his face, with the idea of warding off the glance of the Evil Eye. The barber's servant who carries his master's sign (*i.e.*, the *ḥaml*, which is a wooden case, with four short legs, ornamented with pieces of looking glass, and embossed brass), and a few musicians, walk in front of the house. In purely Muḥammadan schools the education of boys is very simple; they learn to declare the unity of God and their belief in Muḥammad as His Prophet, to hate Christians, to read parts or the whole of the Ḳur'ân, the ninety-nine Beautiful Names of God, and sometimes they learn writing and arithmetic. In learning the Ḳur'ân, the beautiful introductory chapter (Fâtiḥah) is first committed to memory, then the last chapter, then the last but one, and so on backwards until the second is reached; the reason of this being that the chapters successively decrease in length from the second to the last. Girls used to learn to read and write but rarely, and very few even learnt to say their

* Strabo remarks, τὰ γεννώμενα παιδία καὶ τὸ περιτέμνειν καὶ τὰ θήλεα ἐκτέμνειν; Bk. xvii., 2, § 4, Didot's edition, p. 699).

prayers. Certain fanatical Muḥammadans will hardly allow girls or women to touch the Ḳur'ân, and on the borders of Persia the writer has bought manuscripts of the book from widows who had wrapped them in cloth and buried them under their houses, because they regarded them as too sacred for them to handle.

Marriage. Among the Muḥammadans it is thought to be the duty of every man possessing sufficient means to marry. Girls are betrothed at the age of seven or eight years, a few are married at ten, but many not until twelve or thirteen; few remain unmarried after the age of sixteen. Marriages are arranged by a go-between, the deputy of the bride, and by the relatives of the parties, and as long as the girl is quite a child, her parents may betroth her to whom they please. The amount of the dowry varies from £10 to £50, according to the position of the parties, and the dowry of a widow, or divorced woman, is less than that of a maiden. Two-thirds of the dowry are paid immediately before the marriage contract is made, and the remaining third is held in reserve by the bridegroom to be paid to the wife in the event of his divorcing her against her consent, or of his own death. The marriage takes place in the evening about eight or ten days after the contract has been made, and the day usually chosen is Thursday or Sunday. On the Wednesday or Saturday the bride is conducted to the bath, and is accompanied by her friends and relatives, and musicians; she walks under a canopy of silk, which is open in front, but she herself is covered with a Kashmîr shawl of some bright colour. After the bath she returns to her house, and that evening the nails of her hands and feet are stained yellow with ḥenna. The same evening the bridegroom entertains his friends lavishly, and the next day the bride goes in state to his house, and partakes of a meal. At sunset the bridegroom goes to the bath, and a few hours later to the mosque, after which he is escorted to his house by friends and relatives, bearing lamps, and by musicians. Marriage ceremonies may be elaborate or simple, according to the taste or position of the bride or bridegroom, and if a woman merely says to a man who wishes to marry her, "I give myself to thee," even without the presence of witnesses, she becomes his legal wife. Usually a man in Egypt prefers to marry a girl who has neither mother nor any female relative. A part of the house is specially reserved (ḥarîm) for women, *i.e.*, wife or wives, daughters, and female slaves, so that these may not be seen by the male servants and strange men unless properly veiled. A Muḥammadan may possess four wives and a number of female slaves, and he may rid himself of a wife by merely saying, "Thou art divorced." He may divorce a wife twice, and each time receive her back without further ceremony, but he cannot legally take her back again after a third divorce until she has been married to and divorced by another man; a triple divorce may be conveyed in a single sentence. Mr. Lane (*Modern Egyptians*, vol. I., p. 231), commenting on the depraving effects of divorce upon the sexes, says that many men, in a period of ten years, have married twenty or thirty wives, and that women not far advanced in age have been known to be wives to a dozen or more men successively. The abuse of divorce among the lower classes in Egypt is perhaps the greatest curse of the country, and its mental, moral, and physical effects are terrible.

Death. As soon as a man dies, the women begin to lament loudly, and often professional wailing women are sent for to beat their tambourines and utter cries of grief; the relatives join them in their cries, and with dishevelled hair beat their faces and rend their garments. If a man dies in the morning he is buried before night, but if he dies in the afternoon or later he is not buried until the next day. The body is carefully washed and sprinkled with rose water, etc., the eyes are closed, the jaw is bound up, the ankles are tied together, the hands are placed on the breast, and the ears and nostrils are stopped with cotton. The style and quality of the cere-cloths vary with the position and means of the deceased; when dressed, the body is laid upon a bier and covered with a Kashmîr shawl. The funeral procession is composed of six poor men, mostly blind, who walk slowly and chant, "There is no god but God, and Muḥammad is the Apostle of God. God bless and save him!" Next come the male friends and relatives of the deceased; then two or more dervishes, with the flags of the sect to which they belong; then three or four school-boys, one of whom carries upon a palm-stick desk a copy of the Ḳur'ân covered with a cloth, singing a poem on the events of the Last Day, the Judgment, etc. Next comes the bier, borne head-foremost, and then the female mourners; the bier is carried by friends in relays of four into a mosque, and is set down in the place of prayer, with the right side towards Mecca; both men and women from the procession enter the mosque, and prayers are then said ascribing majesty to God, and beseeching mercy for the dead. In the longest prayer the leader of prayer says, "O God, verily this is thy servant, and the son of thy servant: he hath departed from the repose of the world, and from its amplitude, and from whatever he loved, and from those by whom he was loved in it, to the darkness of the grave, and to what he experienceth. He did testify that there is no deity but Thou alone; that Thou hast no companion; and that Muḥammad is Thy servant and Thine Apostle; and that Thou art all-knowing respecting him. O God, he hath gone to abide with Thee, and Thou art the best with whom to abide. He hath become in need of Thy mercy, and Thou hast no need of his punishment. We have come to Thee supplicating that we may intercede for him. O God, if he were a doer of good, over-reckon his good deeds; and if he were an evil-doer, pass over his evil-doings; and of

Thy mercy grant that he may experience Thine acceptance; and spare him the trial of the grave and its torment; and make his grave wide to him; and keep back the earth from his sides; and of Thy mercy grant that he may experience security from Thy torment, until Thou send him safely to Thy Paradise, O Thou most merciful of those who show mercy" (Lane's translation). After the other prayers have been said, the leader in prayer, addressing those present, says, "Give your testimony respecting him," and they reply, "He was of the virtuous." The bier is then taken up, and the procession re-forms in the same order as before, and the body is taken to the grave. In the case of well-to-do people the grave is an oblong brick vault, which is sufficiently high to allow the deceased to sit upright when being examined by the two angels Munkar and Nakîr; over the vault a low, oblong monument is built, having an upright stone at the head and foot. On the stone at the head are inscribed the name of the deceased, the date of death, and a verse from the Ḳur'ân. The body is taken from the bier, its bandages are untied, and it is then laid in the vault on its right side with the face towards Mecca; a little earth is gently laid upon the body, and the vault is closed. But the pious Muḥammadans have imagined it to be possible for the deceased to forget what he ought to say when the angels Munkar and Nakîr come to examine him, therefore, in many cases, an instructor of the dead takes his seat near the tomb after the body has been laid therein, and tells the deceased what questions he will be asked and what answers he is to make. After the burial, food and drink are distributed among the poor, who come in large numbers to the burial of a man of means and position. The soul is thought to remain with the body on the night of burial, and afterwards to depart to its appointed place to await the day of doom. Men do not wear mourning in any case, but women dye their garments blue with indigo as a sign of grief, for everyone except an old man; they also leave their hair unplaited, and omit to put on certain of their ornaments.

The **Fâtiḥah.**—As mention has been made above of the Fâtiḥah, the opening chapter of the Ḳur'ân, a version of it is here given:—"In the Name of God, the Merciful, the Gracious. Praise be unto God, the Lord of the worlds, the Merciful, the Gracious, the Ruler of the day of judgment. Thee do we worship, and of Thee do we beg assistance. Direct us in the right way, in the way of those to whom Thou hast been gracious, upon whom there is no wrath, and who have not erred." It is to the Muḥammadans what the Lord's Prayer is to Christians.

The **Call to Prayer,** which is usually sung from the gallery of the minaret (Arab. *manârah*) by the mueddin of the mosque, is as follows:—"God is great. God is great. God is great. God is great. I bear witness that there is no god but God. I bear witness that there is no god but God. I bear witness that Muḥammad is the Apostle of God. I bear witness that Muḥammad is the Apostle of God. Come to prayer. Come to prayer. Come to service. Come to service. God is great. God is great. There is no god but God." At certain large mosques two other calls to prayer are cried during the night, the first a little after midnight, and the second about an hour before daybreak.

Muḥammadan **Calendar.**—The Muḥammadans reckon their era from the 16th of July, 622, *i.e.*, the day following the Flight (*al-Ḥijra*) of the Prophet from Mecca to Medîna. Their year is lunar, and always consists of twelve lunar months, beginning with the approximate new moon, without any intercalation to keep them in the same season with respect to the sun, so that they retrograde through all the seasons in about 32½ years. Their years are divided into cycles of 30 years, 19 of which contain 354 days, and the other 11 are intercalary years, having an extra day added to the last month. The mean length of the year is 354 days 8 hours 48 minutes; a mean lunation = 29 days 12 hours 44 minutes; the difference between a mean lunation and an astronomical lunation will amount to a day in about 2,400 years. The names of the months are:—Muḥarram (30 days), Ṣafar (29 days), Rabî'a al-awwal (30 days), Rabî'a al-âkhir (29 days), Gumâda al-awwal (30 days), Gumâda al-âkhir (29 days), Ragab (30 days), Sha'bân (29 days), Ramaḍân (30 days), Shawwâl (29 days), Dhu'il-ḳa'dah (30 days), and Dhu'l-ḥiggah (29 days).

Muḥammadan **Weights** and **Measures**:—

Pik or Dirâ' (of the country) = 24 ḳirrâṭ (plur. ḳarârîṭ) = 23·01 inch = ·585 metre.

Pik (Turkish and Indian) = 26⅓ inches = ·66 metre.

Pik (used in building), 29·53 inches = ·75 metre.

Ḳaṣabah = 11 feet 8 inches = 3·55 metre.

Square Pik (used in building) = 6·43 square feet = 562 square metres.

Cubic Pik (used in building) = 14·90 cubic feet = ·42 cubic metre.

Square ḳaṣabah = 13·04 square yards = 12·60 square metres.

Sâ'a (*literally*, hour), like malaḳa, a march, any distance between 2½ and 4½ miles. Very old measures of length are:—*Fitr*, the space between the thumb and first finger when extended; *Shibr*, the space between the thumb and little finger when extended, *i.e.*, a span; the *Ḳabdah*, the measure of a man's fist with the thumb erect.

Ḳamḥah, grain of wheat = ¾ grain.

Ḥabbah, grain of barley = 1 grain.

Ḳirrâṭ, *i.e.*, carat = 3 grains (Troy).

Dirham = 16 ḳirrâṭs = 48·15 grains (Troy) = ·11 ounce = 3·12 grammes.

Mithḳâl = 1½ dirhams = 24 ḳirrâṭs = 72·22 grains (Troy) = 4·68 grammes.

Uḳîya = 12 dirhams = 1·32 ounces = ·066 pint = = 37·44 grammes.

Roṭl = 12 uḳîya = 144 dirhams = ·99 pound = 450 grammes = ·79 pint.

Uḳḳa = 400 dirhams = 2·77 roṭls = 2·19 pints = 2·75 pounds = 1·25 kilogrammes.

Ḳanṭâr = 100 roṭls = 36 oḳḳa = 99·05 pounds = 44·93 kilogrammes.

Ardeb = 3 ḳanṭârs = 43·95 gallons = 5·49 bushels = 198 litres = 300 pounds = 108 oḳḳa. The ardeb = 6 wêba = 12 kîla = 24 rub'a = 48 mahva = 96 kada.

LOWER EGYPT.

ALEXANDRIA.

Alexandria was founded B.C. 332 by Alexander the Great, who began to build his city on the little town of Rakoti, just opposite to the island of Pharos. King Ptolemy I. Soter made this city his capital: and having founded the famous library and museum, he tried to induce the most learned men of his day to live there. His son and successor Ptolemy II. Philadelphus continued the wise policy of his father, and Alexandria became famous as a seat of learning. The keeper of the museum during the reign of Ptolemy III. Euergetes I. was Aristophanes of Byzantium. During the siege of the city by the Romans in the time of Cæsar, B.C. 48, the library of the museum was burnt; but Antony afterwards gave Cleopatra a large collection of manuscripts which formed the nucleus of a second library.* In the early centuries of our era the people of Alexandria quarrelled perpetually among themselves,† the subjects of dispute

* This collection numbered 200,000 MSS., and formed the famous Pergamenian library founded by Eumenes II., king of Pergamus, B.C. 197.

† ". . . . . the Alexandrian rabble took on the slightest pretext to stones and to cudgels. In street uproar, says an authority, himself Alexandrian, the Egyptians are before all others; the smallest spark suffices here to kindle a tumult. On account of neglected visits, on account of the confiscation of spoiled provisions, on account of exclusion from a bathing establishment, on account of a dispute between the slave of an Alexandrian of rank and a Roman foot-soldier as to the value or non-value of their respective slippers, the legions were under the necessity of charging among the citizens of Alexandria . . . . . In these riots the Greeks acted as instigators . . . . . but in the further course of the matter the spite and savageness of the Egyptian proper came into the conflict. The Syrians were cowardly, and as soldiers the Egyptians were so too; but in a street tumult they were able to develope a courage worthy of a better cause." (Mommsen, *Provinces of the Roman Empire*, Vol. II., p. 265.)

being matters connected with Jews and religious questions. St. Mark is said to have preached the Gospel here. Meanwhile the prosperity of the town declined and the treasury became empty.

Alexandria was captured by Chosroes (A.D. 619), and by 'Amr ibn el-'Âṣi, a general of 'Omar, A.D. 641. The decline of Alexandria went on steadily, until it became in the Middle Ages little more, comparatively, than a moderate sized sea-port town, with a population of some thousands of people. In the present century a little of its prosperity was restored by Muḥammad 'Ali, who in 1819 built the Maḥmûdîyeh canal to bring fresh water to the town from the Rosetta arm of the Nile. Its population to-day is about 300,000, and includes large and wealthy colonies of Jews and Greeks.

The Christians were persecuted at Alexandria with great severity by Decius (A.D. 250), by Valerianus (A.D. 257), and by Diocletian (A.D. 304). For a large number of years the city was disturbed by the fierce discussions on religious dogmas between Arius and Athanasius, George of Cappadocia and Athanasius, the Anthropomorphists and their opponents, and Cyril and Nestorius. The Christian sects supported their views by violence, and the ordinary heathen population of the town rebelled whenever they could find a favourable opportunity.

The **Lighthouse** or **Pharos,** one of the seven wonders of the world, was built by Sostratus of Cnidus, for Ptolemy Philadelphus, and is said to have been about 600 feet high. All traces of this wonderful building have now disappeared. The embankment or causeway called the **Heptastadium*** (from its length of seven stades) was made either by Ptolemy Philadelphus or his father Ptolemy Soter; it divided the harbour into two parts. The eastern port is only used by

* The Heptastadium joined the ancient town and the Island of Pharos; a large part of the modern town is built upon it.

native craft, on account of its sandy shoals; the western port is the Eunostos Harbour, which at present is protected by a breakwater about one mile and three-quarters long. The **Museum** and **Library of Alexandria** were founded by Ptolemy I., and greatly enlarged by his son Ptolemy Philadelphus. When this latter king died the library was said to contain 100,000 manuscripts. These were classified, arranged, and labelled by Callimachus; when it was burnt down in the time of Julius Cæsar, it is thought that more than 750,000 works were lost. Copies of works of importance were made at the expense of the State, and it is stated that every book which came into the city was seized and kept, and that a copy only of it was returned to the owner. Antony handed over to Cleopatra about 200,000 manuscripts (the Pergamenian Library), and these were made the foundation of a second library. Among the famous men who lived and studied in this library were Eratosthenes, Strabo, Hipparchus, Archimedes, and Euclid. The **Serapeum** was built by Ptolemy Soter, and was intended to hold the statue of a god from Sinope, which was called by the Egyptians 'Osiris-Apis,' or Serapis. It stood close by Rakoti to the east of Alexandria near 'Pompey's Pillar,' and is said to have been one of the most beautiful buildings in the world; it was filled with remarkable statues and other works of art. It was destroyed by the Christian fanatic Theophilus,* Patriarch of Alexandria, during the reign of Theodosius II. The **Library** of the Serapeum is said to have contained about 300,000 manuscripts, which were burnt by 'Amr ibn el-'Âṣi at the command of the Ḳhalif 'Omar, A.D. 641; these were sufficiently numerous, it is said, to heat the public baths of Alexandria for six

* ". . . the perpetual enemy of peace and virtue; a bold, bad man, whose hands were alternately polluted with gold and with blood." (Gibbon, *Decline*, Chap. xxvii.)

months.* The **Sôma** formed a part of the Cæsareum, and contained the bodies of Alexander the Great and the Ptolemies, his successors. The **Theatre,** which faced the island of Antirhodus, the Sôma, and the Museum and Library, all stood in the royal buildings in the Bruchium quarter of the town, between Lochias and the Heptastadium. The stone sarcophagus (now in the British Museum, No. 10), which was thought to have belonged to Alexander the Great, was made for Nectanebus I., the first king of the XXXth

* "The spirit of Amrou ('Amr ibn el-'Âṣi) was more curious and liberal than that of his brethren, and in his leisure hours the Arabian chief was pleased with the conversation of John, the last disciple of Ammonius, who derived the surname of *Philoponus* from his laborious studies of grammar and philosophy. Emboldened by this familiar intercourse, Philoponus presumed to solicit a gift, inestimable in *his* opinion, contemptible in that of the Barbarians: the royal library, which alone, among the spoils of Alexandria, had not been appropriated by the visit and the seal of the conqueror. Amrou was inclined to gratify the wish of the grammarian, but his rigid integrity refused to alienate the minutest object without the consent of the caliph; and the well-known answer of Omar was inspired by the ignorance of a fanatic. 'If these writings of the Greeks agree with the book of God, they are useless and need not be preserved: if they disagree, they are pernicious and ought to be destroyed.' The sentence was executed with blind obedience: the volumes of paper or parchment were distributed to the 4,000 baths of the city; and such was their incredible multitude that six months were barely sufficient for the consumption of this precious fuel." (Gibbon, *Decline and Fall*, chap. li.) The chief authority for this statement is Bar-Hebraeus (born A.D. 1226, died at Marâghah in Âdhôrbâîjân, July 30th, 1286), and it has been repeated by several Arabic writers. Both Gibbon and Renaudot thought the story incredible, but there is no reason why it should be. Gibbon appears to have thought that the *second* Alexandrian library was pillaged or destroyed when Theophilus, Patriarch of Alexandria, destroyed the image of Serapis; there is, however, no proof that it was, and it seems more probable that it remained comparatively unhurt until the arrival of 'Amr ibn el-'Âṣi. See the additional notes in Gibbon, ed. Smith, Vol. III., p. 419, and Vol. VI., p. 338.

dynasty, B.C. 378. The **Paneum,** or temple of Pan, is probably represented by the modern Kôm al-Dîḳḳ. The JEWS' QUARTER lay between the sea and the street, to the east of Lochias. The NECROPOLIS was situated at the west of the city. The GYMNASIUM stood a little to the east of the Paneum, on the south side of the street which ends, on the east, in the Canopic Gate.

Pompey's Pillar was erected by Pompey, a Roman prefect, in honour of Diocletian, some little time after A.D. 302.* It is made of granite brought from Aswân; the shaft is about 70 feet, and the whole monument, including its pedestal, is rather more than 100 feet high. The fragments of the columns which lie around the base of this pillar are thought to have belonged to the Serapeum.

A few years ago there were to be seen in Alexandria the two famous granite obelisks called **Cleopatra's Needles.** They were brought from Heliopolis during the reign of the Roman Emperor Augustus, and set up before the Temple of Cæsar. Until quite lately one of them remained upright; the other had fallen. They are both made of Aswân granite; one measures 67 feet in height, the other 68½ feet; the diameter of each is about 7½ feet. The larger obelisk was given by Muḥammad 'Ali to the English early in this century, but it was not removed until 1877, when it was transported to England at the expense of Sir Erasmus Wilson, and it now stands on the Thames Embankment. The smaller obelisk was taken to New York a few years later. The inscriptions show that both were made during the reign of Thothmes III., about B.C. 1600, and that Rameses II., who lived about 250 years later, added lines of inscriptions recording his titles of honour and greatness.

* The Greek inscription recording this fact is published in Boeckh, *Corpus Inscriptionum Græcarum*, t. iii., p. 329, where it is also thus restored: Τὸν [ὁσ]ιώτατον Αὐτοκράτορα, τὸν πολιοῦχον 'Αλεξανδρείας, Διοκλητιανὸν τὸν ἀνίκητον πο[μπήϊ]ος ἔπαρχος Αἰγύπτου. . . . . .

The **Catacombs**, which were built early in the fourth century of our era, are on the coast near the harbour and on the coast near the new port.

The **Walls** of the city were built by Muḥammad 'Ali, and appear to have been laid upon the foundation of ancient walls.

On the south side of Alexandria lies Lake Mareotis, which in ancient days was fed by canals running from the Nile. During the Middle Ages the lake nearly dried up, and the land which became available for building purposes in consequence was speedily covered with villages. In the year 1801, the English dug a canal across the neck of land between the lake and the sea, and flooded the whole district thus occupied. During the last few years an attempt has been made to pump the water out; it would seem with considerable success.

Among archæologists of all nationalities for some years past the conviction has been growing that systematic excavations should be undertaken at Alexandria: it was felt that but little of a serious nature had been done, and that unless work were begun soon the few sites available for excavation would be built over, and that the chance of the discovery either of new information or "finds" would be lost for ever. As it is, building operations have advanced with extraordinary rapidity, and what the builder leaves the sea claims. There seems little chance of discovering any portions of the great libraries which flourished at Alexandria in its palmy days, and there is equally little chance that any of its famous buildings remain to be discovered; the utmost that may be hoped for is the recovery of monuments and inscriptions of the late Græco-Roman period. The cuttings of the Alexandria-Ramleh railway, and private diggings made for laying foundations of houses and drains, have yielded a number of interesting objects, but they have added comparatively little to our knowledge. To preserve these remains in a systematic manner, the municipality of Alexandria founded a museum, the direction of which has been placed under the able care of M. Botti; here are exhibited a most interesting series of monuments typical of Egypto-Græco art during the period of the rule of the Ptolemies and during the early centuries of the Christian era. The collection has been added to steadily, and learned bodies in Europe have enriched it by gifts of casts of important objects preserved in their museums and by donations of books with the view of founding a suitable library. Quite recently Mr. D. G. Hogarth, under the auspices of the Egypt Exploration Fund, assisted by Messrs. E. F. Benson and E. R. Bevan of the British School of Archæology at Athens, during two months' work at Alexandria made a series of experimental borings about the central quarter of the ancient city, including the region of Fort Kôm-al-Diḳḳ, the reputed site of the Sôma, and in the eastern cemeteries. Mr. Hogarth's conclusions are, he says, definite, though negative. The results of his work show that an uninteresting deposit, from 15 to 20 feet thick, of the Arab period, lies over all the central part of the Roman town; that the remains of the Roman town are in bad condition, and that their appearance indicates that they have been ruined systematically; that immediately below, and even above the Roman level, water is tapped, and that the stratum earlier than the Roman must be submerged, the soil having subsided. Such definite facts do away, once and for all, with any hope of the discovery of papyri.

Between Alexandria and Cairo are the following important towns:—

I. **Damanhûr,***(Eg.,  Ṭemài en-Ḥeru,

* It is called ϯⲙⲓⲛϩⲱⲣ by the Copts.

'Town of Horus,' the capital of the Mudîrîyeh of Beḥêreh. This was the Hermopolis Parva of the Romans.

II. **Kafr ez-zaiyât,** on the east side of the river, situated among beautiful and fertile fields.

III. **Ṭanṭa,** the capital of Gharbîyeh, situated between the Rosetta and Damietta arms of the Nile. This town is celebrated for three *Fairs*, which are held here in January, April, and August, in honour of the Muḥammadan saint Sayyid el-Bedawi, who was born at Fez about A.D. 1200, and who lived and died at Ṭanṭa. Each fair lasts eight days, and the greatest day in each fair is the Friday; the most important fair is that held in August.

IV. **Benha el-'Asal,** 'Benha of the Honey,' the capital of Ḳalyûb. It obtained this name because a Copt called the Maḳawḳas * sent, among other gifts, a jar of honey to Muḥammad the Prophet. The Arabic geographers state that the best honey in Egypt comes from Benha. Quite close to this town are the ruins of the ancient city of Athribis.

About forty miles to the east of Alexandria lies the town of Rosetta, not far from the ancient Bolbitane. It was

* The Maḳawḳas was "Prince of the Copts," and "Governor of Alexandria and Egypt"; he was a Jacobite, and a strong hater of the Melkites or "Royalists." He was invited to become a follower of Muḥammad the Prophet, but he declined. When Egypt was captured by 'Amr ibn el-'Âṣi he betrayed the Copts, but by means of paying tribute he secured to himself the liberty of professing the Christian religion, and he asked that, after his death, his body might be buried in the church of St. John at Alexandria. He sent, as gifts to the Prophet, two Coptic young women, sisters, called Maryam and Shîrîn; two girls, one eunuch, a horse, a mule, an ass, a jar of honey, an alabaster jar, a jar of oil, an ingot of gold, and some Egyptian linen. (Gagnier, *La vie de Mahomet*, pp. 38, 73.) Maḳawḳas, مقوقس, appears to be the Arabic transcription of the Greek μεγαυχής "famous," a title which was bestowed upon George, the son of Menas Parkabios, who was over the taxes of Egypt, and who was addressed by Muḥammad the Prophet as "Prince of the Copts."

founded towards the end of the ninth century, and was once a flourishing seaport; it has become famous in modern times on account of the trilingual inscription, called the '**Rosetta Stone**,' which was found here in 1799 by a French officer called Boussard. This inscription was inscribed on a block of basalt, and contained a decree by the Egyptian priests in honour of Ptolemy V., Epiphanes, dated in the eighth year of his reign (B.C. 196). The hieroglyphic, demotic, and Greek texts enabled Young and Champollion to work out the phonetic values of a number of the hieroglyphic characters employed to write the names of the Greek rulers. The stone is preserved in the British Museum (No. 32).

SUEZ AND THE SUEZ CANAL.

The town of Suez practically sprang into existence during the building of the Suez Canal, which was opened in 1869; before that time it was an insignificant village with a few hundred inhabitants. Ancient history is almost silent about it, even if it be identified with Clysma* Praesidium. It is situated at the north end of the Gulf of Suez, and is now important from its position at the south end of the Suez Canal. A fresh-water canal from Cairo to Suez was built in 1863, but before the cutting of this canal the inhabitants obtained their water either from the Wells of Moses (about eight miles from Suez) or Cairo. It was at one time considered to be near the spot where the Israelites crossed the 'Sea of Sedge'; there is little doubt, however, that the passage was made much nearer the Mediterranean.

The neck of land which joins Asia to Africa, or the Isthmus of Suez, is nearly one hundred miles wide; on the south side is the Gulf of Suez, on the north the Mediterranean. The Red Sea and the Mediterranean appear to have been united in ancient days. Modern investigations have proved that so far back as the time of Rameses II. or earlier a canal was cut between Pelusium and Lake Timsaḥ, and it is almost certain that it was well fortified. The Asiatics who wished to invade Egypt were compelled to cross the Isthmus of Suez, and a canal would not only serve as a water barrier against them, but be useful

* Clysma, in Arabic Ḳulzum, is said by the Arab geographers to have been situated on the coast of the sea of Yaman, on the Egyptian side, at the far end, three days from Cairo and four days from Pelusium. (Juynboll, *Lex. Geog. Arab.*, t. ii., p. ۴۲۴.)

as a means of transport for troops from one point to another. The name of the place Ḳanṭara, 'a bridge,' a little to the north of Isma'ilîya, seems to point to the fact of a ford existing here from very early times. Nekau (B.C. 610) began to make a canal at Bubastis, between the Nile and the Red Sea, but never finished it; it was continued in later times by Darius, and Ptolemy Philadelphus made a lock for it; still later we know that the Mediterranean and Red Seas were joined by a canal. The emperor Trajan made a canal from Cairo to the Red Sea, which, having become impassable, was re-opened by 'Omar's general, 'Amr ibn el-'Âṣi, after his capture of Egypt.

In the Middle Ages various attempts were made in a half-hearted manner to cut a new canal across the Isthmus, but although several royal personages in and out of Egypt were anxious to see the proposed work begun, nothing was seriously attempted until 1798, when Napoleon Bonaparte directed M. Lepère to survey the route of a canal across the Isthmus. M. Lepère reported that the difference between the levels of the Red Sea and Mediterranean was thirty-three feet, and, that, therefore, the canal was impossible.* Although several scientific men doubted the accuracy of M. Lepère's conclusion, the fact that the level of the two seas is practically the same was not proved until M. Linant Bey, Stephenson, and others examined the matter in 1846. It was then at once evident that a canal *was* possible. M. de Lesseps laid the plans for a canal before Sa'îd Pasha in 1854; two years afterwards they were sanctioned, and two years later the works began. The original plan proposed to make a

* This was the opinion of some classical writers: compare Aristotle, *Meteorologica*, i. 14, 27; Diodorus, i. 23; and Strabo, xvii. 1, 25. The Arab writer Mas'ûdi relates that a certain king tried to cut a canal across this isthmus, but that on finding that the waters of the Red Sea stood at a higher level than those of the Mediterranean, he abandoned his project. (*Les Prairies d'Or*, t. iv. p. 97.)

canal from Suez to Pelusium, but it was afterwards modified, and by bringing the northern end into the Mediterranean at Port Sa'îd, it was found possible to do away with the lock at each end, which would have been necessary had it embouched at Pelusium. The **fresh-water canal** from Bûlâḳ to Suez, with an aqueduct to Port Sa'îd, included in the original plan, was completed in 1863. The filling of the Bitter Lakes with sea-water from the Mediterranean was begun on the 18th March, 1869, and the whole canal was opened for traffic on November 16th of the same year. The cost of the canal was about £19,000,000.

The buoyed channel which leads into the canal at the Suez end is 300 yards across in the widest part. The average width of the dredged channel is about 90 feet, and the average depth about 28 feet. At Shalûf et-Terrâbeh the excavation was very difficult, for the ground rises about twenty feet above the sea-level, and the elevation is five or six miles long. A thick layer of hard rock 'cropped' up in the line of the canal, and the work of removing it was of no slight nature. On a mound not quite half-way between Suez and Shalûf are some granite blocks bearing traces of cuneiform and hieroglyphic inscriptions recording the name of Darius. They appear to be the remains of one of a series of buildings erected along the line of the old canal which was restored and probably completed by Darius. At Shalûf the width of the canal is about 90 feet, and shortly after leaving this place the canal enters the Small Bitter Lake, which is about seven miles long. Before reaching the end of it is, on the left, another mound on which were found the ruins of a building which was excavated by M. de Lesseps. Granite slabs were found there inscribed with the name of Darius in Persian cuneiform characters and in hieroglyphics. The canal next passes through the Great Bitter Lake (about fifteen miles long), and a few kilomètres farther along it passes by the rock, upon which was built by Darius another monument to tell passers-by that he it was who made the canal. The track of the canal through the Bitter Lakes is marked by a double row of buoys; the distance between each buoy is 330 yards, and the space between the two rows is about thirty yards. At a little distance to the north of the Bitter Lake is Ṭusân, which may be easily identified by means of the tomb of the Muḥammadan saint Ennedek. Shortly after Lake Timsaḥ, or the 'Crocodile Lake,' is reached, on the north side of which is the town of Isma'îlîya, formerly the head-quarters of the staff in charge of the various works connected with the construction of the canal. The canal channel through the lake is marked by buoys as in the Bitter Lakes. Soon after re-entering the canal the plain of El-Gisr, or the 'bridge,' is entered; it is about fifty-five feet above the level of the sea. Through this a channel about eighty feet deep had to be cut. Passing through Lake Balâḥ, el-Ḳanṭara, 'the bridge,' a place situated on a height between the Balâḥ and Menzaleh Lakes, is reached. It is by this natural bridge that every invading army must have entered Egypt, and its appellation, the 'Bridge of Nations,' is most appropriate. On the east side of the canal, not far from el-Ḳanṭara, are some ruins of a building which appears to have been built by Rameses II., and a little beyond Ḳanṭara begins Lake Menzaleh. About twenty miles to the east are the ruins of Pelusium. The canal is carried through Lake Menzaleh in a perfectly straight line until it reaches Port Sa'îd.

The town of Port Sa'îd is the product of the Suez Canal, and has a population of about 12,000. It stands on the island which forms part of the narrow tract of land which separates Lake Menzaleh from the Mediterranean. The first body of workmen landed at the spot which afterwards became Port Sa'îd in 1859, and for many years the place was nothing but a factory and a living-place for workmen.

The harbour and the two breakwaters which protect it are remarkable pieces of work; the breakwater on the west is lengthened yearly to protect the harbour from the mud-carrying current which always flows from the west, and which would block up the canal but for the breakwater. Near the western breakwater is the lighthouse, about 165 feet high; the electric light is used in it, and can be seen for a distance of twenty miles. The port is called Sa'îd in honour of Sa'îd Pasha. The fresh water used is brought in iron pipes laid along the western side of the canal from Isma'îlîya. The choice fell upon this spot for the Mediterranean end of the canal because water sufficiently deep for ocean-going ships was found within two miles of the shore. The total length of the canal, including the buoyed channel at the Suez end, is about one hundred miles.

In 1898 the number of vessels which passed through the Suez Canal was 3,503, and the gross tonnage was 12,962,632 tons; of these 2,295 ships were British, 356 German, 221 French, 193 Dutch, 85 Austrian, 46 Japanese, 48 Russian, 49 Spanish, 47 Italian, 47 Norwegian, 54 Turkish, 8 Danish, 10 Egyptian, 4 Chinese, 4 American, 2 Greek, 1 Rumanian, 2 Swedish, 3 Portuguese, and 1 belonging to the Argentine Republic. In 1893 the number of ships which passed through it was 3,341, and the receipts £2,826,694; in 1894, 3,352 ships, and the receipts were £2,951,073; in 1895, 3,434 ships, and the receipts were £3,124,149; in 1896, 3,409 ships, and the receipts were £3,182,800; in 1897, 2,986 ships, and the receipts were £2,913,222; in 1901, 3,699 ships, and the receipts over £4,000,000. The number of passengers in 1898 was 219,671. The state of the capital account (see *Statesman's Year Book*, 1900, p. 1138) was as follows, on December 31, 1898:—

	Francs.
Capital 400,000, at 500 francs ...	200,000,000
Consolidation of unpaid coupons ...	34,000,000
Loan 1867–68	99,999,900
Loan 1871	12,000,000
Loan 1880	26,999,962
Loan 1887	91,100,965
	464,100,827
Revenue applied to improvement of canal	151,174,307
	615,275,134

There were, in addition, 100,000 founders' shares, with the right to participate in the surplus profits under certain conditions. In 1898 the net profits amounted to 48,789,818 francs, and the total amount distributed among the shareholders was 46,618,028 francs. In 1875 Ismâ'îl Pâsha sold 176,602 Suez Canal Shares to the British Government for £3,976,582 sterling; these shares are now worth £25,000,000 sterling. The Suez Canal Company's Steam Tramway, which runs from Port Sa'îd to Isma'îlîya, is 80 kilomètres long; stations are passed at Râs al-'Êsh (رأس العس, kilomètre 15), at kilomètre 24, at kilomètre 34, at Al-Ḳanṭarah, (القنطرة, kilomètre 45, with 579 inhabitants), at kilomètre 55, and at Al-Ferdân (الفردان, kilomètre 65).

CAIRO TO SUEZ.

On the line between Cairo and Suez the following important places are passed :—

I. **Shibîn el-Kanâṭir,** the stopping place for those who wish to visit the 'Jewish Hill' or Tell el-Yahûdîyeh, where

Onias, the high priest of the Jews, built a temple by the permission of Ptolemy Philometor, in which the Egyptian Jews might worship. The site of the town was occupied in very early times by a temple and other buildings which were set up by Rameses II. and Rameses III.; a large number of the tiles which formed parts of the walls of these splendid works are preserved in the British Museum.

II. **Zaḳâzîḳ,** the capital of the Sherḳîyeh province, is a town of about 40,000 inhabitants; the railway station stands about one mile from the mounds which mark the site of the famous old city of Bubastis,* or **Tell Basṭa.** The chief article of commerce here is cotton. Not far from Zaḳâzîḳ flows the Fresh-water Canal from Cairo to Suez, which in many places exactly follows the route of the old canal which was dug during the XIXth dynasty.

Bubastis, Bubastus, or Tell Basṭa (the Pibeseth = "House of Bast" of Ezekiel xxx. 17), was the capital of the Bubastites nome in the Delta, and was situated on the eastern side of the Pelusiac arm of the Nile. The city was dedicated to the goddess Bast, the animal sacred to whom was the cat, and was famous for having given a dynasty of kings (the XXIInd) to Egypt. To the south of the city were the lands which Psammetichus I. gave to his Ionian and Carian mercenaries, and on the north side was the canal which Nekau (Necho) dug between the Nile and the Red Sea. The city was captured by the Persians B.C. 352, and the walls, the entire circuit of which was three miles, were dismantled. Recent excavations, by M. Naville, have shown beyond doubt that the place was inhabited during the earliest dynasties, and that many great kings of Egypt delighted to build temples there. The following description by Herodotus of the town

* From the hieroglyphic  *Per-Bast*, Coptic ⲡⲟⲩⲃⲁⲥϯ; it was the metropolis of the 18th nome of Lower Egypt, "where the soul of Isis lived in [the form of] Bast."

and the festival celebrated there will be found of interest:—

"Although other cities in Egypt were carried to a great height, in my opinion, the greatest mounds were thrown up about the city of Bubastis, in which is a temple of Bubastis well worthy of mention; for though other temples may be larger and more costly, yet none is more pleasing to look at than this. Bubastis, in the Greek language, answers to Diana. Her sacred precinct is thus situated: all except the entrance is an island; for two canals from the Nile extend to it, not mingling with each other, but each reaches as far as the entrance of the precinct, one flowing round it on one side, the other on the other. Each is a hundred feet broad, and shaded with trees. The portico is sixty feet in height, and is adorned with figures six cubits high, that are deserving of notice. This precinct, being in the middle of the city, is visible on every side to a person going round it: for as the city has been mounded up to a considerable height, but the temple has not been moved, it is conspicuous as it was originally built. A wall sculptured with figures runs round it; and within is a grove of lofty trees, planted round a large temple in which the image is placed. The width and length of the precinct is each way a stade [600 feet]. Along the entrance is a road paved with stone, about three stades in length [1800 feet], leading through the square eastward; and in width it is about four plethra [400 feet]: on each side of the road grow trees of enormous height; it leads to the temple of Mercury."*

The goddess Bast who was worshipped there is represented as having the head of a cat. She wore a disk, with an uræus, and carried the sceptre  or . She was, at times, identified with Sekhet, female counterpart of Ptaḥ, a

* Herodotus, ii. 137, 138 (Cary's translation).

member of the triad of Memphis. Sekhet  is called 'Lady of Heaven,' and 'The great lady, beloved of Ptaḥ.'* The nature of the ceremony on the way to Bubastis, says Herodotus,† is this :—

"Now, when they are being conveyed to the city Bubastis, they act as follows : for men and women embark together, and great numbers of both sexes in every barge ; some of the women have castanets on which they play, and the men play on the flute during the whole voyage ; the rest of the women and men sing and clap their hands together at the same time. When in the course of their passage they come to any town, they lay their barge near to land, and do as follows : some of the women do as I have described ; others shout and scoff at the women of the place ; some dance, and others stand up and behave in an unseemly manner ; this they do at every town by the river-side. When they arrive at Bubastis, they celebrate the feast, offering up great sacrifices ; and more wine is consumed at this festival than in all the rest of the year. What with men and women, besides children, they congregate, as the inhabitants say, to the number of seven hundred thousand."

The fertile country round about Zaḳâzîḳ is probably a part of the Goshen of the Bible.

III. Abu Ḥammâd, where the Arabian desert begins.

IV. Tell el-Kebîr, a wretched village, now made famous by the victory of Lord Wolseley over Arabi Pasha in 1882.

V. Maḥsamah, which stands on the site of a town built by Rameses II. Near this place is Tell el-Maskhûta, which

* She was a form of Hathor, and as wife of Ptaḥ was the mother of Nefer-Ȧtmu and I-em-ḥetep. She was the personification of the power of light and of the burning heat of the sun ; it was her duty to destroy the demons of night, mist and cloud, who fought against the sun.

† Book II. 60.

some have identified with the Pithom which the Israelites built for the king of Egypt who oppressed them.

VI. Isma'îlîya (see p. 259).

VII. Nefîsheh. Here the fresh water canal divides into two parts, the one going on to Suez, and the other to Isma'îlîya.

TANIS.

The town which the Greeks called *Tanis*, and the Copts ⲦⲀⲚⲈⲰⲤ or ϪⲀⲚⲎ was named by the ancient Egyptians  *Sekhet Tchā*, or  *Sekhet Tchānt* (which is accurately translated "Field of Zoan,"* שְׂדֵה־צֹעַן, in Psalm lxxviii. 12, 43) and  *Tchart;* it was the capital of the fourteenth nome of Lower Egypt, 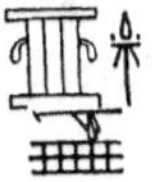 Khent-âbt. The two determinatives  indicate that the place was situated in a swampy district, and that foreigners dwelt there. The Arabs have adopted the shorter name of the town, and call it Ṣân. Dr. H. Brugsch endeavoured to show that Tanis represented the town of Rameses, which was built by the Israelites, but his theory has not been generally accepted, although there is no doubt whatever that Tchar and Tanis are one and the same town. The other names of Tanis given by Dr. Brugsch in his great *Dictionnaire Géographique* are "Mesen, Mesen of the North, Teb of the North, and Beḥuṭet of the

* Zoan must have been considered a place of great importance by the Hebrews, for they date the founding of Hebron by it (Numbers, xiii. 22), and Isaiah, describing the future calamities of Egypt, says, "Surely the princes of Zoan are fools.' (Isaiah xix. 11.)

North." Tanis was situated on the right or east bank of the Tanaïtic branch of the Nile, about thirty miles nearly due west of the ancient Pelusium; and as it was near the north-east frontier of Egypt, it was always one of the towns which formed the object of the first attack of the so-called Hyksos, Syrians, Assyrians, Greeks, Arabs, and Turks. The excavations which have been made in the ruins round about Ṣân by Mariette and Petrie prove that Tanis must have been one of the largest and most important cities in the Delta. The earliest monuments found here date from the time of Pepi I., VIth dynasty, about B.C. 3233; the next oldest are the black granite statues of Usertsen I. and Åmenemḥāt II., a sandstone statue of Usertsen II., an inscribed granite fragment of Usertsen III., and two statues of Sebek-ḥetep III. Following these come the most interesting black granite sphinxes, which are usually said to be the work of the so-called Hyksos, but which are, in the writer's opinion, older than the period when these people ruled over Lower Egypt. The cartouches inscribed upon them only prove that many kings were anxious to have their names added to these monuments. The greatest builder at Tanis was Rameses II., who erected a temple with pylons, colossal statues, obelisks and sphinxes. Pasebkhānu, Shashanq I. and Shashanq III. repaired and added to the buildings in Tanis, and they took the opportunity of usurping sphinxes, obelisks, etc., which had been set up by earlier kings. The famous red granite "Tablet of four hundred years" was found at Ṣân. The inscription upon it, which is of the time of Rameses II., is dated in the four hundredth year of a Hyksos king named "Āa-peḥ-peḥ-Set, son of the Sun, Nub-Set"  , which appears to prove that this king reigned 400 years before the time of Rameses II.

The last native king of Egypt whose name is mentioned

at Tanis is Nectanebus II., and after him come the Ptolemies. The stele, commonly called the "Decree of Canopus," which was set up in the ninth year of Ptolemy III., Euergetes I. (B.C. 238), was found here. The trilingual inscription in hieroglyphics, Greek, and Demotic, mentions at some length the great benefits which this king had conferred upon Egypt, and states what festivals are to be celebrated in his honour and in that of Berenice. The priests assembled at Canopus from all parts of Egypt resolved that these things should be duly inscribed upon stelæ, of which one should be placed in every large temple in Egypt to commemorate their resolution.

Under the Roman Empire Tanis still held a high position among the towns of the Delta, and the Egyptians considered it of sufficient importance to make it an episcopal see. In the list of the bishops who were present at the Council of Chalcedon (A.D. 451), the name of Apollonius, Bishop of Tanis, is found. Tanis must not be confounded with Tennis, the sea-port town which grew and increased in importance as Tanis declined; and it is difficult to understand why Tanis should have dwindled away, considering that Arab writers have described its climate as being most salubrious, and its winter like summer. Water was said to flow there at all times, and the inhabitants could water their gardens at their will; no place in all Egypt, save the Fayyûm, could be compared with it for fertility, and for the beauty of its gardens and vines. In the sixth century of our era the sea invaded a large portion of Tanis territory, and it went on encroaching each year little by little, until all its villages were submerged. The inhabitants removed their dead to Tennis, and established themselves there; Tennis was evacuated by its inhabitants A.D. 1192, and the town itself was destroyed A.D. 1226.

CAIRO.

Cairo (from the Arabic Ḳâhira, 'the Victorious,' because the planet Ḳâhir or Mars was visible on the night of the foundation of the city) is situated on the right or eastern bank of the Nile, about ten miles south of the division of the Nile into the Rosetta and Damietta branches. It is called in Arabic Maṣr *: it is the largest city in Africa, and its population must be now over 570,000 souls. Josephus says that the fortress of the Babylon of Egypt, which stood on the spot occupied by old Cairo or Fosṭâṭ, was founded by the Babylonian mercenary soldiers of Cambyses, B.C. 525; Diodorus says that it was founded by Assyrian captives in the time of Rameses II., and Ctesias is inclined to think that it was built in the time of Semiramis. The opinions of the two last mentioned writers are valuable in one respect, for they show that it was believed in their time that Babylon of Egypt was of very ancient foundation. During the reign of Augustus it was the headquarters of one of the legions that garrisoned Egypt, and remains of the town and fortress which these legionaries occupied are still to be seen a little to the north of Fosṭâṭ. The word Fosṭâṭ † means a 'tent,' and the place is so called from the tent of 'Amr ibn el-'Âṣi, which was pitched there when he invaded Egypt, A.D. 638, and to which he returned after his capture of Alexandria. Around his tent lived a large number of his followers, and

* Maṣr is a form of the old name Mîṣri (Hebrew *Miṣraim*), by which it is called in the cuneiform tablets, B.C. 1450.

† Arab. فُسْطَاط, another form of فُسَّاط, = Byzantine Greek Φοσσάτον.

these being joined by new comers, the city of Fosṭâṭ at length arose. It was enlarged by Aḥmed ibn Ṭulûn, who built a mosque there; by Khamarûyeh, who built a palace there; but when the Fâṭimite Khalif Mu'izz conquered Egypt (A.D. 969), he removed the seat of his government from there, and founded Maṣr el-Ḳâhira, "Maṣr the Victorious," near Fosṭâṭ. Fosṭâṭ, which was also known by the name of Maṣr, was henceforth called Maṣr el-'Atîḳa. During the reign of Ṣalâḥeddîn the walls of the new city were thoroughly repaired and the citadel was built. Sulṭân after Sulṭân added handsome buildings to the town, and though it suffered from plagues and fires, it gained the reputation of being one of the most beautiful capitals in the Muḥammadan empire. In 1517 it was captured by Selim I., and Egypt became a pashalik of the Turkish empire, and remained so until its conquest by Napoleon Bonaparte in 1798. Cairo was occupied by Muḥammad 'Ali in 1805, and the massacre of the Mamelukes took place March 1, 1811.

COPTIC CHURCHES IN CAIRO.*

The Church of MÂR MÎNÂ lies between Fosṭâṭ and Cairo; it was built in honour of St. Menas, an early martyr, who is said to have been born at Mareotis, and martyred during the persecution of Galerius Maximinus at Alexandria. The name Mînâ, or Menâ, probably represents the Coptic form of Menà, 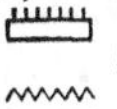, the name of the first historical king of Egypt. The church was probably founded during the fourth century, and it seems to have been restored in the eighth century; the first church built

* The authorities for the following facts relating to Coptic Churches are Butler's *Coptic Churches of Egypt*, 2 vols., 1884; and Curzon, *Visits to Monasteries in the Levant.*

to Mâr Mînâ was near Alexandria. The church measures 60 feet × 50 feet; it contains some interesting pictures, and a very ancient bronze candelabrum in the shape of two winged dragons, with seventeen sockets for lighted tapers. On the roof of the church is a small bell in a cupola.

About half-a-mile beyond the Dêr * containing the church of St. Menas, lies the Dêr of Abu's Sêfên, in which are situated the churches al-'Aḍhra (the Virgin), Anba Shenûti, and Abu's Sêfên. The last-named church was built in the tenth century, and is dedicated to St. Mercurius, who is called "Father of two swords," or Abu's Sêfên. The church measures 90 feet × 50 feet, and is built chiefly of brick; there are no pillars in it. It contains a fine ebony partition dating from A.D. 927, some interesting pictures, an altar casket dating from A.D. 1280, and a marble pulpit. In this church are chapels dedicated to Saints Gabriel, John the Baptist, James, Mâr Buḳṭor, Antony, Abbâ Nûb, Michael, and George. Within the Dêr of Abu's Sêfên is the "Convent of the Maidens"; the account of Mr. Butler's discovery of this place is told by him in his *Coptic Churches of Egypt*, Vol. I. p. 128. The church of the Virgin was founded probably in the eighth century.

The church of Abu Sargah, or Abu Sergius, stands well towards the middle of the Roman fortress of Babylon in Egypt. Though nothing is known of the saint after whom it was named, it is certain that in A.D. 859 Shenûti was elected patriarch of Abu Sargah; the church was most probably built much earlier, and some go so far as to state that the crypt (20 feet × 15 feet) was occupied by the Virgin and her Son when they fled to Egypt to avoid the wrath of Herod. "The general shape of the church is, or was, a nearly regular oblong, and its general structure is basilican. It consists of narthex, nave, north and south

* Arabic دير "convent, monastery."

aisle, choir, and three altars eastward each in its own chapel: of these the central and southern chapels are apsidal, the northern is square ended...... Over the aisles and narthex runs a continuous gallery or triforium, which originally served as the place for women at the service. On the north side it stops short at the choir, forming a kind of transept, which, however, does not project beyond the north aisle...... On the south side of the church the triforium is prolonged over the choir and over the south side-chapel. The gallery is flat-roofed while the nave is covered with a pointed roof with framed principals like that at Abu's Sêfên...... Outside, the roof of Abu Sargah is plastered over with cement showing the king-posts projecting above the ridge-piece. Over the central part of the choir and over the haikal the roof changes to a wagon-vaulting; it is flat over the north transept, and a lofty dome overshadows the north aisle chapel...... The twelve monolithic columns round the nave are all, with one exception, of white marble streaked with dusky lines...... The exceptional column is of red Assuân granite, 22 inches in diameter...... The wooden pulpit...... is of rosewood inlaid with designs in ebony set with ivory edgings...... The haikal-screen projects forward into the choir as at Al 'Aḍra...... and is of very ancient and beautiful workmanship; pentagons and other shapes of solid ivory, carved in relief with arabesques, being inlaid and set round with rich mouldings...... The upper part of the screen contains square panels of ebony set with large crosses of solid ivory, most exquisitely chiselled with scrollwork, and panels of ebony carved through in work of the most delicate and skilful finish." (Butler, *Coptic Churches*, Vol. I., pp. 183–190, ff.) The early carvings representing St. Demetrius, Mâr George, Abu's Sêfên, the Nativity, and the Last Supper are worthy of careful examination.

The Jewish synagogue near Abu Sargah was originally a Coptic church dedicated to St. Michael, which was sold to the Jews by a patriarch called Michael towards the end of the ninth century; it measures 65 feet × 35 feet, and is said to contain a copy of the Law written by Ezra.

A little to the south-east of Abu Sargah is the church dedicated to the Virgin, more commonly called El-Mu‘allaḳah, or the ‘hanging,’ from the fact that it is suspended between two bastions, and must be entered by a staircase. The church is triapsal, and is of the basilican order. It originally contained some very beautiful screens, which have been removed from their original positions and made into a sort of wall, and, unfortunately, modern stained glass has been made to replace the old. The cedar doors, sculptured in panels, are now in the British Museum. The cedar and ivory screens are thought to belong to the eleventh century. The church is remarkable in having no choir, and Mr. Butler says it is "a double-aisled church, and as such is remarkable in having no transepts." The pulpit is one of the most valuable things left in the church, and probably dates from the twelfth century; in the wooden coffer near it are the bones of four saints. Authorities differ as to the date to be assigned to the founding of this church, but all the available evidence now known would seem to point to the sixth century as the most probable period; at any rate, it must have been before the betrayal of the fortress of Babylon to ‘Amr by the Monophysite Copts in the seventh century.

A little to the north-east of Abu Sargah is the church of St. Barbara, the daughter of a man of position in the East, who was martyred during the persecution of Maximinus; it was built probably during the eighth century. In the church is a picture of the saint, and a chapel in honour of St. George. At the west end of the triforium are some mural paintings of great interest.

Within the walls of the fortress of Babylon, lying due north of Abu Sargah, are the two churches of Mâr Girgis and the Virgin.

To the south of the fortress of Babylon, beyond the Muḥammadan village on the rising ground, lie the Dêr of Bablûn and the Dêr of Tadrus. In the Dêr el-Bablûn is a church to the Virgin, which is very difficult to see. It contains some fine mural paintings, and an unusual candlestick and lectern; in it also are chapels dedicated to Saints Michael and George. This little building is about fifty-three feet square. Dêr el-Tadrus contains two churches dedicated to Saints Cyrus and John of Damanhûr in the Delta; there are some fine specimens of vestments to be seen there.

A short distance from the Mûski is a Dêr containing the churches of the Virgin, St. George, and the chapel of Abu's Sêfên. The church of the Virgin occupies the lower half of the building, and is the oldest in Cairo. The chapel of Abu's Sêfên is reached through a door in the north-west corner of the building, and contains a wooden pulpit inlaid with ivory. The church of St. George occupies the upper part of the building, and is over the church of the Virgin.

In the Greek (Byzantine) quarter of Cairo is the Dêr el-Tadrus, which contains the churches of St. George and the Virgin.

The Coptic churches of Cairo contain a great deal that is interesting, and are well worth many visits. Though the fabrics of many of them are not older than the sixth, seventh, or eighth century of our era, it may well be assumed that the sites were occupied by Coptic churches long before this period.

The Mosques of Cairo.

Speaking generally, there are three types of mosque * in

* The word "mosque" is derived from the Arabic مَسْجِد a "place of prayer."

Cairo: 1, the court-yard surrounded by colonnades, as in the Mosques of 'Amr and ibn-Ṭulûn; 2, the court-yard surrounded by four gigantic arches, as in the Mosque of Sulṭân Ḥasan, etc.; and 3, the covered yard beneath a dome, as in the Mosque of Muḥammad 'Ali.

The Mosque of **'Amr** in Fosṭâṭ, or Old Cairo, is the oldest mosque in Egypt, its foundation having been laid A.H. 21 = A.D. 643. The land upon which it was built was given by 'Amr ibn el-'Âṣi and his friends after they had become masters of the fortress of Babylon. Of 'Amr's edifice very little remains, for nearly all the building was burnt down at the end of the ninth century. Towards the end of the third quarter of the tenth century the mosque was enlarged and rebuilt, and it was subsequently decorated with paintings, etc.; the splendour of the mosque is much dwelt upon by Maḳrîzî. The court measures 350 feet × 400 feet. The building contains 366 pillars—one row on the west side, three rows on the north and south sides, and six rows on the east side; one of the pillars bears the name of Muḥammad. In the north-east corner is the tomb of 'Abdallah, the son of 'Amr.

The Mosque of **Aḥmed ibn Ṭulûn** (died A.D. 884) is the oldest in Maṣr el-Ḳâhira or New Cairo, having been built A.D. 879, under the rule of Khalif Mu'tamid (A.D. 870–892). It is said to be a copy of the Ka'ba at Mecca, and to have taken two or three years to build. The open court is square, and measures about 300 feet from side to side; in the centre is the Ḥanafîyyeh (حَنَفِيَّة) or fountain for the Turks. On the north, west, and south sides is an arcade with walls pierced with arches; on the east side are five arcades divided by walls pierced with arches. The wooden pulpit is a famous specimen of wood carving, and dates from the thirteenth century. Around the outside of the minaret of this mosque is a spiral staircase, which is said to have been suggested by its founder. The mosque is called the "Fortress of the Goat," because it is said to mark the spot where Abraham offered up the ram; others say that the ark rested here.

The Mosque of **Ḥâkim** (A.D. 996-1020), the third Fâṭimite Khalif, was built on the plan of the mosque of ibn Ṭulûn (see above); the date over one of the gates is A.H. 39.' = A.D. 1003. The Museum of Arab art is located here.

The Mosque **El-Azhar** is said to have been founded by Jôhar, the general of Mu'izz, about A.D. 980. The plan of the principal part was the same as that of the mosque of 'Amr, but very little of the original building remains. It was made a university by the Khalif 'Aziz (A.D. 975–996), and great alterations were made in the building by different Sulṭâns in the twelfth, thirteenth, fifteenth, sixteenth, and eighteenth centuries; Sa'îd Pasha made the last, A.D. 1848. The minarets belong to different periods; the mosque has six gates, and at the principal of these, the "Gate of the Barbers," is the entrance. On three of the sides of the open court are compartments, each of which is reserved for the worshippers who belong to a certain country. The Lîwân of the mosque is huge, and its ceiling is supported upon 380 pillars of various kinds of stone; it is here that the greater part of the students of the university carry on their studies. The number of students varies from 10,000 to 13,000, and the education, from the Muḥammadan point of view, is perhaps the most thorough in the whole world.

In the Citadel are:—1. The Mosque of Yûsuf Ṣalâḥeddîn, built A.D. 1171–1198; 2. The Mosque of Sulêmân Pasha or Sulṭân Selîm, built A.H. 391 = A.D 1001.

The Muristân Ḳalaûn, originally a hospital, contains the tomb of El-Manṣûr Ḳalaûn (A.D. 1279–1290), which is decorated with marble mosaics.

The Mosque-tomb of Muḥammad en-Nâṣir (A.D. 1293–1341), son of Ḳalaûn, stands near that of Ḳalaûn.

The Mosque of **Sulṭân Ḥasan**, built of stone taken from the pyramids of Gîzeh, is close to the citadel, and is generally considered to be the grandest in Cairo. It was built by Ḥasan, one of the younger sons of Sulṭân Nâṣir, and its construction occupied three years, A.D. 1356–1358. It is said that when the building was finished the architect's hands were cut off to prevent his executing a similar work again. This story, though probably false, shows that the mosque was considered of great beauty, and the judgment of competent critics of to-day endorses the opinion of it which was prevalent in Ḥasan's time. Ḥasan's tomb is situated on the east side of the building. The remaining minaret* is about 280 feet high, the greatest length of the mosque is about 320 feet, and the width about 200 feet. In the open court are two fountains which were formerly used, one by the Egyptians, and one by the Turks. On the eastern side are still to be seen a few of the balls which were fired at the mosque by the army of Napoleon.

The Mosque of **Barḳûḳ** (A.D. 1382–1399) contains the tomb of the daughter of Barḳûḳ.

The Mosque of **Muaiyyad**, one of the Circassian Mamelukes, was founded between the years 1412–1420; it is also known as the "Red Mosque," from the colour of the walls outside. "Externally it measures about 300 feet by 250, and possesses an internal court, surrounded by double colonnades on three sides, and a triple range of arches on the side looking towards Mecca, where also are situated—as in that of Barḳûḳ—the tombs of the founder and his family. A considerable number of ancient columns have been used in the erection of the building, but the superstructure is so light and elegant, that the effect is agreeable." † The bronze gate in front belonged originally to the mosque of Sulṭân Ḥasan.

* From the Arabic مَنَارَة "place of light."

† Fergusson, *Hist. of Architecture*, Vol. II., p. 516.

The Mosque of **Ḳait** Bey (A.D. 1468–1496), one of the last independent Mameluke sulṭâns of Egypt, is about eighty feet long and seventy feet wide; it has some fine mosaics, and is usually considered the finest piece of architecture in Cairo.

The Mosque el-Ghûri was built by the Sulṭân Kanṣuweh el-Ghûri early in the sixteenth century; it is one of the most beautiful mosques in Cairo.

The Mosque of Sittah Zênab was begun late in the last century; it contains the tomb of Zênab, the granddaughter of the Prophet.

The Mosque begun by Muḥammad 'Ali in the Citadel was finished in 1857 by Sa'îd Pasha, after the death (in 1849) of that ruler; it is built of alabaster from the quarries of Beni Suwêf. As with nearly all mosques built by the Turks, the church of the Hagia Sophia at Constantinople served as the model, but the building is not considered of remarkable beauty. The mosque is a square covered by a large dome and four small ones. In the south-east corner is the tomb of Muḥammad 'Ali, and close by is the minbar (منبر) or pulpit; in the recess on the east side is the Ḳiblah (قِبْلَة), or spot to which the Muḥammadan turns his face during his prayers. The court is square, with one row of pillars on each of its four sides, and in the centre is the fountain for the Turks; the clock in the tower on the western side was presented to Muḥammad 'Ali by Louis Philippe.

The Mosque of El-Ḥasanên, *i.e.*, the mosque of Ḥasan and Ḥusên, the sons of 'Ali the son-in-law of the Prophet, is said to contain the head of Ḥusên who was slain at Kerbela A.D. 680; the head was first sent to Damascus and afterwards brought to Cairo.

In the Mosque of El-Akbar the **dancing dervishes** perform.

THE TOMBS OF THE KHALIFS.*

These beautiful buildings are situated on the eastern side of the city, and contain the tombs of the members of the families of the Circassian Mameluke Sulṭâns who reigned from A.D. 1382–1517. The tomb-mosques of Yûsuf, el-Ashraf, and the tomb of el-Ghûri (A.D. 1501–1516) are to the north-east of the Bâb en-Naṣr; the tomb-mosques of Yûsuf and el-Ashraf are only to be seen by special permission. In the tomb-mosque of Barḳûḳ are buried that sulṭân, his son the Sulṭân Farag (A.D. 1399–1412), and various other members of the family. The limestone pulpit and the two minarets are very beautiful specimens of stone work. To the west of this tomb-mosque is the tomb of Sulṭân Sulêmân, and near that are the tombs of the Seven Women, the tomb-mosque of Bursbey (A.D. 1422–1438), the Ma'bed er-Rifâ'i, and the tomb of the mother of Bursbey. The most beautiful of all these tombs is the tomb-mosque of Ḳait Bey (A.D. 1468–1496), which is well worthy of more than one visit.

THE TOMBS OF THE MAMELUKES.†

Of the builders of these tombs no history has been preserved; the ruins, however, show that they must have been very beautiful objects. Some of the minarets are still very fine.

THE CITADEL.

The Citadel was built by Ṣalâḥeddîn, A.D. 1166, and the

* The word "Khalif," Arabic, خَلِيفَة *Khalîfah*, means "successor" (of Muḥammad) or "vicar" (of God upon earth), and was a title applied to the head of the Muslim world. The last Khalîfah died in Egypt *about* A.D. 1517.

† The word "Mameluke" means a "slave," Arabic مَمْلُوك, plur. مَمَالِيك.

stones used were taken from the pyramids of Gîzeh; it formed a part of the large system of the fortifications of Cairo which this Sulṭân carried out so thoroughly. Though admirably situated for commanding the whole city, and as a fortress in the days before long range cannon were invented, the site was shown in 1805 to be ill chosen for the purposes of defence in modern times by Muḥammad 'Ali, who, by means of a battery placed on the Moḳaṭṭam heights, compelled Khurshîd Pasha to surrender the citadel. In the narrow way, with a high wall, through the Bâb el-Azab, which was formerly the most direct and most used means of access to it, the massacre of the Mamelukes took place by the orders of Muḥammad 'Ali, A.D. 1811. The single Mameluke who escaped is said to have made his horse leap down from one of the walls of the Citadel; he refused to enter the narrow way.

Joseph's Well.

This well is not called after Joseph the Patriarch, as is usually supposed, but after the famous Ṣalâḥeddîn (Saladin), whose first name was Yûsuf or Joseph. The shaft of this well, in two parts, is about 280 feet deep, and was found to be choked up with sand when the Citadel was built; Saladin caused it to be cleared out, and from his time until 1865 its water was regularly drawn up and used. This well was probably sunk by the ancient Egyptians.

The Library.

This valuable institution was founded by Ismâ'îl in 1870, and contains the library of Muṣṭafa Pasha; the number of works in the whole collection is said to be about 24,000. Some of the copies of the Ḳur'ân preserved there are among the oldest known.

Ezbekîyeh Garden.

This garden or "place," named after the Amîr Ezbeki,

the general of Ḳait Bey (A.D. 1468—1496), was made in 1870 by M. Barillet, and has an area of about twenty acres.

The Nilometer in the Island of Rôḍa.

The Nilometer here is a pillar, which is divided into seventeen parts, each representing a cubit, *i.e.*, 21⅓ inches, and each cubit is divided into twenty-four parts. This pillar is placed in the centre of a well about sixteen feet square; the lower end is embedded in the foundations, and the upper end is held in position by a beam built into the side walls. The well is connected with the Nile by a channel. The first Nilometer at Rôḍa is said to have been built by the Khalif Sulêmân (A.D. 715—717), and about one hundred years later the building was restored by Mâmûn (A.D. 813—833). At the end of the eleventh century a dome resting upon columns was built over it. When the Nile is at its lowest level it stands at the height of seven cubits in the Nilometer well, and when it reaches the height of 15⅔ cubits, the shêkh of the Nile proclaims that sufficient water has come into the river to admit of the cutting of the dam which prevents the water from flowing over the country. The difference between the highest rise and the lowest fall of the Nile at Cairo is about twenty-five feet. The cutting of the dam takes place some time during the second or third week in August, at which time there are general rejoicings. When there happens to be an exceptionally high Nile, the whole island of Rôḍa is submerged, and the waters flow over the Nilometer to a depth of two cubits, a fact which proves that the bed of the Nile is steadily rising, and one which shows how difficult it is to harmonize all the statements made by Egyptian, Greek, and Arab writers on the subject. As the amount of taxation to be borne by the people has always depended upon the height of the inundation, attempts were formerly made by the governments of Egypt to prove to the people that there never was a low Nile.

HELIOPOLIS.*

About five miles to the north-east of Cairo stands the little village of Maṭarîyeh †, built upon part of the site of Heliopolis, where may be seen the sycamore tree, usually called the "Virgin's Tree," under which tradition says that the Virgin Mary sat and rested during her flight to Egypt; it was planted some time towards the end of the XVIIth century, and was given to the Empress Eugénie by Isma'îl on the occasion of the opening of the Suez Canal. Beyond the "Virgin's Tree" is the fine Aswân granite obelisk which marks the site of the ancient town of Heliopolis, called "On" in Gen. xli. 45, "House of the Sun" in Jeremiah

* Called in Egyptian , *Ànnu meḥt*, "Annu of the North," to distinguish it from , *Ànnu Qemāu*, "Annu of the South," *i.e.*, Hermonthis.

† مطرية, Juynboll, *op. cit.*, t. iii., p. 110. At this place the balsam trees, about which so many traditions are extant, were said to grow. The balsam tree was about a cubit high, and had two barks; the outer red and fine, and the inner green and thick. When the latter was macerated in the mouth, it left an oily taste and an aromatic odour. Incisions were made in the barks, and the liquid which flowed from them was carefully collected and treated; the amount of balsam oil obtained formed a tenth part of all the liquid collected. The last balsam tree cultivated in Egypt died in 1615, but two were seen alive in 1612; it is said that they would grow nowhere out of Egypt. They were watered with the water from the well at Maṭarîyeh in which the Virgin Mary washed the clothes of our Lord when she was in Egypt. The oil was much sought after by the Christians of Abyssinia and other places, who thought it absolutely necessary that one drop of this oil should be poured into the water in which they were baptized. See Wansleben, *L'Histoire de l'Église d'Alexandrie*, pp. 88–93; *Abd-al-Laṭîf* (ed. de Sacy), p. 88.

xliii. 13, and "Eye or Fountain of the Sun" by the Arabs. Heliopolis was about twelve miles from the fortress of Babylon, and stood on the eastern side of the Pelusiac arm of the Nile, near the right bank of the great canal which passed through the Bitter Lakes and connected the Nile with the sea. Its ruins cover an area three miles square. The greatest and oldest Egyptian College or University for the education of the priesthood and the laity stood here, and it was here that Ptolemy II., Philadelphus, sent for Egyptian manuscripts when he wished to augment the library which his father had founded.

The **obelisk** is sixty-six feet high, and was set up by Usertsen I.  about B.C. 2433; a companion obelisk remained standing in its place until the seventh century of our era, and both were covered with caps of *smu* (probably copper) metal. During the XXth dynasty the temple of Heliopolis was one of the largest and wealthiest in all Egypt, and its staff was numbered by thousands. When Cambyses visited Egypt the glory of Heliopolis was well on the wane, and after the removal of the priesthood and sages of the temple to Alexandria by Ptolemy II. its downfall was well assured. When Strabo visited it (B.C. 24), the greater part of it was in ruins; but we know from Arab writers that many of the statues remained *in situ* at the end of the twelfth century. Heliopolis had a large population of Jews, and it will be remembered that Joseph married the daughter of Pa-ṭā-pa-Rā (Potiphar) a priest of On (Ȧnnu), or Heliopolis. It lay either in or very near the Goshen of the Bible. The Mnevis bull, sacred to Rā, was worshipped at Heliopolis, and it was here that the phœnix or palm-bird brought its ashes after having raised itself to life at the end of each period of five hundred years. Alexander the Great halted here on his way from Pelusium to Memphis. Macrobius says that the Heliopolis of Syria, or Baalbek, was founded by a body of priests who left the ancient city of Heliopolis of Egypt.

THE PYRAMIDS OF GÎZEH.

On the western bank of the Nile, from Abu Roâsh on the north to Mêdûm on the south, is a slightly elevated tract of land, about twenty-five miles long, on the edge of the Libyan desert, on which stand the pyramids of Abu Roâsh, Gîzeh, Zâwyet el-'Aryân, Abuṣîr, Ṣaḳḳâra, Lisht, and Dahshûr. Other places in Egypt where pyramids are found are El-lâhûn* in the Fayyûm, Hawâra, and Kullah near Esneh. The pyramids built by the Nubians or Ethiopians at Ḳurrû, Zûma, Tanḳassi, Gebel-Barkal, Nûri, and Baḳrawîyeh (Meroë), are of various dates and are mere copies, in respect of form only, of the pyramids in Egypt. It is well to state at once that the pyramids were tombs and nothing else. There is no evidence whatever to show that they were built for purposes of astronomical observations, and the theory that the Great Pyramid was built to serve as a standard of measurement is ingenious but worthless. The significant fact, so ably pointed out by Mariette, that pyramids are only found in cemeteries, is an answer to all such theories. Tomb-pyramids were built by kings and others until the XIIth dynasty. The ancient writers who have described and treated of the pyramids are given by Pliny (Nat. Hist., xxxvi. 12, 17). If we may believe some of the writers on them during the Middle Ages, their outsides must have been covered with inscriptions; which were, probably, of a religious nature.† In modern times they have been examined by Shaw (1721),

* *I.e.*,  *Le-ḥent*, "mouth of the canal," Coptic ⲗⲉϩⲱⲛⲓ.

† "......... their surfaces exhibit all kinds of inscriptions written in the characters of ancient nations which no longer exist. No one knows what this writing is or what it signifies." Mas'ûdi (ed. Barbier de Meynard), t. ii., p. 404.

Pococke (1743), Niebuhr (1761), Davison (1763), Bruce (1768), Denon and Jomard (1799), Hamilton (1801), Caviglia (1817), Belzoni (1817), Wilkinson (1831), Howard Vyse and Perring (1837–38), Lepsius (1842–45), and Petrie (1881).

It appears that before the actual building of a pyramid was begun a suitable rocky site was chosen and cleared, a mass of rock if possible being left in the middle of the area to form the core of the building. The chambers and the galleries leading to them were next planned and excavated. Around the core a truncated pyramid building was made, the angles of which were filled up with blocks of stone. Layer after layer of stone was then built around the work, which grew larger and larger until it was finished. Dr. Lepsius thought that when a king ascended the throne, he built for himself a small but complete tomb-pyramid, and that a fresh coating of stone was built around it every year that he reigned; and that when he died the sides of the pyramids were like long flights of steps, which his successor filled up with right-angled triangular blocks of stone. The door of the pyramid was walled up after the body of its builder had been laid in it, and thus remained a finished tomb. The explanation of Dr. Lepsius may not be correct, but at least it answers satisfactorily more objections than do the views of other theorists on this matter. It has been pointed out that near the core of the pyramid the work is more carefully executed than near the exterior, that is to say, as the time for the king's death approached the work was more hurriedly performed.

During the investigations made by Lepsius in and about the pyramid area, he found the remains of about seventy-five pyramids, and noticed that they were always built in groups.

The pyramids of Gîzeh were opened by the Persians during the fifth and fourth centuries before Christ; it is probable that they were also entered by the Romans. Khalif Mâmûn (A.D. 813–833) entered the Great Pyramid, and found that others had been there before him. The treasure which is said to have been discovered there by him is probably fictitious. Once opened, it must have been evident to every one what splendid quarries the pyramids formed, and for some hundreds of years after the conquest of Egypt by the Arabs they were laid under contribution for stone to build mosques, etc., in Cairo. Late in the twelfth century Melik el-Kâmil made a mad attempt to destroy the third pyramid at Gîzeh built by Mycerinus; but after months of toil he only succeeded in stripping off the covering from one of the sides. It is said that Muḥammad 'Ali was advised to undertake the senseless task of destroying them all.

THE GREAT PYRAMID.

This, the largest of the three pyramids at Gîzeh, was built by Khufu  or Cheops, the second king of the IVth dynasty, B.C. 3733, who called it  *Khut.* His name was found written in red ink upon the blocks of stone inside it. All four sides measure in greatest length about 755 feet each, but the length of each was originally about 20 feet more; its height now is 451 feet, but it is said to have been originally about 481 feet. The stone used in the construction of this pyramid was brought from Ṭurra and Moḳaṭṭam, and the contents amount to 85,000,000 cubic feet. The flat space at the top of the pyramid is about thirty feet square, and the view from it is very fine.

The entrance (A) to this pyramid is, as with all pyramids, on the north side, and is about 45 feet above the ground. The passage A B C is 320 feet long, $3\frac{1}{4}$ feet high, and 4 feet

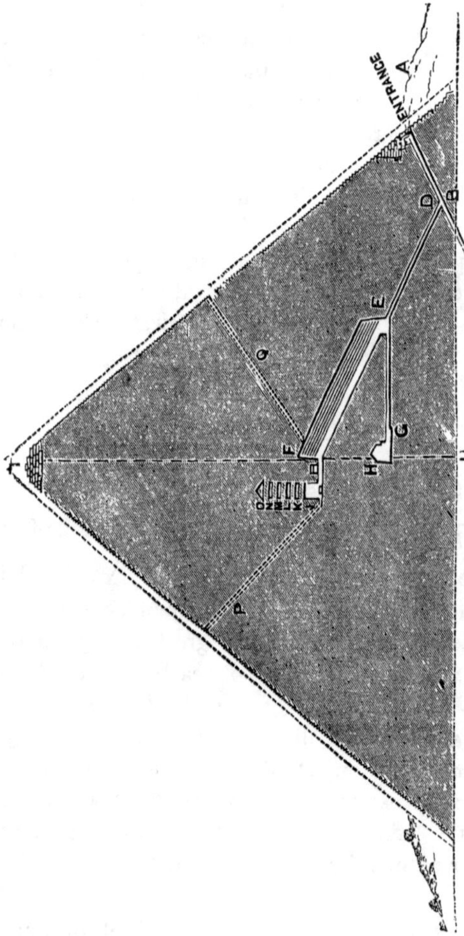

Section of the Pyramid of Cheops at Gîzeh. From Vyse, *Pyramids of Gizeh*, Vol. I., p. 2.

wide; at B is a granite door, round which the path at D has been made. The passage at D E is 125 feet long, and the large hall E F is 155 feet long and 28 feet high; the passage E G leads to the pointed-roofed Queen's Chamber H, which measures about 17 × 19 × 20 feet. The roofing in of this chamber is a beautiful piece of mason's work. From the large hall E F there leads a passage 22 feet long, the ante-chamber in which was originally closed by four granite doors, remains of which are still visible, into the King's Chamber, J, which is lined with granite, and measures about 35 × 17 × 19 feet. The five hollow chambers K, L, M, N, O were built above the King's Chamber to lighten the pressure of the superincumbent mass. In chamber O the name Khufu was found written. The air shafts P and Q measure 234 feet × 8 inches × 6 inches, and 174 feet × 8 inches × 6 inches respectively. A shaft from E to R leads down to the subterranean chamber S, which measures 46 × 27 × 10½ feet. The floor of the King's Chamber, J, is about 140 ft. from the level of the base of the pyramid, and the chamber is a little to the south-east of the line drawn from T to U. Inside the chamber lies the empty, coverless, broken red granite sarcophagus of Cheops, measuring 7½ × 3¼ × 3⅓ feet. The account of the building of this pyramid is told by Herodotus* as follows: "Now, they told me, that to the reign of Rhampsinitus there was a perfect distribution of justice, and that all Egypt was in a high state of prosperity; but that after him Cheops, coming to reign over them, plunged into every kind of wickedness. For that, having shut up all the temples, he first of all forbade them to offer sacrifice, and afterwards he ordered all the Egyptians to work for himself; some, accordingly, were appointed to draw stones from the quarries in the Arabian mountain down to the Nile, others he ordered to receive the stones when transported in vessels across the river, and to drag

* Bk. ii. 124–126.

them to the mountain called the Libyan. And they worked to the number of 100,000 men at a time, each party during three months. The time during which the people were thus harassed by toil, lasted ten years on the road which they constructed, along which they drew the stones, a work in my opinion, not much less than the pyramid; for its length is five stades (3,051 feet), and its width ten orgyæ (60 feet), and its height, where it is the highest, eight orgyæ (48 feet); and it is of polished stone, with figures carved on it: on this road these ten years were expended, and in forming the subterraneous apartments on the hill, on which the pyramids stand, which he had made as a burial vault for himself, in an island, formed by draining a canal from the Nile. Twenty years were spent in erecting the pyramid itself: of this, which is square, each face is eight plethra (820 feet), and the height is the same; it is composed of polished stones, and jointed with the greatest exactness; none of the stones are less than thirty feet. This pyramid was built thus; in the form of steps, which some call crossæ, others bomides. When they had first built it in this manner, they raised the remaining stones by machines made of short pieces of wood: having lifted them from the ground to the first range of steps, when the stone arrived there, it was put on another machine that stood ready on the first range; and from this it was drawn to the second range on another machine; for the machines were equal in number to the ranges of steps; or they removed the machine, which was only one, and portable, to each range in succession, whenever they wished to raise the stone higher; for I should relate it in both ways, as it is related. The highest parts of it, therefore, were first finished, and afterwards they completed the parts next following; but last of all they finished the parts on the ground and that were lowest. On the pyramid is shown an inscription, in Egyptian characters, how much was expended in radishes, onions, and garlic, for the workmen; which the interpreter,* as I well remember, reading the inscription, told me amounted to 1,600 talents of silver. And if this be really the case, how much more was probably expended in iron tools, in bread, and in clothes for the labourers, since they occupied in building the works the time which I mentioned, and no short time besides, as I think, in cutting and drawing the stones, and in forming the subterraneous excavation. [It is related] that Cheops reached such a degree of infamy, that being in want of money, he prostituted his own daughter in a brothel, and ordered her to extort, they did not say how much; but she exacted a certain sum of money, privately, as much as her father ordered her; and contrived to leave a monument of herself, and asked every one that came in to her to give her a stone towards the edifice she designed: of these stones they said the pyramid was built that stands in the middle of the three, before the great pyramid, each side of which is a plethron and a half in length." (Cary's translation.)

THE SECOND PYRAMID.

The second pyramid at Gîzeh was built by Khā-f-Rā, , or Chephren, the third king of the IVth dynasty, B.C. 3666, who called it , *ur*. His name has not been found inscribed upon any part of it, but the fragment of a marble sphere inscribed with the name of Khā-f-Rā,

* Herodotus was deceived by his interpreter, who clearly made up a translation of an inscription which he did not understand. William of Baldensel, who lived in the fourteenth century, tells us that the outer coating of the two largest pyramids was covered with a great number of inscriptions arranged in lines. (Wiedemann, *Aeg. Geschichte*, p. 179.) If the outsides were actually inscribed, the text must have been purely religious, like those inscribed inside the pyramids of Pepi, Tetà, and Unàs.

which was found near the temple, close by this pyramid, confirms the statements of Herodotus and Diodorus Siculus, that Chephren built it. A statue of this king, now in the Gîzeh Museum, was found in the granite temple close by. This pyramid appears to be larger than the Great Pyramid because it stands upon a higher level of stone foundation; it was cased with stone originally and polished, but the greater part of the outer casing has disappeared. An ascent of this pyramid can only be made with difficulty. It was first explored in 1816 by Belzoni (born 1778, died 1823), the discoverer of the tomb of Seti I. and of the temple of Rameses II. at Abu Simbel. In the north side of the pyramid are two openings, one at the base and one about 50 feet above it. The upper opening led into a corridor 105 feet long, which descends into a chamber $46\frac{1}{2} \times 16\frac{1}{3} \times 22\frac{1}{2}$ feet, which held the granite sarcophagus in which Chephren was buried. The lower opening leads into a corridor about 100 feet long, which, first descending and then ascending, ends in the chamber mentioned above, which is usually called Belzoni's Chamber. The actual height is about 450 feet, and the length of each side at the base about 700 feet. The rock upon which the pyramid stands has been scarped on the north and west sides to make the foundation level. The history of the building of the pyramid is thus stated by Herodotus * : "The Egyptians say that this Cheops reigned fifty years; and when he died, his brother Chephren succeeded to the kingdom; and he followed the same practices as the other, both in other respects, and in building a pyramid; which does not come up to the dimensions of his brother's, for I myself measured them; nor has it subterraneous chambers; nor does a channel from the Nile flow to it, as to the other; but this flows through an artificial aqueduct round an island within, in which they say the body of

* Bk. ii. 127.

Cheops is laid. Having laid the first course of variegated Ethiopian stones, less in height than the other by forty feet, he built it near the large pyramid. They both stand on the same hill, which is about 100 feet high. Chephren, they said, reigned fifty-six years. Thus 106 years are reckoned, during which the Egyptians suffered all kinds of calamities, and for this length of time the temples were closed and never opened. From the hatred they bear them, the Egyptians are not very willing to mention their names; but call the pyramids after Philition, a shepherd, who at that time kept his cattle in those parts." (Cary's translation.)

THE THIRD PYRAMID.

The third pyramid at Gîzeh was built by Men-kau-Rā, , the fourth king of the IVth dynasty, about B.C. 3633, who called it , *Ḥer*. Herodotus and other ancient authors tell us that Men-kau-Rā, or Mycerinus, was buried in this pyramid, but Manetho states that Nitocris, a queen of the VIth dynasty, was the builder. There can be, however, but little doubt that it was built by Mycerinus, for the sarcophagus and the remains of the inscribed coffin of this king were found in one of its chambers by Howard Vyse in 1837. The sarcophagus, which measured 8 × 3 × 2½ feet, was lost through the wreck of the ship in which it was sent to England, but the venerable fragments of the coffin are preserved in the British Museum, and form one of the most valuable objects in the famous collection of that institution. The inscription reads: "Osiris, king of the North and South, Men-kau-Rā, living for ever! The heavens have produced thee, thou wast engendered by Nut (the sky), thou art the offspring of Seb (the earth). Thy mother Nut spreads herself over thee in her form as a divine mystery. She has granted thee to be a god, thou shalt nevermore have enemies, O king of the North and South, Men-kau-Rā, living for ever." This formula is one which is found upon coffins down to the latest period, but as the date of Mycerinus is known, it is possible to draw some interesting and valuable conclusions from the fact that it is found upon his coffin. It proves that as far back as 3,600 years before Christ the Egyptian religion was established on a firm base, that the doctrine of immortality was already deeply rooted in the human mind. The art of preserving the human body by embalming was also well understood and generally practised at that early date.

The pyramid of Men-kau-Rā, like that of Chephren, is built upon a rock with a sloping surface; the inequality of the surface in this case has been made level by building up courses of large blocks of stones. Around the lower part the remains of the old granite covering are visible to a depth of from 30 to 40 feet. It is unfortunate that this pyramid has been so much damaged; its injuries, however, enable the visitor to see exactly how it was built, and it may be concluded that the pyramids of Cheops and Chephren were built in the same manner. The length of each side at the base is about 350 feet, and its height is variously given as 210 and 215 feet. The entrance is on the north side, about thirteen feet above the ground, and a descending corridor about 104 feet long, passing through an ante-chamber, having a series of three granite doors, leads into one chamber about 40 feet long, and a second chamber about 44 long. In this last chamber is a shaft which leads down to the granite-lined chamber about twenty feet below, in which were found the sarcophagus and wooden coffin of Mycerinus, and the remains of a human body. It is thought that, in spite of the body of Mycerinus being buried in this pyramid, it was left unfinished at the death of this king, and that a succeeding ruler of

Egypt finished the pyramid and made a second chamber to hold his or her body. At a short distance to the east of this pyramid are the ruins of a temple which was probably used in connexion with the rites performed in honour of the dead king. In A.D. 1196 a deliberate and systematic attempt was made to destroy this pyramid by the command of the Muḥammadan ruler of Egypt.* The account of the character of Mycerinus and of his pyramid as given by Herodotus is as follows: "They said that after him, Mycerinus,† son of Cheops, reigned over Egypt; that the conduct of his father was displeasing to him; and that he opened the temples, and permitted the people, who were worn down to the last extremity, to return to their employments, and to sacrifices; and that he made the most just decisions of all their kings. On this account, of all the kings that ever reigned in Egypt, they praise him most, for he both judged well in other respects, and moreover, when any man complained of his decision, he used to make him some present out of his own treasury and pacify his anger. . . . . . . This king also left a pyramid much less than that of his father, being on each side twenty feet short of three plethra; it is quadrangular, and built half way up of Ethiopian stone. Some of the Grecians erroneously say that this pyramid is the work of the courtesan Rhodopis; but they evidently appear to me ignorant who Rhodopis was; for they would not else have attributed to her the building of such a pyramid, on which, so to speak, numberless thousands of talents were expended; besides, Rhodopis flourished in the reign of Amasis, and not at this time; for she was very many years later than those kings who left these pyramids." (Cary's translation.)

In one of the three small pyramids near that of Mycerinus the name of this king is painted on the ceiling.

* See p. 285.

† Book ii. 129, 134.

THE SPHINX.

The age of the **Sphinx** is unknown, and few of the facts connected with its history have come down to these days. Some years ago it was generally believed to have been made during the rule of the kings of the Middle Empire over Egypt, but when the stele which recorded the repairs made in the temple of the sphinx by Thothmes IV., B.C. 1533, came to light, it became certain that it was the work of one of the kings of the Ancient Empire. The stele records that one day during an after-dinner sleep, Harmachis appeared to Thothmes IV., and promised to bestow upon him the crown of Egypt if he would dig his image, *i.e.*, the Sphinx, out of the sand. At the end of the inscription part of the name of Khā-f-Rā or Chephren appears, and hence some have thought that this king was the maker of the Sphinx; as the statue of Chephren was subsequently found in the temple close by, this theory was generally adopted. An inscription found by Mariette near one of the pyramids to the east of the pyramid of Cheops shows that the Sphinx existed in the time of Khufu or Cheops. The Egyptians called the Sphinx *ḥu*, and he represented the god Harmachis, *i.e.*, *Ḥeru-em-khut*, "Horus in the horizon," or the rising sun, the conqueror of darkness, the god of the morning. On the tablet erected by Thothmes IV., Harmachis says that he gave life and dominion to Thothmes III., and he promises to give the same good gifts to his successor Thothmes IV. The discovery of the steps which led up to the Sphinx, a smaller Sphinx, and an open temple, etc., was made by Caviglia, who first excavated this monument; within the last few years very extensive excavations have been made round it by the Egyptian Government, and several hitherto unseen parts of it have been brought to view. The Sphinx is hewn out of the living rock, but pieces of stone have been added where necessary; the body is about 150 feet long, the paws are 50 feet long, the head is 30 feet long, the face is 14 feet wide, and from the top of the head to the base of the monument the distance is about 70 feet. Originally there probably were ornaments on the head, the whole of which was covered with a limestone covering, and the face was coloured red; of these decorations scarcely any traces now remain, though they were visible towards the end of the last century. The condition in which the monument now appears is due to the savage destruction of its features by the Muḥammadan rulers of Egypt, some of whom caused it to be used for a target. Around this imposing relic of antiquity, whose origin is wrapped in mystery, a number of legends and superstitions have clustered in all ages; but Egyptology has shown I. that it was a colossal image of Rā-Harmachis, and therefore of his human representative upon earth, the king of Egypt who had it hewn, and II. that it was in existence in the time of, and was probably repaired by, Cheops and Chephren, who lived about three thousand seven hundred years before Christ.

The Temple of the Sphinx.

A little to the south-east of the Sphinx stands the large granite and limestone temple excavated by M. Mariette in 1853; statues of Chephren (now at Gîzeh) were found at the bottom of a well or pit in one of its chambers, and hence it has been generally supposed that he was the builder of it. It is a good specimen of the solid simple buildings which the Egyptians built during the Ancient Empire. In one chamber, and at the end of the passage leading from it, are hewn in the wall niches which were probably intended to hold mummies.

The Tomb of Numbers.

This tomb was made for Khā-f-Rā-ānkh, a "royal relative" and priest of Chephren (Khā-f-Rā), the builder of the second pyramid. It is called the "tomb of numbers" because the numbers of the cattle possessed by Khā-f-Rā-ānkh are written upon its walls.

CAMPBELL'S TOMB.

This tomb, named after the British Consul-General of Egypt at that time, was excavated by Howard Vyse in 1837; it is not older than the XXVIth dynasty. The shaft is about 55 feet deep; at the bottom of it is a small chamber in which were found three sarcophagi in niches.

The pyramids of Gîzeh are surrounded by a large number of tombs of high officials and others connected with the services carried on in honour of the kings who built the pyramids. Some few of them are of considerable interest, and as they are perishing little by little, it is advisable to see as many of the best specimens as possible.

THE PYRAMIDS OF ABU ROÂSH.

These pyramids lie about six miles north of the Pyramids of Gîzeh, and are thought to be older than they. Nothing remains of one except five or six courses of stone, which show that the length of each side at the base was about 350 feet, and a passage about 160 feet long leading down to a subterranean chamber about 43 feet long. A pile of stones close by marks the site of another pyramid; the others have disappeared. Of the age of these pyramids nothing certain is known. The remains of a causeway about a mile long leading to them are still visible.

THE PYRAMIDS OF ABUṢÎR.

These pyramids, originally fourteen in number, were built by kings of the Vth dynasty, but only four of them are now standing, probably because of the poorness of the workmanship and the careless way in which they were put together. The most northerly pyramid was built by

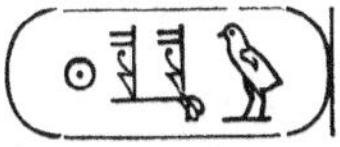 Saḥu-Rā, the second king of the Vth dynasty, B.C. 3533; its actual height is about 120 feet, and the length of each side at the base about 220 feet. The blocks of stone in the sepulchral chamber are exceptionally large. Saḥu-Rā made war in the peninsula of Sinai, he founded a town near Esneh, and he built a temple to Sekhet at Memphis.

The pyramid to the south of that of Saḥu-Rā was built by  "*Usr-en-Rā*, *son of the Sun*, *An*." This king, like Saḥu-Rā, also made war in Sinai. The largest of these three pyramids is now about 165 feet high and 330 feet square; the name of its builder is unknown. Abuṣir is the Busiris of Pliny.

BEDRASHÊN, MEMPHIS, AND ṢAḲḲÂRA.

The ruins of **Memphis** and the antiquities at Ṣaḳḳâra are usually reached by steamer or train from Cairo to Bedrashên. Leaving the river or station the village of Bedrashên is soon reached, and a short ride next brings the traveller to the village of Mît-Rahîneh. On the ground lying for some distance round about these two villages once stood the city of Memphis, though there is comparatively little left to show its limits. According to Herodotus (ii., 99), "Menes, who first ruled over Egypt, in the first place protected Memphis by a mound; for the whole river formerly ran close to the sandy mountain on the side of Libya; but Menes, beginning about a hundred stades above Memphis, filled in the elbow towards the south, dried up the old channel, and conducted the river into a canal, so as to make it flow between the mountains: this bend of the Nile, which flows excluded from *its ancient course*, is still carefully upheld by the Persians, being made secure every year; for if the river should break through and overflow in this part, there would be danger lest all Memphis should be flooded. When the part cut off had been made firm land by this Menes, who was first king, he in the first place built on it the city that is now called Memphis; for Memphis is situate in the narrow part of Egypt; and outside of it he excavated a lake from the river towards the north and the west; for the Nile itself bounds it towards the east. In the next place, *they relate* that he built in it the temple of Vulcan, which is vast and well worthy of mention." (Cary's translation.)

Whether Menes built the town or not, it is quite certain that the city of Memphis was of most ancient foundation.

The reason why the kings of Egypt established their capital there is obvious. From the peoples that lived on the western bank of the river they had little to fear, but on the eastern side they were always subject to invasions of the peoples who lived in Mesopotamia, Syria, and Arabia; with their capital on the western bank, and the broad Nile as a barrier on the east of it, they were comparatively safe. Added to this, its situation at the beginning of the Delta enabled it to participate easily of the good things of that rich country. The tract of land upon which Memphis stood was also fertile and well wooded. Diodorus speaks of its green meadows, intersected with canals, and of their pavement of lotus flowers; Pliny talks of trees there of such girth that three men with extended arms could not span them; Martial praises the roses brought from thence to Rome; and its wine was celebrated in lands remote from it. The site chosen was excellent, for in addition to its natural advantages it was not far from the sea-coast of the Delta, and holding as it were a middle position in Egypt, its kings were able to hold and rule the country from Philæ on the south to the Mediterranean on the north. In the inscriptions it is called  *Men-nefer*,* "the beautiful dwelling,"  *Ḥet-Ptaḥ-ka*, "the temple of the double of Ptaḥ," and  *Àneb-ḥet'*, "the white-walled city." The last name calls to mind the "White Castle" spoken of by classical writers. Tetà, son of Menes, built his palace there, and Ka-Kau 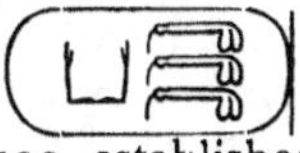, the second king of the IInd dynasty, B.C. 4100, established the worship of Apis there. During the rule of the IIIrd,

* The name Memphis is a corruption of Men-nefer; the city is called by the Arabs *Menûf*, and by the Copts Memfi, Menfi (ⲙⲉⲙϥⲓ, ⲙⲉⲛϥⲓ).

IVth, and VIth dynasties, the kings of which sprang from Memphis, that city reached a height of splendour which was probably never excelled. The most celebrated building there was the temple of Ptaḥ, which was beautified and adorned by a number of kings, the last of whom reigned during the XXVIth dynasty. The Hyksos ravaged, but did not destroy, the city; under the rule of the Theban kings, who expelled the Hyksos, the city flourished for a time, although Thebes became the new capital. When Rameses II. returned from his wars in the east, he set up a statue of himself in front of the temple of Ptaḥ there; Piānkhi the Ethiopian besieged it; the Assyrian kings Esarhaddon and Assurbanipal captured it; Cambyses the Persian, having wrought great damage there, killed the magistrates of the city and the priests of the temple of Apis, and smote the Apis bull so that he died;* he established a Persian garrison there. After the founding of Alexandria, Memphis lost

* "When Cambyses arrived at Memphis, Apis, whom the Greeks call Epaphus, appeared to the Egyptians; and when this manifestation ook place, the Egyptians immediately put on their richest apparel, and kept festive holiday. Cambyses seeing them thus occupied, and concluding that they made their rejoicings on account of his ill success, summoned the magistrates to Memphis; and when they came into his presence, he asked, 'why the Egyptians had done nothing of the kind when he was at Memphis before, but did so now, when he had returned with the loss of a great part of his army.' They answered, that their god appeared to them, who was accustomed to manifest himself at distant intervals, and that when he did appear, then all the Egyptians were used to rejoice and keep a feast. Cambyses, having heard this, said they lied, and as liars he put them to death. Having slain them, he next summoned the priests into his presence; and when the priests gave the same account, he said, that he would find out whether a god so tractable had come among the Egyptians; and having said this, he commanded the priests to bring Apis to him; they therefore went away to fetch him. This Apis, or Epaphus, is the calf of a cow incapable of conceiving another offspring; and the Egyptians say, that lightning descends upon the cow from heaven, and that from thence it brings

whatever glory it then possessed, and became merely the chief provincial city of Egypt. During the reign of Theodosius, a savage attack, the result of his edict, was made upon its temples and buildings by the Christians, and a few hundred years later the Muḥammadans carried the stones, which once formed them, across the river to serve as building materials for their houses and mosques. The circuit of the ancient city, according to Diodorus, was 150 stadia, or about thirteen miles.

The Colossal Statue of Rameses II.

This magnificent statue was discovered by Messrs. Caviglia and Sloane in 1820, and was presented by them to the British Museum. On account of its weight and the lack of public interest in such matters, it lay near the road leading from Bedrashên to Mît Rahîneh, and little by little became nearly covered with the annual deposit of Nile mud; during the inundation the greater part of it was covered by the waters of the Nile. During the winter of 1886–87 Sir Frederick Stephenson collected a sum of money in Cairo for the purpose of lifting it out of the hollow in which it

forth Apis. This calf, which is called Apis, has the following marks: it is black, and has a square spot of white on the forehead; and on the back the figure of an eagle; and in the tail double hairs; and on the tongue a beetle. When the priests brought Apis, Cambyses, like one almost out of his senses, drew his dagger, meaning to strike the belly of Apis, but hit the thigh; then falling into a fit of laughter, he said to the priests, 'Ye blockheads, are there such gods as these, consisting of blood and flesh, and sensible to steel? This, truly, is a god worthy of the Egyptians. But you shall not mock me with impunity.' Having spoken thus, he commanded those whose business it was, to scourge the priests, and to kill all the Egyptians whom they should find feasting. . . . But Apis, being wounded in the thigh, lay and languished in the temple; and at length, when he had died of the wound, the priests buried him without the knowledge of Cambyses."—Herodotus, III, 27–29. (Cary's translation.)

lay, and the difficult engineering part of the task was ably accomplished by Colonel Arthur Bagnold, R.E. This statue is made of a fine hard limestone, and measures about forty-two feet in height; it is probably one of the statues which stood in front of the temple of Ptaḥ, mentioned by Herodotus and Diodorus. The prenomen of Rameses II. 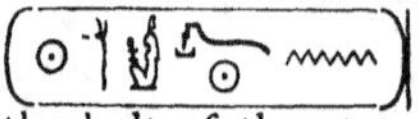 Rā-usr-maāt-setep-en-Rā, is inscribed on the belt of the statue, and on the end of the roll which the king carries in his hand are the words "Rameses, beloved of Åmen." By the side of the king are figures of a daughter and son of Rameses. The famous temple of Ptaḥ founded by Menes was situated to the south of the statue.

Ṣaḳḳâra.

The name Ṣaḳḳâra is probably derived from the name of the Egyptian god Seker , who was connected with the resurrection of the dead. The tract of land at Ṣaḳḳâra which formed the great burial ground of the ancient Egyptians of all periods, is about four and a half miles long and one mile wide; the most important antiquities there are: I. the Step Pyramid; II. the Pyramids of Unås, Tetå, and Pepi, kings of the Vth and VIth dynasties; III. the Serapeum; and IV. the Tomb of Thi. Admirers of M. Mariette will be interested to see the house in which this distinguished *savant* lived.

I. The **Step Pyramid** is generally thought to have been built by the fifth king of the IIIrd dynasty (called , Tcheser in the Tablet of Abydos), who is said to have built a pyramid at Kochome (*i.e.*, Ka-Kam) near Ṣaḳḳâra. Though the date of this pyramid is not known accurately, it is probably right to assume that it is older than the pyramids of Gîzeh. The door which led into the pyramid was inscribed with the name of a king called Rā-nub, and M. Mariette found the same name on one of the stelæ in the Serapeum. The steps of the pyramid are six in number, and are about 38, 36, 34½, 32, 31 and 29½ feet in height; the width of each step is from six to seven feet. The lengths of the sides at the base are: north and south 352 feet, east and west 396 feet, and the actual height is 197 feet. In shape this pyramid is oblong, and its sides do not exactly face the cardinal points. The arrangement of the chambers inside this pyramid is quite peculiar to itself.

II. The **Pyramid of Unȧs** , called in Egyptian Nefer-ȧs-u, lies to the south-east of the Step Pyramid, and was reopened and cleared out in 1881 by M. Maspero, at the expense of Messrs. Thomas Cook and Son. Its original height was about 62 feet, and the length of its sides at the base 220 feet. Owing to the broken blocks and sand which lie round about it, Vyse was unable to give exact measurements. Several attempts had been made to break into it, and one of the Arabs who took part in one of these attempts, "Aḥmed the Carpenter," seems to have left his name inside one of the chambers in red ink. It is probable that he is the same man who opened the Great Pyramid at Gîzeh, A.D. 820. A black basalt sarcophagus, from which the cover had been dragged off, and an arm, a shin bone, some ribs and fragments of the skull from the mummy of Unȧs, were found in the sarcophagus chamber. The walls of the two largest chambers and two of the corridors are inscribed with ritual texts and prayers of a very interesting character. Unȧs, the last king of the Vth dynasty, reigned about thirty years. The Maṣṭabat el-Far'ûn was thought by Mariette to be the tomb of Unȧs, but other scholars thought that the 'blunted pyramid' at Dahshûr was his tomb, because his name was written upon the top of it.

The **Pyramid of Tetȧ** , called in Egyptian

Ṭeṭ-åsu, lies to the north-east of the Step Pyramid, and was opened in 1881. The Arabs call it the "Prison Pyramid," because local tradition says that it is built near the ruins of the prison where Joseph the patriarch was confined. Its actual height is about 59 feet; the length of each side at the base is 210 feet, and the platform at the top is about 50 feet. The arrangement of the chambers and passages and the plan of construction followed is almost identical with that of the pyramid of Unås. This pyramid was broken into in ancient days, and two of the walls of the sarcophagus chamber have literally been smashed to pieces by the hammer blows of those who expected to find treasure inside them. The inscriptions, painted in green upon the walls, have the same subject matter as those inscribed upon the walls of the chambers of the pyramid of Unås. According to Manetho, Tetå, the first king of the VIth dynasty, reigned about fifty years, and was murdered by one of his guards. The Pyramids of Tcheser, Unås, and Tetå belong to the Northern Group at Ṣaḳḳâra.

The **Pyramid of Pepi I.** or  'Rā-meri, son of the Sun, Pepi,' lies to the south-west of the Step Pyramid, and forms one of the central group of pyramids at Ṣaḳḳâra, where it is called the Pyramid of Shêkh Abu Manṣûr; it was opened in 1880. Its actual height is about 40 feet, and the length of the sides at the base is about 250 feet; the arrangement of the chambers, etc., inside is the same as in the pyramids of Unås and Tetå, but the ornamentation is slightly different. It is the worst preserved of these pyramids, and has suffered most at the hands of the spoilers, probably because having been constructed with stones which were taken from tombs ancient already in those days, instead of stones fresh from the quarry, it was more easily injured. The granite sarcophagus was broken to take out the mummy, fragments of which were found lying about on the ground; the cover too, smashed in pieces, lay on the ground close by. A small rose granite box, containing alabaster jars, was also found in the sarcophagus chamber. The inscriptions are, like those inscribed on the walls of the pyramids of Unȧs and Tetȧ, of a religious nature; some scholars see in them evidence that the pyramid was usurped by another Pepi, who lived at a much later period than the VIth dynasty. The pyramid of Pepi I., the third king of the VIth dynasty, who reigned, according to Manetho, fifty-three years, was called in Egyptian by the same name as Memphis, *i.e.*, Men-nefer, and numerous priests were attached to its service. Pepi's kingdom embraced all Egypt, and he waged war against the inhabitants of the peninsula of Sinai. He is said to have set up an obelisk at Heliopolis, and to have laid the foundation of the temple at Denderah. His success as a conqueror was due in a great measure to the splendid abilities of one of his chief officers called Unȧ, who warred successfully against the various hereditary foes of Egypt on its southern and eastern borders.

III. The **Serapeum** or APIS MAUSOLEUM contained the vaults in which all the Apis bulls that lived at Memphis were buried. According to Herodotus, Apis "is the calf of a cow incapable of conceiving another offspring; and the Egyptians say that lightning descends upon the cow from heaven, and that from thence it brings forth Apis. This calf, which is called Apis, has the following marks: it is black, and has a square spot of white on the forehead, and on the back the figure of an eagle; and in the tail double hairs; and on the tongue a beetle." Above each tomb of an Apis bull was built a chapel, and it was the series of chapels which formed the Serapeum properly so called; it was surrounded by walls like the other Egyptian temples, and it had pylons to which an avenue of sphinxes led. This remarkable place was excavated in 1850 by M. Mariette, who having seen in various parts of Egypt sphinxes upon which were written the names of Osiris–Apis, or Serapis, concluded that they must have come from the Serapeum or temple of Serapis spoken of by Strabo. Happening, by chance, to discover one day at Ṣaḳḳâra a sphinx having the same characteristics, he made up his mind that he had lighted upon the remains of the long sought-for building. The excavations which he immediately undertook, brought to light the Avenue of Sphinxes, eleven statues of Greek philosophers, and the vaults in which the Apis bulls were buried. These vaults are of three kinds, and show that the Apis bulls were buried in different ways at different periods: the oldest Apis sarcophagus laid here belongs to the reign of Amenophis III., about B.C. 1500. The parts of the Apis Mausoleum in which the Apis bulls were buried from the XVIIIth to the XXVIth dynasty are not visible ; but the new gallery, which contains sixty-four vaults, the oldest of which dates from the reign of Psammetichus I., and the most modern from the time of the Ptolemies, can be seen on application to the guardian of the tombs. The vaults are excavated on each side of the gallery, and each was intended to receive a granite sarcophagus. The names of Amāsis II., Cambyses, and Khabbesha are found upon three of the sarcophagi, but most of them are uninscribed. Twenty-four granite sarcophagi still remain in position, and they each measure about 13 × 8 × 11 feet. The discovery of these tombs was of the greatest importance historically, for on the walls were found thousands of dated stelæ which gave accurate chronological data for the history of Egypt. These votive tablets mention the years, months, and days of the reign of the king in which the Apis bulls, in whose honour the tablets were set up, were born and buried. The Apis tombs had been rifled in ancient times, and only two of them contained any relics when M. Mariette opened them out.

IV. The **Tomb of Thi** lies to the north-east of the Apis Mausoleum, and was built during the Vth dynasty, about B.C. 3500. Thi 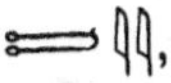, was a man who held the dignities of *smer*, royal councillor, superintendent of works, scribe of the court, confidant of the king, etc.; he held also priestly rank as prophet, and was attached to the service of the pyramids of Abuṣîr. He had sprung from a family of humble origin, but his abilities were so esteemed by one of the kings, whose faithful servant he was, that a princess called Nefer-ḥetep-s was given him to wife, and his children Thi and Tamut ranked as princes. Thi held several high offices under Kakaȧ  and User-en-Rā 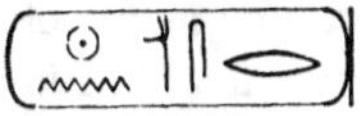 kings of the Vth dynasty. The tomb or maṣṭaba of Thi is now nearly covered with sand, but in ancient days the whole building was above the level of the ground. The chambers of the tomb having been carefully cleared, it is possible to enter them and examine the most beautiful sculptures and paintings with which the walls are decorated. To describe these wonderful works of art adequately would require more space than can be given here; it must be sufficient to say that the scenes represent Thi superintending all the various operations connected with the management of his large agricultural estates and farmyard, together with illustrations of his hunting and fishing expeditions.

The **Necropolis** of Ṣaḳḳâra contains chiefly tombs of the Ancient Empire, that is to say, tombs that were built during the first eleven dynasties; many tombs of a later period are found there, but they are of less interest and importance, and in many cases small, but fine, ancient tombs have been destroyed to make them. As our knowledge of Egyptian architecture is derived principally from tombs and temples, a brief description of the most ancient tombs now known will not be out of place here; the following observations on them are based upon the excellent articles of M. Mariette in the *Revue Archéologique*, S. 2ième, t. xix. p. 8 ff. The tombs of the Ancient Empire found at Ṣaḳḳâra belong to two classes, in the commoner of which the naked body was buried about three feet deep in the sand. When the yellowish-white skeletons of such bodies are found to-day, neither fragments of linen nor pieces of coffins are visible; occasionally one is found laid within four walls roughly built of yellow bricks made of sand, lime, and small stones. A vaulted brick roof covers the space between the walls; it is hardly necessary to say that such tombs represent the last resting places of the poor, and that nothing of any value is ever found inside them. The tombs of the better sort are carefully built, and were made for the wealthy and the great; such a tomb is usually called by the Arabs *maṣṭăba** (the Arabic word for 'bench'), because its length in proportion to its height is great, and reminded them of the long, low seat common in Oriental houses, and familiar to them. The maṣṭaba is a heavy, massive building, of rectangular shape, the four sides of which are four walls symmetrically inclined towards their common centre. Each course of stones, formed by blocks laid upon each other, is carried a little behind the other. The largest maṣṭaba measures about 170 feet long by 86 feet wide, and the smallest about 26 feet by 20 feet: they vary in height from 13 to 30 feet. The ground on which the maṣṭabas at Ṣaḳḳâra are built is composed of rock covered with sand to the depth of a few feet; their foundations are always on the rock. Near the pyramids of Gîzeh they are arranged in a symmetrical manner; they are oriented astronomically to the true north, and their larger axes are always towards the north. Though they have, at first sight, the appearance of unfinished pyramids, still they have nothing in common with pyramids except their orientation towards the true north. Maṣṭăbas

* Pronounced *maṣṭăba*, Arabic مَصْطَبَة, compare Gr. στιβάς.

are built of two kinds of stone and of bricks, and they are usually entered on the eastern side; their tops are quite flat. The interior of a maṣṭaba may be divided into three parts; the chamber, the *sirdâb*,* or place of retreat, and the pit. The entrance is made through a door in the middle of the eastern or northern side, and though the interior may be divided into many chambers, it is usual only to find one. The walls of the interior are sometimes sculptured, and in the lower part of the chamber, usually facing the east, is a stele; the stele alone may be inscribed and the walls unsculptured, but no case is known where the walls are sculptured and the stele blank. A table of offerings is often found on the ground at the foot of the stele. A little distance from the chamber, built into the thickness of the walls, more often to the south than the north, is a high, narrow place of retreat or habitation, called by the Arabs a *sirdâb*. This place was walled up, and the only communication between it and the chamber was by means of a narrow hole sufficiently large to admit of the entrance of the hand. One or more statues of the dead man buried in the maṣṭaba were shut in here, and the small passage is said to have been made for the escape of the fumes of incense which was burnt in the chamber. The pit was a square shaft varying in depth from 40 to 80 feet, sunk usually in the middle of the larger axis of the maṣṭaba, rather nearer the north than the south. There was neither ladder nor staircase, either outside or inside, leading to the funereal chamber at the bottom of the pit, hence the coffin and the mummy when once there were inaccessible. This pit was sunk through the maṣṭaba into the rock beneath. At the bottom of the pit, on the south side, is an opening into a passage, about four feet high, which leads obliquely to the south-east; soon after the passage increases in size in all

* A سِرْدَاب is, strictly speaking, a lofty, vaulted, subterranean chamber, with a large opening in the north side to admit air in the hot season.

directions, and becomes the sarcophagus chamber, which is thus exactly under the upper chamber. The sarcophagus, rectangular in shape, is usually made of limestone, and rests in a corner of the chamber; at Ṣaḳḳâra they are found uninscribed. When the mummy had been laid in the sarcophagus, and the other arrangements completed, the end of the passage near the shaft leading to the sarcophagus chamber was walled up, the shaft was filled with stones, earth, and sand, and the friends of the deceased might reasonably hope that he would rest there for ever. When M. Mariette found a maṣṭaba without inscriptions he rarely excavated it entirely. He found three belonging to one of the first three dynasties; forty-three of the IVth dynasty; sixty-one of the Vth dynasty; twenty-three of the VIth dynasty; and nine of doubtful date. The Egyptians called the tomb "the house of eternity," 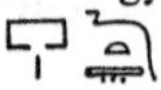, *per t'etta.*

Mariette's House.—This house was the headquarters of M. Mariette and his staff when employed in making excavations in the Necropolis of Ṣaḳḳâra. It is not easy to properly estimate the value to science of the work of this distinguished man. It is true that fortune gave him the opportunity of excavating some of the most magnificent of the buildings of the Pharaohs of all periods, and of hundreds of ancient towns; nevertheless it is equally true that his energy and marvellous power of work enabled him to use to the fullest extent the means for advancing the science of Egyptology which had been put in his hands. It is to be hoped that his house will be preserved on its present site as a remembrance of a great man who did a great work.

The TOMB OF PTAḤ-ḤETEP, a priest who lived during the Vth dynasty, is a short distance from Mariette's house, and well worthy of more than one visit.

The Pyramids of Dahshûr.

These pyramids, four of stone and two of brick, are 3½ miles from the Maṣṭabat el-Far'ûn, once thought to be the Pyramid of Unas. The largest stone pyramid is about 326 feet high, and the length of each side at the base is about 700 feet; beneath it are three subterranean chambers. The second stone pyramid is about 321 feet high, and the length of its sides at the base is 620 feet; it is usually called the "Blunted Pyramid," because the lowest parts of its sides are built at one angle, and the completing parts at another. The larger of the two brick pyramids is about 90 feet high, and the length of the sides at the base is about 350 feet; the smaller is about 156 feet high, and the length of its sides at the base is about 343 feet. The brick pyramids have recently been excavated by M. de Morgan.

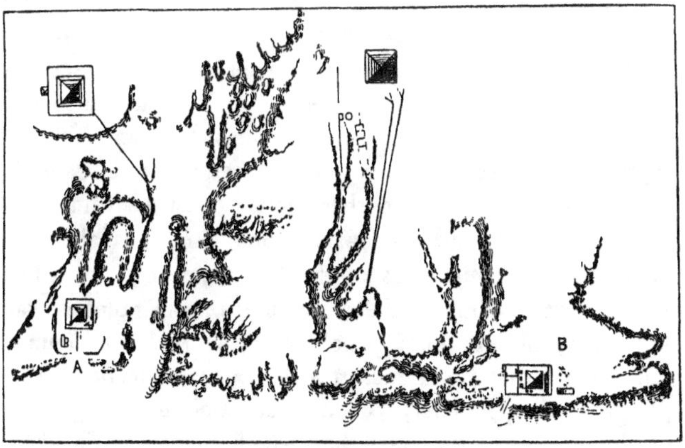

The Necropolis at Dahshûr.
A The Northern Pyramid, built of bricks.
B The Southern Pyramid, built of bricks.

The northern pyramid is built of bricks laid without mortar, in place of which sand is used, and an examination of them shows that they belong to the period of the XIIth dynasty. Soon after the work of clearing had been begun, a stone bearing the cartouche of Usertsen III.  was found, and thus a tolerably exact date was ascertained; on the 26th of February, 1894, the entrance to a pit was found, and in the east corner there appeared an opening which led through a gallery and sepulchral chamber to several tombs. In one chamber were the fragments of a sarcophagus and statue of Menthu-nesu, and in another was the sarcophagus of Nefert-ḥent; it was quite clear that these tombs had been wrecked in ancient days, and therefore to the pit by which they were reached M. de Morgan gave the name, "Pit of the spoilers." Along the principal gallery were four tombs, and in the second of these a queen had been buried; on the lower stage eight sarcophagi were found, but only two were inscribed. Subsequently it was discovered that the burial place of a series of princesses had been found, and in consequence M. de Morgan called the place "Gallery of Princesses." In one of the tombs (No. 3) a granite chest containing four uninscribed alabaster Canopic jars was found, and in another similar chest a worm-eaten wooden box, containing four Canopic jars, was also discovered. The four sides of the box were inscribed, but the jars were plain. While the ground of the galleries was being carefully examined, a hollow in the rock was found, and a few blows of the pick revealed a magnificent find of gold and silver jewellery lying in a heap among the fragments of the worm-eaten wooden box which held it. The box was about eleven inches long, and had been inlaid with silver hieroghyphics which formed the name of the princess Hathor-Sat, for whom the ornaments had been made. It would seem that special care had been taken by the friends of the deceased to conceal her jewellery, and thus the ancient spoilers of the tomb had overlooked it. Among the objects found of special interest are the following :—

1. A gold pectoral, in the form of a shrine , inlaid with carnelian, emeralds, and lapis-lazuli. In the centre is the cartouche of Usertsen II. *neteru ḥetep Khā-kheper-Rā*, and on each side is the hawk of Horus, wearing the double crown, and a disk with pendent uræus and "life" . The inlaying and carving are magnificent specimens of the goldsmith's work.
2. Two gold clasps of bracelets, each containing a *ṭeṭ* inlaid with carnelian, emeralds, and lapis-lazuli; the bracelets were set with pearls.
3. Gold collar-clasp, inlaid with carnelian, emeralds, and lapis-lazuli, formed of two lotus flowers, the stems of which intertwine and form a knot, and a head of Hathor.
4. Gold clasp, inlaid as before, formed of the hieroglyphics
5. Gold shells to form necklaces.
6. Six lions .
7. Gold and lapis-lazuli cylindrical pendant, with ring.
8. Amethyst scarab inscribed with the prenomen of Usertsen III. *Khā-kau-Rā*, and line ornaments.
9. White glazed *faïence* scarab inscribed, "Hathor-Sat, royal daughter, lady of reverence"

10. Amethyst scarab inscribed with a double scene of the two Niles tying a cord around the emblem of "unity" .

All the above objects belonged to the princess Hathor-Sat; the following belonged to the princess Merit, and they were placed in a box and hidden in the same manner as those of Hathor-Sat.

1. A gold pectoral in the form of a shrine, inlaid with carnelian, emeralds, and lapis-lazuli; the roof is supported by lotus columns, from each of which springs a lotus flower. In the centre is the prenomen of Usertsen  III., supported upon the right fore-paws of two hawk-headed sphinxes which have on their heads crowns of feathers and horns . Each right fore-paw rests upon the head of a prostrate foe of red coloured skin, and each right hind-paw rests upon the stomach of a negro, thus typifying the sovereignty of the king over the light and dark races. Above the cartouche and sphinxes is a hawk with outstretched wings, holding , the emblem of the sun's orbit and eternity, in each claw. It would be impossible to overpraise the beauty of this wonderful piece of work and the harmonious blending of the colours.

2. Gold pectoral, in the form of a shrine, inlaid as before. In the centre is the inscription

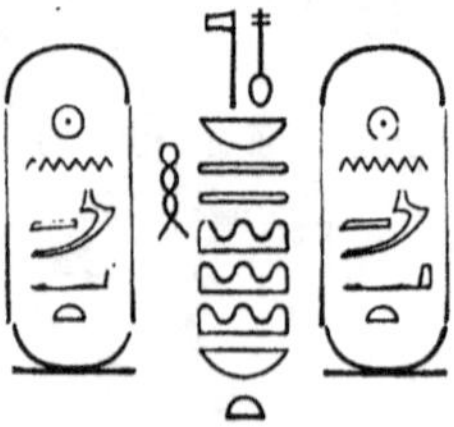

i.e., "Beautiful god, the lord of the North and South, the smiter of all eastern countries, Maāt-en-Rā (Åmen-em-ḥāt III.).[1]

Immediately above this inscription is a vulture with outstretched wings, holding the emblems of "life" and "stability" 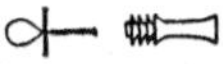 in each claw; she is called 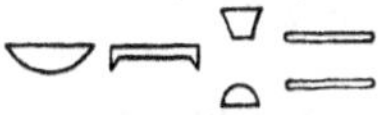 "lady of heaven, and mistress of the North and South." On each side of the inscription is a figure of the king, who stands about to smite with a club a kneeling foe, whose hair he grasps with his right hand. The hieroglyphics read  "the smiter of the Sati (Asiatics) and of the Menti (Africans)." Behind the king is  "life" with human arms and hands moving a fan to waft the breath of "life" to the king. The Menti are armed with daggers and boomerangs.

3. Golden hawk, inlaid, with outstretched wings; in each claw he holds .
4. Necklace formed of ten large gold shells.
5. Necklace formed of eight large gold ornaments, each of which is composed of four lions' heads.
6. Necklace of ninety-eight round and forty-three long pearls.
7. Necklace of amethyst, with spherical gold pendants inlaid with carnelian, emeralds, and lapis-lazuli.
8. Necklace of 252 beautiful amethyst beads.
9. Gold clasp of a bracelet, inlaid as before; the hieroglyphics read 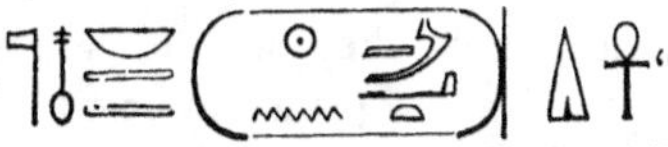 "Beautiful god, the lord of the North and South, Maāt-en-Rā (Ȧmenemḥāt III.), giver of life."
10. Four gold lions, and two pendants in the form of a lion's claws.
11. Two silver mirrors.

12. Gold clasps, inlaid as before, made in the form of the hieroglyphics  *i.e.*, "peace and gladness of heart."

13. Scarab of gold, carnelian, emerald, and lapis-lazuli, forming the bezel of a ring.

14. Scarab inscribed  set in gold.

15. Lapis-lazuli scarab inscribed "Royal daughter, Merret," 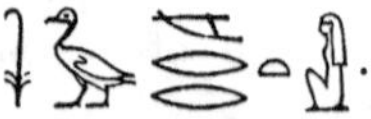.

16. Lapis-lazuli scarab, set in gold, inscribed with the prenomen and titles of Åmenemḥāt III.   "Beautiful god, the lord, creator of things, Maāt-en-Rā, giver of life like the Sun for ever."

17. Yellow glazed *faïence* scarab inscribed with the name of the queen Khnem-nefer-ḥet' 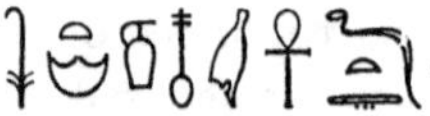.

18. Gold cylindrical stibium tube.

The wooden boats and sledge which were discovered outside the wall enclosing the pyramid are worthy of note, and are of considerable interest.

The southern brick pyramid of Dahshûr is on a lower level than the northern, and much of its upper portion has been removed by the *fellaḥîn*, who treated it as a quarry for the bricks with which they built their houses. It is, however, in a better state of preservation than its fellow, and is still an imposing object in the Egyptian landscape. M. de Morgan's estimate of the length of each side is 125 feet; this pyramid is, like the northern, built of unburnt bricks, and it was surrounded by a wall of unbaked bricks, which enclosed the ground wherein the members of the royal family were buried. While excavating in this spot, M. de

Morgan found some fragments of a base of a statue inscribed with the prenomen of Åmen-em-ḥāt III. 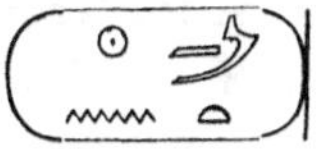, and judging from this fact and from the general appearance of the site, he would ascribe this necropolis to the period of the XIIth dynasty. About 20 feet from the enclosing wall, at the north-east corner of the pyramid, two pits were found, and the second of these proved to be the entrance to a tomb. An inclined brick wall led to a small vaulted door, and in the ruins here the workmen found a small beautifully worked gilded wooden statue, on the base of which was inscribed, "Horus, the son of the Sun, of his body, giver of life," . Near the statue were two Canopic jars of alabaster, inscribed with the prenomen of a new king  Āu-åb-Rā, who it seems was co-regent with Åmenemḥāt IV.; the nomen of this king was  or 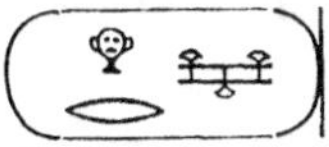 *Ḥeru.* In the tomb of this king were found :—

1. A magnificent wooden shrine for the statue of the *ka*  of king Āu-åb-Kā or Ḥeru.
2. Statue in wood of the *ka* 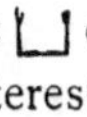 of king Āu-åb-Rā, a unique object of the highest interest ; the execution is simply wonderful. It is worthy of note that there was nothing on this figure to indicate the royal rank of him for whom it was made.
3. Rectangular alabaster stele with an inscription of king Āu-åb-Rā in fourteen lines ; the hieroglyphics are painted blue.
4. Rectangular alabaster stele inscribed with a prayer for funeral offerings for the same king.

5. Alabaster altar inscribed with four lines of hieroglyphics.
6. Two alabaster libation vases inscribed.
7. Small wooden statue of the *ka* of the king, covered with gold leaf; the eyes are of quartz set in silver.
8. Box for holding the sceptres and weapons of the king.

In the coffin the wrecked mummy of the king was found.

On the 15th and 16th February, 1895, M. de Morgan succeeded in bringing to light, in the necropolis of Dahshûr, a further "find" of jewellery. These beautiful and interesting objects were found in the tombs of the princesses Ita and Khnemit, which are situated to the west of the ruined pyramid of Åmenemḥāt II. By good fortune they had been overlooked by the plunderers of tombs in ancient days, and so both the tombs and the coffins inside them remained in the state in which they had been left by the friends of the deceased more than four thousand years ago. Among the objects found were the following:—

1. Bronze dagger, set in a gold handle inlaid with carnelian, lapis-lazuli, and emerald.
2. Pieces of gold and lapis-lazuli from the sheath of the above.
3. Two golden bracelets.
4. Two silver plaques from a necklace.
5. Two gold clasps in the form of 𓊽, inlaid with carnelian, lapis-lazuli, and emerald.
6. A carnelian hawk.
7. Two golden heads of hawks, inlaid with carnelian, etc.
8. One hundred and three gold objects in the form of 𓋹𓊽𓌀, inlaid with carnelian, etc.
9. One hundred and fourteen gold objects in the form of 𓍶 and , inlaid with carnelian, etc.

10. A large number of gold, carnelian, lapis-lazuli, and emerald beads.
11. Two golden crowns inlaid with carnelian, etc.
12. Twenty-four gold amulets, inlaid with carnelian, etc. in the form of the hieroglyphics  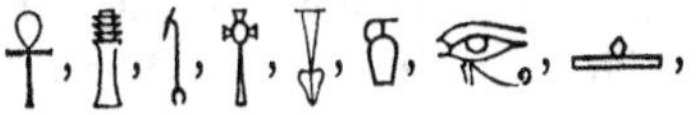, etc.

The Quarries of Ma'ṣara and Ṭurra.

These quarries have supplied excellent stone for building purposes for six thousand years at least. During the Ancient Empire the architects of the pyramids made their quarrymen tunnel into the mountains for hundreds of yards until they found a bed of stone suitable for their work, and traces of their excavations are plainly visible to-day. The Egyptians called the Ṭurra quarry  Re-āu, or Ta-re-āu, from which the Arabic name Ṭurra is probably derived. An inscription in one of the chambers tells us that during the reign of Amenophis III. a new part of the quarry was opened. Unȧ, an officer who lived in the reign of Pepi I., was sent to Ṭurra by this king to bring back a white limestone sarcophagus with its cover, libation stone, etc., etc.

The Pyramid of Mêdûm.

This pyramid, called by the Arabs *El-Haram el-Kaddab*, or "the False Pyramid," is probably so named because it is unlike any of the other pyramids known to them; it was probably built by Seneferu , the first king of the IVth dynasty, for the name of this king is found at various places in and about it. The pyramid is about 115 feet high, and consists of three stages: the first is 70, the second 20, and the third about 25 feet high. The stone for this building was brought from the Moḳaṭṭam hills, but it was never finished; as in all other pyramids, the entrance is on the north side. When opened in modern times the sarcophagus chamber was found empty, and it would seem that this pyramid had been entered and rifled in ancient days.* On the north of this pyramid are a number of maṣṭăbas in which 'royal relatives' of Seneferu are buried; the most interesting of these are those of Nefermat, one of his feudal chiefs ( erpā ḥā), and of Atet his widow. The sculptures and general style of the work are similar to those found in the maṣṭăbas of Ṣaḳḳâra.

* The results of Mr. Petrie's diggings here are given in his *Medum*, London, 1892.

UPPER EGYPT.

CAIRO TO ASWÂN BY THE UPPER EGYPT RAILWAY.

The journey from Cairo to Luxor by train occupies a few minutes over 14 hours, the distance being about 420 miles; the journey from Luxor to Aswân occupies 10 hours, the distance being about 130 miles. The Nile is crossed at Nag' Ḥamâdî by an iron bridge 1,362 feet long. The ordinary gauge is used from Cairo to Luxor, and a narrower gauge from Luxor to Aswân; this necessitates a change of carriage at Luxor. The following are the stations passed:—

Distance in kilos. and metres from Cairo.	Name of Station.		Province.	Population.
13·331*	Gîzeh	الجيزه	Gîzeh	16,820
27·513	Ḥawâmdîyeh	الحوامديه	,,	1,995
32·180	Bedrashên	البدرشين	,,	5,884
41·330	Maz'ûna	مزغونه	,,	1,542
58·813	Al-'Ayâṭ	العياط	,,	94
64·546	Matânîyeh	المتانيه	,,	1,975
72·814	Kafr 'Ammar	كفر عمار	,,	1,669
83·134	Rikka	الرقه	,,	3,128
91·844	Al-Wasṭa†	الوسطى	Beni-Suwêf	1,644
101·440	Beni Ḥudêr	بنى حدير	,,	1,131

* The formula for converting kilometres into miles is $\left(\frac{K}{2} + \frac{K}{8}\right)$.

† The passenger for the Fayyûm changes carriages here.

Distance in kilos. and metres from Cairo.	Name of Station.		Province.	Population.
107·696	Ashmant	اشمنت	Beni-Suwêf	4,375
115·018	Bûsh	بوش	,,	9,724
123·668	Beni-Suwêf	بنى سويف	,,	15,297
135·504	Beni Mâlû Ṭansa	بنى مالو طنسا	,,	2,096
145·354	Bibâ	ببا	,,	101,340 (district)
159·436	Fashn	الفشن	Minyeh	8,935
168·408	Fant	الفنت	,,	3,281
179·874	Maghâgha	مغاغه	,,	3,542
187·840	Aba al-Waḳf	ابا الوقف	,,	140
197·596	Beni-Mazâr	بنى مزار	,,	5,180
207·855	Maṭâî	مطاى	,,	3,803
216·384	Ḳulûṣnah	قلوصنه	,,	4,263
221·916	Samâlûṭ	سمالوط	,,	6,786
232·014	Eṭsa	اطسا	,,	1,680
247·826	Minyâ (Minyeh)	المنيا	,,	20,404
258·850	Mansafîs	منسفيس	,,	2,770
267·802	Abu Ḳerḳâṣ	ابو قرقاص	,,	6,212
274·078	Atlîdam	اتليدم	Asyûṭ	4,954
287·134	Fâwrîḳa Al-Rôḍa	فاوريقه الروضه	,,	2,136
295·181	Malawî	ملوى	,,	15,471
305·124	Dêr Mawâs	دير مواس	,,	6,204
316·182	Dêrûṭ	ديروط	,,	1,624
330·042	Nazâlî Gânûb	نزالى جانوب	,,	2,450

Distance in kilos. and metres from Cairo.	Name of Station.		Province.	Population.
338·290	Beni Ḳurra	بنى قره	Asyûṭ	1,493
349·575	Manfalûṭ	منفلوط	,,	15,215
362·671	Beni Husên	بنى حسين	,,	2,434
378·080	Asyûṭ	اسيوط	,,	42,012
391·305	Muṭî'ah	المطيعه	,,	7,219
401·644	Abu Tîg	ابو تيج	,,	183
412·419	Ṣadfâ	صدفا	,,	3,841
421·079	Ṭemâ	طما	Girgeh	9,784
427·644	Mashṭâ	مشطا	,,	4,801
438·226	Ṭahṭâ	طهطا	,,	16,223
451·405	Marâghâ	المراغا	,,	2,999
460·930	Shandawîl	شندويل	,,	4,352
469·981	Sûhâg	سوهاج	,,	13,930
485·194	Menshâh	المنشاه	,,	10,451
494·884	Al-'Aṣṣîrât	العصيرات	,,	583
504·782	Girgâ (Girgeh)	جرجا	,,	17,271
513·793	Bardîs	برديس	,,	6,156
521·096	Balyanâ	البلينا	,,	7,232
529·172	Abu Shûshâ	ابو شوشه	,,	374
538·254	Abu Tisht	ابو تشت	,,	2,434
547·986	Farshûṭ	فرشوط	Ḳeneh	9,839
556·284	Nag' Ḥamâdî	نجع حمادى	,,	4,365
563·616	Ḍab'îh	الضبعيه	,,	3,122

Distance in kilos. and metres from Cairo.	Name of Station.		Province.	Population.
575·097	Fâw Ḳiblî	فاو قبلى	Ḳeneh	5,056
580·966	Dashnâ	دشنا	,,	1,217
588·255	Al-Samaṭâ	السمطا	,,	652
595·529	Awlâd 'Amrû	اولاد عمرو	,,	1,713
611·634	Ḳanâ (Ḳeneh)	قنا	,,	24,364
632·215	Ḳufṭ	قفط	,,	4,187
642·332	Ḳûṣ	قوص	,,	12,646
658·315	Khizâm	خزام	,,	2,689
673·305	A'-Uḳṣur (Luxor)	الاقصر	,,	7,018
From Luxor.				
20·798	Armant	ارمنت	,,	10,222
46·142	Aṣfûn al-Maṭâ'na	اصفون المطاعنه	,,	5,600
57·534	Asnâ (Esneh)	اسنا	,,	13,564
85·096	Maḥâmîd	المحاميد	,,	3,609
105·389	Adfu (Edfu)	ادفو	Nubia	4,760
136·463	Salwah	سلوه	,,	7,030
172·944	Darâw	دراو	,,	9,233
197·396	Al-Khaṭṭâra	الخطاره	,,	986
208·896	Al-Gazîra	الجزيره	,,	448
213·134	Aswân	اصوان	,,	13,005
220·309	Shallâl	الشلال	,,	5,049

THE FAYYÛM.

At **Wasṭa**, a town 55 miles from Cairo, is the railway junction for the Fayyûm. The line from Wasṭa runs westwards, and its terminus is at Medînet el-Fayyûm, a large Egyptian town situated a little distance from the site of Arsinoë in the Heptanomis,* called Crocodilopolis† by the Greeks, because the crocodile was here worshipped. The Egyptians called the Fayyûm Ta-she  "the lake district," and the name Fayyûm is the Arabic form of the Coptic Φιομ,‡ "the water." The Fayyûm district has an area of about 850 square miles, and is watered by a branch of the Nile called the Baḥr-Yûsuf, which flows into it through the Libyan mountains. On the west of it lies the **Birket el-Kurûn.** This now fertile land is thought to have been reclaimed from the desert by Àmenemḥāt III., a king of the XIIth dynasty. The Birket el-Ḳurûn is formed by a deep depression in the desert scooped out of the Parisian limestone, which has become covered in great part by thick belts of salted loams and marls. On these Nile mud has been deposited. The Birket el-Ḳurûn is all that is left of the ancient Lake Moeris,§ and its water surface is about 130 feet below sea level. Its cubic contents are estimated at 1,500,000,000 of cubic metres.

* Heptanomis, or Middle Egypt, was the district which separated the Thebaïd from the Delta; the names of the seven nomes were: Memphites, Heracleopolites, Crocodilopolites or Arsinoites, Aphroditopolites, Oxyrhynchites, Cynopolites, and Hermopolites. The greater and lesser Oases were always reckoned parts of the Heptanomis.

† In Egyptian , *Neter ḥet Sebek.*

‡ From the Egyptian , *Pa-iumā.*

§ From the Egyptian  *mu-ur*, or  *mer-ur.*

According to Pliny (v. 9), Lake Moeris was 250 miles (Mucianus says 450 miles) in circumference, and 50 paces deep; and its functions are thus described by Strabo (xvii. 1. §37): "The Lake Moeris, by its magnitude and depth, is able to sustain the superabundance of water which flows into it at the time of the rise of the river, without overflowing the inhabited and cultivated parts of the country. On the decrease of the water of the river, it distributes the excess by the same canal at each of the mouths; and both the lake and the canal preserve a remainder, which is used for irrigation. These are the natural and independent properties of the lake, but in addition, on both mouths of the canal are placed locks, by which the engineers store up and distribute the water which enters or issues from the canal."

The Baḥr-Yûsuf is said by some to have been excavated under the direction of the patriarch Joseph, but there is no satisfactory evidence for this theory; strictly speaking, it is an arm of the Nile, which has always needed cleaning out from time to time, and the Yûsuf, or Joseph, after whom it is named, was probably one of the Muḥammadan rulers of Egypt. Herodotus says* of Lake Moeris, "The water in this lake does not spring from the soil, for these parts are excessively dry, but it is conveyed through a channel from the Nile, and for six months it flows into the lake, and six months out again into the Nile. And during the six months that it flows out it yields a talent of silver (£240) every day to the king's treasury from the fish; but when the water is flowing into it, twenty minæ (£80)."

That Lake Moeris was artificially constructed is attested by many ancient writers, and Herodotus says, "That it is made and dry, this circumstance proves, for about the middle of the lake stand two pyramids, each rising 50 orgyæ above the surface of the water, and the part built

* Bk. II., 149.

under water extends to an equal depth; on each of these is placed a stone statue, seated on a throne." The pyramids here referred to can be no other than the pedestals of two large sandstone statues of Åmen-em-ḥāt III., which were set up either close by or in Lake Moeris; remains of these were found by Prof. Petrie when carrying on excavations at Biyahmu and other places in the neighbourhood in the years 1890 and 1891.

The **Pyramid of Ḥawâra** was the tomb of Åmen-em-ḥāt III.; it is built of sun-dried bricks, and even now is of considerable size. It was entered in 1890 on the south side by Prof. Petrie, who discovered the mummy chamber; the remains of what must have been the funerary temple were also found near the entrance. The Pyramid of **El-lâhûn** was entered by Mr. W. Fraser, who found it to be the tomb of Usertsen II.; like the Pyramid of Ḥawâra it is built of sun-dried bricks. The **Labyrinth** stood on the banks of Lake Moeris, and some have identified the ruins of the funerary temple of Åmen-em-ḥāt with it. Strabo (xvii. 1. § 37) declared that the tomb of the king who built the Labyrinth was near it, and desciibes it thus: "After proceeding beyond the first entrance of the canal about 30 or 40 stadia, there is a table-shaped plain, with a village and a large palace composed of as many palaces as there were formerly nomes. There are an equal number of aulæ, surrounded by pillars, and contiguous to one another, all in one line, and forming one building, like a long wall having the aulæ in front of it. The entrances into the aulæ are opposite to the wall. In front of the entrances there are long and numerous covered ways, with winding passages communicating with each other, so that no stranger could find his way into the aulæ or out of them without a guide. The surprising circumstance is that the roofs of these dwellings consist of a single stone each, and that the covered ways through their whole range were roofed in the same manner with single slabs of stone of extraordinary size, without the intermixture of timber or of any other material. On ascending the roof--which is not of great height, for it consists only of a single story—there may be seen a stone-field, thus composed of stones. Descending again and looking into the aulæ, these may be seen in a line supported by 27 pillars, each consisting of a single stone. The walls also are constructed of stones not inferior in size to them. At the end of this building, which occupies more than a stadium, is the tomb, which is a quadrangular pyramid, each side of which is about four plethra (*i.e.*, about 404 feet) in length, and of equal height. The name of the person buried there is Imandes [Diodorus gives Mendes or Marrus]. They built, it is said, this number of aulæ, because it was the custom for all the nomes to assemble there according to their rank, with their own priests and priestesses, for the purpose of performing sacrifices and making offerings to the gods, and of administering justice in matters of great importance. Each of the nomes was conducted to the aula appointed for it." The account given by Herodotus (II., 148, Cary's translation) is as follows :—

"Yet the labyrinth surpasses even the pyramids. For it has twelve courts enclosed with walls, with doors opposite each other, six facing the north, and six the south, contiguous to one another; and the same exterior wall encloses them. It contains two kinds of rooms, some under ground and some above ground over them, to the number of three thousand, fifteen hundred of each. The rooms above ground I myself went through, and saw, and relate from personal inspection. But the underground rooms I only know from report; for the Egyptians who have charge of the building would on no account show me them, saying, that there were the sepulchres of the kings who originally built this labyrinth, and of the sacred crocodiles. I can therefore only relate what I have learnt by hearsay concerning the lower rooms; but the upper ones, which surpass all human works, I myself saw; for the passage through the corridors, and the windings through the courts, from their great variety, presented a thousand occasions of wonder as

I passed from a court to the rooms, and from the rooms to the hall, and to the other corridors from the halls, and to other courts from the rooms. The roofs of all these are of stone, as also are the walls; but the walls are full of sculptured figures. Each court is surrounded with a colonnade of white stone, closely fitted. And adjoining the extremity of the labyrinth is a pyramid, forty orgyæ (about 240 feet) in height, on which large figures are carved, and a way to it has been made under ground."

A number of its ruined chambers are still visible. During the years 1890, 1891 Mr. Petrie carried out some interesting excavations at Ḥawâra, Biyahmu, El-lâhûn, Mêdûm and other sites in the Fayyûm. The funds for the purpose were most generously provided by Mr. Jesse Haworth and Mr. Martyn Kennard.

Aṭfîḥ, 51 miles from Cairo, on the east bank of the Nile, marks the site of the Greek city of Aphroditopolis, the Per-nebt-ṭepu-āḥ  of the ancient Egyptians, where the goddess Hathor was worshipped.

Beni Suwêf, 73 miles from Cairo, is the capital of the province bearing the same name, and is governed by a Mudîr. In ancient days it was famous for its textile fabrics, and supplied Aḥmîm and other weaving cities of Upper Egypt with flax. A main road led from this town to the Fayyûm.

About twelve miles to the north of Beni Suwêf the Baḥr Yûsuf bends towards the east, and runs by the side of large mounds of ruins of houses, broken pottery, etc.; these mounds cover an area of 360 acres, and are commonly called Umm al-Ḳûmân, or "Mother of Heaps," though the official name is Henassîyeh al-Medîna or Ahnâs. They mark the site of the great city which was called by the Egyptians  Ḥet-Suten-ḥenen, or Ḥenen-suten simply, from which the Copts made their name ϩⲛⲏⲥ; the Greeks made the city the capital of the nome Heracleopolites, and called it **Heracleopolis.** No date can be assigned for the founding of the city, but it was certainly a famous place in the early empire, and in mythological texts great importance is ascribed to it. According to Manetho the kings of the IXth and Xth dynasties were Heracleopolitans, but in the excavations which M. Naville carried on at Henassîyeh or Ahnâs he found nothing there older than the XIIth dynasty. It has been maintained that Ahnâs represents the city of Ḥânês mentioned in Isaiah xxx. 4, but the city referred to by the prophet being coupled with Zoan was probably situated in the Delta. The gods worshipped by the Egyptians at Heracleopolis were Ḥeru-shef, or Ḥeru-shefit, who dwelt in the shrine of Ȧn-ruṭ-f, Shu, Beb, Osiris, and Sekhet; at this place Osiris was first crowned, and Horus assumed the rank and dignity of his father, and the sky was separated from the earth, and from here Sekhet set out on her journey to destroy mankind because they had rebelled against Rā, the Sun-god, who, they declared, had become old and incapable of ruling them rightly. The people of Heracleopolis used to worship the ichneumon, a valuable animal which destroyed the eggs of crocodiles and asps, and even the asps themselves. Strabo declares that the ichneumons used to drop into the jaws of the crocodiles as they lay basking with their mouths open and, having eaten through their intestines, issue out of the dead body.

Maghâghah, 106 miles from Cairo, is now celebrated for its large sugar manufactory, which is lighted by gas, and is well worth a visit; the manufacturing of sugar begins here early in January.

About twenty-four miles farther south, lying inland, on the western side of the Nile, between the river and the Baḥr Yûsuf, is the site of the town of **Oxyrhynchus,** so called by the Greeks on account of the fish which they believed was worshipped there. The Egyptian name of the town was , Per-māt'et, from which came the Coptic Pemge, ⲠⲈⲘϪⲈ, and the corrupt Arabic form **Behnesa.**

The Oxyrhynchus fish was esteemed so sacred that the people of the city were afraid to eat any fish which had been caught with a hook, lest the hook should have injured one of the sacred fish ; the Oxyrhynchus fish was thought to have been produced from the blood of the wounded Osiris (Aelian, *De Nat. Animalium*, x. 46). The Oasis of Baḥrîyeh (Oasis Parva), which is called by Abu Ṣalîḥ "the Oasis of Behnesa," is usually visited by the desert road which runs there from the city. The Arabic writer Al-Maḳrîzî says that there were once 360 churches in Behnesa, but that the only one remaining in his time was that dedicated to the Virgin Mary. In recent years the excavations which have been carried on by Mr. Grenfell at Oxyrhynchus have resulted in the discovery of numerous papyri of a late period.

A little above Abu Girgeh, on the west bank of the Nile, is the town of El-Kais, which marks the site of the ancient **Cynopolis** or "Dog-city"; it was the seat of a Coptic bishop, and is called Kais, ⲔⲀⲒⲤ, in Coptic.

Thirteen miles from Abu Girgeh, also on the west bank ot the Nile, is the town of **Ḳulûṣna,** 134 miles from Cairo, and a few miles south, lying inland, is **Samallûṭ.**

Farther south, on the east bank of the Nile, is **Gebel eṭ-Ṭêr,** or the "Bird mountain," so called because tradition says that all the birds of Egypt assemble here once a year, and that they leave behind them when departing one solitary bird, that remains there until they return the following year to relieve him of his watch, and to set another in his place. As there are mountains called Gebel eṭ-Ṭêr in all parts of Arabic-speaking countries, because of the number of birds which frequent them, the story is only one which springs from the fertile Arab imagination. Gebel eṭ-Ṭêr rises above the river to a height of six or seven hundred feet, and upon its summit stands a Coptic convent dedicated to Mary the Virgin, Dêr al-'Adhrâ, but more commonly called **Dêr al-Baḳarah,** or the "Convent of the Pulley," because the ascent to the convent is generally made by a rope and pulley. Leaving the river and entering a fissure in the rocks, the traveller finds himself at the bottom of a natural shaft about 120 feet long. When Robert Curzon visited this convent, he had to climb up much in the same way as boys used to climb up inside chimneys. The convent stands about 400 feet from the top of the shaft, and is built of small square stones of Roman workmanship; the necessary repairs have, however, been made with mud or sun-dried brick. The outer walls of the enclosure form a square which measures about 200 feet each way; they are 20 feet high, and are perfectly unadorned. Tradition says that it was founded by the Empress Helena,* and there is in this case no reason to doubt it. The church "is partly subterranean, being built in the recesses of an ancient stone quarry; the other parts of it are of stone plastered over. The roof is flat and is formed of horizontal beams of palm trees, upon which a terrace of reeds and earth is laid. The height of the interior is about 25 feet. On entering the door we had to descend a flight of narrow steps, which led into a side aisle about ten feet wide, which is divided from the nave by octagon columns of great thickness supporting the walls of a sort of clerestory. The columns were surmounted by heavy square plinths almost in the Egyptian style. I consider this church to be interesting from its being half a catacomb, or cave, and one of the earliest Christian buildings which has preserved its originality . . . . . it will be seen that it is constructed on the principle of a Latin basilica, as the buildings of the Empress Helena usually were." (Curzon, *Monasteries of the Levant*, p. 109.)

* Died about A.D. 328, aged 80. (Sozomen, *Eccles. Hist.*, II., 2.)

In Curzon's time the convent possessed fifteen Coptic books with Arabic translations, and eight Arabic MSS. As the monks were, and are, extremely poor, they used to descend the rock and swim out to any passing boat to beg for charity; the Patriarch has forbidden this practice, but it is not entirely discontinued.

Abu Ṣalîḥ identifies Gebel al-Kaff, *i.e.*, the "Mountain of the Palm of the Hand," with Gebel eṭ-Ṭêr, and records an interesting tradition concerning our Lord. According to this writer there is at this place the mark of the palm of His hand (hence the name) on the rock in the mountain out of which the church is hewn. The mountain is said to have bowed down in worship before Him, and He grasped the mountain as it worshipped, and set it back in its place, and the mark of His palm remains impressed upon it until this day. In the impression of the hand there is a small hole, large enough to admit a stibium needle, and if the needle be inserted and drawn out, it brings with it a black powder, the mark of which cannot be effaced.

Two or three miles from the convent are some ancient quarries having rock bas-reliefs representing Rameses III. making an offering to the crocodile god Sebek  before Åmen-Rā.

Minyeh, 156½ miles from Cairo, on the west bank of the Nile, is the capital of the province of the same name; its Arabic name is derived from the Coptic Mone, ⲙⲟⲛⲉ, which in turn represents the Egyptian  *Ment* in its old name Khufu-menāt , *i.e.*, the "Nurse of Khufu." There is a large sugar factory here, in which about 2,000 men are employed. A few miles south, on the eastern side of the river, is the village of Zâwiyet al-Mêtîn, near which are the remains of some tombs of the VIth dynasty. They appear to be the tombs of the nobles of the city of Ḥebenu , the capital of the XVIth nome of Upper Egypt.

Beni-Ḥasân, 171 miles from Cairo, on the east bank of the Nile, is remarkable for the large collection of fine historical tombs which are situated at a short distance from the site of the villages known by this name. The villages of the "Children of Hasân" were destroyed by order of Muḥammad 'Ali, on account of the thievish propensities of their inhabitants. The **Speos Artemidos** is the first rock excavation visited here. The king who first caused this cavern to be hewn out was Thothmes III.; about 250 years later Seti I. added his name to several of the half obliterated cartouches of Queen Ḥātshepset, but it seems never to have been finished. The cavern was dedicated to the lion-headed goddess Sekhet, who was called Artemis by the Greeks; hence the name "cavern of Artemis." The Arabs call the cavern the "Stable of 'Anṭar," a famous Muḥammadan hero. The portico had originally two rows of columns, four in each; the cavern is about 21 feet square, and the niche in the wall at the end was probably intended to hold a statue of Sekhet.

The famous **Tombs of Beni-Ḥasân** are hewn out of the living rock, and are situated high up in the mountain; they are about thirty-nine in number, and all open on a terrace, somewhat similar to the terrace outside the tombs at Aswân. Each tomb preserves the chief characteristics of the maṣṭăbas of Ṣaḳḳâra, that is to say, it consists of a hall for offerings and a shaft leading down to a corridor, which ends in the chamber containing the sarcophagus and the mummy. The tombs were hewn out of a thick layer of fine, white limestone, and the walls were partly smoothed, and then covered with a thin layer of plaster, upon which the scenes in the lives of the wealthy men who ordered them to be made might be painted. Lower down the hill are some scores of mummy pits, with small chambers attached, wherein, probably, the poorer class of people who lived near were buried. Of the 39 tombs at Beni-Ḥasân only twelve contain inscriptions, but it is clear from these that the men who made the necropolis there were well-born, independent, and almost feudal proprietors of the land in the neighbourhood, who filled various high offices in the city of Menāt-Khufu, which was situated not far off, and that they flourished during the XIth and XIIth dynasties. Of the twelve inscribed tombs, eight are of governors of the nome Meḥ, two are of princes of Menāt-Khufu, one is of the son of a prince, and one is of a royal scribe. The 39 tombs were divided by Lepsius into two groups, northern and southern; in the former are 13 and in the latter 26 tombs. Six of the inscribed tombs belong to the reigns of Ȧmenemḥāt I., Usertsen I., and Usertsen II., and the other six were probably made during the rule of the kings of the XIth dynasty.

No. 2. Tomb of Ȧmeni 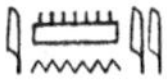 **or Ȧmenemḥāt** , Ȧmeni was the governor of the XVIth nome of Upper Egypt, called Meḥ by the Egyptians and Antinoë by the Greeks, and he flourished in the reign of Usertsen I. He was by birth the hereditary prince of the district, and he held the rank of "ḥā" or "duke," and the office of priest to various gods and goddesses; he seems to have combined in his own person the offices of almost every high state official in the nome. Architecturally his tomb is of great interest, and it is instructive to find examples of the use of octagonal and polyhedral pillars in the same tomb; the shrine is at the east end of the hall, and two shafts, which lead to mummy chambers below, are on one side of it. The inscription shows that Ȧmeni was buried in the 43rd year of the reign of Usertsen I., on the 15th day of the second month of the inundation, *i.e.*, about the end of May; the feudal lords of the nome seem to have had an epoch of their own by which to reckon, for we are told that the 43rd year of Usertsen I. was the equivalent of "year 25 of the nome of Meḥ." Åmeni makes an appeal to those who visit his tomb to pray that abundant funeral offerings may be made to his *ka* (*i.e.*, double), in these words:—"O ye who love life, and who hate death, say ye, 'Thousands of [cakes of] bread and [vessels of] beer, and thousands of oxen and feathered fowl be to the *ka* of the prince and duke* Åmeni, triumphant.'" He then goes on to say that he went with his lord to Ethiopia on an expedition against the peoples of that land, that he set the bounds of Egyptian territory further to the south, that he brought back tribute from the conquered peoples, and that there was no loss among his soldiers. His success was so great that his praise "ascended even into the heavens," and soon afterwards he sailed up the river with 400 chosen men on a second expedition to bring back gold for his lord; his mission was successful, and he was sent up once more, but this time with 600 men, and he returned in peace, having done all that he had been ordered to do. It is a great pity that we are not told how far south he went. In the rest of the inscription Åmeni tells of the excellent way in which he ruled the nome under his charge. He says, "I was a gracious and a compassionate man, and a ruler who loved his city. I have passed [my] years as ruler of the nome of Meḥ, and all the works of the palace came under my hand. The cattle owners of the nome gave me 3,000 of their cattle, and I received praise therefor in the palace; at the appointed seasons I brought the proceeds of their toil to the palace, and nought remained due to him. I journeyed through the nome from one end to the other, making inspections frequently. I have never made the daughter of a poor man to grieve,

* Here follow other titles.

I have never defrauded the widow, I have never oppressed the labourer, and I have never defrauded the owner of cattle. I have never impressed for forced labour the labourers of him who only employed five men; there was never a person in want in my time, and no one went hungry during my rule, for if years of leanness came, I [made them] to plough up all the arable land in the nome of Meḥ up to its very frontiers on the north and south [at my expense]. Thus I kept its people alive and obtained for them provisions, and so there was not a hungry person among them. To the widow I gave the same amount as I gave to her that had a husband, and I made no distinction between the great and the little in all that I gave. And afterwards, when the Nile floods were high, and wheat, and barley, and all things were abundant, I made no addition to the amounts due from them." The pictures on the walls represent the working of flint weapons, the making of bows, the making of a bier, working in metal, the making of pottery and stone vessels, the weaving of rope, ploughing, reaping, the treading of corn, the making of wine, the netting of birds and fish, musicians playing the harp and rattling the sistrum, the hunting of wild animals, games of wrestling, the attack of a fortress, the sailing of boats laden with men and women, the slaughter of the sacrificial bull, the bringing of offerings, etc. The name of Ȧmeni's father is unknown; his mother was called Ḥennu , his wife Ḥetepet, 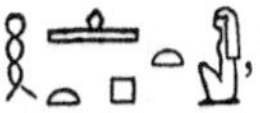, and his son Khnemu-ḥetep 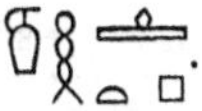.

No. 3. Tomb of Khnemu-Ḥetep II. 

Khnemu-ḥetep was the governor of the Eastern Mountains, *i.e.*, of the land on the eastern side of the nome of Meḥ as far as the Arabian mountains; and he flourished in the reign of Usertsen II. He was by birth the hereditary prince of the district, and he held the rank of "ḥā" or "duke," and the office of priest to various gods and goddesses. On the door-posts and lintel of his tomb is an inscription which records his name and titles, and gives a list of the days on which funeral services are to be performed at the tomb, and offerings made. On the jambs of the doorway are two short inscriptions in which "those who love their life and who hate death," and "those who love a long life, and would be brought to a state of fitness for heaven," are entreated to pray that thousands of meat and drink offerings may be made to the *ka* of Khnemu-ḥetep II. From the inscriptions it is clear that Khnemu-ḥetep II. was the son of Neḥerȧ , the son of Sebek-Ānkh ; his father was a feudal prince, *erpā* , and he held the rank of "ḥā" or "duke." The mother of Khnemu-ḥetep was Baqet , the daughter of a prince called Khnemu-ḥetep I., and of his wife Satȧp, each of whom was of princely rank. His wives were called Khati  and Tchat, ; by the first he had four sons and three daughters, and by the second two sons and one daughter. In the great inscription of 222 lines Khnemu-ḥetep II. records his biography. After stating that he built his tomb in such wise that his name, and those of his officers, might endure in the land for ever, he goes on to tell how in the 19th year of  "Nub-kau-Rā, son of the Sun, Ȧmen-em-ḥāt [II.]," he was made prince of the city of Menāt-Khufu, and governor of the eastern desert, and generally raised to the rank of his maternal grandfather. Following this up, Khnemu-ḥetep II. tells the story of how his maternal grandfather, who seems to have been called Khnemu-ḥetep I., was made lord of Menāt-Khufu in the half-nome of Tut-Ḥeru, and of the nome of Meḥ by  Se-ḥetep-ȧb-Rā, son of the Sun, Ȧmen-em-ḥāt [I.]. The maternal grandfather was succeeded by his eldest son Nekht I., the uncle of the builder of this tomb. The next section of the text tells how greatly Khnemu-ḥetep II. was honoured by his king, and how his sons Nekht II., and Khnemu-ḥetep III. were made governor of a nome, and governor of the foreign lands respectively. In the rest of the inscription Khnemu-ḥetep says that he restored the inscriptions on the tombs of his ancestors which had become defaced; that he built a funeral chapel for himself, even as his father had done in the city of Mernefert, and made doors both for it and for the shrine within it; and that he made near it a tank of water, and made arrangements for a supply of flowers for the festivals which were celebrated in the tomb. It is interesting to note that the name of the official who superintended these works is given—Baqet. The scenes painted on the walls of this tomb are of great interest, and represent:—(*West Wall, over the doorway*) a shrine with a statue of the deceased being drawn to the tomb; (*south side*) carpenters, washers of clothes, boat-builders, potters, weavers, bakers, and others at work, and (*middle row*) the wives and family of Khnemu-ḥetep sailing in boats to Abydos; (*north side*) the storage and registration of grain, reaping, treading of corn, ploughing, gathering of grapes and other fruit, watering the garden, oxen fording a river, a fishing scene, and (*middle row*) the passage of the mummy of the deceased to Abydos. (*North Wall*) Khnemu-ḥetep, armed with bow and arrows, and his sons hunting in the desert; with him went the scribe Menthu-ḥetep, who kept an account of the bag made. On the right is a large figure of Khnemu-ḥetep, who is accompanied by one of his sons,

A deputation of thirty-seven members of the Āāmu people bringing eye paint to Khnemu-ḥetep II. in the reign of Usertsen II.

and by an attendant, and by three dogs, and the four lines of text above him state that he is inspecting his cattle and the produce of his lands. Of the four rows of figures before him, the first is perhaps the most important, for it illustrates a procession of foreign people who visited him in his capacity of governor of the nome. The procession consists of 37 persons of the Āāmu, a Semitic people or tribe, and they are introduced by Nefer-ḥetep, a royal scribe, who holds in his hand a papyrus roll, on which is inscribed, "Year 6, under the majesty of Horus, the leader of the world, the king of the South and North, Rā-Khā-Kheper (*i.e.*, Usertsen II.). List of the Āāmu, brought by the son of the Duke Khnemu-ḥetep, on account of the eye-paint, Āāmu of Shu; a list of 37 [persons]." Behind the scribe stands the official Khati, and behind him the Āāmu chief, or desert shêkh; these are followed by the other members of the foreign tribe. The men of the Āāmu wear beards, and carry bows and arrows, and both men and women are dressed in garments of many colours. The home of the Āāmu was situated to the east of Palestine. In this picture some have seen a representation of the arrival of Jacob's sons in Egypt to buy corn, but there is no evidence for the support of this theory; others have identified the Āāmu with the Hyksos. The company here seen are probably merchants who brought eye-paint, spices and the like from their own country, and sold their wares to the rich officials of Egypt. On the East and South Walls is a series of scenes in which Khnemu-ḥetep is depicted hunting the hippopotamus, and snaring birds, and spearing fish, and receiving offerings.

No. 13. Tomb of Khnemu-hetep III., a royal scribe, the son ot Neteru-ḥetep. This tomb consists of one small, rectangular chamber with one mummy pit. The inscriptions record the name and titles of the deceased, and petitions to those who visit the tomb to pray that abundant offerings may be made to him. This is one of the oldest tombs at Beni-Ḥasân, and was probably made long before the site became a general burial ground for the nobles of Menāt-Khufu.

No. 14. Tomb of Khnemu-ḥetep I., the governor of the nome of Meḥ, and prince of the town of Menāt-Khufu. His father's name and titles are unknown, and the rank of his mother Baqet is also unknown; his wife was called Satȧp, and his son Nekht succeeded to his rank, title, and dignities. He flourished during the reign of Ȧmen-em-ḥāt I. On the south-west wall of the main chamber of this tomb is an inscription which contains the cartouches of Ȧmen-em-ḥāt I., and which states that Khnemu-ḥetep I. went on an expedition with his king in boats to some country, probably to the south. The paintings in the tomb are much faded, but the remains of the figures of the foreigners represented are of considerable interest.

No. 15. Tomb of Baqet III., governor of the nome of Meḥ. Baqet held the rank of "ḥā" or "duke," and flourished before the rule of the kings of the XIIth dynasty. This tomb contains seven shafts leading to mummy chambers. The North Wall is ornamented with some interesting scenes in which men and women are seen engaged in various handicrafts and occupations, and the deceased is seen enjoying himself hunting in the desert, and fishing in the Nile. On the East Wall wrestling scenes are painted, and over two hundred positions are illustrated; below these are illustrations of the events of a pitched battle. On the South Wall are scenes connected with the work on Baqet's estates, and pictures of men engaged in their work or amusements.

No. 17. Tomb of Khati, governor of the nome of Meḥ, and commandant of the Eastern Desert; the main chamber is crossed by two rows of three quatrefoil columns of the lotus bud type, and of these two remain perfect. Each column represents four lotus stems, with unopened buds, tied together below the buds, and is brilliantly painted in red, blue, and yellow. This tomb contains two shafts leading to mummy chambers, and is decorated with a large number of scenes which have, however, much in common with those in the other tombs already described.

Other inscribed tombs are:—No. 21, Tomb of Nekhtȧ, uncle of Khnemu-ḥetep II., and governor of Meḥ; No. 23, Tomb of Neter-nekht, governor of the Eastern Desert, and son of the priestess Ārit-ḥetep, and husband of Ḥer-ȧb; No. 27, Tomb of Re-mu-shentȧ, chief of the nome of Meḥ; No. 29, Tomb of Baqet I., chief of the nome of Meḥ; and No. 33, Tomb of Baqet II., who held the same office.*

Rôḍa, 182 miles from Cairo, and the seat of a large sugar manufactory, lies on the west bank of the river, just opposite Shêkh 'Abâdeh, or **Antinoë,** a town built by Hadrian, and named by him after Antinous,† who was drowned here in the Nile. To the south of Antinoë lies the convent of **Abu Honnês** (Father John), and in the districts in the immediate neighbourhood are the remains of several Coptic buildings which date back to the fifth century of our era. A little to the south-west of Rôḍa, lying inland, are the remains of the city of Hermopolis Magna, called in Egyptian 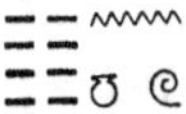, or 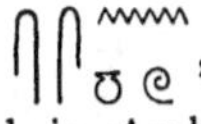, *Khemennu*, in Coptic Shmûn, ϣⲙⲟⲩⲛ, and in Arabic Eshmûnên; the tradition which attributes the building of this city to Eshmûn, son of Miṣr, is worthless. The Greeks called it Hermopolis, because the Egyptians there worshipped Thoth, , the scribe of the gods, who was named by the Greeks Hermes. A little

* Full descriptions of all the above tombs are given by Messrs. Newberry and Fraser in *Beni Hasan*, 4 parts, London, 1893–1899.

† A Bithynian youth, a favourite of the Emperor Hadrian.

distance from the town is the spot where large numbers of the ibis, a bird sacred to Thoth, were buried.

Eshmûnên is sometimes called an "Island" by Arabic writers; this is because it has the Nile on the east, the Baḥr Yûsuf or Al-Manhî on the west and south, and a connecting canal on the north. An old legend says that on the highest point of this town there was a cock, and beneath it a row of dromedaries, and that when a stranger approached, the cock crew, and the dromedaries went forth to destroy the stranger. When our Lord entered this town by the eastern gate these creatures worshipped Him and were straightway turned into stone. It is said that there were three hundred villages in the district, and many Christian churches. The most famous was the church dedicated to the Virgin Mary, which contained several altars and marble pillars, on one of which was the mark of the hand of our Lord. Outside it stood a tree bearing fruit of a dark purple colour which resembled a plum, and is called *sebestan*; when our Lord passed by it, this tree is said to have bowed its head in adoration before Him. About five miles south of Antinoë, and seven miles from Eshmûnên in a direct line across the Nile, on the north side of the rocky valley behind the modern **Dêr Al-Nakhleh,** is a very important group of ancient Egyptian tombs at the place called **Al-Bersheh.** The most important of these is the **Tomb of Teḥuti-hetep** 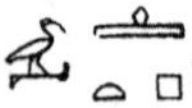, the chief of , the XVth nome of Upper Egypt, who flourished during the reigns of Ȧmen-em-ḥat II., Usertsen II., and Usertsen III., in the XIIth dynasty. The façade consists of two fine columns with palm leaf capitals, supporting a massive architrave, all coloured pink, and marbled with pale green to represent rose granite; the ceiling is painted blue and studded with quatrefoils, and the walls were sculptured with hunting and other scenes. The main chamber measures 25 × 20 × 13½ feet, and on the upper part of the left hand wall is the famous painting of the "Colossus on a sledge," in which we see a huge alabaster statue of the deceased being dragged along by nearly two hundred men. This statue, we are told in the inscriptions, was 13 cubits in height, *i.e.*, nearly 21 feet, and it must have weighed about 60 tons; the work of transporting this mass from the mountain many miles distant, where it was quarried, must have been enormous. Of Teḥuti-ḥetep's career little is known, but the wealth and position of the man are sufficiently indicated by the fact that he was able to undertake such a work. The tomb was discovered by Messrs. Mangles and Irby about August 26, 1817.*

MELÂWÎ AL-'ARÎSH.

Melâwî, 188 miles from Cairo, is situated on the west bank of the river; it is the ⲙⲁⲛⲗⲁⲩ of Coptic writers, and there were many Christian churches in the town, among others one dedicated to Abatir, one to Mercurius, one to Saint George, one to Gabriel the Archangel, one to Raphael the Archangel, and two to the Virgin and to Michael the Archangel.

Haggi Kandil, or **Tell el-'Amarna**, 195 miles from Cairo, lies on the east bank of the river, about five miles from the ruins of the city built by Khut-en-àten, 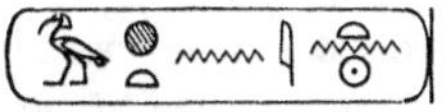, or Amenophis IV., the famous "heretic" king of the XVIIIth dynasty, whose prenomen was 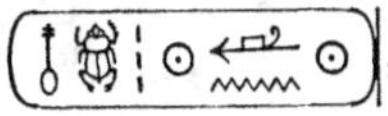, Nefer-kheperu-Rā uā-en-Rā.

* Full descriptions of the tombs at Al-Bersheh, with plans, etc., have been published by Messrs. Newberry and Fraser, in *El-Bersheh*, 2 parts, London (no date).

Amenophis IV. was the son of Amenophis III., by a Mesopotamian princess called Thi, who came from the land of Mitani. When the young prince Amenophis IV. grew up, it was found that he had conceived a rooted dislike to the worship of Ȧmen-Rā, the king of the gods and great lord of Thebes, and that he preferred the worship of the disk of the sun to that of Ȧmen-Rā; as a sign of his opinions he called himself "beloved of the sun's disk," instead of the usual and time-honoured "beloved of Ȧmen." The native Egyptian priesthood disliked the foreign queen, and the sight of her son with his protruding chin, thick lips, and other characteristic features of a foreign race, found no favour in their sight; that such a man should openly despise the worship of Ȧmen-Rā was a thing intolerable to the priesthood, and angry words and acts were, on their part, the result. In answer to their objections the king ordered the name of Ȧmen-Rā to be chiselled out of all the monuments, even from his father's names. Rebellion then broke out, and Khut-en-ȧten thought it best to leave Thebes, and to found a new city for himself at a place between Memphis and Thebes, now called Tell el-Amarna. The famous architect Bek, whose father Men served under Amenophis III., designed the temple buildings, and in a very short time a splendid town with beautiful granite sculptures sprang out of the desert. As an insult to the priests and people of Thebes, he built a sandstone and granite temple at Thebes in honour of the god Harmachis. When Khut-en-ȧten's new town, Khut-ȧten, "the splendour of the sun's disk," was finished, his mother Thi came to live there; and here the king passed his life quietly with his mother, wife, and seven daughters. He died leaving no male issue, and each of the husbands of his daughters became king.

As long as the "heretic king" lived the city prospered and grew, and many wealthy people took up their abode in it; sculptors and artists and skilled workmen of every kind found abundant employment, therefore their patrons were determined to be buried in the mountains close by. Beautifully decorated houses and tombs became the order of the day, and the sculpture, and painting, and indeed art generally prove that artists of all kinds who settled there at that time threw off many of the old trammels and conventionalities of their professions, and indulged themselves in new designs, and new forms, and new treatment of their subjects. Indeed it is to the buildings of the city of Khut-âten and their decorations that we owe many ideas of the possibilities of Egyptian art. The new styles of sculpture and artistic decoration, however, only flourished as long as the king was alive, and as soon as he died the inhabitants of all classes drifted back to Thebes, and by degrees the city of Khut-âten became deserted; tradition and obedience to custom proved to be too strong for the would-be followers of the heretic king. The length of the king's reign does not seem to have been more than twelve or fifteen years, and certainly long before the reign of Rameses II. the beautiful city which he built had been made to fall into ruins. Fortunately, however, the ruins are very instructive, and they allow visitors to follow its plan with success. In 1887 a number of important cuneiform tablets were found by a native woman near the palace, and most of these may be seen in the Museums of London, Berlin, and Cairo. They are inscribed with letters and despatches from kings of countries in and about Mesopotamia and from governors of cities in Palestine and Syria, and those from the last named countries show that, whilst the heretic king was occupying himself with theological problems and artistic developments, his Empire was falling to pieces. In 1892 Mr. Petrie carried on excavations at Tell el-Amarna, and uncovered several painted plaster pavements of an unusual character. In the neighbourhood of the town are a number of inscribed tombs of considerable interest, by reason of the religious texts that are found in them. In form and arrangement they have much in common with the tombs of the XIIth dynasty, but their decoration is characteristic of the period of Khut-Åten. Among them of special interest are:—(*Northern Group*) No. 1. Tomb of **Pa-nehsi**, which seems to have been used as a church by the Copts; No. 2. Tomb of **Pentu**, inscribed with a hymn to Aten; No. 3. Tomb of **Meri-Rā**, which is probably the most characteristic of the period, with sacrificial scenes, hymns to Åten, plans of houses, and scenes of the crowning of officials; No. 4. Tomb of **Åāḥmes**, with a hymn to Åten; No. 5. Tomb of an unknown official which was being built when King Rā-seāa-ka came to the throne; and No. 7, a tomb which mentions the receipt of tribute from vassal nations. The scenes and portraits in this tomb are of great interest. (*Southern Group*), the Tomb of **Tutu**, with hymns to Åten; and the Tomb of **Ai**, the successor of King Khut-en-Åten. The **Tomb of Khut-en-Åten** lies at a considerable distance from the river, and it is chiefly interesting on account of the scenes of sun-worship which are depicted in it.

Gebel Abu Fêdah.—Seventeen miles south of Haggi Ḳandîl, 212 miles from Cairo, on the east side of the river, is the range of low mountains about twelve miles long known by this name. Lying a little distance inland is the village of **Al-Kusîyeh**, which marks the site of the Greek City of **Cusae**, the Qes  of the hieroglyphic texts, and the capital of the XIVth nome of Upper Egypt. The name seems to mean, "the town of the mummy bandages." According to Aelian (H.A. x. 27), the goddess of the city was worshipped under the form of a white cow. Towards the southern end of this range there are some crocodile mummy pits.

Manfalûṭ, 223½ miles from Cairo on the west bank of

the Nile, occupies the site of an ancient Egyptian town. Leo Africanus says that the town was destroyed by the Romans, and adds that it was rebuilt under Muḥammadan rule. In his time he says that huge columns and buildings inscribed with hieroglyphs were still visible. The Coptic name Manbalot, ⲙⲁ ⲛ̀ ⲃⲁⲗⲟⲧ "place of the sack," is the original of its Arabic name to-day.

Asyûṭ, 249½ miles from Cairo, is the capital of the province of the same name, and the seat of the Inspector-General of Upper Egypt; it stands on the site of the ancient Egyptian city called  *Seut*, whence the Arabic name Siûṭ or Asyûṭ, and the Coptic ⲥⲓⲱⲟⲩⲧ. The Greeks called the city Lycopolis, or "wolf city," probably because the jackal-headed Anubis was worshipped there. In ancient Egyptian times the sacred name of the city was Per-Ȧnpu , and it formed the capital of the XVIIth or Anubis nome, 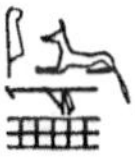, of Upper Egypt. Asyûṭ is a large city, with spacious bazaars and fine mosques; it is famous for its red pottery and for its market, held every Sunday, to which wares from Arabia and Upper Egypt are brought. The **American Missionaries** have a large establishment, and the practical, useful education of the natives by these devoted men is carried on here, as well as at Cairo, on a large scale. The Asyûṭ Training College was specially established to provide and prepare workers to carry on the educational and evangelistic operations of the Evangelical community in Egypt, and nearly all the male teachers, in number 215, have been trained in it. At the end of 1898 there were 604 boarders and day scholars in the institution, who represented 112 towns and villages, and came from all parts of Egypt. In the same year the American Mission had in all Egypt 180 schools with 11,872 pupils, and 295 teachers, and of its Protestant community 365 per 1,000 knew how to read, as against 48 per 1,000 of the entire population in Egypt. If the evangelical community is deducted from the entire population, the latter figure would become smaller still. Of the males of the evangelical community in Egypt, 521 per 1,000 know how to read, and of the females, 200 per 1,000. The number of stations belonging to the Mission, including churches, is 207, and in 1898 the pupils paid 26,741 dollars in tuition fees. The Arabic geographers described Asyûṭ as a town of considerable size, beauty, and importance, and before the abandonment of the Sûdân by the Khedive all caravans from that region stopped there. In the hills to the west of the town are a number of ancient Egyptian tombs, which date back as far as the XIIth dynasty. A large number have been destroyed during the present century for the sake of the limestone which forms the walls. When M. Denon stayed here he said that the number of hieroglyphic inscriptions which cover the tombs was so great that many months would be required to read, and many years to copy them. The disfigurement of the tombs dates from the time when the Christians took up their abode in them.

Fifteen miles farther south is the Coptic town of **Abu Tîg**, the name of which appears to be derived from ΑΠΟΘΗΚΗ, a "granary"; and 14½ miles beyond, 279 miles from Cairo, is **Kau el-Kebîr** (the ⲦⲔⲰⲞⲨ of the Copts), which marks the site of **Antaeopolis**, the capital of the Antaeopolite nome in Upper Egypt. The temple which formerly existed here was dedicated to Antaeus,* the Libyan wrestler, who fought with Hercules. In the plain close by it is said by Diodorus that the battle between Horus, the son of Osiris and Isis, and Set or Typhon, the murderer of Osiris, took

* He was the son of Poseidon and Ge, and was invincible as long as he remained in contact with his mother earth.

place; Typhon was overcome, and fled away in the form of a crocodile. In Christian times Antaeopolis was the seat of a bishop.

Ṭahṭah, 291½ miles from Cairo, contains some interesting mosques, and is the home of a large number of Copts, in consequence of which, probably, the town is kept clean.

Sûhâg, 317½ miles from Cairo, is the capital of the province of Girgeh; near it are the White and Red Monasteries.

The Dêr el-Abyaḍ or "**White Monastery,**" so called because of the colour of the stone of which it is built, but better known by the name of Amba Shenûdah, is situated on the west bank of the river near Sûhâg, 317½ miles from Cairo. "The peculiarity of this monastery is that the interior was once a magnificent basilica, while the exterior was built by the Empress Helena, in the ancient Egyptian style. The walls slope inwards towards the summit, where they are crowned with a deep overhanging cornice. The building is of an oblong shape, about 200 feet in length by 90 wide, very well built of fine blocks of stone; it has no windows outside larger than loopholes, and these are at a great height from the ground. Of these there are twenty on the south side and nine at the east end. The monastery stands at the foot of the hill, on the edge of the Libyan desert, where the sand encroaches on the plain. . . . . . . The ancient doorway of red granite has been partially closed up." (Curzon, *Monasteries of the Levant*, p. 131.) There were formerly six gates; the single entrance now remaining is called the "mule gate," because when a certain heathen princess came riding on a mule to desecrate the church, the earth opened and swallowed her up. The walls enclose a space measuring about 240 feet by 133 feet. The convent was dedicated to Shenûti,*

* Shenûdah, Coptic ϣⲉⲛⲟⲩϯ Shenûti, was born A.D. 333; he died at midday on July 2, A.D. 451.

a celebrated Coptic saint who lived in the fourth century of our era. Curzon says (*op. cit.*, p. 132) . . . . . . "The tall granite columns of the ancient church reared themselves like an avenue on either side of the desecrated nave, which is now open to the sky, and is used as a promenade for a host of chickens. . . . . The principal entrance was formerly at the west end, where there is a small vestibule, immediately within the door of which, on the left hand, is a small chapel, perhaps the baptistery, about twenty-five feet long, and still in tolerable preservation. It is a splendid specimen of the richest Roman architecture of the latter empire, and is truly an imperial little room. The arched ceiling is of stone; and there are three beautifully ornamented niches on each side. The upper end is semi-circular, and has been entirely covered with a profusion of sculpture in panels, cornices, and every kind of architectural enrichment. When it was entire, and covered with gilding, painting, or mosaic, it must have been most gorgeous. The altar on such a chapel as this was probably of gold, set full of gems; or if it was the baptistery, as I suppose, it most likely contained a bath of the most precious jasper, or of some of the more rare kinds of marble, for the immersion of the converted heathen, whose entrance into the church was not permitted until they had been purified with the waters of baptism in a building without the door of the house of God" (p. 135). The library once contained over a hundred parchment books, but these were destroyed by the Mamelukes when they last sacked the convent.

In this monastery the bodies of Saint Bartholomew and Simon the Canaanite are said to be buried, but the body of its founder was laid in the monastery which stood on the Mountain of Athribis, a name derived from the Egyptian Ḥ-erpāt, .

The Dêr el-Aḥmar or "**Red Monastery,**" so called because of the red colour of the bricks of which it is built, was also built by the Empress Helena; it is smaller and better preserved than the White Monastery, and was dedicated to the Abba Bêsa, the disciple and friend of Shenûti. The pillars of both churches were taken from Athribis, which lay close by; the orientation of neither church is exact, for their axes point between N.E. and N.E. by E. The ruined church of Armant near Thebes is built on the same model.

A few miles south of Sûhâg, on the east bank of the river, lies the town of **Akhmîm,** called Shmin or Chmim, ϣⲙⲓⲛ, ϫⲙⲓⲙ, (hence **Khemmis**) by the Copts, and Panopolis by the Greeks; Strabo and Leo Africanus say that it was one of the most ancient cities of Egypt. The ithyphallic god Åmsu, identified by the Greeks with Pan, was worshipped here, and the town was famous for its linen weavers and stone cutters. Its Egyptian name was  Åpu. Of this city Herodotus (ii, 91) says: "There is a large city called Chemmis (*i.e.*, Panopolis), situate in the Thebaic district, near Neapolis, in which is a quadrangular temple dedicated to Perseus, the son of Danaë. Palm-trees grow around it, and the portico is of stone, very spacious, and over it are placed two stone statues. In this enclosure is a temple, and in it is placed a statue of Perseus. The Chemmites affirm that Perseus has frequently appeared to them on earth, and frequently within the temple, and that a sandal worn by him is sometimes found, which is two cubits in length, and that after its appearance all Egypt flourishes. They adopt the following Grecian customs in honour of Perseus: they celebrate gymnastic games, embracing every kind of contest, and they give as prizes cattle, cloaks, and skins. When I enquired why Perseus appeared only to them, and why they differed from the rest of the Egyptians in holding gymnastic games, they answered, 'Perseus derived his origin from their city for that Danaus and Lynceus, who were both natives of Chemmis, sailed from there into Greece; and tracing the descent down from them they came to Perseus'; and that he coming to Egypt, for the same reason as the Greeks allege, in order to bring away the Gorgon's head from Libya, they affirmed that he came to them also and acknowledged all his kindred; and that when he came to Egypt he was well acquainted with the name of Chemmis, having heard it from his mother. They add that by his order they instituted gymnastic games in honour of him." Akhmîm is still famous for its linen weavers, who seem to have inherited the skill of their predecessors in making many-coloured woven fabrics. The city is also famous as the birth-place of Nonnus, the poet, A.D. 410, and as the burial-place of Nestorius, A.D. 450. This wretched man was banished first to Petra, in Arabia, and then to the Oasis of Khârgeh in 435; he was seized by the Blemmyes and carried off, but eventually found his way to Panopolis. He was again banished and tortured by sufferings and privations, and at length died of a disease in the course of which his tongue was eaten by worms; his religious opponents declared that rain never fell on his tomb. In ancient days Akhmîm had a large population of Copts, and large Coptic monasteries stood close by.

Menshîyeh, on the west bank of the river, 328½ miles from Cairo, stands on the site of a city which is said to have been the capital of the Panopolite nome; its Coptic name was Psôi, ⲯⲱⲓ. In the time of Shenûti the Blemmyes, a nomad warlike Ethiopian tribe, invaded Upper Egypt, and having acquired much booty, they returned to Psôi or Menshîyeh, and settled down there.

Girgeh, on the west bank of the river, 341½ miles from Cairo, has a large Christian population, and is said to occupy the site of the ancient This, whence sprang the first dynasty of historical Egyptian kings.

ABYDOS.*

The Ruins of Abydos. (*After Mariette*).

A Ancient town. B Temple of Seti I.
C Temple of Rameses II. D Temple of Osiris.
E Coptic convent.

Abydos,† in Egyptian Ȧbṭu, Coptic ЄⲂⲰⲦ, Arabic ʻArâbat el-Madfûnah, on the wes bank of the Nile, was one of the most renowned cities ot ancient Egypt; it was famous as the chief seat of the worship of Osiris in Upper Egypt, because the head of this god was supposed to be buried here. The town itself was dedicated to Osiris, and the temple in it, wherein the most solemn ceremonies connected with the worship of this god were celebrated, was more revered than any other in the land. The town and its necropolis were built side by side, and the custom usually followed by the Egyptians in burying their dead

* The Temples at Abydos are visited by Messrs. Cook's travellers on the return journey to Cairo.

† Greek Ἄβυδος; see Pape, *Wörterbuch*, p. 4. That the name was pronounced Abydos, and not Abȳdos, is clear from:—

καὶ Σηστὸν καὶ Ἄβυδον ἔχον καὶ δῖαν Ἀρίσβην.

Iliad, ii., 836.

away from the town in the mountains was not followed in this case. Though the hills of fine white stone were there ready, the people of Abydos did not make use of them for funereal purposes; the sandy plain interspersed every here and there with rocks was the place chosen for burial. The town of Abydos, a small town even in its best time, was built upon a narrow tongue of land situated between the canal, which lies inland some few miles, and the desert. It owed its importance solely to the position it held as a religious centre, and from this point of view it was the second city in Egypt. Thebes, Abydos, and Heliopolis practically represented the homes of religious thought and learning in Egypt. The necropolis of Abydos is not much older than the VIth dynasty, and the tombs found there belonging to this period are of the maṣṭaba class. During the XIth and XIIth dynasties the tombs took the form of small pyramids, which were generally built of brick, and the ancient rectangular form of tomb was revived during the XVIIIth dynasty. Abydos attained its greatest splendour under the monarchs of the XIth and XIIth dynasties, and though its plain was used as a burial ground as late as Roman times, it became of little or no account as early as the time of Psammetichus I. It has often been assumed that the town of Abydos is to be identified with This, the home of Menes, the first historical king of Egypt; the evidence derived from the exhaustive excavations made by M. Mariette does not support this assumption. No trace of the shrine of Osiris, which was as famous in Upper Egypt as was the shrine of the same god at Busiris in Lower Egypt, has been found in the temple; neither can any trace be discovered of the royal tombs which Rameses II. declares he restored. Plutarch says that wealthy inhabitants of Egypt were often brought to Abydos to be buried near the mummy of Osiris, and curiously enough, the tombs close to certain parts of the temple of Osiris are more carefully executed than those elsewhere. Of Abydos Strabo says (Bk. XVII., cap. i., sec. 42), "Above this city (Ptolemaïs) is Abydos, where is the palace of Memnon, constructed in a singular manner, entirely of stone, and after the plan of the Labyrinth, which we have described, but not composed of many parts. It has a fountain situated at a great depth. There is a descent to it through an arched passage built with single stones of remarkable size and workmanship. There is a canal which leads to this place from the great river. About the canal is a grove of Egyptian acanthus, dedicated to Apollo. Abydos seems once to have been a large city, second to Thebes. At present it is a small town. But if, as they say, Memnon is called Ismandes by the Egyptians, the Labyrinth might be a Memnonium, and the work of the same person who constructed those at Abydos and at Thebes; for in those places, it is said, are some Memnonia. At Abydos Osiris is worshipped; but in the temple of Osiris no singer, nor player on the pipe, nor on the cithara, is permitted to perform at the commencement of the ceremonies celebrated in honour of the god, as is usual in rites celebrated in honour of the gods." (Bk. XVII. 1, 44, Falconer's translation.) The principal monuments which have been brought to light by the excavations of M. Mariette at Abydos are:—

I. The **Temple of Seti I.,*** and the **Temple of Rameses II.**

The **Temple of Seti I.**, better known as the **Memnonium**, is built of fine white calcareous stone upon an artificial foundation made of stone, earth and sand, which has

* The plans of the temples of Abydos, etc., printed in this book are copied from those which accompany the *Rapport sur les Temples Égyptiens adressé à S.E. Le Ministre des Travaux Publics* par Grand Bey. This gentleman's plans are more complete than the more elaborate drawings given by Lepsius in his *Denkmäler*, and by other *savants*.

been laid upon a sloping piece of land ; it was called Men-māt-Rā,* after the prenomen of its builder. The Phœnician

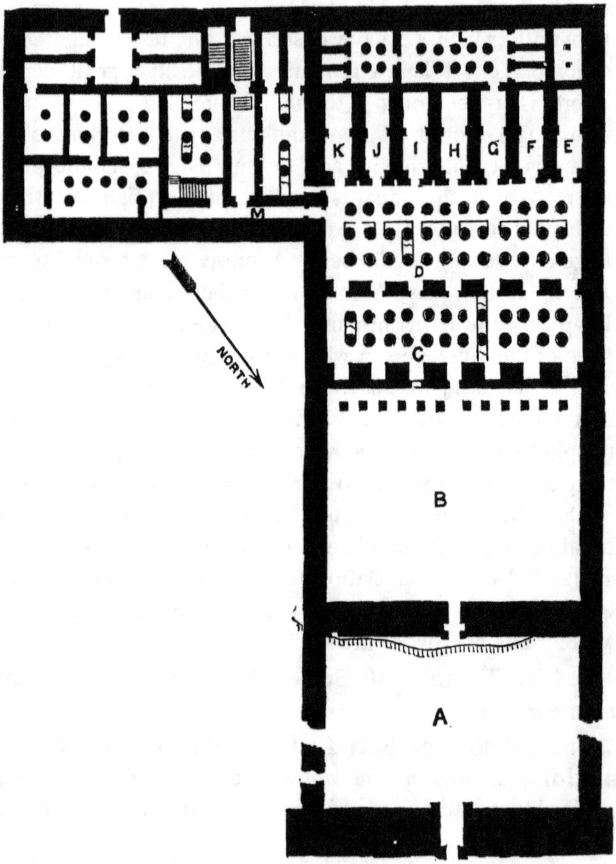

Plan of the Temple of Seti I. at Abydos.

graffiti show that the temple must have ceased to be used at a comparatively early period. It would seem that it was

* 

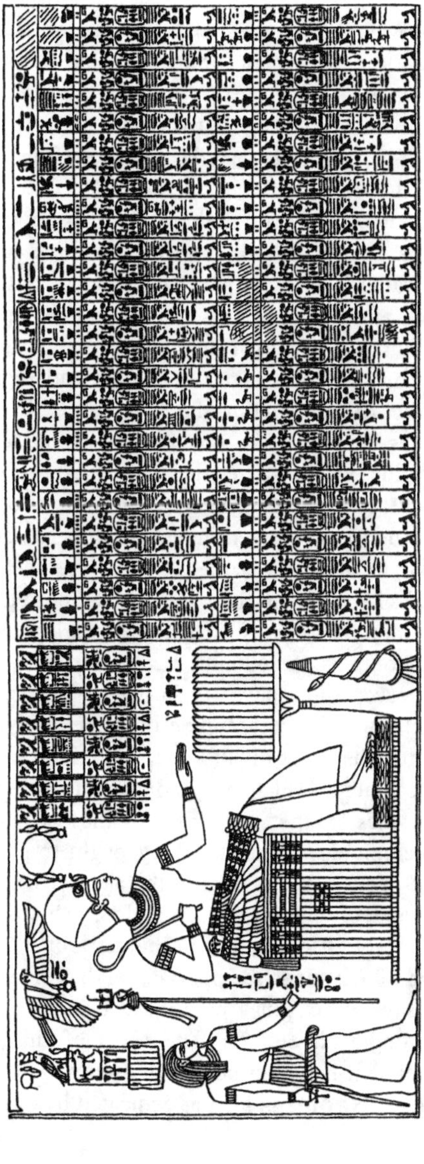

Sculptured relief in which King Seti I. is represented seated before a table of offerings; behind him is the king's KA or "double" bearing his Horus name. The hieroglyphic text consists of a series of addresses to the king, each containing the mention of a gift made to him by the "Eye of Horus."

nearly finished when Seti I. died, and that his son Rameses II. only added the pillars in front and the decoration. Its exterior consists of two courts, A and B, the wall which divides them, and the façade; all these parts were built by Rameses II. The pillars are inscribed with religious scenes and figures of the king and the god Osiris. On the large wall to the south of the central door is an inscription in which Rameses II. relates all that he has done for the honour of his father's memory, how he erected statues of him at Thebes and Memphis, and how he built up the sacred doors. At the end of it he gives a brief sketch of his childhood, and the various grades of rank and dignities which he held. In the interior the first hall, C, is of the time of Rameses II., but it is possible to see under the rough hieroglyphics of this king the finer ones of Seti I.; this hall contains twenty-four pillars arranged in two rows. The scenes on the walls represent figures of the gods and of the king offering to them, the names of the nomes, etc., etc. The second hall, D, is larger than the first, the style and finish of the sculptures are very fine, the hieroglyphics are in relief, and it contains 36 columns, arranged in three rows. From this hall seven short naves dedicated to Horus, Isis, Osiris, Amen, Harmachis, Ptaḥ, and Seti I. respectively, lead into seven vaulted chambers, E, F, G, H, I, J, K, beautifully shaped and decorated, which are dedicated to the same beings. The scenes on the walls of six of these chambers represent the ceremonies which the king ought to perform in them; those in the seventh refer to the apotheosis of the king. At the end of chamber G is a door which leads into the sanctuary of Osiris, L, and in the corridor M is the famous **Tablet of Abydos** (see pp. 626, 627), which gives the names of seventy-six kings of Egypt, beginning with Menes and ending with Seti I. The value of this most interesting monument has been pointed out on p. 3.

The **Temple of Rameses II.** was dedicated by this king

to the god Osiris; it lies a little to the north of the temple of Seti I. Many distinguished scholars thought that this was the famous shrine which all Egypt adored, but the excavations made there by M. Mariette proved that it was not. It would seem that during the French occupation of Egypt in the early part of this century this temple stood almost intact; since that time, however, so much damage has been wrought upon it, that the portions of wall which now remain are only about eight or nine feet high. The fragment of the second Tablet of Abydos, now in the British Museum,

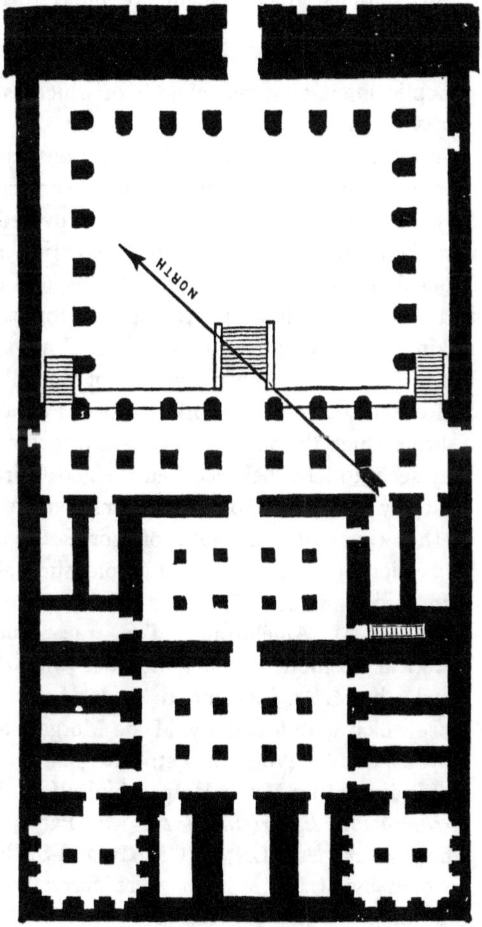

Plan of the Temple of Rameses II. at Abydos.

came from this temple. The few scenes and fragments of inscriptions which remain are interesting but not important.

A little to the north of the temple of Rameses II. is a Coptic monastery, the church of which is dedicated to Amba Musas.

In recent years a number of excavations which have been productive of important results have been carried on near Abydos. In 1896 M. de Morgan discovered a number of remarkable tombs of the Neolithic Period at Al-'Amrah, about three miles to the east of Abydos, and in 1895, 1896, and 1897 M. Amélineau excavated the tombs of a number of kings of the first three dynasties at Umm al-Ḳa'ab, which lies to the west of the necropolis of the Middle Empire; and in the course of his work at Abydos he also discovered a shrine which the ancient Egyptians placed on a spot where they seem to have believed that the god Osiris was buried, or at any rate where some traditions declared he was laid. In the winter of 1899-00 Professor Petrie also carried on excavations on M. Amélineau's old sites at Abydos, and recovered a number of objects of the same class as those found by M. Amélineau. The true value and general historical position of the antiquities which were found at Abydos by M. Amélineau and M. de Morgan, as well as of those which were found by M. de Morgan at Naḳâda and Abydos, and by Professor Petrie at Ballas and Tûkh, were first indicated by M. de Morgan himself in his volumes of *Recherches sur les Origines de l'Égypte*, Paris, 1896 and 1897. The royal names ṬEN, ATCHAB, and SMERKHAT, discovered by M. de Morgan, were correctly identified with the kings of the 1st Dynasty who are usually called Ḥesepti, Merbapen, and Semen-Ptaḥ, by Herr Sethe in the *Aegyptische Zeitschrift*, Bd. 35, p. 1, ff. 1897. M. Jéquier rightly identified PERÅBSEN with Neter-baiu, a king of the 2nd dynasty, and Professor Petrie has correctly identified QĀ with the king of the 1st dynasty who is usually called Qebḥ. The identifications of ĀḤĀ with Menes, and NARMEK with Tetà, and TCHA with Ateth, and MER-NIT with Ata, kings of the 1st dynasty, at present need further evidence. Some of these are more probably pre-dynastic kings.

Farshût, 368 miles from Cairo, on the west bank of the river, called in Coptic Ⲃⲉⲣϭⲟⲟⲩⲧ, contains a sugar factory.

At **Nag' Ḥamâdi**, 373 miles from Cairo, is the iron railway bridge across the Nile.

Ḳaṣr eṣ-Ṣayyâd, or "the hunter's castle," 376 miles from Cairo, on the east bank of the river, marks the site of the ancient Chenoboscion, *i.e.*, the "Goose-pen," or place where geese were kept in large numbers and fattened for market. The Copts call the town ϣⲉⲛ ⲉⲥⲏⲧ, which is probably a corruption of some old Egyptian name, meaning the place where geese were fattened. The town is famous in Coptic annals as the place where Pachomius (he died about A.D. 349, aged 57 years) embraced Christianity, and a few miles to the south of it stood the great monastery of Tabenna, which he founded. In the neighbourhood are a number of interesting tombs of the Early Empire.

ḲENEH AND THE TEMPLE OF DENDERAH.*

Ḳeneh, 405½ miles from Cairo, on the east bank of the river, is the capital of the province of the same name.

* The Greek Tentyra, or Tentyris, is derived from the Egyptian 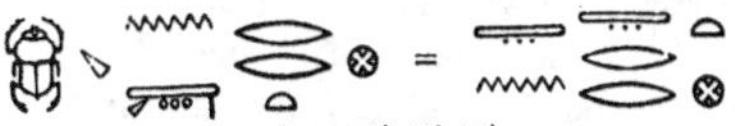 *Ta-en-ta-rert*; the name is also written 

This city is famous for its dates, and the trade which it carries on with the Arabian peninsula.

A short distance from the river, on the west bank, a little to the north of the village of Denderah, stands the **Temple of Denderah**, which marks the site of the classical Tentyra or Tentyris, called ⲦⲈⲚⲦⲰⲢⲈ by the Copts, where the goddess Hathor was worshipped. During the Middle Empire quantities of flax and linen fabrics were produced at Tentyra, and it gained some reputation thereby. In very ancient times Khufu, or Cheops, a king of the IVth dynasty, founded a temple here, but it seems never to have become of much importance,* probably because it lay so close to the famous shrines of Abydos and Thebes. The wonderfully preserved Temple now standing there is probably not older than the beginning of our era; indeed, it cannot, in any case, be older than the time of the later Ptolemies: hence it must be considered as the architectural product of a time when the ancient Egyptian traditions of sculpture were already dead and nearly forgotten. It is, however, a majestic monument, and worthy of careful examination.† Strabo says (Bk. xvii., ch. i. 44) of this town and its inhabitants: "Next to Abydos is . . . . . . the city Tentyra, where the crocodile is held in peculiar abhorrence, and is regarded as the most odious of all animals. For the other Egyptians, although acquainted with its mischievous disposition, and hostility towards the human race, yet worship it, and abstain

* M. Mariette thought that a temple to Hathor existed at Denderah during the XIIth, XVIIIth and XIXth dynasties.

† "Accessible comme il l'est aujourd'hui jusque dans la dernière de ses chambres, il semble se présenter au visiteur comme un livre qu'il n'a qu'à ouvrir et à consulter. Mais le temple de Dendérah est, en somme, un monument terriblement complexe. . . . Il faudrait plusieurs années pour copier tout ce vaste ensemble, et il faudrait vingt volumes du format (folio !) de nos quatre volumes de planches pour le publier. —Mariette, *Dendérah*, *Description Générale*, p. 10.

from doing it harm. But the people of Tentyra track and destroy it in every way. Some, however, as they say of the Psyllians of Cyrenæa, possess a certain natural antipathy to snakes, and the people of Tentyra have the same dislike to crocodiles, yet they suffer no injury from them, but dive and cross the river when no other person ventures to do so. When crocodiles were brought to Rome to be exhibited, they were attended by some of the Tentyritæ. A reservoir was made for them with a sort of stage on one of the sides, to form a basking place for them on coming out of the water, and these persons went into the water, drew them in a net to the place, where they might sun themselves and be exhibited, and then dragged them back again to the reservoir. The people of Tentyra worship Venus. At the back of the fane of Venus is a temple of Isis; then follow what are called Typhoneia, and the canal leading to Coptos, a city common both to the Egyptians and Arabians." (Falconer's translation.)

On the walls and on various other parts of the temples are the names of several of the Roman Emperors; the famous portraits of Cleopatra and Cæsarion her son are on the end wall of the exterior. Passing along a dromos for about 250 feet, the portico, A, open at the top, and supported by twenty-four Hathor-headed columns, arranged in six rows, is reached. Leaving this hall by the doorway facing the entrance, the visitor arrives in a second hall, B, having six columns and three small chambers on each side. The two chambers C and D have smaller chambers on the right and left, E was the so-called sanctuary, and in F the emblem of the god worshipped in the temple was placed. From a room on each side of C a staircase led up to the roof. The purposes for which the chambers were used are stated by M. Mariette in his *Dendérah, Descrip. Gén. du Grand Temple de cette ville.* On the ceiling of the portico is the famous "Zodiac," which was thought to have been made in ancient Egyptian times; the Greek inscription=A.D. 35, written in the twenty-first year of Tiberius, and the names of the Roman Emperors, have clearly proved that, like that at Esneh, it belongs to the Roman time. The Zodiac from Denderah, now at Paris, was cut out, with the permission of Muḥammad 'Ali, in 1821, from the small temple of Osiris, generally called the "Temple on the Roof."

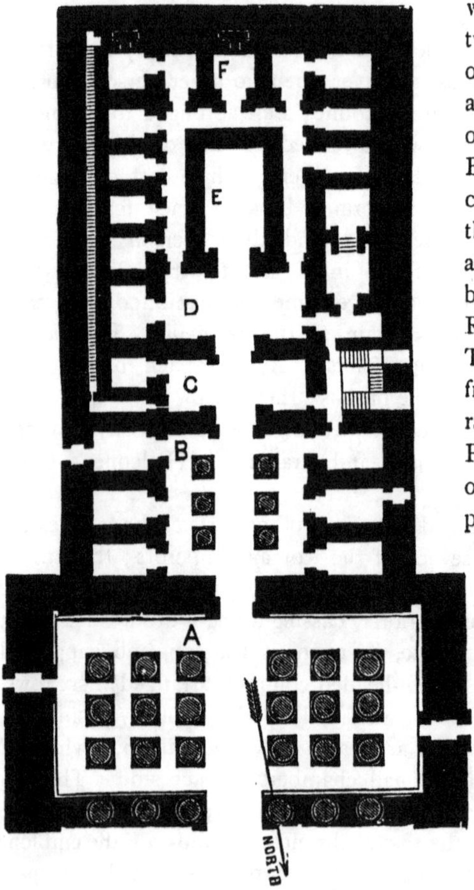

Plan of the Temple at Denderah.

The **Iseium** is situated to the south of the temple of Hathor, and consists of three chambers and a corridor; near by is a pylon which was dedicated to Isis in the 31st year of Cæsar Augustus.

The **Mammisi**, , *Per-mestu*, or "house of giving birth," also built by Augustus, is the name given to the celestial dwelling where the goddess was supposed to have brought forth the third person of the triad which was adored in the temple close by.

The **Typhonium** stands to the north of the Temple of Hathor, and was so named because the god Bes , figures of whom occur on its walls, was confused with Typhon; it measures about 120 feet × 60 feet, and is surrounded by a peristyle of twenty-two columns.

The Temple of Denderah was nearly buried among the rubbish which centuries had accumulated round about it, and a whole village of wretched mud-huts actually stood upon the roof! The excavation of this fine monument was undertaken and completed by M. Mariette, who published many of the texts and scenes inscribed upon its walls in his work mentioned above.

The crocodile was worshipped at Kom Ombo, and Juvenal gives an account of a fight which took place between the people of this place and those of Denderah, in which one of the former stumbled, while running along, and was caught by his foes, cut up, and eaten.

A few miles beyond Denderah, on the east bank of the river, lies the town of **Ḳufṭ**, the  *Qebt* of the hieroglyphics, and ⲕⲉϥⲧ of the Copts; it was the principal city in the Coptites nome, and was the Thebaïs Secunda of the Itineraries. From Ḳofṭ the road which crossed the desert to Berenice on the Red Sea started, and the merchandise which passed through the town from the east, and the stone from the famous porphyry quarries in the Arabian desert must have made it wealthy and important. It held the position of a port on the Nile for merchandise from a very early period; and there is no doubt that every Egyptian king who sent expeditions to Punt, and the countries round about, found Ḳufṭ most usefully situated for this purpose. A temple dedicated to the ithyphallic god Àmsu, Isis and Osiris, stood here. It was nearly destroyed by Diocletian A.D. 292. A copy of a medical papyrus in the British Museum states that the work was originally discovered at Coptos during the time of Cheops, a king of the IVth dynasty; it is certain then that the Egyptians considered this city to be of very old foundation.

Ḳûṣ, 425 miles from Cairo, on the east bank of the Nile, marks the site of the city called Apollinopolis Parva by the Greeks, and Qeset 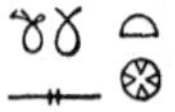 by the Egyptians. To the west of the city stood the monastery of Saint Pisentius, who flourished in the VIIth century, and the well of water which is said to have been visited by our Lord and the Virgin Mary and Joseph; the Copts built numbers of churches in the neighbourhood.

Naḳâdah, 428 miles from Cairo, on the west bank of the river, nearly opposite the island of Maṭarah, was the home of a large number of Copts in early Christian times, and several monasteries were situated there. The four which now remain are dedicated to the Cross, St. Michael, St. Victor, and St. George respectively, and tradition says that they were founded by the Empress Helena; the most important of them is that of St. Michael. The church in this monastery "is one of the most remarkable Christian structures in Egypt, possessing as it does some unique peculiarities. There are four churches, of which three stand side by side in such a manner that they have a single continuous western wall. Two of the four have an apsidal haikal with rectagular side chapels, while the other two are entirely rectangular; but the two apses differ from all other apses in Egyptian churches by projecting . . . beyond the eastern wall and by showing an outward curvature. They form a solitary exception to the rule that the Coptic apse is merely internal, and so far belong rather to Syrian architecture than to Coptic. The principal church shows two other features which do not occur elsewhere in the Christian buildings of Egypt, namely, an external atrium surrounded with a cloister, and a central tower with a clerestory . . . . . Possibly the same remark may apply to the structure of the iconostasis, which has two side-doors and no central entrance, though this arrangement is not quite unparalleled in the churches of Upper Egypt, and may be a later alteration. It will be noticed that the church has a triple western entrance from the cloisters." (Butler, *Ancient Coptic Churches of Egypt*, Vol. I., p. 361.) In 1897 M. de Morgan carried on some important excavations here, and discovered a large number of pre-historic tombs, and the tomb of a king called Āḥā, who has, by some, been identified with Menȧ, the first king of the Ist dynasty.

LUXOR (EL-UḲṢUR) AND THEBES.

Luxor, 450 miles from Cairo, on the east bank of the river, is a small town with a few thousand inhabitants, and owes its importance to the fact that it is situated close to the ruins of the temples of the ancient city of Thebes. The name Luxor is a corruption of the Arabic name of the place, El-Uḳṣûr, which means "the palaces." Ancient Thebes stood on both sides of the Nile, and was generally called in hieroglyphics , Uast; that part of the city which was situated on the east bank of the river, and included the temples of Karnak and Luxor, appears to have been called Ȧpet,* whence the Coptic ⲧⲁⲡⲉ and the name Thebes have been derived. The cuneiform inscriptions and Hebrew Scriptures call it No (Ezek. xxx. 14) and No-Amon † (Nahum iii. 8), and the Greek and Roman writers Diospolis Magna. When or by whom Thebes was founded it is impossible to say. Diodorus says that it is the most ancient city of Egypt; some say that, like Memphis, it was founded by Menes, and others, that it was a colony from Memphis. It is certain, however, that it did not become a city of the first importance until after the decay of Memphis, and as the progress of Egyptian civilization was from north to south, this is only what was to be expected. During the early dynasties no mention is made of Thebes, but we know that as early as the XIIth dynasty some kings were buried there.

The spot on which ancient Thebes stood is so admirably adapted for the site of a great city, that it

* *I.e.*, "throne ity."

† In Revised Version, = *Nut-Ȧmen.*

would have been impossible for the Egyptians to overlook it. The mountains on the east and west side of the river sweep away from it, and leave a broad plain on each bank of several square miles in extent. It has been calculated that modern Paris could stand on this space of ground. We have, unfortunately, no Egyptian description of Thebes, or any statement as to its size; it may, however, be assumed from the remains of its buildings which still exist, that the descriptions of the city as given by Strabo and Diodorus are on the whole trustworthy. The fame of the greatness of Thebes had reached the Greeks of Homer's age, and its "hundred gates" and 20,000 war chariots are referred to in Iliad IX, 381. The city must have reached its highest point of splendour during the rule of the XVIIIth and XIXth dynasties over Egypt, and as little by little the local god Åmen-Rā became the great god of all Egypt, his dwelling-place Thebes also gained in importance and splendour. The city suffered severely at the hands of Cambyses, who left nothing in it unburnt that fire would consume. Herodotus appears never to have visited Thebes, and the account he gives of it is not satisfactory; the account of Diodorus, who saw it about B.C. 57, is as follows: "Afterwards reigned Busiris, and eight of his posterity after him; the last of which (of the same name with the first) built that great city which the Egyptians call Diospolis, the Greeks Thebes; it was in circuit 140 stades (about twelve miles), adorned with stately public buildings, magnificent temples, and rich donations and revenues to admiration; and he built all the private houses, some four, some five stories high. And to sum up all in a word, made it not only the most beautiful and stateliest city of Egypt, but of all others in the world. The fame therefore of the riches and grandeur of this city was so noised abroad in every place, that the poet Homer takes notice of it. . . . . . Although there are some that say it had not a hundred gates; but that there were many large porches to the temples, whence the city was called *Hecatompylus*, a hundred gates, for many gates: yet that it was certain they had in it 20,000 chariots of war; for there were a hundred stables all along the river from Memphis to Thebes towards Lybia, each of which was capable to hold two hundred horses, the marks and signs of which are visible at this day. And we have it related, that not only this king, but the succeeding princes from time to time, made it their business to beautify this city; for that there was no city under the sun so adorned with so many and stately monuments of gold, silver, and ivory, and multitudes of colossi and obelisks, cut out of one entire stone. For there were there four temples built, for beauty and greatness to be admired, the most ancient of which was in circuit thirteen furlongs (about one and a half miles), and five and forty cubits high, and had a wall twenty-four feet broad. The ornaments of this temple were suitable to its magnificence, both for cost and workmanship. The fabric hath continued to our time, but the silver and the gold, and ornaments of ivory and precious stones were carried away by the Persians when Cambyses burnt the temples of Egypt. . . . There, they say, are the wonderful sepulchres of the ancient kings, which for state and grandeur far exceed all that posterity can attain unto at this day. The Egyptian priests say that in their sacred registers there are 47 of these sepulchres; but in the reign of Ptolemy Lagus there remained only 17, many of which were ruined and destroyed when I myself came into those parts." (Bk. I., chaps. 45, 46, Booth's translation, pp. 23, 24.)

Strabo, who visited Thebes about B.C. 24, says:—"Next to the city of Apollo is Thebes, now called Diospolis, 'with her hundred gates, through each of which issue 200 men, with horses and chariots,' according to Homer, who mentions also its wealth; 'not all the wealth the palaces of Egyptian Thebes contain.' Other writers use the same anguage, and consider Thebes as the metropolis of Egypt. Vestiges of its magnitude still exist, which extend 80 stadia (about nine miles) in length. There are a great number of temples, many of which Cambyses mutilated. The spot is at present occupied by villages. One part of it, in which is the city, lies in Arabia; another is in the country on the other side of the river, where is the Memnonium. Here are two colossal figures near one another, each consisting of a single stone. One is entire; the upper parts of the other, from the chair, are fallen down, the effect, it is said, of an earthquake. It is believed that once a day a noise as of a slight blow issues from the part of the statue which remains in the seat and on its base. When I was at those places with Ælius Gallus, and numerous friends and soldiers about him, I heard a noise at the first hour (of the day), but whether proceeding from the base or from the colossus, or produced on purpose by some of

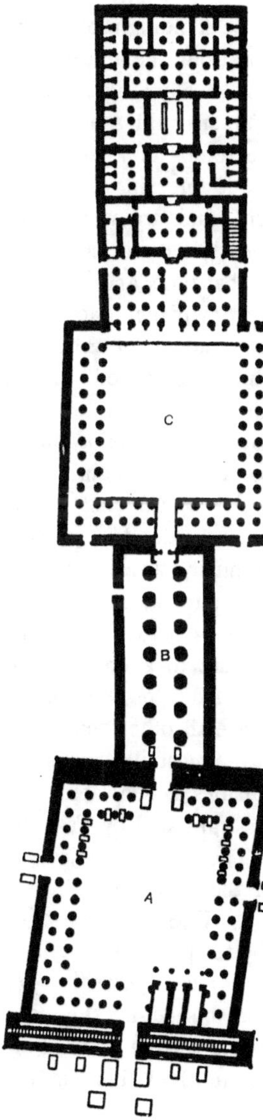

The Temple of Luxor.

those standing around the base, I cannot confidently assert. For from the uncertainty of the cause, I am disposed to believe anything rather than that stones disposed in that manner could send forth sound. Above the Memnonium are tombs of kings in caves, and hewn out of the stone, about forty in number; they are executed with singular skill, and are worthy of notice. Among the tombs are obelisks with inscriptions, denoting the wealth of the kings of that time, and the extent of their empire, as reaching to the Scythians, Bactrians, Indians, and the present Ionia; the amount of tribute also, and the number of soldiers, which composed an army of about a million of men. The priests there are said to be, for the most part, astronomers and philosophers. The former compute the days, not by the moon, but by the sun, introducing into the twelve months, of thirty days each, five days every year. But in order to complete the whole year, because there is (annually) an excess of a part of a day, they form a period from out of whole days and whole years, the supernumerary portions of which in that period, when collected together, amount to a day.* They ascribe to Mercury (Thoth) all knowledge of this kind. To Jupiter, whom they worship above all other deities, a virgin of the greatest beauty and of the most illustrious family (such persons the Greeks call pallades) is dedicated" . . . . (Bk. XVII, chap. 1, sec. 46, translated by Falconer.)

The principal objects of interest on the east or right bank of the river are:—

1. The Temple of Luxor. Compared with Karnak the temple of Luxor is not of the greatest importance, and until recent years the greater part of its courts and chambers was buried by the accumulated rubbish and mud upon which a large number of houses stood. The excavation of the ruins of this temple was begun by M. Maspero, who,

* See page 142.

with the help of several hundred pounds collected by public subscription in England, began the work in the winter of 1883, and it was prosecuted with such vigour, that the natives almost resisted by force the removal of the soil upon which their houses stood. In 1887 M. Grébaut, the successor of M. Maspero, continued the clearing, and shortly afterwards M. Grand Bey, an official who has carried out at Luxor and Karnak works of the highest value for the preservation of the temples, was appointed to report on the means which ought to be taken to prevent the collapse of the temple remains, which was beginning to take place owing to the removal of the earth from the walls and pillars. In 1888 and the following years much clearing was done, and many portions of the building were strengthened with modern masonry, and now it is possible for the visitor to walk about in the temple and get an idea of its general plan. The temple is built of sandstone, and stands, probably, upon the site of an earlier religious edifice; it formed an important part of the sacred buildings of Thebes, which were dedicated to the Theban triad of Àmen-Rā 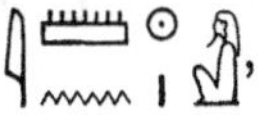, Mut,  and Khonsu, , and was called "The House of Àmen in the Southern Apt," to distinguish it from "The House of Àmen in the Northern Apt," *i.e.*, Karnak. It was built by Amenophis III. about B.C. 1500, and was at that time the most beautiful temple in Egypt; it was nearly 500 feet long and about 180 feet wide, and was connected with Karnak by means of a paved way, on each side of which was arranged a row of rams with their faces turned towards its main axis. Soon after the death of Amenophis III. his son, the heretic king Amenophis IV., ordered the name and figure of the god Àmen to be erased throughout the temple, and built a small shrine or chapel near his father's great work in honour of the god Åten. The building was not popular among the Egyptians, for on the death of Amenophis IV. it was pulled down, and the stones were employed in other parts of the main edifice. Ḥeru-em-ḥeb and Seti I. added a number of bas-reliefs, and Rameses II. built the large colonnade, a large courtyard with porticoes, a pylon, two obelisks, and some colossal statues. This last king, in building the courtyard and pylon, made their axes be in continuation of that of the paved way which led to Karnak, instead of that of the colonnade and other parts of the temple. During the rule of the Persians over Egypt the temple was sacked and burnt, but under the Ptolemies the damage was partially made good; in B.C. 27 the temple was greatly damaged by the earthquake which wrecked many a noble temple and tomb in Egypt, and a little later the stones which had been thrown down from the walls and columns were employed in building a barrier to keep out the waters from the city. But the damage wrought by the Christians in the Luxor temple was, as at Dêr el-Baḥarî, terrible, for not content with turning certain sections of it into churches, the more fanatical among them smashed statues, and disfigured bas-reliefs, and wrecked shrines with characteristic savage and ignorant zeal. When the Christians could afford to build churches for themselves they forsook the temple, and then the inhabitants of the town began to build mud houses for themselves in the courtyard and other parts of the building. As these fell down year by year the natives, who never repair a building if they can help it, built new ones on the old sites, and thus the temple became filled with earth and rubbish. In the XVth century a mosque was built in the large courtyard of Rameses II. by the descendants of a Muḥammadan saint, who is said to have flourished near Mecca either during the life of Muḥammad the Prophet or shortly after; this saint was called Abu Hagag, and several families now living at Luxor claim him as an ancestor.

The **Obelisk,** hewn out of fine Aswân granite, is one of a pair which stood before the pylon of the temple and proclaimed the names and titles of Rameses II.; it is nearly 82 feet high, and weighs a little less than 250 tons. The companion obelisk now stands in the Place de la Concorde in Paris. The front of the temple was ornamented with six colossal statues of Rameses II., four standing and two seated, but of the former three have been destroyed. The seated statues, one on each side of the door, were of black granite, and on the side of the throne of the one which now remains are conventional representations of members of vanquished nations. The top of the **pylon** when first built was about 80 feet above the ground, and its width was nearly 100 feet; each of its towers was hollow, and in their front walls were channels with sockets in the ground, in which large poles with flags flying from them were placed when Thebes was keeping a festival. The face of the pylon is covered with sculptures and texts which refer to the dedication of the pylon to Åmen-Rā, and to the victory of Rameses I. over the Kheta. The battle, which took place near the city of Kadesh on the Orontes, resulted in the overthrow of a great confederation of Syrian tribes, and Rameses was greatly elated at his victory. Among the texts on the pylon is a description of the fight written by one Pen-ta-urt, and this poetical narrative of the momentous event was so much esteemed by the king, that he ordered it to be inscribed on stelæ and many public buildings throughout the country. The outsides of the walls built by Rameses II. are covered with scenes relating to the same campaign and describing the return of the king in triumph. The doorway of the **Court** of Rameses II. (A) contains reliefs by Shabaka, a king of the XXVth dynasty, and in the north-west corner are the ruins of a small chapel which Rameses II. built against the pylon; a portico with two rows of pillars runs round most of the four sides. Of the reliefs on the walls some date from the reign of Amenophis III. and Ḥeru-em-ḥeb, but most of them have been usurped by Rameses II.; here also are figures of personifications of geographical localities bearing offerings, and in the south-west corner are figures of seventeen of the sons of Rameses II., who are making offerings at the ceremony of dedication of the pylon. These are followed by a number of sacrificial scenes. The columns of the portico are 72 in number and have lotus capitals; on each is a relief representing Rameses II. making an offering either to Ȧmen-Rā, or Ȧmsu, and some goddess. The little chapel in the north-west corner contains three chambers, which are dedicated respectively to Ȧmen-Rā, Mut, and Khonsu. On each side of the doorway which leads into the colonnade Rameses II. placed a huge black granite statue of himself, and between the columns close by were eleven statues of himself in red granite; on the side of each of these last is a figure of one of his wives. The **Colonnade** (B) beyond the courtyard of Rameses II. is a part of the original building of Amenophis III., though the names of many other kings are found in it; but it is doubtful if any of the reliefs on the walls were made by him; the scenes represent the celebration of the festival of Ȧmen-Rā, the procession of sacred boats to the Nile and back, the ceremonies in the shrine, etc., and many of them date from the time of Ḥeru-em-ḥeb. The lotus columns, 14 in number, are massive but beautifully proportioned; they are about 51 feet high, and about 11 feet in diameter.

The **Court of Amenophis III.** (C) is next reached. Round three sides of this runs a colonnade with two rows of columns, and the walls are decorated with reliefs belonging to various periods, from that of Amenophis III. to that of

Alexander and Philip. Beyond this courtyard is a hall containing 32 columns; the walls are ornamented with reliefs of various periods, and the occurrence of the names of several kings in this portion of the building shows that, in parts, it has been often repaired. To the left, between the two last columns, is an altar of the Roman period, with a Latin inscription dedicating it to the Emperor Augustus. Passing through the doorway, a chamber which originally had eight columns is entered; this was altered in several ways, and turned into a church by the Christians, who plastered over the interesting reliefs of the time of Amenophis III. with lime, and then painted it with elaborate designs in bright colours. On each side of this chamber is a small chapel; that on the left was dedicated to Mut, and that on the right to Khensu. Leaving the chamber which was turned into a Christian church, and passing through a smaller chamber with four columns, the **shrine of Alexander the Great** is reached. In the time of Amenophis III. it contained four columns, but these Alexander removed, and turned it into a shrine in place of the old shrine which was originally in the last room of the building. In the centre a rectangular building open at both ends was built, and within this was carefully preserved the sacred boat of Rā, wherein was seated a figure of the god. The walls of this shrine are ornamented with reliefs, in which Amenophis III. is seen adoring the various gods of Thebes; the ceiling is decorated with figures of vultures and a large number of five-rayed stars painted in yellow on a blue ground. Through a doorway on the left in the sanctuary, and through a second doorway immediately on the left of it, the chamber on which is depicted the **Birth of Amenophis III.** is reached; the roof of the chamber is supported by three columns with lotus capitals. Here on the west wall are the following scenes, arranged in three rows:—

First or *Lowest Row*. 1. Khnemu, seated opposite Isis, fashioning the body of the young king and his *ka* or double upon a potter's wheel; he predicts that the child shall be king of Egypt. 2. Åmen and Khnemu holding converse. 3. Åmen and Mut-em-ua, wife of Thothmes IV., and mother of Amenophis III., holding converse in the presence of the goddesses Selq, or Serq, and Neith. In the text the god Åmen declares that he had taken the form of the husband of Mut-em-ua and that he is the father of the child who is to be born. 4. Åmen and Thothmes IV. 5. Mut-em-ua being embraced by the goddess Isis in the presence of Åmen. *Second* or *Middle Row*. 1. Thoth telling the queen that Åmen has given her a son. 2. The queen being great with child, is being sustained by Khnemu and Isis, who make her to breathe "life." 3. The child is born in the presence of Thoueris, the goddess of children, and Bes, the driver away of evil spirits from the bed of birth. 4. Isis offering the child to Åmen, who addresses him as "son of the Sun." 5. The child Amenophis III. seated on the knees of Åmen, whilst his destiny is being decreed in the presence of Isis or Hathor; Mut offers to him a palm branch, at the end of which is the emblem of festivals. Åmen declares that he will give him "millions of years, like the Sun." *Third* or *Top Row*. 1. The queen seated on the bed of birth, and the child being suckled by Hathor in the form of a cow. 2. The seven Hathors (?) and two goddesses. 3. The Niles of the South and North purifying the child. 4. Horus presenting the king and his *ka* to Åmen. 5. The gods Khnemu and Anubis. 6. The king and his *ka* seated and standing before Åmen. 7. Amenophis seated on his throne. The scenes on the south wall refer to the acknowledgment of his sovereignty by the gods of Egypt. The remaining chambers of the temple are not of any special interest. It will be noted that the idea of the scenes of the Birth

Chamber is copied from the temple of Ḥātshepset at Dêr el-Baḥarî.

II. The **Temple at Karnak.** The ruins of the buildings at Karnak are perhaps the most wonderful of any in Egypt, and they merit many visits from the traveller. It is probable that this spot was "holy ground" from a very early to a very late period, and we know that a number of kings from Thothmes III. to Euergetes II. lavished much wealth to make splendid the famous shrine of Åmen in the Åpts, and other temples situated there. The temples of Luxor and Karnak were united by an avenue about 6,500 feet long and 80 feet wide, on each side of which was arranged a row of sphinxes; from the fact that these monuments are without names, M. Mariette thought that the avenue was constructed at the expense of the priests or the wealthy inhabitants of the town, just as in later days the pronaos of the temple at Denderah was built by the people of that town. At the end of this avenue, to the right, is a road which leads to the so-called **Temple of Mut,*** which was also approached by an avenue of sphinxes. Within the enclosure there stood originally two temples, both of which were dedicated to Åmen, built during the reign of

* In the Temple of Mut, by permission of the authorities, Miss Margaret Benson carried out some excavations, and in the first court discovered an almost perfect black granite squatting statue of a scribe called Åmen-em-ḥāt. On the front were several lines of well cut hieroglyphics containing prayers to the various great gods of Thebes, and the cartouches on it of Amenophis II. show that the deceased flourished during the first half of the XVIIIth dynasty, about B.C. 1550. The statue is about two feet high, and probably stood in a prominent place in the temple with which he was associated. This site had been dug through more than once by Mariette and by natives, and Miss Benson's "find" indicates that the neighbouring ground should be explored once again. Further excavations by Miss Benson brought to light about forty Sekhet figures, and cartouches of Rameses II., Rameses III., Rameses IV., Rameses VI., and Shishak I. inscribed upon statues and walls.

Amenophis III.; Rameses II. erected two obelisks in front of the larger temple. To the north-west of these a smaller

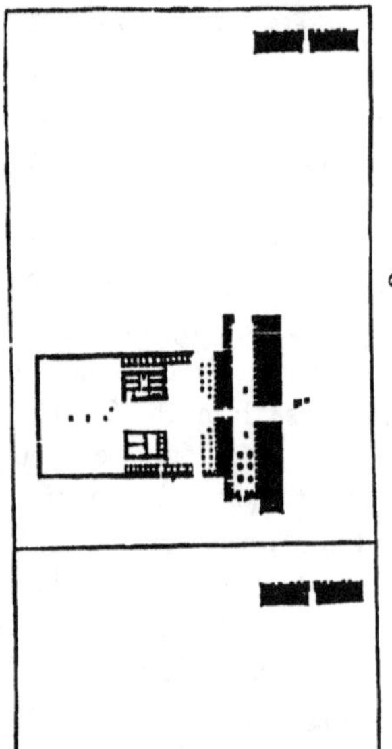

PLANS OF KARNAK—1-3.

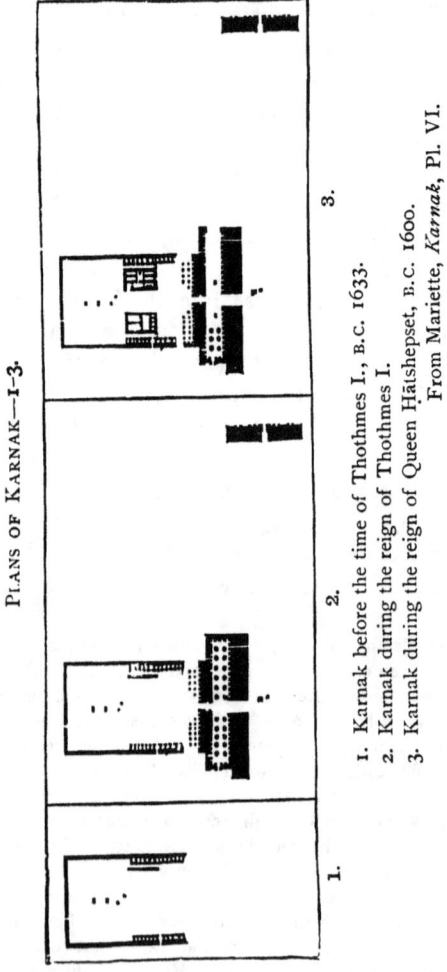

1. 2. 3.

1. Karnak before the time of Thothmes I., B.C. 1633.
2. Karnak during the reign of Thothmes I.
3. Karnak during the reign of Queen Hātshepset, B.C. 1600.

From Mariette, *Karnak*, Pl. VI.

temple was built in Ptolemaic times, and the ruins on one side of it show that the small temples which stood there were either founded or restored by Rameses II., Osorkon, Thekeleth, Sabaco, Nectanebus I., and the Ptolemies. Behind the temple enclosure are the remains of a temple dedicated to Ptaḥ of Memphis by Thothmes III.; the three doors behind it and the courts into which they lead were added by Sabaco, Tirhakah, and the Ptolemies.

Returning to the end of the avenue of sphinxes which leads from Luxor to Karnak, a second smaller avenue ornamented with a row of ram-headed sphinxes on each side is entered; at the end of it stands the splendid pylon built by Ptolemy IX. Euergetes II. Passing through the door, a smaller avenue of sphinxes leading to the temple built by Rameses III. is reached; the small avenue of sphinxes and eight of its columns were added by Rameses XIII. This temple was dedicated to Khonsu, and appears to have been built upon the site of an ancient temple of the time

Ptolemaïc gateway at Karnak.
(From a photograph by A. Beato, of Luxor.)

of Amenophis III. To the west of this temple is a smaller temple built by Ptolemy IX. Euergetes II.

The great Temple of Karnak fronted the Nile, and was approached by means of a small avenue of ram-headed sphinxes which were placed in position by Rameses II.

PLAN OF KARNAK—4.

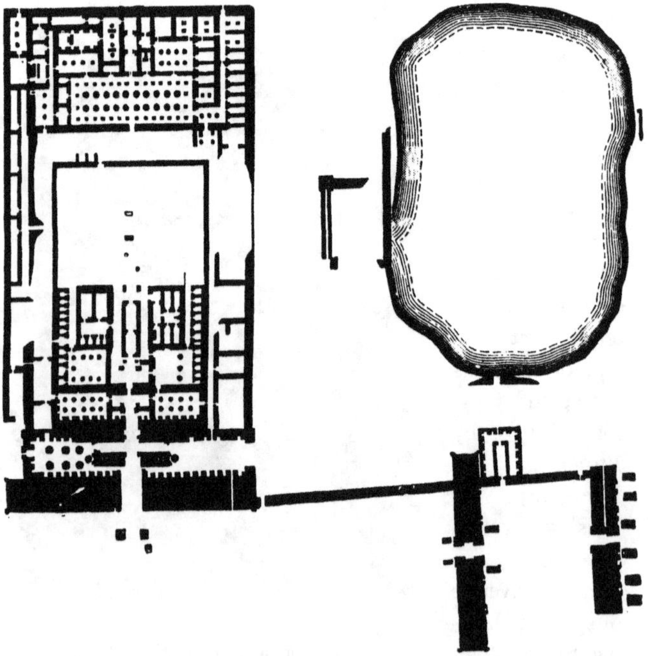

Karnak during the reign of Thothmes III., B.C. 1600.
From Mariette, *Karnak*, Pl. VI.

Passing through the first propylon, a court or hall, having a double row of pillars down the centre, is entered; on each side is a corridor with a row of columns. On the right hand (south) side are the ruins of a temple built by

Rameses III., and on the left are those of another built by Seti II. This court or hall was the work of Shashanq, the first king of the XXIInd dynasty. On each side of the steps leading through the second pylon was a colossal statue of Rameses II.; that on the right hand has now disappeared. Passing through this pylon, the famous "**Hall of Columns**" is entered. The twelve columns forming the double row in the middle are about sixty feet high and about thirty-five feet in circumference; the other columns, 122 in number, are about forty feet high and twenty-seven feet in circumference. Rameses I. set up one column, Seti I., the builder of this hall, set up seventy-nine, and the remaining fifty-four were set up by Rameses II. It is thought that this hall was originally roofed over. At the end of it is the third propylon, which was built by Amenophis III., and served as the entrance to the temple until the time of Rameses I. Between this and the next pylon is a narrow passage, in the middle of which stood two obelisks which were set up by Thothmes I.; the southern one is still standing, and bears the names of this king, but the northern one has fallen,* and its fragments show that Thothmes III. caused his name to be carved on it. At the southern end of this passage are the remains of a gate built by Rameses IX. The fourth and fifth pylons were built by Thothmes I. Between them stood fourteen columns, six of which were set up by Thothmes I., and eight by Amenophis II., and two granite obelisks; one of the obelisks still stands. They were hewn out of the granite quarry by the command of Ḥātshepset,† the daughter of Thothmes I., and

* It was standing when Pococke visited Egypt in 1737–1739.

† "Scarcely had the royal brother and husband of Hashop (*sic*) closed his eyes, when the proud queen threw aside her woman's veil, and appeared in all the splendour of Pharaoh, as a born king. For she laid aside her woman's dress, clothed herself in man's attire, and adorned herself with the crown and insignia of royalty." (Brugsch's *Egypt under the Pharaohs*, *Vol. I.*, p. 349.)

sister of Thothmes II. and Thothmes III. This able woman set them up in honour of "father Åmen," and she relates in the inscriptions on the base of the standing obelisk that she covered their tops with *smu* metal, or copper, that they could be seen from a very great distance, and that

PLAN OF KARNAK—5.

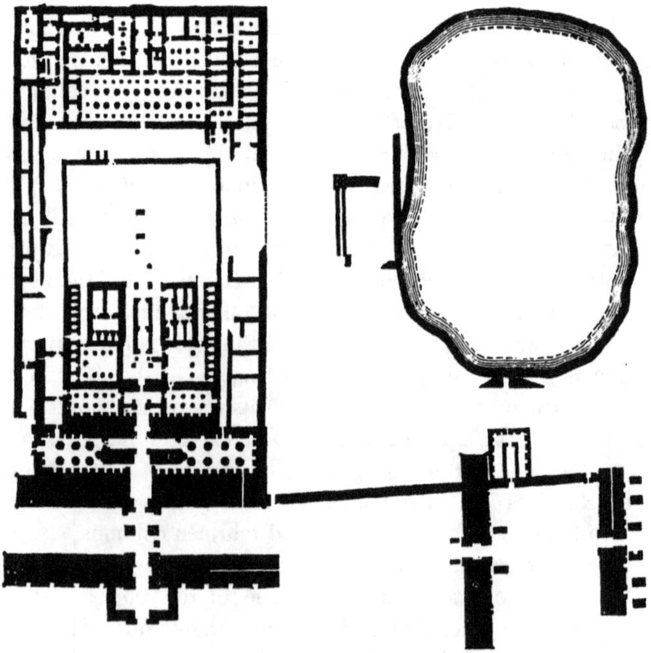

Karnak during the reign of Amenophis III., B.C. 1500.
From Mariette, *Karnak*, Pl. VI.

she had them hewn and brought down to Thebes in about seven months. These obelisks were brought into their chamber from the south side, and were 98 and 105 feet high respectively; the masonry round their bases is of the time of Thothmes III. The sixth pylon and the two walls which flank it on the north and south are the work of Thothmes III., but Seti II., Rameses III., and Rameses IV. have added their cartouches to them. On this pylon are inscribed a large number of geographical names of interest. Passing through it, the visitor finds himself in a vestibule which leads into a red granite oblong chamber, inscribed with the name of Philip III. of Macedon, which is often said to have formed the sanctuary. In the chambers on each side of it are found the names of Amenophis I., Thothmes I., Thothmes II., Ḥātshepset, and Thothmes III. The sanctuary stood in the centre of the large court beyond the two oblong red granite pedestals. In ancient days, when Thebes was pillaged by her conquerors, it would seem that special care was taken to uproot not only the shrine, but the very foundations upon which it rested. Some fragments of columns inscribed with the name of Usertsen I. found there prove, however, that its foundation dates from the reign of this king. Beyond the sanctuary court is a large building of the time of Thothmes III. In it was found the famous **Tablet of Ancestors,** now in Paris, where this king is seen making offerings to a number of his royal ancestors. On the north side of the building is the chamber in which he made his offerings, and on the east side is a chamber where he adored the hawk, the emblem of the Sun-god Rā; this latter chamber was restored by Alexander IV. Behind the great temple, and quite distinct from it, was another small temple. On the south side of the great temple was a lake which was filled by infiltration from the Nile; it appears only to have been used for processional purposes, as water for ablutionary and other purposes was drawn from the well on the north side of the interior of the temple. The lake was dug during the reign of Thothmes III., and its stone quays probably belong to the same period.

Passing through the gate at the southern end of the

passage in which stands the obelisk of Ḥātshepset, a long avenue with four pylons is entered; the first was built by

PLAN OF KARNAK—6.

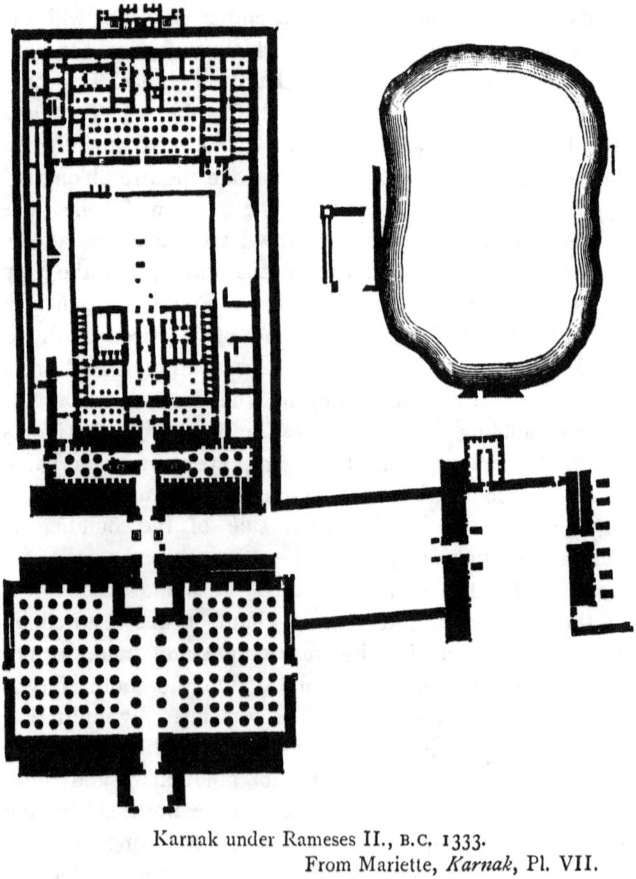

Karnak under Rameses II., B.C. 1333.
From Mariette, *Karnak*, Pl. VII.

Thothmes III., the second by Thothmes I., and the third and fourth by Ḥeru-em-ḥeb. Between these last two, on the east side, stood a temple built by Amenophis II. On the north side of the Great Temple are the ruins of two smaller buildings which belong to the time of the XXVIth dynasty.

The outside of the north wall of the Great Hall of Columns is ornamented with some interesting scenes from the battles of Seṭi I. against the peoples who lived to the north-east of Syria and in Mesopotamia, called Shasu, Rutennu, and Kharu. The king is represented as having conquered all these people, and returning to Thebes laden with much spoil and bringing many captives. It is doubtful if the events really took place in the order in which they are depicted; but the fidelity to nature, and the spirit and skill with which these bas-reliefs have been executed, make them some of the most remarkable sculptures known. The scene in which Seti I. is shown grasping the hair of the heads of a number of people, in the act of slaying them, is symbolic.

The outside of the south wall is ornamented with a large scene in which Shashanq (Shishak), the first king of the XXIInd dynasty, is represented smiting a group of kneeling prisoners; the god Åmen, in the form of a woman, is standing by presenting him with weapons of war. Here also are 150 cartouches, surmounted by heads, in which are written the names of the towns captured by Shishak. The type of features given to these heads by the sculptor shows that the vanquished peoples belonged to a branch of the great Semitic family. The hieroglyphics in one of the cartouches were supposed to read "the king of Judah," and to represent Jeroboam, who was vanquished by Shishak it has now been proved conclusively that they form the name of a place called Iuta-melek. Passing along to the east, the visitor comes to a wall at right angles to the first, upon which is inscribed a copy of the poem of Pen-ta-urt, celebrating the victory of Rameses II. over the Kheta, in the fifth year of his reign; and on the west side of the

PLAN OF KARNAK—7.

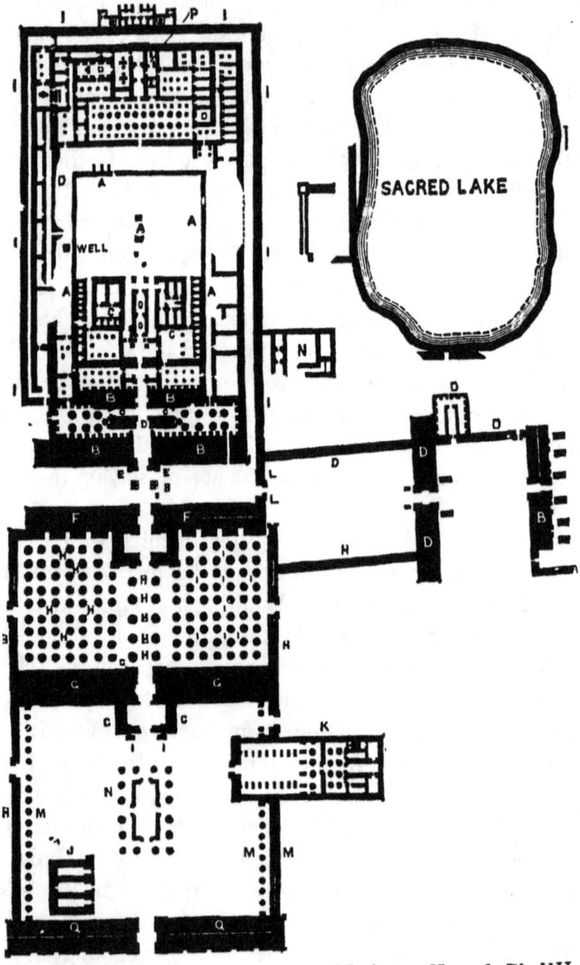

Karnak under the Ptolemies. From Mariette, *Karnak*, Pl. VII.

A. Walls standing before the time of Thothmes I.
B. Pylons built by Thothmes I.
C. Walls and obelisks of Hātshepset.
D. Walls, pylon, etc., of Thothmes III.
E. Gateway of Thothmes IV.
F. Pylon of Amenophis III.
G. Pylon of Rameses I.
H. Walls and columns of Seti I.
I. Columns, walls and statues of Rameses II.
J. Temple of Seti II.
K. Temple of Rameses III.
L. Gateway of Rameses IX.
M. Pillars and walls of the XXIInd dynasty.
N. Pillars of Tirhakah.
O. Corridor of Philip III. of Macedon.
P. Chamber and shrine of Alexander II.
Q. Pylon built by the Ptolemies.

wall is a stele on which is set forth a copy of the offensive and defensive treaty between this king and the prince of the Kheta.

The inscriptions on the magnificent ruins at Karnak show that from the time of Usertsen I., B.C. 2433, to that of Alexander IV., B.C. 312 (?), the religious centre* of Upper Egypt was at Thebes, and that the most powerful of the kings of Egypt who reigned during this period spared neither pains nor expense in adding to and beautifying the temples there. In fact, it was as much a pleasure as a duty for a king to repair the old buildings of the famous shrine of Karnak, or to build new ones, for the walls and pylons of that ancient sanctuary constituted a book of fame in the best and greatest sense in the opinion of the Egyptians. The fury of the elements, the attacks of Egypt's enemies, and the yearly rise of the Nile have all contributed powerfully towards the destruction of these splendid buildings; but what has helped most of all to injure them is the weakness of the foundations of their walls and columns, and the insufficiency of their bases. As long as the columns were partly buried in earth and rubbish, very little strain was put upon them, and they appeared sound enough; but when the masses of earth which surrounded their bases were removed, experts declared that a number of them would fall. In 1899 eleven of the columns in the Great Hall at Karnak *did* fall, and an examination of their foundations showed the reasons, viz., insufficiency of base, poor foundations, and to these may be added, as Sir W. Garstin said, unstable equilibrium of the soil caused by alteration of the levels of the Nile. Much injury has, of course, also been caused to the stones of the columns by the salts which were

* The short-lived heresy of the worship of the disk of the Sun instead of that of Åmen-Rā would not interfere with the general popularity of Theban temples.

present in the masses of earth which formerly surrounded them. If funds could be found, and M. Grand Bey were enabled to increase the scale of the good work upon which he has been engaged at Karnak for so many years, the damage could probably be repaired in two or three years. Many parts of the building have, no doubt, suffered through the shock of the fall of these columns, and exhaustive repairs ought to be taken in hand at once. The work is, naturally, too great and costly for private enterprise, and we must therefore hope that Lord Cromer will find a means of restoring Karnak as effectually as he has revivified Egypt.

On the **west bank** of the river the following are the most interesting antiquities:—

I. The **Temple of Ḳûrnah.** This temple was built by Seti I. in memory of his father Rameses I.; it was completed by Rameses II., by whom it was re-dedicated to the memory of his father Seti I. Two pylons stood before it, and joining them was an Avenue of Sphinxes. This temple was to all intents and purposes a cenotaph, and as such its position on the edge of the desert, at the entrance to a necropolis, is explained. In the temple were six columns, and on each side were several small chambers. The sculptures on the walls represent Rameses II. making offerings to the gods, among whom are Rameses I. and Seti I. According to an inscription there, it is said that Seti I. went to heaven and was united with the Sun-god before this temple was finished, and that Rameses II. made and fixed the doors, finished the building of the walls, and decorated the interior. The workmanship in certain parts of this temple recalls that of certain parts of Abydos; it is probable that the same artists were employed.

II. The **Ramesseum**. This temple, called also the MEMNONIUM and the tomb of Osymandyas (Diodorus I., iv), was built by Rameses II., in honour of Åmen-Rā. As at Ḳûrnah, two pylons stood in front of it. The first court had a single row of pillars on each side of it; passing up a flight of steps, and through the second pylon, is a second court, having a double row of round columns on the east and west sides, and a row of pilasters, to which large figures of Rameses II. under the form of

B

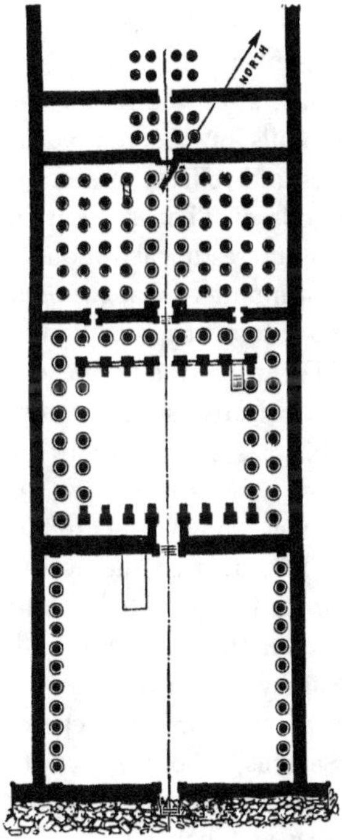

A

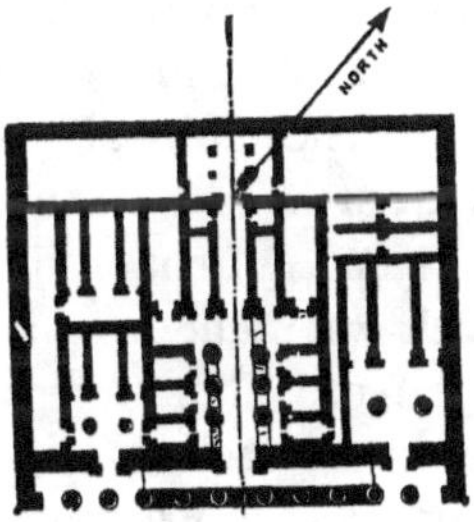

A. Plan of the Temple at Ḳûrnah.

B Plan of the Ramesseum at Ḳûrnah.

Osiris are attached, on the north and south sides. Before the second pylon stood a colossal statue of Rameses II., at least sixty feet high, which has been thrown down (by Cambyses?), turned over on its back, and mutilated. In the hall are twelve huge columns, arranged in two rows, and thirty-six smaller ones arranged in six rows. On the interior face of the second pylon are sculptured scenes in the war of Rameses II. against the Kheta, which took place in the fifth year of his reign; in them he is represented slaying the personal attendants of the prince of the Kheta. Elsewhere is the famous scene in which Rameses, having been forsaken by his army, is seen cutting his way through the enemy, and hurling them one after the other into the Orontes near Kadesh. The walls of the temple are ornamented with small battle scenes and reliefs representing the king making offerings to the gods of Thebes. On the ceiling of one of the chambers is an interesting astronomical piece on which the twelve Egyptian months are mentioned.

III. The **Colossi**.—These two interesting statues were set up in honour of Amenophis III., whom they represent; they stood in front of the pylon of a calcareous stone temple which was built by this king; this has now entirely disappeared. They were hewn out of a hard grit-stone, and the top of each was about sixty feet above the ground; originally each was monolithic. The statue on the north is the famous **Colossus of Memnon**, from which a sound was said to issue every morning when the sun rose. The upper part of it was thrown down by an earthquake, it is said, about B.C. 27; the damage was partially repaired during the reign of Septimius Severus, who restored the head and shoulders of the figure by adding to it five layers of stone. When Strabo was at Thebes with Ælius Gallus he heard "a noise at the first hour of the day, but whether proceeding from the base or from the colossus, or produced on purpose by some of those standing round the base, I cannot confidently assert." It is said that after the colossus was repaired no sound issued from it. Some think that the noise was caused by the sun's rays striking upon the stone, while others believe that a priest hidden in the colossus produced it by striking a stone. The inscriptions show that many distinguished Romans visited the "vocal Memnon" and heard the sound; one Petronianus, of a poetical turn of mind, stated that it made a sighing sound in complaining to its mother, the dawn, of the injuries inflicted upon it by Cambyses. The inscriptions on the back of the colossi give the names of Amenophis III.

IV. **Medînet Habû.**—This village lies to the south of the colossi, and its foundation dates from Coptic times. The early Christians established themselves around the ancient Egyptian temple there, and having carefully plastered over the wall sculptures in one of its chambers, they used it as a chapel. Round and about this temple many Greek and Coptic inscriptions have been found, which prove that the Coptic community here was one of the largest and most important in Upper Egypt.

The Egyptian name of the site was Åat-tcha-Mutet , which the Copts turned into ϫⲏⲙⲉ. The principal buildings at Medînet Habû are:— The Little Temple, the chapels built by royal personages in the XXVIth dynasty, the "Pavilion of Rameses III.," and the Great Temple. The collection of buildings which forms the **Little Temple** belongs to various periods, the oldest dating from the reigns of the early kings of the XVIIIth dynasty (Thothmes II. and III.), and the most recent from the time of the Roman rule over Egypt. The paved courtyard (A) is the work of the Roman period, and in it are inscriptions which record the addresses made to various gods by the Emperor Antoninus. The pylon (C), which was built by Ptolemy X. and Ptolemy XIII., is reached by crossing a smaller court (B), also of the Roman period; the reliefs upon it represent these kings making offerings to the great gods of Egypt, and below them is the text of a hymn to the Sun. This pylon leads to the court-

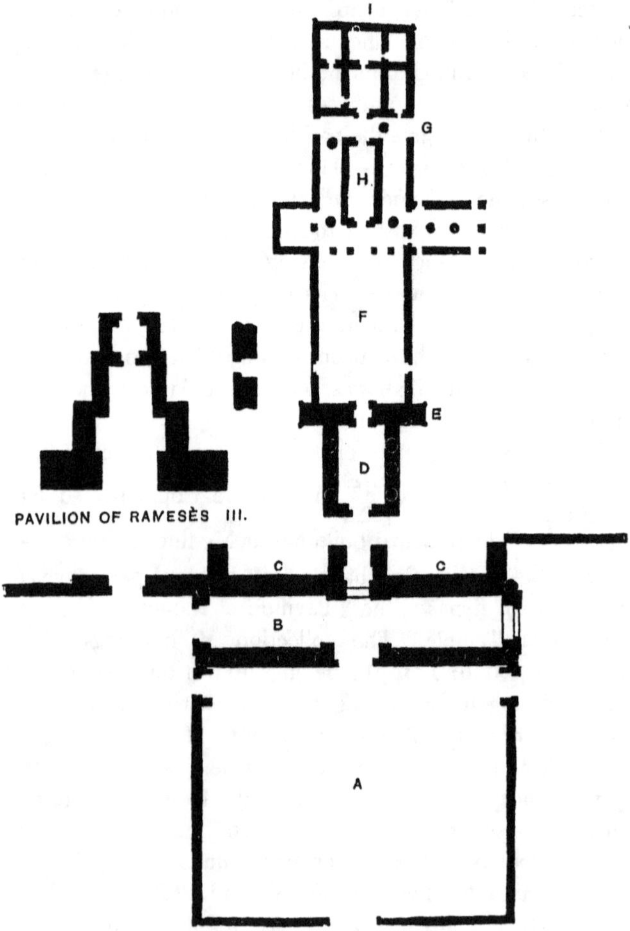

The Little Temple of Thothmes II. at Medînet Habû.

yard built by Nectanebus II. (D), and to the pylon built at the end of it by royal Ethiopian personages (E). The scenes on the walls of the court of Nectanebus represent the king slaughtering prisoners, processions of the personifications of nomes, the king making offerings, etc. The pylon was built by Shabaka, and additions were made by Tirhakah, Nectanebus II., and Ptolemy X. Beyond this pylon is another courtyard, of uncertain date, containing 16 pillars, eight on each side (F). The oldest part of the building is the XVIIIth dynasty temple (G), which consists of a shrine chamber (H), open at each end, and surrounded by an open gallery, and a group of six small chambers beyond: (I) The royal name most frequently found on the temple is that of Rameses III., who added several reliefs, in which he is represented making offerings to the gods. In the open gallery are the names of Thothmes III., Ḥeru-em-ḥeb, Seti I. and Ptolemy Physkon; on one of the pillars is a text showing that Thothmes III. dedicated the temple to Menthu, the lord of Thebes. Repairs were carried out on some of the pillars in this gallery by Queen Ȧmenȧrṭȧs and Achoris. On the walls of the shrine chamber Thothmes III. and Ptolemy Physkon are depicted making offerings to the gods of Thebes, and the inscriptions show that the chamber was rebuilt by the latter king. In one of the chambers beyond is an unfinished red granite shrine in which the boat or emblem of the god Ȧmen-Rā was kept. The Little Temple was, like all other temples, enclosed within a wall of unbaked bricks, but its extent and position were modified at different periods to suit the rearrangements made by the various kings who restored old buildings or added new ones to the site.

To the left of the Little Temple and the Pavilion of Rameses III. lie the **Temple of Queen Ȧmenȧrṭȧs**, the daughter of Kashta, and three small chapels dedicated by Shep-en-ȧp, daughter of Piānkhi, Meḥt-en-usekht, wife of

Psammetichus I., and Nit-âqert (Nitocris), daughter of Psammetichus I. The scenes on the walls of the chapels are of the same class as those on the Temple of Åmenârṭâs, and, though interesting, are of no great importance.

The **Pavilion of Rameses III.** is a most interesting and instructive building, for it represents an attempt to reproduce in Egypt a small fort or strong city of the class with which the Egyptians must have become familiar in their campaigns against the Kheta and other allied peoples in Northern Syria. It seems to have been designed to take the place of a pylon, and to have been intended to add to the dignity and grandeur of the Great Temple of Rameses III., which lay beyond it. It was approached through an opening in the eastern side of the great unbaked mud brick wall, some 30 feet high and 30 feet thick, with which this king surrounded the temple buildings at Medînet Ḥabû. In front of the building was a stone crenelated wall, nearly ten feet thick and eleven feet high, with a doorway nearly five feet wide, and in each side of this was a small room which served as a guard chamber. On the outside of these chambers are scenes representing Rameses III. and Rameses IV. making offerings to the gods. The Pavilion consists of two large rectangular towers, about 26 feet wide, and, when complete, their height must have been about 72 feet; the distance between them is about 22 ft. 6 in. The walls behind them open out and form a small court, but they soon contract, and becoming still narrower, at length the two wings of the building unite; in the portion where they unite is a door, above which are two windows. On each side of the stone walls which remain were a number of chambers built of brick, and it appears that these filled the whole of the thickness of the great mud brick wall which enclosed all the temple buildings. The wall of the front of the pavilion slopes backwards, and its lower part rests upon a low foundation wall which slopes rapidly. On the south tower are reliefs representing Rameses III. clubbing his enemies in the presence of Harmachis, who hands him a sword. The peoples depicted here are the Ethiopians and the tribes that lived in the deserts to the west of the Nile; and those on the north tower are the Kheta, the Ameru, the Tchakari, the Shardana of the sea, the Shakalasha, the Tursha of the sea, and the Pulasta, *i.e.*, the sea-coast dwellers of Phœnicia and the neighbouring coasts and islands (?). The scenes on the towers represent the king bringing his prisoners before Åmen-Rā, and the texts give the words spoken by the god and the king and the chiefs of the vanquished peoples. In the widest part of the space between the towers are scenes depicting Rameses III. making offerings to the gods Ånḥur-Shu, Tefnut, Temu, Iusåāset, Ptah, Sekhet, Thoth, etc. On the walls further in the king is being led to Åmen by Menthu and Temu, and he receives a crown from Åmen, whilst Thoth inscribes his name upon a palm-branch for long years of life. The entrance to the upper rooms was by a staircase in the south tower. The walls of the rooms are decorated with scenes in which the king is seen surrounded by naked women, who play tambourines, and bring him fruit and flowers, and play draughts with him.

The **Great Temple of Rameses III.** is one of the most interesting of the funerary chapels on the western bank of the Nile at Thebes, and was built by this king to his own memory; its length is nearly 500 feet, and its width about 160 feet. The upper parts of the towers of the first pylon have neither texts nor sculptures, but the lower parts have both. The reliefs on both sides of the doorways are, substantially, the same. Here we see Rameses III. clubbing a number of representatives of vanquished peoples, and near these are 86 captives with their names enclosed within ovals upon their bodies. It is clear from some of the names that the peoples here represented lived in Syria, Phœnicia, Cyprus, and parts of Africa. Here also is the god Thoth, who inscribes the king's name upon the leaves of a tree, probably a kind of celestial acacia, for which the neighbourhood was in ancient days famous; and close by are Amen, Mut, and Khonsu, before whom the king kneels. The text on the north side is a poetical description of the king's conquest of the Libyans. To the right of one of the flag-pole channels, on the south side, is a stele, dated in the 12th year of the king, in which his benefactions to the temples are extolled, and a speech of the god Ptaḥ is reported. The door leading to the **First Court** is decorated with reliefs in which Rameses III. is seen adoring various gods. The first court (A), which measures 111 feet by 136 feet, contains two porticoes; that on the right has seven rectangular pillars, in the front of each of which is a statue of the king, nearly 20 feet high, in the form of Osiris, and that on the left has eight columns. On the back of the pylon leading into this courtyard the defeat of the Libyans and the triumph of the Egyptians are depicted; in one portion of the relief on the right side the hands of the dead are being cut off, and the numbers of men killed and mutilated, as well as lists of the spoil, are set forth with evident care. The accompanying text of course describes the battle, and the great valour of Rameses III. The seven rectangular pillars of the north portico are ornamented with battle scenes and representations of the king making offerings to the gods, etc.; in the statues the king has all the attributes of Osiris, and by the side of the legs are small statues of the sons and daughters of Rameses III. The eight columns with cup-shaped capitals of the south portico have each a double relief representing the king slaying prisoners in the presence of Ȧmen-Rā or Menthu. On the north side of the face of the second pylon is a long inscription recording the triumph of the king over some tribes of Western Asia, and on the south side is a representation of Rameses III. reviewing his army and battle scenes, etc. The **Second Court** (B) is about the same size as the first, and on each of the four sides is a portico; on the north and south sides the roof is supported by five columns with lotus capitals, and on the east and west sides by eight rectangular pillars, each of which had a statue of the king as Osiris in front of it. The walls on

Court at Medînet Habû.
(From a photograph by A. Beato, of Luxor.)

the **south-east** side are decorated with reliefs of battle scenes, among them being:—The Theban triad giving the king victory over the invaders of Egypt; defeat of northern tribes by the Egyptians; counting the hands (3,000!) cut off from dead enemies; Rameses leading three rows of captives; and captives being offered to Amen; the accompanying text celebrates the king's victories. On the **north-east** are representations of religious processions at

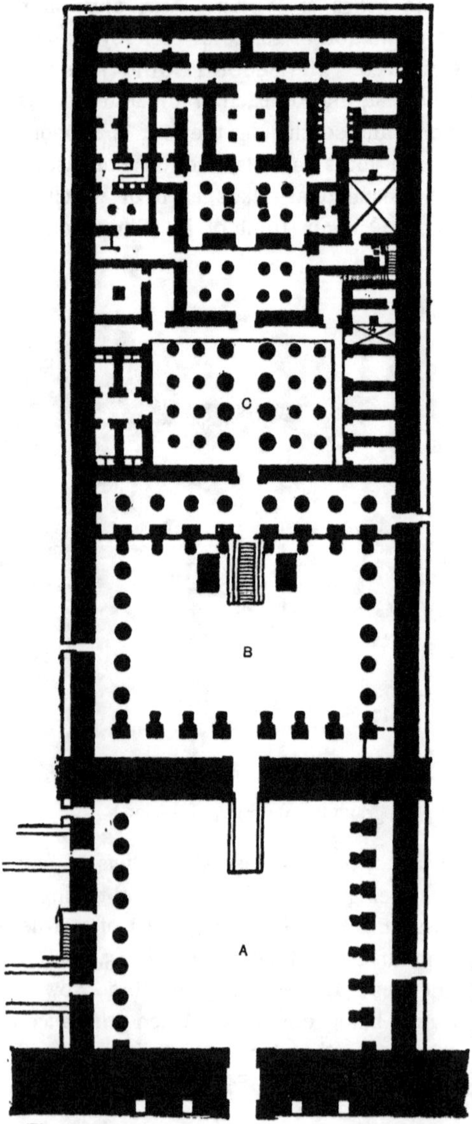

The Temple of Rameses III. at Medînet Habû.

the festival of Seker, the festival of Åmen, and the festival of Åmsu; these reliefs are of great interest. This courtyard was turned into a church by the Copts, who removed the middle column of the northern portico, and built an altar against the wall behind it. On the west wall are figures of a number of the king's sons. Passing into the Hall of Columns (C) it is seen that this part of the temple is not as well preserved as the First and Second Courts, for of the 24 columns which supported the roof, only the bases remain. This damage is said to have been wrought by the earthquake of B.C. 27, and the portions of the overthrown columns were probably used by the Copts and Arabs to make stones for corn mills. This hall measures about 87 feet by 62 feet. On the walls are reliefs in which the king is seen making offerings of various kinds to the gods of Thebes. On the south side are five small chambers wherein the treasures of the temple were kept. After the Hall of Columns come two small chambers, each with eight columns; the first, the reliefs of which are destroyed, measures about 56 feet by 27 feet. On each side are a number of small chambers, the walls of which are decorated with mythological, astronomical, and other scenes, and some were clearly set apart for the service of special gods; in most of them are sculptured figures of the king adoring the gods. The spaces left hollow by the foundation walls, and commonly called crypts, were often used as tombs. On the outside of the temple walls are series of reliefs which refer to :—1. Calendar of Festivals (*South Wall*); 2. Wars against the people of the Sûdân, etc. (*West Wall*); and 3. Wars against the Libyans and peoples of Asia Minor (*North Wall and part of West Wall*). For a full account of the temple, see M. Daressy's excellent *Notice Explicative des Ruines de Médinet Habou*, Cairo, 1897.

THE TEMPLE OF QUEEN ḤĀTSHEPSET AT DÊR EL-BAḤARÎ.

V. The unique and famous Temple of Dêr el-Baḥarî was built in terraces on a wide, open space, bounded at its further end by the semi-circular wall of cliffs which divides this space from the valley of the Tombs of the Kings; it is approached from the plain on the western side of the river through a narrow gorge, the sides of which are honey-combed with tombs. At the end of the last century (1798)

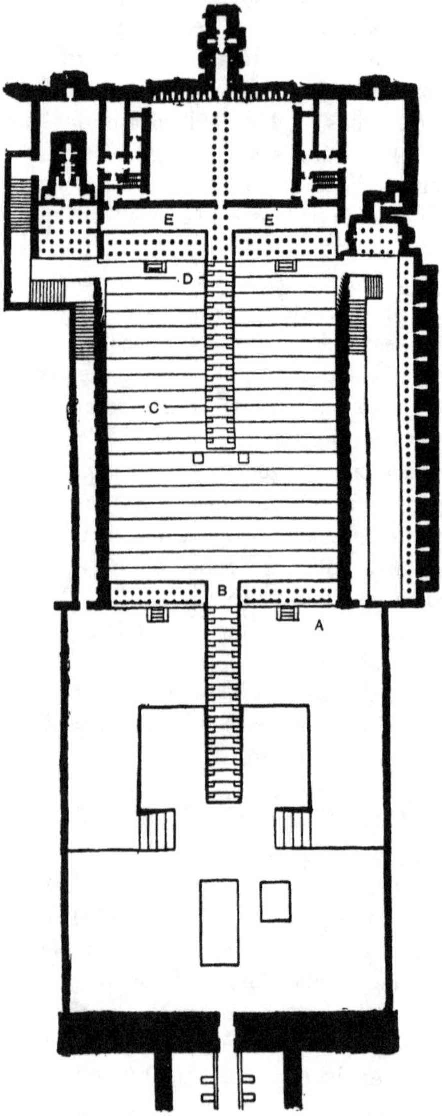

The Temple of Ḥātshepset at Dêr el-Baḥarî.

MM. Jollois and Devilliers visited it, and made a plan of the ruins as they found them; they declared that the approach from the plain was by an Avenue of Sphinxes, and that the avenue was about 42 feet wide, and 437 yards long, omitting to count a break of 54 yards; but they, apparently, did not know the building, which they imperfectly described, by the name it now bears, "Dêr el-Baḥarî," *i.e.*, the Northern Monastery. In 1827 Wilkinson made excavations on the site, and Lepsius seems to have done the same, but no serious clearance of the ruins was begun until Mariette began to work at them in 1858, in which year he uncovered the bas-reliefs which depict the Expedition to Punt. At an early stage in his labours he recognized that Hātshepset's temple was, like many another temple on the western bank of the Nile at Thebes, a funerary temple, and that it must be classed with buildings like the Ramesseum and the great temple at Medînet Habû. In other words, the temple of Dêr el-Baḥarî was a huge private chapel which was built by the great queen for the express purpose that offerings might be made to her *ka*, or "double," on the appointed days of festival, and to that of her father, Thothmes I. The site which she chose for the temple was holy ground, for ruins of a building, which was probably a funerary temple of Menthu-ḥetep II. a king of the XIth dynasty, were found to the south-west of the open space on which the queen built her temple. The whole temple was surrounded by an enclosing wall, most of which has disappeared, and was approached by means of an avenue of sphinxes. It was entered through a pylon, in front of which stood two obelisks. Passing through this pylon the visitor, following the pathway, arrived at an incline which led to the raised colonnade of the Eastern Terrace (A). The bas-reliefs on its wall were protected by a roof (B), supported by one row of rectangular pillars, and by one row of polygonal pillars. From the centre of this platform (C) an inclined plane or flight of steps led to the Western Terrace (D), and the face of the supporting wall was protected by a portico (E), formed by two rows of square pillars. At each end of the portico are rock-cut shrines, which are approached through a twelve-columned portico, the roof of which is in perfect preservation. The Northern Shrine is decorated with religious scenes, and the Southern or Hathor Shrine, which is entered through a covered vestibule having pillars with Hathor-headed capitals, contains scenes relating to the rejoicings which took place at Thebes on the return of the queen's successful expedition to Punt. Everywhere will be seen the marks of the erasure of the queen's name which was carried out by Thothmes III. her ward, who hated Ḥātshepset with a deadly hatred; in many places will be found marks of the vandalism of Amenophis IV., who erased the name and figure of the god Ȧmen from the walls because he hated this god and preferred to worship Ȧten; and everywhere will be seen the cartouche of Rameses II. who, because in places he tried to repair the mischief done by Amenophis IV., added his own name wherever possible. At the end of the building is a small rectangular court, which is entered through a granite gateway, and directly opposite it is a rock-hewn shrine with a vaulted roof. The plan of the temple given on p. 404 is from Mariette's work,* and will be found useful; from it, however, the reader would think that the northern part of the buildings on the Western Terrace was similar to that on the south, but this is not so. The total length of the whole building, not including the Avenue of Sphinxes, was about 800 feet.

Ḥātshepset, the builder of the temple, was the daughter of Thothmes I. and of his half-sister Ȧāḥmes, and the granddaughter of Amenophis I. and one of his wives; her father, however, had two other wives, Mut-nefert, called Senseneb, who bore him a son, Thothmes II., and Ȧset, or Isis, a woman of low rank, who also bore him a son, Thothmes III. Ḥātshepset was half-sister to Thothmes II. and Thothmes III., and she became the wife of the former and the guardian of the latter, their half-brother. The inscriptions on her temple record that she was associated with her father, Thothmes I., in the rule of the kingdom, and that she herself was enthroned at a very early age. From her childhood she is always represented in *male* attire, and in the inscriptions, masculine pronouns and

* *Deir-el-Bahari*, Leipzig, 1877.

verbal forms are used in speaking of her, and masculine attributes, including a beard, are ascribed to her; only when considered as a goddess is she represented in female form. She reigned for about 16 years, and the chief event of her reign, omitting the building of the temple, was the famous **expedition to Punt,** a general name of the land on both sides of the Red Sea as far south as, and including, Somaliland. The queen sent five ships to the coast of Africa, and M. Maspero believes that they were sailed by their crews up the Elephant River, near Cape Guardafui, and made fast near one of the native villages inland. Then followed the exchange of objects brought from Egypt for native produce, and the natives appear to have given large quantities of gold in return for almost valueless articles. The bas-reliefs which illustrate these scenes are found on the southern half of the wall which supports the Western Terrace, and it is easy to see that what the natives are giving to the Egyptians is both valuable and bulky. The chief of Punt, called Pa-rehu, carries a boomerang and wears a dagger in his belt; he is followed by his wife, a lady with a remarkable figure, who wears a single yellow garment and a necklace, and by his two sons and a daughter. The following drawing illustrates this scene.

Pa-rehu, the Prince of Punt, his wife and his two sons, and a daughter. (This portion of the relief was stolen from the temple, and has not been recovered.)

The native products given by the Prince of Punt to the Egyptians consisted of aromatic woods, spices, incense, ānti, rare trees and plants, which were afterwards planted in the gardens of Åmen at Thebes, gold, etc. : these things

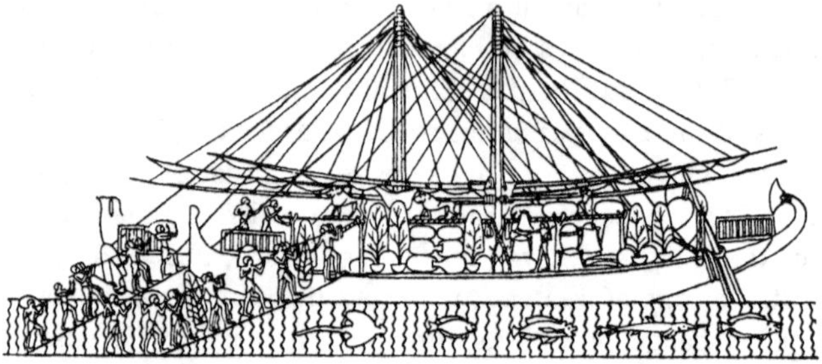

An Egyptian ship being loaded by the people of Punt. (After Mariette.)

were given to the Egyptians in such large quantities that their boats were filled with them, and they formed a very substantial offering to the god Åmen. Among the gifts of the Prince of Punt were leopards, panthers, and other wild animals. Ḥātshepset seems to have been a capable ruler and administrator, but the conquests of foreign lands during her reign were few. Her husband, Thothmes II., waged war against the nomad, raiding tribes of the Eastern Desert, and he conducted a campaign of considerable importance in Nubia; he seems to have died while he was comparatively young. After his death Ḥātshepset associated Thothmes III. with her in the rule of the kingdom, but, as after her death he always obliterated her name from her temple, it seems that the relations between the rulers were not always happy. M. Naville thinks that Thothmes III. hated Ḥātshepset because her husband, Thothmes II., had not raised his (Thothmes III.'s) mother Åset to royal rank, and that he was jealous of his mother's honour; Ḥātshepset had no son, and she seems to have been obliged to associate Åset's son with her in the rule of the kingdom. Thothmes III. seems to have married first Neferu-Rā, a daughter of

Ḥātshepset, and secondly, another daughter of the great queen called Ḥātshepset-meri-Rā. It would be unjust to the memory of a great man and a loyal servant of Ḥātshepset if we omitted to mention the name of **Senmut**, the architect and overseer of works of Dêr el-Baḥarî. There is little doubt that the plan of the temple was his, but it says much for the good sense of the ablest woman who ever sat on the throne of Egypt, that she gave this distinguished architect the opportunity of building the unique and beautiful temple, which has shed glory on the name, both of the subject and of his great sovereign. The visitor to the temple of Dêr el-Baḥarî owes the ease with which he is able to visit every part of it to the labours of M. Naville, assisted by Mr. Hogarth, who spent three winters in clearing it at the expense of the Egypt Exploration Fund. An idea of the vastness of the work may be gleaned from the fact that in two winters the enormous amount of 60,000 cubic metres of rubbish and stones were removed from the site and carried away to a distance of 200 yards. This temple now presents a striking appearance, whether seen from the Luxor or Ḳûrna side, and every visitor will much appreciate the excellent results which have attended the completion of the undertaking.* Archæologists will be interested to know that the newly found fragments of the wall upon which the expedition to Punt is depicted all agree in pointing to the eastern side of Africa as the country which the Egyptians called Punt; some of the animals in the reliefs are identical with those found to this day on the Abyssinian coast, and the general products of the two countries are the same. Punt was famous for its ebony, and all tradition agrees in making Abyssinia, and the countries south and east of it, the home of the ebony

* M. Naville's description of the temple has been published under the title, "*The Temple of Deir el Bahari*," 4 parts, London, 1894–1898.

tree. The tombs at Dêr el-Baḥarî were opened many, many years ago, and a very large number of the coffins with which Mariette furnished the first Egyptian Museum at Bûlâk came from them; since that time the whole site has been carefully searched by diggers for antiquities, hence comparatively few antiquities have been unearthed by M. Naville. In the course of the work he discovered an interesting mummy-pit, and in a small chamber hewn in the solid rock, about twelve feet below the pavement, he found three wooden rectangular coffins (each containing two inner coffins), with arched lids, wooden hawks and jackals, wreaths of flowers, and a box containing a large number of *ushabtiu* figures. These coffins contained the mummies of a priest called Menthu-Teḥuti-àuf-ānkh, and of his mother and of his aunt; they belong to the period of the XXVIth dynasty, or perhaps a little earlier.

The great interest which attaches to the name of the able queen Ḥātshepset, and the romantic circumstances under which she lived and reigned, have induced many to endeavour to discover her mummy and her tomb; up to the present however, all search has failed to bring either to light. During his excavations M. Naville has kept this fact steadily before him, and he eventually found a place which, he says, was not improbably her tomb. In the passage between the retaining wall of the middle platform and the enclosure he came upon an inclined plane cut in the rock and leading to the entrance of a large tomb. The rubbish was untouched; the slope had evidently been made for a large stone coffin; beyond the entrance he found a long sloping shaft which ended in a large chamber. The plain coffin containing bones which he found therein had never been intended for such a tomb, and his conclusion is that the body for whom the tomb was made was never laid in it. It may be that it was prepared for Ḥātshepset herself.

During the last days of the excavations at Dêr el-Baḥarî

M. Naville's workmen came upon a very interesting "foundation deposit" which they discovered in a small rock-hewn pit. It consisted of fifty wooden hoes, four bronze slabs, a hatchet, a knife, eight wooden models of adzes, eight wooden adzes with bronze blades, fifty wooden models of an implement of unknown use, ten pots of alabaster, and ten baskets; above these were a few common earthenware pots, and over all were some mats. All the objects bear the same inscription, *i.e.*, the prenomen and titles of queen Ḥātshepset.

VI. **Dêr el-Medînet**. The temple built in this place owes its name to the Coptic Dêr, or Monastery, which stood near here when Thebes was the home of a flourishing Coptic community, and was dedicated to Saint Paul of Pikolol, of whom, however, nothing is known. The monastery must have contained a society of considerable size, for it is said to have possessed *two* stewards. The small Egyptian temple which stands between the Colossi and Medînet Habû, was begun by Ptolemy IV., Philopator, and continued by Ptolemy VII., Philometor, and finished by Ptolemy IX., Euergetes II. It is built of the ordinary sandstone of the district, and though in many respects it resembles most of the funeral temples built by the Ptolemies, it is a beautiful little example of its class. It appears to have been dedicated to more than one of the goddesses of the underworld, but Hathor was regarded as its tutelary deity. The capitals of some of the columns are Hathor-headed, and over the doorway of the large chamber are the heads of the Seven Hathors, who, in their forms of cows, supplied the deceased with food in the underworld. In one of the chambers is a relief representing the Judgment Scene, which forms the Vignette of the CXXVth Chapter of the Book of the Dead, and has been described above. (See pp. 150–156.) The chief interest of the scene here is that it proclaims the nature of the building, and proves how anxious the Ptolemies were to officially adopt, and to maintain the principal religious views of the Egyptians. The temple was much visited by travellers in ancient times, as the number of names written on the walls testify, and by both Greeks and Copts it was regarded as very holy.

THE DISCOVERY OF THE ROYAL MUMMIES AT DÊR EL-BAḤARÎ.†

In the summer of the year 1871 an Arab, a native of Ḳûrna, discovered a large tomb filled with coffins heaped one upon the other. On the greater number of them were visible the cartouche and other signs which indicated that the inhabitants of the coffins were royal personages. The native, who was so fortunate as to have chanced upon this remarkable "find," was sufficiently skilled in his trade of antiquity hunter to know what a valuable discovery he had made; his joy must however have been turned into mourning, when it became evident that he would need the help of many men even to move some of the large royal coffins which he saw before him, and that he could not keep the knowledge of such treasures locked up in his own breast. He revealed his secret to his two brothers and to one of his sons, and they proceeded to spoil the coffins of *ushabtiu* ‡ figures, papyri, scarabs and other antiquities which could be taken away easily and concealed in their *abbas* (ample outer garments) as they returned to their houses. These precious objects were for

† A minute and detailed account of this discovery is given by Maspero in "Les Momies Royales de Déïr el Bahari" (Fasc. I., t. IV., of the *Mémoires* of the French Archæological Mission at Cairo).

‡ *Ushabtiu* figures made of stone, green or blue glazed Egyptian porcelain, wood, &c., were deposited in the tombs with the dead, and were supposed to perform for them any field labours which might be decreed for them by Osiris, the king of the under-world, and judge of the dead.

several winters sold to chance tourists on the Nile, and the lucky possessors of this mine of wealth replenished their stores from time to time by visits made at night to the tomb. As soon as the objects thus sold reached Europe, it was at once suspected that a "find" of more than ordinary importance had been made. An English officer called Campbell showed M. Maspero a hieratic Book of the Dead written for Pi-net'em; M. de Saulcy sent him photographs of the hieroglyphic papyrus of Net'emet; M. Mariette bought at Suez a papyrus written for the Queen Ḥent-taiu, and Rogers Bey exhibited at Paris a wooden tablet upon which was written a hieratic text relating to the *ushabtiu* figures which were to be buried with the princess Nesi-Khonsu. All these interesting and most valuable objects proved that the natives of Thebes had succeeded in unearthing a veritable "Cave of Treasures," and M. Maspero, the Director of the Bûlâḳ Museum, straightway determined to visit Upper Egypt with a view of discovering whence came all these antiquities. Three men were implicated, whose names were learnt by M. Maspero from the inquiries which he made of tourists who purchased antiquities.

In 1881 he proceeded to Thebes, and began his investigations by causing one of the dealers, 'Abd er-Rasûl Aḥmad, to be arrested by the police, and an official inquiry into the matter was ordered by the Mudîr of Ḳeneh. In spite of threats and persuasion, and many say tortures, the accused denied any knowledge of the place whence the antiquities came. The evidence of the witnesses who were called to testify to the character of the accused, tended to show that he was a man of amiable disposition, who would never dream of pillaging a tomb, much less do it. Finally, after two months' imprisonment, he was provisionally set at liberty. The accused then began to discuss with his partners in the secret what plans they should adopt, and how they should act in the future. Some of them thought that all trouble was over when 'Abd er-Rasûl Aḥmad was set at liberty, but others thought, and they were right, that the trial would be recommenced in the winter. Fortunately for students of Egyptology, differences of opinion broke out between the parties soon after, and 'Abd er-Rasûl Aḥmad soon perceived that his brothers were determined to turn King's evidence at a favourable opportunity. To prevent their saving themselves at his expense, he quietly travelled to Ḳeneh, and there confessed to the Mudîr that he was able to reveal the place where the coffins and papyri were found. Telegrams were sent to Cairo announcing the confession of 'Abd er-Rasûl Aḥmad, and when his statements had been verified, despatches containing fuller particulars were sent to Cairo from Ḳeneh. It was decided that a small expedition to Thebes should at once be made to take possession of and bring to Cairo the antiquities which were to be revealed to the world by 'Abd er-Rasûl Aḥmad, and the charge of bringing this work to a successful issue was placed in the hands of M. Émile Brugsch. Although the season was summer, and the heat very great, the start for Thebes was made on July 1, 1881. At Ḳeneh M. Brugsch found a number of papyri and other valuable antiquities which 'Abd er-Rasûl had sent there as an earnest of the truth of his promise to reveal the hidden treasures. A week later M. Brugsch and his companions were shown the shaft of the tomb, which was most carefully hidden in the north-west part of the natural circle which opens to the south of the valley of Dêr el-Baḥari, in the little row of hills which separates the Bibân el-Mulûk from the Theban plain. According to M. Maspero, the royal mummies were removed here from their tombs in the Bibân el-Mulûk by Āauputh, the son of Shashanq, about B.C. 966, to prevent them being destroyed by the thieves, who were sufficiently numerous and powerful to defy the government of the day. The pit which led to the tomb was about forty feet deep, and the passage, of irregular level, which led to the tomb, was about 220 feet long; at the end of this passage was a nearly rectangular chamber about twenty-five feet long, which was found to be literally filled with coffins, mummies, funereal furniture, boxes, *ushabtiu* figures, Canopic jars,* bronze vases, etc., etc. A large number of men were at once employed to exhume these objects, and for eight and forty hours M. Brugsch and Aḥmad Effendi Kamal stood at the mouth of the pit watching the things brought up. The heavy coffins were carried on the shoulders of men to the river, and in less than two weeks everything had been sent over the river to Luxor. A few days after this the whole collection of mummies of kings and royal personages was placed upon an Egyptian Government steamer and taken to the Museum at Bûlâḳ.

When the mummies of the ancient kings of Egypt arrived at Cairo, it was found that the Bûlâḳ Museum was too small to contain them, and before they could be exposed to the inspection of the world, it was necessary for additional rooms to be built. Finally, however, M. Maspero had glass cases made, and, with the help of some cabinets borrowed from his private residence attached to the Museum, he succeeded in exhibiting, in a comparatively suitable way, the mummies in which such world-wide interest had been taken. Soon after the arrival of the mummies at Bûlâḳ M. Brugsch opened the mummy of Thothmes III., when it was found that the Arabs had attacked it and plundered whatever was valuable upon it.

* The principal intestines of a deceased person were placed in four jars, which were placed in his tomb under the bier; the jars were dedicated to the four children of the Horus, who were called Mesthȧ, Ḥāpi, Tuamāutef āud Qebḥsennuf. The name "Canopic" is given to them by those who follow the opinion of some ancient writers that Canopus, the pilot of Menelaus, who is said to have been buried at Canopus in Egypt, was worshipped there under the form of a jar with small feet, a thin neck, a swollen body, and a round back.

In 1883 the mummy of Queen Mes-Ḥent-Themeḥu, , emitted unpleasant odours, and by M. Maspero's orders it was unrolled. In 1885 the mummy of Queen Ȧāḥmes Nefertȧri, 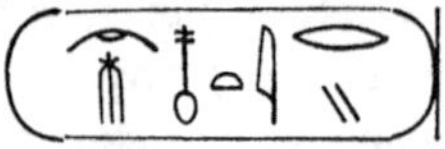, was unrolled by him, and as it putrefied rapidly and stank, it had to be buried. Finally, when M. Maspero found that the mummy of Seqenen-Rā, , was also decaying, he decided to unroll the whole collection, and Rameses II. was the first of the great kings whose features were shown again to the world after a lapse of 3,200 years.

Such are the outlines of the history of one of the greatest discoveries ever made in Egypt. It will ever be regretted by the Egyptologist that this remarkable collection of mummies was not discovered by some person who could have used for the benefit of scholars the precious information which this "find" would have yielded, before so many of its objects were scattered; as it is, however, it would be difficult to over-estimate its historical value.

The following is a list of the names of the principal kings and royal personages which were found on coffins at Dêr el-Baḥari and of their mummies:—

XVIIth Dynasty, before B.C. 1700.

King Seqenen-Rā, coffin and mummy.

Nurse of Queen Nefertȧri Rāȧ, coffin only. This coffin contained the mummy of a queen whose name is read Ȧn-Ḥāpi.

XVIIIth Dynasty, B.C. 1700–1400.

King Ȧāḥmes (Amāsis I.), coffin and mummy.

Queen Ȧāḥmes Nefertȧri, coffin.

King Ȧmenḥetep I., coffin and mummy.

The Prince Sa-Ȧmen, coffin and mummy.

The Princess Sat-Åmen, coffin and mummy.
The Scribe Senu, chief of the house of Nefertåri, mummy.
Royal wife Set-ka-mes, mummy.
Royal daughter Mesḥentthemḥu, coffin and mummy.
Royal mother Åāḥ-ḥetep, coffin.
King Thothmes I., coffin usurped by Pi-net'em.
King Thothmes II., coffin and mummy.
King Thothmes III., coffin and mummy.
Coffin and mummy of an unknown person.

XIXth Dynasty, B.C. 1400–1200.

King Rameses I., part of coffin.
King Seti I., coffin and mummy.
King Rameses II., coffin and mummy.

XXth Dynasty, B.C. 1200–1100.

King Rameses III., mummy found in the coffin of Nefertåri.

XXIst Dynasty, B.C. 1100–1000.

Royal mother Net'emet.
High-priest of Åmen, Masahertha, coffin and mummy.
High-priest of Åmen, Pi-net'em III., coffin and mummy.
Priest of Åmen, T'eṭ-Ptaḥ-åuf-ānkh, coffin and mummy.
Scribe Nebseni, coffin and mummy.
Queen Maāt-ka-Rā, coffin and mummy.
Princess Åset-em-khebit, coffin and mummy.
Princess Nesi-Khonsu.

VIII. **The Tombs of the Kings**, called in Arabic Bibân el-Mulûk, are hewn out of the living rock in a valley, which is reached by passing the temple at Ḳûrna; it is situated about three or four miles from the river. This valley contains the tombs of the kings of the XIXth and XXth dynasties, and is generally known as the Eastern Valley; a smaller valley, the Western, contains the tombs of the last kings of the XVIIIth dynasty. These tombs consist of long inclined planes with a number of chambers or halls receding into the mountain sometimes to a distance of 500 feet. Strabo gives the number of these royal tombs as 40, 17 of which were open in the time of Ptolemy Lagus; in 1835 21 were known, but the labours of M. Mariette were successful in bringing four more to light. The most important of these tombs are:—

No. 17. **Tomb of Seti I.,** B.C. 1366, commonly called "Belzoni's Tomb," because it was discovered by that brave traveller in the early part of this century; it had already been rifled, but the beautiful alabaster sarcophagus, which is now preserved in the Soane Museum in London, was still lying in its chamber at the bottom of the tomb. The inscriptions and scenes sculptured on the walls form parts of the "Book of being in the under-world"; it is quite impossible to describe them here, for a large number of pages would be required for the purpose. It must be sufficient to draw attention to the excellence and beauty of the paintings and sculptures, and to point out that the whole series refers to the life of the king in the under-world. The tomb is entered by means of two flights of steps, at the bottom of which is a passage terminating in a small chamber. Beyond this are two halls having four and two pillars respectively, and to the left are the passages and small chambers which lead to the large six-pillared hall and vaulted chamber in which stood the sarcophagus of Seti I. Here also is an inclined plane which descends into the mountain for a considerable distance; from the level of the ground to the bottom of this incline the depth is about 150 feet; the length of the tomb is nearly 500 feet. The designs on the walls were first sketched in outline in red, and the alterations by the master designer or artist were made in black; it would seem that this tomb was never finished. The mutilations and destruction which have been committed

I.

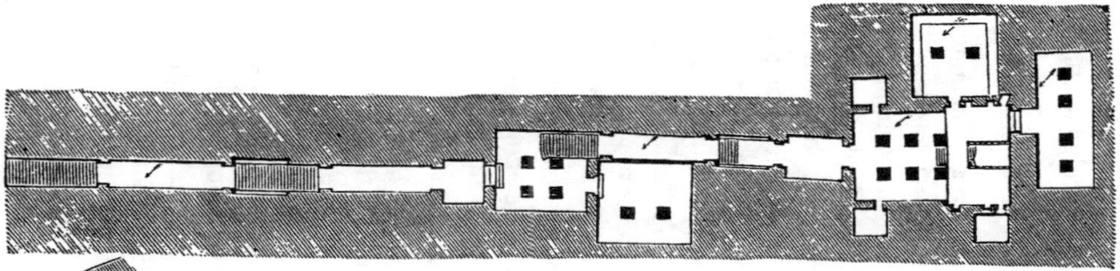

II.

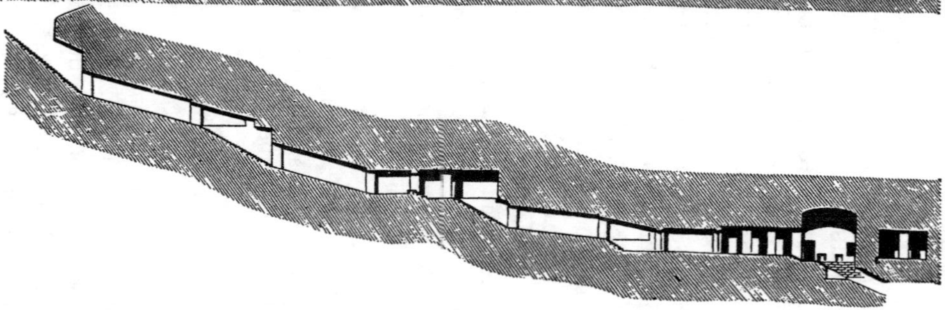

I. Ground plan of the Tomb of Seti I., B.C. 1366.
II. Section of the Tomb of Seti I.
(From Lepsius, *Denkmäler*, Abth. I., Bl. 96.)

here during the last twenty-five years are truly lamentable. The mummy of Seti I., found at Dêr el-Baḥarî, is preserved in the Gîzeh Museum.

No. 11. **Tomb of Rameses III.,** B.C. 1200, commonly called "Bruce's Tomb," because it was discovered by this traveller, and the "Tomb of the Harper," on account of the scene in it in which men are represented playing harps. The architect did not leave sufficient space between this and a neighbouring tomb, and hence after excavating passages and chambers to a distance of more than 100 feet, he was obliged to turn to the right to avoid breaking into it. The flight of steps leading into the tomb is not as steep as that in No. 17, the paintings and sculptures are not so fine, and the general plan of ornamentation differs. The scenes on the walls of the first passage resemble those in the first passage of No. 17, but in the other passages and chambers warlike, domestic, and agricultural scenes and objects are depicted. The body of the red granite sarcophagus of Rameses III. is in Paris, the cover is in the Fitzwilliam Museum, Cambridge, and the mummy of this king is at Gîzeh. The length of the tomb is about 400 feet.

No. 2. The **Tomb of Rameses IV.,** about B.C. 1166, though smaller than the others, is of considerable interest; the granite sarcophagus, of colossal proportions, still stands *in situ* at the bottom. Having seen the beautiful sculptures and paintings in the Tomb of Seti I., the visitor will probably not be disposed to spend much time in that of Rameses IV.

No. 9. The **Tomb of Rameses VI.,** or "Memnon's Tomb," was considered of great interest by the Greeks and Romans who visited it in ancient days; the astronomical designs on some of the ceilings, and the regular sequence of its passages and rooms are interesting. The fragments of the granite sarcophagus of this king lie at the bottom of the tomb.

No. 6. The **Tomb of Rameses IX.** is remarkable for

the variety of sculptures and paintings of a nature entirely different from those found in the other royal tombs; they appear to refer to the idea of resurrection after death and of immortality, which is here symbolized by the principle of generation.

The **Tomb of Rameses I.**, father of Seti I., is the oldest in this valley; it was opened by Belzoni.

Tombs of Thothmes III. and **Amenophis II.** During the spring of 1898 M. V. Loret, the successor of M. de Morgan, reported the discovery of the tombs of Thothmes III. and Amenophis II., kings of the XVIIIth dynasty, about B.C. 1600 or 1550. The tomb of the former king is situated at a distance of about 325 feet from the tomb of Rameses III., and is as interesting as any now known. The walls of the various chambers are ornamented with figures of the gods and inscriptions, among others being a long list of gods, and a complete copy of the "Book of that which is in the Underworld." The sarcophagus was, of course, found to be empty, for the king's mummy was taken from Dêr el-Baḥarî, where it had been hidden by the Egyptians during a time of panic, to the Gîzeh Museum about eighteen years ago. On a column in the second chamber we see depicted Thothmes followed by his mother Åset, his wife Mert-Rā, his wives Åāḥ-sat and Nebt-kheru, and his daughter Nefert-åru. It is to be hoped that steps will at once be taken to publish the texts and inscriptions in this tomb.

The tomb of Amenophis II., the son and successor of Thothmes III., in many respects resembles that of his father; the walls are covered with figures of the gods, the text of the "Book of that which is in the Underworld," and scenes similar to those in the older tomb. Among the numerous objects found in the tomb may be mentioned:—Three mummies, each with a large hole in the skull, and a gash in the breast; fragments of a pink leather cuirass worn by the king; a series of statues of Sekhet, Anubis, Osiris, Horus, Ptah, etc.; a set of alabaster Canopic vases, a collection of amulets of all kinds; and a large series of alabaster vessels; and a number of mummies of kings and royal personages among whom are Thothmes IV., Amenophis III., Seti II., Khu-en-âten, Sa-Ptah, Rameses IV., Rameses V., and Rameses VI. In the tomb of Amenophis II. we have then, another hiding-place of royal mummies similar to that of Dêr el-Baḥarî, and an examination of the mummies and other objects found in it ought to yield much information on many points connected with the history of the XVIIIth dynasty. It is much to be hoped that the Egyptian Government will undertake the publication of the literary compositions written on the walls of the tombs as soon as possible.

The **Tomb*** **of Rekhmàrā** is situated in the hill behind the Ramesseum called Shêkh 'Abd al-Ḳûrnah; it is one of the most interesting of all the private tombs found at Thebes. The scenes on the walls represent a procession of tribute bearers from Punt carrying apes, ivory, etc., and of people from parts of Syria and the shores of the Mediterranean bringing to him gifts consisting of the choicest products of their lands, which Rekhmàrā receives for Thothmes III. The countries can in many cases be identified by means of the articles depicted. The scenes in the inner chamber represent brickmaking, ropemaking, smiths' and masons' work, etc., etc., superintended by Rekhmàrā, prefect of Thebes; elsewhere are domestic scenes and a representation of Rekhmàrā sailing in a boat, lists of offerings, etc.

Tomb of Nekht at Shêkh 'Abd al-Ḳûrnah. This beautiful little tomb was opened out in the year 1889, but there is little doubt that it was known to the inhabitants of Ḳûrnah some time before. Though small,

* No. 35, according to Wilkinson, and No. 15, according to Champollion.

it is of considerable interest, and the freshness of the colours in the scenes is unusual; it is, moreover, a fine example of the tomb of a Theban gentleman of the Middle Empire. As the paintings and inscriptions are typical of their class, they are here described at some length. The tomb of Nekht consists of two chambers, but the larger one only is ornamented; the ceiling is painted with a wave pattern, and the cornice is formed of the *χakeru* pattern . On the left end wall a granite stele is painted, and upon it are the following inscriptions :—

View in the tomb of Nekht.
(From a photograph by A. Beato of Luxor.)

1. 

ṭā *suten* *ḥetep* *Åusår* *Un-neferu,* *neter* *āa* *neb*
Grant royal oblation Osiris Unnefer, god great, lord

Abṭu *ṭā - f* *āq* *it*
of Abydos, may he grant a coming in [and] a going out

em *Neter-χert* *àn* *χesef* *ba* *em*

from the underworld, not being repulsed the soul

en *ka* *en* *un* [*nut*]

{[at the gates of the underworld]}, to the double of the {temple-servant [Nekht]}

maāχeru

triumphant!

2. 

ṭā *suten* *ḥetep* [*Ḥeru-χuti*] *ṭā* - *f* *maa*

Grant royal oblation [Harmachis], may he grant a view

neferu - *f* *hru neb* *pert* *em* *ta*

of his splendours every day, and a coming forth upon earth

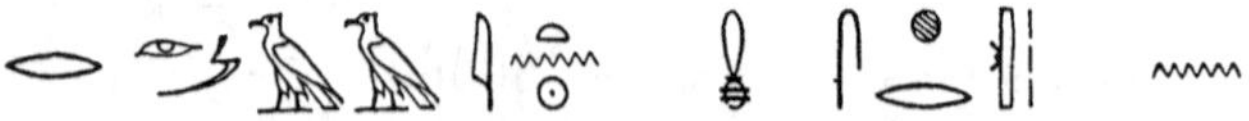

er *maa* *àten* *mà* *seχeru* *en*

to see the Disk according to [his] wont when

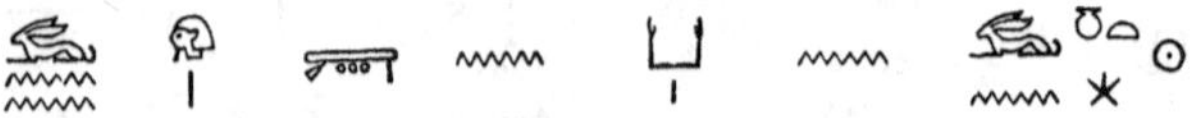

unen *ṭep* *ta* *en* *ka* *en* *unnut*

living upon earth, to the double of the temple-servant

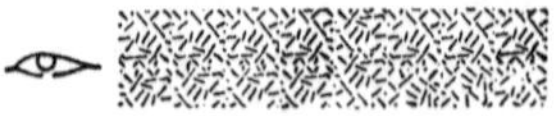

. . . . [Nekht, triumphant]!

3. 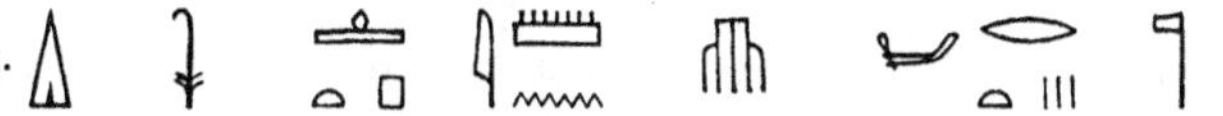

ṭā suten ḥetep Åmen χent sert neter

Grant royal oblation Åmen, president of the . . . . . god

āa ḥer Uast χet hru neb

great, chief of Thebes, . . . [may he grant] things day every

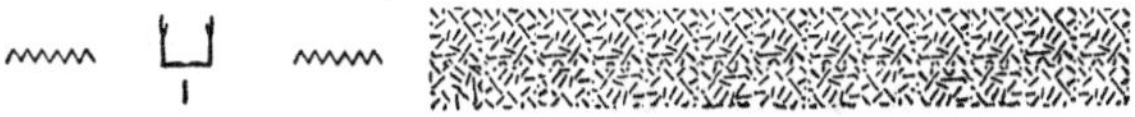

en ka en

to the double of [the temple-servant Nekht, triumphant]!

4. 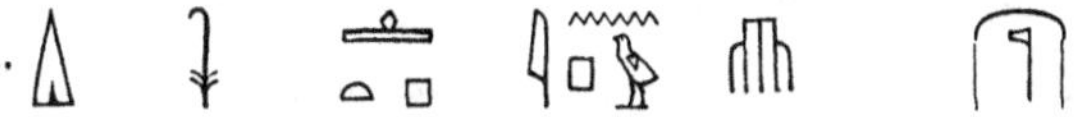

ṭā suten ḥetep Ånpu χent neter seḥ

Grant royal oblation Anubis, chief of the divine hall,

ṭā - f χu em pet χer Rā us em

may he grant glory in heaven with Rā, power upon

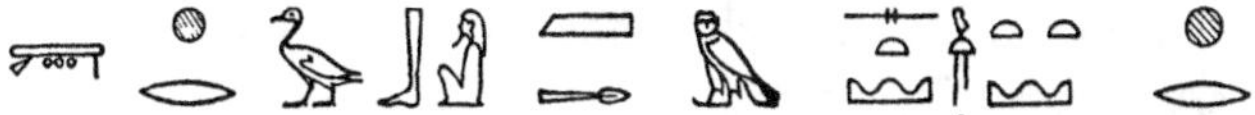

ta χer Seb maāχeru em Set-Åmentet χer

earth with Seb, triumph in the underworld with

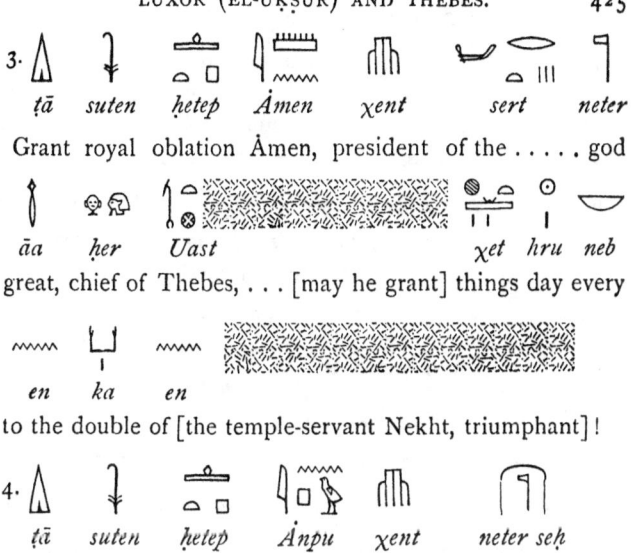

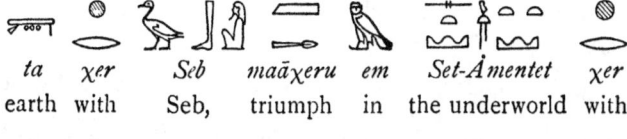

Un-nefer en ka en unnut Nekht

Unnefer, to the double of the temple-servant Nekht.

On the upper part of the stele the deceased Nekht and his sister and wife Taui, a lady of the College of Åmen, are represented sitting before a table of offerings; the inscription reads, "a coming forth always to the table of the lords of eternity every day, to the *ka* of the temple servant, Nekht, triumphant, and to his sister, the lady of the house, triumphant!" Beneath this scene are two *utchats* facing each other , and the signs . The four perpendicular lines of inscription state that the deceased is "watchfully devoted" to the four children of Horus, whose names are Mesthȧ 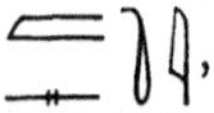, Qebḥsennuf 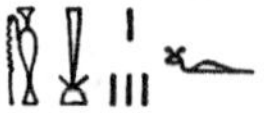, Ḥāpi , and Ṭuamāutef .

On the right of the stele are:—

1. Kneeling figure of a man offering , and the legend, 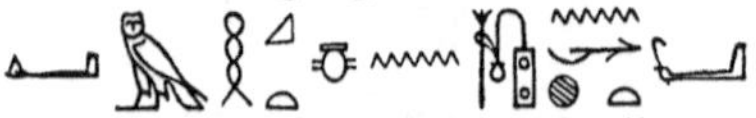 *ṭā em ḥeqt en ān Nekht*, "the giving of beer to the scribe Nekht."

2. Kneeling figure of a man offering two vases 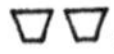, and the legend 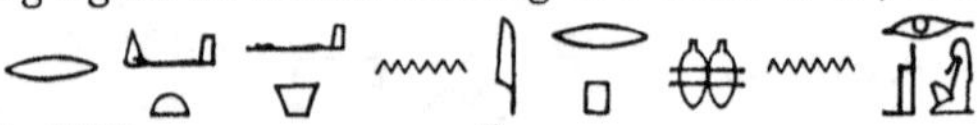 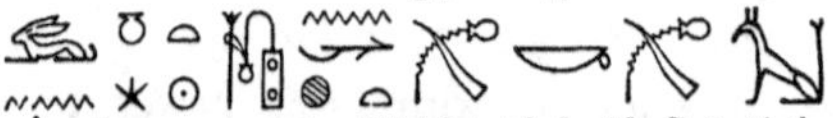 *erṭāt āb en ȧrp en Ȧusȧr unnut ān Nekht āb-k āb Set*, "the giving of a vase of wine to Osiris the temple-servant, the scribe Nekht. Thou art pure, Set is pure."

3. Kneeling figure of a man offering , and the legend  *erṭāt menχ ḥebs en Ȧusȧr ān Nekht*, "the giving of linen bandages to Osiris, the scribe Nekht."

On the left of the stele are:—

1. Kneeling figure offering 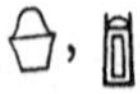, *etc.*, and the legend 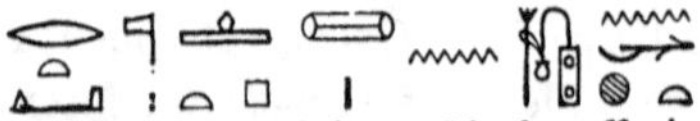 *erṭāt neter ḥetep en ān Nekht*, "the giving of holy offerings to the scribe Nekht."

2. Kneeling figure of a man offering , and the legend
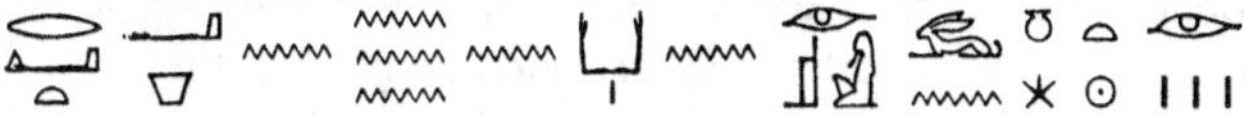
 *erṭāt āb en mu en ka en Ȧusȧr unnut en Ȧmen ān Nekht maāχeru āb-k āb Ḥeru*, "the giving of a vase of water to the double of Osiris, the temple-servant of Ȧmen, the scribe Nekht, triumphant! Thou art pure, Horus is pure."

3. Kneeling figure of a man offering , and the legend, 
 *erṭāt met'et uat' mesṭem en ān Nekht maāχeru*, "the giving of fresh unguents and eye-paint to the scribe Nekht, triumphant!"

Beneath the stele is shown a pile of funereal offerings consisting of fruits and flowers, bread and cakes, ducks, haunches of beef, *etc.*; on each side is a female wearing a sycamore, the emblem of the goddess Hathor, upon her head, and holding offerings of fruit, flowers, *etc.*, in her hands, and behind each is a young man bringing additional offerings.

The scene on the wall at the other end of the chamber was never finished by the artist. In the upper division are Nekht and his wife Taui seated, having a table loaded with funereal offerings before them; a priestly official and the nine *smeri* bring offerings of oil, flowers, *etc.* In the lower division also are Nekht and his wife Taui seated, having a table of offerings before them, and four priestly officials are bringing haunches of veal or beef to them.

On the wall to the left of the doorway leading into the smaller chamber are painted the following scenes connected with agriculture:—1. An arm of the Nile or a canal. On one side are two men ploughing with oxen, and labourers breaking up hard sods with mallets, while a third scatters the seed; on the other are seen men digging up the ground with hoes , and the sower sowing seed. At one end sits the deceased Nekht in the *seḥ* hall, , and at the other is a tree having a water-skin on one of the branches, from which a man drinks. 2. Men reaping, a woman gleaning, men tying up sheaves in a sack, women twisting flax. 3. The measuring of the grain. 4. Winnowing the grain. Above the head of Nekht, who sits in a *seḥ* chamber, is the inscription :—

ḥemset *em* *seḥ* *maa* *seχet* - *f* *àn*

Sitting in the seḥ seeth his fields

unnut *en* *maāχeru* *χer*

the temple-servant of [Àmen, Nekht], triumphant before

neter *āā*

the great god.

On the left of the agricultural scenes stands Nekht pouring out a libation over an altar loaded with all manner of funereal offerings; behind him is his wife Taui holding a *menàt* , emblem of joy and pleasure, in her right hand, and a sistrum  in her left. Beneath the altar two priests are sacrificing a bull. The inscription above the whole scene reads :—

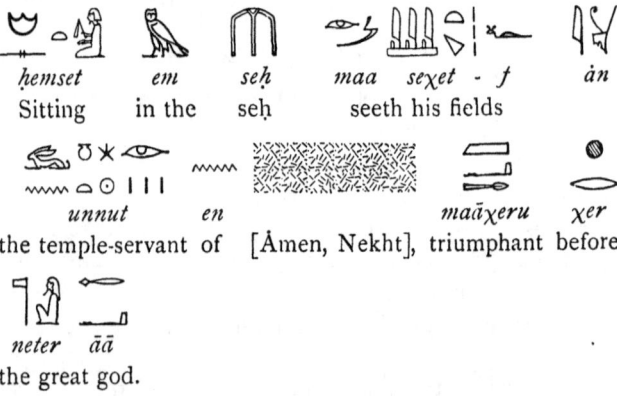

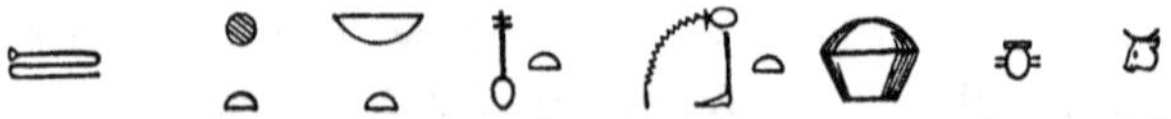

uṭen *χet* *nebt* *nefert* *ābt* *ta* *ḥeq* *àḥ*

Offering of things all beautiful, pure, bread, beer, oxen,

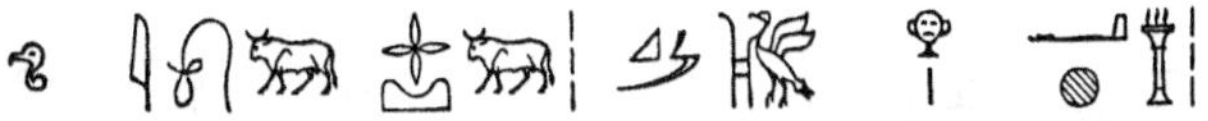

apt *àua* *unṭu* *qema* *ḥer* *āχ*
ducks, heifers, calves, to be made upon the altars

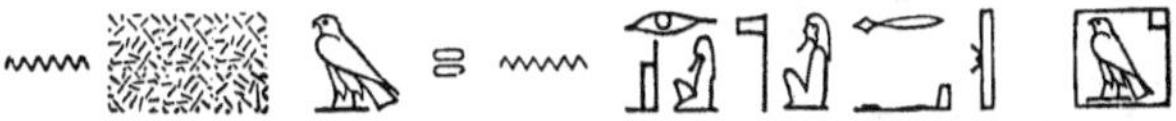

en *Ḥeru-χuti* *en* *Ȧusȧr* *neter* *āā* *Ḥet-Ḥeru*
of . . . . . Harmachis to Osiris, god great, and Hathor

ḥert *set* *en* *Ȧnp* *ḥer*
president of the mountain of the dead, to Anubis upon

ṭu - f *àn* *unnut* *sent - f*
his mountain by the temple-servant . . . . Nekht. His sister,

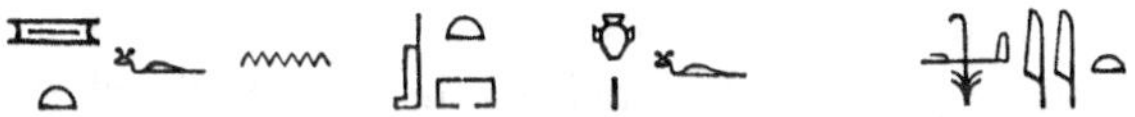

mert - f *en* *àuset* *àb - f* *qemāit*
his darling, of the seat of his heart, the singing priestess

en
of [Ȧmen, Taui, triumphant !]

On the wall to the right of the doorway leading into the smaller chamber are painted the following scenes :—Upper register. Nekht in a boat, accompanied by his wife and children, spearing fish and bringing down birds with the boomerang in a papyrus swamp. Above is the inscription :—

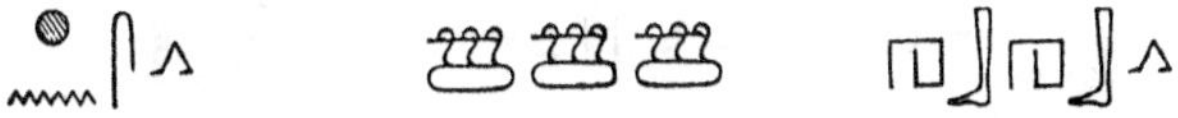

χenes *seś* *hebheb*
Passeth through wild-fowl marshes, traverseth

seś *seχemχem* *satet* *meḥit*

wild-fowl marshes with gladness, speareth fish

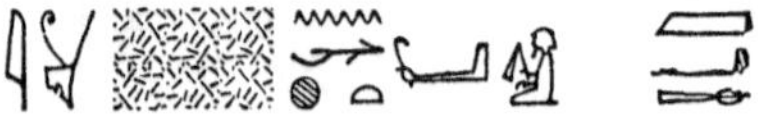

àn *Nekht* *maāχeru*

Nekht, triumphant!

On the bank stand two of Nekht's servants holding sandals, staff, boomerang, *etc.*, and beneath is another servant carrying to Nekht the birds which Nekht himself has brought down. The inscriptions above read :—

1. 

seχemχem *maa* *bu* *nefer* *àri* *seχet*

Rejoiceth, seeth happiness [in] making the chase,

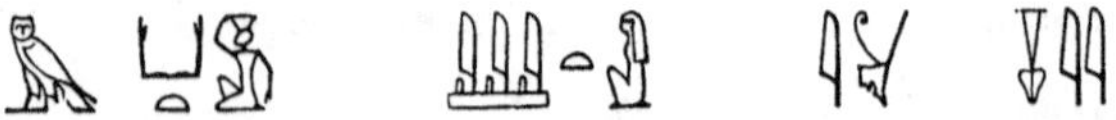

em *kat* *Seχet* *àn* *sami*

[and] in the work of the goddess Sekhet, the friend

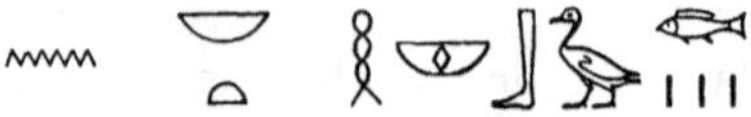 *etc.*

en *nebt* *ḥebu*

of the lady of the chase, the temple-servant, the scribe Nekht, triumphant!

2. 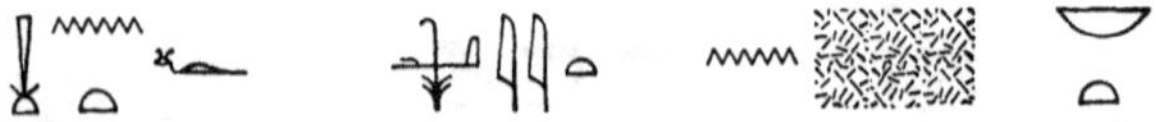

sent - f *qemāit* *en* *nebt*

His sister, the singing priestess of [Àmen], the lady

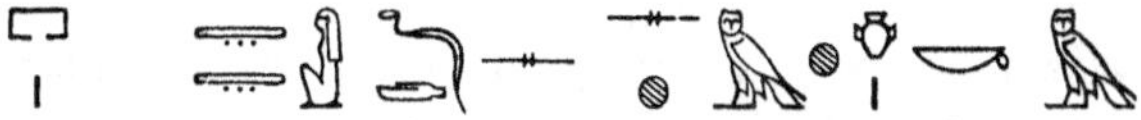

per *Taui* *t'eṭ - s* *seχemχem - k* *em*

of the house, Taui, saith, "Rejoice thou in

kat *Seχet* *qebḥ* *àp - nef*

the work of Sekhet,* [and] the birds [which] he sets apart

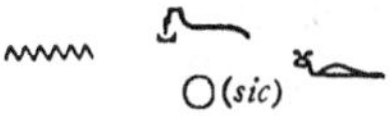

en *setep - f*

for his selection."

3. 

seχemχem *maa* *bu nefer* *em* *ànnu* *en*

Rejoiceth, seeth happiness in the produce of

seχet *ta* *meḥ* *àn* *etc.*

the fields of the land of the north, the temple-
[servant, the scribe Nekht, triumphant !

Lower register. Nekht and his wife sitting in a summer-house "to make himself glad and to experience the happiness of the land of the north" (*i.e.*, Lower Egypt); before them funereal offerings are heaped up. In the upper division of this register are seen Nekht's servants gathering grapes, the treading of the grapes in the wine-press, the drawing of the

* Sekhet was the goddess of the country, and was the wife of the god Khnum. She is represented with the sign for field , upon her head, she wears a girdle of lotus plants round her waist, and upon her hands she bears a plantation filled with all manner of wild fowl. See Lanzone, *Dizionario*, p. 1095.

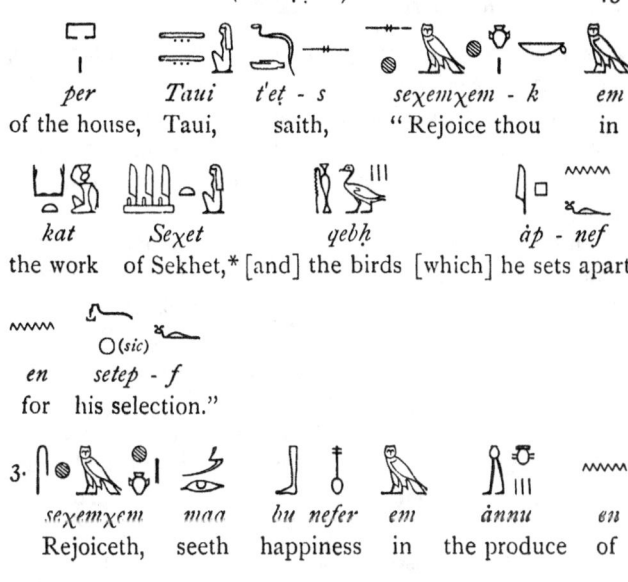

new wine, the jars for holding it, and two servants making offerings to Nekht of birds, flowers, *etc.* In the lower division we see Nekht instructing his servants in the art of snaring birds in nets, the plucking and cleaning of the birds newly caught, and two servants offering to Nekht fish, birds, fruit, *etc.*

In the other scenes we have Nekht, accompanied by his wife Taui, making an offering of *ānta* unguent and incense to the gods of the tomb, and a representation of his funereal feast.

The most ancient necropolis at Thebes is Drah abu'l Neḳḳah, where tombs of the XIth, XVIIth, and XVIIIth dynasties are to be found. The coffins of the Åntef kings (XIth dynasty), now in the Louvre and the British Museum, were discovered here, and here was made the marvellous "find" of the jewellery of Åāḥ-ḥetep, wife of Kames, a king of the XVIIth dynasty, about B.C. 1750. A little more to the south is the necropolis of Asasîf, where during the XIXth, XXIInd, and XXVIth dynasties many beautiful tombs were constructed. If the visitor has time, an attempt should be made to see the fine tomb of Peṭā-Åmen-åpt.

Armant, or Erment, 458½ miles from Cairo, on the west bank of the river, was called in Egyptian 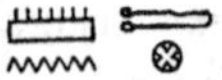 Menth, and  Ånnu qemāt, "Heliopolis of the South"; it marks the site of the ancient Hermonthis, where, according to Strabo, "Apollo and Jupiter are both worshipped."

The ruins which remain there belong to the Iseion built during the reign of the last Cleopatra (B.C. 51–29). The stone-lined tank which lies near this building was probably used as a Nilometer.

Gebelên, *i.e.*, the "double mountain," 468 miles from Cairo, on the west bank of the river, marks the site of the city called by the Greeks, Crocodilopolis, and by the

Egyptians, Neter-ḥet Sebek, . A city must have stood here in very early times, for numerous objects belonging to the Early Empire have been, and are being, continually found at no great distance from the modern village. Below the ruins of the Egyptian town, quite close to the foot of the "double mountain," large numbers of flints belonging to the pre-dynastic period have been found, together with pottery both whole and broken.

Aṣfûn-al-Mata'na, 475 miles from Cairo, on the west bank of the river, marks the site of the city of Asphynis, the Het-sfent  of the Egyptians. In this neighbourhood was **Pathyris,** or Per-Ḥet-ḥert , the capital of the Phatyrites nome, Per-Ḥet-ḥer 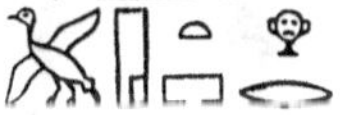.

ESNEH

Esneh, or Asneh, 484½ miles from Cairo, on the west bank of the river, was called in Egyptian 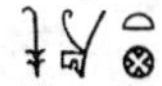 Senet; it marks the site of the ancient Latopolis, and was so called by the Greeks because its inhabitants worshipped the Latus fish. Thothmes III. founded a temple here, but the interesting building which now stands almost in the middle of the modern town is of late date, and bears the names of several of the Roman emperors. The portico is supported by twenty-four columns, each of which is inscribed; their capitals are handsome. The Zodiac here, like that at Denderah, belongs to a late period, but is interesting. The temple was dedicated to the god Khnemu, his wife Nebuut, and their offspring Kaḥrȧ.

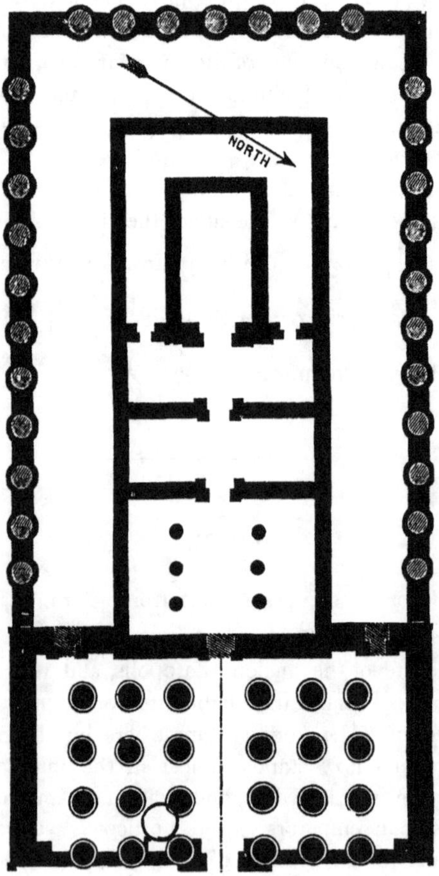

Plan of Temple of Esneh, with restorations by Grand Bey.

El-Kâb, 502 miles from Cairo, on the east bank of the river, was called in Egyptian Nekheb; it marks the site of the ancient Eileithyias. There was a city here in very ancient days, and ruins of temples built by Thothmes IV., Åmenḥetep III., Seti I., Rameses II., Rameses III., Ptolemy IX. Euergetes II. are still visible. A little distance from the town, in the mountain, is the tomb of Åāḥmes (Amāsis), the son of Abana, an officer born in the reign of Seqenen-Rā, who fought against the Hyksos, and who served under Amāsis I., Amenophis I., and Thothmes I. The inscription on the walls of his tomb gives an account of the campaign against some Mesopotamian enemies of Egypt and of the siege of their city. Amāsis was the "Captain-General of Sailors." It is an interesting text both historically and grammatically.

The site of El-kâb is of considerable interest, for it is clear that the little town was at one time fortified in a remarkable manner; the town wall was, in many places, 40 feet thick, and some of the parts of it which still remain are 20 feet high. The tombs found here are of various kinds, *e.g.*, maṣṭăbas either with square shafts or inclines, both made of unbaked brick; and numerous examples of burials in earthenware vessels, *i.e.*, after the manner of the autochthonous inhabitants of Egypt, occur. Mr. Quibell made some extremely interesting excavations here in 1898, and in the course of his work he found a number of diorite bowls inscribed with the name of Seneferu, an early king of the IVth dynasty, a fact which proves that a town was in existence near the spot where they were found in the Early Empire. The small pre-dynastic graves were found chiefly inside the fort of El-kâb, but there were a few outside the walls, and it was evident, from the positions of the bodies, and the style and character of the objects found in the graves, that they belonged to the same class of graves as those which were excavated by Messrs. de Morgan, Amélineau, and Petrie in 1894-95, 1896-97, and 1900 at Abydos, Ballas, and Naḳâda. In the winter of 1892-93, Mr. Somers Clarke and Mr. J. J. Tylor examined and described in an exhaustive manner many of the buildings at El-kâb, and the results of some of their work were published in the *Tomb of Paḥeri*, London, 1894, and in the *Tomb of Sebeknekht*, London, 1896.

The **Tomb of Paḥeri** is a little over 25 feet long, and 11½ feet wide, and when complete consisted of a platform before the entrance in which the shaft leading to the mummy chamber was sunk, a sculptured façade, an oblong chamber with an arched roof, and a shrine, which contained three statues, at the end of the chamber. Subsequently two chambers and a shaft were hewn through the last wall. The shrine contains three life size statues of Paḥeri and his mother and wife. The man for whom the tomb was made was the governor of the Latopolite nome in the reign of Thothmes III., and he was descended from ancestors who had served the State for several generations. His maternal grandfather was the celebrated Ȧāḥmes, the son of Abana, and the inscriptions mention at least seven generations of his family. The scenes in the tomb are worthy of careful examination, and as they are all described in hieroglyphics, they are of peculiar interest. They unfortunately tell us little or nothing of the biography of Paḥeri, who was an Egyptian gentleman of high rank and social position, but one who did little towards making history; that he was a pious man who worshipped the gods of his country diligently, is attested by the sacrificial scenes on the East Wall, and the prayers on the ceiling.

The **Tomb of Sebek-nekht,** a comparatively small tomb, is of considerable interest, because it belongs either to the period of the XIIIth dynasty or a little later. The scenes and inscriptions are characteristic of this period, and illustrate the manners and customs of the time rather than the performance of the religious ceremonies which were depicted on the walls of the tombs of a later date.

UṬFÛ (EDFÛ).

Edfû, 515½ miles from Cairo, on the west bank of the river, was called in Egyptian 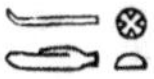 Beḥuṭet, and in Coptic ⲁⲃⲧⲱ; it was called by the Greeks Apollinopolis Magna, where the crocodile and its worshippers were detested. The **Temple of Edfû,** for which alone both the ancient and modern towns were famous, occupied 180 years three months and fourteen days in building, that is to say, it was begun during the reign of Ptolemy III. Euergetes I., B.C. 237, and finished B.C. 57. It resembles that of Denderah in many respects, but its complete condition marks it out as one of the most remarkable buildings in Egypt, and its splendid towers, about 112 feet high, make its general magnificence very striking. The space enclosed by the walls measures 450 × 120 feet; the front of the propylon from side to side measures about 252 feet. Passing through the door the visitor enters a court, around three sides of which runs a gallery supported on thirty-two pillars. The first and second halls, A, B, have eighteen and twelve pillars respectively; passing through chambers C and D, the shrine E is reached, where stood a granite naos in which a figure of Horus, to whom the temple is dedicated, was preserved. This naos was made by Nectanebus I., a king of the XXXth dynasty, B.C. 378. The pylons are covered with battle scenes, and the walls are inscribed with the names and sizes of the various chambers in the building, lists of names of places, etc.; the name of the architect, Ī-em-ḥetep, or Imouthis, has also been inscribed. From the

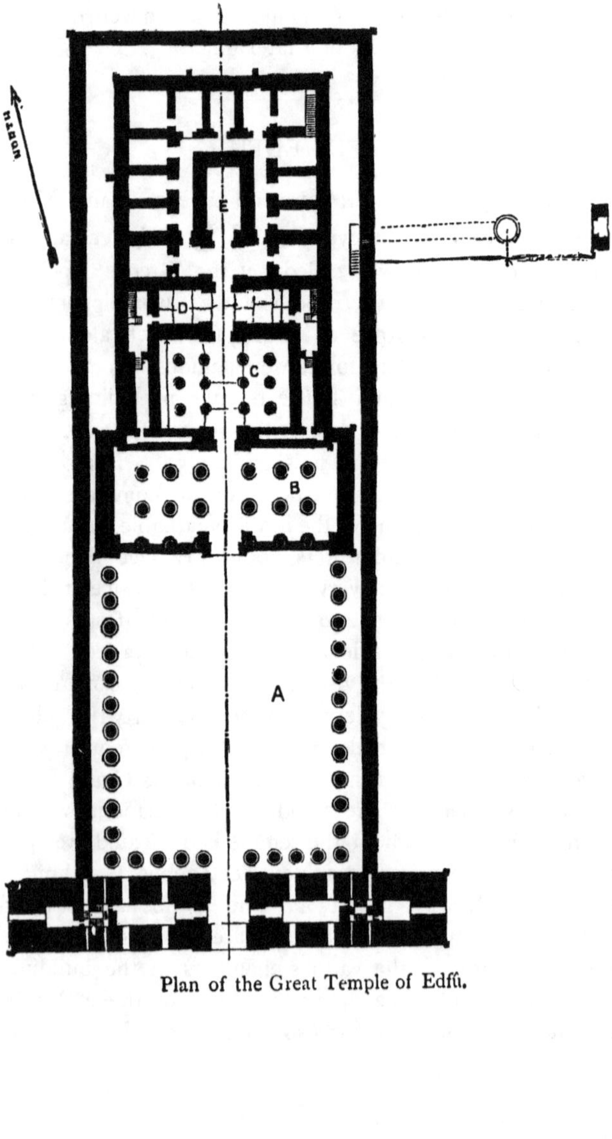

Plan of the Great Temple of Edfû.

south side of the pylons, and from a small chamber on each side of the chamber C, staircases ascended to the roof. The credit of clearing out the temple of Edfû belongs to M. Mariette. Little more than thirty-five years ago the mounds of rubbish outside reached to the top of its walls, and certain parts of the roof were entirely covered over with houses and stables. A few miles to the south of Edfû is the village of **Redesîyeh,** after which a temple of Seti I. has been called; this temple, however, lies at a distance of about 40 miles in a somewhat south-easterly direction from the village.

Hagar (or Gebel) **Silsileh,** 541½ miles from Cairo, on the east and west banks of the river, derives its name probably, not from the Arabic word of like sound meaning "chain," but from the Coptic ϫⲱⲗϫⲉⲗ, meaning "stone wall"; the place is usually called 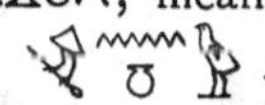 *Khennu* in hieroglyphic texts. The ancient Egyptians here quarried the greater part of the sandstone used by them in their buildings, and the names of the kings inscribed in the caves here show that these quarries were used from the earliest to the latest periods. The most extensive of these are to be found on the east bank of the river, but those on the west bank contain the interesting tablets of Ḥeru-em-ḥeb, a king of the XVIIIth dynasty, who is represented conquering the Ethiopians, Seti I., Rameses II. his son, Meneptaḥ, etc. At Silsileh the Nile was worshipped, and the little temple which Rameses II. built in this place seems to have been dedicated chiefly to it. At this point the Nile narrows very much, and it was generally thought that a cataract once existed here; there is, however, no evidence in support of this view, and the true channel of the Nile lies on the other side of the mountain.

Kom Ombos, 556½ miles from Cairo, on the east bank of the Nile, was an important place at all periods of

Egyptian history; it was called by the Egyptians 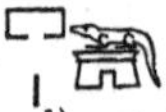, Per-Sebek, "the temple of Sebek" (the crocodile god), and , Nubit, and ⲙ̀ⲃⲱ by the Copts. The oldest object here is a sandstone gateway which Thothmes III. dedicated to the god Sebek.

The ruins of the temple and other buildings at Kom Ombos are among the most striking in Egypt, but until the clearance of the site which M. de Morgan made in 1893-94, it was impossible to get an exact idea of their arrangement. It is pretty certain that a temple dedicated to some god must have stood here in the Early Empire, and we know from M. Maspero's discoveries here in 1882, that Amenophis I. and Thothmes III., kings of the XVIIIth dynasty, carried out repairs on the temple which was in existence in their days; but at the present time no parts of the buildings at Kom Ombos are older than the reigns of the Ptolemies. Thanks to the labours of M. de Morgan, the ruins may be thus classified:—The Mammisi, the Great Temple, and the Chapel of Hathor; and all these buildings were enclosed within a surrounding wall.

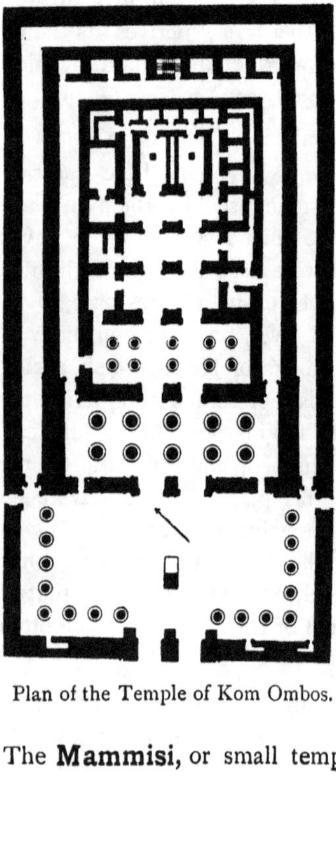

Plan of the Temple of Kom Ombos.

The **Mammisi,** or small temple wherein the festivals of

the birth of the gods were celebrated, stood in front of the great temple, to the left; it consisted of a small courtyard, hall of columns, and the shrine. It was built by Ptolemy IX., who is depicted on the walls making offerings to Sebek, Hathor, Thoth, and other deities. The best relief remaining (see de Morgan, *Kom Ombos*, p. 50) is on the north wall, and represents the king on a fowling expedition through marshes much frequented by water fowl.

The Great Temple. The pylon of the great temple has almost entirely disappeared, and only a part of the central pillar and south half remains. A few of the scenes are in good preservation, and represent the Emperor Domitian making offerings to the gods. Passing through the pylon, the visitor entered a large courtyard; on three sides was a colonnade containing sixteen pillars, and in the middle was an altar. The large hall of ten columns was next entered, and access was obtained through two doors to another, but smaller hall, of ten columns. The shrines of the gods Sebek and Ḥeru-ur, *i.e.*, "Horus the elder" (Haroëris), to whom the temple was dedicated, were approached through three chambers, each having two doors, and round the whole of this section of the building ran a corridor, which could be entered through a door on the left into the second hall of columns, and a door on the right in the first chamber beyond. At the sides and ends of the sanctuary are numerous small chambers which were used probably either for the performance of ceremonies in connection with the worship of the gods, or by the priests. The reliefs on the courtyard represent Cæsar Tiberius

making offerings to Ḥeru-ur, hawk-headed, Sebek, crocodile-headed, Osiris Unnefer, and other gods. The colouring of the relief in which this Emperor is seen making an offering to the lady of Ombos and Khonsu (Column IV) is in an admirable state of preservation. On the façade is an interesting scene in which the gods Horus and Thoth are

The Emperor Tiberius making an offering of land to Sebek and Hathor. (Bas-relief at Kom Ombos, Courtyard, column XVI.)

represented pouring out the water of life over Ptolemy Neos Dionysos. The reliefs in the first hall of columns are very fine examples of the decorative work of the period, and worthy of notice are:—(*West Wall*): The king in the company of Ḥeru-ur, Isis, Nut, and Thoth; the king adoring four mythical monsters, one of which has four lions' heads. (*East Wall*): Harpocrates, seated in the Sun's disk in a boat, accompanied by Shu, Isis, Nephthys, Maāt, Nut, etc.; the 14 *kas* or "doubles" of the king; the king making offerings to the gods. (*Ceiling*): The gods of the stars in boats in the heavens, gods and goddesses, etc. Here it is interesting to note that certain sections of the ceiling are divided by lines into squares with the object of assisting the draughtsman and sculptor, and that the plan of the original design was changed, for unfinished figures of gods may be seen on it in quite different positions. In the small hall of columns are reliefs similar in character to those found in the larger hall. An examination of the great temple shows that the building was carried out on a definite plan, and that the decoration of the walls with reliefs was only begun after the builders had finished their work. The oldest reliefs and texts belong to the period of the Ptolemies, and are found in the main buildings, and begin with the shrines of the gods Sebek and Ḥeru-ur; the reliefs and inscriptions of the courtyard belong to the Roman period. The **Chapel of Hathor** also belongs to the Roman period, and seems not to have been completed. Drawings made in the early part of the XIXth century show that the ruins of the temples and other buildings were in a much better state of preservation than they are at present, and as the ruin which has fallen upon them since that date cannot be justly attributed to the natives, it must be due to the erosion of the bank by the waters of the Nile, which has for centuries slowly but surely been eating its way into it. The building which Amenophis I. erected there was destroyed by the encroachment of its waters, and, according to M. de Morgan, a strip of ground from the front of the temple nearly 20 feet in width has been swallowed up in the waters during the last 60 years, and with it there probably went the greater part of the Mammisi. This being so, all lovers of antiquities will rejoice that a stone platform has been built in front of the temple to prevent the further destruction of it by the Nile.

ASWÂN.

Aswân (or Uswân), the southern limit of Egypt proper, 583 miles from Cairo, on the east bank of the river, called in Egyptian , Coptic ⲥⲟⲩⲁⲛ, was called by the Greeks Syene, which stood on the slope of a hill to the south-west of the present town. Properly speaking, Syene was the island of Elephantine. In the earliest Egyptian inscriptions it is called 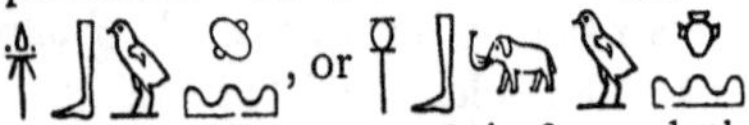, Åbu, *i.e.*, "the district of the elephant," and it formed the metropolis of the first nome of Upper Egypt,  Ta-kens. As we approach the time of the Ptolemies, the name Sunnu, *i.e.*, the town on the east bank of the Nile, from whence comes the Arabic name Aswân, takes the place of Åbu. The town obtained great notoriety among the ancients from the fact that Eratosthenes and Ptolemy considered it to lie on the tropic of Cancer, and to be the most northerly point where, at the time of the summer solstice, the sun's rays fell vertically; as a matter of fact, however, the town lies 0′ 37′ 23″ north of the tropic of Cancer. There was a famous well there, into which the sun was said to shine at the summer solstice, and to illuminate it in every part. In the time of the Romans three cohorts were stationed here,* and the town was of considerable importance. In the twelfth century of our era it was the seat of a bishop. Of its size in ancient days

* It is interesting to observe that the Romans, like the British, held Egypt by garrisoning three places, viz., Aswân, Babylon (Cairo), and Alexandria. The garrison at Aswân defended Egypt from foes on the south, and commanded the entrance of the Nile; the garrison at Babylon guarded the end of the Nile valley and the entrance to the Delta; and the garrison at Alexandria protected the country from invasion by sea.

nothing definite can be said, but Arabic writers describe it as a flourishing town, and they relate that a plague once swept off 20,000 of its inhabitants. Aswân was famous for its wine in Ptolemaic times. The town has suffered greatly at the hands of the Persians, Arabs, and Turks on the north, and Nubians, by whom it was nearly destroyed in the twelfth century, on the south. The oldest ruins in the town are those of a Ptolemaic temple, which are still visible.

The island of **Elephantine** * lies a little to the north of the cataract just opposite Aswân, and has been famous in all ages as the key of Egypt from the south; the Romans garrisoned it with numerous troops, and it represented the southern limit of their empire. The island itself was very fertile, and it is said that its vines and fig-trees retained their leaves throughout the year. The kings of the Vth dynasty sprang from Elephantine. The gods worshipped here by the Egyptians were called Khnemu, Sati and Sept, and on this island Amenophis III. built a temple, remains of which were visible in the early part of this century. Of the famous Nilometer which stood here, Strabo says: "The Nilometer is a well upon the banks of the Nile, constructed of close-fitting stones, on which are marked the greatest, least, and mean risings of the Nile; for the water in the well and in the river rises and subsides simultaneously. Upon the wall

* "A little above Elephantine is the lesser cataract, where the boatmen exhibit a sort of spectacle to the governors. The cataract is in the middle of the river, and is formed by a ridge of rocks, the upper part of which is level, and thus capable of receiving the river, but terminating in a precipice, where the water dashes down. On each side towards the land there is a stream, up which is the chief ascent for vessels. The boatmen sail up by this stream, and, dropping down to the cataract, are impelled with the boat to the precipice, the crew and the boats escaping unhurt." (Strabo, Bk. xvii. chap. i., 49, Falconer's translation.) Thus it appears that "shooting the cataract" is a very old amusement.

of the well are lines, which indicate the complete rise of the river, and other degrees of its rising. Those who examine these marks communicate the result to the public for their information. For it is known long before, by these marks, and by the time elapsed from the commencement, what the future rise of the river will be, and notice is given of it. This information is of service to the husbandmen with reference to the distribution of the water; for the purpose also of attending to the embankments, canals, and other things of this kind. It is of use also to the governors, who fix the revenue; for the greater the rise of the river, the greater it is expected will be the revenue." According to Plutarch the Nile rose at Elephantine to the height of 28 cubits; a very interesting text at Edfû states that if the river rises 24 cubits 3¼ hands at Elephantine, it will water the country satisfactorily.

A mile or so to the north of the monastery stands the bold hill in the sides of which are hewn the tombs which General Sir F. W. Grenfell, G.C.B., excavated; this hill is situated in Western Aswân, the ⲥⲟⲩⲁⲛ ⲙ̀ ⲡⲉⲙⲉⲛⲧ of the Copts, and is the Contra Syene of the classical authors. The tombs are hewn out of the rock, tier above tier, and the most important of these were reached by a stone staircase, which to this day remains nearly complete, and is one of the most interesting antiquities in Egypt. The tombs in this hill may be roughly divided into three groups. The first group was hewn in the best and thickest layer of stone in the top of the hill, and was made for the rulers of Elephantine who lived during the VIth and XIIth dynasties. The second group is composed of tombs of different periods; they are hewn out of a lower layer of stone, and are not of so much importance. The third group, made during the Roman occupation of Egypt, lies at a comparatively little height above the river. All these tombs were broken into at a very early period, and the largest of them formed a common sepulchre for people of all classes from the XXVIth dynasty downwards. They were found filled with broken coffins and mummies and sepulchral stelæ, etc., etc., and everything showed how degraded Egyptian funereal art had become when these bodies were buried there. The double tomb at the head of the staircase was made for Sabbenȧ and Mekhu; the former was a dignitary of high rank who lived during the reign of Pepi II., a king of the VIth dynasty, whose prenomen 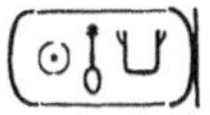 Nefer-ka-Rā is inscribed on the left hand side of the doorway; the latter was a *smer*, prince and inspector, who appears to have lived during the XIIth dynasty. The paintings on the walls and the proto-Doric columns which support the roof are interesting, and its fine state of preservation and position make it one of the most valuable monuments of that early period. A little further northward is the small tomb of 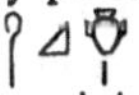 Ḥeqȧb, and beyond this is the fine, large tomb hewn originally for Sa-Renput, one of the old feudal hereditary governors of Elephantine, but which was appropriated by Nub-kau-Rā-nekht. He was the governor of the district of the cataract, and the general who commanded a lightly-armed body of soldiers called "runners"; he lived during the reign of Usertsen I., the second king of the XIIth dynasty, and his tomb must have been one of the earliest hewn there during that period. Another interesting tomb is that of Ḥeru-khuf, who was governor of Elephantine, and an inscription from it (now in the Gîzeh Museum) shows that this official was sent by Pepi II. to bring back a pygmy 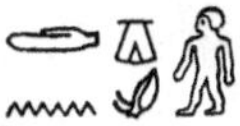 *ṭenḳ* from the interior of Africa. The king promised Ḥeru-khuf that if he brought back a pygmy alive and well, he would confer upon him a higher rank and dignity than that which King Assȧ conferred upon his minister Ba-ur-Ṭeṭṭeṭ, who performed the same office about eighty years before.

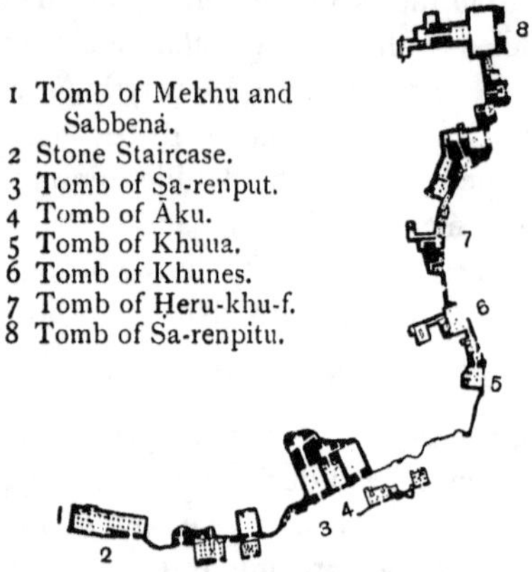

The Tombs at Aswân.

The following is a list of the principal tombs at Aswân :—

No. 1. Tomb of Mekhu and Sabbenȧ, and . In this tomb is an interesting scene of the deceased in a boat spearing fish.

No. 2. Tomb of Ḥeq-ȧb, .

No. 3. Tomb of Sa-renput, , son of Satet-ḥetep. (No. 31.)

No. 4. Tomb of Āku, . (No. 32.)

No. 5. Tomb of Khuuȧ, .

No. 6. Tomb of Khunes (?).

No. 7. Tomb of Khennu-sesu, .

No. 8. Tomb of Ḥer-Khu-f, .

No. 9. Tomb of Pepi-nekht, .

No. 10. Tomb of Sen-mes, .

No. 11. Tomb of Sa-renput, . This tomb is the finest of all the tombs at Aswân. It faces the north, and lies round the bend of the mountain. Before it is a spacious court, which was enclosed by a wall, and the limestone jambs of the door, which were ornamented with reliefs and hieroglyphics, were, until recently, still standing. At the south end of the court was a portico supported by eight rectangular pillars. The first chamber contains four pillars, and leads through a wide corridor to another chamber with two pillars; in this last are two flights of steps which lead to two other chambers. The walls of the court were without reliefs, but the pillars of the portico were decorated with figures of the deceased and with inscriptions on each of their sides. The face of the tomb is inscribed with a long text in which the deceased tells how he "filled the heart of the king" (*i.e.*, satisfied him), and enumerates all the work which he did in Nubia on behalf of his lord; to the left of the doorway is a relief in which Sa-renput is seen in a boat spearing fish (?), and to the right we have a representation of ancestor worship. On

Scene from the shrine in the tomb of Sa-renput.

the wall of the first chamber inside is a long inscription which fortunately enables us to date the tomb, for it mentions the prenomen Kheper-ka-Rā  of Usertsen I., a king of the XIIth dynasty; elsewhere are depicted a number of boats, fishing scenes, etc. The other scenes in the tomb refer to the storage of wheat, jars of wine, etc. When the writer first cleared this tomb for Sir Francis Grenfell in 1886, the shrine, containing a figure of Sa-renput, was *in situ*, and was of considerable interest. In the sand which filled the first chamber almost to the ceiling were found the bodies of two or three Muḥammadans, who appear to have been hastily buried there. The shaft, which is entered from the right side of the second chamber by means of a flight of steps, was cleared out, and two or more small chambers, lined and barricaded with unbaked bricks, were entered. In the floor of one of these an entrance to a further pit was made, but the air was so foul that candles ceased to burn, and the work had to be abandoned.

Lower down in the hill are the following tombs :—

1. Tomb of Sebek-ḥetep 
2. Tomb of Khnemu-khenu 
3. Tomb of Thethȧ 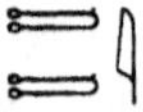
4. Tomb of Sen 
5. Tomb of Ȧba 

The **Monastery of St. Simon**, or Simeon.* On the western bank of the Nile, at about the same height as the southern point of the Island of Elephantine, begins the

* A plan and full description of this building will be found in J. de Morgan's *Catalogue*, vol. 1, Vienna, 1894, page 130 ff.

valley which leads to the monastery called after the name of Saint Simon, or Simeon. It is a large, strong building, half monastery, half fortress, and is said to have been abandoned by its monks in the XIIIth century, but the statement lacks confirmation; architecturally it is of very considerable interest. It was wholly surrounded by a wall from about 19 to 23 feet high, the lower part, which was sunk in the rock, being built of stone, and the upper part of mud brick; within this wall lay all the monastery buildings. The monks lived in the north tower, in the upper storeys, where there were several cells opening out on each side of a long corridor; on the ramparts were a number ofhi ding places for the watchmen, and there are evidences that the building was added to from time to time. The church consisted of a choir, two sacristies, and a nave, the whole being covered with a vaulted roof, which was supported by columns. In the church were the remains of a fine fresco in the Byzantine style, which formerly contained the figures of Christ and twenty-four saints, etc., and also a picture of Christ enthroned. In a small rock-hewn chapel at the foot of the staircase which leads to the corridor, the walls are ornamented with figures of our Lord's Apostles or Disciples. Every here and there are found inscriptions in Coptic and Arabic. The Coptic texts usually contain prayers to God that He may show mercy upon their writers, who regard the visit to the monastery as a meritorious act; the oldest Arabic inscription states that a certain Mutammar 'Ali visited the monastery in the year A.H. 694, *i.e.*, towards the end of the XIIIth century of our era. About a fifth of a mile to the east of the monastery lay the ancient cemetery, which was cleared out about seventeen years ago; the bodies of the monks had been embalmed after a fashion, but they fell to pieces when touched. If the position of the Copts in Egypt in the XIIIth century be considered, it will be seen to be extremely unlikely that the monastery of St.

Simon was flourishing at that time, and it is far more probable that it was deserted many scores of years before. From Abû Ṣalîḥ, the Armenian, we learn that there were several churches and monasteries at Aswân. Thus he says that on the island of Aswân, *i.e.*, Elephantine, there was a church in which was laid the body of Abû Hadrî, and near this church was a monastery, which was in ruins in the days of Abû Salîḥ, with 300 cells for monks. There were also the churches of Saint Mennas, the Virgin Mary, and the archangels Gabriel and Michael. The church of Saint Ibsâdah stood on the citadel of Aswân, on the bank of the Nile, and the saint was said to have the power of walking upon the water. The monastery of Abû Hadrî was "on the mountain on the west," and it is probable that the monastery now called by the name of St. Simon is here referred to.

The **gold mines,** which are often referred to by writers on Aswân, were situated in the Wâdî al-'Alâḳî, to the south-east of Aswân, in the country of the Bishârîn; these appear to be the mines that were worked by the Egyptians in the XVIIIth and XIXth dynasties. The **clay quarries** were situated on the east bank of the Nile, just opposite to Elephantine Island, and were famous for red and yellow ochres, and for a fine clay, called the "clay of art," which was much used in making jars to hold Aswân wine. These quarries were worked in ancient days, and the stratum of clay was followed by the miners to very considerable distances into the mountains; the entrance to the workings is buried under the sand.

Aswân was as famous for its granite, as Silsileh was for its sandstone. The Egyptian kings were in the habit of sending to Aswân for granite to make sarcophagi, temples, obelisks, etc., and it will be remembered that Unȧ was sent there to bring back in barges granite for the use of Pepi I., a king of the VIth dynasty. It is probable that the granite slabs which cover the pyramid of Mycerinus (IVth dynasty) were brought from Aswân. The undetached obelisk, which still lies in one of the quarries, is an interesting object.

Near the quarries are two ancient Arabic cemeteries, in which are a number of sandstone grave-stones, many of them formed from stones taken from Ptolemaïc buildings, inscribed in Cufic * characters with the names of the Muḥammadans buried there, and the year, month, and day on which they died. We learn from them that natives of Edfû and other parts of Egypt were sometimes brought here and buried.

The first **Cataract**, called Shellâl by the Arabs, begins a little to the south of Aswân, and ends a little to the north of the island of Philæ; six great cataracts are found on the Nile, but this is the most generally known. Here the Nile becomes narrow and flows between two mountains, which descend nearly perpendicularly to the river, the course of which is obstructed by huge boulders and small rocky islands and barriers, which stand on different levels, and cause the falls of water which have given this part of the river its name. On the west side the obstacles are not so numerous as on the east, and sailing and rowing boats can ascend the cataract on this side when the river is high. The noise made by the water is at times very great, but it has been greatly exaggerated by both ancient and modern travellers, some of whom ventured to assert that the "water fell from several places in the mountain more than two hundred feet." Some ancient writers asserted that the fountains of the Nile were in this cataract, and Herodotus†

* A kind of Arabic writing in which very old copies of the Ḳor'ân. etc., are written: it takes its name from Kûfah, الكوفة *El-Kûfa*, a town on the Euphrates. Kûfah was one of the chief cities of 'Irâḳ, and is famous in the Muḥammadan world because Muḥammad and his immediate successors dwelt there. Enoch lived here, the ark was built here, the boiling waters of the Flood first burst out here, and Abraham had a place of prayer set apart here.

† Bk. ii., chap. 28

reports that an official of the treasury of Neith at Sais stated that the source of the Nile was here. Many of the rocks here are inscribed with the names of kings who reigned during the Middle Empire; in many places on the little islands in the cataract quarries were worked. The island of **Sehêl** should be visited on account of the numerous inscriptions left there by princes, generals, and others who passed by on their way to Nubia. On February 6th, 1889, Mr. Wilbour was fortunate enough to discover on the south-eastern part of this island a most important stele consisting of a rounded block of granite, eight or nine feet high, which stands clear above the water, and in full view from the river looking towards Philæ. Upon it are inscribed thirty-two lines of hieroglyphics which form a remarkable document, and contain some valuable information bearing upon a famous seven years' famine. The inscription is dated in the eighteenth year of a king whose name is read by Dr. Brugsch as Tcheser , , or , who reigned early in the IIIrd dynasty; but internal evidence proves beyond a doubt that the narrative contained therein is a redaction of an old story, and that it is, in its present form, not older than the time of the Ptolemies. In the second line we are told :—

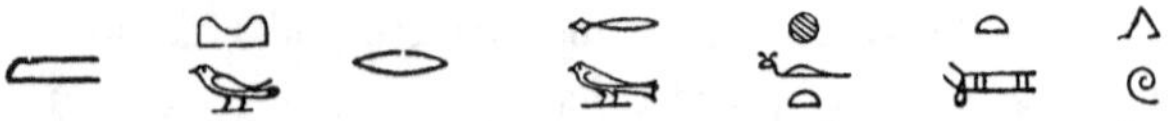

em	ṭu	er	āa ur	χeft	tem	iu
By	*misfortune*	*the*	*very greatest*		*not had*	*come forth*

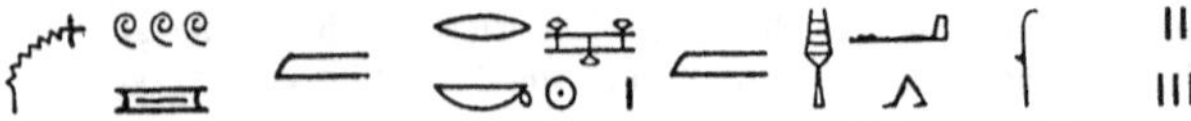

Ḥāpu	em	rek	em	āḥā	renpit	seχef
the Nile	*during*	*a period*		*lasting*	*years*	*seven.*

ket nepi uśer renp

Scarce [was] grain, lacking [was] vegetable food,

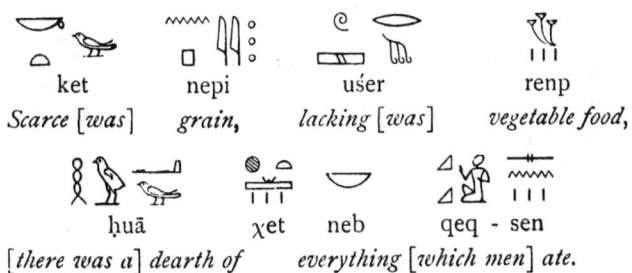

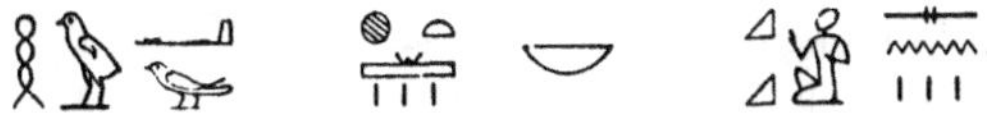

ḥuā χet neb qeq - sen

[there was a] dearth of everything [which men] ate.

In this time of distress the king despatched a messenger to Matar, the governor of Elephantine, informing him of the terrible state of want and misery which the country was in, and asking him to give him information about the source of the Nile, and about the god or goddess who presided over it, and promising to worship this deity henceforth if he would make the harvests full as of yore. Matar informed the messenger concerning these things, and when the king had heard his words he at once ordered rich sacrifices to be made to Khnemu, the god of Elephantine, and decreed that tithes of every product of the land should be paid to his temple. This done the famine came to an end and the Nile rose again to its accustomed height. There can be no connection between this seven years' famine and that recorded in the Bible, for it must have happened some two thousand years before Joseph could have been in Egypt; but this remarkable inscription proves that from time immemorial the people of Egypt have suffered from periodic famines. The village of Mahâtah, on the east bank of the river, is prettily situated, and worth a visit.

PHILÆ.

Philæ is the name given by the Greeks and Romans to the two islands which are situated at the head of the First Cataract, about six miles south of Aswân; the larger island is called **Biggeh,** the Senemet 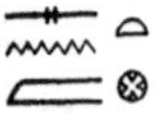 of the Egyptian texts, and the name Philæ now generally refers to the smaller island, on which stands the group of ancient buildings of the Ptolemaic and Roman periods. The name Philæ is derived from the Egyptian words P-á-lek, , *i.e.*, "the Island of Lek," or 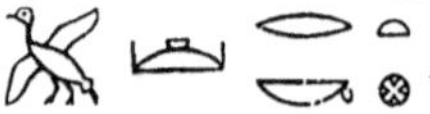; from these words the Copts formed the name ⲡⲓⲗⲁⲕϩ, and the Arabs the name Bilâķ, بلاق. A well-known name for Philæ in the inscriptions is "the city of Isis," and one text speaks of it as the "interior of heaven," ; that it was held to be a most holy site is evident from its titles, Åuset ābt , and P-á-āb , *i.e.*, "Holy House" and "Holy Island" respectively. Of the history of the Island of Philæ during the Early and Middle Empires nothing is known; only it is certain that the Egyptians made use of it for military purposes in very early times. Whether they built forts upon it cannot be said, but the site was an excellent one for a garrison. Judging by analogy, shrines to local gods, or temples, must have stood upon one or both of the islands, for it is impossible to imagine that such a well-protected and picturesque spot for a temple or temples should have remained unoccupied. The early travellers in Egypt declare that slabs of granite and sandstone inscribed with the names of Amenophis II., Amenophis III., and Thothmes III., were visible on this island, as well as on that of Biggeh; but it is certain that nothing of the kind remains there now. We shall be probably correct in assuming that the first temple of any great importance was built there in the XVIIIth dynasty,

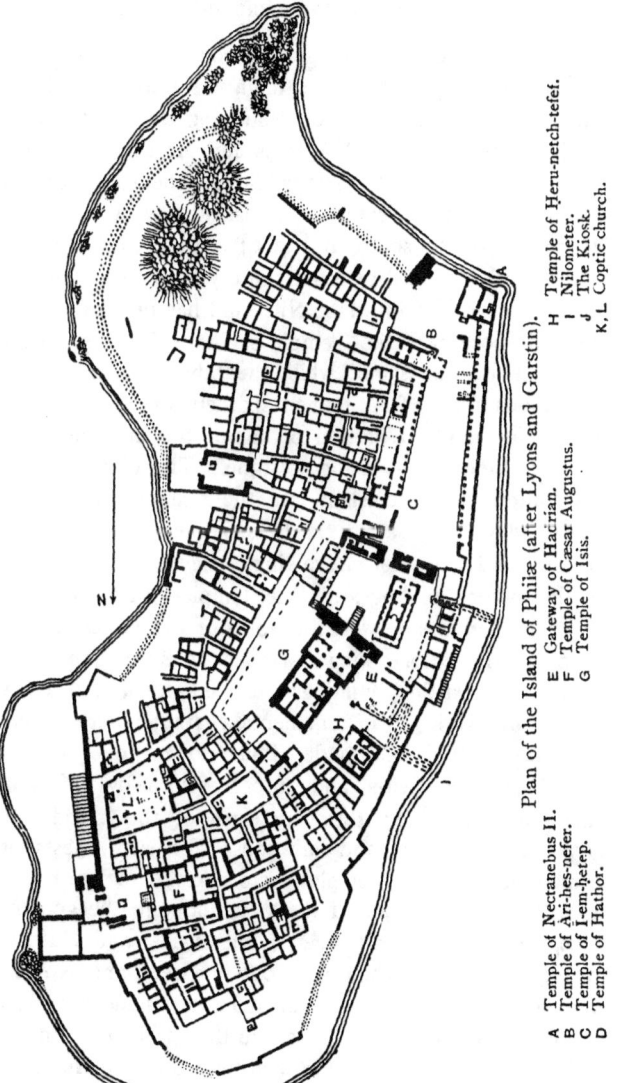

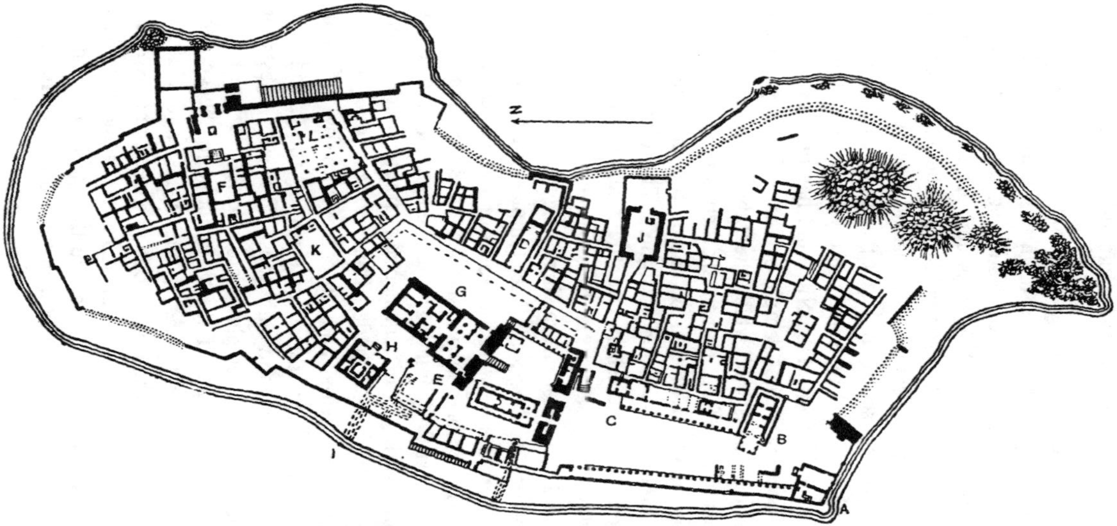

Plan of the Island of Philæ (after Lyons and Garstin).

A Temple of Nectanebus II.
B Temple of Àri-hes-nefer.
C Temple of Ì-em-ḥetep.
D Temple of Hathor.
E Gateway of Hadrian.
F Temple of Cæsar Augustus.
G Temple of Isis.
H Temple of Ḥeru-netch-tefef.
I Nilometer.
J The Kiosk.
K, L Coptic church.

and that the sides of the granite rock which forms the island were scarped that walls might be built upon them. This would have the effect of destroying the rough graffiti which the troops of the Usertsens and Ȧmenemḥāts must have chiselled upon it, as they did on the rocks on the cataract on their way south. The island is 1,418 feet long, *i.e.*, from north to south, and 464 feet wide, *i.e.*, from east to west, and is formed by a mass of crystalline rock, mainly hornblendic granite, on which Nile mud has been deposited. The main portion of the Temple of Isis is founded on the solid rock of the island, while the other buildings have foundations usually from four to six metres in depth, which rest on Nile mud; a portion of one of the buildings rests upon an artificial quay made of stone. The oldest portion of a building on the island are the remains of a small edifice which was set up at the southern end of it by Nectanebus II., the last native king of Egypt (B.C. 358–340). Of the other buildings, all the temples date from the Ptolemaïc period, and were the works of the Ptolemies and of one or two Nubian kings. Under the Roman emperors a few of the existing buildings were enlarged, and a few architectural works of an ornamental character were added. An ancient tradition made Philæ to be one of the burial places of Osiris, and an oath sworn by Osiris of Philæ was inviolable; the very earth of the island was considered to be holy, and only those who were priests, or were employed in the temples, were allowed to live there. In early times the gods of the Cataract were the gods of Philæ, *i.e.*, Khnemu and Satet, Khnemu-Rā, and Hathor, Anuqet, Ptaḥ and Sekhet, etc.; but in Greek and Roman times the deities chiefly worshipped in the island were Isis and Osiris, and the gods who were in their train, *i.e.*, Horus, Nephthys, etc. In connection with the worship of Isis and Osiris a number of ceremonies were performed, in which the death and mutilation of the body of Osiris, the gathering together of his scattered limbs, the reconstruction of the body by Isis, and its revivification by means of the words of power which Thoth had taught her, formed very prominent scenes. Together with such ceremonies, a number of others connected with the worship of Osiris as the god of life and fecundity were also celebrated at Philæ, something after the manner of a miracle play, and there is no doubt that great crowds would be drawn to the spot by such performances. Primarily, such ceremonies would most appeal to the Egyptians, who, seeing that the great, and probably original, shrine of Osiris at Abydos had fallen into decay, endeavoured to make Philæ its successor; but in Ptolemaïc times and later the Greeks and Romans flocked to the spot, the former to worship Osiris, and the latter to worship Isis. The form of Osiris which the Greeks revered was Serapis, *i.e.*, Ȧusȧr-Ḥāpi, "Osiris-Apis," to whom they ascribed all the attributes of Pluto, the Greek god of Hades. The Egyptian priests, of course, approved of the introduction of the god into the national collection of gods as long as it could be effected by identifying him with an ancient god of the country, and thus the Egyptian and Greek priests found a deity which could satisfy the religious aspirations of both peoples. The introduction of the god was made in the reign of Ptolemy Soter; but in a few generations the attributes of Pluto were forgotten, and the worship of Serapis became identical with that of Osiris. This having been brought about, and Philæ being recognized as one of the most holy shrines of the god, the palmy days of the island began, and as long as the Ptolemies could keep the tribes quiet on the south and west of Egypt, all went well, and the shrine became very rich. In B.C. 22, however, Candace seized Philæ, Aswân, and Elephantine, and in A.D. 250 the Blemmyes followed her example; in the reign of Diocletian the Blemmyes invaded the neighbourhood so frequently that this Emperor was obliged to come to terms with them, and eventually ceded Nubia to them on the understanding that they allowed no inroads upon Egypt from the south. Meanwhile, Christianity had spread into Egypt, and was making its way into Nubia, but the worship of Osiris and Isis was continued at Philæ, apparently without much interruption. In A.D. 380 Theodosius the Great issued the edict for establishing the worship of the Trinity, and a year later he prohibited sacrifices, and ordered some of the temples to be turned into Christian churches, and the rest to be shut; but in spite of everything, sacrifices were offered at Philæ, and the worship of Osiris was carried on there, just as was the worship of the gods of Greece and Rome in Italy and elsewhere, until nearly the end of the Vth century. In Christian times the Copts built at Philæ one church in honour of Saint Michael and another in honour of Saint Athanasius, and recent excavations have shown that many small churches were built there. Abu Ṣalîḥ says that there are "many idols and temples" on the island, and that on the west bank of the river there were several churches overlooking the cataract, but adds that they were in ruins in his day.

When Strabo visited Philæ he says that he came from Syene (Aswân) in a waggon, through a very flat country. "Along the whole road on each side we could see, in many places, very high rocks, round, very smooth, and nearly spherical, of hard black stone, of which mortars are made; each rested upon a greater stone, and upon this another; they were like unhewn stones, with heads of Mercury upon them. Sometimes these stones consisted of one mass. The largest was not less than 12 feet in diameter, and all of them exceeded this size by one-half. We crossed over to the island in a pacton, which is a small boat made of rods, whence it resembles woven-work. Standing there in the water (at the bottom of the boat), or sitting upon some little planks, we easily crossed over, with some alarm, indeed, but without good cause for it, as there is no danger if the boat is not overturned." Of Philæ itself he says, "A little above the cataract is Philæ, a common settlement, like Elephantina, of Ethiopians and Egyptians, and equal in size, containing Egyptian temples, where a bird, which they call hierax (the hawk), is worshipped; but it did not appear to me to resemble in the least the hawks of our country nor of Egypt, for it was larger, and very different in the marks of its plumage. They said that the bird was Ethiopian, and is brought from Ethiopia when its predecessor dies, or before its death. The one shown to us when we were there was sick and nearly dead."—(Strabo, xvii., 1–49, Falconer's translation.)

In 1893 the project for a dam and reservoir at Aswân was submitted to the Government of Egypt, and the scheme, if carried out, would have entailed the partial submersion of the temples at Philae for a portion of the year. The project was very severely criticised at the time, and in the discussion which followed it was often forgotten that the Irrigation Engineers were only animated by a desire to give a better and more regular water supply to Egypt, and to increase the revenue of the country—which things it was their *duty* to do. Subsequently, however, the plan was modified in such a way that the level of the water in the reservoirs will never be high enough to flood the temples on the island, or to damage any of the buildings there. In order to obtain an accurate idea of the stability of the temples, etc., Sir W. Garstin, K.C.M.G., caused an exhaustive examination of the island to be made by Major H. G. Lyons, R.E., whose labours prove that, contrary to the general practice of the ancient Egyptian architects, the foundations of all the main buildings go down to the bed-rock, and that consequently there is nearly as great a depth of masonry below the ground as there is above it. In the course of his excavations Major Lyons discovered a trilingual inscription in hieroglyphics, Greek, and Latin, recording the suppression of a revolt mentioned in Strabo (xvii., i, § 53) by Cornelius Gallus, the first prefect of the country in the reign of Augustus Cæsar. The principal objects of interest on the island are:—

1. The **Temple of Nectanebus II.**, the last native king of Egypt, which was dedicated to Isis, the lady of Philæ; it contained 14 columns with double capitals, but few of them now remain. The columns were joined by stone walls, on which were reliefs, in which Nectanebus is depicted making offerings to the gods of Philæ. The southern part of the temple either fell into the river, or was removed when the quay wall was built across the south end of the island, cutting off the remainder of the court, and leaving only the front portion to mark the place of the original temple. The present building rests on a course of blocks which formed part of an earlier wall, and the cartouches prove that it was repaired by Ptolemy II. Philadelphus.

2. The **Temple of Ȧri-ḥes-nefer,** . Ȧri-ḥes-nefer was the son of Rā and Bast, and this temple was dedicated to him by Ptolemy IV.; it was restored or repaired by Ptolemy V., the Nubian king Ergamenes, and the Emperor Tiberius, all of whom are represented in the reliefs on the walls. The present building stands upon the site of an older temple, and part of it was turned into a church by the Copts; a number of the stone blocks from its walls were used in the building of some Coptic houses which stood near.

3. The **Temple of Ī-em-ḥetep,** which was finished in the reign of Ptolemy V. Epiphanes. In later times, when the east colonnade was built against it, a forecourt was added, with a narrow chamber on the east side of it; and in still later times the Copts lived in some portions of it.

4. The **Temple of Hathor,** which was dedicated to this goddess by Ptolemy VII., Philometor, and Ptolemy IX. Euergetes II. The forecourt was added in Roman times, and it contained columns with Hathor-headed capitals. The Copts destroyed the forecourt and built a church of the stones of which it was made. On the south side are the ruins of houses which were built before the temple was destroyed. Over the door of the one remaining room of the temple is a dedicatory inscription of Ptolemy IX. in Greek.

5. The **Gateway of Hadrian.** This gateway stands on a portion of the enclosing wall of the Temple of Isis, on the western side, and was connected with the temple by two parallel walls, which were added at a later time. On the lintels are reliefs in which the Emperor Hadrian is depicted standing before a number of the gods of Philæ, and inside the gateway is a scene representing Marcus Aurelius, who must have repaired the gateway, making offerings to Isis and Osiris.

6. The **Temple of Cæsar Augustus,** which was built about A.D. 12, and is thought to have been destroyed by an earthquake in Coptic times. In the centre of the paved court in front of it were found in the north-west and south-west corners the two halves of a stele which was inscribed in hieroglyphics and in Greek and Latin, with the record of a revolt against the Romans, which was suppressed by Cornelius Gallus about B C. 22. The temple was built of sandstone, with granite columns and pedestals, and diorite capitals, and was dedicated to the Emperor by the people of Philæ and of that part of Nubia which was under the rule of the Romans.

7. The **Temple of Isis.** The buildings of this edifice consist of:—1. A pylon, decorated with reliefs of Nectanebus II., Ptolemy VII., Ptolemy IX., and Ptolemy XII. Neos Dionysos; 2. A court containing the Mammisi and a colonnade, and decorated with reliefs of Ptolemy IX.,

Ptolemy XIII., and of the Emperors Augustus and Tiberius; 3. A second pylon, ornamented with reliefs by Ptolemy IX. and Ptolemy XIII. (at the foot of the right tower a portion of granite bed rock projects, and the inscription upon it records the dedication of certain lands to the temple by Ptolemy VII.); 4. A temple which consists of the usual court, hypostyle hall, and shrine. In the various parts of this temple are the names of Ptolemy II., Ptolemy III., Ptolemy IX., and the Emperor Antoninus. Of special interest is the **Osiris Chamber**, wherein are reliefs referring to ceremonies which were connected with the death and resurrection of Osiris. The texts on the outside of this group of buildings mention the names of the Emperors Tiberius and Augustus.

8. The **Temple of Ḥeru-netch-tef-f**, which consisted of a court, having four columns on the eastern face, and a large chamber in which stood the shrine, with a narrow passage running round it. It was built on a part of the old surrounding wall of the Temple of Isis, and the greater number of its stones were removed by the Copts, who built a church with them.

9. The **Nilometer.** The doorway leading to the Nilometer is in the old surrounding wall of the temple, and the hinge and the jamb can still be seen. Three scales are cut in the walls, two on the north wall, and one on the south; the oldest is probably the vertical line chiselled on the face of the north wall, and showing whole cubits only, which are marked by horizontal lines. The average length of the cubit in each portion of the scale except the second is about ·520 metre. In the second scale on the north wall the cubit is divided into 7 palms, and each palm into 4 digits; two of the cubits are marked by Demotic numerals. The third scale, which is on the south wall, is in a perfect state of preservation; the mean length of the 17 cubits marked is ·535 metre. Over the 16th cubit is cut the sign

☥ *ankh*, *i.e.*, "life." This sign probably indicates that when the waters of the inundation rose to the height marked by it, there would be abundance and prosperity in the land. The river level of the tops of scales Nos. 1, 2, and 3 are 99·654, 99·890, and 99·990 metres respectively, and the river level of the present time is 99·200 metre; therefore Major H. G. Lyons, R.E., who made these measurements, concludes that there is very little difference between the flood level of to-day and that of about 2000 years ago.

10. The "**Kiosk**," which is one of the most graceful objects on the island, and that by which Philæ is often best remembered; the building appears to be unfinished. Its date is, perhaps, indicated by the reliefs in which the Emperor Trajan is depicted making offerings to Isis and Horus, and standing in the presence of Isis and Osiris.

THE NILE BETWEEN THE FIRST AND SECOND CATARACTS.

The country which is entered on leaving Philæ is generally known by the name of Ethiopia, or Nubia; the latter name has been derived by some from *nub*, the Egyptian word for gold, because in ancient days much gold was brought into Egypt from that land. In the hieroglyphics, Nubia, or Ethiopia, is generally called 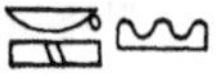 Kesh (the Cush of the Bible) and 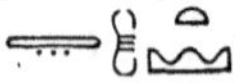 Ta-kenset; from the latter name the Arabic El-Kenûs is derived. It is known that, as far back as the VIth dynasty, the Egyptians sent to this country for certain kinds of wood, and that all the chief tribes that lived round about Korosko hastened to help the Egyptian officer Unȧ in the mission which he undertook for King Pepi I. It seems pretty certain too, if we may trust Unȧ's words, that the whole country was made to acknowledge the sovereignty of the Egyptian king. From the VIIth to the XIth dynasty nothing is known of the relations which existed between the two countries, but in the time of Usertsen I., the second king of the XIIth dynasty, an expedition was undertaken by the Egyptians for the purpose of fixing the boundaries of the two countries, and we know from a stele set up at Wâdî Ḥalfah by this king, that his rule extended as far south as this place. Two reigns later the inhabitants of Nubia or Ethiopia had become so troublesome, that Usertsen III. found it necessary to build fortresses at Semneh and Kummeh, south of the second cataract, and to make stringent laws forbidding the passage of any negro ship unless it was laden with cattle or merchandise.

The Hyksos kings appear not to have troubled greatly about Nubia. When the XVIIIth dynasty had obtained full power in Egypt, some of its greatest kings, such as Thothmes III. and Åmenḥetep III., marched into Nubia and built temples there; under the rulers of the XIXth dynasty, the country became to all intents and purposes a part of Egypt. Subsequently the Nubians appear to have acquired considerable power, and as Egypt became involved in conflicts with more Northern countries, this power increased until Nubia was able to declare itself independent. For several hundreds of years the Nubians had had the benefit of Egyptian civilization, and all that it could teach them, and they were soon able to organize war expeditions into Egypt with success.

After leaving Philæ, the first place of interest passed is **Dâbûd** دابود, on the west bank of the river, 599½ miles from Cairo. At this place, called  Ta-ḥet in the inscriptions, are the ruins of a temple founded by Åt'a-khar-Åmen,* a king of Ethiopia, who reigned about the middle of the third century B.C. The names of Ptolemy VII. Philometor and Ptolemy IX. Euergetes II. are found engraved upon parts of the building. Dâbûd probably stands on the site of the ancient Parembole, a port or castle on the borders of Egypt and Ethiopia, and attached alternately to each kingdom. During the reign of Diocletian it was ceded to the Nubæ by the Romans, and it was frequently attacked by the Blemmyes from the east bank of the river. At Ḳartassi, on the west bank of the river, 615 miles from Cairo, are the ruins of a temple and large quarries; seven miles further

* 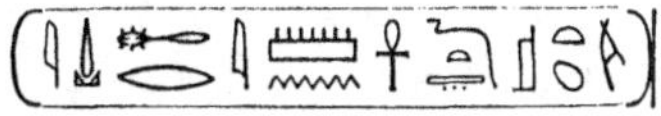 "*Åt'a-khar-Åmen*, living for ever, beloved of Isis," with the prenomen 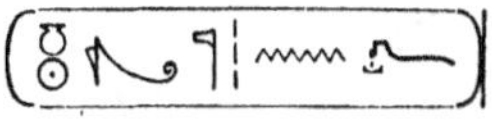 *Åt-nu-Rā, setep-en-neteru.*

south, on the west bank of the river, is **Wâdî Tâfah,** the ancient Taphis, where there are also some ruins; they are, however, of little interest. Contra-Taphis lay on the east bank.

Kalâbshah كلابشه, on the west bank of the river, 629 miles from Cairo, stands on the site of the classical Talmis, called in hieroglyphics 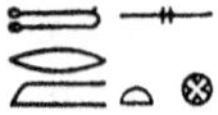 Thermeset, and  *Ka-ḥefennu;* it was for a long time the capital of the country of the Blemmyes. It stands immediately on the Tropic of Cancer. The god of this town was called  Merul or Melul, the Mandulis or Malulis of the Greeks. At Kalâbshah there are the ruins of two temples of considerable interest. The larger of these, which is one of the largest temples in Nubia, appears to have been built upon the site of an ancient Egyptian temple founded by Thothmes III., B.C. 1600, and Amenophis II., B.C. 1566, for on the pronaos this latter monarch is representing offering to the god Àmsu and the Ethiopian god Merul or Melul. It seems to have been restored in Ptolemaïc times, and to have been considerably added to by several of the Roman emperors—Augustus, Caligula, Trajan, etc. From the appearance of the ruins it would seem that the building was wrecked either immediately before or soon after it was completed; some of the chambers were plastered over and used for chapels by the early Christians. A large number of Greek and Latin inscriptions have been found engraved on the walls of this temple, and from one of them we learn that the Blemmyes were defeated by Silko, king of the Nubæ and Ethiopians, in the latter half of the sixth century of our era.

At **Bêt el-Walî,** *i.e.*, the "house of the Saint," a short distance from the larger temple, is the interesting rock-hewn temple which was made to commemorate the victories of Rameses II. over the Ethiopians. On the walls of the court leading into the small hall are some beautifully executed sculptures, representing the Ethiopians bringing before the king large quantities of articles of value, together with gifts of wild and tame animals, after their defeat. Many of the objects depicted must have come from a considerable distance, and it is evident that in those early times Talmis was the great central market to which the products and wares of the Sûdân were brought for sale and barter. The sculptures are executed with great freedom and spirit, and when the colours upon them were fresh they must have formed one of the most striking sights in Nubia. Some years ago casts of these interesting sculptures were taken by Mr. Bonomi, at the expense of Mr. Hay, and notes on the colours were made; these two casts, painted according to Mr. Bonomi's notes, are now set up on the walls in the Fourth Egyptian Room in the British Museum (Northern Gallery), and are the only evidences extant of the former beauty of this little rock-hewn temple, for nearly every trace of colour has vanished from the walls. The scenes on the battle-field are of great interest.

Between Kalâbshah and **Dendûr,** on the west bank of the river, 642 miles from Cairo, there is nothing of interest to be seen; at Dendûr are the remains of a temple built by Augustus,  Per-āa, where this emperor is shown making offerings to Åmen, Osiris, Isis, and Sati. At **Garf Ḥusên** جرف حسين, on the west bank of the river, 651 miles from Cairo, are the remains of a rock-hewn temple built by Rameses II. in honour of Ptaḥ, Sekhet, Ta-Tenen, Hathor, and Aneq; the work is poor and of little interest. This village marks the site of the ancient Tutzis.

Dakkeh الدكّه, on the west bank of the river, 662½ miles from Cairo, marks the site of the classical Pselchis, the  P-selket of the hieroglyphics. About B.C. 23 the Ethiopians attacked the Roman garrisons at Philæ and Syene, and having defeated them, overran Upper Egypt. Petronius, the successor of Ælius Gallus, marching with less than 10,000 infantry and 800 horse against the rebel army of 30,000 men, compelled them to retreat to Pselchis, which he afterwards besieged and took. "Part of the insurgents were driven into the city, others fled into the uninhabited country; and such as ventured upon the passage of the river, escaped to a neighbouring island, where there were not many crocodiles on account of the current. Among the fugitives were the generals of Candace,* queen of the Ethiopians in our time, a masculine woman, and who had lost an eye. Petronius, pursuing them in rafts and ships, took them all, and despatched them immediately to Alexandria." (Strabo, XVII., 1, 54.) From Pselchis Petronius advanced to Premnis (Ibrîm), and afterwards to Napata, the royal seat of Candace, which he razed to the ground. As long as the Romans held Ethiopia, Pselchis was a garrison town.

The temple at Dakkeh was built by 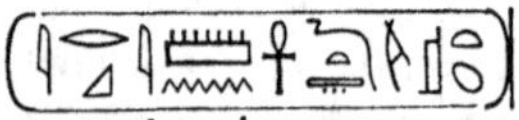 *Årq-Åmen ānkh t'etta mer Auset*, "Årq-Åmen, living for ever, beloved of Isis," having the prenomen 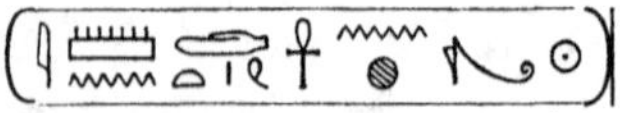 "*Åmen ṭet ānkh tåa Rā*." In the sculptures on the ruins which remain Årq-Åmen is shown standing between Menthu-Rā, lord of Thebes, and Åtmu the god of Heliopolis, and sacrificing to Thoth, who promises to give him a long and prosperous life as king. Årq-Åmen (Ergamenes) is called the "beautiful god,

* Candace was a title borne by all the queens of Meroë.

son of Khnemu and Osiris, born of Sati and Isis, nursed by Aneq and Nephthys," etc. According to Diodorus, the priests of Meroë in Ethiopia were in the habit of sending, "whensoever they please, a messenger to the king, commanding him to put himself to death; for that such is the pleasure of the gods; . . . and so in former ages, the kings without force or compulsion of arms, but merely bewitched by a fond superstition, observed the custom; till Ergamenes (Årq-Åmen), a king of Ethiopia, who reigned in the time of Ptolemy II., bred up in the Grecian discipline and philosophy, was the first that was so bold as to reject and despise such commands. For this prince . . . marched with a considerable body of men to the sanctuary, where stood the golden temple of the Ethiopians, and there cut the throats of all the priests." (Bk. III., chap. vi.) Many of the Ptolemies and some Roman emperors made additions to the temple at Dakkeh.

On the east bank of the river opposite Dakkeh is **Ḳubbân,** called  Baka, in the hieroglyphics, a village which is said to mark the site of Tachompso or Metachompso, "the place of crocodiles." As Pselchis increased, so Tachompso declined, and became finally merely a suburb of that town; it was generally called Contra-Pselchis.

The name Tachompso is derived from the old Egyptian name of the town, Ta-qemt-sa,  or 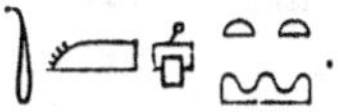. Tachompso was the frontier town which marked the limit on the south of the district which lay between Egypt and Ethiopia, and derived its name, "Dodecaschoenus," from the fact that it comprised twelve schonoi; the schoinos is said by Herodotus (ii. 6) to be equal to sixty stades, but other writers reckon fewer stades to the schoinos. The stade equals one-eighth of a mile.

During the XIIth, XVIIIth and XIXth dynasties this place was well fortified by the Egyptians, and on many blocks of stone close by are found the names of Thothmes III., Ḥeru-em-ḥeb, and Rameses II. It appears to have been the point from which the wretched people condemned to labour in the gold mines in the desert of the land of Akita set out; and an interesting inscription on a stone found here relates that Rameses II., having heard that much gold existed in this land, which was inaccessible on account of the absolute want of water, bored a well in the mountain, twelve cubits deep, so that henceforth men could come and go by this land. His father Seti I. had bored a well 120 cubits deep, but no water appeared in it.

At **Ḳûrta** قورتة,  *Karthet*, a few miles south of Dakkeh, on the west bank of the river, are the remains of a temple which was built in Roman times upon a site where a temple had stood in the days of Thothmes III.

Opposite **Miḥarraḳah** محرقة, about 675 miles from Cairo, on the west bank of the river, lie the ruins of Hierasycaminus, the later limit on the south of the Dodecaschoenus.

About 20 miles from Dakkeh, and 690 from Cairo, on the west bank of the river, is **Wâdî Sabû'a,** or the "Valley of the Lions," where there are the remains of a temple partly built of sandstone, and partly excavated in the rock; the place is so called on account of the dromos of sixteen sphinxes which led up to the temple. On the sculptures which still remain here may be seen Rameses II., the builder of the temple, "making an offering of incense to father Âmen, the king of the gods," who says to him, "I give to thee all might, and I give the world to thee, in peace." Elsewhere the king is making offerings to Tefnut, lady of heaven, Nebt-ḥetep, Horus and Thoth, each of whom promises to bestow some blessing upon him. On another part is a boat containing a ram-headed god, and Harmachis seated in a shrine, accompanied by Horus, Thoth, Isis, and Maāt; the king kneels before him in adoration, and the god says that he will give him myriads of years and festivals; on each side is a figure of Rameses II. making an offering Beneath this scene is a figure of a Christian saint holding a key, and an inscription on each side tells us that it is meant to represent Peter the Apostle. This picture and the remains of plaster on the walls show that the chambers of the temple were used by the early Christians as chapels.

Kuruskau (Korosko) كرسكو, on the east bank of the river, 703 miles from Cairo, was from the earliest times the point of departure for merchants and others going to and from the Sûdân, viâ Abu Ḥamed; from the western bank there was a caravan route across into north Africa. In ancient days the land which lay to the east of Korosko was called  Uaua, and as early as the VIth dynasty the officer Unȧ visited it in order to obtain blocks of acacia wood for his king Pepi I. An inscription, found a few hundred yards to the east of the town, records that the country round about was conquered in the XIIth dynasty by Ȧmenemḥāt I. .

A capital idea of the general character of Nubian scenery can be obtained by ascending the mountain, which is now, thanks to a good path, easily accessible.

At **'Amâda,** عماده, on the west bank of the river, 711 miles from Cairo, is a small but interesting temple, which appears to have been founded in the XIIth dynasty by Usertsen II., who conquered Nubia by setting fire to standing crops, by carrying away the wives and cattle, and by cutting down the men on their way to and from the wells. This temple was repaired by Thothmes III. and other kings of the XVIIIth dynasty.

At **Dêrr,** on the east bank of the river, 715 miles from Cairo, is a small, badly executed rock-hewn temple of the time of Rameses II., where the usual scenes representing the defeat of the Ethiopians are depicted. The king is accompanied by a tame "lion which follows after his majesty, 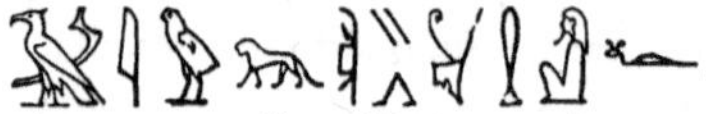, *maȧu ṡesi en ḥen-f*, to slay . . . . . ." Close to the temple is the rock stele of the prince Åmen-em-ḥeb of the same period; the temple was dedicated to Åmen-Rā. The Egyptian name of the town was , *Per-Rā pa ṭemȧi*, "the town of the temple of the sun."

Thirteen miles beyond Dêrr, 728 miles from Cairo, also on the east bank of the river, stands **Ibrîm,** which marks the site of the ancient Primis, or Premnis, called in the Egyptian inscriptions , Måāmam. This town was captured during the reign of Augustus by Petronius on his victorious march upon Napata. In the first and third naos at Primis are representations of Neḥi, the governor of Nubia, with other officers, bringing gifts before Thothmes III., which shows that these caves were hewn during the reign of this king; and in another, Rameses II. is receiving adorations from Setau, prince of Ethiopia, and a number of his officers. At Anibe, just opposite Ibrîm, is the grave of Penni, the governor of the district, who died during the reign of Rameses VI. About three miles off is the battle-field of Toski, on the east bank of the Nile, where Sir Francis Grenfell, G.C.B., slew Wad en-Negûmî and utterly defeated the dervishes on August 4, 1891.

ABÛ SIMBEL.*

Abû Simbel, on the west bank of the river, 762 miles from Cairo, is the classical Aboccis, and the place called

* The spelling of this name is doubtful.

II.

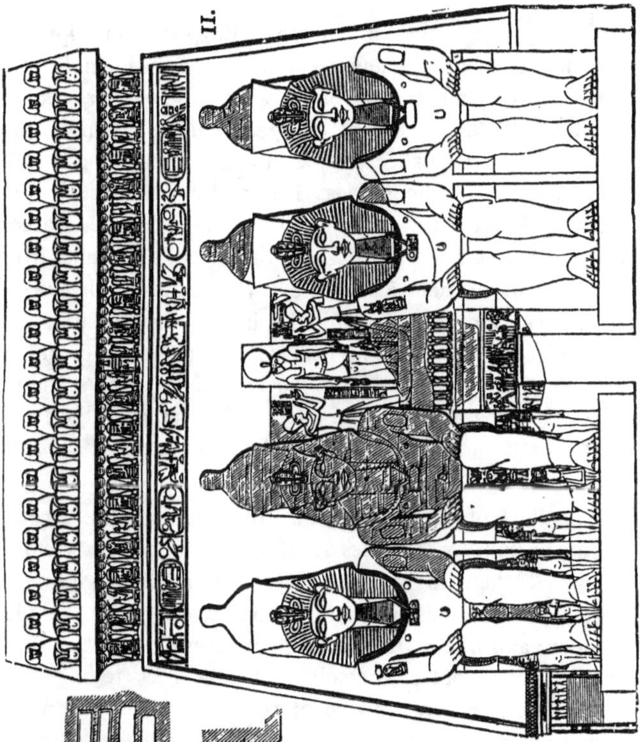

I

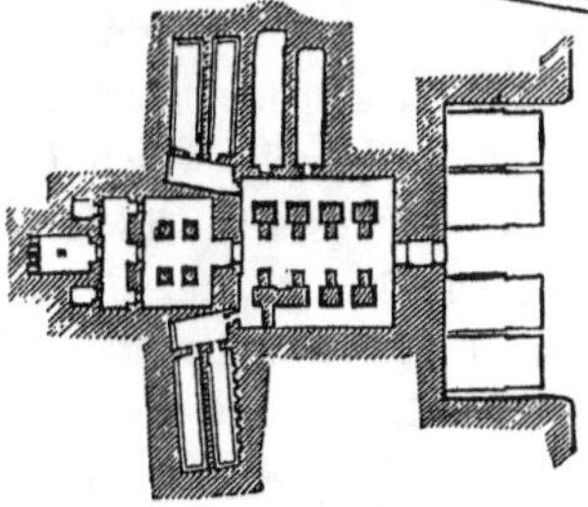

I. Plan of the Temple of Rameses II. at Abû Simbel.
II. The seated Colossi and front of the Temple at Abû Simbel.
From Lepsius' *Denkmäler*, Bd. iii., Bl. 185.

 Åbshek in the Egyptian inscriptions. Around, or near the temple, a town of considerable size once stood; all traces of this have, however, disappeared. To the north of the great temple, hewn in the living rock, is a smaller temple, about 84 feet long, which was dedicated to the goddess Hathor by Rameses II. and his wife Nefert-Åri. The front is ornamented with statues of the king, his wife, and some of his children, and over the door are his names and titles. In the hall inside are six square Hathor-headed pillars also inscribed with the names and titles of Rameses and his wife. In the small chamber at the extreme end of the temple is an interesting scene in which the king is making an offering to Hathor in the form of a cow; she is called the "lady of Åbshek," and is standing behind a figure of the king.

The chief object of interest at Abû Simbel is the **Great Temple** built by Rameses II. to commemorate his victory over the Kheta in north-east Syria; it is the largest and finest Egyptian monument in Nubia, and for simple grandeur and majesty is second to none in all Egypt. This temple is hewn out of the solid grit-stone rock to a depth of 185 feet, and the surface of the rock, which originally sloped down to the river, was cut away for a space of about 90 feet square to form the front of the temple, which is ornamented by four colossal statues of Rameses II., 66 feet high, seated on thrones, hewn out of the living rock. The cornice is, according to the drawing by Lepsius, decorated with twenty-one cynocephali, and beneath it, in the middle, is a line of hieroglyphics, , *ṭā-nȧ nek ānkh usr neb*, "I give to thee all life and strength," on the right side of which are four figures of Rā, , and eight cartouches containing the prenomen of Rameses II., with an uræus on each side; on the left side are four figures of

Ȧmen, , and eight cartouches as on the right. The line of boldly cut hieroglyphics below reads, "The living Horus the mighty bull, beloved of Maāt, king of the North and South, Usr-Maāt-Rā setep en-Rā, son of the Sun, Rameses, beloved of Ȧmen, beloved of Harmachis the great god. Over the door is a statue of Harmachis, , and on each side of him is a figure of the king offering . Each of the four colossi had the name of Rameses II. inscribed upon each shoulder and breast. On the leg of one of these are several interesting Greek inscriptions, which are thought to have been written by troops who marched into Ethiopia in the days of Psammetichus I.

The interior of the temple consists of a large hall, in which are eight columns with large figures of Osiris about 17 feet high upon them, and from which eight chambers open; a second hall having four square columns; and a third hall, without pillars, from which open three chambers. In the centre chamber are an altar and four seated figures, viz., Harmachis, Rameses II., Ȧmen-Rā, and Ptaḥ; the first two are coloured red, the third blue, and the fourth white. In the sculptures on the walls Rameses is seen offering to Ȧmen-Rā, Sekhet, Harmachis, Ȧmsu, Thoth, and other deities; a list of his children occurs, and many small scenes of considerable importance. The subjects of the larger scenes are, as was to be expected, representations of the principal events in the victorious battles of the great king, in which he appears putting his foes to death with the weapons which Harmachis has given to him. The accompanying hieroglyphics describe these scenes with terse accuracy.

One of the most interesting inscriptions at Abû Simbel is that found on a slab, which states that in the fifth year of the reign of Rameses II., his majesty was in the land of

Tchah, not far from Kadesh on the Orontes. The outposts kept a sharp look-out, and when the army came to the south of the town of Shabtûn, two of the spies of the Shasu came into the camp and pretended that they had been sent by the chiefs of their tribe to inform Rameses II. that they had forsaken the chief of the Kheta,* and that they wished to make an alliance with his majesty and become vassals of his. They then went on to say that the chief of the Kheta was in the land of Khirebu to the north of Tunep, some distance off, and that they were afraid to come near the Egyptian king. These two men were giving false information, and they had actually been sent by the Kheta chief to find out where Rameses and his army were; the Kheta chief and his army were at that moment drawn up in battle array behind Kadesh. Shortly after these men were dismissed, an Egyptian scout came into the king's presence bringing with him two spies from the army of the chief of the Kheta; on being questioned, they informed Rameses that the chief of the Kheta was encamped behind Kadesh, and that he had succeeded in gathering together a multitude of soldiers and chariots from the countries round about. Rameses summoned his officers to his presence, and informed them of the news which he had just heard; they listened with surprise, and insisted that the newly-received information was untrue. Rameses blamed the chiefs of the intelligence department seriously for their neglect of duty, and they admitted their fault. Orders were straightway issued for the Egyptian army to march upon Kadesh, and as they were crossing an arm of the river near that city the hostile forces fell in with each other. When Rameses saw this, he "growled at them like his father Menthu, lord of Thebes,"

* The Kheta have, during the last few years, been identified with the Hittites of the Bible; there is no ground for this identification beyond the slight similarity of the names. The inscriptions upon the sculptures found at Jerâbîs still remain undeciphered.

and having hastily put on his full armour, he mounted his chariot and drove into the battle. His onset was so sudden and rapid that before he knew where he was he found himself surrounded by the enemy, and completely isolated from his own troops. He called upon his father Åmen-Rā to help him, and then addressed himself to a slaughter of all those that came in his way, and his prowess was so great that the enemy fell in heaps, one over the other, into the waters of the Orontes. He was quite alone, and not one of his soldiers or horsemen came near him to help him. It was only with great difficulty he succeeded in cutting his way through the ranks of the enemy. At the end of the inscription he says, "Every thing that my majesty has stated, that did I in the presence of my soldiers and horsemen." This event in the battle of the Egyptians against the Kheta was made the subject of an interesting poem by Pen-ta-urt; this composition was considered worthy to be inscribed upon papyri, and upon the walls of the temples which Rameses built.

A little to the south of the Great Temple is a small building of the same date, which was used in connexion with the services, and on the walls of which are some interesting scenes. It was re-opened some years ago by Mr. McCallum, Miss Edwards and party.

In 1892, at the instance of Mr. Willcocks, **Capt. J. H. L. E. Johnstone, R.E.,** and a detachment of soldiers arrived at Abû Simbel with a view of carrying out certain repairs to the face and side of the great rock temple. They began by clearing away several enormous masses of overhanging rock which, had they fallen in, must have inflicted very great damage on the colossal statues below; and having broken them into smaller pieces, Captain Johnstone used them for building two walls at the head of the valley to prevent the drift sand from burying the temple again, and for making a hard, stone slope. The cynocephali which form the ornament of the cornice were carefully repaired and strengthened, and the original rock was in many places built up with stone and cement. The whole of the sand and broken stones which had become piled up in front of the entrance to the small chamber re-opened by Mr. McCallum some years before was cleared away, and any dangerous break in the rock was carefully repaired. All lovers of Egypt will rejoice at the excellent way in which Captain Johnstone has performed his difficult task, and we may now hope that it will not be long before the repairs which are urgently needed by temples and other buildings in other parts of Egypt are undertaken by the able officers of the Royal Engineers.

The village of **Wâdî Ḥalfah**, on the east bank of the Nile, 802 miles from Cairo, marks the site of a part of the district called  Buhen in the hieroglyphic inscriptions, where, as at Dêrr and Ibrîm, the god Harmachis was worshipped. On the plain to the east of the village some interesting flint weapons have been found, and a few miles distant are the fossil remains of a forest. On the western bank of the river, a little further south, are the remains of a temple which, if not actually built, was certainly restored by Thothmes III. It was repaired and added to by later kings of Egypt, but it seems to have fallen into disuse soon after the Romans gained possession of Egypt. The excavations recently carried out here by Major H. G. Lyons, R.E., and Mr. Somers Clarke, have brought to light the ruins of temples built by a king of the XIIth dynasty and Thothmes IV. A few miles south of Wâdî Ḥalfah begins the second cataract, a splendid view of which can be obtained from the now famous rock of Abûṣîr on the west bank of the river. Nearly every traveller who has visited Abû Simbel has been to this rock and inscribed his name upon it; the result is an interesting collection of names and dates, the like of which probably exists nowhere else.

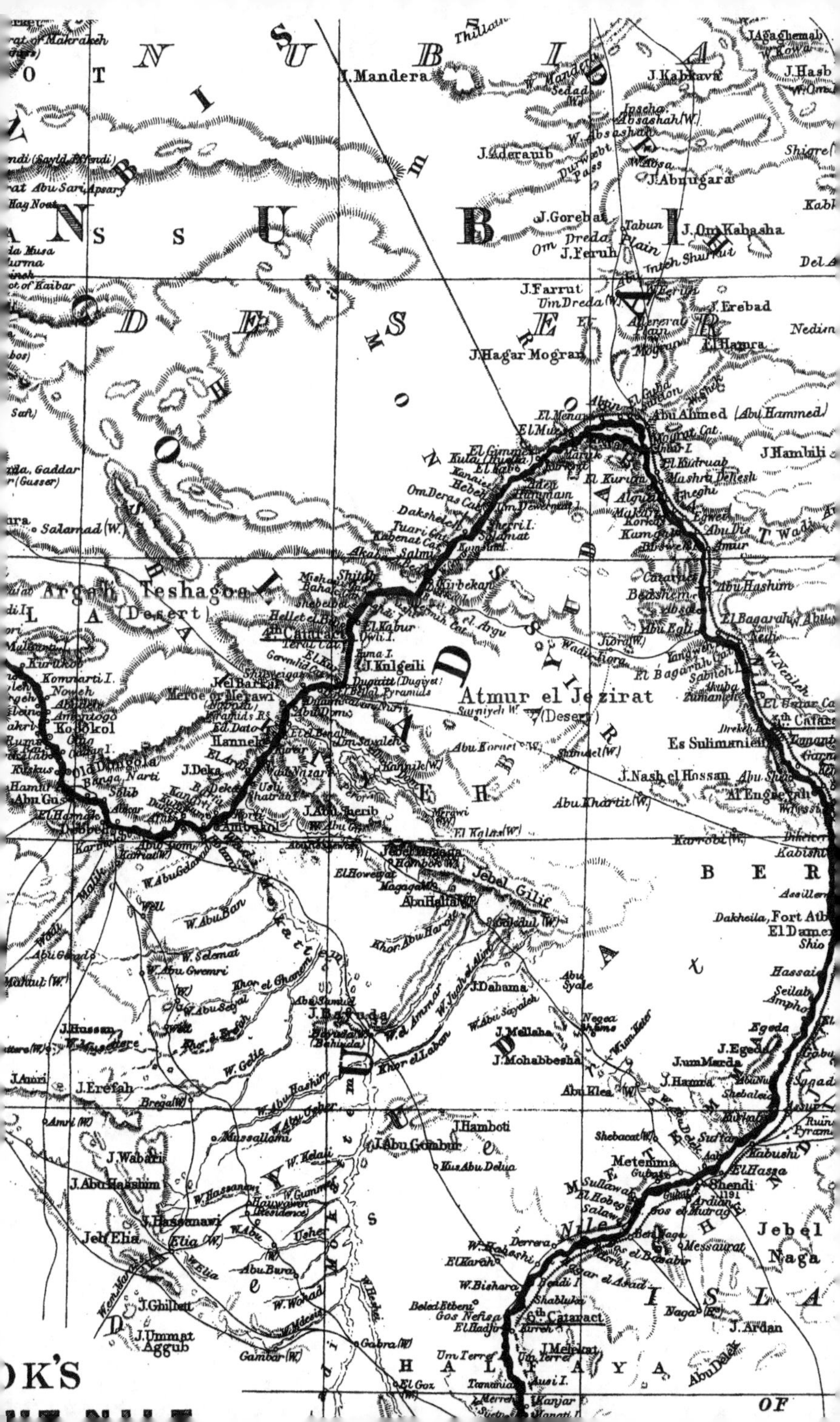
J. Mandera
J. Kabkava
J. Aderaub
Durweebt Pass
J. Abnugara
J. Gorebat
J. Om Kabasha
J. Feruh
J. Farrut
Um Dreda (W.)
J. Erebad
J. Hagar Mogran
El Hamra
Abu Ahmed (Abu Hammed)
J. Hambili
Argah Teshagon
(Desert)
4th Cataract
J. Kulgeili
Meroe or Merawi
Atmur el Jezirat
(Desert)
Es Sulimanieh
Old Dongola
J. Deka
J. Nash el Hossan
Abu Khartit (W.)
Jebel Gilif
Korti
Ambukol
J. Abu Sherib
Abu Halfa
Khor Abu Harad
J. Dahama
J. Bayuda
W. Abu Ban
J. Mellaha
J. Mohabbesha
J. Hussan
J. Erefah
Abu Klea
Khor el Laban
J. Hamboti
J. Abu Gomhur
Metemma
Shendi
J. Wabari
J. Abu Hashim
J. Hassanawi
Jebel Elia
Nile
Jebel Naga
Messaurat
6th Cataract
J. Ghillett
J. Ummat Aggub
J. Ardan
Naga
Abu Delek
B E R
Fort Atb
Salamad (W.)
Dakhella
Old Dongola
H A L F A Y A
OF
OK'S

WÂDÎ ḤALFAH TO KHARṬÛM.

History.—Speaking generally, the town of Wâdî Ḥalfah marked the limit of the rule of the ancient Egyptians on the south, and the famous forts of Semneh and Kummeh, which lie at a distance of 35 miles up the Second Cataract, can in reality only be regarded as advanced outposts. We know from the tomb of Ḥeru-khu-f at Aswân that, in the Early Empire, certain kings sent their officials as far south as the Land of the Pygmies to bring back to the Pharaohs specimens of this remarkable people, and it is probable that a brisk commerce between the Nubians and the Egyptians was carried on at a still earlier period. In the XIIth dynasty we hear of expeditions to the south, and the faces of the rocks from the First to the Third Cataract proclaim that the Egyptian kings sent their officers "to enlarge the borders of Egypt" in that direction. The peoples and tribes south of Wâdî Ḥalfah caused the great kings of the XVIIIth and XIXth dynasties much trouble, and it is very doubtful if they had any effective dominion beyond the Fourth Cataract. The "royal son of Kesh" (Cush) was, no doubt, a great official, but Kesh, or "Ethiopia," as the word is generally translated, was a geographical expression with limited signification, and that the country of his rule included the whole country which is now called Ethiopia is an unwarranted assumption. The fact is that the Second and Third Cataracts and the terrible, waterless Eastern desert proved almost insuperable barriers in the way of moving large masses of men from Egypt to the south, for the cataracts could only be passed in boats during a few weeks at the period of the inundation, and the desert between Korosko and Abu Ḥamed, and that between Wâdî Ḥalfah, or Buhen, to use the Egyptian name, struck terror into the hearts of those who knew the character of the roads and the fatigues of travelling upon them. As long as the natives were friendly and rendered help, small bodies of troops might pass to the south either by river or desert, but any serious opposition on their part would invariably result in their destruction. As long as trade was brisk and both buyer and seller were content, and the nation to which each belonged could hold its own, wars were unnecessary; but as soon as the tribes of the South believed it possible to invade, conquer, and spoil Egypt, they swooped down upon it in much the same fashion as the followers of the Mahdi and Khalîfa did in recent years. They saw the power of Egypt waning under the kings of the XXIst and XXIInd dynasties, and the people of an important district of Southern Nubia, whose capital was Napata, and who had been foremost in adopting the civilization, and gods, and hieroglyphic writing of the Egyptians, became the dominant power in the country, and extended their rule even north of Aswân. Their king Piānkhi, at a favourable moment, *i.e.*, when Taf-nekht, prince of Saïs and Memphis, revolted, swooped down upon Egypt, and overcoming all opposition, advanced as far north as Memphis, which he assaulted and captured, and so became master of Egypt, about B.C. 760. Less than one hundred years later another king of Napata marched north to Memphis, and succeeded in driving out the Assyrians who had found foothold there under Esarhaddon, king of Assyria, B.C. 681–668. After Egypt had fallen under the rule of the Persians and Macedonians, the princes of Napata continued to be their own masters; but at a later period, probably whilst the Ptolemies were reigning over Egypt, they either moved their capital further south to a site on the fertile plain which is bounded by the Atbara and the Nile and the Blue Nile, and is commonly called the "Island of Meroë," or were succeeded in their sovereignty by another branch of the same race as they themselves, who were indigenous to the province. The princes of Meroë built temples with ante-chapels, pylons, courts, hypostyle halls, sanctuary chambers, etc., taking as their models the temples of Napata, which in turn were copied from the temples of Egypt, and they decorated them with bas-reliefs and scenes, and inscriptions, chiefly in the hieroglyphic character. Their buildings lack the beauty and finish of the temples of Egypt, but many of them must have been grand and impressive. In the time of the Romans, and probably long before, the rule of the kingdom of Meroë seems to have been in the hands of a series of queens, or queen-mothers, each of whom bore the title "Candace." Thus certain legends say that Alexander the Great was entertained in Ethiopia by a queen called Candace; we have also a Candace mentioned in Acts viii. 27; Strabo (Bk. XVII., chap. 1, § 54) speaks of the "officers of Candace"; and mentioning Meroë, Pliny says (Bk. VI., 30), "a female, whose name was Candace, ruled over the district, that name having passed from queen to queen for many years." In B.C. 22 the Romans made war upon one Candace who had seized Philæ, the Island of Elephantine, and Syene, and enslaved the inhabitants. The Roman general attacked her forces with 10,000 infantry and 800 horse, and, having captured one city after another, advanced as far as Napata, at the foot of the Fourth Cataract, *i.e.*, nearly 700 miles from Syene. Both Strabo (XVII., 1, § 54) and Pliny (VI., 35) say that he destroyed Napata, but the former declares that he then returned to Alexandria, whilst the latter tells us that the extreme distance to which he penetrated beyond Syene was "DCCCLXX. mil. passuum," or about 970 miles. If Petronius marched so far, he must have reached the Island of Meroë. Napata having been laid waste, it seems that the Nubian princes withdrew further south, and either consolidated an old kingdom or founded a new one at Meroë. The Romans appear to have maintained garrisons at certain points on the Nile between the Third and Fourth Cataracts, *e.g.*, Donḳola and Napata, for at each of these places considerable remains of the walls ot their forts exist to this day; such forts, however, were neither as large nor as strong as those which existed between Philæ and Wâdî Ḥalfah. During the early centuries of our era the princes of Meroë ruled their country without much interference from the Romans, and the large groups of pyramids, and the ruins of their temples and other buildings which are found on the eastern bank of the Nile between the Atbara and Kharṭûm, indicate that their kingdom lasted for some hundreds of years. In the fifth century there were many Christians in Nubia, and about A.D. 545 the Nubians (or Nobadæ), under their Christian king Silko, defeated the Blemmyes and founded a kingdom at Donḳola. After the conquest of Egypt by the Arabs in 640, the Muḥammadans entered Nubia, but the Christians held their ground, and the kingdom founded by Silko lasted for several centuries. In the 14th century the Arabs conquered the Nubians, and they were obliged to become followers of the Prophet. For centuries before this date, however, the Nubians intermarried with tribes that came into the Nile valley from Arabia, and with the dwellers in the south and to the west of the Nile, and there was no chief who was powerful enough to make himself king over the whole of their country.

Of the manners and customs of the Nubians or Ethiopians classical writers do not speak very highly. Strabo (XVII., 2, § 2 ff.) says that they went naked for the most part; that they were nomadic shepherds of sheep, goats, and oxen, which were very small. They lived on millet and barley, from which also a drink was prepared, and made use of butter and fat instead of oil. They fought with bows and arrows, and some of their soldiers were armed with leather shields. They worshipped Hercules, Isis and Pan (by which we may understand Åmen-Rā, Mut, and Khonsu), and believed in one god who was immortal, and in another who was mortal and without a name. It is clear though that Strabo often refers to tribes and peoples who lived south of Kharṭûm, and that he treats them all as Ethiopians or Nubians.

The traveller wishing to visit Kharṭûm from Wadî Ḥalfah may do so by two routes. He may either travel there direct by the Sûdân Military Railway, or he may go to Kerma by rail, by steamer from Kerma to Kassingar at the foot of the Fourth Cataract, by horse or camel to Abu Ḥamed, and thence to Kharṭûm by the Sûdân Military Railway. The distance by the former route is about 560 miles, and by the latter about 880 miles. A glance at the map will show how much time and distance are saved by the Sûdân Railway, which, in going direct to Abu Ḥamed, cuts off the great bend of the Nile between Korosko and Abu Ḥamed; on the other hand, the traveller who goes direct to Kharṭûm from Wâdî Ḥalfah will see little of the temples and other remains which still stand in certain parts of the Cataracts and at Kurru, Zûma, Gebel Barkal, Nûri, and on the "Island of Meroë."

The **Sûdân Military Railway** consists of two sections: the older section runs from Wâdî Ḥalfah to Kerma, at the head of the Third Cataract, a distance of about 201 miles, and the newer section runs from Wâdî Ḥalfa to a spot on the east bank of the Nile, just opposite Khartûm, a distance of about 560 miles. The gauge throughout in both sections is 3 feet 6 inches. The older section was begun in the days of the Khedive Ismâ'îl, who had the line laid as far as Sarras, a distance of 33 miles, and it was continued by the British to Akasheh, 55 miles further south, in 1884. In 1896, when the reconquest of the Sûdân was ordered by the British Government, Lord Kitchener determined to carry the line on to the head of the Third Cataract. It was found that the original piece of line had been badly laid; that the Dervishes had torn up 55 miles of it, and burnt the sleepers and twisted the rails; that only two engines were capable of moving; and that practically an entirely new line from Wâdî Ḥalfah to Kerma would have to be built. This wonderful work was done in thirteen months by a few young Royal Engineer officers under Lieut. Girouard, R.E. On March 21 the Sirdar ordered the advance; by June 4 the line was working to Ambuḳûl Wells, 68 miles from Wâdî Ḥalfah; on August 4 it reached Kosheh, 108 miles from Wâdî Ḥalfah; and on May 4 it reached Kerma, 201 miles from Wâdî Ḥalfah. Of the thirteen months occupied in its construction, five had been almost wasted for want of engines and material, and in repairing the damage caused by rain storms, and meanwhile, at intervals, the Sirdar, Lord Kitchener, fought and defeated the Dervishes at Ferket (June 7) and elsewhere, and reconquered the Donḳola province. The line from Wâdî Ḥalfah to Abu Ḥamed, a distance of 232 miles, was begun on May 15, 1897, and reached Abu Ḥamed on October 31 of the same year; the average daily progress was about 1¼ miles, but 3¼ miles were made in one day early in October. The line was laid during the hottest time of the year, through a previously unmapped and waterless desert, and the work was so well done that trains carrying 200 tons of stores and supplies, drawn by engines weighing, without tender, 50 tons, could travel over it in safety at the rate of 25 miles per hour. The survey camp was always six miles in advance of railhead, the embankment party, 1,500 strong, followed at the average rate mentioned above, and the plate-laying party, 1,000 strong, came next. One section of the last party unloaded the sleepers, and another laid and spaced them, a third party adjusted them, a fourth party fixed and spiked the rails, and a fifth party levelled the line with levers. This done, the engine and train advanced, and so kept supplies of material at hand for the workers in front, whilst gangs of men behind straightened, levelled, graded, and ballasted the line. The camp moved forward about six miles every four days, and rations and water were supplied from Wâdî Ḥalfah. Every 20 miles a loop siding was made to allow trains to pass each other, and each station had a station-master, two pointsmen, and a telephone clerk. Between Wâdî Ḥalfah and Abu Ḥamed the line rises about 1,200 feet. The stations are nine in number, and the various sections of the line may be thus described:—

Wâdî Ḥalfah to No. 1	17½	miles,	up-hill the whole way.
No. 1 to „ 2	21	„	with short up-gradients.
„ 2 to „ 3	23	„	ditto
„ 3 to „ 4	23	„	ditto
„ 4 to „ 5	25½	„	11 miles level, the rest steep and curved.
„ 5 to „ 6	23	„	all down hill.
„ 6 to „ 7	21	„	slight down gradient.
„ 7 to „ 8	25	„	fairly level.
„ 8 to „ 9	28	„	slight down gradient
„ 9 to Abu Ḥamed	32	„	irregular, with curves.

At No. 4 station are three wells, two of which yield water from a depth of 90 feet, and a reservoir was made there; at No. 6 station are two wells, 84 feet deep, which join each other, and there is no reservoir. The water is pumped up by Worthington pumps. At other places in the desert small supplies of water were found, but they were too highly charged with mineral salts to be used in the engine boilers. Nos. 2, 4, 6, and 9 are coaling stations, but all coals have to be brought up from Alexandria. The head shop for railway repairs is at Wâdî Ḥalfah, where there are lathes, drilling machines, planing machines, steam hammer, lathe for turning up the 5-feet wheels of the American engines, etc.; in 1899 the number of workmen was 150, of all nationalities, the heads of departments being all Royal Engineers. The locomotives and rolling stock are of all kinds and classes, but in recent years many substantial additions to both have been made; the upkeep of engines has always been a serious matter, for it is difficult to make the native clean and oil the running parts regularly. Thirty-six quarts of oil are allowed for running between Wâdî Ḥalfah and the Atbara, and six pounds of tallow. In 1899 the Sûdân Military Railway possessed about 40 locomotives, varying in weight from 30 to 70 tons. The most powerful type of locomotive on the line is that built by Neilson, of Glasgow, which is said to be able to haul 600 tons at the rate of 15 miles per hour; it was used in laying the greater part of the Wâdî Ḥalfah—Atbara line, but it is useless on the Wâdî Ḥalfah—Kerma line, because of the curves. The sight of one of these "steamers on wheels," as the natives call them, hauling its tender, and water tanks, and a long row of trucks piled up with 400 tons dead weight of railway material across the desert at night, and breathing forth fire and smoke like a genuine 'Afrît in the Arabian Nights, impressed the imagination of the dwellers in the desert with the idea of Lord Kitchener's "magic" more than did the British soldier. When the first locomotive reached Berber, many of the natives hastened to touch its oily and dusty tender, believing it to possess magical powers, and some of them declared that the touch had cured their ailments! The revenue from the Sûdân Railway in 1899 was £31,000, and the telegraphs and post office, which are worked chiefly through it, £E.10,000 more. There are no antiquities in the desert between Wâdî Ḥalfah and Abu Ḥamed, and as the route of the railway may be described as containing nothing but sand, rock, a few desert trees, and blazing sunshine, the principal places of interest between Wâdî Ḥalfah and Kharṭûm, travelling by the Wâdî Ḥalfah—Kerma Railway and river may be thus described:—

Leaving Wâdî Ḥalfah, the train proceeds slowly past the signal box and points, and keeping to the track on the right, after a few miles enters a very rocky gorge in the mountains on the east bank of the Nile, at the foot of the **Second Cataract.** Every here and there glimpses are caught of little patches of cultivated ground on the banks of the river, and (in European eyes) of the miserable huts in which the natives live. Eight miles from Wâdî Ḥalfah is **Abkeh,** or Amkeh, which was the advanced post of the Dervishes in 1886, and a few miles further on is **Gemai,** which was a Dervish base at that time. Thirty-three miles from Wâdî Ḥalfah is **Sarras,** from which place the Dervishes raided the country round; it was taken and re-occupied by the Egyptian troops at the end of August, 1889, shortly after the crushing defeat of the Dervishes under Wad* en-Negûmî at Tushkeh (Toski) on August 4. Forty miles from Wâdî Ḥalfah is the **Semneh Road** station, where the traveller may alight and visit **Semneh** and **Kummeh,** which mark the site of an ancient Egyptian settlement that dates from the time of the XIIth dynasty.

Here are inscriptions dated in the 8th and 16th years of the reign of Usertsen III., who conquered Nubia as far south as this point, and made stringent laws to regulate the entry of the Nubians into the territory newly acquired by Egypt; it seems that only traders and merchants were allowed to bring their boats north of Semneh. Of special interest also are the series of short inscriptions which mark the levels of the waters of the Nile during the inundations in a number of years of the reign of Àmemenḥāt III., the famous constructor of Lake Moeris. These inscriptions show that at that time the river level during the inundation was about 26 feet higher than it is at the present time, and they seem to indicate that Àmenemḥāt III. set to work in a systematic manner to endeavour to understand the effects upon the agriculture of Egypt caused by inundations of

* Wad = Weled, *i.e.*, "son of."

varying heights. The ruins at Semneh and Kummeh are of considerable interest from many points of view, and especially because they represent buildings which were primarily fortresses of great strength. The two buildings, that of Semneh on the left bank, and that of Kummeh on the east bank of the Nile, occupied positions of extreme strategical importance, and when well garrisoned must have formed a formidable obstacle to the progress north of the raiding river tribes. Inside the fortifications at Semneh are the ruins of a temple which was founded by Usertsen III., and restored by Thothmes III. and Amenophis III.; it consisted of a single chamber measuring about 30 feet by 12 feet, with an extremely plain front. Inside the fortifications at Kummeh are the ruins of a larger temple which date from the period of Thothmes II. and Thothmes III. The most recent investigator of these ruins is Mr. Somers Clarke, who has prepared scale plans of them all.

The traveller now finds himself journeying through the mountainous district called the Baṭn al-Ḥagar, *i.e.*, the "Stone Belly," and a more terrible desert it would be difficult to find blackened rocks and bright yellow sand meet the eye in every direction, and the heat and glare in the afternoon even in the winter months are very fierce. The next station on the line is **Mughrât Wells,** about 6 miles from the river, and 44 miles from Wâdî Ḥalfah; about seven miles further on is the **Ambuḳûl Road Station,** and 14 miles more bring us to **Ambuḳûl Wells Station,** 64 miles from Wâdî Ḥalfah. Here died "Roddy" Owen, of cholera, in July, 1896; on his tombstone in the desert was inscribed, "Under the shadow of the sword is Paradise." At **'Uḳmeh** in the Cataract, 20 miles from Ambuḳûl, and 2 miles north of Akasheh, is a sulphur spring. At **Akasheh,** 88 miles from Wâdî Ḥalfah, an action was fought between 240 of the Egyptian Cavalry and the Dervishes, on May 1st, 1896; the Egyptians routed the Dervish force of 1,300 men, 300 of whom were mounted, and killed 18 and wounded 80. At **Ferket,** 103 miles from Wâdi Ḥalfah, a famous battle was fought on June 7th, 1896. The Sirdar (Lord Kitchener) attacked the Dervishes at 5 a.m., killed and wounded about 1,000 of them, including 40 amîrs, or chiefs, and took 500 prisoners, his own loss being 20 killed and 80 wounded; the battle was over in two hours. The Second Cataract begins at Ferket. At **Kôsheh,** 109 miles from Wâdî Ḥalfah, died Captain Fenwick and Surgeon-Captain Trask, of cholera, in July, 1896. On the **Island of Sai,** about 130 miles from Wâdî Ḥalfah, are the remains of a small temple with inscriptions of Thothmes III. and Amenophis II., and a number of gray granite pillars from a Coptic church, on which are cut the Coptic cross. At the north end of the island, on the east bank, are the ruins of the **Temple of Amârah.** The foundations are of brick, but the columns eight in number, are of sandstone, and are $3\frac{1}{2}$ feet in diameter. The temple measured about 54 feet by 30 feet, and the doorway, which had a column on each side, was 19 feet wide. It was built by an Ethiopian king whose pyramid-tomb is at Meroë, on the top of the hill behind Baḳrawîyeh. Six miles further south is **Sedênga,** where there are the ruins of a temple built by Amenophis III., and a broken statue. A little to the north, on the east bank of the Nile, is **Suarda,** which became the Sirdar's advanced outpost after the Battle of Ferket. Six miles to the south of Sedênga is **Gebel Dûsh** (Doshe), a mass of sandstone in which was hewn a tomb in the reign of Thothmes III. ; the spot is extremely picturesque. One mile further south is **Soleb,** near which are the remains of a large and magnificent temple which was built by Amenophis III. ; they are the best preserved ruins of a temple and undoubtedly the most interesting of all the ancient Egyptian remains south of Semneh. The Egyptian name of the city of Soleb was Menen-en-khā-em-maāt 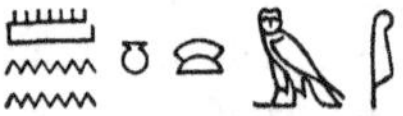, and the temple was built there to commemorate the king's victories over the Nubians, many of the names of the tribes of which are found inscribed on its walls. The temple was approached through two pylons. The court between the two pylons measured about 70 ft. by 45 ft., and contained six columns ; the second pylon, 167 ft. wide, was approached by steps. The second court measured about 90 ft. by 113 ft., and a colonnade ran round all four sides ; the columns, 28 in number, are $6\frac{1}{2}$ feet in diameter. The sanctuary was approached through two hypostyle halls, the second of which measured 78 ft. by 113 ft., and contained 32 columns $5\frac{3}{4}$ feet in diameter. Almost opposite the railway "triangle" at **Dalgo,** about 150 miles from Wâdî Ḥalfah, on the west bank of the Nile, lie the ruins of the Temple of **Sesebi,** which bear inscriptions of Seti I., about B.C. 1370. On the **Island of Tombos,** near Kerma, and on the banks of the river, at the head of the **Third Cataract,** 201 miles from Wâdî Ḥalfah, are gray granite quarries, in one of which the two statues, now lying on the Island of Arḳaw (Argo), were quarried; nearly 70 years ago Mr. Hoskins saw lying here a broken statue of the same material 12 feet long.

Al-Ḥafîr, about six miles to the south of Kerma, on the left bank of the river, is famous in Anglo-Egyptian annals as the scene of the action between the Egyptian artillery and gunboats and the Dervishes on September 19, 1896. The Dervishes had made along the river a long line of shelter trenches, with loopholed mud walls, and they had five small guns, which were well worked by ex-gunners of the Egyptian army. The Sirdar's gunboats, *Tamaai*, *Abu Klea*, and *Metammeh*, attacked the forts; the Egyptian artillery kept up a strong fire, but it was the fire from three batteries of artillery and a Maxim battery, which were landed on the Island of Artaghasi, that silenced the Dervish guns. On the **Island of Arḳaw**, which is about 20 miles long, are two gray granite statues, which, together with the pedestals, must have stood about 24 feet high; they seem not to have been finished. One is broken, and the other has lost part of an arm. Lepsius assigned the statues to the Hyksos period, but this is clearly impossible; and there is no reason for doubting that they belong to the period when the Nubian kingdom of Napata or of Meroë was flourishing. From their positions it appears that they were set up in front of the temple, the ruins of which lie close by, after the manner of the colossal statues of kings that were placed before the pylons of temples in Egypt. The temple which stood on this island must have been of considerable size. On the right bank of the Nile, near Arḳaw, at **Ḳarmân**, are the ruins of a very large town, and in the necropolis are the remains of two rectangular mud brick tombs which, in Lepsius' day, measured 150 × 66 × 40 feet, and 132 × 66 × 40 feet respectively; they are called **Dafûfa** and **Ḳarmân**.

Al-Urdî, or **New Donḳola**, a little over 60 miles from

Kerma, on the west bank of the Nile, was re-occupied by Egyptian troops on September 23, 1896. In the western desert, at no great distance from the town, are large quantities of salt deposit. During the revolt of the Mahdi this town, under the rule of Mustafa Yawir, who doubted the divinity of the Mahdi, remained loyal for a long time, and its people actually defeated the Dervishes at Ḳûrta (Korti); finally, however, it was compelled to submit to the rebel, and the loss of the Donḳola Province was a serious blow to Egypt. The town was large and prosperous, but, like every place which fell under Dervish rule, was destroyed.

Old Donḳola is situated on the east bank of the Nile, and is 155 miles from Kerma. At the present time it is simply a deserted town, filled with the ruins of mud-brick houses, and containing about 30 able-bodied men. The people belonging to it usually live on a little island in the Nile close by, and on the western bank. It is built on a rocky height overlooking the river and the Eastern Desert, and has always been of great strategic importance, from its commanding position. The current is very strong here, and the steamer in which the writer passed it in September, 1897, with difficulty made one mile in an hour. A fine stele, dated in the 8th year of the Nubian king **Nâstasenen** 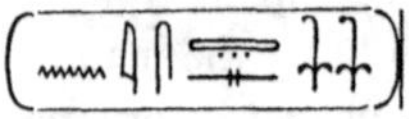 which was found here some years ago, proves that the town was of considerable size and importance long before the Christian era began, and in the second half of the sixth century A.D. the Christian king Silko, who defeated the Blemmyes, adopted the town as his capital. Abu Ṣalîḥ describes it as a large city, and says that it "contains many churches, and large houses, and wide streets. The king's house is lofty, with several domes of red brick, and resembles the buildings in Al-'Irâḳ; and this novelty was introduced by Raphael, who was king of Nubia A.H. 392, *i.e.*, A.D. 1002." The Nubians are said to have been star-worshippers, and the first who was converted to Christianity was Baḥriyâ, the son of the king's sister, who built many churches and monasteries in Nubia, some on the river banks, and some in the desert. The northern frontier of Nubia was at Aswân, which was said to be distant a journey of 40 days, and was called Marîs, a name derived from two ancient Egyptian words meaning the "south land." The south wind is commonly called "Marîsîyeh," المريسيّة, as belonging to the south. The king of Nubia had dominion over Mâḳurrah and 'Alwah The Mosque at Old Donḳola was dedicated to the service of God A.D. 1317; it stands in a prominent place, and commands the country and the river.

Abu Gûs, 86 miles from New Donḳola, is the starting point of the great Kordofân and Darfûr caravan road.

Al-Dabbah (Debbeh), 101½ miles from New Donḳola, originally a small village, was turned into a fortified place by the Turks; at this point the Nile is 750 yards wide. Debbeh is the starting point of the direct caravan road to Omdurmân.

Ḳûrta (Korti), 138 miles from New Donḳola, on the west bank of the river, was the headquarters of Lord Wolseley's expedition to rescue General Gordon in 1884; nearly all the forces were concentrated there on Christmas Day of that year, and the withdrawal from the place began in March, 1885. From this point on the Nile to Matammah is a distance of 176 miles. Water is first met with 37 miles from Korti or Ambuḳul, and 18 miles further on are the Wells of Al-Ḥuwêyât; 100 miles from Ambuḳûl are the Gakdûl Wells, which are situated in one of the spurs of the Gebel Gillif range. The wells are water-worn basins at the bottom of a granite gorge, and the largest of the pools measures 180 feet by 30 feet; the water is sweet. At the distance of 150 miles from Ambuḳûl are the Wells of Abu

Klea, and 18 miles further on is the Well of Shabakat, which is 12 feet in diameter and 50 feet deep.

At **Kurru, Zuma** (east bank), and **Tanḳassi** (west bank), 7 to 10 miles from Marawî, are the remains of large groups of pyramids, but the stone casings have been removed by many generations of Muḥammadans for building their tombs, and for making the foundations of the supports of their water-wheels. The cores of most of these pyramids were built of mud bricks, but in each pyramid field are the ruins of at least one well-built step pyramid made of stone.

Marawî (east bank), and **Ṣanam Abu-Dôm** (west bank), 170 miles from New Donḳola, mark the site of the ancient and famous city of **Napata**, the  Nept, or  Nepita, of the Egyptian inscriptions. The ancient city seems to have been situated on the west bank, over which, on account of the bend in the river, the sun rises. It must have been a city of very considerable size, for whenever any excavations were made for the purpose of building block-houses, etc., in 1897, when Ṣanam Abu-Dôm was the head-quarters of the Frontier Field Force of the Egyptian Army, remains of buildings and portions of large sandstone columns were generally found at the depth of a few feet below the surface. Away in the low hills on the west bank, a few miles from the river, are the remains of a number of rock-hewn tombs, and on the east bank, about three or four miles up-stream from Ṣanam Abu-Dôm, lie the pyramids and ruins of the temples of Napata. The name Ṣanam Abu-Dôm means "the place of graven images which is situated among *dôm* palms," and proves that there were ancient ruins of one or more temples in the immediate neighbourhood. At Marawî, just opposite, are the ruins of one of the brick and stone forts which are so common in the country, and a mosque, and close by is a settlement of the brave Shaiḳia Arabs, whose ancestors several centuries ago came from Arabia and possessed considerable power in the country. Next comes the village of Shibba, and straight ahead is the striking mountain called **Gebel Barkal** by the Arabs, and Ṭu-āb, [hieroglyphs], the "Holy (*or* Pure) Mountain" in the Egyptian inscriptions. This mountain is 302 feet high, and is about five-eighths of a mile long; it is the most prominent object in the landscape, and can be seen for many miles round. On the plain by the side of the mountain are the ruins of eight or nine pyramids, and on the crest of the rising ground are

Scene from the Chapel of a Pyramid at Gebel Barkal.

eight more; they are, however, much dwarfed in appearance by the huge mass of the mountain. The pyramids in the plain vary in size from 23 feet to 88 feet square; those on the hill vary from 33 feet to 65 feet square, and from 35 to 60 feet in height. Before each pyramid there stood a chapel containing one or more chambers, the walls inside being decorated with reliefs, in which the deceased was represented standing in adoration before the gods of the Holy Mountain, and receiving offerings of incense, etc., from priests and others. The above illustration, taken from Cailliaud's *Voyage*, will give a good idea of the class of reliefs found in the chapels, but the slabs from which it was first drawn at Gebel Barkal have long since disappeared. The general characteristics are, of course, Egyptian, but the details of treatment are peculiar to the artists and sculptors of Nubia. The writer excavated the shafts of one of the pyramids here in 1897, and at the depth of about 25 cubits found a group of three chambers, in one of which were a number of bones of the sheep which was sacrificed there about 2000 years ago, and also

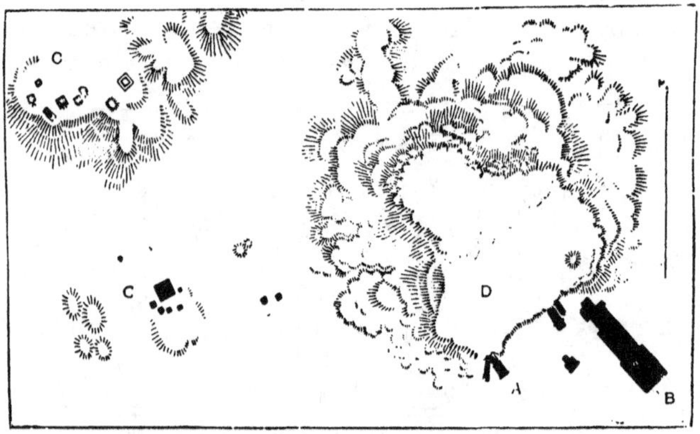

The Pyramids and Temples of Gebel Barkal. (Drawn from Lepsius.)

A Temple of Tirhakhah.
B Temple of Piānkhi.
C Pyramids.
D Gebel Barkal.

portions of a broken amphora which had held Rhodian wine. A second shaft, which led to the mummy chamber, was also emptied, but at a further depth of 20 cubits it was found to be full of water; and having no means for pumping it out, the mummy chamber could not be entered. The principal ruins of temples are:—

1. The **Temple of Tirhakah.** (A.) Taharqa, the Tirhakah of the Bible, was the third king of the XXVth dynasty; he began to reign about B.C. 693, and reigned

over 25 years. From the excavations which Mr. Hoskins made at Gebel Barkal, it is clear that four pillars of a porch or portico stood before the pylon, which was 11 feet deep and 63 feet wide. The court, which measured about 59 feet by 50 feet, contained 16 columns, 8 round and 8 square; their diameter was about 3½ feet, and their height 18 feet. A small hypostyle hall with 8 columns led into the sanctuary, wherein was the shrine of the god and his companions; on the west side of the sanctuary is one room, and on the east are two. The total length of the temple was about 120 feet. The chambers are decorated with reliefs, in which the king is depicted worshipping the gods of Gebel Barkal; many of the reliefs were painted with bright colours. Since Hoskins and Lepsius were at Gebel Barkal, a huge mass of rock crashed down from the top of the mountain, and did great damage to the ruins of this temple. Between the temples of Tirhakah and Piānkhi are the ruins of a small temple building which consisted of two chambers, the first containing 4 columns, and the second an altar; about 250 yards to the north of these are the ruins of the pylon of a temple which was decorated with sculptured scenes.

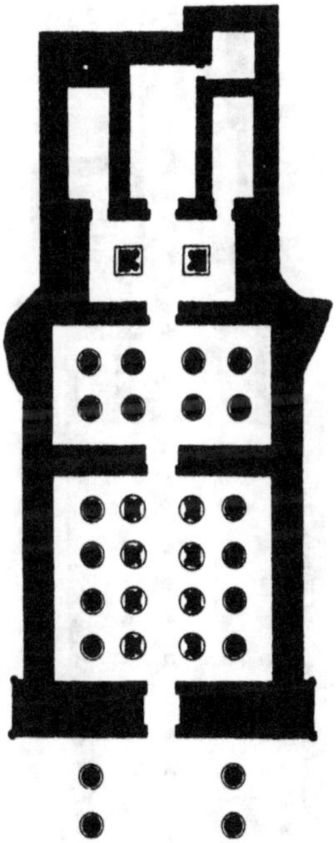

Temple of Tirhakah at Gebel Barkal. (Drawn from Lepsius.)

2. The **Temple of Piānkhi** (B.) Piānkhi ruled at Napata in the last quarter of the VIIIth century B.C., and

is famous as the Nubian monarch who invaded and conquered all Egypt. His temple, according to the figures of Mr. Hoskins, measured 500 feet in length and 135 feet in width. The first court, which contained 26 columns about 6 feet in diameter, measured 150 feet by 135 feet; the second court, which contained 46 columns about 5½ feet in diameter, measured 125 feet by 102 feet; the hypostyle hall, which contained 10 columns about 4 feet in diameter, measured 51 feet by 56 feet; the chamber leading to the sanctuary measured 40 feet by 28 feet; and the sanctuary, which contained three shrines, probably for Åmen-Rā, Mut, and Khonsu, 37 feet by 21½ feet. The pylon which divided the two courts was decorated with battle scenes, processions, and the like. Close in under the hill are the remains of a temple which seems to have been built and added to by later Nubian kings, for the reliefs which were on its walls belong to the class which is found in the island of of Meroë, further south. An idea of the style of the reliefs in this temple will be gained from the following illustration, which is taken from Cailliaud's *Voyage*. Here we see the Nubian king, who calls himself "the pacifier of the two lands, king of the South and North, Se-kheper-ren-Rā, the son of the sun, the lord of diadems, Senka-Åmen-seken,

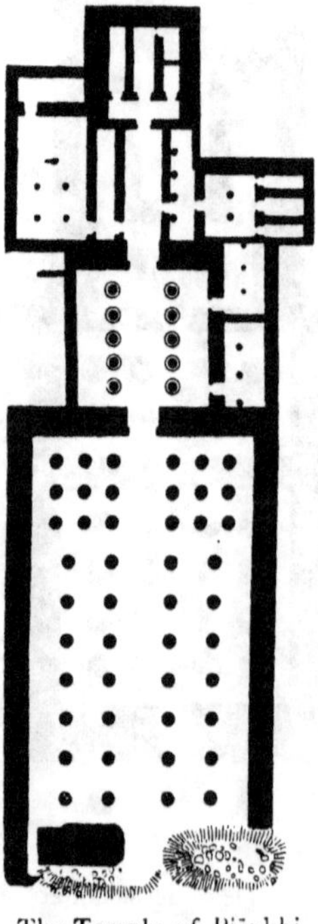

The Temple of Piānkhi at Gebel Barkal.
(Drawn from Lepsius.)

giver of life, like the sun." The prenomen of this king, Se-kheper-ren-Rā,  means, "Rā createth name" (*or* renown), and his nomen shows that he was a devotee of the god Åmen-Rā. He is here depicted in the act of clubbing the representatives of a number of vanquished peoples in the presence of the god Åmen, who is offering him a short sword. An interesting collection of stelæ containing inscriptions of Piānkhi and Ḥeru-sa-tef,

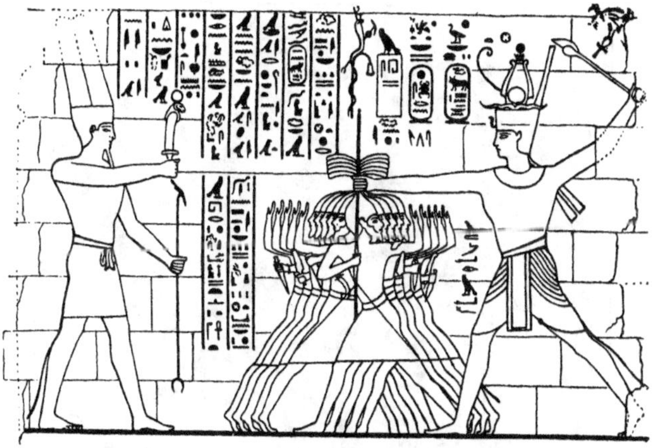

Senka-Åmen-seken, king of Nubia, clubbing his foes.
(Drawn from Cailliaud.)

and the texts of the histories of the Dream, and the Enthronement, and the Excommunication, drawn up for certain Nubian kings, was found some years ago among the ruins of the great temple of Piānkhi at Gebel Barkal; all these are now in the Gîzeh Museum. The condition of the ruins at Gebel Barkal renders it extremely difficult to gain any exact idea of the appearance of the temples as a whole, but they can never have impressed the beholder with the sense of massiveness and dignity which seems to be the peculiar attribute of the great temples of Egypt.

The temple remains at Gebel Barkal are naturally not to be compared with those of Soleb, but the site is one of great historic interest, for there is little reason to doubt that the Egyptian occupation of the country is certainly as old as the time of the kings of the XIIth dynasty.

At **Nûri**, or Nurri, 7½ miles from Marawî, on the west bank of the Nile, are the remains of 35 pyramids, which probably formed the tombs of the kings and royal person-

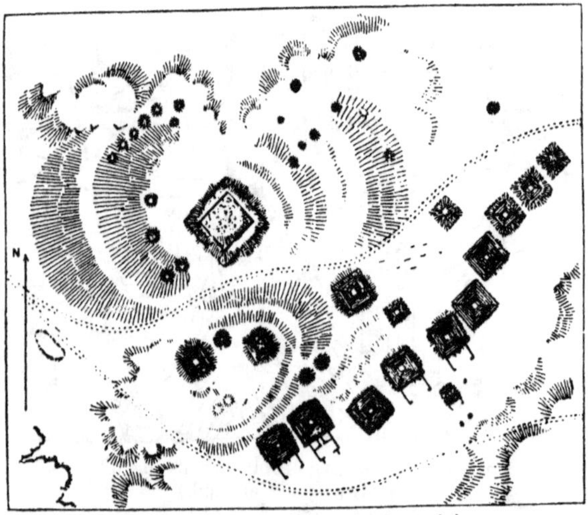

The Pyramids of Nûri at the foot of the Fourth Cataract.

ages of Napata. These pyramids are better and more solidly built than any others which the writer has seen in the Sûdân, and in very few cases do their cores consist of anything besides well-hewn sandstone blocks laid in regular courses. Each pyramid had orginally a chapel in front of its face on the south-east side, but every building of the kind has long since disappeared, and there is not an inscription or bas-relief left by which any of them may be dated. The style of building suggests the Middle Empire, but only excavations of an extensive character can decide this question. The remains of two temples are to be found there, and the ruins of buildings which are found all the way between Ṣanam Abu-Dôm and Nûrî prove that in the flourishing times of the kingdom of Nubia a great city must have extended nearly the whole way between these places. The whole district could, under an honest government, become very flourishing, but it will need many years to recover from the misery and desolation caused in the first place by the incapacity, cruelty, and dishonesty of the officials who represented the Turkish Government, and secondly by the Mahdi and the Khalîfa.

At Bĕlăl, or Bellal, 8½ miles from Marawî, is the foot of the **Fourth Cataract**, which extends to Abu Ḥamed, a distance of 120 miles. A few miles beyond Bĕlăl, on the west bank, are the remains of a Coptic building, part monastery and part fortress, which contained a church, and opposite Hamdab Island, about 6 miles further on, are the ruins of a pyramid. The journey from Bĕlăl to Abu Ḥamed is difficult, but the following places in the Cataract will always possess interest for the British. **Birti,** 51 miles from Marawî, the headquarters of the River Column in the Nile Expedition of 1884; **Kirbekan,** 59 miles from Marawî, where the British defeated the Dervishes, February 10, 1885, and General Earle was killed by a Dervish who "sniped" him from a hut; **Salamat,** 90 miles from Marawî, which was occupied by the British on February 17; and **Hebbeh,** 101 miles from Marawî. On the 18th of September, 1884, the steamer "Abbas," with Colonel Stewart on board, was run aground on the west side of the Island of Hebbeh, and every one of the 44 men on board, except four, were treacherously murdered by the arrangement of Sulêman Wad Gamr, the shêkh of the Munassir tribe. The British troops, on February 17, 1885, destroyed the house and palm-trees and water-wheels of this shêkh, and three days later the property of Fakri Wad Atman, in whose house at Hebbeh Colonel Stewart had been murdered, was also destroyed. The ill-fated steamer was seen tightly fixed on a rock about 200 yards from the river, with her bottom about 20 feet above low-water level; she was pitted with bullet marks and rent by fragments of shell.

At **Abu Ḥamed,** 560 miles from Wâdî Ḥalfah by river and about 232 by rail, is the head of the Fourth Cataract. On August 7, 1897, the village was captured by General Sir A. Hunter, and about 1,200 men of the Dervish garrison there were slain; at this battle Major Sidney and Lieut. FitzClarence were killed. Abu Ḥamed derives its name from a local shêkh who is buried here, and whose memory is greatly venerated in the neighbourhood, and it owes its importance entirely to the fact that the caravans, which crossed the Nubian desert, started from it. It is said that any article left at the tomb of the shêkh by a traveller on his departure, will be found there uninjured on his return! On the railway between Abu Ḥamed and **Berber** the traveller will pass the following stations:—**Mushra ad-Dakêkh,** 14 miles from Abu Ḥamed; **Abu Dês,** 33 miles from Abu Ḥamed; **Sherêkh,** 60 miles from Abu Ḥamed **Abu Sellem,** 74½ miles from Abu Ḥamed; **Al-Obêda,** 118 miles from Abu Ḥamed; and Berber is reached at mile 135. For the first 70 miles the line runs close to the Nile, it then turns sharply into the desert, in which it runs for 20 miles, when it returns to the Nile bank, along which it runs into Berber. Before Abu Ḥamed and Berber were connected by railway, the journey was made partly by river and partly by land, the reason being that between Nadi, 168 miles from Abu Ḥamed, and Bashtanab, the navigation was impeded for 4 miles by rocks, and by the **Fifth Cataract,** which extended from Umm Hashîya to Ganê-netta, a distance of about 14 miles. Nadi is at the foot of the Abu Sinûn Cataract, better known as the Al-Baḳara Rapid; the Fifth Cataract is called Shellâl al-Ḥimâr, or the "Cataract of the wild ass[es]," and the end of it is about 88 miles from Abu Ḥamed.

Berber, or Al-Makerif (latitude north 18° 1′), on the east bank of the river, marks the northern boundary of the country of the Barabara, which extended as far south as Abyssinia, and included all the land on the east bank of the Nile between the Niles and the Red Sea. To this point on the Nile, from very ancient times, the products of the Sûdân, gum, ivory, ebony, gold, curious animals, slaves, etc., have been brought on their road to the coast of the Red Sea at Suâkin, and it is probable that, for many reasons, the Sûdân boatmen were not in the habit of proceeding further north. The country round about Berber is rich, and was, and still is, with care, capable of producing large crops of grain of various kinds, which are sufficient for the needs of a city of considerable size; the city, however, owed its importance, not to the grain-producing qualities of the neighbourhood, but to its position on the great caravan routes to and from the Sûdân, and the facilities which it offered for traffic and barter. The distance from Berber to Suâkin is about 245 miles. Two principal routes are laid down by the Intelligence Department of the Egyptian Army, but the ordinary caravan route is *viâ* Obak, 57 miles from Berber, Ariab, 111 miles from Berber, Kokreb, 145 miles from Berber, Dissibil, 200 miles from Berber, and Tambuk, 219 miles from Berber. The old town of Berber is described as having been much like a town of Lower Egypt, with dusty, unpaved streets, and houses built of unbaked bricks, and having flat roofs; in the early years of the XIXth century it possessed a few large mosques, and abundant palm and acacia trees. Under Turkish rule the town lost much of its prosperity, and the Dervishes ended what the Turkish officials began. The new town lies to the north of the old town, and contained many large well-built houses, but most of them have been without tenants for years, and are now in ruins. Old and new Berber straggle along the river bank for a distance of six miles. Captain Count Gleichen estimated the population of Berber in 1897 at 12,000, of which 5,000 were males. Berber fell into the hands of the Mahdi's forces on May 26, 1884, but it was re-occupied by the Egyptian troops on September 6, 1897, and a week later General Sir A. Hunter entered the town with his army. From Berber the railway continues to Darmali (14 miles), and to the river Atbara, 23 miles from Berber; the distance from Berber to Kharṭûm is about 200 miles.

The river **Atbara**, or Muḳrân, the Astaboras of Strabo, which flows into the Nile on the east bank, is at this point about 450 yards wide, and in the rainy season has a depth of water in it which varies from 25 to 30 feet. It brings down the entire drainage of Eastern Abyssinia, and has four tributaries, the Setit, Royân, Salâm and Anḳareb rivers; it carries into the Nile more soil than any other of the Nile tributaries, and the dark brown colour of its waters has gained for it the name of Baḥr al-Aswad or "Black River." For more than 150 miles before its junction with the Nile its bed is perfectly dry from the beginning of March to June, and the late Sir Samuel Baker says that "at intervals of a few miles there are pools or ponds of water left in the deep holes below the general average of the river's bed. In these pools, some of which may be a mile in length, are congregated . . . . crocodiles, hippopotami, fish, and large turtle in extraordinary numbers, until the commencement of the rains in Abyssinia once more sets them at liberty by sending down a fresh volume of water." The rainy season begins in Abyssinia in May, but the torrents do not fill until the middle of June. From June to September the storms are terrific, and every ravine becomes a raging torrent, and the Atbara becomes a vast river. "Its waters are dense with soil washed down from most fertile lands far from its point of junction with the Nile; masses of bamboo and driftwood, together with large trees and frequently the dead bodies of elephants and buffaloes, are hurled along its muddy waters in wild confusion." The rains cease about the middle of September, and in a very short time the bed of the Atbara becomes a "sheet of glaring sand," and the waters of its great tributaries, though perennial streams, are absorbed in its bed and never reach the Nile. The velocity of the Atbara current is so great, and its waters so dense, that in flood it forces the water of the Nile across on to the western bank. The railway is carried over the Atbara by means of an iron bridge of six spans of 200 feet each, the piers of which are built upon the rock, which was reached at a depth of about 30 feet below the bed of the river. The **Battle of the Atbara** was fought on April 8, 1898, at a place called Nakhila, about 37 miles from the junction of the river with the Nile, on the right bank. The Dervish force numbered about 14,000 men, and of these about 3,000 were killed and wounded, and 2,000 were made prisoners. The Anglo-Egyptian loss was 5 officers and 78 men killed, and 475 officers and men wounded; large numbers of swords, spears, rifles, 100 banners, and 10 guns, fell into the victors' hands, and Maḥmûd, the Dervish general, was captured.

Having crossed the Atbara the traveller now enters the country which Strabo (xvii. 2. § 2) calls the **Island of Meroë**; the name "island" was probably given to it because it is, generally speaking, bounded by the Atbara, the Nile, and the Blue Nile. Strabo says that its shape is that of a shield, and goes on to mention that it is "very mountainous and contains great forests"; but from this statement and the fact that he speaks of the "mines of copper, iron, gold, and various kinds of precious stones," we may conclude that he is referring to the country south of Kharṭûm. Of the early history of the country nothing is known, and the statements made by Greek writers about its peoples and their manners and customs must have been derived from the garbled traditions left by ancient Egyptian officials who travelled to the south, and perhaps from merchants who were not well informed, and soldiers who were quartered in Nubia. The name given to the chief city of the Island by the Egyptians is Mârâuat 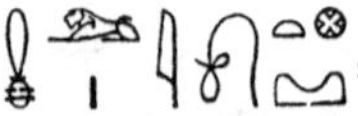, whence the name Meroë clearly is derived. The last determinative indicates that the town was built in a mountainous district, and lends support to Lepsius' derivation of the name from a Berber word *mêrua*, or *méraui*, "white rocks," "white stones." If this derivation be correct, it would rather point to Napata opposite Gebel Barkal as the original city of Meroë.

A little above the mouth of the Atbara, on the right bank, are the ruins of the once flourishing little town of **Ad-Dâmar**, which was famous, like Marawî near Gebel Barkal, as a seat of Muḥammadan learning. From this place to Shendi the east bank is flat and covered with a thick growth of scrub, thorn bushes and ḥalfah grass, which have swallowed up everything, and the strip of cultivable ground is of considerable width; on the west bank the ground is also flat, and the strip is less wide. Here and there ravines, or "khors," run back from the river, and in flood time these must be filled with water. The whole district bears emphatic testimony to the results of the misgovernment of the Turkish Governors-General, and the rule of the Dervishes, which was, of course, the only possible result of such misgovernment of fanatical, superstitious, and warlike Muḥammadans. When the writer first visited the neighbourhood in 1897–98 there were hardly any people to be seen no cattle existed, only here and there was a water wheel at work, and only here and there were a few sheep or goats to be seen ; the gazelles in the desert were almost as numerous as the sheep. Not a donkey could be obtained for many miles, and the very dogs had been exterminated by the Dervishes. Scores of houses in each village were empty and desolate, and at the sight of them the traveller might wonder what would have been the fate of Egypt at the hands of the Dervishes, whom some described as "brave men fighting for their independence."

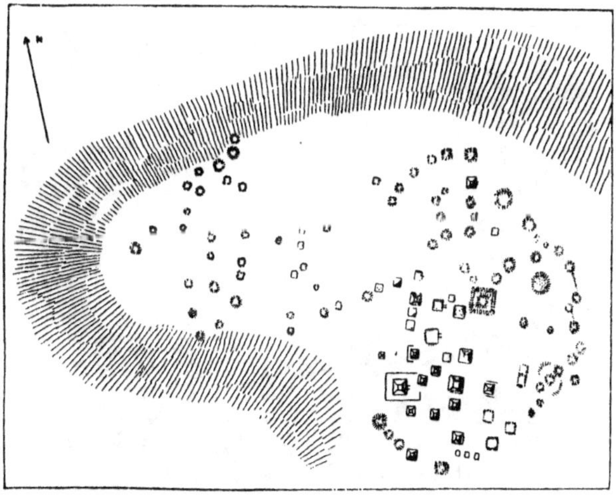

The largest group of Pyramids at Meroë.
(Drawn from the plan of Lepsius.)

At a distance of about 40 miles from the mouth of the Atbara the district of **Baḳrawîyeh*** is reached, and from this point a visit may be made to three groups of pyramids, commonly called the **Pyramids of Meroë**, the most distant of which lie about three miles from the river. These pyramids are the tombs of the kings and royal personages who reigned over the Island of Meroë in the

* Hoskins calls it Bagromeh.

capital city, which seems to have stood near the modern town of Shendi, and are also called the Pyramids of As-sur. The general arrangement of the largest group, which is in the plain, about 1¾ miles from the river, is illustrated by the following plan; nearly all are in ruins, for the stone casings have been removed by generations of natives. At no great distance from these pyramids are the ruins of a temple and the remains of an artificial depression, which seems to mark the site of the sacred lake of the temple.

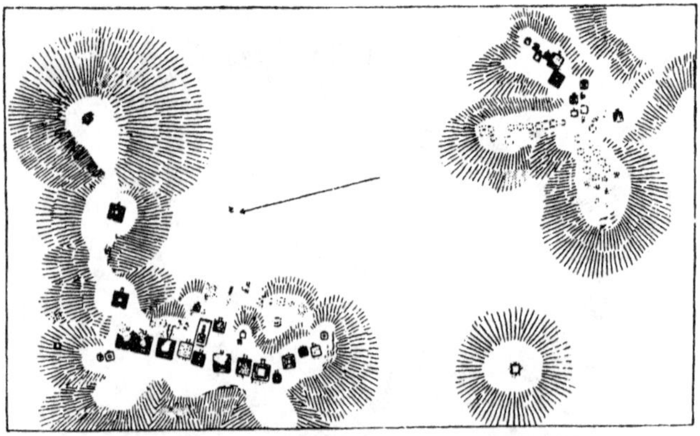

The second and third group of Pyramids at Meroë,
(Drawn from the plan of Lepsius.)

The other two groups of pyramids are situated further to the east, and are built on low hills, the smaller group lying to the south-east of the larger; and some of their pyramids are quite in ruins. The most interesting group is that which is built on a comparatively high hill, and which at the beginning of the XIXth century was in a good state of preservation, as the plates which illustrate Cailliaud's *Voyage* prove. The 29 pyramids of this group vary in size at the base from 20 feet to 63 feet. In front of each pyramid was a chapel which consisted of one or more chambers, the walls of which were decorated with reliefs, in which kings and queens were depicted worshipping the local gods and making offerings to them. There is little doubt that the sites of these groups of pyramids were used as burial grounds from an extremely early period, but the inscriptions of the pyramids now standing there show that they belong to a period which lies between about B.C. 400 and A.D. 250. Both reliefs and inscriptions prove that the Nubians, or Ethiopians as they are often called, were *borrowers* from, and not the *originators* of, the Egyptian civilization, with its gods and religion, and system of writing, as some, following Diodorus, have thought. The royal names found in some of the chapels are those of the builders of the great temples at Nâga, and others are those which are known from buildings at Dakkeh and Gebel Barkal. In them also are inscriptions in the character called Meroïtic, which, in some respects, resembles the Demotic, and Lepsius had no doubt that they were contemporaneous. It is not at present possible to arrange the royal names of the Nubian or Ethiopian kings in chronological order, especially as many of them seem to be peculiar to certain parts of the old kingdom of Meroë, and it is possible that many of their owners were contemporary. It is, however, evident that when this kingdom was in its most flourishing state, the rule of its kings extended from the Blue Nile to Aswân. In 1834 an Italian doctor called Ferlini selected one of the largest pyramids on the crest of the hill at Baḳrawîyeh (*i.e.*, the one marked F in Cailliaud's plan, and the most westerly of the group), and began to pull it down. In the course of the work an entrance to a chamber was accidentally discovered, wherein were found a dead body and a large quantity of jewellery, boxes, etc., of a most interesting character.* This treasure was not

* His account of the discovery is so interesting, that an extract from the French version of it is here given :—

"Monté au sommet de la pyramide, avec quatre ouvriers, pour mettre

buried, as one would expect, in a chamber below the surface of the ground, but in a small chamber within the masonry of the pyramid. One good result attended this lucky "find," for it became certain that the period when the jewellery was placed in the pyramid was Roman, and the inscriptions showed that the queen for whom the pyramid was built was the great queen who is depicted on the walls of the ruins at Nâga with rich decorations and pointed nails almost an inch long. The ill result that followed the discovery was the destruction of several pyramids by treasure seekers, and Lepsius relates that when he was there Osman Bey, who was leading back his army of 5,000 men from Taka, offered him the help of his battalions to pull down all the pyramids, in order to find treasure as Ferlini had done. The few natives found by the writer at Baḳrawîyeh would hardly approach the pyramids by day,

---

la main à l'ouvrage, je reconnus au premier coup-d'œil que la démolition pouvait se faire fort facilement, vu que le monument tombait déjà de vétusté ; les premières pierres enlevées, je relevais mes ouvriers. Pendant qu'on jetait par terre les pierres des gradins, ne pouvant plus résister à l'ardeur du soleil, dont les brûlans rayons donnaient jusq'à 48° de Réaumur, [*i.e.*, 60° Centigrade, and 140° Fahrenheit], j'allai me reposer avec M. Stefani à l'ombre d'une pyramide voisine. Tout-à-coup je fus appelé par mon fidèle domestique. J'accourus avec mon ami au haut du monument . . . et je sentis déjà mon cœur s'ouvrir à la douce espérance . . . Je vois mon domestique couché sur son ventre, sur l'emplacement qu'il avait pratiqué, et cherchant à couvrir de son corps l'ouverture qui venait d'être découverte. Les noirs, poussés par la cupidité, voulaient à toute force chasser mon domestique et plonger leurs mains avides dans le fond de l'ouverture . . . Nous fîmes bonne contenance, et les armes à la main, nous les forçâmes de descendre ; nous appellâmes d'autres domestiques de confiance, et nous fîmes continuer la fouille en notre présence. L'ouverture nous laissait entrevoir un vide qui contenait des objets que nous ne pouvions distinguer. Ce vide, ou cellule, était formé de grandes pierres grossièrement assemblées. Nous fîmes enlever les pierres les plus larges qui couvraient le plan supérieur, et

far less in the evening or by night, and the shêkh Muḥammad Amîn, who had been in the employ of General Gordon, declared that it was "not nice" to intrude upon the "spirits of the kings who were taking their rest in the mountain." Seen from the river at sunset, the western sides of the pyramids appear to be of a ruddy crimson colour.

Shendi, on the east bank of the river, 95 miles from the Atbara, was once a large town, containing several thousands of inhabitants, and possessed a considerable trade with the northern and southern provinces on the east bank of the Nile. In the year 1820 Muḥammad 'Ali sent his son Ismâ'îl Pâsha with 5,000 soldiers to conquer Sennaar, and another force of about the same strength to conquer Kordofân. Ismâ'îl was successful in his mission, but the year following he was invited by Nimr the Nubian king to a banquet in his palace at Shendi, and during the

---

nous reconnûmes une cellule ayant la forme d'un carré long et composée de grosses pierres superposées qui formaient les quartre mun latéraux correspondant aux gradins de la pyramide. Cette cellule avait quatre pieds de hauteur sur six ou sept de longueur. La première chose qui frappa nos regards ce fut un grande corps couvert d'un tissu en coton d'une éclatante blancheur qui, à peine touché, tomba en poussiére. C'était une espèce de table ou autel, soutenue par quatre pieds cylindriques et entourée d'une balustrade de barreaux en bois, grands et petits alternativement placés. Ces barreaux étaient sculptés et représentaient des figures symboliques. C'est sous cette table que se trouva le vase en bronze . . . qui contenait les objets précieux enveloppés dans du linge semblable à celui dont je viens de parler. Près du vase et sur le plan de la cellule, étaient symétriquement disposés, au moyen de fils, des colliers, des pâtes en verre, des pierres de couleur, etc. Il y avait aussi quelques talismans, de petites idoles, un étui cylindrique en métal, de petites boîtes travaillées au tour remplies d'une matière pulvérisée dont je donne plus loin l'analyse, une scie, un ciseau, et plusieurs autres objets dont j'ai donné la description dans mon catalogue."—J. Ferlini, *Relation Historique des fouilles opérées dans la Nubie* ; Rome, 1838.

course of the entertainment the palace was set on fire and the Egyptian prince was burned to death. Muḥammad Bey at once marched to Shendi, and having perpetrated awful cruelties upon nearly all its inhabitants, destroyed houses and gardens and property of every kind. Shendi was a Dervish stronghold for some years, but it was re-occupied by the Egyptian troops on March 26th, 1898.

Maṭammah, on the west bank of the Nile, 98 miles from the Atbara, had, in 1885, about 3,000 inhabitants, two or more mosques, and a market twice a week. In 1897 the Gaalîn Arabs in and about the town revolted against the Khalîfa's authority, and having fortified the place they awaited the result. Maḥmûd, by the Khalîfa's orders, attacked it on July 1st, and after a three days' fight, all their ammunition being expended, the Gaalîn were compelled to submit, for Maḥmûd had surrounded the town with his troops. The victors promptly slew 2,000 men, and women and children were massacred mercilessly; the prisoners were drawn up in a line and treated thus: the first was beheaded, the second lost a right hand, the third his feet, and so on until every man had been mutilated. The Gaalîn chief, 'Abd-Allah wad Sûd, was walled up at Omdurmân in such a position that he could neither stand nor sit, and was thus left to die of hunger and thirst (Royle, *op. cit.*, p. 521). General Sir A. Hunter bombarded the town on October 16, 17, and November 3, 1897, and it was evacuated by Maḥmûd in March, 1898.

About 20 miles south of Shendi, on the east bank, is the entrance to the Wâdî Ben-Nâga, and near it is a little village called **Ben-Nâga**; three miles down the river are the ruins of a small ancient Nubian temple, which, according to Hoskins, measured about 150 feet in length; it contained 6 pilasters about 5 feet square. The principal remains are two columns on which are figures of Bes in relief. Travelling in a south-easterly direction, and passing Gebel Buerib, after a journey of ten hours, the ruins of **Nâga** are reached; these are usually called by the natives of the district, Muṣawwarât* an-Nâga, *i.e.*, the "sculptures of Nâga," as opposed to the Muṣawwarât al-Kirbekân, *i.e.*, the sculptures of Ben-Nâga in the Wâdî Kirbekân, and the Muṣawwarât aṣ-Ṣufra, *i.e.*, the sculptures of the Wâdî aṣ-Ṣufra. The ruins consist of the remains of at least four temples, and there is no doubt that they belong to the late Ptolemaïc or early Roman period. The reliefs here will illustrate how closely the architects and masons tried to copy Egyptian models, and the cartouches show that the kings, whoever they were, adopted prenomens formed on the same lines as those used by the old kings of Egypt. The gods worshipped were the same as those of Napata and other Nubian cities, but there is here in addition to them a god with three lions' heads. Before satisfactory plans of the temples here could be drawn, excavations and clearances on a large scale would have to be made. Twelve miles from Nâga, in a north-easterly direction, is a comparatively small circular valley, which, because it resembles in shape a circular brass tray, is called Aṣ-Ṣufra. Here are the **Muṣawwarât aṣ-Ṣufra**, or ruins of a group of buildings enclosed within walls, without inscriptions and without reliefs, which, according to Hoskins, measured 760 feet by 660 feet; there were no entrances on any side except the north-west, where there were three. The walls enclosed five or six small temples, in one of which were several pillars. Cailliaud thought that the ruins of the main building were those of a school, and Hoskins of a hospital, while Lepsius offered no opinion; but it is useless to theorise until systematic excavations have shown what the plan of the group of buildings actually was. About 1½ miles distant are the ruins of a small

*Arabic مُصَوَّرَات sculptures, bas-reliefs, images, paintings, and the like.

temple with reliefs, [on which men are depicted riding elephants, lions, panthers, and other wild animals; all the ruins in this neighbourhood seem to belong to a Christian period. From Shendi an almost direct route runs to Nâga, distance about 30 miles, and there is another to Aṣ-Ṣufra, distance about 26 miles.

About 50 miles from Shendi begins the **Sixth Cataract,** commonly called the Shabluka Cataract; it begins at the north end of Mernat Island, on which General Gordon's steamer, the "Bordein," was wrecked on January 31, 1885, and extends to Gebel Rawyan, a distance of 11 miles. At the entrance to the Shabluka gorge, the channel turns sharply to the east, and is only 200 yards wide; in July the rate of the current through this channel exceeds 10 miles per hour. The Dervishes guarded the northern end of the channel by five forts, four on the western, and one on the eastern bank. From this point to Omdurmân there is little to be seen of general interest. The hills of Kerreri, seven miles from Omdurmân on the east bank, mark the site of the great **Battle of Omdurmân**, on Friday, September 2, 1898, when the Khalifâ's army was practically annihilated; on the same day the Sirdar marched into the city of Omdurmân, and the rule of the Khalifâ was at an end.

The city of **Omdurmân,** 200 miles from the Atbara, on the west bank of the Nile, was originally a small village of no importance, which General Gordon fortified with the view of resisting the advance of the Mahdi's troops. The village was then called Omdurmân Fort, and was defended by a rocket battery and a small force under Faragallah Pâsha. This brave man held out during the last months of 1884, but in December the Dervishes entrenched themselves between the Fort and the river, and so stopped his supplies; on January 5th, when he and his garrison were starving, he surrendered, and was well treated by the

Mahdi. After the fall of Kharṭûm the Mahdi took up his abode in Omdurmân, and gradually the people flocked there, until a city measuring 5 miles by 2 came into being. Its population was estimated at 400,000. The chief buildings were the Great Mosque, the Mahdi's Tomb, the Khalîfa Abdallah's Palace, and the Palace of Ya'ḳûb, his son. The Mosque was enclosed by a brick wall, several hundreds of yards round; the Mahdi's tomb was built by the Khalîfa, is close to the Mosque, and was surmounted by a dome ending in three brass balls and a spear head, and its height was about 70 feet. The dome was badly injured in the bombardment of Omdurmân on September 2nd, and since the building was the symbol of, up to a certain point, successful rebellion and fanaticism, and was certain to become a goal for pilgrimages, and the home of fraudulent miracles, it was destroyed by charges of guncotton. For the same reasons the Mahdi's body was burnt, and the ashes thrown into the river, and this was done on the advice of Muḥammadan officers and notables; the Mahdi's head is said to have been buried at Wâdî Ḥalfah. Omdurmân was defended by a stone wall, which varied in height from 11 to 30 feet, and from 9 to 12 feet in thickness. The Arsenal was about 1½ miles from the Mosque; the Bêt al-Mâl, or Treasury, lay on the river bank, to the north of the town; the Slave Market was to the south of it, and the prison was on the river bank, about the centre of the town. Communication was kept up with Kharṭûm by means of a submarine cable worked by ex-Government officials.*

Five miles up stream from Omdurmân, on the tongue o land formed by the union of the Blue and White Niles, stands **Kharṭûm**, and just below the junction is **Tuti Island**, which has the Blue Nile on two of its sides, and

* Plans of Omdurmân and Kharṭûm by Sir Rudolf Slatin Pâsha will be found in his "*Fire and Sword in the Sudan*," London, 1896.

the White Nile on the third. The difference in the colour of the waters of the two Niles is very marked. The town of Kharṭûm (latitude 15° 36′ 38″ north) was built on the northern face of the tongue of land, and all the Government buildings, and most of the residences of the Consuls, were situated along the river front. On Sunday, September 4th, 1898, the Sirdar and his Staff crossed over to Kharṭûm, which was in ruins, followed by representatives of every corps belonging to the expedition, and when the troops were landed, they were formed up into three sides of a square, facing the front of General Gordon's ruined palace. The Sirdar gave a signal, whereupon the British and Egyptian flags were simultaneously hoisted on the flag-staffs which had been erected on the palace, and the bands played "God Save the Queen," and the Khedivial Hymn, whilst the gunboat fired a royal salute of 21 guns, the officers and men all standing at attention. After cheers had been given for the Queen and the Khedive, the bands played the Dead March in *Saul*, etc., and a solemn service was performed by the various chaplains, which concluded with Gordon's favourite hymn, "Abide with me," played by the Sudanese band.

LIST OF EGYPTIAN KINGS.

It should be borne in mind that the Egyptians never divided their kings into dynasties, and that this arrangement is due to Manetho.

Dynasty I., from Thinis, B.C. 4400.

1. 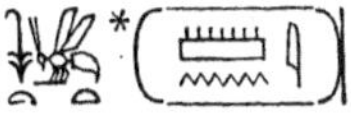
Menȧ.

2. 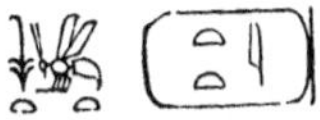
Tetȧ.

3. 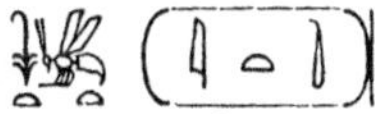
Ȧte*o*.

4. 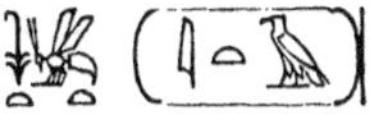
Ȧta.

5. 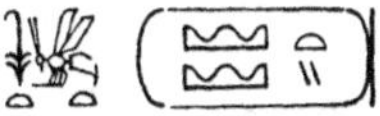
Sem-ti.

6. 
Mer-ba-pen (Mer-p-ba)

7.  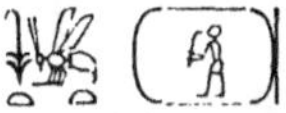
Semsu, or Ḥu (or Nekht)?

8. 
Qebḥ.
(Originally Sen, mistaken for Qebḥ.)

Dynasty II., from Thinis, B.C. 4133.

9. 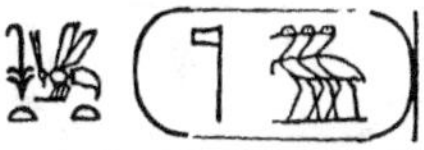
Neter-baiu (Besh, Betchau?)

10. 
Ka-kau.

11. 
Ba-en-neter.

12. 
Uat'-nes.

13. 
Senṭȧ.

14. 
Per-ȧb-sen.

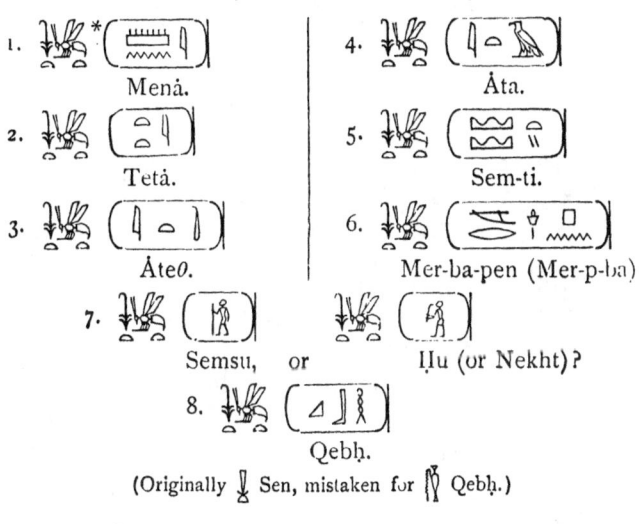

* = *suten net*, "King of the North and South."

15. 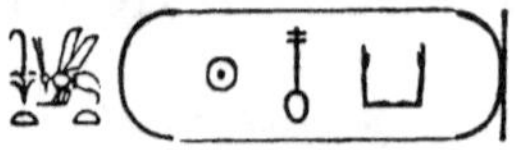
Nefer-ka-Rā.*

16. 
Nefer-ka-seker.

17. 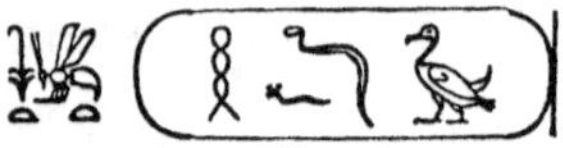
Ḥet'efa.

Dynasty III., from Memphis, B.C. 3966.

18. 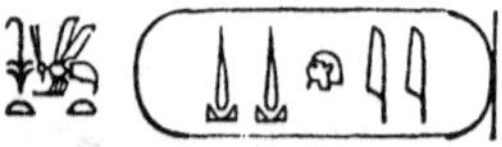
T'at'ai.

19. 
Neb-ka.

20. 
Tcheser

21. 
Tetȧ (Ḥen-nekht)

22. 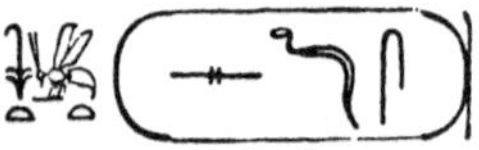
Set'es.

23. 
Tcheserteta

24. 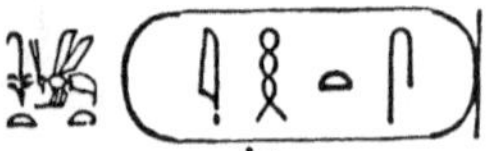
Ȧḥtes.

25. 
Neb-ka-Rā.

26. 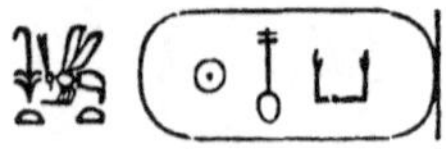 
Nefer-ka-Rā, son of the Sun, Ḥuni.

Dynasty IV., from Memphis, B.C. 3766.

27. 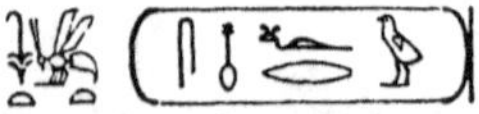
Senefeiu.

28. 
χufu.
(Cheops.)

* Though ⊙ Rā is generally placed first in the cartouche, it is generally to be read last.

†  = *Se Rā*, "son of the Sun."

29. 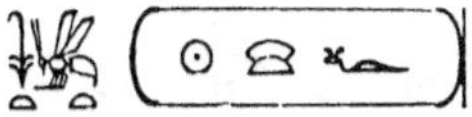

χā-f-Rā.
(Chephren.)

30. 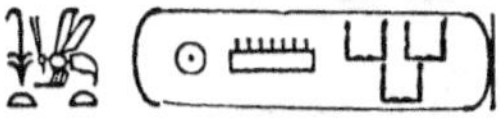

Men-kau-Rā.
(Mycerinus.)

31. 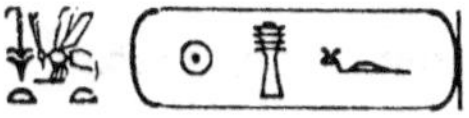

Ṭeṭ-f-Rā.

32. 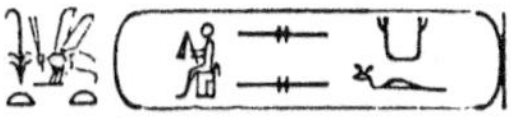

Shepses-ka-f.

33. 

Sebek-ka-Rā.

34. 

I-em-ḥetep.

Dynasty V., from Elephantine, B.C. 3366.

35. 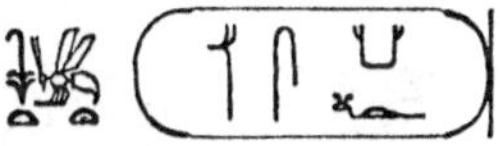

Usr-ka-f.

36. 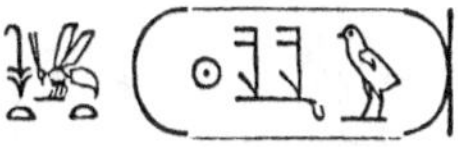

Saḥ-u-Rā.

37. 

Nefer-ka-ȧri-Rā, son of the Sun, Kakaȧ.

38. 

Nefer-f-Rā, son of the Sun, Shepses-ka-Rā.

39. 

Nefer-χā-Rā, son of the Sun, Ḥeru-ȧ-ka-u

40. 

Usr-en-Rā, son of the Sun, Ȧn.

41. 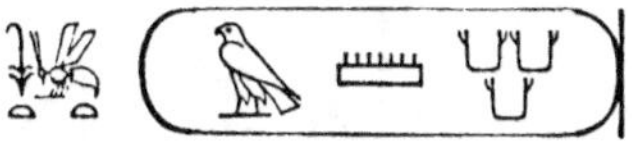

Men-kau-Ḥeru.

42. 

Ṭeṭ-ka-Rā, son of the Sun, Åssà.

43.  Unås.

DYNASTY VI., FROM MEMPHIS, B.C. 3266.

44. 

Tetà. or Tetà-mer-en-Ptaḥ.
(Teta beloved of Ptaḥ.)

45. 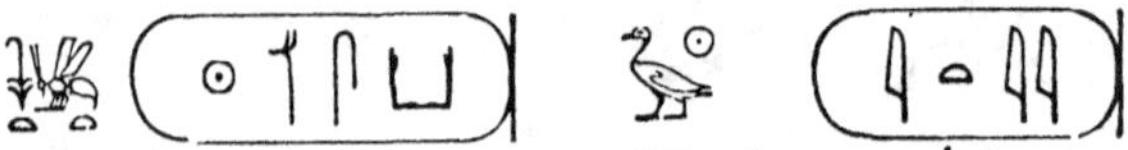

Usr-ka-Rā, son of the Sun, Åti.

46. 

Meri-Rā, son of the Sun, Pepi (I.).

47. 

Mer-en-Rā, son of the Sun, Ḥeru-em-sa-f.

48. 

Nefer-ka-Rā, son of the Sun, Pepi (II.).

49.  50. 

Rā-mer-en-se (?)-em-sa-f Neter-ka-Rā.

51 

Men-ka-Rā, son of the Sun, Netàqerti.
(Nitocris.)

DYNASTIES VII. AND VIII., FROM MEMPHIS; DYNASTIES IX. AND X., FROM HERACLEOPOLIS, B.C. 3100.

52. 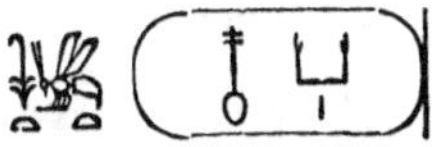
Nefer-ka.

53. 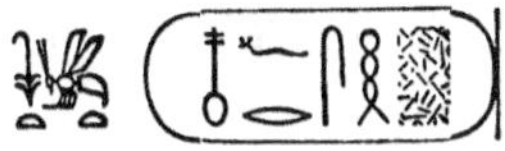
Nefer-seḥ . . . .

54. 
Åb.

55. 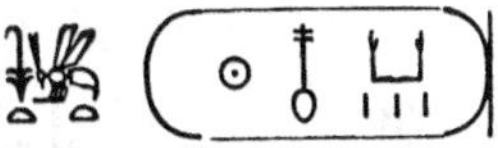
Nefer-kau-Rā.

56. 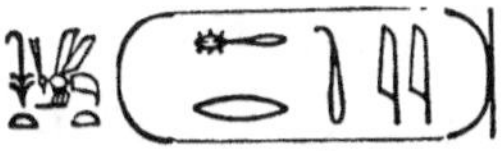
χarθi.

57. 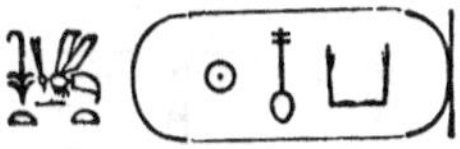
Nefer-ka-Rā.

58. 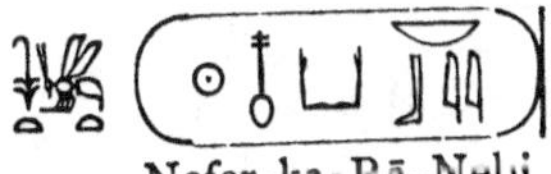
Nefer-ka-Rā-Nebi.

59. 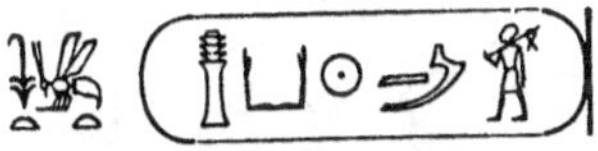
Ṭeṭ-ka-Rā-maā . . . . .

60. 
Nefer-ka-Rā-χenṭu.

61. 
Mer-en-Ḥeru.

62. 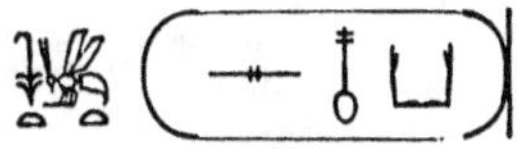
Senefer-ka.

Or 
Se-nefer-ka-Rā.

63. 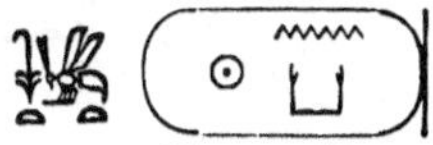
Ka-en-Rā.

64. 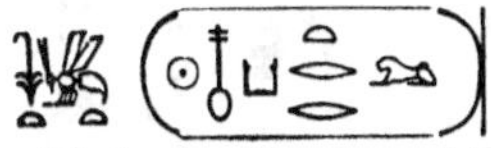
Nefer-ka-Rā-t-rer-l (?).

65. 
Nefer-ka-Ḥeru.

66. 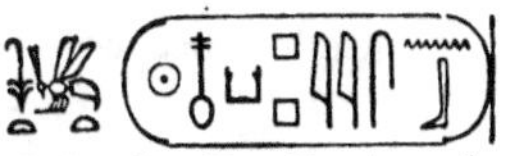
Nefer-ka-Rā-Pepi-senb.

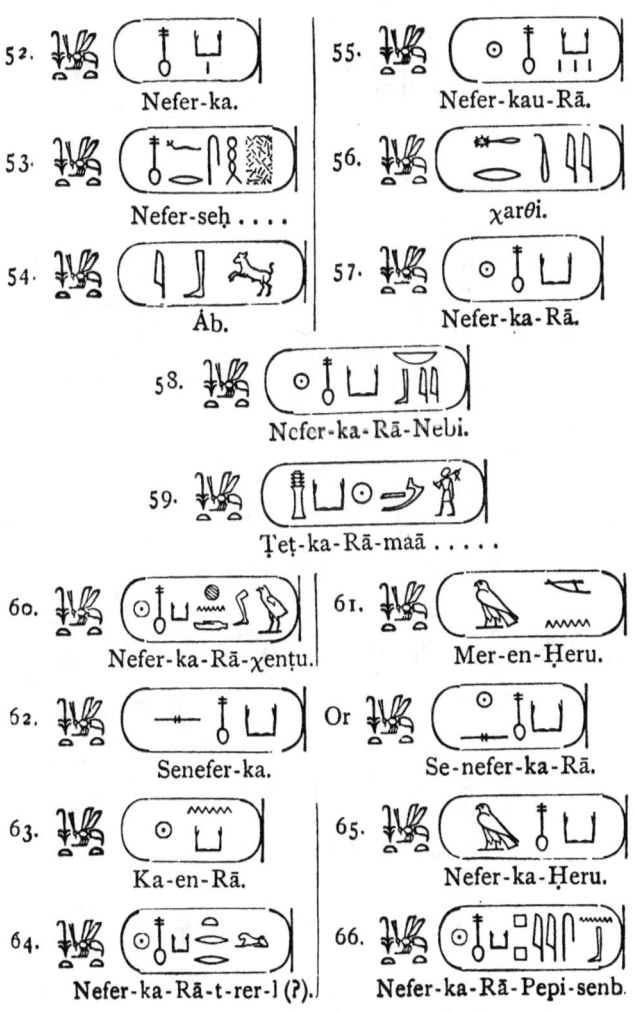

67. Nefer-ka-Rā-ānnu.*

68. Nefer-kau-Rā.

69. Nefer-kau-Ḥeru.

70. Nefer-ka-ȧri-Rā.

DYNASTY XI., FROM THEBES.

71. Erpā† Ȧntef.

72. Men-[tu-ḥetep].

73. Ȧntef.

74. Ȧntef.

75. Ȧntef (?).

76. Neter nefer, Ȧntef.
    Beautiful god, Antef.

77. Son of the Sun Ȧntef.

78. Son of the Sun Ȧn-āa.

79. Nub-χeper-Rā, son of the Sun, Ȧntuf.

---

* After this name the tablet of Abydos has
... kau-Ra.

† Erpā, usually translated "hereditary prince" or "duke," is one of the oldest titles of nobility in Egypt.

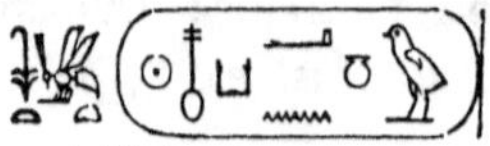

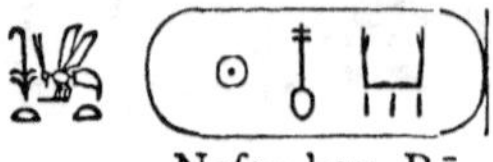

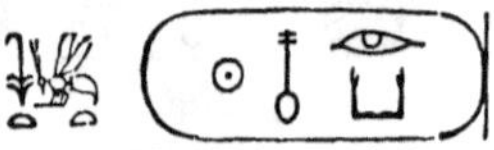

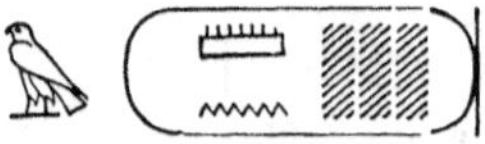

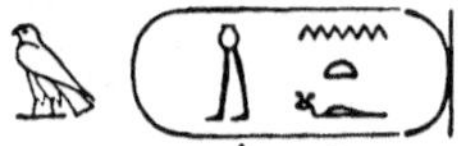

80. 

Āḥā-Ḥeru-Rā-ȧpu-maāt, son of the Sun, Ȧntuf-āa.

81. 

Āḥā-renpit-Rā-ȧput-maāt, son of the Sun, Ȧntef-āa.

82. 

Ṭeṭ-Rā-her-ḥer-maāt, son of the Sun, Ȧntef.

83. 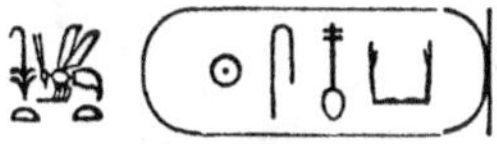

Senefer-ka-Rā.

84. 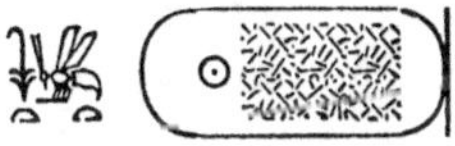

Rā . . . . . .

85. 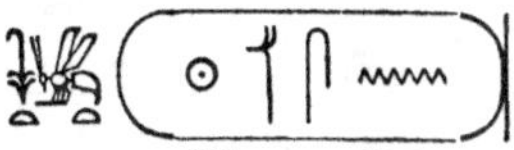

Usr-en-Rā.

86. 

Neb-nem-Rā.

87. 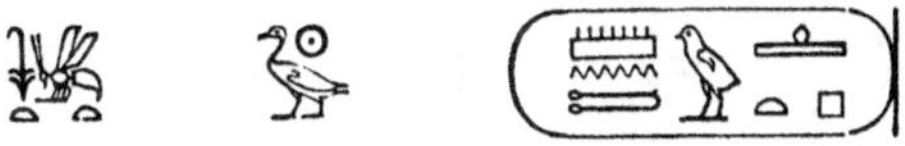

Son of the Sun, Menθu-ḥetep (I.).

88. 

Se-Rā-Menθ-ḥetep (II.).

89. 

Neb-ḥetep-Rā, son of the Sun, Menθ-ḥetep (III.).

90. 

Neb-taiu-Rā, son of the Sun, Menθ-ḥetep (IV.).

91. 

Neb-χeru-Rā, son of the Sun, Menθ-ḥetep (V.).

92. 

Se-ānχ-ka-Rā.

DYNASTY XII., FROM THEBES, B.C. 2466.

93. 

Seḥetep-ȧb-Rā, son of the Sun, Åmen-em-ḥāt (I.).

94. 

χeper-ka-Rā, son of the Sun, Usertsen (I.).

95. 

Nub-kau-Rā, son of the Sun, Åmen-em-ḥāt (II.).

96. 

χeper-χā-Rā, son of the Sun, Usertsen (II.).

97. 

χā-kau-Rā, son of the Sun, Usertsen (III.).

98. 

Maāt-en-Rā, son of the Sun. Åmen-em-ḥāt (III.).

99. 

Maā-χeru-Rā, son of the Sun, Ȧmen-em-ḥāt (IV.).

100. 

Sebek-neferu-Rā.

DYNASTY XIII., B.C. 2233.

101. 

χu-taiu-Rā.

102. 

χerp-ka-Rā.

103. 

. . . . em-ḥāt.

104. 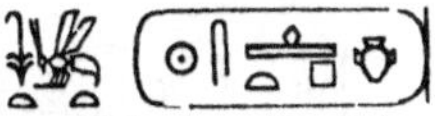

Seḥetep-ȧb-Rā.

105. 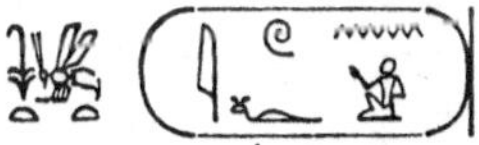

Ȧuf-nȧ.

106. 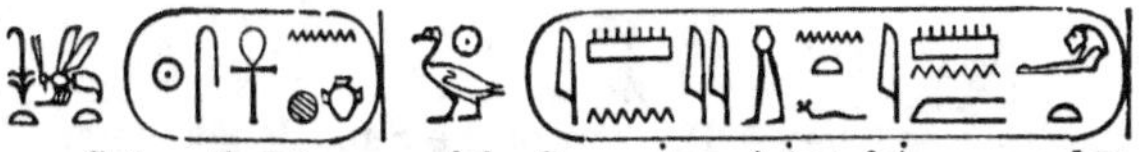

Seānχ-ȧb-Rā, son of the Sun, Ȧmeni-Ȧntef-Ȧmen-em-ḥāt.

107. 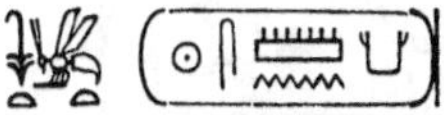

Semen-ka-Rā.

108. 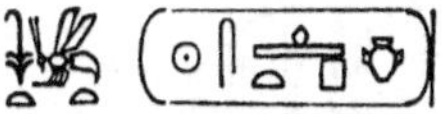

Seḥetep-ȧb-Rā.

109. 

. . . . . ka.

110. 

Net'em-ȧb-Rā.

111. 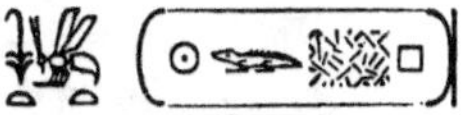

Sebek-[ḥete]p-Rā.

112. 

Ren . . . . . .

113. 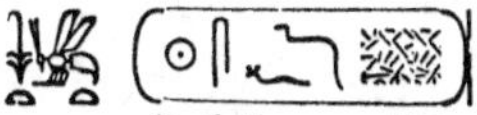

Set'ef . . . . Rā.

114. 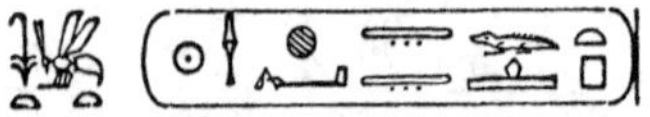

Rā-χerp (?)-χu-taiu Sebek-ḥetep (I.).

115. 

Semenχ-ka-Rā, son of the Sun, Mer-menfitu.

116. 

χerp-seuat'-taiu-Rā, son of the Sun, Sebek-ḥetep (II.).

117. 

χā-seχem-Rā, son of the Sun, Nefer-ḥetep.

118. 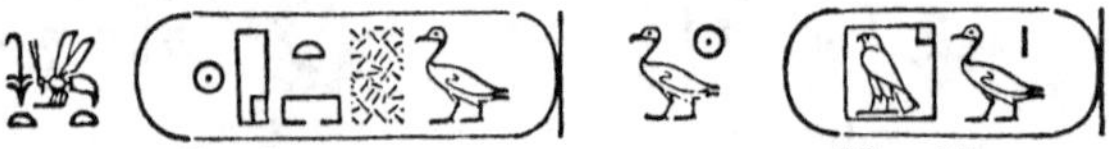

Rā-ḥet . . . . se, son of the Sun, Ḥet-Ḥeru-se-

119. 

χā-nefer-Rā, son of the Sun, Sebek-ḥetep (III.).

120. 

χā-ḥetep-Rā, son of the Sun, Sebek-ḥetep (IV.).

121. 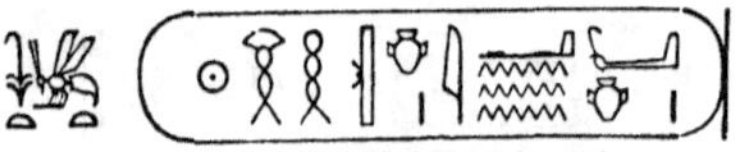

Uaḥ-àb-Rā-àā-àb.

122. 

χāā-χeru-Rā.

123. 

Neb-f-ā (?) a-mer-Rā.

124. 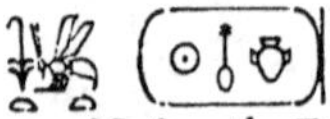

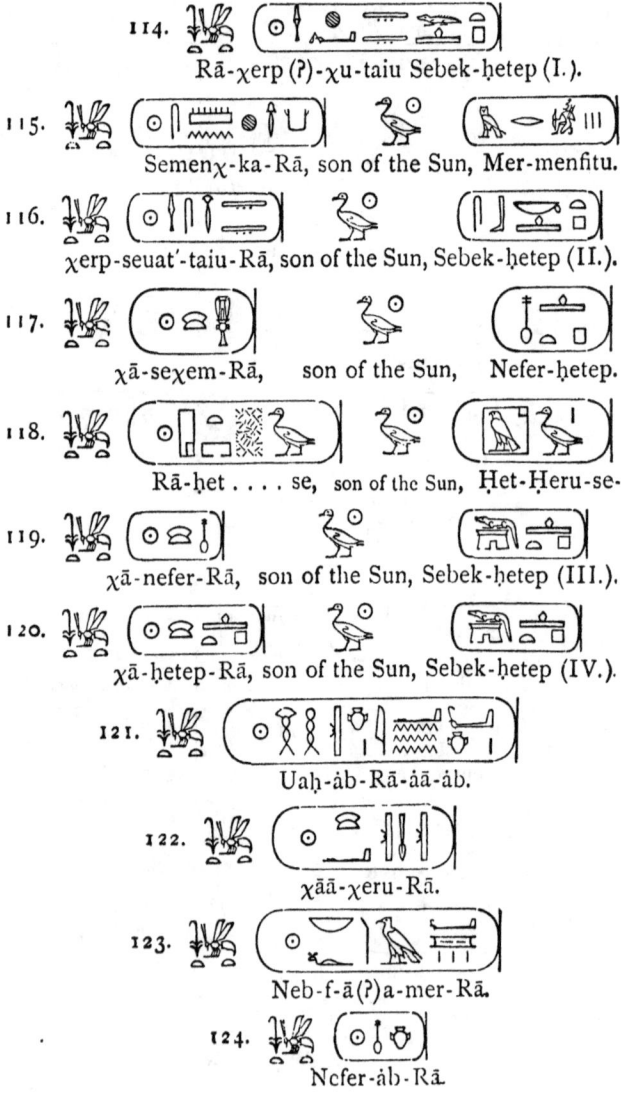

Nefer-àb-Rā.

125. 

χā-ānχ-Rā, son of the Sun, Sebek-ḥetep (V.).

126. 

Mer-χerp-Rā.

127. 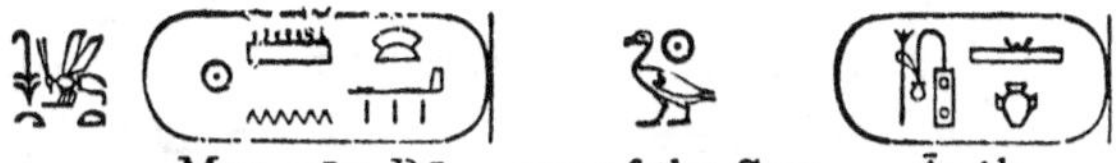

Men-χāu-Rā, son of the Sun, Ānȧb.

128. 

χerp-uat'-χāu-Rā, son of the Sun, Sebek-em-sa-f (I.).

129. 

χerp-seśeṭ-taiu-Rā, son of the Sun, Sebek-em-sa-f (II.).

130. 

Sesusr-taiu-Rā,

131. 

χerp (?)-Uast-Rā.

132. 

χerp-uaḥ-χā-Rā, son of the Sun, Rā-ḥetep.

Dynasty XIV.

133. 

Mer-nefer-Rā, son of the Sun, Ȧi.

134. 

Mer-ḥetep-Rā, son of the Sun, Ȧnȧ.

135. 

Seānχenseḥtu-Rā.

136. 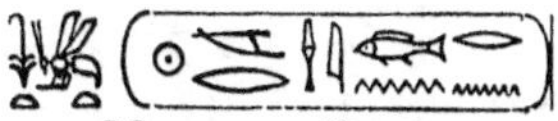

Mer-χerp-Rā-ȧn-ren.

137. 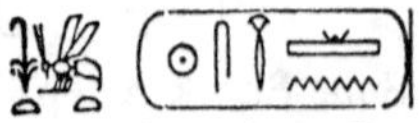

Seuat'-en-Rā

138. 

χā-ka-Rā.

139. 

Ka-meri-Rā

neter nefer Mer-kau-Rā.

140. 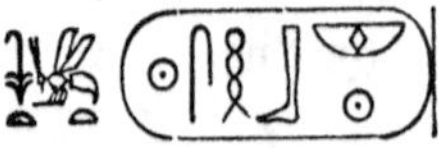

Seḥeb-Rā.

141. 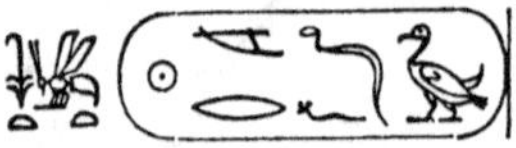

Mer-t'efa-Rā.

142. 

Sta-ka-Rā.

143. 

Neb-t'efa-Rā Rā (*sic*).

144. 

Uben-Rā.

145. 

Her-ȧb-Rā.

146. 

Neb-sen-Rā.

147. 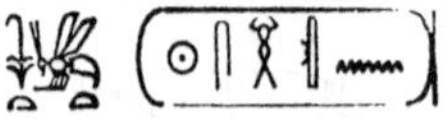

Seuaḥ-en-Rā.

148. 

Seχeper-en-Rā.

149. 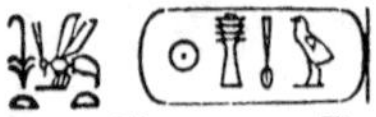

Ṭeṭ-χeru-Ra.

Dynasty XV., "Shepherd Kings."

150. 

Āa-peḥ-peḥ-Set, son of the Sun, Nub-Set (?).

151. 

. . . Bȧnān.

152. 

Ȧbeḥ (?)-en-χepeś.

152*. 

Se-user-en-Rā, son of the Sun, Khian.

153. 

Ȧpepȧ.

DYNASTY XVI., "SHEPHERD KINGS."

154. 

Neter nefer Beautiful god, Āa-ȧb-taiu-Rā, son of the Sun, Ȧpepȧ.

or neter nefer Āa-qenen-Rā.

DYNASTY XVII., FROM THEBES.

155. 

Seqenen-Rā, son of the Sun, Tau-āa.

156. 

Seqenen-Rā, son of the Sun, Tau-āa-āa.

157. 

Seqenen-Rā, son of the Sun, Tau-āa-qen.

158. 

Uat'-χeper-Rā, son of the Sun, Kames.

159. 

Suten ḥemt — Royal wife. Āāh-ḥetep.

160. 

Āāh-mes-se-pa-āri.

Dynasty XVIII., from Thebes, B.C. 1700.

161. 

Neb-peḥ-peḥ-Rā, son of the Sun, Āāḥmes. (Amāsis I.)

162. 

Neter ḥemt — Divine wife. Āāh-mes-nefert-āri.

163. 

Ser-ka-Rā, son of the Sun, Āmen-ḥetep. (Amenophis I.)

164. 

Āa-χeper-ka-Rā, son of the Sun, Teḥuti-mes. (Thothmes I.)

165. 

Āa-χeper-en-Rā, son of the Sun, Nefer-χāu-Teḥuti-mes. (Thothmes II.)

166. 

Māt-ka-Rā, son of the Sun, Ḥāt-shepset-χnem-Ȧmen. (Queen Hatshepsu.)

167. 

Men-χeper-Rā, son of the Sun, Teḥuti-mes. (Thothmes III.)

168. 

Āa-χeperu-Rā, son of the Sun, Ȧmen-ḥetep neter ḥeq Ȧnnu. (Amenophis II.)

169. 

Men-χeperu-Rā, son of the Sun, Teḥuti-mes χā-χāu. (Thothmes IV.)

170. 

Neb-māt-Rā, son of the Sun, Ȧmen-ḥetep ḥeq-Uast. (Amenophis III.)

171. 

Suten ḥemt θi.

(The Mesopotamian wife of Amenophis III.).

172. 

Nefer-χeperu-Rā-uā-en-Rā,, son of the Sun, Ȧmen-ḥetep neter ḥeq Uast (Amenophis IV.).

or χu-en-Ȧten.

173. 

Suten ḥemt urt Nefer neferu-àten Neferti-iθ.
Royal wife, great lady.

174. 

Ānχ-χeperu-Rā, son of the Sun, Seāa-ka-neχt-χeperu-Rā

175. 

Neb-χeperu-Rā, son of the Sun, Tut-ānχ-Àmen ḥeq Ànnu resu (?)

176. 

χeper-χeperu-māt-àri-Rā, son of the Sun, Atf-neter Ài neter ḥeq Uast.

177. 

Ser-χeperu-Rā-setep-en-Rā, son of the Sun, Àmen-meri-en Ḥeru-em-ḥeb.

Dynasty XIX., from Thebes, B.C. 1400.

178. 

Men-peḥtet-Rā, son of the Sun, Rā-messu.
(Rameses I.)

179. 

Men-māt-Rā, son of the Sun, Ptaḥ-meri-en-Seti.
(Seti I.)

180. 

Usr-māt-Rā setep-en-Rā, son of the Sun, Rā-messu-meri-Àmen.
(Rameses II.)

181. 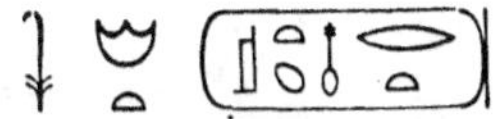

Suten ḥemt Ȧuset-nefert.
Royal wife.

182. 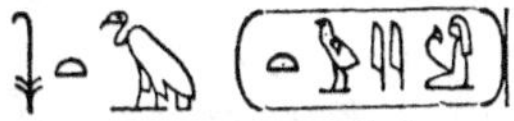

Suten mut Tui.
Royal mother.

183. 

Ba-Rā-meri-en-Ȧmen, son of the Sun, Ptaḥ-meri-en-ḥetep-ḥer-māt.
(Meneptah I.)

184. 

Men-mȧ-Rȧ setep-en-Rā, son of the Sun, Ȧmen-meses-ḥeq-Uast.
(Amen-meses.)

185. 

Usr-χeperu-Rā meri-Ȧmen, son of the Sun, Seti-meri-en-Ptaḥ.
(Seti II).

186. 

χu-en-Rā setep-en-Rā, son of the Sun, Ptaḥ-meri-en-se-Ptaḥ.
(Meneptah II.)

187. 

Usr-χāu-Rā setep-en-Rā meri-Ȧmen, son of the Sun, Rā-meri Ȧmen-merer Set-neχt.
(Set-Neχt.)

DYNASTY XX., FROM THEBES, B.C. 1200.

188. 

Usr-māt-Rā-meri-Ȧmen, son of the Sun, Rā-meses-ḥeq-Annu.
(Rameses III.)

189. 

Usr-māt-Rā setep-en-Ȧmen, son of the Sun, Rā-meses-meri-Ȧmen-Rā ḥeq māt. (Rameses IV.)

190. 

Usr-māt-Rā s-χeper-en-Rā, son of the Sun, Rā-mes-meri-Ȧmen-Ȧmen suten-f. (Rameses V.)

191. 

Rā-Ȧmen-māt-meri-neb, son of the Sun, Rā-Ȧmen-meses neter ḥeq Ȧnnu. (Rameses VI.)

192. 

Rā-usr-Ȧmen-meri-setep-en-Rā, son of the Sun, Rā-Ȧmen-meses-tȧ neter-ḥeq-Ȧnnu. (Rameses VII.)

193. 

Rā-māt-usr-χu-en-Ȧmen, son of the Sun, Rā-Ȧmen-meses-meri-Ȧmen. (Rameses VIII.)

194. 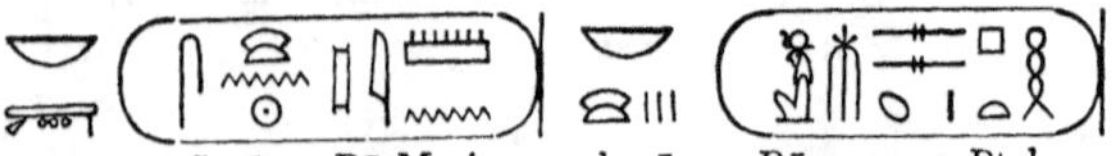

Neb ta Lord of the land, S-χā-en-Rā Meri-Ȧmen, neb χāu lord of crowns, Rāmeses-se-Ptaḥ. (Rameses IX.)

195. 

Nefer-kau-Rā setep-en-Rā, son of the Sun, Rā-meses-merer-Ȧmen-χā-Uast (?). (Rameses X.)

196. 

Rā-χeper-māt setep-en-Rā, son of the Sun, Rā-mes suten (?) Åmen. (Rameses XI.)

197. 

Usr-māt-Rā setep-nu-Rā. son of the Sun, Åmen mer-Rā-meses. (Rameses XII.)

198. 

Men-māt-Rā setep-en-Rā, son of the Sun, Rā-meses-merer-Åmen χā Uast (?) neter ḥeq Ånnu. (Rameses XIII.)

DYNASTY XXI., FROM TANIS, B.C. 1100.

I.

199. 

Rā-neter-χeper setep-en-Åmen, son of the Sun, Se-Åmen meri-Rā. (Se-Åmen.)

200. 

Rā-āa-χeper setep-en-Åmen, son of the Sun, Åmen-meri Pa-seb-χā-nu. (Pasebχānu I.)

201. 

Āa-seḥ-Rā, son of the Sun, Nefer-ka-Rā-meri-Åmen.

202. 

User-Maāt-Rā setep-en-Åmen, son of the Sun, Meri-Åmen Åmen-em-åpt. (Amenemapt.)

203. 

Ḥet′ ḥeq . . . . son of the Sun, Meri-Åmen Pa-seb-χā-nu. (Pasebχānu II.)

DYNASTY XXI., FROM THEBES, B.C. 1100.

II.

204. 

Neter-ḥen-ṭep en-Åmen, Prophet first of Amen, son of the Sun, Ḥer-Ḥeru-se-Åmen. (Ḥer-Ḥeru.)

205. 

Neter ḥen ṭep en Åmen Pa - ānχ

Prophet first of Åmen Pa - ānχ.

206. 

Pai-net′em (I).

207. 

χeper-χā-Rā setep-en-Åmen, son of the Sun, Åmen-meri-Pai-net′em (II).

208. 

Suten mut Ḥent-taiu.

Royal mother, Ḥent - taiu.

209. 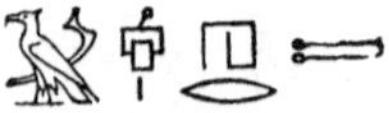

Prophet first of Amen, Masaherθ.

210. 

Prophet first, Men-χeper-Rā, {child Royal, or son of King.} Åmen-meri Pai-net′ em.

211. 

Neter ḥen ṭep en Āmen-Rā, Pai-net'em (III.)
Prophet first of Āmen-Rā.

212. 

Neter ḥemt en Āmen suten sat, suten ḥemt Māt-ka-Rā.
Divine wife of Āmen, royal daughter, royal wife.

DYNASTY XXII., FROM BUBASTIS, B.C. 966.

213. 

χeper-ḥet'-Rā setep-en-Ra, son of the Sun, Āmen-meri-Shashanq. (Shashanq I.)

214. 

χerp-χeper-Ra setep-en-Rā, son of the Sun, Āmen-meri Uasārken. (Osorkon I.)

215. 

Usr-Maāt-Rā, son of the Sun, Thekeleth.

216. 

Rā-usr-māt setep-en-Āmen, son of the Sun, Āmen-meri sa-Bast Uasārken. (Osorkon II.)

217. 

χeper-seχem-Rā setep-en-Āmen, son of the Sun, Āmen-Rā-meri Shash[anq]. (Shashanq II.)

218. 

Ḥet'-Rā-setep-en-Åmen neter ḥeq Uast, son of the Sun, Åmen-meri Auset-meri θekeleθ. (Takeleth II.)

219. 

Usr-māt-Rā setep-en-Rā, son of the Sun, Åmen-meri-Shashanq ḥeq neter Ånnu. (Shashanq III.)

220. 

Usr-māt-Rā setep-en-Åmen, son of the Sun, Åmen-meri Pa-mȧi. (Pa-mai.)

221. 

Āa-χeper-Rā son of the Sun, Śaśanq. (Shashanq IV.)

Dynasty XXIII., from Tanis, b.c. 766.

222. 

Se-her-ȧb-Rā, son of the Sun, Peṭā-se-Bast.

223. 

Āa-χeper-Rā setep-en-Åmen, son of the Sun, Rā-Åmen-meri Uasarkenȧ. (Osorkon III.)

Dynasty XXIV., from Sais, b.c. 733.

224. 

Uaḥ-ka-Rā, son of the Sun, Bakenrenf.

Dynasty XXIV., from Ethiopia, b.c. 733.

225. 

Suten King Kasta. Kashta.

226. 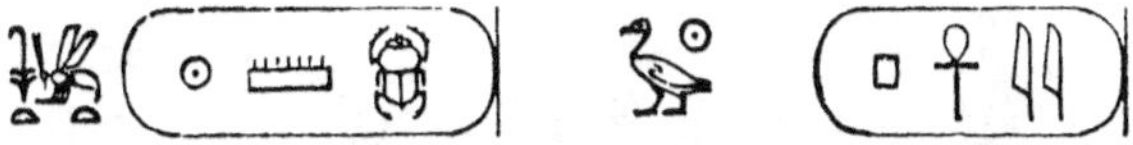

Men-χeper-Rā, son of the Sun, P-ānχi.

227. 

Àmen-meri P-ānχi, son of the Sun, P-ānχi.

DYNASTY XXV., FROM ETHIOPIA, B.C. 700.

228. 

Nefer-ka-Rā, son of the Sun, Shabaka.
(Sabaco.)

229. 

Ṭeṭ-kau-Rā, son of the Sun, Shabataka.

230. 

Rā-nefer-tem-χu, son of the Sun, Tahrq.
(Tirhakah.)

231. 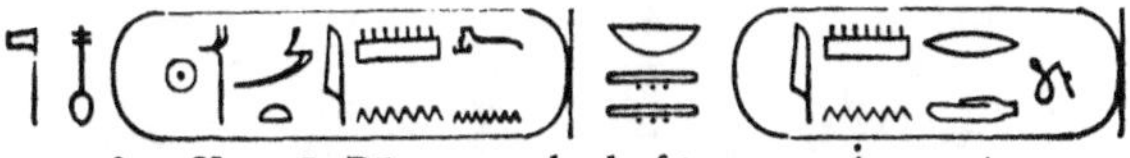

Neter nefer God beautiful, Usr-māt-Rā setep-en-Àmen, lord of two lands, Àmenruṭ.

DYNASTY XXVI., FROM SAIS, B.C. 666.

232. 

Uaḥ-àb-Rā, son of the Sun, Psemθek.
(Psammetichus I.)

233. 

Nem-àb-Rā, son of the Sun, Nekau.
(Necho II.)

234. 

Nefer-àb-Rā, son of the Sun, Psemθek.
(Psammetichus II.)

235. 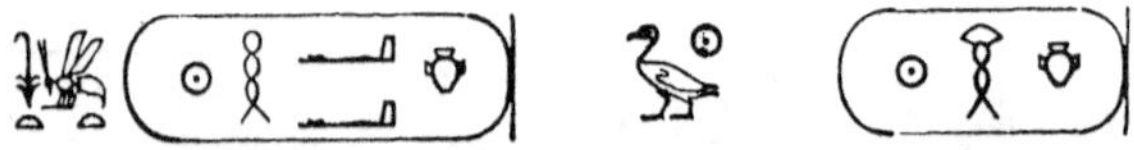

Ḥāā-àb-Rā, son of the Sun, Uaḥ-àb-Rā.
(Apries.)

236. 

χnem-àb-Rā, son of the Sun, Åḥmes-se-net.
(Amāsis II.)

237. 

Ānχ-ka-en-Rā, son of the Sun, Psemθek.
(Psammetichus III.)

Dynasty XXVII. (Persian), B.C. 527.

238. 

Mesuθ-Rā, son of the Sun, Kembàθet.
(Cambyses.)

239. 

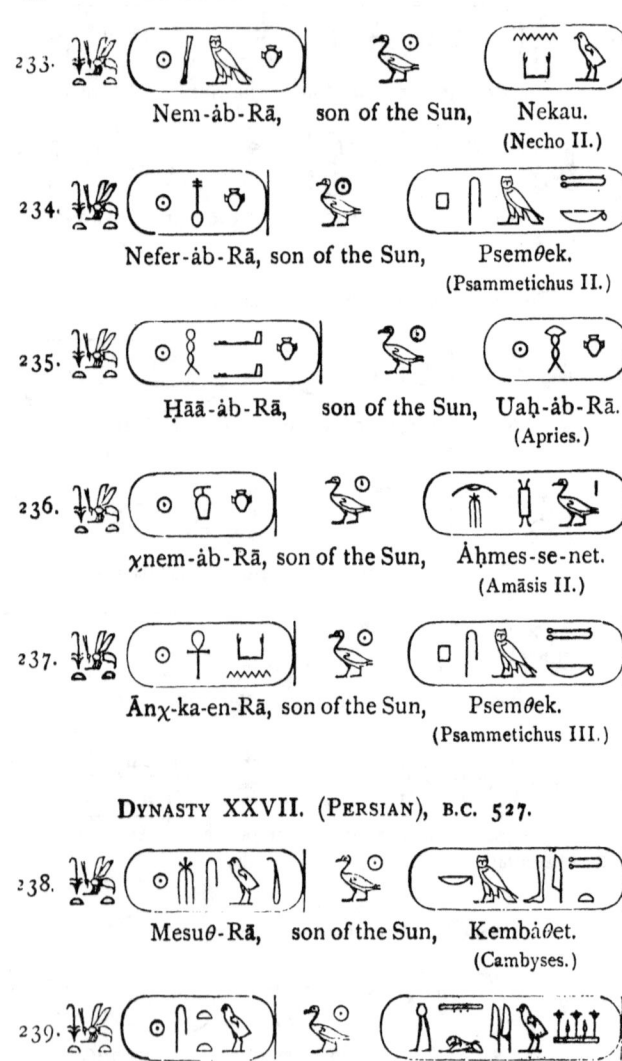

Settu-Rā. son of the Sun, Àntariusha.
(Darius Hystaspes.)

240. 

Lord of two lands, χshaiarsha.
(Xerxes the Great.)

241. 

Artaχshashas.
(Artaxerxes.)

242. 

Rā-meri-Åmen, son of the Sun, Ånθeriruṭsha.
(Darius Xerxes.)

DYNASTY XXVIII., FROM SAIS.

243. 

Senen-en-Ptaḥ-Mentu-setep, son of the Sun, (χabbesha.)

DYNASTY XXIX., FROM MENDES, B.C. 399.

244. 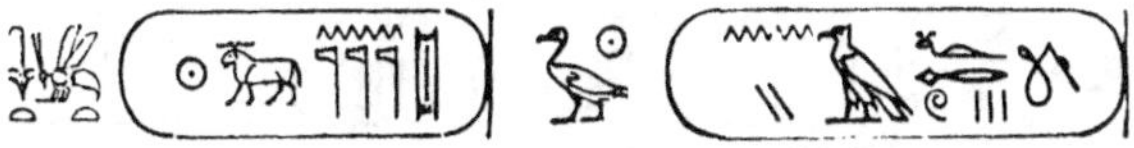

Ba-en-Rā neteru-meri, son of the Sun, Niafāaaruṭ.

245. 

χnem-māt-Rā, son of the Sun, Haḳer.

246. 

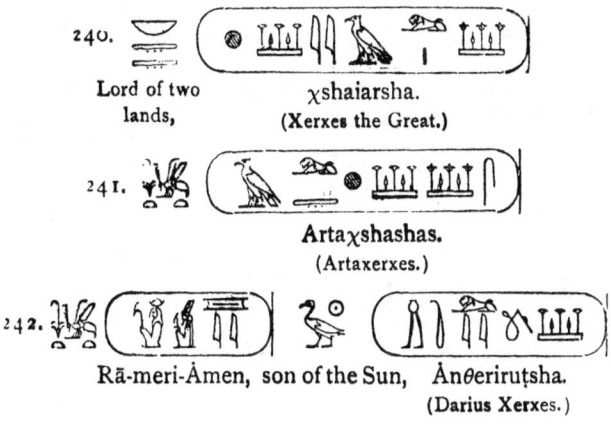

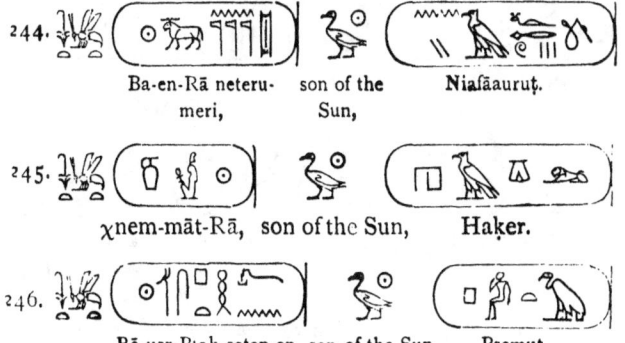

Rā-usr-Ptaḥ-setep-en, son of the Sun, Psemut.

DYNASTY XXX., FROM SEBENNYTUS, B.C. 378.

247. 

S-net'em-ȧb-Rā setep-en-Ȧmen, son of the Sun, Neχt-Ḥeru-ḥebt-meri-Ȧmen. (Nectanebus I.)

248. 

χeper-ka-Rā, son of the Sun, Neχt-neb-f. (Nectanebus II.)

DYNASTY XXXI.,* PERSIANS.

DYNASTY XXXII., MACEDONIANS, B.C. 332.

249. 

Setep-en-Rā-meri-Ȧmen, son of the sun, Aleksȧnṭres (Alexander the Great.)

250. 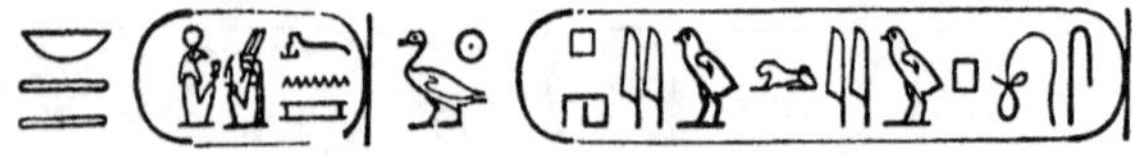

neb taiu Setep-en-Rā-meri-Ȧmen, son of the Sun, Phiuliupuas (Philip Aridaeus.)

251. 

Rā-qa-ȧb-setep-en-Ȧmen, son of the Sun. Aleksȧnṭres. (Alexander IV.)

* The word "dynasty" is retained here for convenience of classification.

DYNASTY XXXIII., PTOLEMIES, B.C. 305.

252. 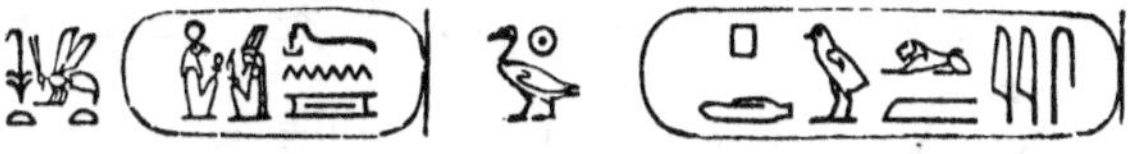

Setep-en-Rā-meri-Ȧmen, son of the Sun, Pṭulmis (Ptolemy I. Soter I.)

253. 

Neter mut, Bareniḳet.
Divine Mother (Berenice I.)

254. 

Rā-usr-ka-meri-Ȧmen, son of the Sun, Ptulmis (Ptolemy II. Philadelphus.)

255. 

Sutenet set suten sent suten ḥemt neb taiu Ȧrsanat
Royal daughter, royal sister, royal wife, lady of the two lands (Arsinoë)

256. 

Suten set suten sent Pilatra.
Royal daughter, royal sister (Philotera).

257. 

Neteru-senu-uā-en-Rā-setep-Ȧmen-χerp (?)-en-ānχ, son of the Sun,

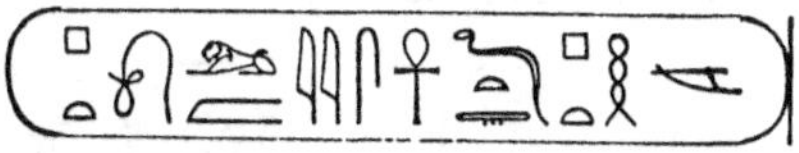

Ptualmis ānχ t'etta Ptaḥ meri
Ptolemy (III. Euergetes I.), living for ever, beloved of Ptah.

258. 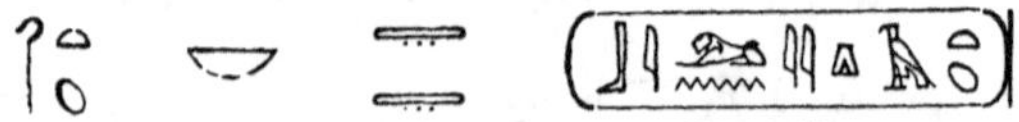

Ḥeqt nebt taiu, Bārenikạt

Princess, lady of the two lands, (Berenice II.)

259. 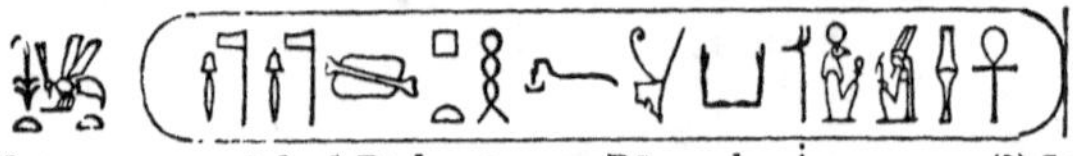

Neteru-menχ-uā-[en]-Ptaḥ-setep-en-Rā-usr-ka-Āmen-χerp (?) ānχ,

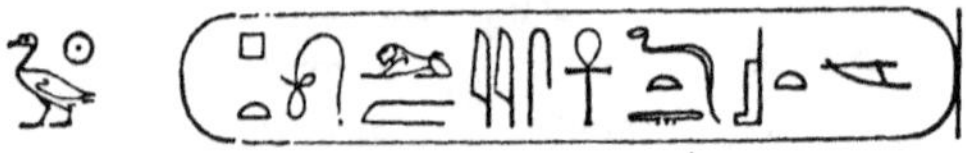

son of the Sun Ptualmis ānχ t'etta Āuset meri

Ptolemy (IV. Philopator,) living for ever, beloved of Isis.

260. 

Suten set suten sent ḥemt urt nebt taiu

Royal daughter, royal sister, wife, great lady, lady of the two lands

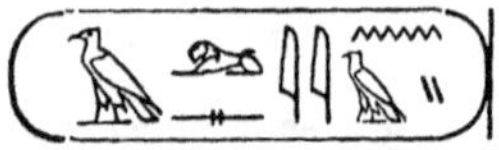

Arsinai.

Arsinoë (III., wife of Philopator I.)

261. 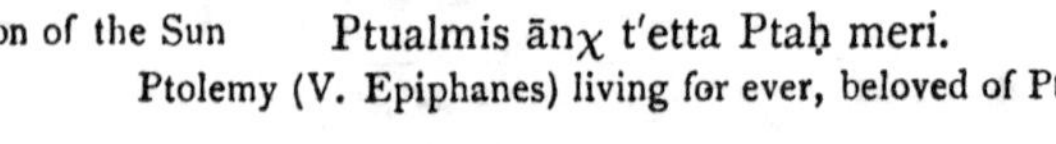

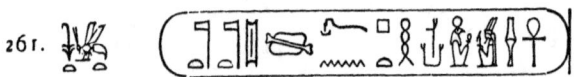

Neteru-meri-uā-en-Ptaḥ-setep-Rā-usr-ka-Āmen-χerp-ānχ,

son of the Sun Ptualmis ānχ t'etta Ptaḥ meri.

Ptolemy (V. Epiphanes) living for ever, beloved of Ptaḥ.

262. Ptolemy VI. Eupator, wanting.

263.

Suten set sen ḥemt Qlauapeṭrat.

Royal daughter, sister, wife, (Cleopatra I).

264. 

Neteru-χu (?)-uā-Ptaḥ-χeper-setep-en-Rā-Ȧmen-ȧri-māt (?),

son of the Sun. Ptualmis ānχ t'etta Ptaḥ meri.

Ptolemy (VII. Philometer I.), living for ever, beloved of Ptaḥ.

265. 

Sutenet set suten sent ḥemt suten mut neb taiu

Royal daughter, royal sister, wife, royal mother, lady of the two lands,

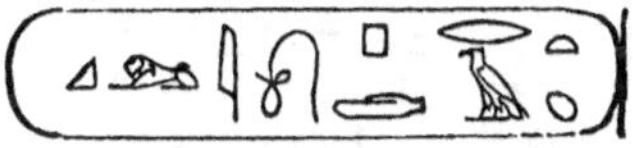

Qlȧuapeṭrat.

(Cleopatra II. wife of Philometor I.).

266. Ptolemy VIII. Philopator II. wanting.

267. 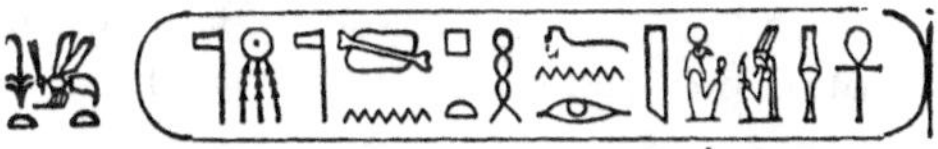

Neteru-χu (?)-uā-en-Ptaḥ-setep-en-Rā-Ȧmen-ȧri-māt χerp ānχ

son of the Sun. Ptualmis ānχ t'etta Ptaḥ meri.

Ptolemy (IX. Euergetes II.), living for ever, beloved of Ptaḥ.

268. 

Suten net

King of North and South, lord of two lands,

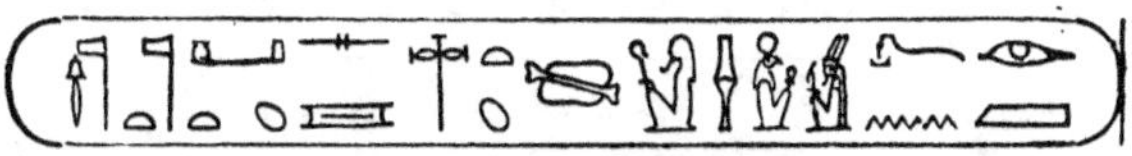

Neteru-menχ-māt-s-meri-net-uā-Ptaḥ-χerp (?)-setep-en-Rā Ȧmen-ȧri-māt.

Rā-se neb χāu — Ptualmis ānχ t'etta Ptaḥ meri.

Son of the Sun, lord of diadems, — Ptolemy X. (Soter II. Philometor II.).

269. 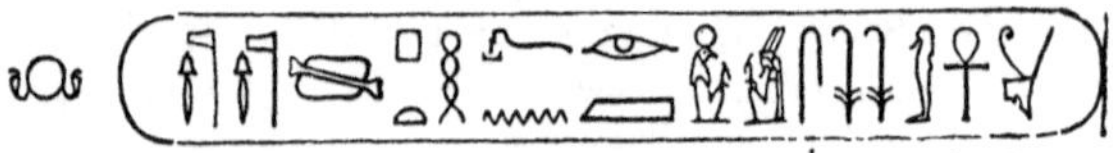

Suten net, — Neteru-menχ-uā-Ptaḥ-setep-en-Rā-Åmen-ȧri-māt-senen-Ptaḥ-ānχ-en,

King of North and South,

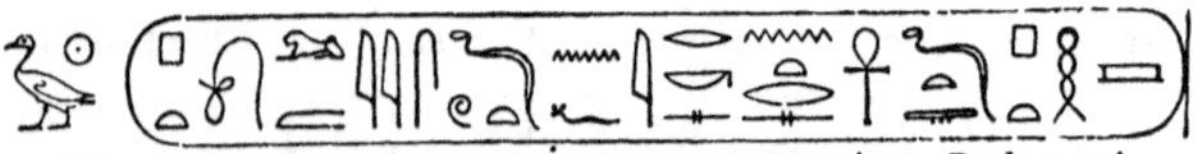

son of the Sun. — Ptualmis t'etu-nef Åleksentres ānχ t'etta Ptaḥ meri

Ptolemy (XI.) called is he Alexander, living for ever, beloved of Ptaḥ.

270. 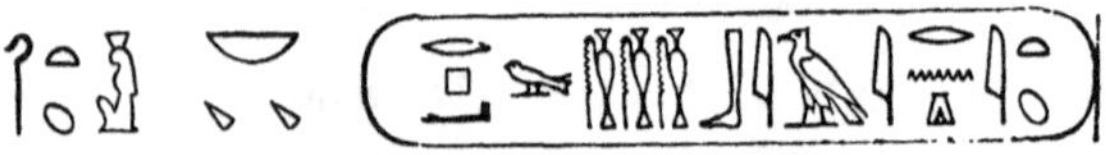

Ḥeqt neb taiu — Erpā-ur-qebḥ-Bȧaȧrenekȧt.

Princess, lady of two lands, — Berenice (III.)

271. Ptolemy XII. (Alexander II.), wanting.

272. 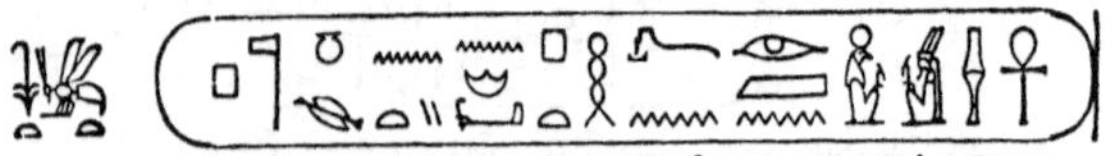

P-neter-n-uā-enti-neḥem-Ptaḥ-setep-en-ȧri-māt-en-Rā-Åmen-χerp-ānχ

son of the Sun. — Ptualmis ānχ t'etta Ptaḥ Åuset meri.

Ptolemy (XIII.), living for ever, beloved of Isis and Ptaḥ.

273. 

Neb taiu — Qlapeṭrat t'eṭtu-nes Ṭrapenet.

Lady of two lands, — Cleopatra (V.), called is she Tryphaena.

274. 

Ḥeqt taiu Qluapeter.

Queen of two lands, Cleopatra (VI.)

275. 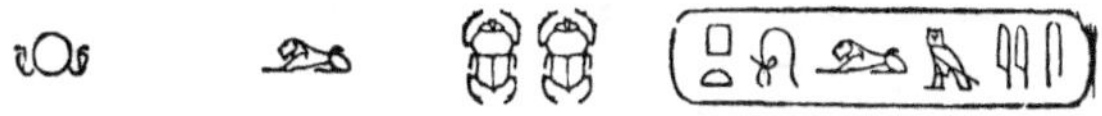

Suten net neb taiu Ptualmis.

King of North and South, lord of two lands, Ptolemy (XIV.)

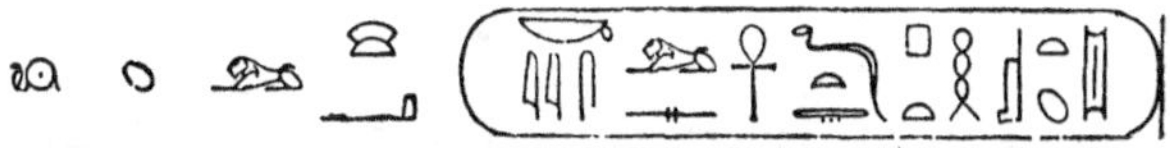

Rā se neb χāā Kiseres ānχ t'etta Ptaḥ Åuset meri

son of the Sun, lord of diadems, Cæsar, living for ever, of Ptaḥ and Isis beloved.

DYNASTY XXXIV ROMAN EMPERORS. B.C. 27.

276. 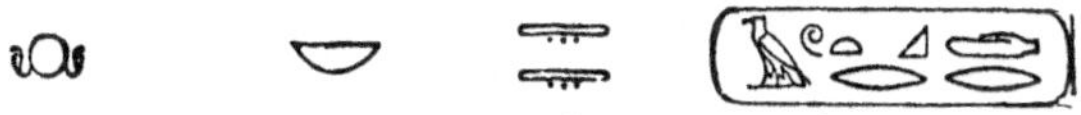

Suten net neb taiu Auteqreṭer

King of North and South, lord of two lands, Autocrator,

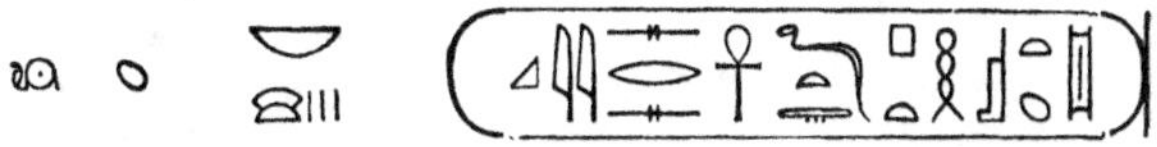

Rā se neb χāu Kiseres ānχ t'etta Ptaḥ Åuset meri

Sun's son, lord of crowns. Cæsar (Augustus), living for ever, of Ptaḥ and Isis beloved.

277. 

Suten net neb taiu Auteqreṭer Rā se neb χāu

Autocrator, son of the Sun, lord of diadems,

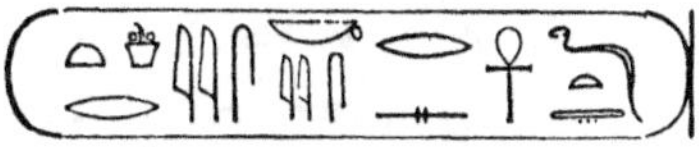

Tebaris Kiseres ānχ t'etta

Tiberius Cæsar living for ever.

278. 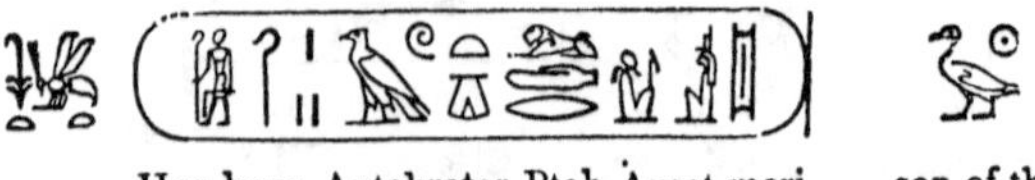

Ḥeq ḥequ Auteḳreṭer Ptaḥ Ȧuset-meri — son of the Sun.
King of kings, Autocrator, of Ptaḥ and Isis beloved, — Sun.

Qais Kaiseres Kermeniqis.
Gaius (Caligula) Cæsar Germanicus.

279. 

Suten net neb taiu — Auteqreṭer Kiseres
Autocrator Cæsar,

Rā se neb χāu — Qlutes Ṭibaresa.
Sun's son, lord of crowns, — Claudius Tiberius.

280. 

neb taiu — Ḥeq ḥequ-setep-en-Ȧuset meri Ptaḥ
King of North and South, — lord of two lands, — Ruler of rulers, chosen one of Isis, beloved of Ptaḥ.

se Rā — neb χāu — Auteḳreṭer Anrȧni.
Sun's son, — lord of crowns, — (Autocrator Nero).

281. 

Merqes Auθunes (Marcus Otho).

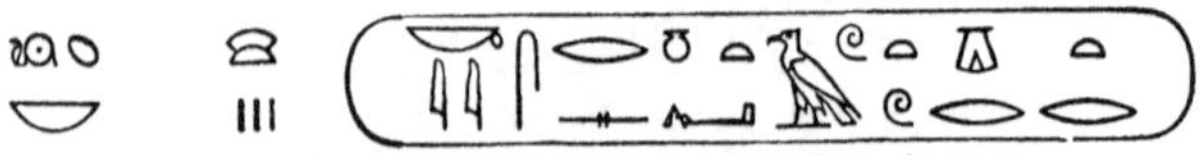

Sun's son, — lord of crowns, — Kiseres ent χu Autuḳreter.
Cæsar he who defendeth Autocrator.

282. Vitellius (wanting).

283. 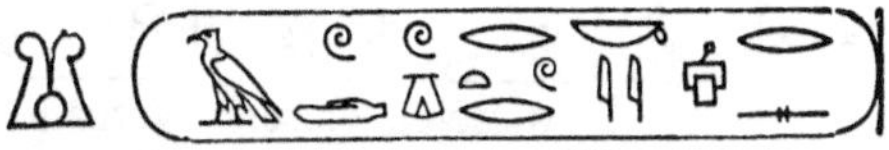

Suten net (?) Auṭuḳretur Kisares
Autocrator Cæsar

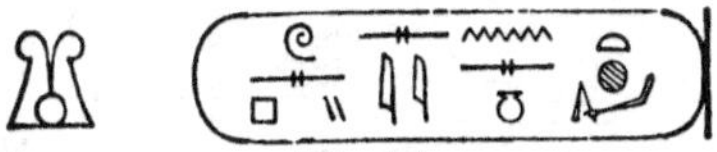

Suten net (?) Uspisines ent χu
Vespasianus, he who defendeth.

284. 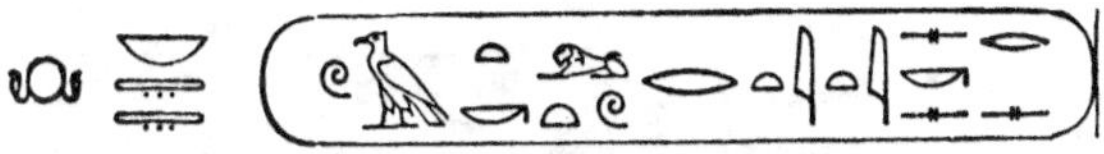

Autekretur Tetis Keseres
Autocrator Titus Cæsar,

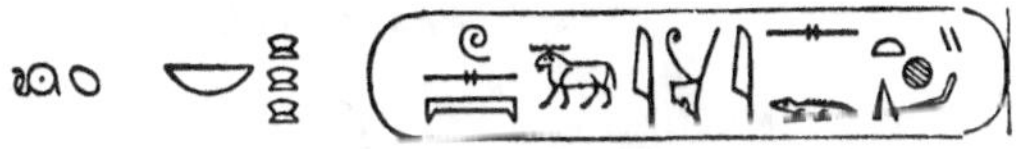

Sun's son, lord of crowns, Uspesines ent χu
Vespasianus, he who defendeth.

285. 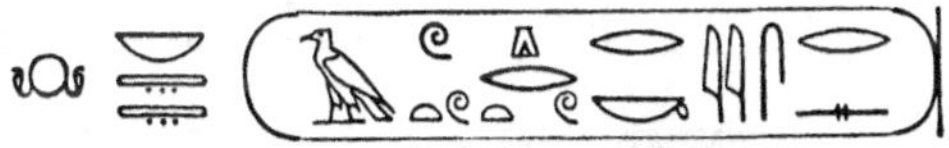

Autuḳretur Kiseres
Autocrator Cæsar,

Sun's son, lord of crowns, Tumetines ent χu
Domitianus, he who defendeth.

286 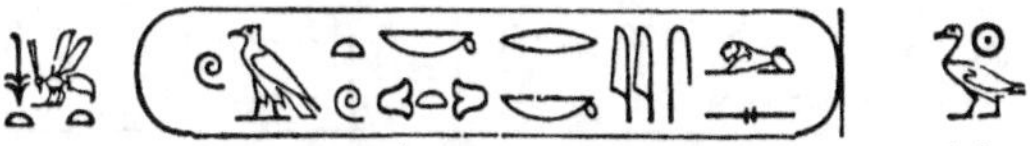

Autukreter Kiseres
Autocrator Cæsar,

son of the Sun,

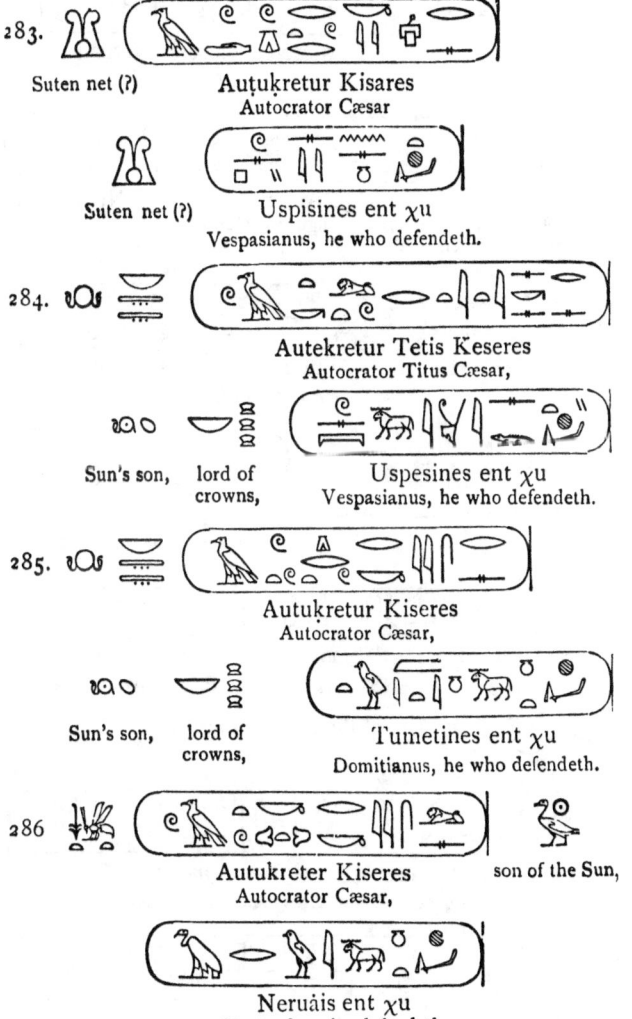

Neruȧis ent χu
Nerva, he who defendeth.

287. 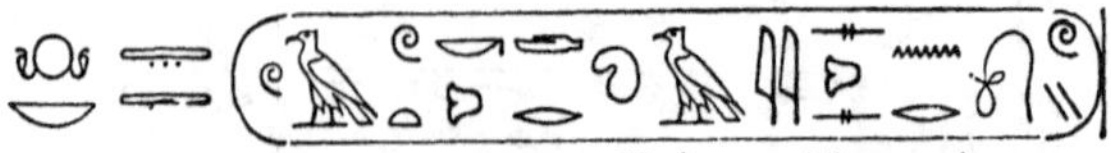

Autukreṭer Kaiseres Neruaui
Autocrator Cæsar Nerva,

the Sun's son, lord of crowns, Trāianes ent χu Arsut Kermineqsa Nteḳiques.
Trajan, he who defendeth, (Augustus) Germanicus Dacicus.

288. 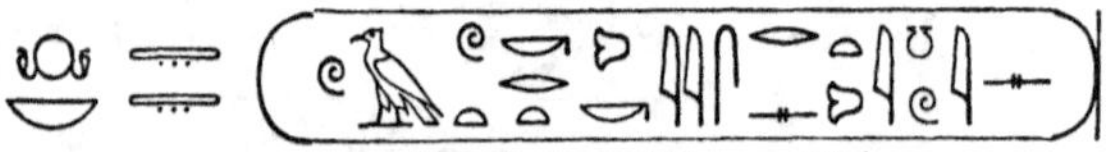

Autukreter Kiseres Trinus
Autocrator Cæsar Trajan,

 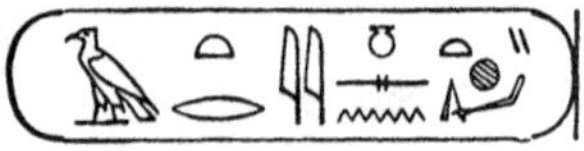

the Sun's son, lord of crowns. Atrines ent χu.
Hadrian, he who defendeth.

289. 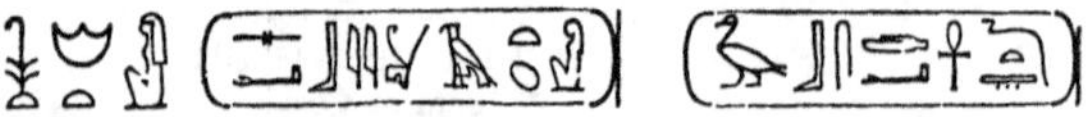

Suten ḥemt Sābinat Sebesṭā ānχ t'etta.
Royal wife, Sabina, Sebaste living for ever.

290. 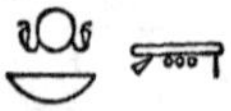 King of the North and South, lord of the world,

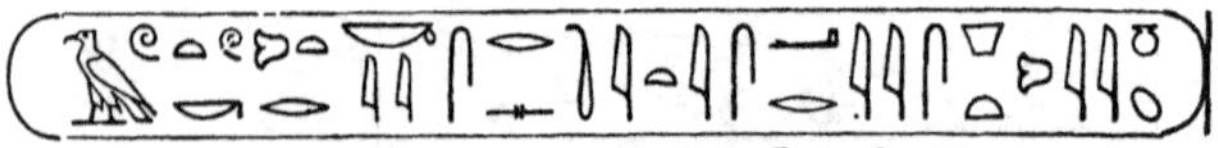

Autukreter Kiseres Θites Ālis Ātrins
Autocrator Cæsar Titus Aelius Hadrianus,

 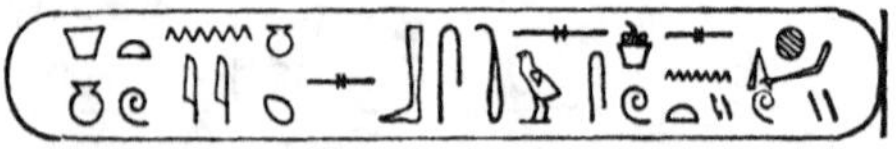

the Sun's son, lord of crowns. Āntunines Sebesθesus Baus enti χui.
Antoninus Augustus Pius, he who defendeth.

291. 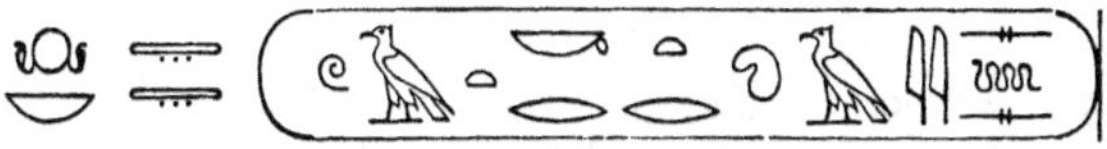

Autekreter Kaiseres
Autocrator Cæsar,

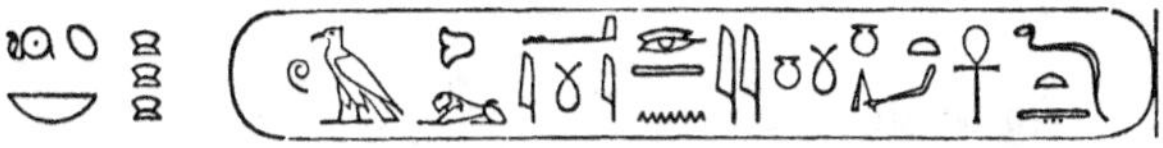

the Sun's son, lord of crowns, Aurelāis Antinines ent χu ānχ t'etta
Aurelius Antoninus, he who defendeth, living for ever.

292. 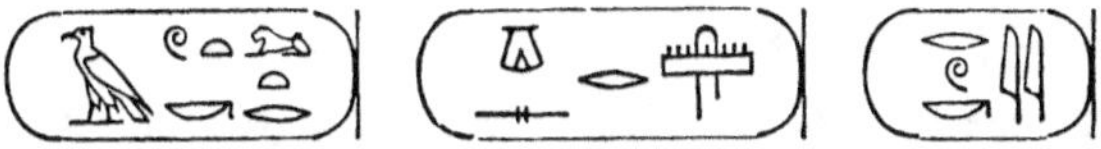

Autekreter — Ḳesers — Luki
Autocrator — Cæsar — Lucius

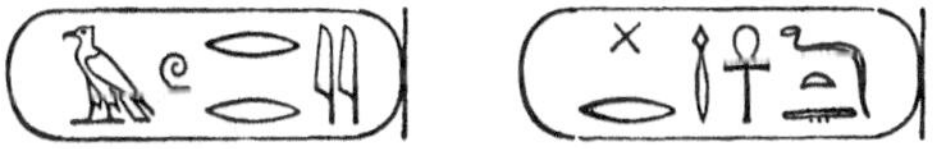

Aulli — Uarā ānχ 'tetta
Aelius — Verus, living for ever.

293. 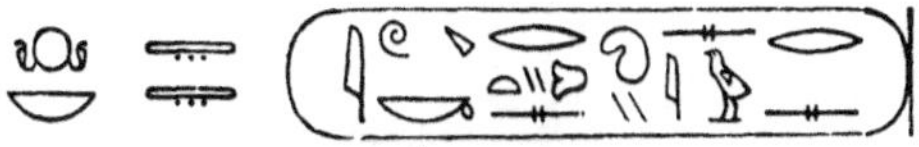

Åutekretirs Kisåures
Autocrator Cæsar,

the Sun's son, lord of crowns, Kāmṭāus Ā-en-ta-nins enti χu.
Commodus. Antoninus, he who defendeth.

294. Autocrator Cæsar 

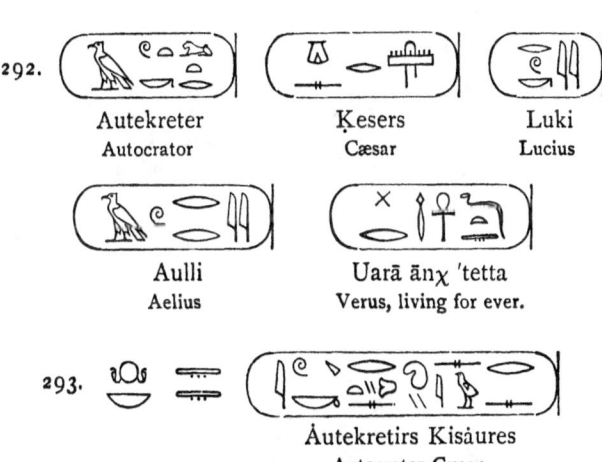

Sāuris enti χu.
Severus, he who defendeth

295. Autocrator Cæsar 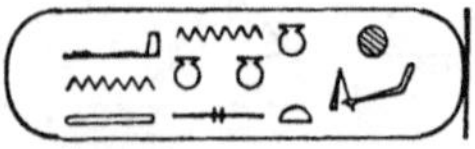

Āntanenes ent χu.

Antoninus [Caracalla] he who defendeth.

296. Autocrator Cæsar 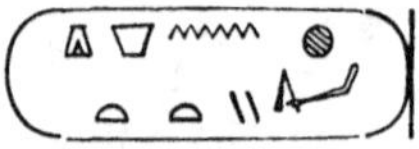

Ḳāt enti χu.

Geta he who defendeth.

297. Autocrator Cæsar 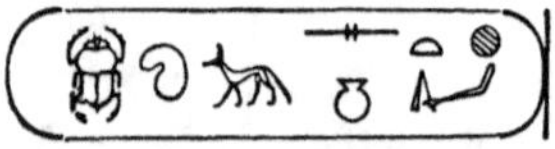

Taksas enti χu.

Decius he who defendeth.

THE EGYPTIAN MUSEUM AT GÎZEH.

The Khedivial collection of Egyptian antiquities, formerly exhibited in the Museum at Bûlâḳ, is now arranged in a large number of rooms in the **Palace at Gîzeh**, a building which is, in most ways, unsuitable for the purpose. This edifice, which is pleasantly situated in spacious grounds close to the river, was opened by H.H. the Khedive on January 12, 1890.

For many years the condition and arrangement of the antiquities exhibited in the Bûlâḳ and Gîzeh Museums have been notorious subjects for complaint on the part of the Egyptologist and the tourist. The Egyptologist could obtain no trustworthy information about the antiquities which he knew were being acquired year by year, and the tourist visited the collection time after time and winter after winter, and went away on each occasion feeling that nothing had been done to help him to understand the importance of a number of objects, which guide-books and experts told him were famous and of the greatest value to the artist, ethnographer, philologist, and historian. That marvellous man Mariette had gathered together from all parts a series of unique specimens of Egyptian sculpture and art of the earliest dynasties, and had, owing to the parsimony of the Egyptian government, been obliged to house them in the buildings of an old post-office at Bûlâḳ, and thither, for several years, the curious of all nations bent their steps. As his great excavations went on, the collection at Bûlâḳ became larger, until at last it was found necessary to store coffins, sarcophagi, mummies, stelæ, stone statues, *etc.*, in the sheds attached to the buildings like boxes of preserved meats in a grocer's shop. With the arrival of the Dêr el-Baḥari mummies and coffins the crowding of objects became greater, for the civilized world demanded that a

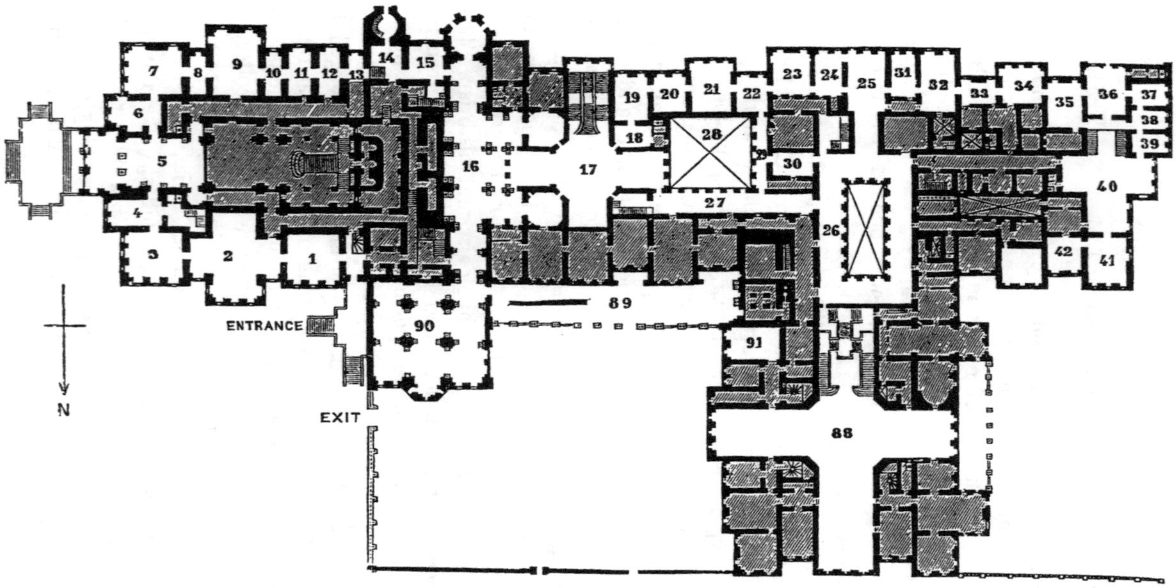

PLAN OF THE GROUND FLOOR OF THE GÎZEH MUSEUM.

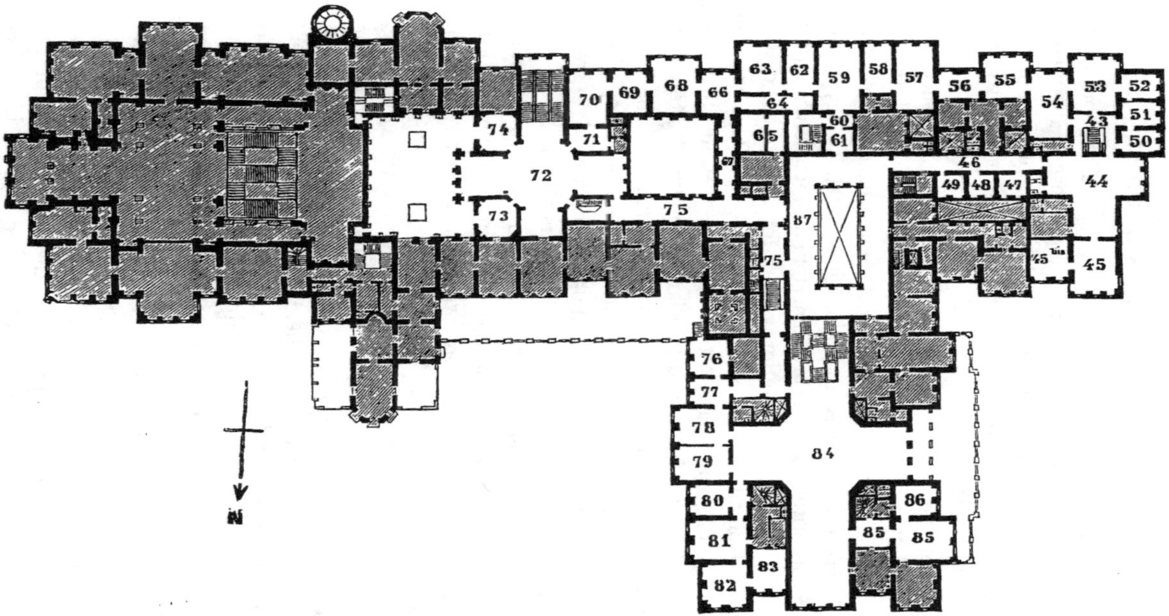

Plan of the First Floor of the Gîzeh Museum.

place of honour should be afforded to the well-preserved mummy of Rameses the Great, and to those of the mighty kings who were his ancestors and successors. For one object laid by in the "magazine" two new ones arrived to claim its place.

Under the beneficent rule of M. Maspero, the successor of Mariette in the direction of the Museum, and that of E. Brugsch Bey, Mariette's colleague, excavations were undertaken by natives and others in all parts of Egypt, and the authorities of the Museum found themselves called upon to provide exhibition rooms for antiquities of the Greek, Roman, Arabic, and Coptic periods. This was an impossibility, and at last it became certain that the antiquities must be moved to a larger building. Moreover, many people viewed with alarm the situation of the Bûlâḳ Museum itself. On the one side flowed the Nile, which more than once during the inundation threatened to sweep the whole building away, and the waters of which, on one occasion, actually entered the courtyard; and on the other were a number of warehouses of the flimsiest construction, filled with inflammable stores which might at any moment catch fire and burn down the Museum. In the early winter mornings the building was often full of the white, clinging, drenching mist which is common along the banks of the river, and it was no rare thing to see water trickling down inside the glass cases which held the mummies of the great kings of Egypt. With all its faults, however, there was much to be said for the old Bûlâḳ Museum, and the arrangement of the antiquities therein. Every important object was numbered, and the excellent catalogue of M. Maspero gave the visitor a great deal of information about the antiquities. Had M. Maspero remained in Egypt he would, no doubt, have added to his catalogue, and every important change in the arrangement of the rooms would have been duly chronicled. After his retirement, however, a policy was inaugurated which is difficult either to understand or describe. The influx of objects during Maspero's reign at Bûlâḳ was great—so great that it would have been impossible for him to incorporate them all, even if he had had the necessary space; we now know that many of them were exceedingly fine, yet after his departure no attempt was made to exhibit them. This might, in many cases, have been done easily, for poor specimens could have been relegated to the "magazine," and fine ones exhibited in their stead.

With the increase of accommodation for tourists and of facilities for travelling after the occupation of Egypt by the British, public opinion grew and waxed strong, and the advisers of the late Khedive found it necessary to consider the task of the removal of the Egyptian antiquities from Bûlâḳ to a safer and larger resting-place. The Egyptian Government had no funds at their disposal with which to build a new Museum, and after much discussion it was decided to transfer the antiquities to the large palace at Gîzeh, which is said to have cost five millions sterling. The usual irresponsible opposition to the scheme was offered by those who should have known better, but there seems to be little doubt that this decision was the best that could have been arrived at under the circumstances in which the Egyptian Government was placed. The fabric of the Gîzeh palace is flimsy, and the appearance of the building is not that which those who are acquainted with European museums are accustomed to associate with Egyptian antiquities; it is, nevertheless, a large building, and the fact that it would cost nothing must have been a great inducement to transform the palace into a museum. Much was said at first about danger to the antiquities from fire, but it is quite certain that the danger from fire at Bûlâḳ was greater than it is at Gîzeh. Some excellent alterations in the building and arrangements to prevent fire were made by Sir Francis Grenfell, and now that the further contemplated precautions have been taken the Museum is as safe from fire as any building, half French, half Oriental, can be in the East. The specially arranged fire-proof building which is being constructed in Cairo will more effectually protect the priceless relics of a great early civilization. Here the antiquities will be better arranged and better guarded in every way, and it is probable that the income which will be derived from the increased number of visits made by tourists, will in a short time form an important contribution towards the original outlay.

The decision to remove the antiquities from Bûlâḳ to Gîzeh was carried out in 1889 in the most praiseworthy manner. Gangs of men toiled from morning till night, and behind the trucks or carts containing the most precious objects M. Grébaut, the director of the Museum, and Brugsch Bey might be seen directing the workmen. During the hottest months of the summer and during the hottest hours of the day, under an exposure to the sun such as the ancient Coptic monks considered to be an adequate preparation for the lake of fire in Gehenna, the work went on; nothing of value was injured or broken, and the authorities declare that no object was lost. When the antiquities had been moved from Bûlâḳ, every lover of Egyptian art hoped that the statues, etc., which had been acquired during the last seven or eight years would be incorporated with those with which he was familiar, that each object would be numbered, that brief labels would be added, and that a chronological arrangement would be attempted. Owing to ill-health, however, M. Grébaut failed to continue the good work which he had begun, and for a long period but little new was done. Early in the year 1892 it was reported that M. Grébaut was about to resign, and for once rumour was correct. M. Grébaut was succeeded by M. Jacques de Morgan, who at once began the task of re-arranging the collection and of examining the contents of the "magazine" with the view of increasing the number of exhibited objects. During the past years the work has been pushed on with great energy, and we believe that the visitors to the Gîzeh Museum will greatly appreciate what the staff has done. It will be remembered that of the rooms in the palace, only some thirty-eight contained antiquities in 1895; now, however, about eighty-seven are used for exhibition purposes, and, for the first time, it is possible to see of what the Egyptian collection really consists. On the ground floor the positions of several of the large monuments have been changed, and the chronological arrangement is more accurate than before. In one large handsome room are exhibited for the first time several fine maṣṭăba stelæ, which were brought from Saḳḳârah by M. J. de Morgan. The brightness of the colours, the vigour of the figures, and the beauty of the hieroglyphics upon these fine monuments of the early dynasties, will, we believe, make them objects of general interest and attraction. On the same floor the visitor will also examine with wonder two splendid colossal statues of the god Ptaḥ, which were excavated by M. de Morgan at Memphis in 1892. In a series of rooms are arranged the coffins and mummies of the priests of Åmen which M. Grébaut brought down from Thebes in the winter of 1890–91. The coffins are of great interest, for they are ornamented with mythological scenes and figures of the gods which seem to be peculiar to the period immediately following the rule of the priest-kings of Thebes, *i.e.*, from about B.C. 1000–800.

A new and important feature in the arrangement of the rooms on the upper floor is the section devoted to the exhibition of papyri. Here in flat glazed cases are shown at full length fine copies of the Book of the Dead, hieratic texts, including the unique copy of the "Maxims of Ani," and many other papyri which have been hitherto inaccessible to the ordinary visitor. Now that these precious works cannot be reached by damp, their exhibition in a prominent place is a wise act on the part of the direction of the Museum. To certain classes of objects, such as scarabs, blue glazed *faïence*, linen sheets, mummy bandages and clothing, terra-cotta vases and vessels, alabaster jars, *etc.*, special rooms are devoted, and the visitor or student can see at a glance which are the most important specimens of each class. The antiquities which, although found in Egypt, are certainly not of Egyptian manufacture, *e.g.*, Greek and Phœnician glass, Greek statues, tablets inscribed in cuneiform, found at Tell el-Amarna, are arranged in groups in rooms set apart for them; and the monuments of the Egyptian Christians or Copts are also classified and arranged in a separate room. The antiquities have now been arranged and numbered on an intelligent system by the exertion of MM. de Morgan and Brugsch, and the excellent work which has been done during the past years is, we hope and believe, an earnest of what will be done in the immediate future. The growing prosperity of Egypt is an accomplished fact,* and it seems that the Museum of

* The following table shows the revenue from 1887–1897:—

	Revenue from direct taxation.	Revenue from indirect taxation.	Revenue from Railways, Telegraphs, Post Office, etc.	Total.
	£	£	£	£
1887	5,474,503	2,246,182	1,579,719	9,616,358
1888	5,456,791	2,277,217	1,551,158	9,661,436
1889	5,463,470	2,354,275	1,597,303	9,718,958
1890	5,480,752	2,712,551	1,688,813	10,236,612
1891	5,272,667	3,003,623	1,905,439	10,539,460
1892	5,224,378	2,741,300	1,974,717	10,297,312
1893	5,121,648	2,854,917	1,907,731	10,241,866
1894	4,747,487	3,072,298	2,033,978	10,161,318
1895	5,080,442	3,029,171	1,983,046	10,431,265
1896	5,023,697	3,219,939	2,074,013	10,693,577
1897	5,049,386	3,398,854	2,225,686	11,092,564

From Lord Cromer, *Egypt*, No. 1 (1898), p. 51. The surplus in 1898 was £E1,376,000, and, in 1899, £E1,848,000.

Egyptian Antiquities should participate in this prosperity and receive a larger grant of money, both for making purchases and excavations, for the attraction of the antiquities of the country is a very real and genuine matter, and induces travellers to visit it again and again. When the antiquities have been removed to the new museum at Cairo, we may be certain that the English advisers of the Khedive will never allow the progress of an institution which draws much money into the country, and which is now doing splendid work, to be hampered for the sake of a few thousand pounds a year.

The founding of the Bûlâḳ Museum was due to the marvellous energy and perseverance of **F. Auguste Ferdinand Mariette.** This distinguished Frenchman was born at Boulogne-sur-Mer on February 11th, 1821.* His grandfather was the author of several poetical works, short plays, etc., but his father was only an employé in the Registrar's Office of his native town. He was educated at Boulogne, and was made professor there when he was twenty years of age; here too he lived until 1848. Side by side with the duties of his professorship he devoted himself in turn to journalism, painting, novel-writing, etc., and in addition to these matters he found time to study archæology. Some of his early studies were devoted to classical archæology, and here, according to M. Maspero, he exhibited "power of discussion, clearness and vigour of style, and keen penetration," qualities for which in after-life he was famous. His attention was first drawn to the study of Egyptian

* For full accounts of the life of Mariette, see *Inauguration du Monument élevé à Boulogne-sur-Mer en l'honneur de l'Égyptologue Auguste Mariette*, le 16 Juillet, 1882, par Aug. Huguet, Mayor of Boulogne, Boulogne, 1882; and Wallon, *Notice sur la vie et les travaux de F. A. F. Mariette Pasha*, Paris, 1883, 4to., with portrait of Mariette as frontispiece; and Maspero, *Guide au Musée de Boulaq*, Cairo, 1884, pp. 12–23.

archæology by the examination of a collection of Egyptian antiquities which had been made by Vivant Denon, one of the artists attached to the French Expedition in Egypt, and his first work on Egyptian archæology seems to have been a notice of a coffin in this collection, which he drew up for the instruction of those who came to inspect it in the municipal buildings where it was exhibited. Soon after this he wrote a paper on the classification of the cartouches inscribed upon the **Tablet of Karnak,*** a most valuable monument which was discovered at Karnak by Burton, and taken by Prisse d'Avennes to Paris, where it is now preserved in the Bibliothèque Nationale. This work was addressed to Charles Lenormant, a pupil of the famous Champollion, and this gentleman, together with Maury, de Saulcy and Longpérier, advised him to come to Paris, where by the kind intercession of Janron, he obtained an appointment on the staff of the Louvre in 1848. As the salary paid to the young man was not sufficient to keep him, he resolved to ask the French Government to provide him with the necessary funds to go to Egypt, where he wished to try his fortune. In his application to the Government he stated that the object of his proposed mission was to study the Coptic and Syriac manuscripts† which still remained in the monasteries of the Nitrian desert. and if possible to acquire them for the nation, and with his application he sent in an essay on Coptic bibliography. The petition was favourably received, and he set out for Egypt in the summer of 1850. Having arrived in Egypt, he found that it was not easy to obtain access to the libraries of the monasteries, for the Patriarch had insisted that they should

* See page 3.

† The reader interested in the history of Dr. Tattam's acquisition of MSS. from the Monastery of St. Mary Deipara, in the Natron Valley, should read the article in the Quarterly Review for December, 1845, and the preface to Cureton, *Festal Letters of Athanasius*, London, 1848.

be carefully guarded from strangers. Profiting by the delays caused by the Patriarch's orders, he began to visit the sites of ancient Egyptian buildings in the neighbourhood of Cairo. While at Saḳḳârah one day he discovered by accident a sphinx, on which were inscribed the names of Ȧusȧr-Ḥāpi or Osiris-Apis (Serapis), similar to one he had seen at Cairo. He remembered that the Serapeum at Memphis was described by ancient authors as standing on a sandy plain,* and he believed that he had really found the spot where it stood and its ruins. Neglecting the original object of his expedition, he collected workmen, and in 1850 set to work to dig; two months' work revealed one hundred and forty sphinxes, two chapels, a semi-circular space ornamented with Greek statues, etc. Through the jealousy of certain people who united the profession of politics with wholesale trading in antiquities, the Egyptian Government of the day issued an order to suspend the excavations, and the work was stopped. Soon after, however, the French National Assembly voted 30,000 francs for excavation purposes, and towards the end of the year Mariette was enabled to enter the Serapeum, where he found sixty-four Apis bulls, stelae, etc. As the dates when the bulls were placed in the Serapeum are stated, they afford a valuable help in fixing the chronology of Egypt as far back as the XVIIIth dynasty. The year 1852 was spent in clearing out the Serapeum, and early in 1853 he came to the Pyramids of Gîzeh, where he carried on excavations for the Duc de Luynes; in the latter year he discovered a granite temple near Gîzeh. About this time he was appointed Assistant-Curator at the Louvre.

In 1854, 'Abbâs Pasha, who had suspended Mariette's excavations two or three years before, died; he was succeeded by Sa'îd Pasha, who at once conferred the honour of Bey upon Mariette, and commissioned him to found an Egyptian Museum at Bûlâḳ. Mariette proceeded to work

* Ἔστι δὲ καὶ Σαράπιον ἐν ἀμμώδει τόπῳ σφόδρα, Strabo, xvii. i. 32.

out a plan for the complete excavation of ancient Egyptian sites, and it is said that he began to work at thirty-seven places at once; his work literally extended from "Rakoti (Alexandria) to Syene." At Tanis he brought to light valuable monuments belonging to the XIIIth, XIVth, XIXth and XXIst dynasties, among which must be specially mentioned the statues and the sphinx which he attributed to the Hyksos; he explored hundreds of maṣṭăbas in the cemeteries at Gîzeh, Saḳḳârah, and Mêdûm; he opened the *Maṣṭăbat el-Far'ûn*; at Abydos, which he practically discovered, he cleared out the temple of Seti I., two temples of Rameses II., and a large number of tombs; at Denderah, a temple of Hathor; at Thebes he removed whole villages and mountains of earth from above the ruins of the temples at Karnak, Medînet-Habû and Dêr el-Baḥari; and at Edfû he removed from the roof of the temple a village of huts, and cleared out its interior. Mariette was appointed Commissioner of the Paris Exhibition of 1867, and upon him devolved the task of removing to Paris several of the most beautiful and valuable antiquities from the collection under his charge at Bûlâḳ. In 1870 he was overtaken by severe domestic troubles, and a disease which had some years before fastened upon him now began to show signs of serious progress. Notwithstanding his infirmities, however, he continued to edit and publish the texts from the monuments which he had discovered, and remained hard at work until his death, which took place at Cairo on January 17th, 1881. His body was entombed in a marble sarcophagus which stood in the courtyard of the Bûlâḳ Museum, and which has since been removed to Gîzeh, together with the antiquities of the Museum.

The following is a list of the most important of Mariette's works:—

Abydos, description des fouilles exécutées sur l'emplacement de cette ville. 3 tom. Paris, 1869–1880. Fol.

Album du Musée de Boulaq. Cairo, 1871. Fol.
Aperçu de l'histoire d'Égypte. Cairo, 1874. 8vo.
Choix de Monuments et de dessins découverts ou exécutés pendant le déblaiement du Sérapéum de Memphis. Paris, 1856. 4to.
Deir el-bahari. Leipzig, 1877. 4to.
Dendérah—Description générale. Paris, 1875.
Dendérah—Planches. Paris. 5 tom. 1870–74.
Itinéraire de la Haute-Égypte. Alexandria, 1872.
Karnak—Étude Topographique. Leipzig, 1875. 4to.
Karnak—Planches. Leipzig, 1875. 4to.
Les Mastaba de l'ancien empire. Paris, 1889. Fol.
Les Papyrus Égyptiens du Musée de Boulaq. Paris, 1872.
Monuments divers. Paris, 1872. Fol.
Le Sérapéum de Memphis. Paris, 1857. Fol.
Voyage dans la Haute Égypte. Cairo, 1878. Fol.

Mariette was succeeded as Director of the Bûlâḳ Museum by **M. Maspero**, who proved an able administrator, and who carried on many of the works which Mariette had left unfinished at his death. Mariette had formulated a theory that none of the pyramids was ever inscribed inside, and consequently never attempted to open the Pyramids of Saḳḳârah, although he lived at their feet for some thirty years; M. Maspero, however, dug into them, and was rewarded by finding inscribed upon the walls a series of religious texts of the greatest importance for the history of the religion of Egypt. M. Maspero was, in 1886, succeeded by **M. Grébaut**, who, in turn, was, in 1892, succeeded by **M. de Morgan.**

Jacques Jean Marie de Morgan, Ingénieur civil des Mines, was born on June 3rd, 1857, at the Château de Bion, Loir-et-Cher, and is descended from a family which came originally from Wales. For more than twenty years he has devoted himself to the study of archæology, but he is, nevertheless, a distinguished pupil of the School of Mines at Paris, and is eminent as a geologist and mathematician. To the exactness induced by the study of mathematics, and to his scientific training as a geologist and observer of nature, his works entirely owe their value, for he arranges his historical, geographical, and other facts in a logical manner, and does not confound fact with theory or assumption with evidence. In 1882 he made a tour through India for scientific purposes, and in the same year he published his *Géologie de la Bohême*, 8vo. In 1884 he undertook an expedition to Siam and the neighbouring countries, and in the following year he published some account of his work in *Exploration dans la presqu'île Malaisie*, Rouen, 1885. In this year we also find him contributing articles to the newspaper *L'Homme*; and in 1886 he published in the *Annales des Mines* an important article entitled, *Note sur la géologie et l'industrie minière du royaume de Perak.* During the years 1886–1889 he was employed on a mission to Turkey-in-Asia, the Caucasus and Armenia, and he published the scientific results of his travels in two volumes, large 8vo., entitled *Mission Scientifique au Caucase. Études archéologiques et historiques*, Paris, 1889. In this work M. de Morgan shows that he is well acquainted with the statements about these countries made by classical writers, that he is familiar with the best works upon general archæology, such as those of Sir John Evans, Montelius and Mourier, and also that he knows well the works of Brugsch, Maspero, George Smith, and of other scholars of Assyriology and Egyptology at first hand. From 1889 to the beginning of 1892 M. de Morgan made an expedition to Persia, Kurdistan and Luristan, and the results of his travels in these countries have appeared in due course.

During the first years of his work as Director of Antiquities, M. de Morgan carried out the following works:—At Aswân, the sand was cleared away from the tombs which were discovered by Sir Francis Grenfell, G.C.B., and the tomb of Se-renput has been entirely cleared. At Kom Ombos the whole temple has been excavated; at Luxor the works have been carried on with great activity; at Ṣaḳḳârah the tomb of Ti has been restored and cleared; at Dahshûr two brick pyramids and several *maṣṭăba* tombs have been excavated; and at Gîzeh and Memphis important excavations have been made. M. de Morgan was, in 1897, succeeded by **M. Loret.**

Victor Loret was born at Paris on September 1, 1859. He has been a Member of *Institut Français d'archéologie Orientale au Caire* since its foundation in 1879; and he was "Maître de conférences d'Égyptologie à l'Université de Lyon" in April, 1886. He is the author of *Manuel de la langue Égyptienne* (Paris, 1891); *La Flore pharaonique* (Paris, 1892); and of articles in the various publications devoted to Egyptology. Towards the end of 1899 it became generally known that M. Loret was to be succeeded as Director of the Gîzeh Museum by **M. G. Maspero,** who had done such excellent work at the old Bûlâḳ Museum after the death of Mariette. This eminent scholar is the author of a large number of important works on Egyptian philology, history, archæology, etc., and is undoubtedly the greatest of the Egyptologists who have directed the National Museum of Egyptian Antiquities. The remembrance of his wise and liberal policy at Bûlâk in the past, and his archæological experience and knowledge, lead all to believe that the interests of the great museum, both from a material and a scholarly point of view, will be well guarded under his renewed rule. The various Directors of the Museum have been most ably seconded in all their endeavours by **Emil Brugsch Bey,** the Conservator of the Museum, to whom the arrangement and classification of the collections therein are chiefly due. He holds the traditions of the great Mariette, having been his fellow-worker, and possesses an unrivalled knowledge of sites and of matters relating to excavations; his learning and courtesy are too well known to need further mention.

The national **Egyptian collection at Gîzeh** surpasses every other collection in the world, by reason of the number of the monuments in it which were made during the first six dynasties, and by reason of the fact that the places from which the greater number of the antiquities come are well ascertained. It contains also a large number of *complete* monuments and statues, which it owes chiefly to the fact that MM. Mariette, Maspero, E. Brugsch-Bey and Grébaut were present at the sites when they were found, and superintended their transport to the Museum. The collection of scarabs is of little importance, and many a private collector, not to mention the great museums of Europe, now possesses collections of more importance historically, and of more value intrinsically.

In the **Garden of the Museum** are exhibited:—

6008. Red granite **Sphinx**, inscribed with the cartouches of Rameses II.; excavated by Mariette at Tanis in the Delta. The Egyptians called the Sphinx *ḥu* , and he represented the god Harmachis, *i.e.*, "Horus in the horizon." (See p. 294.)

6628. Upper portion of an **obelisk** or pyramidion of the XVIIth dynasty, before B.C. 1700; from Karnak.

Marble sarcophagus on a pedestal of masonry, containing the body of **F. A. F. Mariette,** the founder of the Egyptian Museum at Bûlâḳ; the sphinxes round about it come from the Serapeum.

Among the most interesting of the antiquities in the Museum are:—

Ground Floor. Room I.—Monuments of the first six Dynasties.

261. Table of offerings of the scribe **Setu,** sculptured with grapes, bread, chickens, etc., in relief; the hollow for

holding the libations offered is divided into a series of cubits to represent the height of the water in the Nilometer at Memphis: 22 cubits in the spring, 23 in the autumn, and 25 in the winter.

VIth dynasty. From Dahshûr.

1. Black granite statue of a priest kneeling. A remarkable example of early work, probably before the IVth dynasty. From Saḳḳârah.

2. Panels of wood for inlaying upon the false doors of the tomb of **Ḥesi-Rā**; they are splendid examples of the delicate and accurate work executed by Egyptian carvers in wood during the IVth dynasty. From Saḳḳârah.

962. Round, white alabaster table of offerings made for **Khu-ḥetep-heres**, prophet of the goddess Maāt of Nekhen. Vth dynasty. From Saḳḳârah.

3. Layer of clay and plaster painted in water colours, with a scene in which geese are represented walking along. The artist has depicted the birds with great fidelity to nature, and was evidently a very accomplished draughtsman. This fragile object was brought from a ruined maṣṭăba at Mêdûm by M. Vassali, and dates probably from the IVth dynasty.

4, 5. Two libation tables found in a tomb near the Step Pyramid (see page 302) of Saḳḳârah. A slab, resting on the backs of a pair of lions, has a trench cut in it for carrying off the liquid into a bowl, which stands between the tails of the two lions.

IVth dynasty. From Saḳḳârah.

6. Double statue of **Rā-ḥetep** and his wife Nefert, "a royal connexion," found in a maṣṭăba near the Pyramid of Mêdûm, which is generally thought to have been built by Seneferu the first king of the IVth dynasty. The eyes are filled with quartz or rock crystal. Mariette placed the period when this statue was made in the IIIrd dynasty, but Maspero thinks that it belongs to the XIIth dynasty.

8, 9. Stelæ of **Setu.** IVth dynasty. From Gîzeh.

11, 12. Two door-posts from the tomb of **Seker-khā-baiu,** inscribed with figures of the lady Hathor-nefer-ḥetep, who was surnamed Tepes.
Before the IVth dynasty. From Saḳḳârah.

13. Stele, in the form of a false door, from the tomb of **Sherȧ,** a priest who lived during the reign of **Senṭ,** the fifth king of the IInd dynasty, about B.C. 4000. A stele of this Sherȧ is preserved in the Ashmolean Museum at Oxford. From Saḳḳârah.

16. Stele in the form of a door from the tomb of **Seker-khā-baiu.** Before the IVth dynasty. From Saḳḳârah.

Room II.—Monuments of Dynasties IV.–VI.

17. Limestone statue of **Rā-nefer,** a priest with shaven head. Vth dynasty. From Saḳḳârah.

18. Limestone statue of **Rā-nefer,** a priest wearing a wig. These two statues are generally admitted to be the best examples of the work of the Vth dynasty, and they exhibit an amount of skill in sculpture which was never surpassed at any subsequent period in the history of Egyptian art. From Saḳḳârah.

19. Wooden statue of a man, originally covered with a thin layer of plaster and painted; the feet are restored. His hair is cut short, his eyes are formed of pieces of quartz set in bronze lids, each having a piece of bright metal driven through it to hold it in position and to give the rock-crystal pupil in front of it an animated appearance; he wears an apron only, and holds in one hand an unpeeled stick. It is quite evident that we have here a portrait statue which possesses the greatest possible fidelity to life, and a startling example of what the ancient Egyptian artist could attain to when he shook

off the fetters of conventionality. The countenance possesses the peaceful look of the man who is satisfied with himself, and contented with the world. This statue is commonly known by the name of **Shêkh el-Beled**, or "Shêkh of the Village," because of the likeness which it was thought to bear to a native shêkh at Saḳḳârah by Mariette's workmen when they found it in the tomb of the man in whose honour it was made.

Vth dynasty. From Saḳḳârah.

20. Statue of **Antkha**, a priest.

21. Statue of **Atep**, a master of funereal ceremonies.

23, 28. Stelæ of **Rā-en-kau.**

Vth dynasty. From Saḳḳârah.

24. Statue of **Ḥeses**, an overseer of public works.

From Saḳḳârah.

25. Stele of **Sesha.** VIth dynasty. From Abydos.

29, 30. Portions of the shrine from the tomb of **Sabu**, a large land-owner. On No. 881 are represented Sabu receiving funereal offerings, statues of the deceased being brought to the tomb, the slaughter of animals for the funereal feast, boats bringing furniture for the tomb, etc. On No. 1046 are given the names of the various foods which are to form the meal of the deceased, and Sabu is seen sitting at a table loaded with offerings.

Vth dynasty. From Saḳḳârah.

35. Upper part of a wooden statue of a female which was found in the tomb with the **Shêkh el-Beled.**

Vth dynasty. From Saḳḳârah.

Room III.—Monuments of Dynasties IV.-VI.

33. Diorite statue of **Mycerinus**, builder of the third pyramid at Gîzeh, IVth dynasty, B.C. 3633.

From Mît-Rahîneh.

37. Alabaster statue of a king, name unknown.
From Mît-Rahîneh.

38. Alabaster statue of **Men-kau-Ḥeru**, Vth dynasty, B.C. 3400. From Mît-Rahîneh.

39. Red granite statue of **User-en-ka**, Vth dynasty, B.C. 3433. From Mît-Rahîneh.

41. Alabaster statue of **Chephren**, builder of the second pyramid at Gîzeh, IVth dynasty, B.C. 3666.
From Mît-Rahîneh.

42. Green basalt statue of **Chephren**, IVth dynasty. B.C. 3666. Found in a well in the temple at Gîzeh.

43. Limestone statue of **Ȧtetȧ**, surnamed Ānkhares.
Vth or VIth dynasty. From Saḳḳârah.

48. Portion of a grey granite shrine, inscribed with the name of **Saḥu-Rā**. Vth dynasty.

49. Limestone slab from the tomb of **Unȧ**, a high official who served under the kings **Tetȧ, Pepi I. and Mer-en-Rā**, of the VIth dynasty, about B.C. 3300–3233. Unȧ was a man of humble birth, and began life in the royal service as a "crown bearer"; he was next made overseer of the workmen, and was soon after sent to Ṭurrah to bring back a block of stone for the sarcophagus of the king. He was then made governor of the troops, and was set at the head of an expedition against the Āāmu and the Ḥerushā. On five different occasions did Unȧ wage war successfully against Egypt's foes, and having wasted their countries with fire and sword, he returned to Memphis crowned with glory. The inscription is of the greatest importance for the history of the period, and is interesting as showing that a man of very humble birth could attain to the highest dignities at the Egyptian court. From Abydos.

51. Slab from the tomb of **Tchāu**, the uncle of Pepi II.
VIth dynasty. From Abydos.

54. Limestone stele, inscribed with a text recording the **building of the temple of Isis**, lady of the pyramid, by Khufu, or Cheops, the builder of the Great Pyramid, IVth dynasty, B.C. 3733. This stele is not a contemporaneous monument, but was probably set up by a later king after the XXth dynasty.

55. Black granite stele of **User.** From Karnak.

Room IV.—Stelæ, etc., of Dynasties IV.-VI.

In this room are arranged stelæ found at Gîzeh and Saḳḳârah.

62. In the centre of the room is a seated limestone statue of Heken, a lady belonging to the royal family.

Room V.—Statues, etc., of Dynasties IV.-VI.

64. Green diorite statue of **Chephren**, the builder of the second Pyramid at Gîzeh. This full-sized portrait statue of the king is one of the most remarkable pieces of Egyptian sculpture extant. Chephren is seated upon a throne, the arms of which are ornamented with lions' heads; on the sides are depicted the papyrus, , and the lotus, , intertwined about , forming the device  emblematic of the union of Upper and Lower Egypt. The king holds in his hand a roll of papyrus, and above his head is a hawk, the visible emblem of the god Horus, his protector, with outspread, sheltering wings. On the pedestal, by the feet, is inscribed, "The image of the Golden Horus, Chephren, beautiful god, lord of diadems." IVth dynasty.
Found in a well in the granite temple at Gîzeh.

65. Limestone stele from the tomb of **Ankheftka**; see Room VII., No. 86.
Vth dynasty. From Saḳḳârah.

66. Stele of **Ankhmàra,** a priest of the kings Saḥu-Rā and User-ka-f. From Saḳḳârah.

70. Limestone stele of **Ptaḥ-ḥetep.** Vth dynasty. From Saḳḳârah.

74. Granite sarcophagus of **Ḥeru-baf,** a descendant or relative of Cheops. IVth dynasty. From Gîzeh.

926. Red granite seated statue of **Ma-nefer,** a scribe. Vth dynasty. From Gîzeh.

The seated statues of the **scribes** near the door are good examples of the work of this period.

Room VI.—Stelæ of Dynasties IV.–VI.

In this room are arranged stelæ and statues found at Gîzeh and Saḳḳârah.

Room VII.—Statues, etc., of Dynasties IV.–VI.

77. Limestone statue of **Ti.** Found in her tomb. Vth dynasty. From Saḳḳârah.

78. Statue of the dwarf **Khnum-ḥetep.** IVth dynasty. From Saḳḳârah

79. Limestone statue of **Nefer.** Vth dynasty. From Saḳḳârah.

81. Limestone statues of **Nefer-ḥetep** and the lady **Tentetȧ.** Vth dynasty. From Saḳḳârah.

1033. Limestone statue of **Seten-Maāt.** Vth dynasty. From Saḳḳârah.

82. Limestone bas-relief on which the high official **Apa,** seated in a chair, making a tour of inspection of his farm, is depicted. The operations of harvest, and the slaughter of animals for the funereal meal are also represented. At the table Apa is accompanied by his wife **Senbet** and daughter **Pepi-ānkh-nes.** VIth dynasty. From Saḳḳârah.

83. Limestone slab, sculptured with scenes in which are depicted the threshing and winnowing of wheat, the baking of bread, the carving of a statue, glass blowing, and working in gold.

85. Limestone group of three figures. The decoration of the woman is curious and worthy of note.

86. Bas-relief from the tomb of **Ānkheftka.**

From Saḳḳârah.

87. Statue of a man carrying a sack or bag over his left shoulder. Vth dynasty. From Saḳḳârah.

88. Limestone figures of a man and woman kneading dough.

IVth dynasty. From Saḳḳârah.

89. Limestone statue of a scribe kneeling.

Vth dynasty. From Saḳḳârah.

All the small statues exhibited in the wall-cases of this room are worth careful study.

Room VIII.—Bas-reliefs, etc., from Gîzeh and Saḳḳârah.

95. Wooden statue of **Tep-em- nkh.**

Vth dynasty. From Saḳḳârah.

Among the bas-reliefs should be noticed :—quarrel of boatmen ; servants making bread and bottling wine ; flocks crossing a river or canal ; bulls being led to slaughter ; ape biting a man's leg ; pasturing of flocks, etc. ; cleaning and grinding of corn (Nos. 91, 92, 93, 94).

All these are from Saḳḳârah.

Room IX.—Sarcophagi, Wooden Objects, etc.

96. Red granite sarcophagus of **Khufu-Ānkh,** a priest of Isis, and "Clerk of the Works." The cover is rounded, and at each end are "ears" or projections for lifting it on

and off; its sides are inscribed with the usual prayer to the god **Åp-uat,** and record the names of a large number of festivals. The sides of the sarcophagus are ornamented with false doors, etc., and resemble the architectural decorations of the maṣṭăbas.

IVth dynasty. Found near the Great Pyramid.

97. Red granite sarcophagus of the royal son **Ka-em-sekhem.** IVth dynasty. From Gîzeh.

98. Limestone stele of **Tep-em-ānkh,** a priestly official who held offices connected with the pyramids of Cheops, Chephren, Mycerinus, Seneferu, Saḥu-Rā, and Userkaf. From Saḳḳârah.

99. Stele of **Sebu,** a minister of art education under king Tetå. From Saḳḳârah.

100. Limestone stele of **Ptaḥ-kepu,** who lived in the reign of king Asså. From Saḳḳârah.

103. Models of granaries. The grain was carried on to the roof and poured into the different chambers through holes therein; in the front are rectangular openings with sliding shutters through which it could be taken out. From Akhmîm (Panopolis).

104. Model of a house. From Akhmîm (Panopolis).

105. Box containing models of an altar, vases, a granary, boats, etc. VIth dynasty. From Saḳḳârah.

6229. Small ivory statue. Vth dynasty. From Gîzeh.

6235. Model of a boat for carrying the dead. From Akhmîm.

Room X.—Royal Mummies, etc.

106. **Mummy** of king **Mentu-em-sa-f.** VIth dynasty. Found in a pyramid at Saḳḳârah, 1881.

107. Fragments of the **mummy** of King **Unȧs.**
Vth dynasty. Found in his pyramid at Saḳḳarah.

109. Portion of the tomb of **Tesher** (re-constructed).
VIth dynasty. From Dahshûr.

Rooms XI.-XIII.—Stelæ, etc., belonging to Dynasties IV.-XI., from Upper Egypt.

In these rooms are arranged a number of stelæ chiefly from Abydos, Akhmîm and Thebes. The stelæ from each place have their special characteristics, and afford most valuable information for dating the period of each step in the development of the decoration of the funereal stele from its oldest and simplest to its full and final form. They afford excellent material for hieroglyphic palæography.

The three wooden sarcophagi (Nos. 6301, 6302, 6608). from Akhmîm (Panopolis) are very interesting as examples of local art and decoration.

Rooms XIV.-XVI.—Stelæ, Royal Statues, Hyksos Monuments.

111. Limestone stele of a prince called **Ȧntefȧ.**
XIth dynasty (or earlier). From Thebes.

112. Stele of **Ȧntef IV.**, sculptured with a figure of his son, and five dogs. XIth dynasty. From Thebes.

113. Bas-relief in which king **Mentu-ḥetep** is represented slaying the Sati (Asiatics), the Tahennu (Libyans), and other peoples. From Gebelên

114. Tomb of **Ḥeru-ḥetep.** This interesting monument was discovered and broken into in the early part of this century; it was brought to Bûlâḳ in 1883 by M. Maspero.
XIth dynasty. From Dêr el-Baḥari.

115. Mummy of **Ament,** priestess of Hathor. The body of the deceased is in the attitude in which it was when overtaken by death. It was found by M. Grébaut in a stone chest at the bottom of a small uninscribed chamber at Dêr el-Bahâri; the necklaces and rings which were upon it are exhibited in Room LXX, case E.

116, 117. Outer and inner coffins of Ament, priestess of Hathor.

118. Stele of **Men-khāu-Rā**; the king adoring the god Ȧmsu. XIVth dynasty. From Abydos.

122. Granite seated statue of **Nefert,** wife of Usertsen I. XIIth dynasty. From Tanis.

123. Sandstone table of offerings inscribed with the name of **Ȧmeni-Ȧntef-Amenemḥāt.** XIIIth dynasty. From Karnak.

125. Grey granite bust of a colossal statue of a king usurped by Meneptah. Middle Empire From Alexandria

127. Stele of Se-ḥetep-ȧb, an officer of Ȧmenemḥāt III. XIIth dynasty. From Abydos.

128. Granite statue of **Sebek-em-sa-f.** XIIIth dynasty. From Abydos.

129. Statue of King **Ī-ȧn-Rā,** excavated at Zaḳâziḳ in 1888 by M. Naville. XIVth or XVth dynasty.

130. Alabaster table of offerings made for the princess Neferu-Ptaḥ. From the Pyramid of Hawâra.

131. Grey granite altar inscribed with the name of Usertsen III. XIIth dynasty. From Thebes.

132. Two figures making offerings of water-fowl, fish, and flowers. This interesting monument is supposed to be the work of the period of the "Shepherd Kings," although the cartouche of Pa-seb-khā-nut is found upon it.

133. Black granite table of offerings dedicated to the temple at Tanis by **Àpepȧ**.

XVIIth dynasty. From Tanis.

134. Black granite **Sphinx** excavated at Tanis by Mariette in 1863. The face of this remarkable monument has given rise to much discussion, and the theories propounded on the subject of the origin of the monument have been many. Mariette believed it to have been made by the so-called Hyksos, or "Shepherd Kings," and saw in the strange features of the face, and short, thick-set lion's body, a proof of their Asiatic origin. Some have seen a likeness to a Turanian original in the features, and others have insisted, probably rightly, that the king for whom the monument was originally made was a foreigner. Judging from the style of the work and the form of the lion's body, we should probably attribute it to a period anterior to B.C. 2000; that the name of the so-called Hyksos king Àpepȧ is inscribed upon it proves nothing except that this king, in common with many others, had his name inscribed on the statue. On the right shoulder, almost effaced, is the name of Àpepȧ; on the left shoulder is the name of Meneptah I.; on the right-hand side and front of the pedestal are the cartouches of Rameses II.; and on the breast is the cartouche of Pasebkhānet.

135. Head of a sphinx, similar to No. 107, inscribed with the name of **Meneptah**. This object is older than the time of the king whose name it bears.

136. Black granite table of offerings dedicated to the temple at Luxor by Usertsen III. From Thebes.

137. Grey granite head of a king. From the Fayyûm.

139. Limestone fragments of a sphinx. XIIth dynasty (?). From El-Ḳâb.

140. Limestone sarcophagus of Tagi.

XIth dynasty. From Thebes.

Room XVII.—Rectangular wooden sarcophagi of the XIth and XIIth dynasties.

142. Wooden sarcophagus of Kheper-ka.

143. Alabaster table of offerings bearing the cartouches of Usertsen I. Found near the Pyramid of Mêdûm.

Room XVIII.—Panels of a sarcophagus of the Middle Empire.

Room XIX.—Sarcophagi from Akhmîm and stelæ from Abydos.

Rooms XX and XXI.—Sarcophagi, stelæ, etc.

144. Black granite sphinx inscribed with the name of Sebek-ḥetep III. XIIIth dynasty.

Room XXII.—Stelæ, etc.

145. Fragment of a limestone bas-relief inscribed with the name of Rameses II. The hieroglyphics are painted blue, and the figures of the gods are decorated with gold. XIXth dynasty. From Abydos.

146, 147. Red granite fore-arms of a colossus. XIXth dynasty. From Luxor.

148. Colossal red granite scarab.

Room XXIII.—Stelæ, reliefs, etc.

149. Limestone bas-relief in which Amenophis IV. is represented making an offering to the solar disk. XVIIIth dynasty. From Tell el-Amarna.

153. Red granite seated figures of the god Harmachis and his beloved, Rameses II. Excavated at Memphis by M. de Morgan in 1892.

154. Red granite statue of a man carrying offerings. From Karnak.

Room XXIV.

155. Colossal red granite model of the sacred boat of Ptaḥ. A remarkably fine object.

Excavated at Memphis by M. de Morgan in 1892.

Room XXV.—Stelæ from Ethiopia, etc.

160. Red granite **Stele of Piānkhi**, King of Ethiopia, about B.C. 750. The text gives a detailed account of the expedition of this king into Egypt and of his conquest of that country. It was reported to Piānkhi in the 21st year of his reign, that the governors of the northern towns had made a league together and had revolted against his authority. He set out for Egypt with his soldiers, and when he arrived at Thebes he made offerings to Ȧmen-Rā, and commanded his soldiers to pay proper homage to the god. Passing northwards from Thebes he captured city after city, and finally besieged Memphis, which he soon captured, and thus made himself master of Egypt. The details of the capture of the towns, the speeches of the king and of his vassal princes, and the general information contained in the narrative, give this inscription an importance possessed by few others.

From Gebel Barkal.

161. Greygranite **Stele of Ḥeru-se-ȧtef**, King of Ethiopia, about B.C. 580, dated in the 35th year of his reign. The text records that this king made war expeditions in the 3rd, 5th, 6th, 11th, 16th, 23rd and 33rd years of his reign against various peoples living to the south and east of Nubia, and that he returned from them in triumph. It also sets forth at great length a list of the various articles which he dedicated to the temple of Ȧmen-Rā at Napata, or Gebel Barkal, on his return from each expedition. From Gebel Barkal.

162. Grey granite **Stele of the Dream.** The text here inscribed records that an Ethiopian king, whose name is read provisionally Nut-meri-Åmen, and who reigned about B.C. 650, had a dream one night in which two snakes appeared to him, one on his right hand, and the other on his left. When he awoke he called upon his magicians to explain it, and they informed him that the snakes portended that he should be lord of the lands of the North and South. His majesty went into the temple of Åmen-Rā at Napata, or Gebel Barkal, and having there made rich offerings to the god, he set out for the north. Sailing down the river he made offerings to Khnemu-Rā, the god of Elephantine, and to Åmen-Rā of Thebes, and the people on both sides of the river shouted "Go in peace." When he arrived at Memphis the people thereof made war upon him, but he defeated them and entered the town. He went into the temple of Ptaḥ and made rich offerings to Ptaḥ-Seker and to Sekhet, and gave orders to build a temple to Åmen. He then set out to conquer the chiefs in the Delta, and having succeeded by the help of Åmen, he returned to Nubia. From Gebel Barkal.

163. Grey granite **Stele of the Coronation.** The text gives an account of the ceremonies which were performed at the coronation of a king of Ethiopia, whose names are erased; this king was probably called **Åspaleta**

From Gebel Barkal.

164. Black granite head of **Tirhakah,** King of Ethiopia. XXVth dynasty; about B.C. 693.

165. Red granite **Stele of the Excommunication.** The text records that a king of Ethiopia, whose name has been carefully chiselled out, went into the temple of Åmen-Rā of Napata to drive out a set of people whose

custom was to eat the sacrificial meat raw, and who had made a resolve to kill all those who ate it cooked. The king passed an edict forbidding those men and their posterity to enter the temple for ever, and it seems that he burnt some of the heretics with fire.

From Gebel Barkal.

166. Black granite head of a colossal statue of **Rameses II.** From Luxor.

167. Group inscribed with the name of **Meneptah.**

168. Limestone stele of **Rameses IV.** From Abydos.

169, 171, 172. Bas-reliefs from the tomb of **Ptaḥ-mai.** XVIIIth dynasty. From Saḳḳârah.

174. Alabaster statue of **Åmenårṭās** , daughter of Kashta , sister of Shabaka , wife of Piānkhi , and mother of Shep-en-åpt , the wife of Psammetichus I. A very beautiful piece of sculpture.

XXVth dynasty. From Karnak.

Room XXVI.

177. Granite bust of Rameses IV.

XXth dynasty. From Bubastis.

178. Granite dog-headed ape from the foundations of the obelisk of Luxor. XIXth dynasty.

179. Seated group, brother and sister. Fine work.

XIXth dynasty. From Memphis.

180. Alabaster shaft of a column from the temple of Rameses III. at Tell el-Yahûdîyyeh.

182. Grey granite pillar inscribed on its four faces with scenes representing Rameses II. making offerings to Åmen and Mentu-Rā.

184. Limestone stele inscribed with a prayer of Rameses IV. to the gods of Abydos.

185, 186. Two sandstone colossal statues of Ptaḥ, one of the primeval gods of Egypt; they were set up by Rameses II., and in the inscriptions upon them the god promises to give to the king "all life, health, and strength," and long years of existence and an unlimited posterity. These wonderful objects are as beautiful for the delicacy of their work as for their size. They were discovered by M. de Morgan in the temple of Ptaḥ of Memphis, in 1892.

188. Grey granite fragment of a statue of Amenophis II.
From Karnak.

190. Granite head of a statue of a nobleman.
XIIIth dynasty. From Karnak.

192. Red granite bust of Thothmes III.
XVIIIth dynasty. From Karnak.

193. Limestone stele of Åmen-mes.
XVIIIth dynasty. From Saḳḳârah.

196. Grey granite colossal statue usurped by Rameses II.
XII–XVth dynasty. From Tanis.

198. Limestone head, thought by Mariette to belong to a statue of Queen Thi.
XVIIIth dynasty. From Karnak.

200. Black granite shrine, containing a figure of Ptaḥ-Mes, a priest who lived in the reign of Thothmes III.

202. Red granite statue of Thothmes III. From Karnak.

205. Limestone statue of a scribe, seated, reading from a roll of papyrus spread out upon his knees.
XVIIIth dynasty. From Ḳûrnah

206. Limestone statue of Amenophis II.

210. Grey granite statue of the lion-headed goddess Sekhet, who represented the destructive heat of the sun; this monument bears the name of Amenophis III.

From the temple of Mut at Karnak.

213. Black granite stele inscribed with a poetical account of the victories of Thothmes III. The text is a speech of the god Åmen-Rā addressed to Thothmes. After describing the glory and might which he has attached to his name, he goes on to mention the countries which he had made his son Thothmes to conquer. The countries enumerated include Tchah and Ruthen in northern Syria, Phœnicia and Cyprus, Mathen or Mitani on the borders of Mesopotamia by the Euphrates, the countries along the Red Sea, the land of Nubia and the countries lying to the south of it, and the northern parts of Africa. Although Thothmes wasted and destroyed these lands, it cannot be said that he was successful in imposing the yoke of Egypt upon them permanently, for history shows that on the accession to the throne of each of his successors it was necessary to re-conquer them. Many of the phrases are stereotyped expressions which we find repeated in the texts of other kings. This monument was found at Karnak, on the site of the famous temple of Åmen of the Apts, and shows marks of erasures made by the order of Amenophis IV., the king who vainly tried to upset the national religion of Egypt. XVIIIth dynasty.

214. Black granite seated statue of **Thothmes III.**

XVIIIth dynasty.

Room XXVII. The Tablet of Saḳḳârah, Stelæ, etc.

218. The **Tablet of Saḳḳârah** was found by Mariette in the tomb of a high official named Tanurei, at Saḳḳârah, in 1861. It is a valuable document, for it contained when complete the names of fifty-six kings; this list agrees tolerably well with that on the Tablet of Abydos, but there are many omissions. The list begins with Merbapen, the sixth king of the Ist dynasty, instead of with Menȧ, and ends with Rameses II.

Courtyard XXVIII.—Sphinxes and Colossal Statues.

221, 222. Red granite sphinxes inscribed with the names and titles of **Thothmes III.**
XVIIIth dynasty. From Karnak.

223. Colossal statue of **Usertsen I.** From Abydos.

224. Red granite statue usurped by Rameses II.
From Tanis.

225. Red granite statue usurped by Rameses II.
From Abûkîr.

226. Black granite seated statue of a king, usurped by **Rameses II.** XIVth dynasty. From Tanis.

Gallery XXIX.—Bas-reliefs of the XVIIIth and XXth dynasties.

228, 229. Limestone slabs from the tomb of Ḥeru-em-ḥeb.
XIXth dynasty. From Saḳḳârah.

Room XXX.

231. Painted limestone statue of Mut-nefert, the mother of Thothmes II.
From the ruins of a little temple near the Ramesseum.

232. Limestone funereal box made for the lady Ta-maut.
XVIIIth dynasty. Excavated by M. de Morgan at Memphis in 1892.

234. Limestone fragment of a stele in which Thothmes III. pays honour to his father Thothmes I.

236. Limestone wall fragment upon which is a figure of the Queen of Punt. From Dêr el-Baḥari.

237. The donkey of the Queen of Punt.

Room XXXI.—Monuments of the Saïte Period.

241. Granite sarcophagus inscribed with the cartouches of Psammetichus II. From Damanhûr.

242. Limestone table of offerings inscribed with the cartouches of Hophra.

243. Red granite slab inscribed with the cartouches of Anput.

245. Black granite shrine inscribed with the name of Shabaka, King of Ethiopia. From the temple of Esneh.

246. Red granite bas-relief inscribed with the cartouches of Nectanebus I. From Bubastis.

249. Black granite shrine inscribed with the cartouches of Nectanebus II. XXXth dynasty.

250. Black granite headless statue inscribed with the names of Shabataka and Tirhakah. XXVth dynasty.

Room XXXII.

253. Black granite shrine inscribed with the name of Nectanebus I.

256. Sandstone bas-relief inscribed with the cartouche of Queen Nitocris. XXVIth dynasty. From Karnak.

257. Sandstone cornice inscribed with the cartouches of Queens Shep-en-åp and Åmenarṭās. XXVIth dynasty. From Karnak.

Room XXXIII.—Stelæ from Saḳḳârah, Heliopolis, Abydos, etc.

261. Sandstone shrine inscribed with the cartouches of Psammetichus I., Shep-en-åp, and Nitocris; for the green basalt statue of the goddess Thoueris, which was found in it, see Room LXXII.

262. Basalt statue of the god Osiris. XXVIth dynasty. From Saḳḳârah.

Room XXXIV.—Stelæ, chiefly from Abydos.

Room XXXV.—Antiquities of late Periods.

271. Fragment of a granite obelisk set up in honour of Ȧmen-Rā at Napata in Nubia by the Ethiopian king Atalnarsa.

Room XXXVI.

278. "Stele of Pithom." Excavated at Tell el-Maskhuta by M. Naville.

283. Black granite stele dated in the seventh year of Alexander II., son of Alexander the Great, and set up by Ptolemy Lagus. The text records victories in Syria and on the North coast of Africa, and the restoration of the temple of Buto.

284. Limestone stele of the Ram of Mendes, discovered by E. Brugsch Bey on the site of the ancient city of Mendes.

Room XXXVII.—Monuments inscribed in Demotic.

Room XXXVIII.—Stelæ from about B.C. 100—A.D. 300.

Room XXXIX.—Græco-Roman Antiquities.

Room XL.

290. White limestone stele generally known as the "Stele of Canopus." It is inscribed in hieroglyphics, Demotic and Greek, with a decree made at Canopus by the priesthood assembled there from all parts of Egypt, in honour of Ptolemy III., Euergetes I. It mentions the great benefits which he had conferred upon Egypt, and states what festivals are to be celebrated in his honour and in that of Berenice, *etc.*, and concludes with a

resolution ordering that a copy of this inscription in hieroglyphics, Greek, and Demotic shall be placed in every large temple of Egypt.

291. White limestone stele of Canopus (duplicate). A third copy of the decree is in the Louvre at Paris.

304. Black granite "Stele of Menshiah," inscribed with the name of the emperor Trajan.

306. White marble head of Jupiter Olympus.
From Crocodilopolis.

308. Red granite colossal statue of a Macedonian king.
From Karnak.

Rooms XLI, XLII.

The monuments exhibited in these rooms illustrate the work of the Egyptian Christians or Copts.

Room XLIII.

In five cases in this room are exhibited Græco-Roman terra-cotta figures of Harpocrates, Bes, Aphrodite, Isis, Serapis, *etc.*; moulds for casting figures; lamps, pieces of glass, *etc.*

Room XLIV.—Mummies, from Akhmîm, the Fayyûm, etc.

334. Mummy with portrait painted upon linen.

335. Mummy with portrait painted upon wood.

337. Mummy, with portrait, from the Fayyûm. IIIrd century A.D.

350. Glazed faïence "mummy label."

355. Mummy of Artemidora. From the Fayyûm.

359. Fine gilded mummy mask inlaid with enamel. From Meir.

All the mummies in this room are of interest.

Room XLV.—Græco-Roman Antiquities.

363. Black granite inscribed slabs from the temple of Coptos.

395. Wooden sarcophagus ornamented with some curious paintings.

Gallery XLVI.—Coptic Linen Work.

Room XLVII.

Here are exhibited Coptic inscriptions upon papyrus, leather, wood, terra-cotta, *etc.*; bronze lamps, candlesticks, censers, basins, cymbals and other objects employed in Coptic churches; bottles bearing upon them figures of Saint Mina; and many small objects of Coptic work.

Room XLVIII.

This room contains Coptic pottery and inscriptions, and three remarkable Coptic mummies.

Room XLIX.

431. Wooden coffin with an inscription in the Himyaritic character.

The **Tell el-Amarna Tablets** exhibited in this room are a portion of a collection of about 320 documents which were found at Tell el-Amarna, the site of the town built by **Khu-en-àten** or Amenophis IV., which is situated about 180 miles south of Memphis. The Berlin Museum * ac-

* The cuneiform texts of the tablets at Berlin and Gîzeh are published by Abel and Winckler, *Der Thontafelfund von El-Amarna*, Berlin, 1889–1890; and the texts of those in the British Museum by Bezold, with an introduction and summary of contents by Bezold and Budge, *The Tell El-Amarna Tablets in the British Museum*. Printed by Order of the Trustees, 1892.

quired 160, a large number being fragments, the British Museum 82, and the Gîzeh Museum 55. These documents were probably written between the years B.C. 1500–1450.

The Tell el-Amarna tablets supply entirely new information concerning the political relations which existed between the kings of Egypt and the kings of Western Asia, and prove that an important trade between the two countries existed from very early times. They also supply facts concerning treaties, alliances, religious ceremonies, etc., which cannot be derived from any other source, and they give us for the first time the names of Artatama, Artashumara, and Tushratta, kings of Mitani (the Māthen of the Egyptian inscriptions), and of Kadashman-Bêl (?), King of Karaduniyash. The dialect in which these inscriptions are written has a close affinity to the language of the Old Testament.

The first conquest of Syria by the Egyptians took place in the reign of Amāsis I., B.C. 1700. Thothmes I., B.C. 1633, conquered all Palestine and Syria, and set up a tablet at Ruthen to mark the boundary of Egypt. Thothmes III., B.C. 1600, marched through Palestine and Syria and made himself master of all the country from Gaza to the Euphrates. At Tunip he established the Egyptian religion, and at Ruthen, in the 33rd year of his reign, he set up a tablet by the side of that of Thothmes I. The cuneiform tablets call him

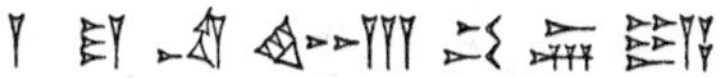

D.P. Ma - na - akh - bi - ir - ya

a very close imitation of the pronunciation of this king's prenomen Men-Kheper-Rā 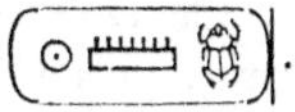.

Amenophis II., B.C. 1566, marched to Nî on the Euphrates, and slew seven kings in Ruthen, and brought their bodies to Egypt. Amenophis III. was not a great conqueror in the strict sense of the word, but he was proclaimed conqueror of Kadesh, Tunip, Sankar, and north-western Mesopotamia, to which country he was in the habit of going to shoot lions. Now we know from a scarab that a lady called Thi , the daughter of Iuáa  and Thuáa , came to Egypt to become the wife of Amenophis in the tenth year of his reign. We know also that she became the "great Queen of Egypt," and as she is depicted with a fair complexion and blue eyes, there is no doubt that she is to be identified with the lady called Tī , in the inscriptions on the Tell el-Amarna tablets, who came from the country to the north-east of Syria. Tī was the mother of Amenophis IV., the "heretic king." Besides this lady, we learn from the tablets that Amenophis married at least five other ladies from Mesopotamia, viz., a sister and two daughters of Kadashman-Bêl (?), King of Karaduniyash, and a sister and daughter of Tushratta, King of Mitani; but none of these ladies was acknowledged as "Queen of Egypt." In the time of Amenophis III., a Mesopotamian princess was honoured by marriage with the King of Egypt, but when Kadashman-Bêl (?) wished to marry an Egyptian princess, Amenophis replied haughtily, "the daughter of the King of the land of Egypt hath never been given to a nobody"; yet in the reign of Khu-en-áten we learn that an Egyptian princess was given in marriage to Burraburiyash, King of Karaduniyash, a proof that the Egyptian power was waning in Mesopotamia. The greater number of the tablets are addressed to "the King of Egypt," either Amenophis III. or his son Amenophis IV., and they reveal a state of disorganization and rebellion in the Egyptian dependencies in Palestine and Syria which cannot be understood unless we assume that for some years before the death of Amenophis III. the Semitic peoples of Western Asia were being encouraged to reject the rule of the Egyptians by their kinsfolk living in Egypt.

A list of the letters preserved at Gîzeh is as follows :—

*1. Letters from Kadashman-Bêl (?).

9. Letter from Ashur-uballiṭ, King of Assyria, B.C. 1400.

10. Letter from Amenophis III. to Tarḫundaradush, King of Arzapi.

11, 12, 14. Letters from the King of Alashiya.

40. Letter from Aziru.

60, 61, 62, 63, 65, 78, 79, 83. Letters from Rib-Adda.

94. Letter from Zatadna.

96. Letter from Namyawiza.

98, 99. Letters from Abu-Milki.

100. Letter from Shuardata.

109. Letter from Milkili.

115. Letter from Biridiwi.

116, 117. Letters from Shubandi.

118, 121. Letters from Widya.

124. Letter from Yabnî ili.

125. Letter from Arzawya.

127. Letter from Dashru.

131. Letter from Shamu-Adda.

138. Letter from the lady 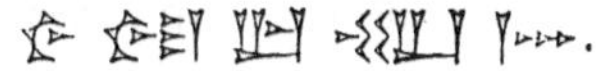.

150. Letter from Nurtuwi . . . . (?)

151. Letter from the governor of the city of Nazima.

152. Letter from Ara . . . . . of the city of Kumiṭi.

153. Letter from Pu-Addu.

154. Letter from Addu-asharid.

195. Letter from Bayawi.

196. Letter from Aba . . . . zi.

239. Part of a legend.

5, 17, 18, 20, 197-209. Letters from unknown writers.

436. Table of offerings with Meroïtic inscription.

441, 442. Phœnician and Aramean papyri.

* These numbers refer to Winckler's edition of the texts.

443. Terra-cotta cylinders of Nebuchadnezzar II., King of Babylon, B.C. 605–562.

445. The Lord's Prayer in Syriac.

Room L.—Weights, Measures, etc.

446. Alabaster vase, of the capacity of 21 *hin*, inscribed with the cartouches of Thothmes III.

447. Grey granite weight of 300 *uten*, in the form of a calf's head; the cartouches are those of Seti I.

449-451. Squares and plumb-line from the tomb of Sennetchem. XXth dynasty. From Thebes.

455. Goldsmith's scales.

In Case B are masons' and carpenters' mallets, models of houses, a window-screen, *etc.*

467. Painted wooden door from the tomb of Sennetchem.

Room LI.

The cases in this room contain fine examples of glazed *faïence* from Tell el-Yahûdîyyeh; bricks stamped with royal names; a collection of bronzes from Saïs, *etc.*

Room LII.

The cases in this room contain wooden beds, chairs, stools and boxes; plaques inlaid with ivory; granite, limestone, and *faïence* legs of beds, or couches; a pillow; wooden spindles and distaffs; hanks of thread, cushions, *etc.*

Room LIII.—Chairs, Stools and other furniture.

Room LIV.

This room contains a large number of thin slices of limestone upon which are traced in black and red curious and interesting designs of royal personages, gods, animals, etc.

Room LV.—Sculptors' Models, terra-cotta Moulds, etc.

Room LVI.—Inscribed Ostraka, etc.

Room LVII.—Inscribed Papyri.

587. Papyrus of Ḥerub, a priestess of Mut, daughter of Pai-netchem and Åuset-em-khebit.

XXIst dynasty. From Dêr el-Baḥari.

589. Copy of a work written by a scribe called **Ani**, who gives his son Khensu-ḥetep advice as to judicious behaviour in all the varied scenes of life; the following are taken from his precepts:—

"If a man cometh to seek thy counsel, let this drive thee to books for information.

"Enter not into the house of another; if a man maketh thee to enter his house it is an honour for thee.

"Spy not upon the acts of another from thy house.

"Be not the first to enter or to leave an assembly lest thy name be tarnished.

"The sanctuary of God abhorreth noisy declamations. Pray humbly and with a loving heart, whose words are spoken silently. God will then protect thee, and hear thy petitions, and accept thy offerings.

"Consider what hath been. Set before thee a correct rule of life as an example to follow. The messenger of death will come to thee as to all others to carry thee away; yea, he standeth ready. Words will profit thee nothing, for he cometh, he is ready! Say not, 'I am a child, wouldst thou in very truth bear me away?' Thou knowest not how thou wilt die. Death cometh to meet the babe at his mother's breast, even as he meeteth the old man who hath finished his course.

"Take heed with all diligence that thou woundest no man with thy words.

"Keep one faithful steward only, and watch his deeds, and let thy hand protect the man who hath charge of thy house and property.

"The man who having received much giveth little, is as one who committeth an injury.

"Be not ungrateful to God, for He giveth thee existence.

"Sit not while another standeth if he be older than thou, or if he is thy superior.

"Whosoever speaketh evil receiveth no good.

"When thou makest offerings to God, offer not that which He abominateth. Dispute not concerning His mysteries. The god of the world is in the light above the firmament, and his emblems are upon earth; it is unto those that worship is paid daily.

"When thou hast arrived at years of maturity, and art married and hast a house, forget never the pains which thou hast cost thy mother, nor the care which she hath bestowed upon thee. Never give her cause to complain of thee, lest she lift up her hands to God in heaven, and He listen to her complaint.

"Be watchful to keep silence."

This work has much in common with the Maxims of Ptaḥ-ḥetep * and the Book of Proverbs.

590. Papyrus inscribed with a treatise on the geography of the Fayyûm and of the country round about. The concluding part is in the possession of a Mr. Hood, residing in England. Greek period. From Dêr el-Medîneh.

In the wall cases are exhibited the Egyptian scribes' palettes of wood, ivory, limestone, *etc.*, and specimens of the reeds and colours with which they wrote.

* The maxims of Ptaḥ-ḥetep are inscribed upon the Prisse papyrus, which was written about B.C. 2500; they were composed during the reign of Ȧssȧ the eighth king of the Vth dynasty, about B.C. 3366.

Room LVIII.—Funereal Objects.

In this room are exhibited:—Network for placing upon mummies; painted and gilded masks for mummies; hypocephali in terra-cotta, bronze and cartonnage, the object of which, by means of the texts inscribed upon them, was to preserve some heat in the body until the day of the resurrection; linen shrouds inscribed with funereal scenes; pads for the feet of the dead; sandals; wooden figures of the god Osiris in which papyri were deposited; pectorals in the form of pylons in which scarabs are embedded between figures of the goddesses Isis and Nephthys; symbolic eyes or *utchats* ; green basalt scarabs inscribed with Chapter 30B of the Book of the Dead, *etc.*

Room LIX.

In Case A is arranged a fine collection of small sepulchral figures called in Egyptian *ushabtiu*. They are made of stone, alabaster, wood, glazed *faïence*, and are in the form of the god Osiris, who is here represented in the form of a mummy. They were placed in the tomb to do certain agricultural works for the deceased, who was supposed to be condemned to sow the fields, to fill the canals with water, and to carry sand from the East to the West. They are usually inscribed with the VIth Chapter of the Book of the Dead. As many travellers buy *ushabtiu* figures in Egypt, the following version of the chapter may be of interest to them.

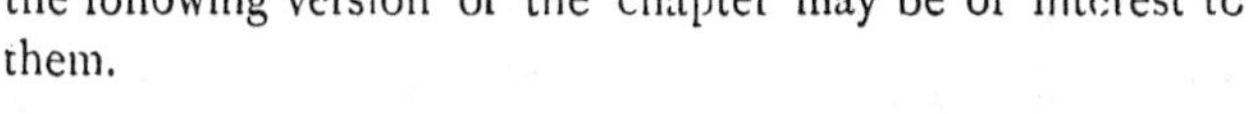

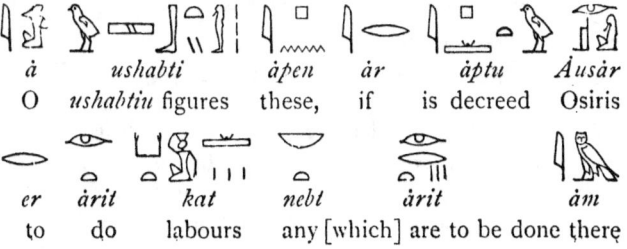

à *ushabti* *àpen* *àr* *àptu* *Àusàr*

O *ushabtiu* figures these, if is decreed Osiris

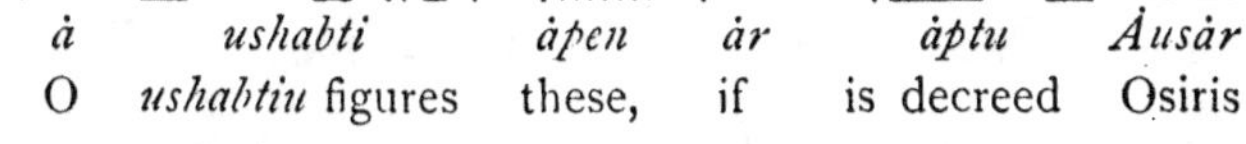

er *àrit* *kat* *nebt* *àrit* *àm*

to do labours any [which] are to be done there

em *neter χert* *àstu* *ḥu - nef*
in the underworld, behold, be there smitten down for him

set'ebu *àm* *em* *se* *er* *χert - f*
obstructions there for a person beneath him.

māku - à *ka - ten* *àp - tu - ten*
Here am I [when] call ye. Watch ye

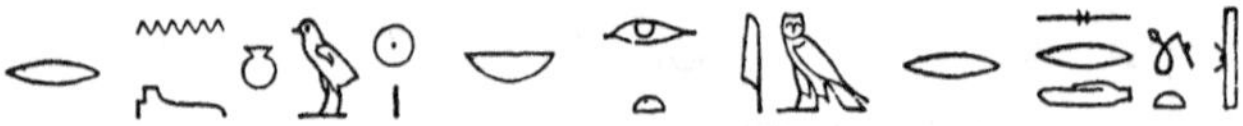

er *ennu* *neb* *àrit* *àm* *er* *serutet*
at moment every to work there, to plough

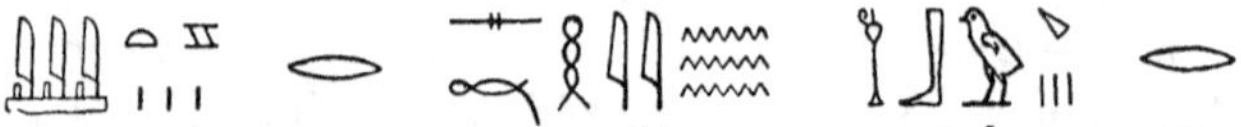

seχet *er* *semeḥi* *utebu* *er*
the fields, to fill with water the canals, to

χen *šā* *en* *Abtet* *er* *Àmentet*
carry sand of the east to west.

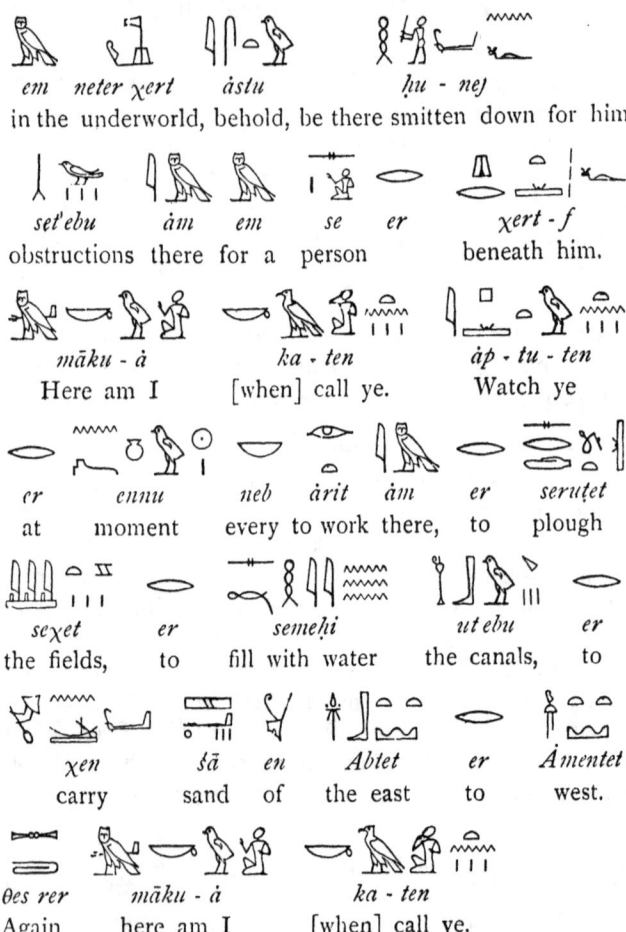

θes rer *māku - à* *ka - ten*
Again here am I [when] call ye.

That is to say, the deceased addresses each figure and says, "O *ushabtiu* figures, if the Osiris," that is, the deceased, "is decreed to do any work whatsoever in the underworld, may all obstacles be cast down in front of him!" The figure answers and says, "Here am I ready when thou callest." The deceased next says, "O ye figures, be ye ever watchful to work, to plough and sow the fields, to water the canals, and to carry sand from the east to the west." The figure replies, "Here am I ready when thou callest."

In Case D is an interesting set of collections of wooden tablets, pillows, *etc.*

In Case G is a collection of sets of limestone and alabaster "Canopic Jars."

Each jar of a set was dedicated to one of the four genii of the underworld, who represented the cardinal points, and each jar was provided with a cover which was made in the shape of the deity to whom it was dedicated. The jar of Mesthà is man-headed; that of Ḥāpi is dog-headed; that of Ṭuamāutef is jackal-headed; and that of Qebḥsennuf is hawk-headed. They represented the south, north, east, and west respectively, and in them were placed the stomach and large intestines, the small intestines, the lungs and heart, and the liver and gall-bladder.

Room LX.

Here are arranged funereal figures from the "find" of the priests of Åmen at Dêr el-Baḥari.

Room LXI.—Funereal Figures, Canopic Vases, etc.

Room LXII.—Papyri.

683. Fragment of a Book of the Dead written for Mapui.

684. Papyrus of Tchet-Khonsu-auf-ānkh. From Dêr el-Baḥari.

686. Papyrus of the Princess Nesi-Khonsu, inscribed in fine hieratic characters. From Dêr el-Baḥari.

687. Papyrus of Queen Maāt-ka-Rā. From Dêr el-Baḥari.

Room LXIII.

688. Green basalt slab of Ṭirhaka.

694. Blue glazed *faïence* sistrum, inscribed with the cartouche of Darius.

698. Limestone figure of Amenophis I. Fine work.
From Medînet-Habu.

700. Four alabaster vases found with the mummy of Queen Àāḥ-ḥetep. XVIIIth dynasty.

701a. Stele of Hophra, with Carian (?) inscription.

710. Blue glazed faïence *ushabti* figure of Rameses IV.

716. *Ushabti* figure of Nectanebus I.

717. *Ushabti* figure of Nectanebus II.

721. Bronze lion, inscribed with the name of Hophra.

738. Papyrus of Pi-netchem.

740. Blue paste scarab, inscribed with the cartouches of Hophra.

742. Steatite scarab, made to celebrate the marriage of Amenophis III. with the Mesopotamian lady Thi.

742a. Steatite scarab, recording the slaughter by Amenophis III. of 102 lions during the first ten years of his reign.

743. Blue paste scarab inscribed with the name of Nekau (Necho). XXVIth dynasty.

744. Bronze axe-head, inscribed with the cartouches of Kames, a king of the XVIIth dynasty; it is set in a horn handle.

In this room are also exhibited a series of amulets, the principal of which are as follows :—

1. The **Buckle** or Tie, , usually made of some red stone, the colour of which was intended to represent the blood of Isis, was placed on the neck of the mummy which it

was supposed to protect. It was often inscribed with the 156th chapter of the Book of the Dead.

2. The **Tet**, , which had sometimes plumes, disk and horns, , attached to it, was also placed on the neck of the mummy, and was often inscribed with the 155th chapter of the Book of the Dead.

3. The **Vulture**, , was placed upon the neck of the mummy on the day of the funeral, and brought with it the protection of the "mother" Isis.

4. The **Collar**, , was placed upon the neck of the mummy on the day of the funeral.

5. The **Papyrus Sceptre**, , was placed upon the neck of the mummy, and typified the green youth which it was hoped the deceased would enjoy in the nether world.

6. The **Pillow**, , usually made of hæmatite, was generally inscribed with the 166th chapter of the Book of the Dead.

7. The **Heart**, , represented the "**soul of Kheperȧ**."

8. The **Ānkh**, , represented "Life."

9. The **Utchat**, or Symbolic Eye, , typified "good health and happiness," and was a very popular form of amulet in Egypt.

10. The **Nefer**, , represented "good-luck."

11. The **Sam**, , represented "union."

12. The **Menȧt**, , represented "virility."

13. The **Neha**, , represented "protection."

14. The **Serpent's Head**, , was placed in mummies to prevent their being devoured by worms.

15. The **Frog,** , represented "fertility" and "abundance."

16. The **Stairs,** , the meaning of which is unknown to me.

17. The **Fingers,** index and medius, found inside mummies, represented the two fingers which the god Horus stretched out to help the deceased up the ladder to heaven.

Rooms LXIV, LXV.

Here are exhibited tables of offerings; models of boats and rowers (see particularly No. 760, a boat with a sail); boxes for *ushabtiu* figures; mummies of animals sacred to the gods *; models of funereal bread in terra-cotta, *etc.*

Room LXVI.—Vessels in alabaster, bronze, etc.

Room LXVII.—Weapons and Tools.

Room LXVIII.—Pottery, etc.

Room LXIX.—Articles of Clothing.

Room LXX.

In this room are exhibited bronze mirrors, musical instruments, draught boards, dolls, necklaces of precious stones, vases of coloured glass, statuettes of fine work, spoons, perfume boxes, a broken ivory figure from a tomb of the Vth dynasty (No. 912), fans, *etc.*

922. Collection of silver vases found among the ruins of Mendes.

* The principal animals sacred to the gods were the ape to Thoth, the hippopotamus to Thoueris, the cow to Hathor, the lion to Horus, the sphinx to Harmachis, the bull to Apis or Mnevis, the ram to Ȧmen-Rā, the cat to Bast, the jackal to Anubis, the hare to Osiris, the sow to Set, the crocodile to Sebek, the vulture to Mut, the hawk to Horus, the ibis to Thoth, the scorpion to Serqet, and the beetle to Ḳheperȧ.

The jewellery of Åāḥ-ḥetep, the wife of Seqenen-Rā, mother of Kames, and grandmother of Amāsis I., the first king of the XVIIIth dynasty, was found in the coffin of that queen by the fellâḥîn at Drah abu'l-Neḳḳa in 1860. Among the most beautiful objects of this find are :—

943. Gold bracelet, inlaid with lapis-lazuli, upon which Amāsis I. is shown kneeling between Seb and other gods.

944. Gold head-dress, inlaid with precious stones, inscribed with the name of Amāsis I.

945. Gold chain, terminated at each end by a goose's head; from the chain hangs a scarab made of gold and blue paste.

948. Part of a fan made of wood covered with gold, upon which Kames is shown making an offering to Khonsu.

949. Mirror of Åāḥ-ḥetep set in an ebony handle.

950. Cedar haft of an axe, plated with gold, into which a bronze axe, also plated with gold, inscribed with the cartouche of Amāsis I., has been fastened with gold wire.

951. Gold dagger, inscribed with the cartouche of Amāsis I. (?), and gold sheath inlaid with lapis-lazuli and other precious stones.

953. Gold pectoral, inlaid with precious stones, upon which Amāsis I. is represented standing in a sacred bark between the gods Åmen and Rā, who pour water upon him.

955. Gold model of the sacred bark of the dead, in the centre of which is seated Amāsis I. The rowers are made of silver, the body of the chariot of wood, and the wheels of bronze.

956. Silver bark and seven men found with the jewellery of Åāḥ-ḥetep.

958. Bronze dagger, set in a silver handle in the form of a circle.

962. Gold necklace.

963. Gold bracelet inlaid with lapis-lazuli, carnelian, and other precious stones.

963a. Gold bracelet inlaid with lapis-lazuli, carnelian, and other precious stones, inscribed with the prenomen of Amāsis I.

965. Bronze head of a lion inscribed with the prenomen of Amāsis I.

966. Nine small gold and silver axes.

967. Gold chain and three flies.

982. Gold figure of Ptaḥ.

983. Gold figure of Ȧmen.

All the other ornaments in this case are worth careful examination.

Room LXXI.—Scarabs, Amulets, etc.

Scarab or scarabæus (from the Greek *σκάραβος*) is the name given by Egyptologists to the myriads of models of a certain beetle, which are found in mummies and tombs and in the ruins of temples and other buildings in Egypt, and in other countries the inhabitants of which from a remote period, had intercourse with the Egyptians. M. Latreille considered the species which he named *Ateuchus Aegyptiorum*, or ἡλιοκάνθαρος, and which is of a fine greenish colour, as that which especially engaged the attention of the early Egyptians, and Dr. Clarke affirmed that it was eaten by the women of Egypt because it was considered to be an emblem of fertility. In these insects a remarkable peculiarity exists in the structure and situation of the hind legs, which are placed so near the extremity of the body, and so far from each other, as to give them a most extraordinary appearance when walking. This peculiar formation is, nevertheless, particularly serviceable to its possessors in rolling the balls of excrementitious matter in which they enclose their eggs. These balls are at first irregularly shaped and soft, but by degrees, and during the process of rolling along, become rounded and harder; they are propelled by means of the hind legs. Sometimes these balls are an inch and a half or two inches in diameter, and in rolling them along the beetles stand almost upon their heads, with the heads turned from the balls. They do this in order to bury their balls in holes which they have already dug for them, and it is upon the dung thus deposited that the larvæ when hatched feed. Horapollo thought that the beetle was self-produced, but he made this mistake on account of the females being exceedingly like the males, and because both sexes appear to divide the care of the preservation of their offspring equally between them.

The Egyptians called the scarabæus Kheperà  , and the god represented by this insect also Kheperà 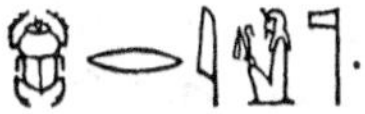. The god Kheperà was supposed to be the "father of the gods," and the creator of all things in heaven and earth; he made himself out of matter which he himself had made. He was identified with the rising sun and thus typified resurrection. The verb *Kheper* , which is usually translated "to exist, to become," also means "to roll," and "roller," or "revolver," was a fitting name for the sun. In a hieratic papyrus in the British Museum (No. 10,188), the god Khepera is identified with the god Neb-er-tcher, who, in describing the creation of gods, men, animals and things, says:—"I am he who evolved himself under the form of the god Kheperà. I, the evolver of evolutions, evolved myself, the evolver of all evolutions, after a multitude of evolutions and developments* which came forth from my mouth (or at my command). There was no heaven, there was no earth, animals which move upon the earth and reptiles existed not at all in that place. I constructed their forms out of the inert mass of watery matter. I found no place there where I could stand. By the strength which was in my will I laid the foundation [of things] in the form of the god Shu [see page 189], and I created for them every attribute which they have. I alone existed, for I had not as yet made Shu to emanate from me, and I had not ejected the spittle which became the god Tefnut; there existed none other to work with me. By my own will I laid the foundations of all things, and the evolutions of the things, and the evolutions which took place from the evolutions of their births which took place through the evolutions of their offspring, became multiplied. My shadow was united with me, and I produced Shu and Tefnut from the emanations of my body, ... thus from being one god I became three gods . . . . I gathered together my members and wept over them, and men and women sprang into existence from the tears which fell from my eye." Scarabs may be divided into three classes :—1. Funereal scarabs; 2. Scarabs worn for ornament; 3. Historical scarabs. Of **funereal scarabs**

* The duplicate copy of this chapter reads, "I developed myself from the primeval matter which I made. My name is Osiris, the germ of primeval matter. I have worked my will to its full extent in this earth, I have spread abroad and filled it . . . . . . I uttered my name as a word of power, from my own mouth, and I straightway developed myself by evolutions. I evolved myself under the form of the evolutions of the god Khepera, and I developed myself out of the primeval matter which has evolved multitudes of evolutions from the beginning of time. Nothing existed on this earth [before me], I made all things. There was none other who worked with me at that time. I made all evolutions by means of that soul which I raised up there from inertness out of the watery matter."

the greater number found measure from half an inch to two inches, and are made of steatite glazed green, or blue, or brown; granite, basalt, jasper, amethyst, lapis-lazuli, carnelian, and glass. The flat base of the scarab was used by the Egyptians for engraving with names of gods, kings, priests, officials, private persons, monograms and devices. Scarabs were set in rings and worn on the fingers by the dead or living, or were wrapped up in the linen bandages with which the mummy was swathed, and placed over the heart. The best class of funereal scarabs were made of a fine, hard, green basalt, which, when the instructions of the rubric concerning them in the Book of the Dead were carried out, were set in a gold border, and hung from the neck by a fine gold wire. Such scarabs are sometimes joined to a heart on which is inscribed, "life, stability, and protection" . Funereal scarabs were also set in pectorals, and were in this case ornamented with figures of the deceased adoring Osiris. Scarabs of all kinds were kept in stock by the Egyptian undertaker, and spaces were left blank in the inscriptions * to add the names of the persons for whom they were bought. **Scarabs worn for ornament** exist in many thousands. By an easy transition, the custom of placing scarabs on the bodies of the dead passed to the living, and men and women wore the scarab probably as a silent act of homage to the creator of the world, who was not only the god of the dead, but of the living also. **Historical scarabs** appear to be limited to a series of four, which were made during the reign of **Amenophis III.** to commemorate certain historical events, *viz.*, 1. The slaughter of 102 lions by Amenophis during the first ten years of his reign. 2. A description of the boundaries of the Egyptian Empire, and the names of the

* The chapter usually inscribed upon these scarabs is No. 30 B.

parents of Queen Thi. 3. The arrival of Thi and Gilukhipa in Egypt together with 317 women. 4. The construction of a lake in honour of Queen Thi.

Room LXXII.—Figures of the Gods and of Animals sacred to them.

1006. Black granite vase in the shape of a heart, dedicated to the god Thoth by Hophra.

1007. Bronze figure of a goddess.

1008. Bronze *lepidotus* fish.

In the standard and wall cases are arranged a very fine collection of **figures of the gods** of Egypt, and of the animals, birds, and reptiles, sacred to them. These interesting objects are made of glazed faïence, hard stone, bronze, glass, etc., and among them are some splendid specimens of excellent design and workmanship. Figures of gods are found among the ruins of houses, and in tombs and temples. Those found in the ruins were either placed in shrines, and represented the gods worshipped by the family, or were buried in niches in the walls, and were supposed to be able to protect the family by their supernatural influence. It is thought that the Egyptians believed that the gods inhabited the statues placed in the temples in their honour. Figures of gods were also buried in the sand round about houses and tanks with the view of guarding them from the influences of demons. The principal gods exhibited in this room are Ȧmen, Ȧmen-Rā, Ȧmsu, Anhur, Anubis, Apis, Ȧtmu, Bast, Bes, Ḥāpi, Harpocrates, Hathor, Horus, Horus-beḥuṭet, Ī-em-ḥetep (Imouthis), Isis, Khnemu (Chnoumis), Khensu, Maāt, Mahes, Mehit, Meḥ-urit, Mentu, Mut, Neḥebka, Nephthys, Nit (Neith), Nefer-Ȧtmu, Osiris, Ptaḥ, Ptaḥ-Seker-Osiris, Rā, Rā-Harmachis, Sebek, Set, Serqet, Shu, Ta-urt (Thoueris), and Thoth.

1015. Bronze statatues of the goddess Sekhet. From Saïs.

1016. Green basalt figure of the goddess **Ta-urt** (Thoueris), in the form of a hippopotamus; this is one of the finest examples of the work of the period.

1017. Green basalt table of offerings inscribed with the name of **Psammetichus**, an official.
XXVIth dynasty. From Karnak.

1018. Green basalt seated statue of **Osiris**, judge of the dead. XXVIth dynasty.

1019. Green basalt seated statue of **Isis**, wife of Osiris.
XXVIth dynasty.

1020. Green basalt statue of a cow, sacred to **Hathor**, the goddess of Åmentet or the underworld, in front of which stands the official **Psammetichus**, in whose honour this beautiful group was made. XXVIth dynasty.

Room LXXIII.—Collection of Egyptian Plants, Seeds, etc., classified and arranged by Dr. Schweinfurth.

Room LXXIV.

In this room M. de Morgan himself intended to arrange a mineralogical collection.

Galleries LXXV.—Sarcophagi of the XXVIth dynasty.

Room LXXVI.—Priests of Åmen.

1135. Cartonnage of Pameshon, high-priest of Åmen.

1136. Case inscribed with the name of Khonsu-em-ḥeb, "divine father" and scribe of the estates of Åmen-Rā at Thebes.

Room LXXVII.—Priests of Ȧmen.

1137, 1138. Coffins of children.

1140. Coffin of Ānkhes-nesit, a lady in the college of Ȧmen-Rā at Thebes.

1141. Coffin of Tanneferef, a "divine father" of Ȧmen.

Room LXXVIII.—Priests of Amen.

1142. Coffin of Nesi-neb-taui, a lady in the college of Ȧmen-Rā at Thebes.

Room LXXIX.—Priests of Ȧmen.

1144. Coffin of Peṭā-Ȧmen, a "divine father" and priest of the highest rank.

1145. Coffin of Ṭirpu, a lady in the college of Ȧmen-Rā.

1146. Coffin of Ānkh-f-en-Mut, a "divine father," which originally belonged to a lady whose name still stands upon it.

1147. Coffin of Ānkh-f-en-Mut, a priest of Mut, and scribe of the estates of Ȧmen, and priest of the Queen Ȧāḥ-ḥetep.

1148 a and b. Covers of coffins of Peṭā-Ȧmen, a scribe of the granaries of Ȧmen-Rā.

Room LXXX.—Priests of Ȧmen.

1150. Cover of a coffin of Pa-khare, surnamed Kha-nefer-Ȧmen, a "divine father."

1151 a and b. Coffins of Nesesta-pen-her-tahat, fourth prophet of Ȧmen.

1152. Coffin of Peṭā-Ȧmen, an official of Ȧmen, Mut and Khonsu.

Room LXXXI.—Priests of Ȧmen.

1153. Coffin of Ānkh-f-en-Khonsu, chief of the metal-workers of Ȧmen.

1154. Coffin of Nes-pa-nefer-ḥrȧ, a "divine father" of Ȧmen and Mut.

1155. Cartonnage of Ȧmen-nut-nekhtu, a metal-worker of Ȧmen.

1156. Cartonnage of Mert-Ȧmen, a lady in the college of Ȧmen-Rā.

1157 a and b. Covers of the inner coffin of Mert-Ȧmen.

1158. Coffin of Nesi-Ȧmen-ȧpt, a high-priest of Ȧmen, director of the offerings in the chamber of Anubis, *etc.*

Room LXXXII.—Priests of Ȧmen.

1160. Coffin of Peta-Ȧmen, a priest who held many high offices at Thebes.

1161. Coffin of Masha-sebeket, a lady attached to the service of Ȧmen-Rā, Mut, Hathor and Khonsu.

1162. Coffin of Pennest-taui, a scribe of the estates of Ȧmen.

1163. Coffin of Ta-nefer, a "divine father" of the goddess Maāt.

1164. Cartonnage of Khonsu-en-renp, a priest, "divine father," and scribe.

1165. Coffin of Nesi-pa-her-an, a "divine father" of Ȧmen, and scribe.

Room LXXXIII.—Priests of Ȧmen.

1166. Coffin of Ta-nefer, third prophet of Ȧmen-Rā, prophet of Mentu and Khnum, superintendent of the "flocks of the sun," *etc.*

1167 a and b. Cartonnage and coffin of Maāt-ka-Rā, a lady of the college of Ȧmen.

1168. Coffin of Heru, prophet of Åmen-Rā, Hathor, Khonsu, Anubis, *etc.*

1169. Coffin of Katsheshni, daughter of the first prophet of Åmen.

1170. Coffin of Men-kheper-Rā, son of Tcha-nefer, third prophet of Åmen.

1171. Coffin of Herub, second prophetess of the goddess Mut, *etc.*, daughter of Men-Kheper-Rā and Āuset-em-khebit.

Room LXXXIV.—The Der el-Baḥari Mummies.*

XVIITH DYNASTY, B.C. 1700.

1174. Coffin and mummy of **Seqenen-Rā.** This king was killed in battle.

XVIIITH DYNASTY, B.C. 1700–1400.

1172. Cartonnage mummy-case, inscribed with the name of Aāḥmes-nefert-åri, wife of Amāsis I.

1173. Mummy-case of Queen Åāḥ-ḥetep, wife of Amenophis I.

1175. Mummy and coffin of Amāsis I.

1176. Mummy and coffin of Se-Åmen, son of Amāsis I.

1177. Mummy and coffin of Amenophis I.

1178, 1188a. Coffin and mummy of Thothmes II.

1179, 1188. Coffin of **Thothmes III.** The mummy of this king when brought up from the pit at Dêr el-Baḥari was found to be in a very bad condition, and examination showed that it had been broken in three places in ancient times. The large scarab which was laid over the heart when the body of the king was being mummified is now in the British Museum.

* For an account of finding the mummies, see pp. 412–417.

XIXTH DYNASTY, B.C. 1400–1200.

1180. Coffin and **mummy of Seti I.**, father of Rameses II.

1181. Coffin and **mummy of Rameses II.**

XXTH DYNASTY, B.C. 1200–1100.

1182. Mummy of Rameses III., found in the coffin of Queen Åāḥmes-nefert-åri.

XXIST DYNASTY, B.C. 1100–1000

1183. Coffin of Pinetchem I.

1184. Coffin of Queen Åuset-em-khebit 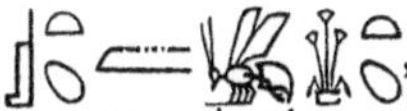, the daughter of Masahertha. The mummy is that of Nessu (*or* Nesi) Khensu.

1185. Coffin of Set-Åmen, daughter of Amāsis I.

1187, 1190. Coffins of Masahertha 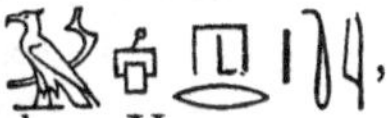, high-priest of Åmen, and son of Pinetchem II.

1189. Coffins of Tcheṭ-Ptaḥ-åuf-ānkh , priest and "divine father" of Åmen-Rā.

1191. Outer coffin of Åuset-em-khebit.

1192. Outer coffin of Maāt-ka-Rā (see No. 1198).

1193. Coffin and mummy of Nebseni , a scribe, the son of Pa-ḥeri-åb , and Ta-mesu .

1194. An excellent reproduction of the leather canopy of Åuset-em-khebit by E. Brugsch Bey and M. Bouriant.*

1195. Coffin of Netchemet , mother of the priest-king "Ḥer-Ḥeru, the son of Åmen" 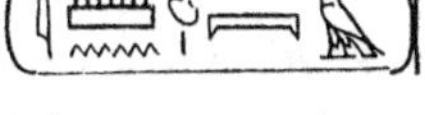.

* This interesting object is reproduced in Maspero, *Les Momies Royales de Déir el-Baharî* (*Mémoires de la Mission Archéologique Française*, Paris, 1887, p. 585).

1196. Coffin of Nessu-Khensu 

1198. Coffin and mummies of Queen Maāt-ka-Rā, daughter of Pa-seb-khā-nut, and her infant daughter Mut-em-ḥāt . It is thought that the queen died in giving birth to her daughter.

1199. Coffins of Nesi-ta-neb-âsher  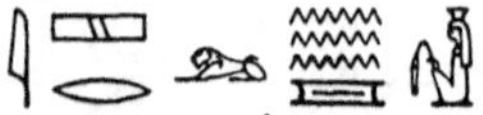, daughter of Nesi-Khensu, and priestess of Åmen.

1204. Cover of the coffin of Queen Netchemet.

1206. Box containing the wig of Princess Åuset-em-khebit.

1208. Small chest inscribed with the name of Rameses IX.

1212. Oars found with the mummy of Thothmes III.

1214. Coffin of Pi-netchem II., son of Åuset-em-khebit.

1216. Coffin, which originally belonged to Thothmes I., and mummy of Pi-netchem I.

1217. Gilded cover of the outer coffin of Queen Åuset-em-khebit.

Case E. Cover of the coffin of Thothmes I.

Case F. Cover of the coffin of Masahertha.

1225. Wooden plaque inscribed in hieratic with the assurances of the god Åmen concerning the welfare of the Princess Nesi-Khonsu. A duplicate of this plaque is preserved in the British Museum.

Case H. Cover of the coffin of Maāt-ka-Rā.

Case I. Cover of the coffin of Nesi-Khonsu.

Case K. Cover of the outer coffin of Nesi-ta-neb-âsher.

Case L. Cover of the coffin of Amenophis I.

1234, 1235. Cover and cartonnage of the coffin of Pi-netchem II.

1236. Cover of the coffin of Queen Ḥent-taui.

1237. Coffin of Rameses II.

1238. Mummy of Åuset-em-khebit.

Case O. Cover of the coffin of Rameses II.

Rooms LXXXV and LXXXVI.—Mummies of the Priests of Amen.

On the landing of the staircase leading to Room LXXXVII, is:

1251. Gilded cover of the coffin of Åāḥ-ḥetep I., the queen whose jewellery is exhibited in Room No. LXX.

Room LXXXVII.

1252. Gilded coffin of Ḥeru-se-Åuset, prophet of Horus of Beḥuṭet.

1253. Coffin of Åuset, mother of Sen-netchem.

1254. Funereal sledge of Khonsu, found in the coffin of Sen-netchem.

1256. Coffin and mummy of Tripi (?).
1st century A.D. From Thebes.

1258. Coffin of Amenårṭās.

1259. Funereal sledge of Sennetchem.

1260. Coffin of Sennetchem. From Dêr el-Medîneh.

1261. Mummy of a woman. Greek period.

1264, 1265. Portraits painted upon wax laid upon pieces of wood, which were fastened by bandages over the faces of mummies. From the Fayyûm.

1266. Portrait painted on a mummy wrapping.

1272. Painted wooden mummy-bier.

The other coffins exhibited in this room are worthy of careful examination.

Room LXXXVIII.

1278. Granite sarcophagus of Queen Nitocris.
From Dêr el-Medîneh.

1280. Grey granite sarcophagus inscribed with the name of Psammetichus.

1281–1284. Sarcophagi of the Greek period.

1285. Grey granite sarcophagus of Ānkh-Ḥāpi.
From Saḳḳârah.

1286. Limestone Sarcophagus of Tche-ḥrȧ.

1299, 1300. Grey granite sarcophagi of two brothers, each of whom was called Tchaho.

1302 a and b. Basalt sarcophagus of Ḥeru-em-ḥeb.

1304. Black granite sarcophagus of Un-nefer.

1305. Grey basalt sarcophagus of Ī-em-ḥetep, a priest.

1308. Grey basalt sarcophagus of Bataita, mother of the brothers Tchaho.

Whether the art of mummifying was known to the aboriginal inhabitants of Egypt, or whether it was introduced by the newcomers from Asia, is a question which is very difficult to decide. We know for a certainty that the stele of a dignitary preserved at Oxford was made during the reign of Senṭ, the fifth king of the IInd dynasty, about B.C. 4000. The existence of this stele, with its figures and inscriptions, points to the fact that the art of elaborate sepulture had reached a high pitch in those early times. The man for whom it was made was called  Sherȧ, and he held the dignity of  *neter ḥen*, or "prophet"; the stele also tells us that he was  *suten reχt*, or "royal kinsman." The inscriptions contain prayers asking for the deceased in the nether-world "thousands of oxen, linen bandages, cakes, vessels of wine, incense, etc.," which fact shows that religious belief, funereal ceremonies, and a hope for a life after death had already become a part of the life of the people of Egypt. During the reign of King Senṭ the redaction of a medical papyrus was carried out. As this work presupposes many years of experiment and experience, it is clear that the Egyptians possessed ample anatomical knowledge for mummifying a human body. Again, if we consider that the existence of this king is proved by papyri and contemporaneous monuments, and that we know the names of some of the priests who took part in funereal ceremonies during his reign, there is no difficulty in acknowledging the great antiquity of such ceremonies, and that they presuppose a religious belief in the revivification of the body, for which hoped-for event the Egyptian took the greatest possible care to hide and preserve his body.

"Mummy" is the term which is generally applied to the body of a human being or animal which has been preserved from decay by means of bitumen, spices, gums, and natron. As far as can be discovered, the word is neither a corruption of the ancient Egyptian word for a preserved body, nor of the more modern Coptic form of the hieroglyphic name. The word "mummy" is found in Byzantine Greek and in Latin, and indeed in almost all European languages. It is derived from the Arabic مُوميَا *mûmîâ*, "bitumen"; the Arabic word for mummy is مُوميّة *mûmîyyet*, and means a "bitumenized thing," or a body preserved by bitumen.

We obtain our knowledge of the way in which the ancient Egyptians mummified their dead from Greek historians and from an examination of mummies. According to Herodotus (ii. 86) the art of mummifying was carried on by a special guild of men who received their appointment by law. These men mummified bodies in three different ways, and the price to be paid for preserving a body varied according to the manner in which the work was done. In the first and most expensive method the brain was extracted through the nose by means of an iron probe, and the intestines were removed entirely from the body through an incision made in the side with a sharp Ethiopian stone. The intestines were cleaned and washed in palm wine, and, having been covered with powdered aromatic gums, were placed in jars. The cavity in the body was filled up with myrrh and cassia and other fragrant and astringent substances, and was sewn up again. The body was next laid in natron for seventy days,* and when these were over, it was carefully washed, and afterwards wrapped up in strips of fine linen smeared on their sides with gum. The cost of mummifying a body in this fashion was a talent of silver, *i.e.*, about £240, according to Diodorus (i. 91, 92).

In the second method of mummifying the brain was not removed at all, and the intestines were simply dissolved and removed in a fluid state. The body was also laid in salt or natron which, it is said, dissolved everything except the skin and bones. The cost of mummifying in this manner was 20 minae, or about £80.

The third method of embalming was employed for the poor only. It consisted simply of cleaning the body by injecting some strong astringent, and then salting the body for seventy days. The cost in this case was very little.

The account given by Diodorus agrees generally with that of Herodotus. He adds, however, that the incision was made on the left side of the body, and that the "dissector" having made the incision fled away, pursued and stoned by those who had witnessed the ceremony. It would seem that the dissector merely fulfilled a religious obligation in fleeing away, and that he had not much to fear. Diodorus goes on to say that the Egyptians kept the

* In Genesis l. 3, the number is given as forty.

bodies of their ancestors in splendid chambers, and that they had the opportunity of contemplating the faces of those who died before their time. In some particulars he is right, and in others wrong. He lived too late (about B.C. 40) to know what the well-made Theban mummies were like, and his experience therefore would only have familiarised him with the Egypto-Roman mummies, in which the limbs were bandaged separately, and the contour of their faces, much blunted, was to be seen through the thin and tightly drawn bandages which covered the face. In such examples the features of the face can be clearly distinguished underneath the bandages.

An examination of Egyptian mummies will show that the accounts given by Herodotus and Diodorus are generally correct, for mummies with and without ventral incisions are found, and some are preserved by means of balsams and gums, and others by bitumen and natron. The skulls of mummies which may be seen by hundreds in caves and pits at Thebes contain absolutely nothing, a fact which proves that the embalmers were able not only to remove the brain, but also to take out the membranes without injuring or breaking the nose in any way. The heads of mummies are found, at times, to be filled with bitumen, linen rags, or resin. The bodies which have been filled with resin or some such substance are of a greenish colour, and the skin has the appearance of being tanned. Such mummies, when unrolled, perish rapidly and break easily. Usually, however, the resin and aromatic gum process is favourable to the preservation of the teeth and hair. Bodies from which the intestines have been removed and which have been preserved by being filled with bitumen, are quite black and hard. The features are preserved intact, but the body is heavy and unfair to look upon. The bitumen penetrates the bones so completely that it is sometimes difficult to distinguish what is bone and what is bitumen. The arms, legs, hands, and feet of such mummies break with a sound like the cracking of chemical glass tubing; they burn freely. Speaking generally, they will last for ever.

When a mummy has been preserved by natron, that is, a mixture of carbonate, sulphate, and muriate of soda, the skin is found to be very hard, and it hangs loosely from the bones in much the same way as it hangs from the skeletons of the dead monks preserved in the crypt beneath the Capuchin convent at Floriana in Malta. The hair of such mummies usually falls off when touched.

When the friends of a dead Egyptian were too poor to pay for the best method of embalmment, the body could be preserved by two very cheap methods; one method was to soak it in salt and hot bitumen, and the other in salt only. In the salt and bitumen process every cavity of the body was filled with bitumen, and the hair disappeared. Clearly it is to the bodies which were preserved in this way that the name "mummy," or bitumen, was first applied.

The salted and dried body is easily distinguishable. The skin is like paper, the features and hair have disappeared, and the bones are very brittle and white.

The art of mummifying arrived at the highest pitch of perfection at Thebes. The mummies of the first six dynasties drop to pieces on exposure to the air, and smell slightly of bitumen; those of the XIth dynasty are of a yellowish colour and very brittle; those of the XIIth dynasty are black. The method of embalming varied at different periods and places. From the XVIIIth to the XXIst dynasties the Memphis mummies are black, while those made at Thebes during the same period are yellowish in colour, and have the nails of the hands and feet dyed yellow with the juice of the *henna* plant. After the XXVIth dynasty the mummies made at both places are quite black and shapeless; they are also very heavy and tough, and can only be broken with difficulty.

What the mummies which were made three or four hundred years after Christ are like, the writer never having seen one unrolled, is unable to say. About B.C. 100 the Greeks began to paint the portrait of the dead upon the wrappings which covered the face.

The art of mummifying was carried on in Egypt for nearly five hundred years after the birth of Christ, for the Greeks and Romans adopted the custom freely. We may then say that we know for a certainty that the art of embalming was known and practised for about five thousand years.

In the account of embalming given us by Herodotus, we are told that the internal organs of the body were removed, but he omits to say what was done with them. We now know that they also were mummified and preserved in four jars, the covers of which were made in the shape of the heads of the four children of Horus, the genii of the dead, whose names were Mestha, Ḥāpi, Ṭuamāutef, and Qebḥsennuf. These genii have been compared with the four beasts in the Revelation (chap. iv. 7). The jars and the genii to which they were dedicated were under the protection of Isis, Nephthys, Neith, and Serk respectively. They are called "Canopic" jars, because they resemble the vase shape of Osiris called Canopus, and they are made of Egyptian porcelain, marble, calcareous stone, terra-cotta, wood, etc. The jar of Mesthà received the stomach, that of Ḥāpi the smaller intestines, that of Ṭuamāutef the heart, and that of Qebḥsennuf the liver. Each jar was inscribed with a legend stating that the genius to which it was dedicated protected and preserved the part of the dead body that was in it. In the case of poor people, who could not afford a set of canopic jars, it was usual to have a set of wax figures made in the shape of the four genii of the dead, and to place them in the dead body with the intestines, which were put back. In the time of the XXVIth dynasty, and later, poverty or laziness made people consider the interior parts of the body to be sufficiently well guarded if figures of these genii were roughly drawn on the linen bandages. It was sometimes customary to lay a set of these figures, made of porcelain or bead-work, upon the chest of the mummy.

It was the fashion some years ago to state in books of history that the ancient Egyptian was a negro, and some distinguished historians still make this statement, notwithstanding Prof. Owen's distinct utterance, "taking the sum of the correspondence notable in collections of skulls from Egyptian graveyards as a probable indication of the hypothetical primitive race originating the civilised conditions of cranial departure from the skull-character of such race, that race was certainly not of the Australoid type, is more suggestive of a northern Nubian or Berber basis. But such suggestive characters may be due to intercourse or 'admixture' at periods later than [the] XIIIth dynasty; they are not present, or in a much less degree, in the skulls, features, and physiognomies of individuals of from the IIIrd to the XIIth dynasties."* The character of the ancient Egyptian,

* *Journal of the Anthropological Institute of Great Britain and Ireland*, vol. iv., p. 239. The most important scientific examinations of the skeletons of mummified Egyptians in England have been made by the late Sir Richard Owen, Prof. Sir W. Flower, and Prof. Macalister of Cambridge. Some years ago the writer collected for this last-named *savant* beween six and seven hundred Egyptian skulls from Thebes and Aswân (Syene). The greater part of these reached England in excellent condition, and they have been measured and examined by craniological experts. On some of them the skin of the face and neck remains in a perfect condition, and Prof. Macalister has found means whereby he is able to make these dry and withered faces fill out and resume something of the appearance which they wore in life. As all these skulls are of great antiquity, and belonged to high-class Egyptians, priests, and others, the results of his work may be anticipated with great interest by both the ethnographist and Egyptologist.

and of the race to which he belonged, has been vindicated by examinations of the skulls of Egyptian mummies.

If the pure ancient Egyptian, as found in mummies and represented in paintings upon the tombs, be compared with the negro, we shall find that they are absolutely unlike in every important particular. The negro is prognathous, but the Egyptian is orthognathous; the bony structure of the negro is heavier and stronger than that of the Egyptian; the hair of the negro is crisp and woolly, while that of the Egyptian is smooth and fine.

It must be pointed out clearly that the Egyptians originally took trouble to preserve the bodies of the dead because they believed that after a series of terrible combats in the underworld, the soul, triumphant and pure, would once more return to the clay in which it had formerly lived. It was necessary, then, to preserve the body that it might be ready for the return of the soul. It was also necessary to build large and beautiful tombs, in order that the triumphant soul, having revivified its ancient house of clay, might have a fit and proper abode in which to dwell. The pyramid tombs built by the kings of the earlier dynasties, and the vast many-chambered sepulchres hewn in the sides of the Theban hills during the XVIIIth and XIXth dynasties, were not built to gratify the pride of their owners. This belief however, seems to have been considerably modified at a later period, for the evidence now available indicates that the later Egyptians preserved the material body in order that the spiritual body might spring from it, which result was partly due to the ceremonies performed and the words recited at the tomb by the priests and pious persons.

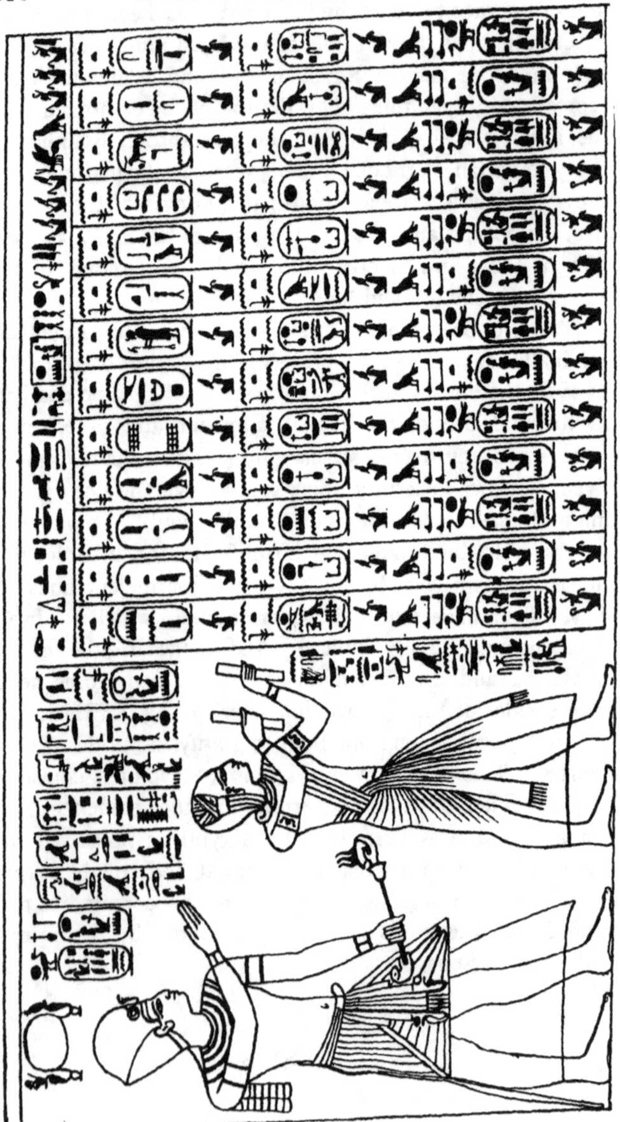

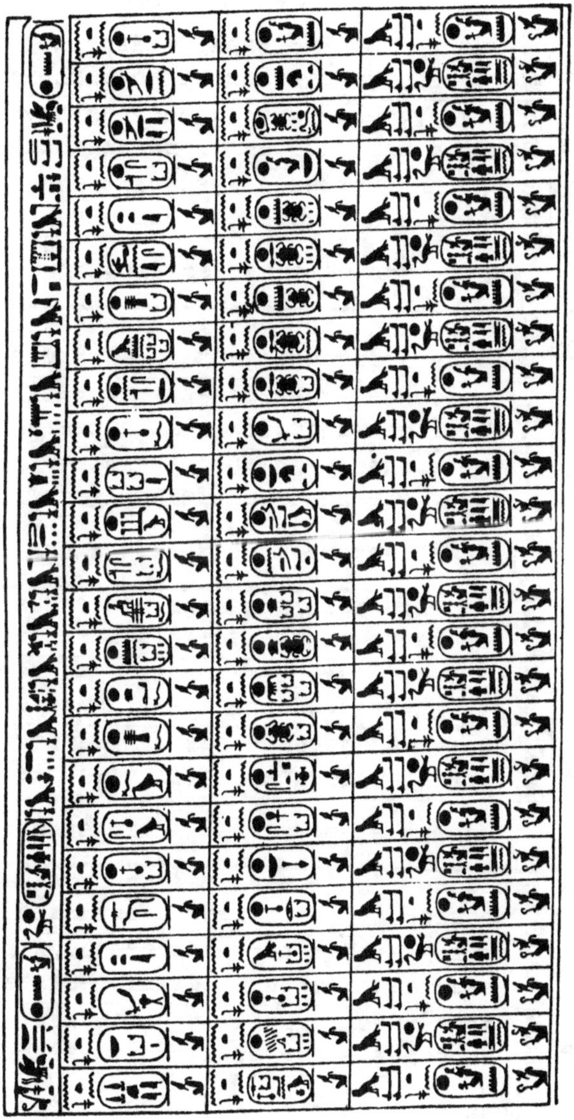

The King List of Abydos.

Comparative Tables showing the RISE OF THE NILE, as registered by the Roda Gauge.

	1901		1900		1899	
	Pics	Kts	Pics	Kts	Pics	Kts
July						
21 ...	12	22	9	22	10	17
22 ...	13	4	10	2	10	17
23 ...	13	4	10	7	10	17
24 ...	13	5	10	16	10	19
25 ...	13	5	11	2	10	21
26 ...	13	6	11	15	10	23
27 ...	13	6	12	5	11	1
28 ...	13	7	12	20	11	4
29 ...	13	8	13	3	11	7
30 ...	13	12	13	5	10	10
31 ...	13	11	13	1	11	13
Aug.						
1 ...	13	13	13	4	11	16
2 ...	13	15	13	5	12	6
3 ...	13	17	13	6	12	8
4 ...	13	18	13	7	12	8
5 ...	13	18	13	7	12	9
6 ...	13	20	13	8	12	10
7 ...	13	21	13	9	12	13
8 ...	14	0	13	9	12	17
9 ...	14	1	13	9	12	20
10 ...	14	2	13	11	12	23
11 ...	14	7	14	16	13	2
12 ...	14	16	15	12	13	3
13 ..	15	7	16	14	13	4
14 ...	15	16	17	19	13	7
15 ...	15	21	18	8	13	17
16 ...	16	3	18	12	14	2
17 ...	16	11	18	15	14	14
18 ...	16	15	18	17	14	23
19 ...	16	22	18	23	15	3
20 ...	17	8	19	4	15	7
21 ...	18	0	19	13	15	8
22 ...	18	18	19	22	15	7
23 ...	19	8	20	0	15	6

	1901		1900		1899	
	Pics	Kts	Pics	Kts	Pics	Kts
Aug.						
24 ...	19	16	20	3	15	6
25 ...	19	20	20	7	15	6
26 ...	19	22	20	4	15	7
27 ...	20	0	20	9	15	7
28 ...	20	0	20	8	15	9
29 ...	20	0	20	8	15	12
30 ...	20	0	20	8	15	17
31 ...	19	23	20	8	15	23
Sept.						
1 ...	20	0	20	12	16	8
2 ...	19	23	20	14	16	15
3 ...	19	23	20	14	16	16
4 ...	19	23	20	13	16	16
5 ...	19	23	20	12	16	15
6 ...	19	21	20	10	16	15
7 ...	19	22	20	7	16	17
8 ...	20	2	20	0	16	19
9 ...	20	9	19	18	16	20
10 ...	20	15	19	13	16	20
11 ...	20	19	19	8	16	19
12 ...	20	22	19	4	16	16
13 ...	20	22	19	0	16	15
14 ...	20	22	18	19	16	11
15 ...	20	22	18	15	16	8
16 ...	20	20	18	10	16	6
17 ...	20	20	18	7	16	5
18 ...	20	17	18	6	16	3
19 ...	20	15	18	8	16	0
20 ...	20	13	18	10	16	0
21 ...	20	17	18	14	15	23
22 ...	21	0	18	19	15	23
23 ...	21	4	19	3	16	0
24 ...	21	6	19	8	16	4
25 ...	21	8	19	12	16	7

	1901		1900		1899	
	Pics	Kts	Pics	Kts	Pics	Kts
Sept.						
26 ...	21	3	19	13	16	9
27 ...	21	2	19	14	16	7
28 ...	21	0	19	12	16	1
29 ...	20	20	19	10	15	23
30 ...	20	14	19	10	15	21
Oct.						
1 ...	20	3	19	12	15	20
2 ...	19	20	19	12	15	19
3 ...	19	20	19	12	15	18
4 ...	19	16	19	9	15	16
5 ...	19	13	19	5	15	16
6 ...	19	7	19	1	15	14
7 ...	19	0	18	20	15	10
8 ...	18	20	18	19	15	9
9 ...	18	15	19	0	15	9
10 ...	18	9	19	11	15	7
11 ...	17	21	19	22	15	5
12 ...	17	18	20	0	15	2
13 ...	18	5	20	0	15	0
14 ...	18	10	20	0	14	21
15 ...	18	10	19	20	14	19
16 ...	18	8	19	22	14	16
17 ...	18	8	20	4	14	14
18 ...	18	8	20	4	14	12
19 ...	18	12	20	7	14	11
20 ...	18	12	20	21	14	8
21 ...	18	15	21	0	14	6
22 ...	18	12	20	22	14	4
23 ...	18	8	20	21	14	2
24 ...	18	5	19	23	13	23
25 ...	18	1	19	13	13	21
26 ...	17	22	18	19	13	18
27 ...	17	17	18	0	13	16
28 ...	17	0	17	7	13	16

	1901		1900		1899	
	Pics	Kts	Pics	Kts	Pics	Kts
Oct.						
29 ...	16	5	16	15	13	13
30 ...	15	20	17	0	13	12
31 ...	15	18	17	4	13	12
Nov.						
1 ...	15	13	17	0	13	10
2 ...	15	9	16	20	13	9
3 ...	15	14	16	23	13	9
4 ...	15	16	16	18	13	9
5 ...	15	14	16	0	13	10
6 ...	15	22	15	21	13	9
7 ...	16	5	15	23	13	9
8 ...	15	22	15	20	13	8
9 ...	15	20	15	14	13	4
10 ...	15	16	15	11	13	1
11 ...	15	13	15	7	12	23
12 ...	15	13	15	3	12	21
13 ...	15	8	15	1	12	20
14 ...	15	4	14	20	12	19
15 ...	15	0	14	15	12	18
16 ...	14	20	14	12	12	16
17 ...	14	18	14	11	12	17
18 ...	14	15	14	11	12	19
19 ...	14	2	14	11	12	19
20 ...	13	23	14	9	12	18
21 ...	13	21	14	7	12	16
22 ...	13	18	14	3	12	15
23 ...	13	17	13	22	12	14
24 ...	13	13	13	18	12	13
25 ...	13	7	13	14	12	12
26 ...	12	23	13	10	12	12
27 ...	12	18	13	5	12	19
28 ...	12	14	13	1	12	19
29 ...	12	12	12	21	12	16
30 ...	12	9	12	18	12	15

INDEX.

The main references are printed in blacker type.]

PAGE

Aāḥ-ḥetep, Queen, Jewellery of 417, **432**, **532**, **605**, 606
Åāḥmes (Amāsis I.), 14, **416**, 532; tomb of **348**
Åāḥmes II. .. **17**, **542**
Åāḥmes, son of Abana 435
Åāḥmes-nefert-åri 416, **532**
Åāḥmes-se-pa-åri ...**532**
Åāḥsat, wife of Thothmes III. 421
Āāmu 341
Āauputh 414
Āa-qenen-Rā **531**
Åat-tcha-Mutet... ...**395**
Åb, king ... **11**, **523**
Åba, tomb of 450
Åba al-Waḳf **322**
Ababdeh Arabs ... 196
Abana 435, 436
Abba Bêsa 353
,, Island of 38, 39, 48, 235
,, Nûb 270

PAGE

'Abbâs, Pâsha, son of Ṭusûn **32**
'Abbâs II. Hilmy ... 45
Abbas, steamer, wreck of **236**
Abbasides **27**
'Abd-Allah } the Khalifa
'Abd-Allahi } ... 213, **238**ff
'Abd-Allah, an officer ... 39
,, son of 'Amr 274
,, wad Sûd ... 514
'Abd al-Laṭîf 281
'Abd al-Muṭṭalib ... 213
'Abd er-Rasûl Aḥmad ... **413** 414
Abdîn Palace 35
Abercromby, Sir R. ... 30
Abkeh (Amkeh) ... 489
Aboccis... ... ...**474**
Abraham, the Patriarch 211, 453
Åbshek **474**
Absorption of Nile water **79**
Abu (Elephantine) ... 442
Abû Bakr 214, 217, 233
Abû Dês 504

PAGE

Abû Girgeh 331
Abû Gûs **495**
Abû Hadrî 452
Abû Hagag 375
Abû Ḥamed ... 46, 47, 486
Abû Ḥamed, Battle of ... 504
Abû Ḥammâd 264
Abû Ḥanîfa 231
Abû Ḥonnes 343
Abû Ḳerḳâṣ 322
Abû Klea ... 41, 42
Abû Kru 42
Abû Mansûr 304
Abû Milki 595
Abû Roâsh, Pyramids of 283, 296
Abû Ṣalîḥ quoted 331, 333, **452**, 460, 494
Abû Salma 215
Abû Sargah 270
Abû Sellem 504
Abû Sinûn, Cataract of 505
Abû Shûsâ 323
Abu's Sêfên 270
Âbû Simbel 59, 109, 114, **474–480**
Abû Ṭâlib ... 213, 214
Abû Tamîm al-Mustanṣir 28
Abû Tîg ... **323, 350**
Abu Tisht 323
Abuḳîr Bay ... 29, 30
Abuṣîr, Pyramids of ... 296
„ Rock of ... 480
Abydos ... 16, 61, 105, 123, 566

PAGE

Abydos, Temples at **357, 360**
„ King List of ... **359**
„ Excavations at ... 362
„ Tablet of **1, 3**, 626, 627
Abyssinia ... 15, 196
„ sources of Nile in ... **73–75**
Achoris 397
Achillas 200
Acre 28, **31**
Adam 219, 220
„ and Eve... ... 227
Ad-Dâmer **508**
Addu-asharid 595
'Adîd Ledînallâh ... 28
Âdhôrbâîjân 250
Adnân 211
Adowa 46
Adrianople, Mahdi of ... 235
Adultery 226
Aelian quoted ... 331, 348
Aelius Gallus 21, 373, 394, 470
Africa 400, 408
Africanus 7
'Afrîts 219
Agathon 204
Āḥā, tomb of ... 363, **369**
Aḥmad Arabi 36
Aḥmad Bey 49
Aḥmad ibn-Tulûn 27, **269**
Aḥmad, Mosque of ... 274
Aḥmad Kamal 415
Âhnâs 329, 330
Âḥtes **520**

PAGE

Ài (XIVth dynasty) ... **529**
Ài (XVIIIth „) ... 534
„ („ „), sarcophagus of 119
Ài (XVIIIth dynasty), tomb of 348
Aird & Co., Messrs. ... 87
Aisha **214**
Akasheh 46, 485, 491
Akerblad 126
Akhmîm (Panopolis) 181, **353**
Aku, tomb of 448
Alabastronpolis 61
Alashiya 595
Al-'Aḍra (Al-'Adhra) ... 270
Al-'Amrah 67
Al-'Arîsh 29
Al-Ashraf Khalîl ... 28
Al-'Aṣṣirât 323
Al-'Ayât... 321
Al-'Azîz 27
Albania 30
Albanians 30
Al-Bersheh 344
Albert-Nyanza 73
Al-Dabbah 495
Alexander the Great 19, 247, 282, 379, 485, **544**
Alexander I. 20
„ II. 20
„ „ stele of ... 590
„ IV. 387, 391, 544
„ , the Patriarch, 202
Alexandria 19, 24, **247**, **255**
„ Library of 19, **124**

PAGE

Alexandria captured by 'Amr, 26; occupied by Napoleon I., 29; Battle of, 30; massacre at, 23; bombardment of ... 37
Al-Ferdân 261
'Ali Bey... 29
'Ali, cousin of Muḥammad 233
Al-Gazîra **324**
Al-Ghûri 28
Al-Ḥafîr... 493
Al-Ḥîra 211
Al-Islâm, see Islâm ... 215
Al-Ḳanṭara **261**
Al-Kaswa 214
Al-Khârgeh, Oasis of ... 94
Al-Khaṭṭâra 324
Al-Ḳur'ân .. 217, 218
Al Ḳusîyeh 348
Almohades 234
Almsgiving 223
Al-Obêda 504
Al-Samaṭâ 324
Al-Uḳṣûr 324
Al-Urdî 493
Al-Uzza... 212
'Alwah 495
Al-Wasṭa 321
'Amâda 473
Āmām 152
'Amârah, Temple of ... 491
Amāsis I. 14, 306, **348**, 406, **416**, **532**
„ II. ... **17**, **542**
Amba Mîna 204

PAGE
Amba Musas 362
Amba Shenûdah ... 351
Ambûkûl (Ambigol) Station 491
„ Wells of 486, 491
Ȧmen } 19, **375**, 171;
Ȧmen-Rā } hymn to, 177, 178
Ȧmen, priests of, **611–614, 617**
Ȧmenȧrṭȧs 397
„ statue of ... 585
„ Temple of 397, 398
Ȧmen-em-ȧpt ... **16**, 537
Ȧmen-em-ḥāt I. 13, 342, **526**
„ II. 13, **526**
„ III. 13, 314–317, **526**
„ Pyramid of, 327; builds Lake Moëris, 325; his works at Semneh, 76, **489**
„ IV. 13, **527**
Ȧmen-ḥetep I. 14, 416, **532**
„ II. ... 14, **533**
„ III. ... 15, **533**
„ IV. ... 15, 533
Ȧmeni-Ȧmenemḥāt **335–337**
Ȧmeni-Ȧntef-Ȧmenemḥāt 527, **580**
Ȧmen-meses 535
Amenophis I. 14, 387, 406, **593**

PAGE
Amenophis II. 14, 385, 388, 389, **593**; tomb of 421
„ III. 5, 15, 306, 319, 385, 394, **594**; birth of, depicted, 379; mummy of, 422; Temples of 375, 492
„ IV. 5, 15, **345–347, 375, 376**, 406, **594**; mummy of, 422; tomb of 348
Ȧmen-ruṭ ... 18, **541**
Ȧmenta 149, 156
Ȧmentuf 12
Amélineau ... 67, **362**
American Missionaries... 55, **206, 349**
Ameru 399
Amkeh 489
Amîna 213
Amnis Trajânus ... 23
'Amr, Khalîfa 195
„ Mosque of ... 274
'Ȧmr ibn al-'Aṣi **26**, 27, **203**, 248, 268
Ȧmsu-Ȧmen 96
Ȧmsu 163, **171, 353**, 368
Amulets... ... **602–604**
Amyrtaeus 18
Ȧn, king 521
Ȧnȧ 529
Ȧn-āa 12, **524**

PAGE
Ānāb 529
Ananius... 200
Ȧn-ȧntef 12
Anastasius, Emperor ... 26
„ of Antioch... 25
Anatomy, work on ... 10
Anba Shenûti 270
Ancient Empire ... 8
Andronicus 203
Aneb-ḥet' 299
Aneq 167, 469
Angels **219**
Ȧn-Hāpi 416
Ani, Papyrus of... 149, **152**, **153**, 162
Ani, Maxims of... 165, 561, **597**, **598**
Ani, a form of Rā ... 174
Anibe 474
Animals, sacred... ... 604
Anḳareb 506
Ānkh-mȧ-Rā 576
Ȧnnu (On, Heliopolis)... 157
Ȧnnu-qemāt 432
Ȧnpu (Anubis) 130, 187
Ȧn-ruṭ-f 330
Antæopolis ... 61, **350**
Antaeus 350
Anṭar 334
Ȧntef kings, the **12**, 432, **524**
Ȧntef-ȧ 579
Ȧntef-āa... ... 12, **525**
Anthony, Saint ... 200, 207
Anthropomorphites 24, 248

PAGE
Antichrist 233
Antinoë... 343
Antinous 343
Antioch ... 10, 25
Antiochus 20
Antiquaries, Society of **126**
Antirhodus 250
Antkha 573
Antoninus **23**, 395, 464, **552**
Antony 21
„ and Cleopatra... 247
Anttenet 159
Ȧntuf 524
Ȧntuf-āa 525
Anubis 145, **149**, 152, **187**, 380
Anuqet 458
Āpep 170, 173
Āpepȧ I. **14**, 531, **581**
„ II. **14**, 531, **581**
Apet 370
Aphroditopolis 61, 62, 186, 329
Apion 7
Apis **10**, 62, **190**, 299, **305**
„ Slain by Cambyses 300
„ Bulls of 565; Mausoleum ... 305, 307
Apollo 357, 432
Apollinopolis Magna 61, **437**
„ Parva ... 368
Apollonius 267
Apostasy 267
Apostles... 220
Apries (Hophra) 17, 524

PAGE

Apt, North } 375
„ South }
Apts, the ... 176, 177
'Arâbat el-Madfûneh ... 355
Arabi Pâsha **36**, 37, 51, **264**
Arabia 12, 211
Arabs **8**, 206, 207, **210–213**
'Arafât 224
Araj, Oasis of 96
Arcadius 24
Archangels, the Four ... 219
Archimedes 249
Argîn 44
Argo (Arḳaw), Island of 38, 493
Ariab 505
Arians 24
Ȧri-ḥes-nefer 462
'Arîsh 26
Aristophanes of Byzantium 247
Aristotle 257
Ȧrit-ḥetep 343
Arius ... 24, **201**, 248
Armant ... 324, 353, 432
Armenians 22, 192, 198
Arq-Ȧmen 470
Arsenal at Omdurmân... 517
Arses 19
Arsinoë... 19, 325, 545, 546
Artaghasi 493
Artashumara 593
Artatama 593
Artaxerxes I. ... 18, 543
„ II. 18

PAGE

Artaxerxes III.... ... 18
Artemis... 334
Arzapi 595
Arzawya 595
Asasîf 432
Ascalon... 28
Ȧset (see Isis)
Ȧset 406, 421
Asfûn al-Mata'na 324, 433
Ashmant 322
Ashur-uballiṭ 595
Asia 15
Askelon 231
Ȧspaleta 584
Asphynis 433
Ȧssȧ 522
As-sur, Pyramids of ... 510
Assur-bani-pal ... 6, 300
Astaboras 506
Assyrian Viceroys ... 7
Assyrians, the 17
Aswân ... 57, 59, **324, 444**
„ Dam and Reservoir at 87, 88, 461
„ Gold Mines ... 452
„ Quarries (clay and granite)... 453
„ Obelisk at ... 453
„ Tombs at ... 103
„ Western ... 446
Asyûṭ ... 60, **63, 323, 349**
„ Dam at 88
Ȧta, king 519
Atbara, River 74, **78**, 482, 484, **506**

PAGE
Atbara, Battle of the 47, 507
Atchab 362
Åtcha-khar-Åmen ... 467
Atep 573
Atet 320
Āṭet Boat 176
Åteta 574
Åteth 519
Aṭfîh 329
Athanasius 23, 201, 202, 248
Athôr, month of ... 181
Athribis 62, **352**
Ati 522
Atlidam 322
Åtmu (Tem, or Temu) **168**, 174, 175, 177, **189**
Åtmu-khepera 177
Åuf-na 527
Augustus Cæsar 251, 366, **379**, 464, 468, **549**
Auletes 20
Aurelian 23
Aurelius 553
Āu-åb-Rā (king) ... 317
Åuset-em-khebit ... 417
Avenue of Sphinxes ... 306
Awlâd 'Amrû 324
'Azâzêl 219
Azd, tribe of 211
Azîru 595
'Azîz 27, 275
Azraêl 219

B

Baalbek 282

PAGE
Bâb-el-Azab 279
Bâb-en-Naṣr 278
Babylon 5, 15, 17
Babylonians 72
Babylon (Cairo) ... 268
„ Fortress of 26, 27, 203
Bacchus 181
Bactria 22
Bactrians 374
Ba-en-neter ... 10, **519**
Badr, Battle of 214
Baghdad 232
Bagnold, Colonel A. ... 302
Bagromeh 509
Baḥr al-Abyaḍ 73
Baḥr al-Aswad 506
Baḥr al-Azraḳ 73
Baḥr al-Ghazal 82
Baḥr Yûsuf 325, 326, 330, 344
Baḳêrah 62
Baḥrite Mamelukes ... 28
Baḥriya, a Nubian ... 495
Baḥrîyah, Oasis of **63**, 96
Baka 471
Baker Pâsha 40
Baker, Sir Samuel 73, 82, 507
Bakenrenf ... 16, **540**
Baḳrawîyeh 283, **509**, **511**, **512**
Ballas 68, 362
Balsam trees 281
Balyanâ 323
Balâḥ 259
Baptism 207, 209

PAGE

Baq 60
Baqet ... 60, 338, 342, 343
Barabara 505
Barbara, Saint 272
Bardîs 323
Bar Hebræus 250
Barillet 280
Barḳûḳ 28, 278 ; Mosque of 276
Barrage (*or* Barrages) 76 ; history of, **83–88** ; cost of 84
Bartholomew, Saint ... 352
Baṭn al-Ḥagar 490
Bashtanab 504
Baṣra 218
Bas-reliefs, Egyptian ... 120
Bast, goddess 169, 262, 263
Bata 130, 167
Battle of Argîn... ... 44
" Atbara ... 507
" Ferket ... 491
" Omdurmân ... 516
" the Pyramids... 29
" Toski... ... 474
Bayawi 595
Beb 330
Bêbars 28
Bedâwin 196 ; number of, 192
Bedrashên ... 298, **321**
Behnesa, Oasis of ... 331
Beḥuṭet 437
Bek 346
Bĕlăl 503
Belbês 27

PAGE

Belzoni 284, 421 ; "tomb" of 418
Benha 32, 58, **62**
" el-'Asal 254
Ben Nâga ... 115, **514**
Beni Ḥasan, tombs of 103, **334–343**
Beni Ḥudêr 321
Beni Ḥusên 323
Beni Kurêba 215
Beni Ḳurra 323
Beni Mâlû Ṭansa ... 322
Beni Mazâr 322
Beni Suwêf **58**, **63**, 277, 322, 329
Benjamin, Patriarch 26, 203
Benson, Miss M. ... 381
Berber 38, 39, 40, 41, 197, **505** ; rail to, 43 ; evacuation of ... 47
Berenice ... 19, 367
" I. 545
" II. 546
" II. 546
" III. 548
Bes 115, 514
Bêt el-Mâl 517
Bêt el-Walî ... 109, 468
Betrothal, Coptic ... 210
Bibâ 322
Bible, Coptic version of 125
Bibân el-Mulûk... 414, 417
Biggeh 455, 456
Bilāḳ 456
Birch, Dr. S. 127

PAGE
Biridiwi 595
Birket el-Ḥagg 231
Birket el-Kurûn ... 325
Birth Chamber of Amenophis III. ... 379–381
Birti 503
Bisharîn 196
Bithynian Sea 22
Bitter Lakes ... 27, 258
Biyahmu ... 327, 329
Black Stone, the 213, **224**
Blasphemy 226
Blemmyes 22, 354, **459**, 467, **484**, **494**
Blue Nile **73**, **517**; rise of 78
Blunted Pyramid ... 101
Bocchoris 16
Boeckh, Chronology of 9
Body, the 145; mummified, 145; spiritual ... 145
Boheiric dialect ... 196
Bôhr 74
Bolbitane ... 125, 254
Bolbitic mouth of Nile 77
Bonomi 469
Book of the Dead 10, 11, 145, **165**
„ of the Underworld 421
Bordein, the 516
Botti, Signor 253
Bouriant 615
Boussard 255
Brown, Major R. H. 83, 85
Bruce 284; tomb of ... 420
Bruchium 250

PAGE
Brugsch, E. 414, 558, 569, 560
„ H. 95, 142, 265, 454; chronology of 9
Bubastis 10, 16, 26, 62, 163, **169**, 257, 262, 264
Buhen 480
Bûlâḳ Museum 32, 414, 415, **555**, **565**
„ Printing Press 32
Buller, Gen. 42
Bunsen, Chronology of... 9
Burges, Major, capture of Osman Diḳna ... 49
Burgite Mamelukes ... 28
Burraburiyash 594
Bursbey 28, 278
Burton 3
Bûsh 322
Bushmur 196
Busiris ... 62, **297**, 356
Butler, A. J. 269, 270, 271, 369
Buto 62
Butus 183
Byblos 182

C

Cæsar Augustus ... 21
„ Julius 247
„ Philippus ... 200
Cæsareum 250
Cæsarion ... 21, 365

PAGE

Cailliaud, 497, 500, 510, 511, 515
Cairo ... 29, **268–279**
Calendar, Muḥammadan 244
Caligula ... 22, 468
Call to Prayer 244
Cambyses, **17**, **268**, 282, 306, 372, 373, 393, **395**, 542
Cambyses and the Apis Bull 300
Campbell ... 296, 413
Canaan 65
Canaanites 65
Canals in Egypt ... 32
Cancer, Tropic of 444, 468
Candace, **21**, 101, **459**, **470**, **483**
Canon of proportion ... 119
Canopic Jars **415**, **601**, 623
Canopic mouth of Nile ... 77
Canopus, city of and pilot 21, 62, 123; Decree of **19**, 122, 267, **590**
Cape Guardafui ... 407
Cappadocians 22
Caracalla ... 23, **554**
Catacombs of Alexandria, 252
Cataract, First ... 76, **453**
" Second 75, **489**
" Third ... 75, 492
" Fourth 75, 503
" Fifth ... 75, 505
" Sixth ... 75, **516**
" Shooting the ... 445
Cavalla 30

PAGE

Caviglia... 284, 294, 301
Census of 1881... ... 192
" 1897... ... 191
" monks ... 204
Cerdo 200
Ceylon 38
Chabas 187
Chaeremon 8
Chalcedon, Councils of, 25, 194, 202
Champollion, le Jeune 2, 126
" 255, 422, 564
" Figeac ... 9
Charthi 11
Chemmis 181, 353, 354
Chenoboscion 363
Cheops, 11, **364**, **368**, **520**, **575**; Pyramid of 285
Chephren, 11, **521**, **575**; Pyramid of, 289; statues of 574
Chinese 121
Chmim 353
Chosroës ... 26, 248
Christianity in Egypt, 22, 24; among the Arabs 211, 212
Christians, number of, in Egypt 192
Christians, persecutions of 23, 200, 202, 204, 205
Christians in Great Oasis 95
" in Nubia ... 484
" in Syria ... 198
Christodoulos 205

PAGE
Chronology, systems of Egyptian 50
Churches, Coptic ... 209
Circassian Mamelukes... 28
Circumcision ... 208, 239
Citadel of Cairo, **278**; assassination of 470 Mamelukes in, 31; Mosque of 277
Clarke, Dr. 606
Clarke, Somers 113, 436, 480, 490
Claudianus 200
Claudius ... 22, **550**
Cleopatra 20, 21, 247, 365, 546
Cleopatra Tryphæna 548, 549
Cleopatra's Needles ... 251
Clock in Citadel Mosque 277
Clot Bey 83
Clysma Præsidium ... 256
Cnidus 248
Codomannus 19
Cœlesyria 20
Colonnade, the... ... 108
Colossi 394, 411
Colossus, tomb of the ... 345
Column, the 114
Commission of Enquiry 33
„ of Indemnities 37
„ of Liquidation 35
Commissioners of Public Debt 53
Commodus ... 23, 553

PAGE
"Completion" of the Nile 92
Confession 209
Constantine ... **23**, 201
Constantinople 25, 28, 31, 194
Constantius 24
Contra-Pselchis. 471
Contra-Taphis 468
Contra-Syene 446
Convent of the Maidens 270
Conversion Economies 53
Cook, Mr. J. M., death of 48, 49
Copt, derivation of name 193
Coptic Alphabet ... 140
„ Churches 462ff.
„ Dialects... ... 196
„ Language ... 195
„ Months 141
„ Year 142
Coptites nome 367
Coptos ... 61, 72, 365, 368
Copts, the 26, 192, **193**
„ education of, 209; dress of, 207; era of, 23; persecution of, 200–210; they embrace Islâm, 205; physical characteristics of, 206, 207; history of, 200–210
Cornelius Gallus 21, 463
Coronation, Stele of ... 584
Corvée **51**, 80
Cos 124
Cosmas 204

PAGE

Council of Chalcedon 25, 194, 202
„ of Nicæa 23, 201
„ Œcumenical ... 194
Court, the Temple ... 108
Creation, the 608
Cretaceous Age ... 57
Crocodile, the 183
„ Lake ... 259
Crocodilopolis ... 325, 432
Crops, summer and winter 93
Cromer, Lord 52, 54, 81, 82
Crusaders 28
Ctesias 268
Cultivated land in Egypt 93
Cureton... 564
Curzon, R. 269, 332, 351, 352
Cusal 61, **348**
Cush 65
Customs, Egyptian ... 54
Cynonpolis 61
Cynopolis 331
Cyprus 400
Cyrenæa 367
Cyrene 124
Cyril of Alexandria 24, 195, 202, 248
Cyrus of Damanhûr ... 273

D

Dab'îh 323
Dâbûd 467
Dafûfa 493

PAGE

Dahshûr, 101; Pyramid of **311**
Daḳhalîyeh 63
Dakkeh... 470
Dâkhel (*or* Dâkhlah), Oasis of ... **63**, 95, 96
Dalgo 492
Dam, cutting of the ... 92
Damanhûr ... **62**, 253
Damascus 28, 112, 218, 277
Damianus 203
Damiette ... 28, 83
Darâw 324
Darius I. Hystaspes, **18**, 95, 258, 259, **542**
„ II. Nothus **18**, 95
„ Xerxes ... 19, 543
David 191
Danæ 353
Darfûr 495
Darmali 506
Darwîsh (Dervish), meaning of name 236
Dashnâ 324
Dashru 595
Davison... 284
Dawkins, Mr., quoted ... 53
Death among Muḥammadans ... 238, 241
Debbeh... ... 46, 495
de Blignières 34
Decius 23, 200, 248, **554**
de Lesseps ... 32, 38, 258
Delta, 13, 58, 330; Greeks settle in, 17; railways in, 32; towns and villages in, 93; width of 77

PAGE
de Luynes, Duc ... 565
Demetrius ... 200, 271
Demi-gods 7
de Morgan **311, 362,** 369, 440, **560**, 561, **567–569**
Demotic writing ... 121
Denderah 61, **363–367**
Dendûr 469
Denon 284, 350
Deposits of sand and gravel in Nile ... 58
Dêr al-ʻAdhrâ 332
Der al-Baḳarah 332
Derby, Lord 33
Dêr el-Aḥmar 353
Dêr el-Bablûn 273
Dêr el-Tadrus 273
Dêr êl-Baḥari ... 376, 381
„ Temple of, 403–411
„ Mummies, 412–417, 614–617
Dêr el-Medînet 411
Dêr Mawâs 322
Dêrr 474
Dervish, *see* Darwîsh.
Dervishes break British square 41
Dervishes, the Dancing ... 277
Dêrûṭ 322
de Sacy, Silvestre ... 126
de Saulcy ... 413, 564
Destiny 152
Determinatives 128
Devilliers 404
Devil, the stoning of ... 224

PAGE
Devourer, the 152
Dhu'l-Ḥiggah 231
Dhu Muwâs 212
Diana 263
Diocletian 23, 200, 248, 251, 368, 459, 467
Diodorus Chronus ... 124
Diodorus Siculus 1, 8, 65, 191, 268, 299, 370, 371, 392, 470, 620 621
Dionysius 200
Dionysos ... 21, 181
Dioscorus 202
Diospolis Parva 61, 62
Diospolis Magna (Thebes), 12, **374**, 371, 372; the kings of 13
Disk-worshippers ... 15
Dissibil 505
Divorce 225
Drah abu'l-Neḳḳah 12, 432, 605
Dream, Stele of 501, 584
Dromos 108
Drunkenness 226
Druses, the 27
Dodecaschœnus **471**, 472
Domitian ... 23, **551**
Donḳola, Old ... 38, 41, 43, 46, 484
„ New ... **493**, 494
Doseh 229
Doshe 492
Dowry 210
Duêm 39

	PAGE
Duffilé	74
Dümichen ...	3, 95, 96
Dykes of the Nile ...	79
Dynasties, Egyptian	8, 519ff

E

Earle, General ...	42, 503
Eater of the Dead ...	152
Earthquake	10
Eber	211
Eclipse	10
Economies Fund ...	53
Edfû 20, 59, 324, **437**; Nilometer at	76
Education	54
Edwards, Miss A. B. ...	479
Egypt, ancient names of, 60; geology of, 57; nomes of, 61; provinces of, 22, 62; gods of, 147 ff; kings of, 519 ff; progress of, under British ...	51
Egyptian Army... ...	34
„ Customs ...	54
„ Dynasties	8, 50
„ Education ...	54
„ Gods	190
„ History ...	1–49
„ Imports, etc.. .	54
„ National Debt	53
„ Post Office ...	54
„ Railways ...	54
„ Religion ...	143
Egyptian Reserve Fund	53
„ Revenue ...	53
„ Unifieds ...	56
„ Writing	121–139
„ Year	142
Egyptians, the Ancient	64–72
„ the Modern	191–199
Eileithyia	61
Eileithyias	435
Elagabalus	23
El-Akbar, Mosque of ...	277
El-Azhar, Mosque of ...	275
Elephantine 11, 22, 61, **445**, **455**, 461; Nilometer at	76
Elephant River... ...	407
El-Fayyûm	13
El-Gisr	259
El-Ḥasanên, Mosque of	277
El-kâb, **435**; Fort of ...	113
El-Kais	331
El-Kenûs	466
El-lâhûn, Pyramid of	283, 327, 329
El-Manṣûr Ḳalaûn ...	275
El-Mu'allaḳah	272
El-'Obêd	39
El-Teb (Et-Teb) ...	40
El tekeh...	6
El-Uḳṣûr (Thebes)	**370** ff
Elysian Fields, the	158, 159
Embâbeh	29
„ Bridge ...	54
Emesa	31
Empire, Ancient ...	8

PAGE

Empire, Middle ... 8
„ New 8
Ennedek 259
Enoch ... 212, 220, 453
Enthronement, stele of... 501
Epaphus 300
Epiphanes 20
Equator... 73
Era of the Martyrs 142, 201
Era of Muḥammadans, *see* Hijra.
Eratosthenes ... 249, 444
Ergamenes 464, 470, 471
Esarhaddon ... 6, 17, 300
Eshmûn... ... 343, 344
Eshmunên ... 343, 344
Esneh 59, 94, 297, 324, **433**; Nilometer at ... 76
Ethiopia 6, 13, 22, **466** ff; Civilization of Egyptian origin ... 65
Ethiopians 17, 21, 206, 399, 484
Eṭsa 322
Eucharist 209
Euclid 249
Euergetes I. 19
„ II. 20
Eumenes 247
Eumenius 200
Eupator... 20
Euphrates 453
European populations in Egypt... 198
Eusebius 7
Eutyches ... 25, 194

PAGE

Eutychians 194
Evaporation of water of Nile 79
Evil Eye 239
Excommunication, stele of 501, 584
Exodus, Pharaoh of ... 15
Exports 54
Ezbeki, Emîr 279
Ezbekîyeh Garden ... 279
Ezekiel 72

F

Fakri, Wad Atman ... 504
Famine, the Seven years' 455
Fant 322
Farâfra, Oasis of 63, 95, 96
Faragallah Pâsha ... 516
Farag Sulṭân 278
Farshûṭ 323, 363
Fashn 322
Fashôda... ... 39, 47, 48
Fasting among the Copts 209
„ „ Muḥammadans 223
Fâtiḥah, the ... 239, 244
Fâṭima 233
Faṭimites ... 27, 28, 234
Fâw Ḳiblî 324
Fâwrîḳa Al-Rôḍa ... 322
Fayyûm, the 63, 96, 164, 188, **325**, 598
„ towns and villages in 9

	PAGE
Feddân, the	93
Fellaḥîn...	193
Female succession to throne	10
Female population of Egypt	192
Fenwick, Captain	46, 491
Ferket, Battle of	46, 486, 491
Ferlini's discovery ...	511 ff
Festivals ...	227, 231
Fez	254
Fitz Clarence, Lieut. ...	504
Flood, the	453
Floriana...	622
Fola Falls	74
Followers of Horus ...	8
Form, the	145
Fossils	59
Fosṭâṭ	27, **268**
Fowler, Sir J.	85
Fraser, General... ...	30
Fraser, Mr. W.	327, 343, 345
France	53
Fresh Water Canal	33, **258**
Fum al-Khalîg	92
Funeral Ceremonies, etc.	147, 148

G

	PAGE
Gaalîn Arabs	514
Gabriel	214
Gaius Germanicus ...	550
Gakdûl Wells	495
Galerius Maximinus ...	269
Gallery of Princesses ...	312
Gallienus	23
Gamilâb	49
Ganênetta	504
Garf Ḥusên	469
Garstin, Sir W. ...	83, 87, 461
Gaza	231, 593
Gazelle River	74
Gebel abu Fêdah ...	348
Gebel al-Kaff	333
Gebel Barkal, 109, 115, 283, 497; Pyramids of	101, 485
Gebel Buerib	514
Gebel Dûsh	492
Gebelên... ...	59, **432**
Gebel Gaddîr ...	48, 235
Gebel Gillif	495
Gebel eṭ-Ṭêr ...	331, 333
Gebel Rawyan	516
Geddîn	39
Gemai	489
George of Cappadocia	24, 248, 271, 273
George, the Maḳawḳas	26, 203, 215
Germanicus ...	21, **191**
Geta	554
Gharbîyeh	63
Ghuzz	30
Gibbon quoted	25, 249, 250
Giegler Pâsha	39
Ginnis	44
Girgâ	323
Girgeh	63, 354
Girouard, Major ...	486

PAGE

Gizeh, 63, 321 ; Museum, 555ff ; Palace of, **555** ; Pyramids of 11, **283–293**
Gleichen, Count ... 506
GOD, the 99 names of ... 239
God-kings 1
Gods of Egypt, 143–190 ; figures of 610
Godfrey de Bouillon ... 28
Goose-pen 363
Gordon, General C. G., **40–42**, **236**, 495, 516, 518 ; head of, 354 ; Memorial Service, 47, **518** ; Relief Expedition ... 48, 49
Goshen 282
Graham, General 40, 43
Granite of Aswân ... 58
Grand Bey ... 375, 392
Grant, Captain 73
Grébaut... 171, 560, 561
Greece 21
Greek Language in Egypt 124, 125
Greeks, settlement of, in Egypt... 17
Grenfell, Gen. Sir F. W. 43, 44, 45, 46, 446, 474, 560, 568
Grenfell, Mr. 331
Gubat 42
Gulf of Suez 58
Gulf of Akaba 58
Gymnasium of Alexandria 251

PAGE

H

Hadendoa 196
Hadramaut 211
Hadrian **23**, 343, **552** ; Gateway of 463
Hafîr 44, 46
Ḥafṣa 214, 217
Hagar 211
Hagar and Ishmael 224, 228
Haggi Ḳandîl 345
Hagia Sophia 277
Haḳar, Haḳer ... 18, **543**
Hâḳim, 27, 28 ; Mosque of 275
Hall of Columns ... 383
Hall of Double Truth ... 149
Ḥalîma 213
Ham 64, 65
Ḥamâmât 12
Hamârûyeh 27
Ḥambal 232
Ḥambalites 231
Hamdab Island ... 503
Hamilton 284
Ḥanafîyeh 274
Ḥanafites 231
Ḥânês 330
Ḥāpi (Nile) 88, 157, 160, 190
Ḥāpi 155, 623
Harmachis **149, 170**, 175, 399
Haroëris 441
Harper, Tomb of the ... 420
Harran 212
Harris Papyrus ... 5, 123

PAGE

Harûn ar-Rashîd ... 27
Ḥasan ... 22, 233, 277, 276
Hashîn 43
Hashîsh 225
Ḥaswa 231
Hathor **149**, 169, **189**, **364**
Hathor-Sat ... 312, 313
Ḥātshepset **14**, 334, **380**, 385, 387, 388, **533**; history of, 406, 407; Temple of 403–411
Ḥawâmdîyeh 321
Ḥawâra 329; Pyramid of 13, 327
Hawk at Philæ... ... 461
Haworth, Mr. J. ... 329
Hay, Drummond ... 469
Heart, the 145
Hebbeh... ... 503, 504
Hebt 94
Hecatompyhis 372
Hekatæus 8
Helena, Empress 332, 351, 353, 368
Heliopolis 10, 13, 16, 26, 62, 105, 157, 162 176, 177, **281**, **282**, **356**
„ (Southern) ... 432
„ of Syria ... 282
Ḥelwân 45
Ḥenassîyeh al-Medîna 329, 330
Ḥenna 207
„ Boat 178
Henoticon 25
Ḥent-taiu ... 413, **538**

PAGE

Heptanomis, nomes of 61, 325
Heptastadium 248
Ḥeq-âb, tomb of ... 448
Ḥequ-Shaâsu (Hyksos)... 14
Ḥer-âb 343
Ḥer-âb-Rā 530
Heracleopolis 61, 179, 330
Heraclius ... **26**, 215
Hercules ... 350, 484
Hermes 184, 343
Hermonthis ... 61, 432
Hermopolis Magna 62, 153, 162, 343
Hermopolis Parva ... 254
Ḥer-Ḥeru ... 16, **538**
Herodotus 1, 7, 8, 191, 262, 264, 326, 353, 371, 453, 619, 621
Ḥeruâkau 521
Ḥeru-baf 576
Ḥeru-em-ḥeb 376, 378, 388, 397, **534**
Ḥeruemsaf 522
Ḥeru-ḥetep, tomb of ... 579
Ḥeru-khuf, tomb of 447, **448**
Ḥeru-netch-tef-f... ... 464
Ḥeru-sa-tef-f ... 501, 583
Ḥeru-shef ... } 330
Ḥeru-shefît ... } 330
Ḥeru-ur (Aroëris) 441, 443
Ḥesepti ... 10, **362**, **519**
Ḥesi, tomb of 119
Ḥesi-Rā... 571
Hess 123
Ḥetchefa 520

PAGE
Ḥeṭepet 337
Heterodox Sects ... 231
Ḥet-ka-Ptaḥ ... 162, 299
Ḥet-Sfent 433
Ḥet-suten-ḥenen ... 179
Hezekiah 17
Hicks Pâsha ...39, 40, 236
Hierasycaminus ... 472
Hieratic Writing ... 121
Hieroglyphic Writing ... 121
Hijâz 211
Hijrah, First 214
„ Second 142, 214, 245
Himyar 211, 212
Hipparchus 249
Hipponon 61
Ḥittin 28
Hittites 478
Holled Smith, Sir C. ... 45
Homer 355, 372
Hophra (Apries) ... 17
Horapollo ... 8, 62, **607**
Horus ... **149**, **170**, 176
„ Sepṭ 155
„ Seker 155
„ and Set ... **183**, **184**, 186, 350
„ Children of ... 155
„ Followers of ... 8
Hoskins, Mr. 493, 499, 500, 509, 514, 515
Houris 222
House, an Egyptian ... 111
Ḥu 149
Ḥunefer 146

PAGE
Ḥuni 520
Hunter, Gen. Sir A. 47, 504, 506, 514
Ḥusên 227, 229, 233, 277
Hymn to Rā 157
Hyksos 1, 14, 187, 266, 300, 435, 467, 493
„ kings, period ... 13
Hypsele... 61
Hypostyle Hall, the ... 108
Hystaspes 11

I

Ī-án-Rā, statue of .. 580
Iblîs 219
Ibrâhîm... 29, 30, 31, 215
Ibrîm 470, 474
Ibsâdeh, Saint 452
Ichneumon 330
Idols of the Arabs ... 212
Ī-em-ḥetep (god) **188**, 438, 462
„ (king) ... 521
Ignorance, period of Arab 212
Iliad 371
Illâhûn, pyramid of ... 13
Imâm Shafêi 229
Imamians 233
Imandes 328
Immortality 625
Imouthis ... 188, 437
Imports, Egyptian ... 54

PAGE

Incarnation, the ... 25
Indians 374
Indiction, the 142
Ink, writing 123
Intelligence, the ... 145
Inundation, the ... 77
Ionia 374
'Irâḳ 453
Irrigation ... 32, 78
Iseium of Denderah ... 366
Ismael 211, 224
Isis, 149; Isis and Serapis at Rome, 23; her marriage, 179; seeks the dead body of Osiris, 182; builds sepulchres for him, 184; her hymn to Osiris, 185; beheaded by Horus 184
Isis, temple of 575
Islâm 205, 209, **219, 233**
Island of Argo (Arḳaw) 493
" of Artaghasi ... 493
" of Biggeh ... 455
" of Elephantine ... 445
" of Mernet ... 516
" of Meroë ... 507
" of Philæ ... 456
" of Rôḍa 280
" of Sai 491
" of Tombos ... 492
Israelites 234
Ismâ'îl, expedition to Sûdân 31

PAGE

Ismâ'îl Pâsha, the Khedive, his debts and extravagance, 33, 34; bribes the Sulṭân, 35; is deposed by telegraph ... 35, 80, 261, 279
Isma'îlîya ... 259, 260
Ismandes 357
Israel 191
Israelites 15
Isrâfêl 219
Issus 19
Isthmus of Suez ... 256
Ita 318
Italians, defeat at Adowa 46
Itinerary of M. Aurelius 23
Iuâa 6, 594
Iuta-melek 389

J

Jacobites ... 202, 203
Ja'fâr 234
Janron 564
Jann 219
Jéquier 70
Jerâbîs 478
Jeremiah 17
Jerusalem 16, 22, 28, 214, 229
Jesus, son of Sirach ... 165
Jews 22, 198, 202; number of in Egypt .. 192
Jiddah 231
Jinn 219, 227

PAGE

Jôhar 234, 275
John the Baptist ... 270
John of Antioch ... 10
John of Damanhûr ... 273
John Philoponus ... 250
Johnstone, Capt. J. H. L. E. 479
Joktan 211
Jollois 404
Jomard 284
Jordan Valley 58
Joseph, Patriarch 304, 455
„ husband of Mary 368
Joseph's Well 279
Josephus ... 7, 8, 268
Josiah 17
Judah 17
Judaism 233; in Arabia 212
Judgment, the 150, 151, **221**
Julian the Apostate 24, 202
Julianus... 200
Jupiter 432
Jupiter Ammon ... 96
Justinian 26
Juvenal **365**, 367
Juwêrya... 215
Juynboll ... 256, 285

K

Ka, *i.e.*, the double **145**, 152
Ka of Osiris 185
Ka'ba 213, 214, 224, 228, **230**, 231
Kabasos 62

PAGE

Kadashman-Bêl 593, 594, 595
Kadesh ... 377, 394, 478
Ka-en-Rā ... 12, 523
Kafr 'Ammar 321
Kafr ez-Zaiyât 254
Ḳâhir 268
Ḳâhira (Cairo) 268
Kaḥra 433
Kâhtân 211
Ḳâit Bey 28, 278, 280
„ „ Mosque of ... 277
Kakaȧ 307, 521
Ka-kam 302
Ka-kau ... **10**, 299, **519**
Kalâbsheh 57, 58, 59, **468**
Ḳalâûn 28, 275
Ḳalyûb 58
Ḳalyubîyeh 62
Kames ... 432, 531, 605
Ḳana (Ḳeneh) 324
Kanṣûweh el-Ghura ... 277
Ḳanṭara 257, 259
Karaduniyash ... 15, **593**
Ḳarmân 493
Karnak **107**, **370**, **375**; Nilometer at, 76; Tablet of, 1, 3, 564; Temple of ... **381** ff
Ḳartassi... 467
Kashta 397, **540**
Ḳaṣr eṣ-Ṣayyâd 363
Kassala 46
Kau el-Kebîr 350
Ḳeneh 57, 63, **363**
Kenem, wine of ... 97
Kenemet, Oasis of ... **94**

PAGE
Kenemmet 163
Kenememti 163
Kennard, Martyn ... 329
Kerbela... ... 227, 277
Kerma 485
Kerreri 516
Kesh **466**, 481
Khabbesha ... 306, 543
Khadîjah ... 213, 214
Khāf-Rā-ānkh 295
Khā-ka-Rā 530
Khā-kheru-Rā 528
Khalîfa, 43, 44; defeat of, **47**; death of, 48 482
Khalifs, Tombs of ... 278
Khalîg (Canal)... ... 92
Khamarûyeh 269
Khârgeh, Oasis of **63**, 354
Kharṭûm, 38, 39, 73, **517**, 518; fall of, 42, 236; rise of Nile at ... 78
Kharu 389
Kharthi... 523
Khati 338, 341
Khêbar 215
Khedive, the title ... 33
Khemennu ... 153, 343
Khemmis 353
Khennu-sesu 448
Kheperà **169**, 174, 607
Kher-āba ... 162, 186
Kher-ḥeb, the 146
Kherp-ka-Rā 527
Kheta 187, **389**, 398, 399, 476
Khirebu 478

PAGE
Khizâm 324
Khnemit 318
Khnemu **167**, 380, 431, 433, 455, 458
Khnemu-Rā 458
Khnemu-ḥetep I. ... 342
" " II. 13, **116**, **337-341**
" " III. ... 341
" " a dwarf 575
Khnemu-khenu ... 450
Khonsu **171**, **188**, 375
Khu-en-Åten 5, 15, **533**, 592
Khufu (Cheops) ... 11
Khufu-menāt 333, 338, 339, 342
Khu-ḥetep-ḥeres ... 571
Khunes, tomb of ... 448
Khurshîd Pâsha ... 279
Khu-taui-Rā 527
Khut-en-Åten, king, 345; city of ... **346**, **347**
Khuzêma 215
Ḳiblā 223, 277
Kilḳipa 6
Kinana 215
King-lists 1
Kiosk at Philæ ... 465
Kirbekan ... 42, 503
Kiswah 230
Kitchener, Lord 44, 46, 485, 488, 491
Kléber, General 29, 30
Kochome 302
Kokreb 505

PAGE
Kôm âd-Diḳḳ ... 251, 253
Kom Ombo 59, 188, 367, **439**, **569**
Koran (Kur'ân), the 217, 218
Kordofân 48, 495, 513
Koreish tribe ... 213, 219
Korosko ... 13, **473**
Korti 41, 42, 46, **494**, 495
Kosheh ... 44, 484, 491
Krôphi 90
Kubbân... ... ... **471**
Kûfa ... 218, 231, 453
Ḳufṭ 324, 367
Ḳulûṣnah ... 322, 331
Kumiṭi 595
Kummeh **466**, 481, **489**
Ḳur'ân, MSS. of ... 279
Kurigalzu 5
Ḳûrnah, Temple of ... 392
Kurru 283, 485
„ Pyramids of ... 496
Ḳûrṭa (Korti in Nubia) 472
„ (Korti in Sûdân) 494, 495
Kuruskaw (Korosko) ... 473
Ḳûs 324, 368
Ḳûsêr (Kosseir) ... 72

L

Labyrinth 13, **327**, 357
Lado **74**, 77, 78
Lagids 190
Lagus 19
Lake Albert ... 73, 74, 77
„ Balâḥ 259
„ Mareotis 252

PAGE
Lake Menzâleh 196, 259
„ Moëris ... 13, **325**, 489
„ No 82
„ Rahad 39
„ Tchestches ... 157
„ Timsaḥ 256
„ Victoria ... 73, 74, 77
Lane, Edward, quoted 91, 210, 227, 241
Lanzone 66, 167, 431
Lascelles 35
Lât 212
Lathyrus 20
Latopolis ... 61, **433**
Latreille 606
Latus Fish 433
Lêlet al-Ḳadr 230
Lêlet al-Nuḳṭa 91
Lemnos... 235
Lenormant, C. 564
Lent, Fast of 209
Leo Alfricanus ... 349, 353
Lepère 257
Lepsius 9, 19, 75, 127, 284, 404, 493, 499, 508, 512, 515
Letopolis 62
Levantines 198
Library of Alexandria ... 249
„ Khedivial ... 279
„ of the Serapeum 249
Libya 21, 22
Libyans... ... 71, 400
Lieblein... 9
Limestone in Nile Valley 58
Linant Pâsha ... 83, 257

PAGE

Lisht, Pyramids of ... 13
Lists of kings 1
Lions in Mesopotamia... 5
Lîwân 275
Lloyd, Col. 46
Lochias 250
Logos, the 201
Londinian formation ... 59
Longpérier 564
Loret, V. ... 421, 569
Lote tree 229
Louis IX. 28
Louis Philippe 277
Louvre... 432
Lucas and Aird ... 43
Lucius Marbanus ... 21
Luck, the 152
Luxor ... **370** ff, 381
„ Hospital 49; Temple of 374
Lycian Sea 22
Lycopolis ... 6, 349
Lyons, Major H. G. 57, 461, 465, 480

M

Maāt 157, **189**
Maāt-ka-Rā (Ḥātshepset) 417, 533
Maā-ka-Rā, a priestess... 539
Ma'bed er-Rifâ'î ... 278
Macalister 624
Macedonians ... 8, **19**
Macrinus **23**
Macrobius 282
Maghâgha ... 322, 330

PAGE

Magianism 212
Magians 218
Mahallet Rûḥ 58
Mahâtah 455
Maḥâmîd 324
Mahdi, the idea of, 232, 233; false Mahdis, 31, 234; Muḥammad the Mahdi, **38, 39**, 482, 516; his death, 43; his body burnt, 47; his head at Wâdî Ḥalfah, 47; his tomb ... 517
Mahdiism 235
Mahdîya, city of ... 234
Maḥmil 228, 230
Maḥmûd, Dervish Emîr 47, 514
Maḥmûd Sami ... 36, 37
Maḥmûdîyeh Canal ... 248
Maḥsamah 264
Maidens, Convent of ... 270
Maḳawḳas, George the 203, 215, 254
Maḳrîzî 274, 331
Mâḳurrah 495
Malawî 322
Malek 231
Male population of Egypt, number of 192
Mamelukes, Baḥrite ... 28
„ Burgite or Circassian, 28, 276, 278, 352
„ Massacre of 31, 266, 279

PAGE
Mamelukes, Tombs of ... 278
Mammisi at Denderah... 367
„ at Kom Ombo 441
Mâmûn, Khalîfa, 280, 285; opened Great Pyramid 27
Man, component parts of 145
Manât 212
Manetho **7**, 8, 13, 19, 124, 143, 291, 304, 330
Manfalût ... **323**, 348
Mangles and Irby ... 345
Mansafîs 322
Manslaughter 226
Manṣûrah ... 28, **63**
Marâghah ... 250, **323**
Marawî 46, **496**
Mâr Buḳṭor 270
Mâr Mînâ 269
Marchand, Major ... 48
Marcianus **25**, 200, 202
Marcus Aurelius **23**, 463
„ Otho 550
„ Silanus... ... 21
Mareb 211
Mârids 219
Mariette, 3, 4, 105, 145, 171, 190, 266, 294, 302, 305, 356, 364, 365, 381, 405, 406, 439, 558, **563-567**; chronology of, 9; house of, 310; sarcophagus of 570
Marîs 495

PAGE
Marîsîyeh 495
Mark, Saint, 22, 125, 193, 200, 248
Marriage of Copts, 210; of Arabs 238
Marrus 328
Martial 299
Martyrs, Era of 142, 201
Mary, the Virgin 25, 368
Maryam... 215
Masaherthà ... 417, **538**
Ma'ṣara 319
Mashṭâ 323
Masmûda 234
Maspero 374, 375, 407, 413, **558, 559**, 567, 569
Maṣr el-'Atîḳa 269
„ el-Ḳâhira ... 27, 269
Massa 235
Maṣṭăba tomb, the 98, 308-310
Maṣṭabat el-Far'ûn 303, 311, 566
Mas'ûdî 257, 283
Maṭâî 322
Merṭânîyeh 321
Maṭammah ... 41, 42, **514**
Matar 455
Maṭarah... 368
Maṭarîyeh 281
Matchau 171, 172, 176
Mâthen 593
Matter carried by Nile to the sea 79
Maury 564

PAGE

Maximus, Patriarch ... 200
Maximinus 272
Maxims of Ani... ... 165
„ Ptaḥ-ḥetep... 165
Mazhar Bey 84
Maz'ûna 321
McCallum ... 479, 480
McNeill, General ... 43
Measures, Muḥammadan 245
Mecca 212, 214, 218, 223, 242, 274, 376
„ Caravan 227, 231
„ Pilgrimage ... 224
Media 22
Medîna ... 27, 214, 218, 232
Medînet el-Fayyûm ... 325
„ Habû 5, 114; temples of ... 395–403
Mediterranean Sea 57, 422
Mêdûm, Pyramid of 11, 101, **319**
Megara 124
Meḥ, the nome of 335 ff
Meḥt-en-usekht... ... 397
Mekhu, tomb of 447, 448
Melâwi al-'Arîsh ... 345
Melik al-'Adîl 28
„ al-Kâmil ... 28, 285
„ aṣ-Ṣâleḥ 28
Melkites 26, 202, **231**
Melul 468
Memfi 299
Memnon, **22**, 357; colossus of, 394; tomb of, 420
Memnonium 15, **357**, **373**, **374**, 392

PAGE

Memphis, 10, 11, **26**, 27, 62, 105, 162, 168, 190, 203, **298**, **299**
Memphitic dialect ... 196
Mêmûna 215
Menȧ (Menes), 3, 8, **10**, **57**
Menas, Saint ... 203, 269
Menāt-Khufu 333, 338, 339
Mendes 18, 62, 328; ram of 590
Mendesian Nile mouth... 77
Menelaus 21
Menen-en-kha-em-Maāt 492
Menes .. 7, 8, **298**, **370**
Meneptah I. 535
„ II. 535
Menḥentthemḥu ... 417
Men-ka-Rā (Nitocris) ... 522
Men-kau-Ḥeru ... 521, 574
Men-kau-Rā 291
Men-khāu-Rā 580
Mennas, Saint 452
Men-nefer 299
Menou 30
Menshâh 323
Menshîyeh 354; stele of 591
Menth (Armant) ... 432
Menthu-ḥetep I. ... 525
„ „ II. ... 525
„ „ III. ... 525
„ „ IV. ... 525
„ „ V. ... 526
Menthu-nesu 312
Menthu-Teḥuti-ȧuf-ānkh 410

PAGE
Mentu-em-sa-f 578
Menûf 63, 299
Menûfîyah 63
Merbapen 3, **362**, **519**
Mercurius 270
Mercury... .. 263, 374
Mer-en-Ḥeru ... 12, 523
Mer-en-Rā ... 11, 522
Mer-en-Teḥuti 124
Meri-Rā 348, 522
Mer-kau-Rā 530
Mer-kherp-Rā 529
Mer-menfitu 528
Mernat Island 516
Mer Nit... 363
Meroë, Island of 283, 492, 482
" ... 483, 484, **507**
" Pyramids of 509 ff.
Merret 316
Mer-tchefa-Rā 530
Mert-Rā... 421
Merul 468
Merv 232
Merwâ 224
Merwân II. ... 27, 218
Mes-Ḥent-Themeku ... 416
Meskhenet 152
Mesopotamia ... 5, 14, 15, 389, 594
Messiah, Arab and Persian ideas of ... 233
Mesthâ 155, **623**
Metachompso 471
Metelis 62

PAGE
Michael, Patriarch ... 204
Middle Empire... ... 8
Miḥarraḳah 472
Miḥrâb 223
Milkili 595
Milner, Sir A. ... 53, 83, 85, 87
Milverton 125
Mina, Valley of ... 224
Minbar 277
Minius 200
Minyâ 322
Minyeh 60, 63, 333
Miocene earth movements... 57
Mirwân 204
Miṣor 65
Miṣraim 65, 268
Mitani ... 15, 346, 593
Mît Rahîneh ... 298, 301
Mixed Tribunals ... 54
Mizraim... 65
Mnevis Bull ... 10, 282
Moḳaṭṭam 279
Mommsen quoted 124, 190, 191, 247
Monastery of St. Simon 450–452
Monophysite doctrine ... 25
Monophysites ... 26, 194
Môphi 90
Morgan, J. de, work at Naḳâda 67
Morocco 234
Mosque at Omdurmân... 517

PAGE

Mosques :—Aḥmad ibn Ṭulûn, 274; Akbar, 277; 'Amr, 274; Azhar, 275; Barḳûḳ, 276; Ghûri, 277; Ḥasan, 276; Ḥasanen, 277; Hâkim, 275; Ḳait Bey, 277; Muaiyyad, 276; Sulêman, 275; Yûsuf (Saladin), 275; Zênab 277
Mother of God 25
Mougel and the Barrage 84–87
Mount 'Ârafât 224
Mouth, opening of ... 146
Muaiyyad, Mosque of ... 276
Mucianus 326
Mughrât Wells 491
Muḥammad the Prophet 195, **211–246**, 376
Muḥammad IV. Sultân 235
Muḥummad Abu-Dhabad 29
Muḥammad Aḥmad, the Mahdi 38, **235–238**
Muḥammad 'Ali **30**, 279, 513, 514; and the Barrage, 83, 84; assassinates Mamelukes, 31; death of 31
Muḥammad 'Ali, shêkh 49
Muḥammad Amîn ... 513
Muḥammad en-Nâṣir ... 275
Muḥammad the Hanafite 234
Muḥammad ibn Ṭumurt 234
Muḥammad Sherîf ... 38
Mu-Ḥāpi 90

PAGE

Muḥarram 227
Muir, Sir W. 224
Mu'izz ... 27, 234, 269, 275
Muḳrâm 506
Mukhtâr 234
Mûlid al-Ḥasamên ... 229
Mûlid al-Nebi 228
Mûmîâ 619
Mummies, Dêr el-Baḥarî 416ff
Mummification, art of 618-623
Munassîr 503
Munkar ... 219, 220, 243
Murâd 29
Murder 226
Muristân Ḳalâûn ... 275
Musailima 217
Muṣawwarât an-Nâga ... 515
„ al-Kirbekân 515
„ aṣ-Ṣufra ... 515
Mushra ad-Dakêkh ... 504
Mûski 273
Muslims, number of in Egypt 192
Muṣṭafa Pâsha 279
Muṣṭafa Yawir 494
Musta'ili 28
Mut **169**, 375; Temple of 381
Mu'tamid 274
Mutammar 'Ali 451
Muṭi'ah 323
Mut-em-ua 380
Mutnefert 406
Mycerinus, 453, **521**; Pyramid of, 291; coffin of, 11; statue of **573**

PAGE

N

Nabopolassar 17
Nadi 504
Nâga 515
Nag' Ḥamâdî ... 323, 363
Naifāarut I. 18
„ II. 18
Nȧk, the fiend ... 157, **173**
Naḳâda 68, 123, **362**, **368**
Nakhîla 507
Nakîr ... 219, 220, 243
Name, the 145
Namyawiza 595
Napata **470**, 481, 483, **496**, 499, 515
Napoleon I. 29, 83, 84, 257, 269
Narmer 363
Nasha 146
Nâṣir, Sulṭân 276
Nasra 212
Nȧstasenen 494
National Debt of Egypt ... 53
Native Tribunals ... 54
Nativity, Fast of ... 209
Natron Valley 96
Naucratis 17
Naville, E. 262, 408, 409, 590
Nazâli Gânûb 323
Nazîma 595
Neb-er-tcher 607
Neb-f-āa-mer-Rā ... 528
Neb-ka 520
Neb-ka-Rā 520
Neb-nem-Rā 525

PAGE

Nebseni ... 156, 161, 417
Neb-sen-Rā 530
Neb-tchefa-Rā-Rā ... 530
Nebt-Ānkh 177
Nebt-Kheru 421
Nebuchadnezzar II. 7, 17, 596
Nebuut 433
Nectanebus I. **18**, 95, 383, 437, **544**
„ II. **18**, 267, 397, 462, **544**
Necho II. ... 17, 542
Necropolis of Alexandria 251
Nefer-ȧb-Rā 528
Nefer-ȧri-ka-Rā 12
Nefer-Ȧtmu 264
Nefer-f-Rā 521
Nefer-ḥetep 188
Nefer-ḥetep-sa 528
Nefer-ka... ... 11, 523
Nefer-ka-ȧri-Rā... 521, 524
Nefer-ka-Ḥeru ... 12, 523
Nefer-ka-Rā 11, 12, 520, 522
Nefer-ka-Rā-Ānnu 12, 524
Nefer-ka-Rā-Khenṭu 12, 523
Nefer-ka-Rā-Meri-Ȧmen 537
Nefer-ka-Rā-Nebi 12, 523
Nefer-ka-Rā-Pepi-senb 12, 523
Nefer-ka-Rā-Seker 10, 520
Nefer-ka-Rā-Tererl 12, 523
Nefer-kau-Ḥeru ... 524
Nefer-kau-Rā 11, 523, 524
Nefer-khā-Rā 521
Nefer-mat 320
Nefer-seḥ ... 11, 523

PAGE

Nefert 571
Nefert-åri ... 421, 476
Nefert-ari-Rāå 416
Nefert-ḥent 312
Nefert-ith 534
Nefer-Temu 164
Neferu-Rā 408
Nefîsheh 265
Negative Confession 162–164
Negroes 192, 197
Neha-ḥra 162
Neḥebka 164
Neḥerå 13, 338
Neith (Nit) **169**, 380, 454
Nekau (Necho) **17**, **257**, 262, 542
Nekheb 435
Nekht I. 339
" II. 339
" " Tomb... 422–432
Nekhtå 343
Nekht-Ḥeru-ḥeb ... 18
Nekht-neb-f 18
Nelson 29
Nemart 4
Neolithic man in Egypt 68
Neos Dionysos 20
" Philopator ... 20
Nephthys 149, 179 ff, **185**, **187**
Nepita 496
Nept 496
Nero 22, 550
Nerva 551
Nesi-Khonsu ... 413, 417

PAGE

Nestorius **24**, 25, 248, **354**; heresy of ... 202
Netåqerti 522
Netchefet 164
Netchemet ... 413, 417
Net'em-āb-Rā 527
Neter baiu 10, **362**, 519
Neter-ḥet-Sebek ... 433
Neter-ka-Rā 522
Neter-nekht, tomb of ... 343
Neter-ta... 172
Netherworld 177, 178, 179
Newberry, Mr. P. 343, 345
New Empire 8
"New" Race, the ... 70
Nî 593
Niaråuat 508
Niafāaruṭ 543
Nicæa 23, 201
Niebuhr... 284
Night of the Drop ... 91
Nile, canal from, to Red Sea, 15, 23; "completion" of, 92; course altered, 10; course described, 73-83; cubic contents of, 79; discharge at Aswân and Cairo, 78; dykes, 79; festival of, 91; flows honey, 10; levels at Kummeh, 489; levels elsewhere, 76; mud, depth of, 58; depth of mud and rate of deposit, 58; North and South,

PAGE

89; Damietta and Rosetta branches of, 77; the Seven mouths of, 77; slope of water, 79; water discharge into the sea, 79; solid matter discharged, 79; works in reign of Åmen-emḥāt, 13; worship of ... 90
Nile Valley, history of ... 57
Nilometer at Aswân ... 445
,, at Edfû ... 76
,, at Elephantine 76
,, at Esneh ... 76
,, at Karnak ... 76
,, at Philæ 76, 464
,, at Rôḍa ... 28
Nimr burns Ismâ'îl to death 31, 513
Nimrod 4
Nineveh, Fast of ... 209
Nit (Neith) 169
Nitåqert... ... 11, 398
Nitocris ... 11, 291, 398
No, No Ammon ... 370
Nomads, number of ... 192
Nobadæ... 484
Nomes of Egypt ... 61
Nonnus 354
Nothus 18
Nu 157
Nu, Papyrus of ... 166
Nubæ 467, 468
Nubar Pâsha 34
Nubia 13, 15, 58, 65, 77, 109, 408, **466**ff.

PAGE

Nubians 197, 484; they worship stars... ... 495
Nubit 440
Nub-Set... ... 266, 530
Nubti 14
Numbers, Egyptian ... 129
Nûri, Pyramids of 101, 283, 485, **502**
Nut **149**, 187
Nut-Åmen 370
Nut-meri-Åmen... ... 584
Nut-ur 158

O

Oases, The 17, **94-97**; banishment to ... 79
Oasis of Kenemet (Khârgeh, Oasis Major Southern) 94, 354; the gods of 95
Oasis of Baḥrîyeh (Northern) 94
Oasis of Sekhet-Åmit ... 94
,, of Sekhet-Ḥemam 94
,, of Ta-Åḥet ... 94
,, of Tchestcheset (Dâkhel, Oasis Minor) 94, 95, 331
Oasis, the ... 94, 96
,, of Behnesa ... 331
Obak 505
'Obêdellâh ... 27, 234
Obelisk at Luxor ... 377
,, at Maṭarîyeh ... 281

PAGE
Ochus 18, 19
Ohrwalder, Father, quoted ... 237, 238
'Okaṣ, Fair of 213
Old Testament, Greek version of, made ... 19
Olympus 25
'Omar, Khalîfa, 26, 214, 217, 233
'Omayyade dynasty ... 27
Ombos 61
Omdurmân, 47, 514; Battle of, 516; Fort of, ... 516, 517
On 281
Onias 262
Opium, use of 225
Ornamentation of tombs, temples, etc. 110
Orontes ... 377, 394, 478
Orthodox sects 232
Osiris, **144**, **153**, 608; chamber of, at Philæ, 464; history of, 179–182; hymn to, 185; judge of the dead, 149; of Philæ, 458; the soul of, 179; Temple of, at Abydos, 3; worship of, at Abydos 555
Osiris-Apis 190, 249, 306, 459
Osiris Pillar 114
„ Unnefer 441
Osman Bey 512
„ Diḳna, 43, **44f**; capture of 49

PAGE
Osman Rifkî 36
Osorkon I. ... 16, 539
„ II. ... 16, 66, 539
„ III. ... 16, 540
Osymandyas 392
'Othmân 27, 217, 233
Owen, Sir Richard ... 624
„ "Roddy" ... 491
Oxyrhynchus 61, 163, 330, 331

P

Pachomius 363
Paḥeri, tomb of ... 436
Pai-netchem I. ... 16, 538
„ II. ... 16, 538
„ III. ... 16, 539
Palace of 'Abdallah ... 517
„ Ya'ḳûb ... 517
Palace, the Egyptian ... 111
Palestine ... 20, 341
Palette, the scribe's ... 123
Palmyra... ... 23, 211
Pamai 16, 540
Pan, 353, 485; Pans ... 181
Paneum... 251
Panic Terrors 182
Panopolis 61, 181, 353
Paoni 91
Pape 355
Papyrus... 123
„ Medical ... 368
„ of Turin ... 1
Papyri, funereal ... 601

PAGE
Paradise, 218, **222**, 227; tree of 229
Parehu 407
Parembole 467
Paris 3
Parisian Strata 60
Parthia 22
Pasebkhanu I. ... 16, 537
„ II. ... 16, 538
Pa-ta-reset 72
Pathros 72
Patriarchs, Coptic 200-201; election of ... 207
Pathyris... ... 72, 433
Peake, Major, and the "sudd" 83
Pelusium 17, 20, 26, 203, 256, 258, 259
Pelusiac mouth of Nile... 77
Pemge 331
Penni 474
Penta-urt 4, 15, 377, 389
Pentu, tomb of... ... 348
Pepi I. 143, 266, 319, 452 **522**; pyramid of (1) 304
Pepi II. 522
Pepi-Nekht, tomb of ... 448
Per-āa (Pharaoh) ... 2
Per-áb-sen ... **362**, 519
Per-Ânpu 349
Per-Bast 262
Pergamenian Library ... 247
Pergamus 247
Per-Ḥet-ḥert 433
Per- Mātchet 331
Perring 284
PAGE
Perrot and Chipiez 105, 114
Per-Sebek 440
Perseus 353
Persia 22
Persian Kings 17
Persians 8; defeat of 18; rule of in Egypt ... 26
Peṭā-Bast 16
Peṭá-sa-Bast 540
Peter, Patriarch... 200, 202
Peter, Saint 473
Petra 354
Petrie, Prof. 68, 284, 362
Petronianus 395
Petronius ... 470, 483
Phakussa 62
Pharaoh... 2
Pharos 19, **248**; Island of 247
Pharsalia 21
Phatnitic mouth of Nile 77
Phatyrites 433
Philadelphus (Ptolemy) 19
Philæ 167, **455–465**; Nilometer at 76
Philetas 124
Philip III. of Macedon 387
Philition 291
Philometor I. 20
„ II. 20
Philopator 2
Philotera 545
Phœnicia ... 5, 15, 65, 400
Phœnicians 399
Physcon 20

PAGE

Piānkhi, priest king ... 16
Piānkhi I. 541
Piānkhi II. 300, 397, 541; his love for horses, 4; Stele of, 4, 583; Temple of ... 499
Pibeseth 262
Pilgrimage to Mecca ... 224
Pillar-stele, the 115
Pillars 114, 115
Pi-netchem (*see* Pai-netchem)
Pisentius 368
Pit of the Spoilers ... 312
Pithom 265, 590
Plants, Egyptian ... 611
Pliny 283, 297, 299, 326, 483
Plutarch ... 7, 8, 356, 446; his history of Osiris... ... 180–182
Pluto 190, 459
Poocke 284
Polygamy 225
Pompey... 21
Pompey's Pillar ... 251
Population of Egypt 93, 191, 192
Port Sa'îd ... 38, 260
Post Office, the Egyptian 54
Potiphar 282
Prayer among Copts ... 209
Prayer among Muḥammadans 222
Prayer, the Call to ... 244
Precepts of Ptaḥ-ḥetep... 11
Premnis... 470

PAGE

Predestination 222
Preserved Table, the ... 218
Priests of Åmen, coffins of 611ff
Primus 200
Prison Pyramid... ... 304
Prisse d'Avennes 3, 114, 564
,, Papyrus ... 122, 123
Probus 23
Proportion, Canon of ... 119
Prophets, the 220
Proterius 202
Proto-Doric pillars ... 115
Proverbs of Solomon ... 165
Provinces, Egyptian, population of... ... 192
Psammetichus I. 17, 262, 398, 541
,, II. 17, 542
,, III. 17, 542
Pselchis... 470
Psemthek I. ... 17, 541
,, II. ... 17, 542
,, III. ... 17, 542
Psemut 18, 543
Psôi 354
Psyllians 363
Ptaḥ, 263; temple of at Memphis 300
Ptaḥ-Seker-Åusår ... 168
Ptaḥ-ḥetep, Maxims of 11, 122, 123, 165
Ptaḥ-ḥetep, tomb of ... 310
Ptolemaïs 357
Ptolemies, the 19
Ptolemy Lagus 418

PAGE
Ptolemy I. 7, 19, 124, 247, 545
„ II. 7, 19, 124, 143, 247, 262, 282, 545
„ III. 19, 267, 247, 545
„ IV. 19, 411, 546
„ V. 20, 255, 546
„ VI. ... 20, 546
„ VII. ... 20, 547
„ VIII. 20, 397, 547
„ IX. 20, 383, 411, 547
„ X. 20, 395, 397, 548
„ XI. ... 20, 548
„ XII. ... 20, 548
„ XIII. 201, 395, 397, 548
„ XIV. ... 21, 548
„ XV. 21
„ XVI. 21
Ptolemy, the geographer 444
Pygmies... ... 447, 481
Pylon 108
Pyramid of Ellâhûn ... 327
„ Ḥawâra ... 327
„ Mêdûm 11, 101, 319
„ Pepi I. ... 303
„ Tetá ... 303
Unás ... 304
„ Cheops, *i.e.*, the "Great Pyramid," 11, 27, 285

PAGE
Pyramid of Chephren ... 289
„ Mycerinus ... 291
„ the "Step" 10, 101, 302
Pyramids, 22; were made for tombs, 100, 102; Battle of, 29; venerated by Arabs, 212; ordered to be destroyed 84
Pyramids of Abuṣîr ... 11
„ of As-sur ... **510**
„ of Dahshûr 101, 311
„ of Gebel Barkal 101, **496**
„ of Gîzeh 11, **283**
„ of Kurru ... 496
„ of Meroë 101, **509**
„ of Nûri 101, **502**
„ of Ṣakkâra, 11, 101, **303**
„ Tankassi ... 496
„ Zûma ... 496
Pu-Addu 595
Pulasta 399
Punt, 12, 14, 65, 185, 368, 405, 409, 422
„ Expedition to 407, 408
„ Prince of 407
„ Queen of 588
Put 65

Q

Qā 363
Qebḥ 363, 519

PAGE

Qebḥ sennuf ... 155, 623
Qebt 367
Qemt 60
Qenqenet 158
Qen-Ḥāpi 90
Qernet 162
Qererti 162
Qeset 368
Quarries 319
Quibell 435, 436

R

Rā, the Sun-god 144, **170**
Rā-en-kau 573
Rā-en-user, Pyramid of 11
Rā-Harmachis ... 160, 295
Rā-ḥetep ... 529, 571
Rā-mer-en-se-em-sa-f ... 522
Rā-nefer 572
Rā-nub 302
Ra'âmah 59
Railways in Egypt 33, 54
Rakoti ... 247, 249, 566
Ramaḍân ... 223, **229**
Ramaḍân Bairam ... 230
Rameses I., 15, 377, 385, 392, 417, 421, **534**
Rameses II., 3, 4, **15**, 191, 301, 369, 376, 377, 385, 389, 392, 393, 406, 417, 469, **534**
Rameses III., **5**, 16, 333, 383, 385, 387, **397-399**, 417 **420**, **535**

PAGE

Rameses IV. 387, 398, **420**, **536**
„ V. ... 422, **536**
„ VI. 420, 422, **536**
„ VII. 536
„ VIII. 536
„ IX. 385, 420, **536**
„ X. 536
„ XI. 537
„ XII. 537
„ XIII. 537
Ramesseum 392
Raphael, king of Nubiȧ 494
Râs al-'Êsh 261
Rashîd Pâsha ... 31, 39
Rauf Pâsha 39
Red Crown, the ... 60
Red Monastery ... 353
Red Mosque 276
Red Sea ... 27, 58, 407
Red Sea Canal... ... 15
Reed pen 123
Rekh-mȧ-Rā 422
Re-mu-shentȧ 343
Renaudot 250
Renenet 152
Reserve Fund 53
Re-stau 162
Resurrection, the 144, 168, **220**
Revenue of Egypt ... 52
Rhamses 22
Rhodopis 293
Rîaz Pâsha 35
Rib-Adda 395

PAGE

Ribton, Mr., killed ... 37
Rikka 321
Ripon Falls 74
Rôda, Island of 280, 343
„ Gauge 628
Rogers Bey 413
Romans, **8**, 20; Emperors, 21; Empire ... 22
Rome 22, 23
Rosellini 127
Rosetta, 123, **254**; branch of Nile, 83; Osman Dikna arrives at 49
Rosetta Stone ... 125, **254**
Rousseau Pâsha ... 85
Royalists 202
Royân 506
Royle quoted 34, 49, 37, 38ff
Rundle, General ... 85
Ru-stau 179
Rutennu 389
Ruthen 593

S

Sa 149
Sa-Âmen 537
Sâba, Dam of 211
Sabaco ... **17**, 383, **541**
Sabaism... 212
Sabbatoi Zevi, false Mahdi 235
Sabbena, tomb of 447, 448
Sabi 212
Sabu 573

PAGE

Sad'îyeh Dervishes ... 228
Sâ el-Hagar 16
Safâ 224
Safia 215
Sahidic Dialect... ... 196
Sahu-Rā ... 521, **574**
„ Pyramid of 11, 297
Sai, Island of 491
Sa'îd Pâsha 32, 80, 257, 275, 277
Saïs 16, 62, 454
„ kings of 17
Sakkâra **298**, 302
„ Necropolis of ... 307
„ Pyramids of ... **101**
„ Tablet of **1**, **3**, 587
Sanam abû Dôm 496, 503
Saladin 28, 279
Salâheddîn 28, 269, 278
„ Mosque of... 275
Salâm 506
Salamat 503
Salt Field 96
Salt Regulations ... 54
Salvolini... 127
Salwah 324
Samâlût 322, **331**
Sa-Mentu 16
Sân 265, 266
Sandstone in the Nile Valley 58
Sanutius 205
Sarras ... 44, 485, **489**
Sa-renput, tombs of 447, 448, 449
Sat-Âmen 417

PAGE

Satans 219
Satáp 338, 343
Satet 458
Sati, goddess ... 167, 470
Sati (Asiatics) 579
Satyrs 181
Sawâ'â 212
Sawwaķîn 40
Sawda 214
Sayyid el-Badawi ... 254
Scarab, the 606
Scarabs, varieties of 607-610
Schweinfurth 611
Schools (see Education) 33
Scorpio 181
Sculpture, Egyptian ... 126
Scythia 22
Scythians 374
Scriptures, the 219
Se-ān-ka-nekht 534
Se-Àmen 416
Se-ānkh-ka-Rā ... **12**, 526
Se-ānkh-en-seḥtu ... 529
Seb ... **149**, 161, 187
Sebaste 552
Sebek 188, 440
Sebek-Ānkh 338
Sebek-em-sa-f I. ... 529
„ II. ... 529
Sebek-ḥetep I. 528
„ II. 528
„ III. ... 266, **528**
„ IV. 528
„ V. 529
„ tomb of ... 450
Sebek-ḥetep-Rā ... 527

PAGE

Sebek-ka-Rā 521
Sebek-neferu-Rā ... 527
Sebek-nekht, tomb of ... 436
Sebennytic mouth of Nile 77
Sebennythos ... } 7, 18, 62
Sebennytus ... } 7, 18, 62
Sedênga... 492
Sects, Muḥammadan ... 231
Seḥeb-Rā 530
Sehêl 454
Se-ḥetep-àb-Rā 527
Seker 302, 402
Seker-khā-baiu 572
Sekheper-en-Rā 530
Sekhet **169**, **264**, 330, **334**, 431
Sekhet-Aanre 160
Sekhit Àmit 96
Sekhet-Ḥemam 96
Sekhet-Ḥetepu ... 153, 158
Sekti Boat ... 176, 178
Seleucids 190
Selmi I. 28, 269
Selq 380
Semen-ka-Rā 527
Semen-Ptaḥ ... 362, **519**
Semiramis 268
Semites 211
Semneh ... 13, **466**, 48, **489**
„ Fortress of ... 113
„ Nile gauge at 75, 76
„ Road Station ... 489
Sen, tomb of 450
Senefer-ka 523
Se-nefer-ka-Rā 12, 523, 525
Seneferu **11**, **319**, 520

PAGE
Senehet 13
Senemet (Biggeh) ... 456
Senet 433
Senka-Åmen-seken ... 500
Sen-mes, tomb of ... 448
Senmut, the architect ... 409
Sennaar 513
Sennacherib ... 6, 17
Senseneb 406
Senṭ ... **10, 572,** 619
Senṭa 519
Senu 417
Senûsi, Mahdi of ... 235
Septimius Severus 23, 394
Septuagint 19
Seqenen-Rā I. **14,** 416, **531**
" " II.... ... 531
" " III. ... 531
Ser (Tcheser) 520
Serapeum 190, **305, 565**
" of Alexandria 249
Serapis **190, 306,** 459, 565
Serdâb 309
Sertetå (Tcheserteta) ... 520
Sesebi 492
Sesha 573
Sesheta 185
Set 176, **186,** 187; Set and Horus, 350; slays Osiris, 179–181; is slain by Horus ... 184
Setau 474
Seti I. 3, **15,** 334, 376, 385, 389, 392, 397, 417, 534; Temple of, 357; Tomb of ... 418

PAGE
Seti II., 15, 535; Mummy of 422
Setit 506
Setches 520
Seth 212, 220
Sethroë 62
Set-ka-mes 417
Set-Nekht 535
Settu-Rā 95
Setu 570
Seuaḥ-en-Rā 530
Seuatch-en-Rā 530
Seven Women, tombs of 278
Severianus 200
Severus 553
Shabaka (Sabaco) **17, 377,** 397, **541**
Shabakat 496
Shabataka ... 17, **541**
Shablûka Cataract ... 516
Shabtîm... 478
Shadow, the 145
Shâfe'i 231
Shâfe'ites 231
Shaiḳiyah Arabs ... 497
Shakalasha 399
Shallâl 324
Shalûf-et-Terrâbeh ... 258
Shamu-Adda 595
Shandawîl 323
Shardana 399
Sharḳîyeh 62
Shashanq I. 16, 266, 385, 389, 539
" II. ... 16, 539
" III. 16, 266, 540

	PAGE
Shashanq IV. ...	16, 540
Shasu	389, 478
Shaw	284
Shêkh 'Abâdeh... ...	343
„ 'abd al-Ḳûrnah ...	422
„ el-Beled ...	28, **573**
Shellâl (Shallâl)... ...	453
„ al-Ḥimâr ...	505
Shendi ...	513, 514, 516
Shenûdah	351
Shenûti ...	351, 353, 354
Shep-en-ȧpt	397
Shepses-ka-f	521
Shepses-ka-kā	521
Sherȧ	572
Sherêkh...	504
Sherîf Pâsha	35
Shesu Ḥeru	8
Shibba	497
Shibîn el-Ḳanaṭîr ...	261
Shî'îtes	233
Ship, Egyptian	408
Shirîn	215
Shishak	16, 389
Shmûn	343
Shmîn	353
Shrine, the temple ...	108
Shu	**149**, 161, **189**, 608
Shuardata	595
Shubandi	595
Sidney, Major ...	46, 504
Signs, Egyptian	127--136
Silko	25, **468**, **484**, **494**
Silsileh	59, **439**
Simon, Saint ...	450, 451
„ the Canaanite	352
Simon, the Syrian ...	204
Sinai	11, **297**
Sinkat	40
Sinn al-Kiddâb	59
Sinope	249
Sirdâb (Serdâb) ...	309
Sirius	142
Sitta Zênab, Mosque of	277
Siûṭ	349
Siwa, Oasis of ...	62, **96**
Slatin Pâsha	49, 236, 238, 517
Slavedealing	54
Slave Market	517
Sloane	301
Smerkhat	362
Smith, Sir Sydney ...	29
Smyrna	35
Soane Museum... ...	418
Sobat (Sawbat) ...	74, 78, 82
Socrates... ...	24, 25, 201
Soleb	492, **502**
Solomon	165
Sôma, the	250
Somâli Coast	65
Somaliland	407
Somerset River... ...	74
Sooshyant	233
Sostratus	248
Soter I.	19
„ II.	20
Sothic Year	142
Soul, the, 145; form of, 152; revisits body, 161; transformations of, 161	
Sozomen	24, 201, 332

PAGE
Spartans 21
Speos Artemidos ... 334
Sphinx, the, 294, 570; from Tanis, 581; Temple of ... 105, **295**
Sphinxes, Avenue of 383, 384, 404
Sta-ka-Rā 530
Steam Tramway at Port Sa'îd 261
Stefani 512
"Step" Pyramid 10, 101, 302
Stephenson, Gen. Sir F. 40, 43, 301
„ Robert ... 257
Stern, L. 196
Stewart, Colonel 43, 236, 503, 504
Stewart, Sir Herbert 41, 42
Stilpo 124
Stoning the Devil ... 224
Strabo 8, 79, 249, 326, 353, 357, 364, 371, 372, 394, 418, 432, 445, 460, 470, 483, 484, 506, 507, 565
Suâkin-Berber road and railway, 40, 41, 43, 44, 45, 49, **505**
Suarda 492
Succoth **191**
Sûdân Expeditions 31, 54
„ Military Railway, 485–488
Sudd, the ... 74, **82**
Suez, 49; Isthmus of, 64

PAGE
Suez Canal ... 256–261
„ „ English shares in 33
Ṣûfism 232
Sûhâg (Sûhâḳ) 59, 323, 351, 353
Sukharti... 15
Sulêmân, Khalîfa ... 280
Sulêman Pâsha, Mosque of 275
Sulêman Wad Gamr 42, **503**
Sumerians 72
Sunnites 233
Suten-ḥenen 329
Syene ... 22, 57, **444**, 566
„ Contra 446
Syria, 19, 203, 389, 400, 422; invasion of ... 31
Syrians 22

T

Tabenna, Monastery of 363
Tablet of Abydos 3, 360
„ of Ancestors ... 387
„ of Four Hundred Years 266
Tablet of Karnak ... 1, 3
„ of Ṣaḳḳâra ... 1, 3
Tachompso 471
Tacitus 191
Taharqa... ... 17, **498**
Taḥennu ... 71, 579
Ta-ḥet 466
Tahrq 541

PAGE

Ṭahṭâ 323, 351
Taif 214
Takeleth I. 16
„ II. 16
Ta-kens 444
Ta-Kenset 466
Tale of Two Brothers 130–132
Tamaai 40, 43, 44
Tamanib 40
Tamarisk Tree 182
Tambuk 505
Ta-Meḥ 60
Ta-Merȧ 60
Ta-Qemā 60
Ta-Res 60
Tanis 62, **265–267**, 566
„ kings of ... 16, 77
Tanäitic mouth of Nile 181
Tangourie River ... 73
Tanḳassi ... 283, **496**
Ṭanṭa 58, 63, 254
Taphis 468
Tarḥundaradush ... 595
Ta-she 164, 325
Ta-Tenen 469
Tattam 564
Taui, wife of Nekht ... 427
Tawfîḳ Pâsha 34, 35, 36, 45
Tcha, Tchah ... 363, 478
Tchakari 399
Tchat 338
Tchatchai 520
Tchāu 574
Tche-ḥer 18

PAGE

Tcheser 10, 302, 304, 454, 520
Tchestcheset, Oasis of... 95
Tcheṭ-Ptaḥ-ȧuf-ānkh ... 417
Tefnut **149**, 161, **189**, 608
Teḥuti-ḥetep, tomb of ... 344
Teḥuti-mes I. 14 (See Thothmes)
„ II. 14 (See Thothmes)
„ III. 14 (See Thothmes)
„ IV. 14 (See Thothmes)
Telegraphs, Egyptian ... 54
Tell-Basta ... 16, **262**
Tell el-Amarna ... 345-348
„ „ tablets of 5, 15, **347**, **592–595**
Tell el-Kebîr ... 38, 49, 264
Tell el Maskhûta ... 264
Tell el-Yahûdîyeh ... 261
Tell Lo 72
Ṭemâ 323
Temple, the Egyptian 105, 107
Temple at Jerusalem ... 16
Temu ... **149**, 164, **168**
Ṭen 362
Tennis 267
Tentyra **363**, 364
Tentyritæ 363
Tentyris ... 363, 364
Tertiary Age 57
Tetȧ ... 10, 143, **519**
„ Pyramid of 11, 303
Tetȧ (IIIrd dynasty) ... 520
Teta (Mer-en-Ptaḥ) ... 522
Ṭet-f-Rā 521
Ṭet-ka-Rā ... 11, 12, 522
Ṭet-ka-Rā-maā 523

PAGE

Teṭ-kheru-Rā 534
Thaḥennu 71
Theatre of Alexandria ... 250
Thebaïd 325
Thebaïs Secunda ... 367
Theban Dialect... ... 196
„ Triad **375**, 378, 379
Thebes, 16, 179, **356**; antiquities, 370 ff; false Mahdi at, 31; visited by Germanicus 21
Theft 226
Thekeleth I. ... 483, 539
„ II. 540
Theoclus 200
Theodore 204
Theodorus 124
Theodosius **24**, 202, 301, 460
„ II. ... 24, 249
Theonas 200
Theophilus ... 24, 202
Theotokos 25
Thermeset 468
Thethȧ, tomb of ... 450
Thi 6, 307, 346, 533, 594
This ... 10, 61, 354, 356
Thoth **149**, 152, **188**, **343**
Thoth Jupiter 374
„ month of ... 186
Thothmes I. 14, 385, 386, 387, 388, 405, 406, 417, 532, 593
„ II. 14, 386, 387, 395, 406, 408, 417, 532

PAGE

Thothmes III. 2, 4, 14, 334, **385–389**, 395, 397, 406, 417, 533, 593; mummy of, 415; stele of ... 5, 587
„ IV. 14, 380, mummy of, 422; and the Sphinx ... 294
Thoueris ... 184, 380
Thuȧa 6, 594
Thuêba 213
Ti, statue of, 576; tomb of 569
Tiberius 22, 366, 462, 464, 549
Timothy 202
Tirhakah 617, **383**, 397, **541**, **584**; Temple of 498
Titus 95
Tobacco, use of ... 225
To-Bedhawîyyeh ... 196
Tofrif 43
Tokar 40, 45, 49
Tombos... 492
Tomb, the Egyptian ... 98
Tombs, pre-dynastic ... 67
Tombs of the Kings 403, **417**
Toṣki ... 45, 474, **489**
Towns of Egypt ... 93
Trajan 23, **257**, 468, **552**, **591**
Trask, Captain 491

PAGE

Tricou, M. 35
Topoli, Mahdi of ... 235
Ṭu-âb (Gebel Barkal) ... 497
Ṭuamāutef ... **155**, 623
Tûkh 362
Ṭûmân Bey 28
Tunep 478, **593**
Turin 2
„ Papyrus of ... 1, 3
Turks ... 8, **30**, 192, **198**
Ṭurra 319
Ṭursha 399
Tusân 259
Tushkeh 489
Tushki 45
Tushratta ... 15, **593**
Ṭusûn 30, 31, 32
Tut-ānkh-Åmen... ... 534
Tuti Island ... 42, **517**
Tutzis 469
Two Natures 24
Tylor, J. J. 436
Typhon 181, 182, 183, 184, 185
Typhoneia 365
Typhonium 367

U

Uaua 13, 473
Uaḥ-åb-Rā 17
Uaḥ-åb-Rā-åā-åb ... 528
Uasarken I. 16
„ II. 16
„ III. 16

PAGE

Uast 370
Uatch-nes 519
Uben-Rā 530
Uhud 214
'Uḳmeh 491
Umm al-Ḳa'ab 362
Umm al-Ḳûmân ... 329
Umm Dabrikât... ... 48
Umm Ḥabûba 215
Umm Hashîya 504
Umm Salma 215
Unȧ 305, 319, 452, 466, 574
Unås ... 11, **143**, **522**
„ mummy ... 302, **579**
„ pyramid of 11, **303**
Unaset 164
Unified Debt 33
Un-nefer ... 160, 441
Upper Egypt Railway ...321ff
Urdamanah 17
Ur-ḥekau 146
User-en-Rā ... 307, 574
Usertsen I. 13, 266, 337, 391, 447, 450, **526**
„ II. 13, 266, **327**, 337, 341, 344, **526**
„ III. 13, 266, 312, 313, 344, 489, **526**
Ushabtiu figures ... 599
Usr-en-Rā, Pyramid of 297, **521**
Usr-ka-f... 521
Usr-ka-Rā 522
Uswân 444
Uṭen 164

PAGE

V

Valerianus ... 23, 248
Valley of Mîna... ... 224
Vassali 571
Veil of Ka'ba door ... 230
Venus 363
Verus 553
Vespasian 22, 191, 551
Victoria Nyanza ... 73
Villages of Egypt ... 93
Village Justice... ... 54
Virgin sacrificed to the Nile 92
Virgin's Tree 281
Vyse 284, 296

W

Waddington ... 33, 212
Wad en-Negûmî 44, 45, 474, 489
Wâdî Ben-Nâga 514, 515
Wâdî Ḥalfah 41, 46, 47, **480**
Wâdî Ma'ârah 11
Wâdî Naṭrûn ... 58, 96
Wâdî Sabû'a 472
Wâdî Tâfah 468
Wâdî Ṭûmîlât 27
Walls of Alexandria ... 252
Wansleben 281
Warriba Mountains ... 49
Wasṭa 63, **325**
Water, yearly discharge of by Nile into the sea... 79
Weights, Muḥammadan 245

PAGE

Wells of Abû Klea ... 496
„ Al-Ḥuwêyât ... 495
„ Gakdûl ... 495
„ Moses... ... 256
„ Shabakat ... 496
White Castle 299
White Crown 60
White Monastery ...351ff
White Nile ... 73, 518
Widya 595
Wiedemann ... 70, 289
Wilbour 454
Wilkinson, Sir G. 192, 284, 404, 422
Willcocks, Major 57, 78, 83, 93; his irrigation schemes, 52; his work on Barrage... 86
William of Baldensel ... 289
Wilson, Sir C. 42
Wilson, Sir Erasmus ... 251
Wilson, Sir Rivers 33, 34
Wine, use of 225
Wingate, Sir F. R., the Sirdar... ... 48, 235
Wisdom of Jesus . . 165
Wodehouse 44
Wolseley, Lord... 38, 495
Women in Paradise ... 222
Writing, various kinds of 121–123

X

Xerxes 18, 543
kings of ... 13, 62

PAGE

Y

Yabni-ili 595
Yaghûth 212
Yaman 72, 211
Yârab 211
Ya'ûḳ 212
Year, the Sothic ... 142
,, the Solar 142
,, the vague ... 142
Yenbo 27
Yôrhôm... 211
Young, Dr. Thomas 125, 126, 255
Yussuf Pâsha 39

Z

Zacharias 205

PAGE
Ẓâhir 28
Zaḳâziḳ 58, 62, 262
Zamzam, Well of ... 228
Zatadna... 595
Zauryet al-Mêtín ... 333
Zêd ibn Thâbit 215, 217
Zedekiah 17
Zênab ... 214, 215, 229, 277
Zeno 25
Zenobia... 23
Zenodotus 124
Zoan, Field of 265
Zodiac 366, 433
Zoroaster 233
Zoroastrianism 233
Zûma ... 283, 485, **496**

For Product Safety Concerns and Information please contact our EU
representative GPSR@taylorandfrancis.com
Taylor & Francis Verlag GmbH, Kaufingerstraße 24, 80331 München, Germany

www.ingramcontent.com/pod-product-compliance
Lightning Source LLC
Chambersburg PA
CBHW071710300426
44115CB00010B/1375

* 9 7 8 1 1 3 8 9 7 7 3 0 3 *